U0935970

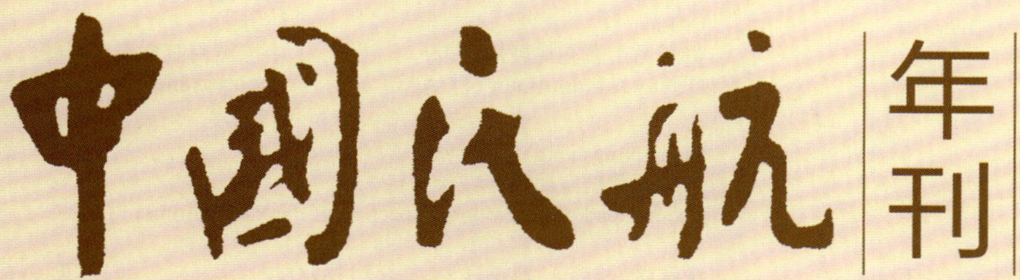

CHINA CIVIL AVIATION ANNUAL REPORT

2011

特约通讯员（按姓氏笔画排序）
Specially Invited Correspondents

丁　明 Ding Ming	马晓晴 Ma Xiaoqing	马　玉 Ma Yu	王建喜 Wang Jianxi	王志伟 Wang Zhiwei	王小林 Wang Xiaolin	王海明 Wang Haiming
王洪秋 Wang Hongqiu	王省谋 Wang Shengmou	包随义 Bao Suiyi	石义刚 Shi Yigang	付立伟 Fu Liwei	刘　瑶 Liu Yao	刘海云 Liu Haiyun
刘占赢 Liu Zhanying	孙霞峰 Sun Xiafeng	杨辛萌 Yang Xinmeng	李　根 Li Gen	李　鑫 Li Xin	李志鸿 Li Zhihong	李晓蕾 Li Xiaolei
李晓晶 Li Xiaojing	李汝义 Li Ruyi	李　静 Li Jing	肖连英 Xiao Lianying	沈宗耀 Shen Zongyao	张　睿 Zhang Rui	陈　卫 Chen Wei
陈　晔 Chen Ye	陈小佳 Chen Xiaojia	陈学伟 Chen Xuewei	陈中妮 Chen Zhongni	金　哲 Jin Zhe	孟宪岭 Meng Xianling	林淑惠 Lin Shuhui
罗顺明 Luo Shunming	郑尼亚 Zheng Niya	侯　佳 Hou Jia	胡晓建 Hu Xiaojian	胡玉萍 Hu Yuping	邱奕文 Qiu Yiwen	陶烨红 Tao Yehong
袁加林 Yuan Jialin	郭振华 Guo Zhenhua	梁　楠 Liang Nan	崔海鹏 Cui Haipeng	彭岚兰 Peng Lanlan	程　琦 Cheng Qi	奥　斌 Ao Bin
訾世平 Zi Shiping	熊　巍 Xiong Wei	潘东华 Pan Donghua	潘力猷 Pan Liyou			

《中国民航年刊》编辑部
China Civil Aviation Annual Report Editorial Department

主　任 Editorial Director	孟庆芬 Meng Qingfen							
副主任 Deputy Editorial Director	何　巍 He Wei	刘乃君 Liu Naijun						
编　辑 Edition	张　洁 Zhang Jie	韩　婕 Han Jie	马松伟 Ma Songwei					
审　校 Revision	杨　澄 Yang Cheng	李　煊 Li Xuan	王向荣 Wang Xiangrong	林建文 Lin Jianwen	梁谚民 Liang Yanmin			
翻　译 Translation	徐文保 Xu Wenbao	杜　建 Du Jian	宋国力 Song Guoli	王堪林 Wang Kanlin	何鄂湘 He Exiang	邴元春 Bing Yuanchun	李　磊 Li Lei	王华玲 Wang Hualing

年刊主管单位　　中国民用航空局
Accountable Authority　　Civil Aviation Administration of China

监　制　　中国民用航空局综合司
Supervision　　Department of General Affairs of CAAC

编辑单位　　中国民用航空局国际合作服务中心
Editing Unit　　International Cooperation and Service Center, CAAC
《中国民航年刊》编辑部
China Civil Aviation Annual Report Editorial Department

地　址（Add）　　北京市东四西大街155号，100710
155 Dongsi Street West, Beijing, 100710, China
电　话（Tel）　　010-84023933　64092309
传　真（Fax）　　010-84023933
邮　箱（E-mail）　　caac@vip.sina.com

目 录

中国民航年刊 2011 CHINA CIVIL AVIATION ANNUAL REPORT

CONTENTS

中国民航年刊 | 2011 CHINA CIVIL AVIATION ANNUAL REPORT

CAH

重庆
呼和浩特
武汉
南昌
天津
北京
长春
哈尔滨
周年
首都机场集团公司 2002－2012
Capital Airports Holding Company(CAH)

倡行中國服務
展示國門形象

李家祥

局 长　李家祥
Administrator Li Jiaxiang

副局长　李　军
Deputy Administrator Li Jun

副局长　李　健
Deputy Administrator Li Jian

副局长　夏兴华
Deputy Administrator Xia Xinghua

党组纪检组组长　梁宁生
Group Head of Discipline Inspection of the Party Group
Liang Ningsheng

中国民用航空局局长致辞

2011年是实施“十二五”规划的第一年。中国民航紧紧围绕科学发展的主题和转变发展方式的主线，做了大量扎实有效的工作，取得了新的成绩，实现了“十二五”规划的良好开局。

航空安全持续稳定。全年全行业未发生航空运输飞行事故和空防安全事故，运输航空严重事故征候万时率下降44.2%。其间狠抓资质能力建设，对10 000余名机长、教员等进行了资质排查。

行业发展稳中向好。全年全行业完成运输总周转量577.44亿吨公里、旅客运输量2.93亿人次、货邮运输量557.5万吨，比上年分别增长7.2%、9.5%和−1.0%。

经济效益基本趋稳。在燃油价格大幅增长和国际航空业仍不景气的情况下，我国民航企业依然保持着较好的经营业绩，全年全行业完成营业收入5 001亿元、利润总额363亿元，比上年分别增长21.2%和−13.9%。

运行质量得以提高。航班延误治理取得明显成效，全年主要航空公司航班正常率为77.9%，同比提高2.1个百分点；京沪、京广航路航班正常率分别提高30和11个百分点。

圆满完成多轮重大紧急运输任务。优质高效地完成了建国以来最大规模的海外紧急航空运输——利比亚撤侨任务，以及赴埃及、日本撤侨任务，彰显了国家实力和民航良好形象，受到党和国家领导人的高度赞扬。此外，还顺利地完成了西安世界园艺博览会、深圳第26届世界大学生夏季运动会、西藏和平解放60周年大庆、中国—亚欧博览会、夏季达沃斯论坛等重大运输任务。

结构调整和深化改革迈出了新的步伐。中国、东方、南方三大航空集团公司和北京、上海、广州、成都等大型机场积极实施战略转型，加快构建航空枢纽和完善航线网络。积极推进联合重组，形成了新的中货航和新的国货航。研究制定国内运价改革方案，以及空管收费改革方案和机场收费并轨方案。

基础建设和科教工作取得了新的进展。全年全行业完成基础设施建设固定资产投资687.7亿元，其中机场建设投资495.4亿元；全国运输机场达到180个。民航局首次编制颁布了《民航业人才队伍建设中长期规划（2010—2020年）》。

回顾2011年，我们感到欣慰和鼓舞；展望2012年，我们信心满怀、斗志弥坚！

2012年是十分关键的一年，我们党将召开第十八次全国代表大会。民航的工作任务十分繁重，责任十分重大。让我们紧密团结在党中央周围，再接再厉、开拓创新、真抓实干、攻坚克难，努力把民航科学发展提高到新的水平，以优异成绩迎接党的十八大胜利召开！■

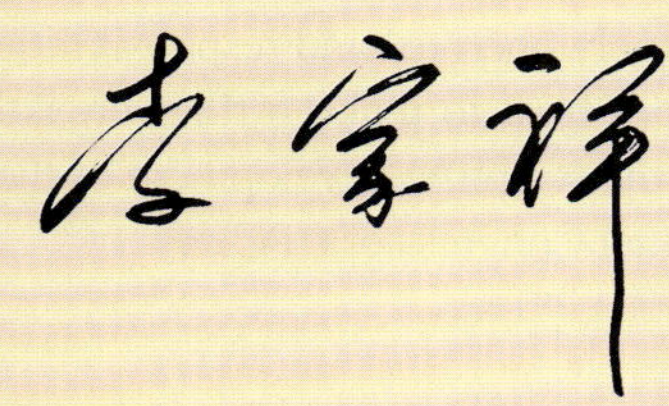

MESSAGE FROM THE ADMINISTRATOR OF CAAC

2011 marked the start for the implementation of the 12th Five-Year Plan. By firmly focusing on the theme of scientific development and following the call of transforming the development pattern, China civil aviation industry did a great deal of solid and effective work with fresh progress, realizing a good beginning for the 12th Five-Year Plan.

Aviation safety remained stable. The whole industry saw no air transport flight accident or aviation security accident in 2011, and the rate of severe transport aviation incidents per 10 000 flight hours decreased by 44.2%. In the meantime, the industry went to great lengths in addressing qualification capability building, screening the qualifications of more than 10 000 captains and instructors.

Civil aviation achieved solid growth. The whole industry delivered a total transport turnover of 57.744 billion ton-km and carried 293 million passengers and 5.575 million tons of cargo and mail in 2011, increasing by 7.2%, 9.5% and -1.0% respectively over those of the previous year.

Financial performance was stabilized on the whole. Despite the hikes in fuel price and the sluggishness in international air transport, China civil aviation industry still maintained a fair financial performance with 500.1 billion yuan in business revenue and 36.3 billion yuan in profit in 2011, year-on-year increases of 21.2% and -13.9% respectively.

Operation quality was improved. Significant progress was made in addressing flight delays, with a flight regularity rate of 77.9% for major airlines, 2.1 percentage points higher than that of 2010; and the flight regularity rates for Beijing-Shanghai and Beijing-Guangzhou routes rose by 30 and 11 percentage points respectively.

The industry impeccably performed multiple major emergency transport tasks. It excellently and efficiently carried out the evacuation of Chinese compatriots from Libya, the largest overseas emergent air transport mission ever since the founding of the P.R.C, as well as the evacuations from Egypt and Japan, demonstrating China's national strength and leaving a good image of the civil aviation industry, which won high applause from leaders of the Party and the State. Besides, it also successfully completed other major transport tasks, such as Xi'an International Horticultural Exposition, Universiade Shenzhen 2011, celebrations for the 60th anniversary of the peaceful liberation of Tibet, China-Eurasia Expo and Summer Davos in Asia, etc.

The industry made new strides in restructuring and reform. The 3 largest airlines, i.e. Air China, China Eastern Airlines and China Southern Airlines and big size airports such as those in Beijing, Shanghai, Guangzhou and Chengdu actively implemented strategic transformation to step up the construction of aviation hubs and improve the route network. The industry vigorously pushed forward mergers and consolidations, creating a new China Cargo Airlines and Air China Cargo. It also worked on the development of the reform plan for domestic fares, the reform plan for ATM charges and the alignment plan for airport charges.

The industry made fresh headways in infrastructure development and scientific and educational work. The whole industry made a total fixed-asset investment of 68.77 billion yuan for infrastructure development in 2011, among which 49.54 billion yuan was earmarked for airport construction, and transport airports in the country numbered 180. CAAC developed and unveiled the first Mid and Long-term Plan for Human Resources Development in Civil Aviation Industry (2010-2020).

Looking back on 2011, we feel pleased and encouraged; and looking ahead to 2012, we are full of confidence and resolve.

2012 is a pivotal year, in which the 18th National Congress of CPC will take place. Tasks for the civil aviation industry are extremely onerous, and responsibilities extremely heavy. Let's unite as one around the CPC Central Committee, continue to work hard to make further breakthroughs and innovations, to make solid efforts and overcome the difficulties and push the scientific development of the civil aviation industry to a new high to embrace the successful opening of the 18th National Congress of CPC. ■

中国民航业发展稳中向好

2011年，中国民航业发展稳中向好，安全形势持续稳定，旅客运输较快增长，通用航空增长加快，经济效益整体良好，运行质量得以提高，圆满完成重大紧急运输任务，结构调整和深化改革迈出新步伐，基础设施建设和科技教育工作取得新进展，实现了“十二五”规划的良好开局。

安全形势持续稳定

全行业牢固树立持续安全理念，切实落实安全主体责任和监管责任。狠抓关键岗位人员资质建设，对10 092名机长、教员等进行资质排查，排查率100%，通过率98.2%；制定《民用航空运输机长职责》，进行机长职责培训；开展飞行签派员、维修人员和空管专业人员资质情况排查摸底。继续推进安全管理体系（SMS）、航空安保管理体系（SeMS）建设和安全审计工作，完善安全信息管理系统。启动对23个支线机场盲降系统和助航灯光系统的建设和改造。完成了全国民航使用坐标系由“北京54”向“WGS-84”的过渡。加快新技术的应用，完成23个机场基于性能导航（PBN）飞行程序设计和试飞；国航、东航、南航、海航均在国外开始了广播式自动相关监视(ADS-B)正式运行；加强飞行标准监管系统（FSOP）建设。认真开展日常安全监察和集中检查，加强薄弱环节，消除安全隐患。增加安全投入，开展航空公司安全保障财务考核，提升保障能力。提高适航管理能力，加快适航审定中心建设。推进美国联邦航空局（FAA）以国产ARJ21飞机为平台开展影子审查。全年全行业未发生航空运输飞行事故和空防安全事故，成功处置一起预谋恐怖袭击事件；运输航空事故征候万时率为0.37，比上年下降0.01，其中人为原因事故征候万时率比上年下降21.7%，严重事故征候万时率下降44.2%；通用航空事故征候万架次率为0.12，比上年下降45.5%。南航等36家航空公司运输飞行事故征候万时率低于行业平均水平，34家航空公司没有发生公司责任的事故征候。

旅客运输较快增长

受国内经济增长减缓和发达国家经济复苏乏力的影响，2011年中国航空运输增速明显下降，特别是航空货运出现了负增长，但旅客运输仍保持了快速增长。全年全行业完成运输总周转量、旅客运输量和货邮运输量577.44亿吨公里、2.93亿人次和557.5万吨，分别比上年增长7.2%、9.5%和下降1.0%。国内航线上述三项指标为380.61亿吨公里、2.72亿人次和379.4万吨，分别比上年增长10.2%、9.5%和2.4%。其中，港澳台地区航线为12.64亿吨公里、0.076亿人次和21万吨，分别比上年增长9.1%、13.1%和下降3.0%。国际航线为196.84亿吨公里、0.21亿人次和178.0万吨，分别比上年增长2.0%、9.7%和下降7.6%。

全年178个通航机场（不含港澳台地区机场）共完成旅客吞吐量6.21亿人次，比上年增长10.0%；完成货邮吞吐量1 157.8万吨，比上年增长2.5%。西部地区、中部地区旅客吞吐量和货邮吞吐量增速远高于东部地区。乌鲁木齐、三亚、沈阳、海口、郑州机场旅客吞吐量首次超过1 000万人次，全国年旅客吞吐量超过1 000万人次机场达21个。北京首都国际机场年旅客吞吐量达7 867.45万人次，在全球机场排名中继续列第2位；上海浦东机场货邮吞吐量达308.53万吨，在全球机场排名中继续列第3位。

截至2011年底，全行业共有定期航班航线2 290条，按不重复距离计算的航线里程为349.06万公里。其中国内航线1 847条，按不重复距离计算的航线里程为199.62万公里（其中：内地至香港、澳门、台湾航线91条，按不重复距离计算的航线里程为13.51万公里）；国际航线443条，按不重复距离计算的航线里程为149.44万公里。定期航班国内通航175个城市（不含香港、澳门、台湾），内地45个城市通航香港，14个城市通航澳门，37个城市通航台湾；国外通航58个国家的126个城市。

全行业运输飞机年末在册架数为1 764架，比上年底增加167架。在册运输飞机平均日利用率为9.26小时，比上年降低0.09小时。平均正班客座率为81.8%，比上年提高1.6个百分点；平均正班载运率为72.0%，比上年提高0.4个百分点。

通用航空增长加快

全行业共完成通用航空飞行50.27万小时，比上年增长28.5%。其中：工农业航空作业完成8.98万小时，比上年下降5.7%；教学培训飞行完成37.22万小时，比上年增长40.8%；其它飞行完成4.07万小时，比上年增长29%。截至2011年底，全行业持有通用航空经营许可证的企业共123家，比上年增加12家，开展非经营性通用航空活动的单位12家；共拥有通用航空机场及临时起降点286个，其中通用航空机场70个，临时起降点216个；通用航空机队在册总数为1 154架，比上年增长14.3%，其中固定翼飞机893架，旋翼航空器238架，气球17架，飞艇6架。

经济效益整体良好

根据财务快报统计，2011年全行业累计实现营业收入5 001亿元，利润总额363亿元，分别比上年增长21.2%和减少13.9%。其中，航空公司实现营业收入3 532亿元，利润总额278亿元，分别比上年增长17.9%和减少17.7%；机场实现营业收入498亿元，利润总额43亿元，分别比上年增长15.7%和减少16.8%；保障企业实现营业收入971亿元，利润总额42亿元，分别比上年增长39%和31.2%。年末航空公司平均资产负债率为76.5%，比上年末下降2.2个百分点。全年全行业客公里收入水平为0.68元/客公里，比上年增加0.05元/客公里；货邮收入水平为1.86元/吨公里，与上年基本持平。

运行质量得以提高

航班延误专项治理成效明显。明确了航空公司航班放行的主体责任，空管、机场、油料等部门保障航班正常的责任，以及监管部门协调督察航班运行的责任。空管系统开展“排堵保畅”工作，加大对京沪、京广两大航路的流量管理力度。建立航班运行的常设协调机构。建立完善大面积航班延误处置的联动机制和信息沟通机制。着重解决旅客机上等待时间过长问题。2011年，全国航班正常率平均为77.15%，同比提高2.2个百分点；京沪、京广航路航班正常率分别提高30个和11个百分点。航班延误后服务明显改善，旅客满意度提高。

强化空管运行管理。对北京、南京、重庆、乌鲁木齐等4个繁忙机场的运行容量进行调整，每周共增加2 700个可用时刻。统一调整了北京、上海高空管制区域管制下限。北京区域管制中心成功接管济南高空空域，首次实现了全国民航跨地区高空管制移交指挥。大幅调整优化了华北地区主要机场及部分干线航路空域结构。郑州、青岛、重庆、杭州等飞行繁忙机场进离场分流工作基本完成。大力开展节能减排工作，通过航路截弯取直、使用临时航路，全年累计缩短飞行距离1 296万公里，减少二氧化碳排放22万吨，节省燃油成本5.3亿元。

圆满完成重大紧急运输任务

2011年，埃及、利比亚等国家先后发生社会动荡，日本强烈地震引发海啸和核辐射，中国民航迅速投入紧急运输。1月底埃及局势动荡，在不到48小时之内，共组织派出8架飞机接回中国公民1 796人；在利比亚政局恶化后，共组织包机182架次，接回中国公民26 240人；3月11日日本东北部强烈地震引起核泄漏后，不到10天共运回中国公民66 500人。三次大规模撤离中国公民的紧急航空运输任务，在中国民航史上尚属首次，彰显了国家实力和中国民航的良好形象。此外，还顺利完成了西安世界园艺博览会、深圳第26届世界大学生夏季运动会、庆祝西藏和平解放60周年、中国—亚欧博览会、在大连召开的夏季达沃斯论坛等重大运输任务，提供了良好保障。

结构调整和深化改革迈出新步伐

国航、东航、南航等大型航空公司和北京、上海、广州、成都等大型机场积极实施战略转型，加快构建航空枢纽和完善航线网络。推进联合重组，东航将原中货航、上货航、长城航重组为新的中货航，国航与国泰合资成立新的国货航。改善机队结构，减少机型种类。烟台新机场管理模式改革试点工作取得进展。深化市场管理改革，实行国内航权和航班网上管理和信息公开。积极推进价格和收费改革，研究制定国内运价改革方案，以及空管收费改革方案和机场收费并轨方案。国家对进口航空煤油免征关税。中航油完成了公司制改革。民航局和所属单位干部人事制度改革力度加大，竞争性选拔全面铺开，交流轮岗和挂职锻炼普遍推行。

基础建设和科教工作取得新进展

全行业完成基础设施建设固定资产投资690亿元，其中机场建设投资460亿元。广东揭阳潮汕（迁建）、甘肃张掖和金昌、内蒙古阿尔山和巴彦淖尔、西藏日喀则、新疆库车（迁建）等7个机场竣工投入使用，全国运输机场达到180个。昆明新机场建设基本完成，南昌、长沙机场扩建竣工。北京新机场建设前期工作取得重大进展，民航局、北京市和空军就此达成协议。空管建设投资18亿元，东部地区和西部主要航路雷达管制工程进展顺利。

实施科教兴业和人才强业战略，民航局首次编制颁布了《民航业人才队伍建设中长期规划（2010—2020年）》。各院校继续扩大办学规模，优化专业设置。飞行学院招生人数大幅度增加，在世界同类院校中名列前茅。全面加强专业技术人员和管理人员在职培训，促进职工队伍综合素质提高。推动民航科研平台建设，重点支持民航强国战略和持续安全战略相关项目研究。组织完成11个民航科研基地建设验收。共鉴定科技成果68项，评选出民航科技进步一等奖3项。大力推进文化建设，行业文化、企业文化和安全文化、服务文化的研究与实践都有新的进展。

2012年是实施“十二五”规划的关键一年。中国民航局确定2012年民航工作的总体要求是：

认真贯彻党的十七大与十七届五中、六中全会和中央经济工作会议精神，紧紧围绕科学发展主题和转变发展方式主线，坚持落实主体责任和加强监督管理并举，确保飞行和空防持续安全；坚持开拓市场和扩容增效并举，促进民航事业平稳较快发展；坚持改革创新、调整结构、科教兴业和文化建设并举，进一步提高发展质量和效益，更好地为经济社会发展和对外开放服务，以优异成绩迎接党的十八大胜利召开。

2012年民航发展的主要预期指标是：

全行业运输总周转量632亿吨公里，旅客运输量3.2亿人，货邮运输量578万吨，分别比上年增长10.1%、10.3%和4.7%。通用航空飞行50万小时，比上年增长10%。其中教学训练及其他飞行37万小时、生产作业飞行13万小时，比上年分别增长7.3%和18%。固定资产投资1 585亿元，其中基础设施建设投资750亿元。

2012年民航安全工作的主要目标是：

杜绝航空运输飞行事故；防止劫机、炸机事件，杜绝空防事故；通用航空事故万架次率不超过0.3；防止重大航空地面事故和特大航空维修事故；运输航空事故征候万时率不超过0.5。

China's Civil Aviation Showed Steady Improvement

In 2011, China's civil aviation industry showed steady improvement, continued stability of safety, rapid increase in passenger traffic, accelerated growth of general aviation, good financial performance and improved quality of operations. Major and emergency transport tasks were fulfilled; new steps were taken in restructuring and reform and new progress was made in infrastructure development, science and technology and education. 2011 represented a good start of the 12th Five-Year Plan Period.

Continued Stability of Safety

The concept of sustained safety was upheld firmly industry-wide. Safety responsibility and regulatory responsibility were fulfilled. Qualifications of personnel in key roles were enhanced. 10 092 captains and instructors were screened for qualifications, at a screening rate of 100% and pass rate of 98.2%. The Functions of of Pilots-in-command in Civil Air Transport was formulated and captains were trained on duties. Qualifications of flight dispatchers, maintenance staff and air traffic controllers were investigated. Development of the safety management system (SMS), the aviation security management system (SeMS) and the safety audit were further pushed ahead and the safety information management system was promoted. The instrument landing system and the airfield lighting system were developed or upgraded at 23 regional airports. The coordination system for civil aviation shifted from Beijing 54 to WGS-84 nationwide. Application of new technologies was accelerated, with the design and trial of performance-based navigation (PBN) flight program completed at 23 airports; Air China, China Eastern Airlines, China Southern Airlines and Hainan Airlines all started formal overseas operation of the automatic dependent surveillance-broadcast (ADS-B); development of the flight standards oversight procedure (FSOP) was enhanced. Day-to-day safety oversight and thorough inspection were duly carried out to improve weaknesses and eliminate potential safety hazards. Safety investment was increased and financial evaluation of safety support at airlines was made to enhance the supporting capacity. Airworthiness management capability was boosted and the development of the Airworthiness Certification Center accelerated. The shadow review by the U.S. Federal Aviation Administration (FAA) based on the local ARJ21 aircraft was pushed forward. In the reporting year, the whole industry recorded no transport flight accidents or aviation security accidents and successfully thwarted a terrorist attack attempt. The rate of transport flight incident per 10 000 hours was 0.37, down 0.01 from the pervious year, of which the rate of human factor induced incident per 10 000 hours was down 21.7% and the rate of severe incident per 10 000 hours down 44.2% from the previous year; the rate of general aviation incident per 10 000 aircraft movements was 0.12, down 45.5% from the previous year. 36 airlines including China Southern Airlines recorded a lower-than-industry-average rate of transport flight incident per 10 000 hours and 34 airlines recorded zero incident for which they were liable.

Passenger Traffic Increased Rapidly

Due to domestic economic slowdown and weak recovery of developed economies, China's air traffic grew at an obviously lower rate in 2011, and, in particular, air cargo traffic declined from last year, but passenger traffic still maintained rapid growth. The whole industry realized a total turnover of about 57.744 billion ton-km and carried 293 million passengers and 5.575 million tons of cargo and mail, up respectively by 7.2%, 9.5% and -1.0% from the previous year. The aforementioned 3 indicators for domestic routes were 38.061 billion ton-km, 272 million passengers and 3.794 million tons, up by

10.2%, 9.5% and 2.4% from the previous year, respectively. Specifically, the indicators for routes connecting Hong Kong, Macao and Taiwan were 1.264 billion ton-km, 7.6 million passengers and 210 000 million tons, up by 9.1%, 13.1% and -3.0% from the previous year respectively and those for international routes stood at 19.684 billion ton-km, 210 million passengers and 1.78 million tons, up by 2.0%, 9.7% and -7.6% respectively from the previous year.

The 178 airports in service (excluding those in Hong Kong, Macao and Taiwan) realized a passenger turnover of 621 million and 11.578 million tons of cargo and mail, increasing by 10.0% and 2.5% from the previous year. The passenger turnover and the cargo and mail turnover in the western and central regions grew much faster than in the eastern region. 21 airports handled over 10 million passengers in the year, including airports in Urumqi, Sanya, Shenyang, Haikou and Zhengzhou that broke the 10 million mark for the first time. Passenger turnover at Beijing Capital International Airport reached 78.674 5 million, still ranking No. 2 among airports around the world; and cargo and mail turnover at Shanghai Pudong Airport stood at 3.085 3 million tons, still ranking the 3rd globally.

By the end of 2011, the whole industry had boasted 2 290 scheduled flight routes, and the total mileage of the routes without overlapped distances reached 3.490 6 million km, among which there were 1 847 domestic routes, whose total mileage excluding overlapped distances stood at 1.996 2 million km (including 91 routes between the Mainland and Hong Kong, Macao and Taiwan, with 135 100 km of non-overlapped mileage); and 443 international routes with 1.494 4 million km of non-overlapped mileage. There were 175 domestic cities with scheduled flight services (excluding Hong Kong, Macao and Taiwan), with 45 cities having flight service for Hong Kong, 14 for Macao and 37 for Taiwan. International flight services connected to 126 cities in 58 countries.

There were 1 764 transport aircrafts on registry industry-wide at the end of the year, which is 167 more than the end of last year. The average daily use rate of transport aircraft on registry was 9.26 hours, 0.09 hour lower than last year; the average passenger load factor for normal flights stood at 81.8%, 1.6 percentage points higher than last year, and the average load factor for normal flights was 72.0%, 0.4 percentage point higher than the previous year.

General Aviation Gained Pace

The whole industry completed 502 700 hours of flight in general aviation, up by 28.5% from the previous year, among which, 89 800 hours were spent on industrial and agricultural aviation tasks, 5.7% lower than last year; 372 200 hours on teaching and training flights, 40.8% higher than last year; and 40 700 hours on others, 29% higher than last year. By the end of 2010, there had been 123 businesses that had won the business licenses for general aviation operations, 12 more than last year. 12 entities engaged in non-profit general aviation activities; there were 286 general aviation airports and temporary airdromes in total, including 70 general aviation airports and 216 temporary airdromes. There had been 1 154 registered aircraft in the general aviation fleet, up 14.3% from the pervious year and consisting of 893 fixed-wing aircraft, 238 rotary-wing aircraft, 17 air balloons and 6 airships.

Good Overall Profit

According to financial reports, the whole industry realized aggregate operating revenue of 500.1 billion yuan in 2011, with profit totaling 36.3 billion yuan, up 21.2% and down 13.9% respectively from the last year. Operating revenue for airlines stood at 353.2 billion yuan, with 27.8 billion in profit, up 17.9% and down 17.7% from the last year; 49.8 billion yuan for airports, with 4.3 billion in profit, up 15.7% and down 16.8% respectively from the previous year; 97.1 billion yuan for supporting enterprises, with 4.2 billion in profit, up 39% and 31.2% respectively. At the end of 2011, average asset-liability ratio of airlines was 76.5%, down 2.2 percentage points from the previous year. The industry-wide passenger-kilometer revenue was 0.68 yuan/passenger-km, up 0.05 yuan/passenger-km from the last year; and the revenue for cargo and mail was 1.86 yuan/ton-km, practically flat with the last year.

Operating Quality Improved

The flight delay rectification campaign delivered good results. Airlines' responsibility for release, air traffic control, airport and fuel suppliers' responsibility for normal flight assurance and regulatory bodies' responsibility for coordinating and supervising flight operations were clarified. The air traffic management system carried out the Eliminating Congestion and Assuring Smoothness campaign to enhance traffic management for the Beijing-Shanghai and Beijing-Guangzhou routes. A permanent coordinating body was created for flight operations. The collaboration mechanism and communication mechanism for massive flight delays were established and improved, with focus placed on the excessive waiting time on board. In 2011, the average flight punctuality rate was 77.15% nationwide, up 2.2 percentage points from the previous year; the flight punctuality rate for Beijing-Shanghai and Beijing-Guangzhou routes increased by 30 and 11 percentage points respectively. Flight delay services were markedly improved and passenger satisfaction was increased.

ATM's operation and management was enhanced. The capacity of four busy airports in Beijing, Nanjing, Chongqing and Urumqi was adjusted to add a total of 2 700 slots a week. The lower limit for the upper control area in Beijing and Shanghai was adjusted. The Beijing Area Control Center successfully took over the upper airspace in Ji'nan, realizing the first cross-regional handover of upper airspace control in China's civil aviation industry. The airspace structure for main airports and selected main routes in Northern China was optimized significantly. Separation of inbound and outbound flights at busy airports in Zhengzhou, Qingdao, Chongqing and Hangzhou was generally completed. Energy conservation and emission reduction were carried out by straightening routes and using temporary routes. The flight distance was shortened by 12.96 million km in the year, reducing 220 000 tons of carbon dioxide emissions and cutting 530 million yuan of fuel cost.

Major and Emergency Transport Tasks Fulfilled

In 2011, China's civil aviation industry made swift emergency transport arrangements during the social turmoil in such countries as Egypt and Libya and after the massive earthquake in Japan that triggered tsunami and nuclear radiation accidents. In the Egyptian turbulence late in January, 8 airplanes were dispatched within 48 hours to bring back 1 796 Chinese citizens. After the Libya situation deteriorated, 182 charter flights were organized to bring back 26 240 Chinese citizens. After the massive earthquake hit the northeastern Japan and triggered nuclear leaks on March 11, 66 500 Chinese citizens were carried back to China in less than 10 days. The three massive emergency air transport tasks to evacuate Chinese citizens were unprecedented in China's civil aviation history, manifesting the national strength and projecting a good image of China's civil aviation. In addition, major transport tasks were all fulfilled for the International Horticultural Expo 2011 Xi'an, the 26th Summer Universiade, the Celebration of the 60th anniversary of peaceful liberation of Tibet, the China-Eurasia Expo and the Summer Davos in Dalian.

New Steps Forward in Restructuring and Reform

Large airlines including Air China, China Eastern Airlines and China Southern Airlines and large airports including those of Beijing, Shanghai, Guangzhou and Chengdu actively sought strategic transformation, stepped up their efforts to establish aviation hubs and improved air route networks. Mergers and reorganizations were pushed forward. China Eastern Airlines reorganized the former China Cargo Airlines, Shanghai Airlines Cargo and Great Wall Airlines into a new China Cargo Airlines; Air China and Cathay Pacific put up the joint venture of the new Air China Cargo. Fleet structure was improved to reduce aircraft types. The new Yantai Airport made progress in the pilot reform of the management model. The market management reform was deepened to implement online management and information disclosure of domestic traffic rights and flights. The price and charge reform was advanced, with the domestic transport price reform plan, the air traffic control charge reform plan and the consolidated airport charge plan formulated. China exempted imported jet fuel from customs duties. China National Aviation Fuel completed the corporate system reform. CAAC and its subordinate entities stepped up the personnel reform by promoting competitive promotion, job rotation and secondment on a full scale.

New Progress in Infrastructure Development, Science and Technolgy and Education

The whole industry completed 69 billion yuan of fixed-asset investment in infrastructure development, including 46 billion yuan of investment in airport construction. Seven airports of Guangdong Jieyang Chaoshan (relocated), Gansu Zhangye and Jinchang, Inner Mongolia Aershan and Bayannur, Tibet Rikaze and Xinjiang Kuche (relocated) were completed and put in service, increasing the number of transport airports to 180 nationwide. The new Kunming airport was largely completed and the expansions of Nanchang and Changsha airports were completed. The new Beijing airport made great progress in preparatory work, within an agreement reached among CAAC, Beijing Municipality and the air force. 1.8 billion yuan was invested in air traffic management. Radar control projects proceeded smoothly for major routes in eastern and western parts of China.

The strategy of education- and talent-driven industry development was implemented. CAAC prepared and issued the Mid and Long-term Plan for Human Resource Development in Civil Aviation Industry (2010-2020) for the first time. Colleges and universities continued to expand the school size and optimize the discipline portfolio. Flight colleges recruited a much larger number of students, ranking among the top few worldwide. On-the-job training of specialists and managers was enhanced to improve overall competency of employees. The civil aviation research platform was further developed, with focus placed on researches relating to the strategy of building a country with a strong civil aviation and the strategy of sustained safety. 11 civil aviation research bases were accepted. 68 research findings were certified and three projects were awarded the First Prize for Civil Aviation Technology Advancement. Cultural development was vigorously pushed forward, with new progress made in the research and practice in the field of industry culture, corporate culture, safety culture and service culture.

2012 is a critical year of the 12th Five-Year Plan period. The overall requirements for civil aviation work identified by CAAC in 2012 are as follows: we should earnestly act upon the guiding principles of the 17th CPC National Congress, the 5th and 6th plenary sessions of the 17th CPC National Congress and the Central Economic Work Meeting; focus closely on the theme of scientific development and the main thrust of transforming development model, we should persistently combine fulfillment of responsibilities with enhancement of supervision to ensure sustained safety of flights and aviation security; combine market development with capacity expansion and efficiency enhancement to promote steady and rapid development of civil aviation; combine reform and innovation, restructuring, research- and education-driven industry development and culture development to further improve quality and efficiency of development, so as to better serve the eco-social development and opening up and embrace the 18th CPC National Congress with outstanding achievements.

Major expectations for the development of civil aviation in 2012 are as follows: 63.2 billion ton-km of total transport turnover, 320 million people for passenger traffic, and 5.78 million tons of cargo and mail turnover, up 10.1%, 10.3% and 4.7% respectively from 2011; 500 000 hours of flight for general aviation, up 10% from 2011, including 370 000 hours of training and other flights and 130 000 hours of commercial flight, up 7.3% and 18% respectively from 2011; and 158.5 billion yuan in fixed-assets investment, including 75 billion yuan in infrastructure investment.

Major objectives for the safety of civil aviation in 2012 are as follows: prevention of major transport flight accidents; prevention of hijacking, aircraft bombing and aviation security accidents; a maximum of 0.3 for the rate of general aviation accident per 10 000 aircraft movements; prevention of major aviation ground accidents and major aircraft maintenance accidents; and a maximum of 0.5 for the rate of transport flight incident per 10 000 hours.

2011年民航行业发展统计公报（摘要）

一、运输航空

2011 年，民航运输发展稳中向好，实现了“十二五”时期的良好开局。

（1）运输总周转量 2011 年，全行业完成运输总周转量 577.44 亿吨公里，比上年增加 38.99 亿吨公里，增长 7.2%，其中旅客周转量 403.53 亿吨公里，比上年增加 43.98 亿吨公里，增长 12.2 %；货邮周转量 173.91 亿吨公里，比上年减少 4.99 亿吨公里，减少 2.8%。

2011 年，国内航线完成运输周转量 380.61 亿吨公里，比上年增加 35.13 亿吨公里，增长 10.2%，其中港澳台航线完成 12.64 亿吨公里，比上年增加 1.05 亿吨公里，增长 9.1%；国际航线完成运输周转量 196.84 亿吨公里，比上年增加 3.87 亿吨公里，增长 2.0%。

（2）旅客运输量 2011 年，全行业完成旅客运输量 29 317 万人次，比上年增加 2 548 万人次，增长 9.5%。国内航线完成旅客运输量 27 199 万人次，比上年增加 2 361 万人次，增长 9.5%，其中港澳台航线完成 760 万人次，比上年增加 88 万人次，增长 13.1%；国际航线完成旅客运输量 2 118 万人次，比上年增加 187 万人次，增长 9.7%。

（3）货邮运输量 2011 年，全行业完成货邮运输量 557.5 万吨，比上年降低 1.0%。国内航线完成货邮运输量 379.4 万吨，比上年增长 2.4%，其中港澳台航线完成 21 万吨，比上年降

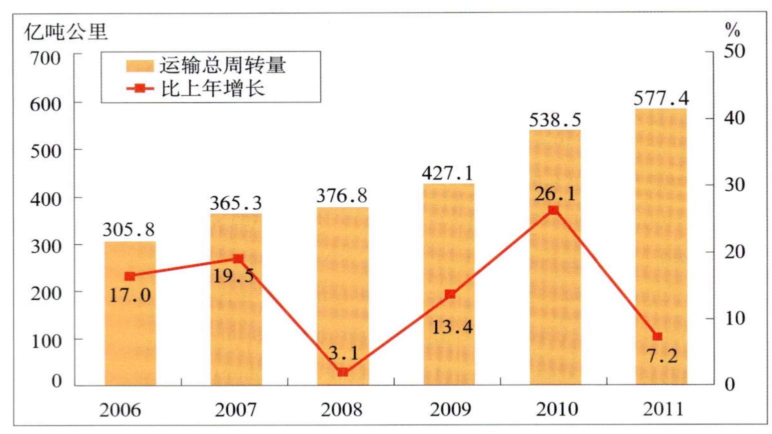

图1 2006—2011年民航运输总周转量

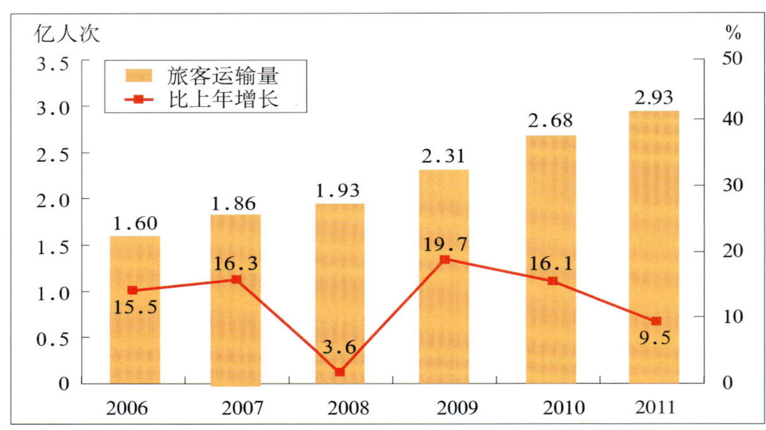

图2 2006—2011年民航旅客运输量

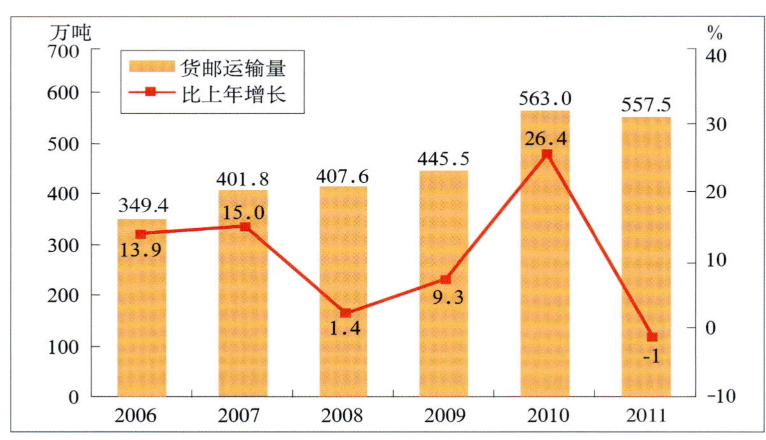

图3 2006—2011年民航货邮运输量

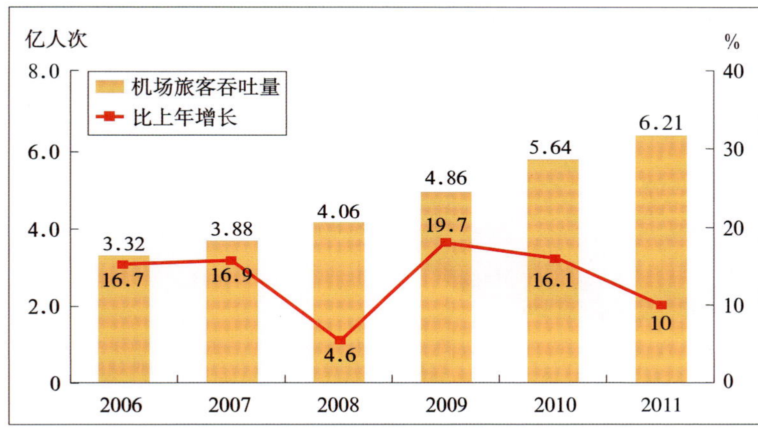

图4 2006—2011年民航运输机场旅客吞吐量

低 3.0%；国际航线完成货邮运输量 178.0 万吨，比上年降低 7.6%。

（4）机场业务量 2011 年，全国民航运输机场完成旅客吞吐量 6.21 亿人次，比上年增长 10.0%。

其中：2011 年东部地区完成旅客吞吐量 3.65 亿人次，东北地区完成旅客吞吐量 0.38 亿人次，中部地区完成旅客吞吐量 0.59 亿人次，西部地区完成旅客吞吐量 1.59 亿人次。

2011 年全国运输机场完成货邮吞吐量 1 157.8 万吨，比上年增长 2.5%。

其中：2011 年东部地区完成货邮吞吐量 905.98 万吨，东北地区完成货邮吞吐量 42.28 万吨，中部地区完成货邮吞吐量 47.47 万吨，西部地区完成货邮吞吐量 162.04 万吨。

2011 年，全国运输机场完成起降架次 597.97 万架次，比上年增长 8.1%。

2011 年，年旅客吞吐量 100 万人次以上的运输机场 53 个，其中北京、上海和广州三大城市机场旅客吞吐量占全部机场旅客吞吐量的 31.9%。

表 1 2011 年旅客吞吐量 100 万人次以上的机场数量

单位：个

年旅客吞吐量	机场数量	比上年增加	吞吐量占全国比例（%）
1 000万人次以上	21	5	75.1
100万~1 000万人次	32	−3	20.1

2011 年，年货邮吞吐量 1 万吨以上的运输机场 47 个，其中北京、上海和广州三大城市机场货邮吞吐量占全部机场货邮吞吐量的 54.9%。

表2 2011年货邮吞吐量万吨以上的机场数量

单位：个

年货邮吞吐量	机场数量	比上年增加	吞吐量占全国比例（%）
10 000吨以上	47	0	98.6

2011 年，北京首都机场完成旅客吞吐量 0.79 亿人次，位列亚洲第一，世界第二；上海浦东机场完成货邮吞吐量 308.5 万吨，位列世界第三。

（5）运输机队 截至 2011 年底，民航全行业运输飞机期末在册架数 1 764 架，比上年增加 167 架。

（6）机场服务能力 截至 2011 年底，我国共有颁证运输机场 180 个，比上年增加 5 个。2011 年新增机场分别为西藏日喀则机场、内蒙古阿尔山伊尔施机场和巴彦淖尔天吉泰机场、甘肃金昌金川机场和张掖甘州机场。另外，迁建完成了库车龟兹机场和揭阳潮汕机场，原库车老机场、汕头外砂机场停止使用。

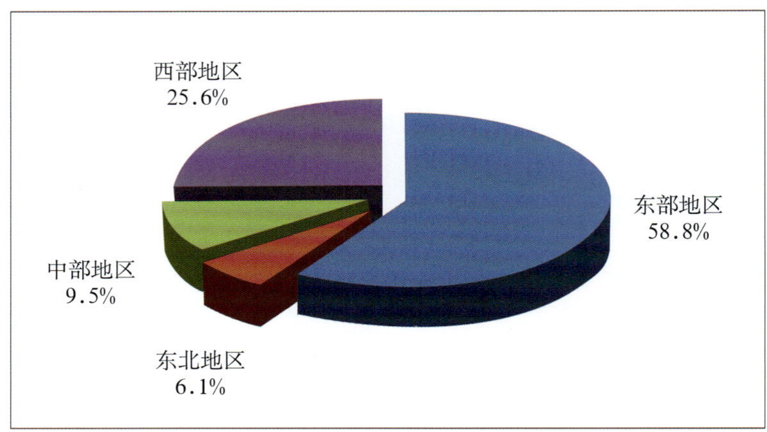

图5 2011年机场旅客吞吐量按地区分布

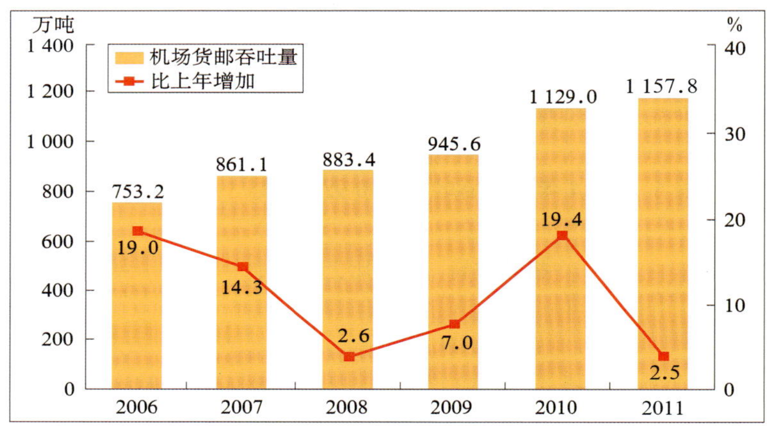

图6 2006—2011年民航运输机场货邮吞吐量

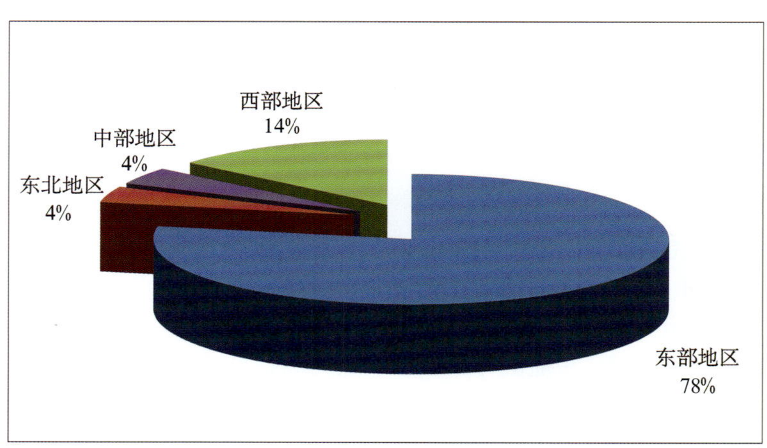

图7 2011年机场货邮吞吐量按地区分布

表3 2011年各地区运输机场数量

单位：个

地区	运输机场数量	占全国比例（%）
全国（不含港澳台）	180	100.00
其中：东北地区	19	10.56
东部地区	46	25.56
西部地区	90	50.00
中部地区	25	13.89

（7）航线网络 截至2011年底，我国共有定期航班航线2 290条，按重复距离计算的航线里程为512.77万公里，按不重复距离计算的航线里程为349.06万公里。

表4 2011年我国定期航班条数及里程

指标（单位）	数 量
航线条数（条）	2 290
国内航线	1 847
其中：港澳台航线	91
国际航线	443
按重复距离计算的航线里程（万公里）	512.77
国内航线	318.00
其中：港澳台航线	13.57
国际航线	194.77
按不重复距离计算的航线里程（万公里）	349.06
国内航线	199.62
其中：港澳台航线	13.51
国际航线	149.44

注：上表数据因四舍五入原因存在与分项合记不等的情况。

截至2011年底，定期航班国内通航城市175个（不含香港、澳门、台湾），定期航班通航香港的内地城市45个，通航澳门的内地城市14个，通航台湾的大陆城市37个。

（8）对外关系 截至2011年底，我国与其他国家或地区签订双边航空运输协定114个，比2010年底增加2个。其中：亚洲43个国家，非洲23个国家，欧洲35个国家，美洲8个国家，大洋洲4个国家，地区组织1个。

（9）运输航空（集团）公司生产 截至2011年底，我国共有运输航空公司47家，按不同类别划分：国有控股公司38家，民营和民营控股公司9家；全货运航空公司11家；中外合资航空公司16家；上市公司5家。

中航集团完成飞行小时154.9万小时，完成运输总周转量181.8亿吨公里，比上年增加3.7%，完成旅客运输量0.78亿人次，比上年增加8.1%，完成货邮运输量174.7万吨，比上年降低3.0%。

东航集团完成飞行小时130.1万小时，完成运输总周转量137.7亿吨公里，比上年增加1.2%，完成旅客运输量0.69亿人次，比上年增加5.9%，完成货邮运输量149.7万吨，比上年降低9.2%。

南航集团完成飞行小时150.7万小时，完成运输总周转量144.7亿吨公里，比上年增加10.4%，完成旅客运输量0.81亿人次，比上年增加5.5%，完成货邮运输量113.5万吨，比上年增加1.6%。

海航集团完成飞行小时68.5万小时，完成运输总周转量63.7亿吨公里，比上年增加11.6%，完成旅客运输量0.36亿人次，比上年增加16.6%，完成货邮运输量55.3万吨，比上年增加5.9%。

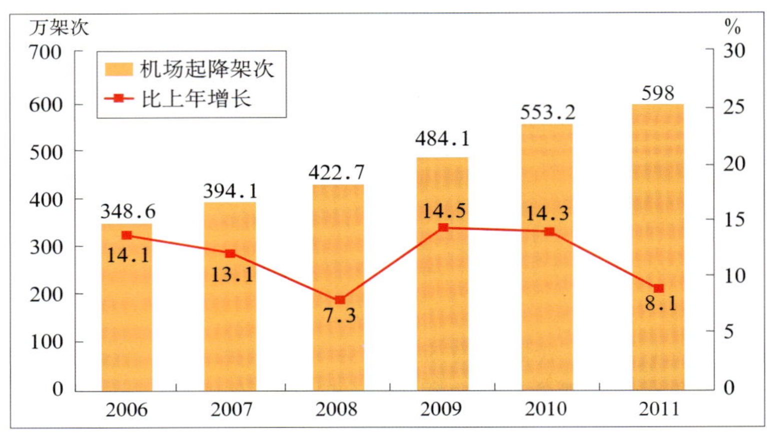

图8　2006—2011年民航运输机场起降架次

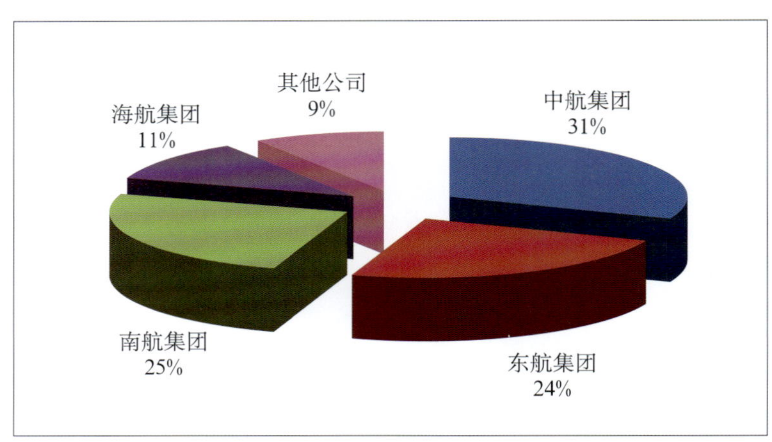

图9　2011年各航空（集团）公司运输总周转量比重

其他航空公司共完成飞行小时 55.3 万小时，完成运输总周转量 49.5 亿吨公里，比上年增加 26.9%，完成旅客运输量 0.30 亿人次，比上年增加 28%，完成货邮运输量 64.4 万吨，比上年增加 18.8%。

二、通用航空

（1）作业时间　2011 年，全行业完成通用航空生产作业飞行 50.27 万小时，比上年增长 28.5%。其中：工业航空作业完成 5.67 万小时，比上年减少 13.4%；农林业航空作业完成 3.32 万小时，比上年增长 11.9%；其他通用航空作业完成 41.29 万小时，比上年增长 39.4%。

（2）通用航空企业　截至 2011 年底，获得通用航空经营许可证的通用航空企业 123 家，其中，华北地区 33 家，中南地区 23 家，华东地区 22 家，东北地区 15 家，西南地区 13 家，西北地区 11 家，新疆地区 6 家。

（3）机队规模　截至 2011 年底，通用航空企业期末在册航空器总数达到 1 124 架，其中教学训练用飞机 303 架。

三、运输效率、经济效益与运输收入水平

（1）运输效率　2011 年，全行业在册运输飞机平均日利用率为 9.26 小时，比上年降低 0.09 小时。其中，大中型飞机平均日利用率为 9.71 小时，比上年降低 0.05 小时，小型飞机平均日利用率为 4.75 小时，比上年降低 0.4 小时。2011 年，正班客座率平均为 81.8%，比上年提高 1.6 个百分点。

2011 年，正班载运率平均为 72.0%，比上年提高 0.4 个百分点。

表5　2011年正班客座率和正班载运率

指　标	指标值(%)	比上年增长(%)
正班客座率	81.8	1.6
国内航线	83.2	2.2
其中：港澳台航线	76.7	1.8
国际航线	76.3	-0.8
正班载运率	72.0	0.4
国内航线	74.0	1.6
其中：港澳台航线	63.5	-0.2
国际航线	68.5	-1.8

（2）经济效益　2011年，全行业累计实现营业收入5 001亿元，比上年增长21.2%，利润总额363亿元，同比下降13.9%。其中，航空公司实现营业收入3 532亿元，比上年增长17.9%，利润总额278亿元，同比下降17.7%；机场实现营业收入498亿元，同比增长15.7%，利润总额43亿元，同比下降16.8%；保障企业实现营业收入971亿元，同比增长39%，利润总额42亿元，同比增长31.2%。2011年，民航全行业应缴税金208亿元，比2010年增长31.7%。

（3）运输收入水平　2011年，全行业运输收入水平为5.83元/吨公里，同比增加0.56元/吨公里。其中国内航线（不含港澳台航线）6.91元/吨公里，同比增加0.69元/吨公里；港澳台航线7.58元/吨公里，同比增加0.08元/吨公里；国际航线3.68元/吨公里，同比增加0.21元/吨公里。

国内航线（不含港澳台航线）客运收入水平为7.74元/吨公里，同比增加0.72元/吨公里；港澳台航线客运收入水平为8.37元/吨公里，同比减少0.06元/吨公里；国际航线客运收入水平为6.59元/吨公里，同比增加0.08元/吨公里。

国内航线（不含港澳台航线）货邮收入水平为1.93元/吨公里，同比增加0.22元/吨公里；港澳台航线货邮收入水平为4.56元/吨公里，同比减少0.1元/吨公里；国际航线货邮收入水平为1.77元/吨公里，同比减少0.08元/吨公里。

全行业客公里收入水平为0.68元/客公里，同比增加0.05元/客公里。其中，国内航线（不含港澳台航线）0.70元/客公里，同比增加0.07元/客公里；港澳台航线0.75元/客公里，同比减少0.01元/客公里；国际航线0.59元/客公里，与上年基本持平。

四、固定资产投资

2011年，民航基本建设和技术改造投资687.7亿元，比上年增长6.4%。

基本建设和技术改造投资按系统划分如下。

（1）机场建设　2011年，机场系统完成固定资产投资总额495.4亿元，比上年增长12.2%。重点建设项目19个，其中：竣工项目有南昌昌北机场扩建工程、长沙黄花机场扩建工程、昆明新机场等工程；续建项目有合肥新机场、杭州萧山机场扩建工程、深圳宝安机场扩建工程、成都双流机场扩建工程、贵阳龙洞堡机场扩建工程、拉萨贡嘎机场扩建工程、西安咸阳机场扩建工程、西宁曹家堡机场扩建工程等；新开工项目有沈阳桃仙机场航站区扩建工程、浦东机场飞行区扩建工程、南京禄口机场扩建工程、南宁机场扩建工程等。

（2）空管建设　2011年，空管系统完成固定资产投资18亿元，比上年减少5.3%。重点建设项目6个，其中：续建项目有成都区域管制中心、西安区域管制中心等；新开工项目有乌鲁木齐区域管制中心等。

（3）其他方面　2011年，民航其他系统完成固定资产投资总额174.3亿元，比上年减少6.3%。其中：民航信息系统建设投资7.5亿元，民航科研、教育系统投资24.3亿元，民航安全保卫系统投资2.2亿元，民航油料系统投资9.3亿元，民航机务维修系统投资9亿元，运输服务系统投资56.2亿元，公共设施系统投资13.3亿元，其他系统投资52.5亿元。（以上数据截止日期为2011年11月底）

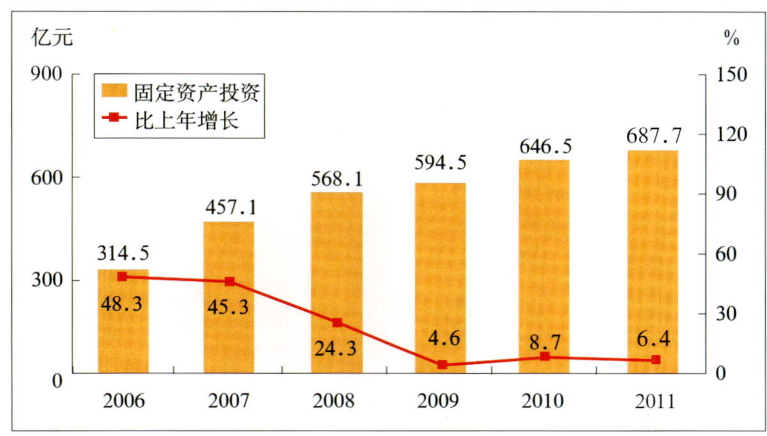

图10　2006—2011年民航基本建设和技术改造投资额

2011 Statistical Bulletin on the Development of China Civil Aviation Industry (Summary)

I. Transport Aviation

In 2011, civil air transport witnessed stable development and won a good start for the 12th Five-Year Plan period.

1) Total Air Traffic. In 2011, the whole industry completed a total air traffic of 57.744 billion tonne-km, an increase of 3.899 billion tonne-km or 7.2% over that of the previous year, of which 40.353 billion tonne-km were for passengers, an increase of 4.398 billion tonne-km or 12.2% over that of the previous year, and 17.391 billion tonne-km for cargo and mail, a decrease of 499 million tonne-km or 2.8% over that of the previous year.

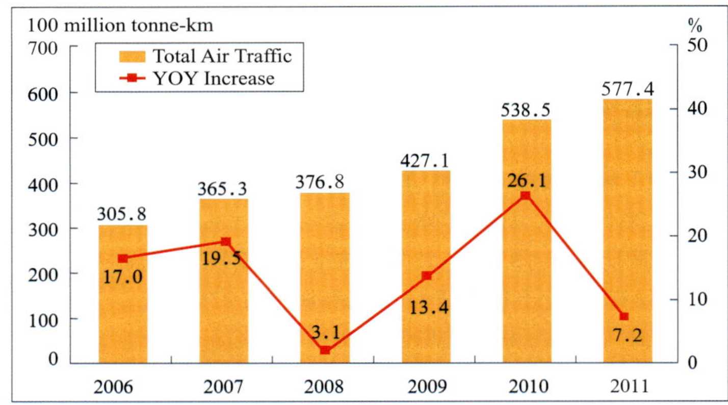

Figure1. Total Air Traffic of Civil Air Transport 2006—2011

In 2011, domestic air routes witnessed a transport turnover of 38.061 billion tonne-km, an increase of 3.513 billion tonne-km or 10.2% over that of 2010, of which 1.264 billion tonne-km was for Hong Kong, Macao and Taiwan routes and 19.684 billion tonne-km for international routes, increasing by 105 million tonne-km or 9.1% and 387 million tonne-km or 2.0% respectively over that of the previous year.

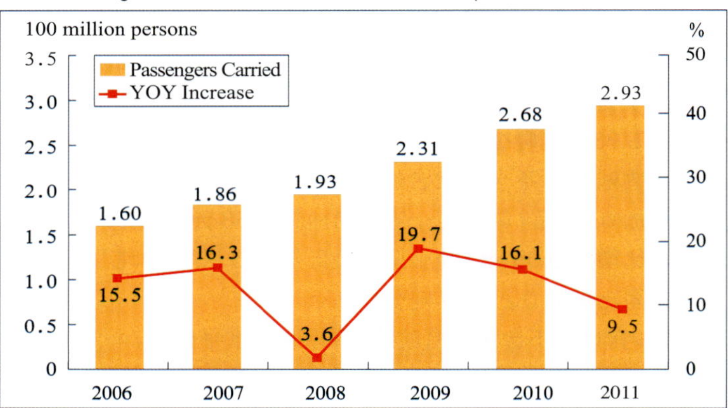

Figure 2. Passengers Carried by Civil Aviation 2006—2011

2) Passengers Carried. In 2011, the whole industry carried 293.17 million passengers, an increase of 25.48 million passengers or 9.5% over that of the previous year, of which 271.99 million were for domestic air routes, 7.6 million were for the air routes of Hong Kong, Macao and Taiwan and 21.18 million were for international air routes, increasing by 23.61 million or 9.5%, 880 000 or 13.1% and 1.87 million or 9.7% respectively over that of the previous year.

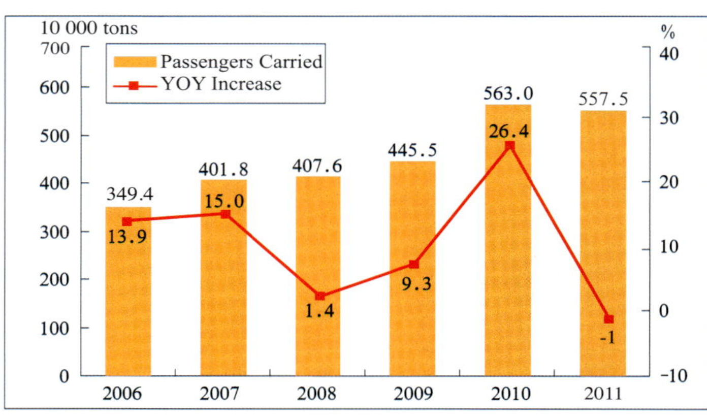

Figure 3. Cargo and Mail Carried by Civil Aviation 2006—2011

3) Cargo and Mail Carried. In 2011, the whole industry carried 5.575 million tons of cargo and mail, a decrease of 1.0% over that of the previous year, of which 3.794 million tons of cargo and mail were for domestic air routes, an increase of 2.4% over that of the previous year, and 210 000 tons were for the air routes of Hong Kong, Macao and Taiwan, and 1.78 million tons of cargo and mail were for international

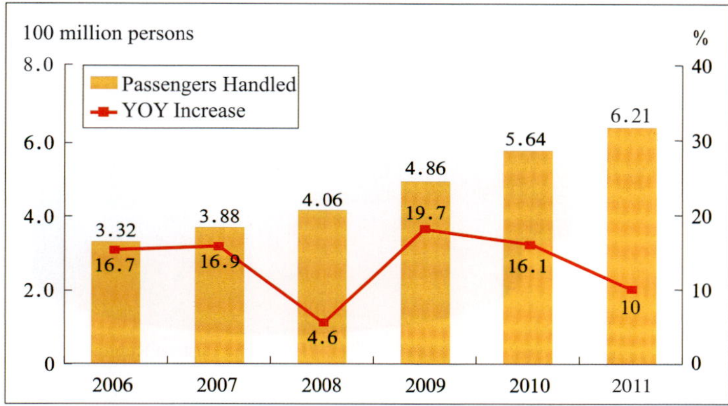

Figure 4. Passengers Handled at Civil Transport Airports 2006—2011

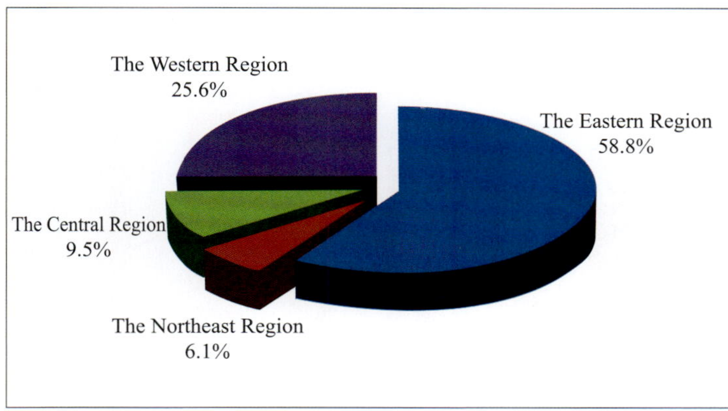

Figure 5. Passengers Handled by Regions in 2011

routes, decreasing by 3.0% and 7.6% respectively over that of the previous year.

4) Airport Turnover. In 2011, civil airports across the country handled 621 million passengers, an increase of 10.0% over that of the previous year.

In 2011, 365 million passengers were handled in the eastern region of China, 38 million in the northeast region, 59 million in the central region and 159 million in the western region.

In 2011, transport airports across the country handled 11.578 million tons of cargo and mail, an increase of 2.5% over that of the previous year.

In 2011, 9.059 8 million tons of cargo and mail were handled in the eastern region, 422 800 tons in the northeast region, 474 700 tons in the central region and 1.620 4 million tons in the western region.

In 2011, transport airports across the country supported 5.979 7 million aircraft movements, an increase of 8.1% over that of the previous year.

In 2011, there were 53 airports that handled more than 1 million passengers, and the passengers handled at airports in the three major cities namely Beijing, Shanghai and Guangzhou accounted for 31.9% of the total.

Table 1. The Number of Airports that Handled Over 1 Million Passengers in 2011

Passengers Handled Annually	Number of Airports	YOY Increase	% of the Total
10 million or above	21	5	75.1
1-10 million	32	-3	20.1

In 2011, there were 47 transport airports that handled more than 10 000 tons of cargo and mail, and the three major cities i.e. Beijing, Shanghai and Guangzhou made up 54.9% of the total.

Table 2. The Number of Airports that Handled Over 10 000 Tons of Cargo and Mail in 2011

Cargo & Mail Handled Annually	Number of Airports	YOY Increase	% of the Total
10 000 tons or above	47	0	98.6

In 2011, Beijing Capital International Airport handled 79 million passengers, ranking the first in Asia and the second in the world; and Shanghai Pudong Airport handled 3.085 million tons of cargo and mail, ranking the third in the world.

5) Transport Aircraft Fleet. By the end of 2011, the whole civil aviation industry had had 1 764 registered transport aircraft, adding 167 to those of the previous year.

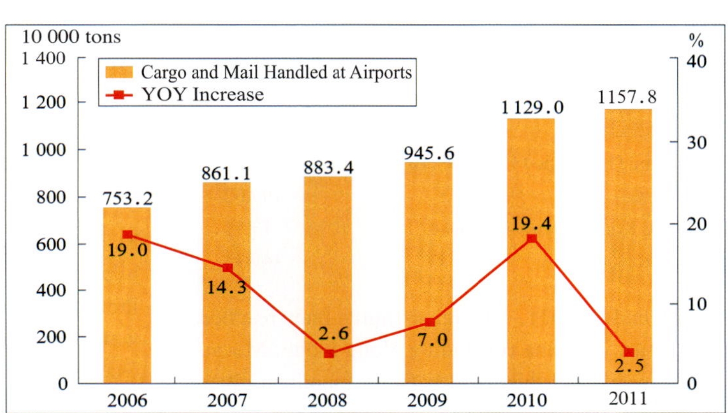

Figure 6. Cargo and Mail Handled at Civil Transport Airports 2006—2011

6) Airport Service Capability. By the end of 2011, China had had a total of 180 certified transport airports, adding 5 to those of the previous year. Airports added in 2011 were Tibet Rigaze Airport, Aershan Airport and Bayannur Tianjitai Airport in Inner Mongolia, and Jinchang Jinchuan Airport and Zhangye Airport in Gansu. In addition, Kuche Qiuci Airport and the Jieyang Chaoshan Airport were relocated, with the old Kuche Airport and Shantou Waisha Airport closed.

Table 3.The Number of Transport Airports by Regions in 2011

Region	Number of Transport Airports	% of the Total
Total (Excluding Hong Kong, Macao and Taiwan)	180	100
Northeast Region	19	10.56
Eastern Region	46	25.56
Western Region	90	50.00
Central Region	25	13.89

Note: The sum of percentages may be not equal to 100% due to the figure rounding.

7) Air Route Network. By the end of 2011, China had had 2 290 air routes for scheduled flights, and the route mileage amounted to 5.127 7 million km including overlapped distance, and 3.490 6 million km excluding overlapped distance.

Table 4. China Scheduled Flight Routes and Mileage in 2011

Item (Unit)	Number of Routes/ Mileage
Total Air Routes	2 290
Domestic	1 847
Hong Kong, Macao & Taiwan	91
International	443
Including Overlapped Distance (10 000 km)	512.77
Domestic	318.00
Hong Kong, Macao & Taiwan	13.57
International	194.77
Excluding Overlapped Distance (10 000 km)	349.06
Domestic	199.62
Hong Kong, Macao & Taiwan	13.51
International	149.44

By the end of 2011, scheduled flights had reached 175 cities in China (excluding Hong Kong, Macao and Taiwan), and there had been 45 mainland cities providing scheduled flights to Hong Kong, 14 to Macao and 37 to Taiwan.

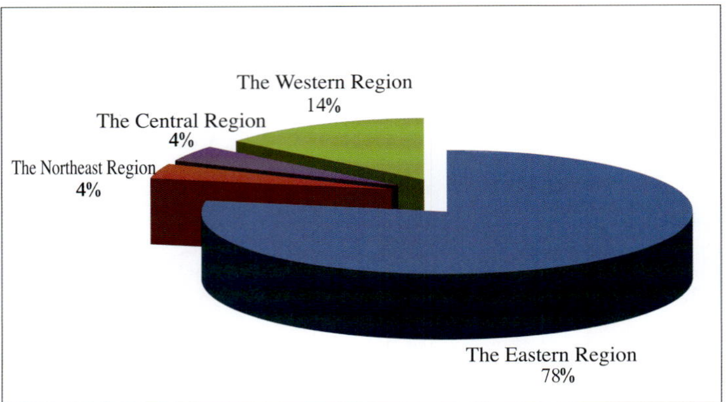

Figure 7. Cargo and Mail Handled by Regions

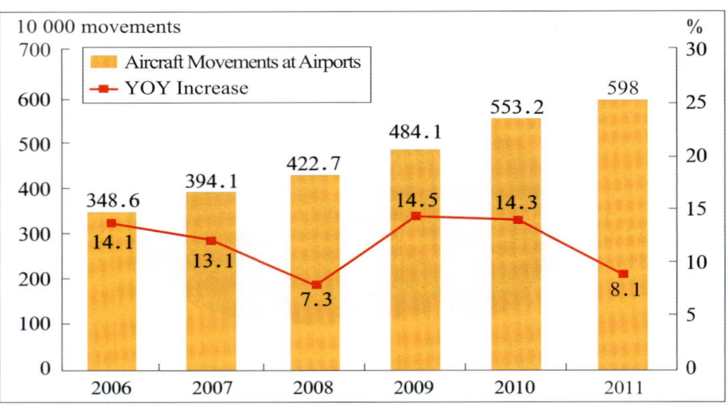

Figure 8. Aircraft Movements Supported at Civil Transport Airports 2006—2010

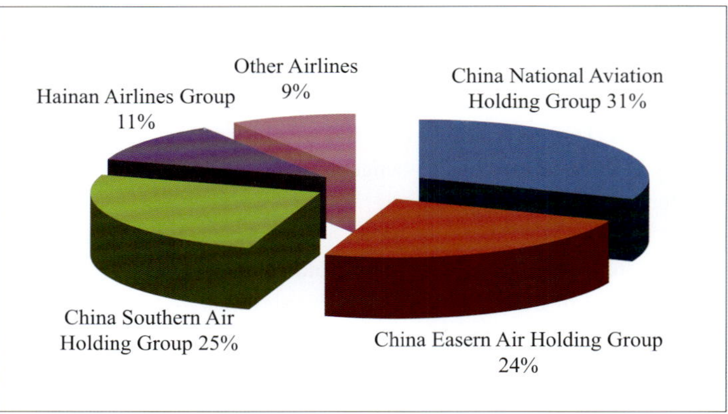

Figure 9. The Proportion of the Total Turnover of Airlines (Group) in 2011

8) Foreign Relations. By the end of 2011, China had signed bilateral air services agreements with 114 countries or regions, increasing by 2 over that at the end of 2010. Among them, 43 were in Asia, 23 in Africa, 35 in Europe, 8 in Americas, 4 in Oceania, and 1 regional organization.

9) Transport Airlines (Group) Performance. By the end of

2011, China had had 47 transport airlines, of which, as classified by categories, 38 were state-owned, 9 were private or private held, 11 were all-cargo carriers, 16 were joint-ventures, and 5 were publicly listed.

China National Aviation Holding Group completed 1.549 million flight hours and a total turnover of 18.18 billion tonne-km, an increase of 3.7% over that of the previous year. 78 million passengers were carried, an increase of 8.1% over that of the previous year and 1.747 million tons of cargo and mail were carried, a decrease of 3.0% over that of the previous year.

China Eastern Air Holding Group completed 1.301 million flight hours and a total turnover of 13.77 billion tonne-km, an increase of 1.2% over that of the previous year. 69 million passengers were carried, an increase of 5.9% over that of the previous year and 1.497 million tons of cargo and mail were carried, a decrease of 9.2% over that of the previous year.

China Southern Air Holding Group completed 1.507 million flight hours and a total turnover of 14.47 billion tonne-km, an increase of 10.4% over that of the previous year. 81 million passengers and 1.135 million tons of cargo and mail were carried, increasing by 5.5% and 1.6% respectively over that of the previous year.

Hainan Airlines Group completed 685 000 flight hours and a total turnover of 6.37 billion tonne-km, an increase of 11.6% over that of the previous year. 36 million passengers and 553 000 tons of cargo and mail were carried, increasing by 16.6% and 5.9% respectively over that of the previous year.

Other airlines completed 553 000 flight hours and a total turnover of 4.95 billion tonne-km, an increase of 26.9% over that of the previous year. 30 million passengers and 644 000 tons of cargo and mail were carried, increasing by 28% and 18.8% respectively over that of the previous year.

II. General Aviation

1) Flight Hours. In 2011, the whole industry completed 502 700 flight hours of general aviation operation, an increase of 28.5% over that of the previous year, among which, 56 700 were for industrial aviation, 33 200 for agriculture and forestry and 412 900 for other purposes, representing increases of -13.4%, 11.9% and 39.4% respectively over those of the previous year.

2) General Aviation Enterprises. By the end of 2011, 123 general aviation enterprises had been issued operation licenses, of which, 33 were in north China region, 23 in central and southern region, 22 in east China region, 15 in northeast region, 13 in southwest region, 11 in northwest region and 6 in Xinjiang region.

3) Aircraft Fleet Size. By the end of 2011, general aviation enterprises had had a total of 1 124 registered aircraft, of which 303 were used for teaching and training.

III. Transport Efficiency, Financial Performance and Transport Revenue

1) Transport Efficiency. In 2011, the average daily utilization rate for all registered transport aircraft of the industry was 9.26 hours, that for large and medium sized aircraft was 9.71 hours and that for small aircraft was 4.75 hours, 0.09, 0.05 and 0.4 hours less respectively than that of the previous year. In 2011, the average passenger load factor of scheduled flights was 81.8%, 1.6 percentage points higher than that of the previous year.

In 2011, the average load factor of scheduled flights was 72.0%, 0.4 percentage point higher than that of the previous year.

Table 5. Passenger Load Factor and Load Factor of Scheduled Flights in 2011

Item	Value (%)	Increase over the Previous Year (%)
Passenger Load Factor of Scheduled Flights	81.8	1.6
Domestic Routes	83.2	2.2
Hong Kong, Macao & Taiwan Routes	76.7	1.8
International Routes	76.3	- 0.8
Load Factor of Scheduled Flights	72.0	0.4
Domestic Routes	74.0	1.6
Hong Kong, Macao & Taiwan Routes	63.5	- 0.2
International Routes	68.5	- 1.8

2) Financial Performance. In 2011, the whole industry garnered a revenue of 500.1 billion yuan, an increase of 21.2% over that of the previous year, and realized a total profit of 36.3 billion yuan, a decrease of 13.9% over that of the previous year. Of the revenue, airlines recorded a revenue of 353.2 billion yuan, an increase of 17.9% over that of the previous year and realized a total profit of 27.8 billion yuan, a decrease of 17.7% over that of the previous year. Airports yielded a revenue of 49.8 billion yuan, an increase of 15.7% over that of the previous year, and realized a total profit of 4.3 billion yuan, a decrease of 16.8% over that of the previous year. Support enterprises yielded a revenue of 97.1 billion yuan, an increase of 39% over that of the previous year, and

realized a total profit of 4.2 billion yuan, an increase of 31.2% over that of the previous year. In 2011, taxes payable by the civil aviation industry were 20.8 billion yuan, an increase of 31.7% over that of 2010.

3) Transport Revenue. In 2011, the transport revenue of the whole industry was 5.83 yuan/tonne-km, an increase of 0.56 yuan/tonne-km over that of the previous year. The revenue on domestic routes (Hong Kong, Macao and Taiwan routes excluded) was 6.91 yuan/tonne-km; that on Hong Kong, Macao and Taiwan routes was 7.58 yuan/tonne-km and that on international routes was 3.68 yuan/tonne-km, increasing by 0.69 yuan/tonne-km, 0.08 yuan/tonne-km and 0.21 yuan/tonne-km respectively over those of the previous year.

The passenger transport revenue on domestic routes (Hong Kong, Macao and Taiwan routes excluded) was 7.74 yuan/tonne-km, that on Hong Kong, Macao and Taiwan routes was 8.37 yuan/passenger-km and that on international routes was 6.59 yuan/tonne-km, an increase of 0.72 yuan/tonne-km, -0.06 yuan/tonne-km and 0.08 yuan/tonne-km respectively over those of the previous year.

The cargo and mail transport revenue on domestic routes (Hong Kong, Macao and Taiwan routes excluded) was 1.93 yuan/tonne-km, that on Hong Kong, Macao and Taiwan routes was 4.56 yuan/tonne-km and that on international routes was 1.77 yuan/tonne-km, an increase of 0.22 yuan/tonne-km, -0.1 yuan/tonne-km and -0.08 yuan/tonne-km respectively over those of the previous year.

The revenue/passenger-km of the whole industry was 0.68 yuan, an increase of 0.05 yuan/passenger-km over that of the previous year. The revenue/passenger-km on domestic routes (Hong Kong, Macao and Taiwan routes excluded) was 0.70 yuan, that on Hong Kong, Macao and Taiwan routes was 0.75 yuan and that on international routes was 0.59 yuan, representing increases of 0.07 yuan/passenger-km, -0.01 yuan/passenger-km and zero respectively over those of the previous year.

IV. Investment in Fixed Assets

In 2011, 68.77 billion yuan was invested in civil aviation infrastructure and technical upgrading, an increase of 6.4% over that of the previous year.

Investments in infrastructure and technical upgrading were systematically classified as follows:

1) Airport Construction. In 2011, the airport system made a total investment of 49.54 billion yuan in fixed assets, an increase of 12.2% over that of the previous year. There were 19 key construction projects. The completed projects were the expansion of the Nanchang Changbei Airport, the expansion of the Changsha Huanghua Airport and the new Kunming Airport, etc.; the ongoing projects were Hefei new Airport, the expansion of the Hangzhou Xiaoshan Airport, the expansion of Shenzhen Bao'an Airport, the expansion of the Chengdu Shuangliu Airport, the expansion of the Guiyang Longdongbao Airport, the expansion of the Lhasa Gonggar Airport, the expansion of Xi'an Xianyang Airport and the expansion of Xining Caojiabao Airport, etc.; and the newly commenced projects were the expansion of the terminal area of the Shenyang Taoxian Airport, the expansion of the aircraft movement area of Pudong Airport, the expansion of Nanjing Lukou Airport and the expansion of Nanning Airport, etc.

2) ATM Construction. In 2011, the ATM system made an investment of 1.8 billion yuan in fixed assets, a decrease of 5.3% over that of the previous year. There were six key projects, of which the ongoing projects included Chengdu area control center and Xi'an area control center, etc.; and the newly commenced projects included Urumqi area control center, etc.

3) Investment in Other Areas. In 2011, other systems in the civil aviation industry made a total investment of 17.43 billion yuan in fixed assets, a decrease of 6.3% over that of the previous year. Of the total, 750 million yuan was used in the construction of information system, 2.43 billion yuan in scientific research and education system, 220 million yuan in aviation security system, 930 million yuan in aviation fuel system, 900 million yuan in aircraft maintenance system, 5.62 billion yuan in transport service system, 1.33 billion yuan in public facilities system and 5.25 billion yuan in other systems. (Statistics in this bulletin were by the end of November 2011.)

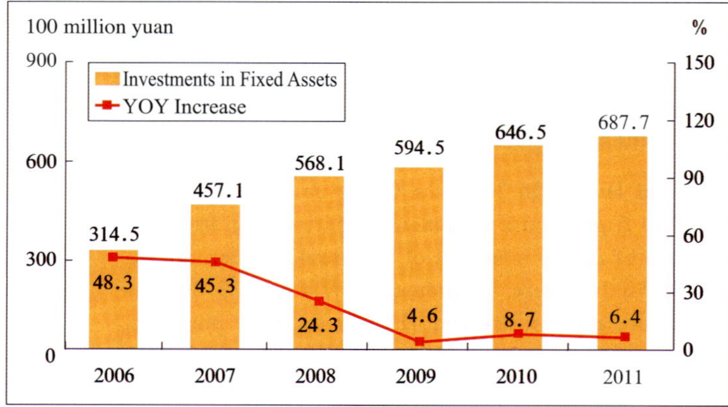

Figure 10. Investments in Civil Aviation Infrastructure and Technical Upgrading 2006—2011

2011年度中国民用航空政策报告
（摘要）

第一部　改革与开放

一、深化改革和调整结构

2011年，民航局紧紧围绕科学发展的主题和转变发展方式的主线，采取切实措施，深化改革，调整结构，实现了航空运输稳中向好的发展。

民航局引导国航、东航、南航等大型航空公司和北京、上海、广州、成都等大型机场积极实施战略转型，加快构建航空枢纽和完善航线网络。积极推进联合重组，东航将原中货航、上货航、长城航重组为新的中货航，国航与国泰合资成立新的国货航。改善机队结构，减少机型种类。改善企业资本结构，航空公司资产负债率逐步下降。烟台新机场管理模式改革试点工作取得进展。深化市场管理改革，实行国内航权和航班网上管理和信息公开。积极推进价格和收费改革，研究制定国内运价改革方案，以及空管收费改革方案和机场收费并轨方案。国家对进口航空煤油免征关税。中航油完成了公司制改革。民航局和所属单位干部人事制度改革力度加大，竞争性选拔全面铺开，交流轮岗和挂职锻炼普遍推行。

二、优化监管机构设置，增强监管力量

为适应民航行业持续快速发展和加强民航安全监管工作的实际需要，根据中央机构编制委员会办公室的批复，民航局在温州、青岛、桂林、三亚、丽江、喀什6个城市增设民航安全监督管理局。

温州、青岛、桂林、三亚监管局的管辖范围为：按照民航华东、中南地区管理局授权，负责其所在市行政区域内的民航行业管理；丽江监管局的管辖范围为：按照民航西南地区管理局授权，负责丽江、迪庆、大理市（州）行政区域内的民航行业管理；喀什监管局的管辖范围为：按照民航新疆管理局授权，负责喀什、克孜勒苏柯尔克孜、和田地区（州）行政区域内的民航行业管理。

新增的6个监管局作为相关管理局的派出机构，隶属相关管理局领导。相关地区管理局可根据实际工作需要，授权相应的省会所在地监管局负责对温州、青岛、桂林、三亚、丽江监管局实施管理。

第二部分　法制建设

为加强民航法制工作，便于各单位更好地贯彻执行规章，提高工作效率，印发了《中国民用航空规章汇编》(2009—2010年卷)。本汇编收集了2009至2010年民用航空局发布并已向国务院法制办公室备案的各项规章。

其中包括民用航空安全信息管理规定（民航局令第194号）、大型飞机公共航空运输承运人运行合格审定规则（民航局令第195号）、中国民用航空应急管理规定（民航局令第196号）、民用航空飞行签派员执照管理规则（民航局令第197号）、民用航空情报工作规则（民航局令第198号）、民用航空情报员执照管理规则（民航局令第199号）、民用航空电信人员执照管理规则（民航局令第200号）、民用航空空中交通管制员执照管理规则（民航局令第201号）、民用航空气象人员执照管理规则（民航局令第202号）、民用航空气象探测环境管理办法（民航局令第203号）、民用航空空中交通管理运行单位安全管理规则（民航局令第204号）、《外商投资民用航空业规定》的补充规定（四）（民航局令第205号）、《外商投资民用航空业规定》的补充规定（五）（民航局令第206号）。

第三部分　安全监管

一、加强综合安全管理和重点监管

——督促落实安全生产主体责任。民航局下发《关于继续做好航空安全责任书签订工作的通知》，明确

运输航空公司对其分（子）公司所承担的安全责任以及子公司的安全主体责任，指导各地区管理局继续做好安全责任书的签订，持续监督辖区生产运行单位安全责任落实情况，通过逐级细化、分解安全生产指标，将主体责任落实到生产运行的各个环节，促进了安全考核评价体系的健全和完善，做到安全绩效与经营绩效相结合、过程管理与细节管理相结合、隐患治理与实际效果相结合，有力推动了各项安全工作的落实。

——明确运输机长职责。为进一步明确机长的有关职责，提高航空安全水平，民航局研究制定了《民用航空运输机长职责》。民用航空运输机长（以下简称机长）是依据中国民用航空规章取得航线运输驾驶员执照，并被航空运输企业聘为机长的飞行员。机长对当班机组负有管理责任，在其职权范围内发布的命令，民用航空器所载人员都应当执行。机长应当模范遵守并督促机组人员执行法律、法规、规章和标准，以及被批准或加入的国际公约。机长发现机组人员不适宜执行飞行任务的，为保证飞行安全，有权提出调整。机长发现民用航空器、机场气象条件等不符合规定，不能保证飞行安全的，有权拒绝起飞。飞行中，对于任何破坏民用航空器、扰乱民用航空器内秩序、危害民用航空器所载人员或者财产安全以及其他危及飞行安全的行为，在保证安全的前提下，机长有权采取必要的适当措施。机长在民用航空器遇险时，有权采取一切必要措施，并指挥机组人员和航空器上其他人员采取应急措施。在必须撤离遇险民用航空器的紧急情况下，首先组织旅客安全离开民用航空器；未经机长允许或旅客未完全撤离航空器的情况下，机组成员不得擅自离开民用航空器；机长应当最后离开民用航空器。

——规范飞行人员执照工作。为规范执照办理工作程序，统一标准，以及针对特定问题作出说明，民航局对《关于飞行人员执照有关问题的说明》（2008年7月14日）以及管理文件MD-FS-2003-03《关于飞行院校学生在学习期间申办执照有关问题的通知》（2003年12月26日）进行修订，明确适用于所有中国民用航空器驾驶员执照持有人及申请人的复杂飞机训练替代要求、增加执照记录页签注代码说明、明确何种监察员实施境外机型考试等内容。

——完善对民航委任代表的管理。根据《民用航空飞行标准委任代表和委任单位代表管理规定》（CCAR-183FS）的规定，民航局审核并委任了航空人员体检委任代表，要求各航空人员体检委任代表应严格按照有关规定履行委任职责，加强临床进修和体检业务培训。同时将中国民用航空局民用航空医学中心门诊部及民航西北航空医学体检中心两家体检委任单位代表信息进行变更。

2011年民航局批准了43名西南地区局方飞行签派检查委任代表，要求代表在局方航务监察员的监督下，按照航空规章要求履行飞行签派员执照考试、训练和技术检查等职责。

——修订机组人员英文水平偏离的限制。根据《大型飞机公共航空运输承运人运行合格审定规则》（CCAR-121），自2008年3月5日起，除经批准外，执照上未取得英语语言能力4级或以上签注的人员，不得在使用英语进行通信的航线上担任机组成员。民航局根据我国目前实际情况和国际民航组织相关要求，修订《使用英语通信的有关要求以及对CCAR-121.479的偏离限制》，新的要求是每个机组仅允许包含最多1名未达到英语4级的驾驶员；对于1960年（不含）以前出生人员，机组应配备至少2名达到英语4级以上机组成员，包括一名机长或者资深副驾驶；对于1960年（含）以后出生人员，应达到英语3级标准，且机组应配备至少2名达到英语4级以上机组成员，包括一名机长或者资深副驾驶。

——修订《民用航空安全检查人员定额定员（试行）》行业标准。近年来，随着民航事业高速发展，民航安检工作的要求和环境发生较大变化，原《民用航空安全检查人员定员定额》行业标准已不适应安检实际工作的需要。为进一步加强对安检工作的科学管理，保证空防安全，2011年民航局对原标准进行了修订。新标准明确规定了安检各岗位（不含管理岗位）设置及其基本定员标准和人员资质要求；为保障安全运行所需最低人员配备标准，各单位不得低于上述标准配备安检人员；人身安检通道劳动定额标准为保障安全运行最高标准，各单位要将单通道小时旅客通过量严格控制在该标准以内。民航局将对标准执行的有关情况进行监督检查，对违规单位按规定予以处理。

——修订《民用航空器事故征候标准》。按照轻重有别、宽严适度的原则，民航局于2011年完成了《民用航空器事故征候标准》修订工作。修订后的标准，完成了在严重事故征候上与ICAO的新版附件13中所列16项条款内容接轨；细化并严格规范了运输航空一般事故征候相关条款；加强了对运输航空公司强化安全管理、提高安全裕度的引导；同时还适当调整放宽了通航事故征候条款，以利于通航发展和训练飞行。

——规范民用航空重大安全事项挂牌督办及整改工作。依据《生产安全事故报告和调查处理条例》(国务院 493 令)和国务院《重大事故查处挂牌督办办法》中相关要求，民航局制定了《民用航空重大安全事项挂牌督办及整改工作暂行办法》。办法主要针对重特大安全隐患的挂牌督办和整改工作，所称民用航空重大安全事项为民用航空器事故、重大和特大安全生产事故隐患。办法明确了民航局负责对跨地区、有争议的或者长期难以解决的重特大安全隐患实施挂牌督办，民航各地区管理局负责对辖区内的重特大安全隐患实施挂牌督办。同时还对挂牌督办和整改工作程序进行了规定。

——制定《民航局安全监管行政约见暂行办法》。依据有关法律法规和《国务院关于进一步加强企业安全生产工作的通知》精神，民航局制定《民航局安全监管行政约见暂行办法》。明确了民航局可予以行政约见民航企事业单位的四种情形，以及行政约见程序，指出行政约见应至少包含以下内容：①指导民航行政相对方正确认识合法行为与非法行为的界限，并充分认识相关安全问题严重性；②明确不规范行为或违法行为的危害性及可能承担的法律责任；③提出整改要求；④视情宣布处理决定。同时，办法还统一了《民航局行政约见通知书(样例)》和《行政约见问题整改通知书(样例)》。

二、飞行标准管理

——制定飞行签派员训练机构合格审定程序。依据《大型飞机公共航空运输承运人运行合格审定规则》(CCAR-121)和《飞行签派员训练手册》(ICAO Doc 7192)，民航局制定了咨询通告《飞行签派员训练机构合格审定程序》，规定有关飞行签派员训练机构合格审定中民航局和地区管理局的职责、管理手册的要求、训练机构和人员的要求、训练机构合格证审定程序、训练大纲的要求、设施、设备和人员的要求以及记录保持的要求等，从而为承担 CCAR-121 部航空承运人飞行签派员训练的机构获得训练机构合格证提供指南。同时为监察员履行运行批准和监督检查职责提供指导。

——制定高性能多发飞机训练要求。为了使获得多发商用驾驶员执照和仪表登记并完成航线运输驾驶员执照理论培训后的飞行学员进入航空公司后适应高空、高速、多人制机组的现代商用飞机的运营，掌握大中型飞机的设备以及应对相应安全威胁，调整和培养飞行员的思维和行为。民航局发布相关咨询通告，明确规定相关的过渡性训练课程的进入条件、训练时间要求、飞行教员要求、航空知识训练、考试要求、训练证书要求等，并提供详细的高性能飞机训练考试标准，为考试提供指南。

——制定大型飞机公共航空运输卫生工作要求。该要求为大型公共航空运输的航空卫生工作提供了专业指导，明确合格证持有人、航空医师、机组成员各自的责任和义务，详细规定了合格证持有人、航空医师以及机组成员的基本要求；航空卫生管理手册的制定要求、航空卫生知识培训和健康指导、健康管理和疾病风险因素控制、机组人员履行职责时的健康管理、机组成员的配餐和用餐要求；同时对机组成员健康档案及医学资料的管理、信息报告、航空器环境卫生、航空食品安全、驻外地点的航空卫生保障、突发公共卫生事件应急处置等进行了规定。

——完善大型飞机公共航空运输机载应急医疗能力。为指导大型飞机公共航空运输承运人或合格证持有人及其代理人载客运行时配备机组应急医疗设备、制定机组成员在运行中对紧急医学事件的处置程序和训练大纲，实施紧急医学事件处置训练，民航局对大型飞机公共航空运输机载应急医疗设备配备和训练要求进行了规定，明确了了机载应急医疗设备的要求、管理、使用和政府监管，紧急医学事件处置训练的要求等。但是不要求合格证持有人及其代理人在载客运行时提供专业的应急医疗服务，紧急医学事件处置训练也不要求机组成员的应急医疗措施取代或者达到有资质的医疗专业人员的应急救护水平。

——继续强化对民用航空机场运行的管理。为提高民用航空全天候运行的安全水平，规范机场运行最低标准的制定与实施，与国际通行准则保持一致；为已建立仪表或目视飞行程序的民用机场及军民合用机场制定民用航空器使用的机场运行最低标准；为 CCAR-91、121、135 部航空运营人制定其运行最低标准和实施细则提供指南，民航局发布《民用航空机场运行最低标准制定与实施准则》，规定了飞机类别、目视运行的最低要求、起飞最低标准、I 类 PA、

APV、NPA、II 类 PA、III 类 PA 以及盘旋进近的最低标准；机场设备故障或降级对运行标准的影响以及对运营人和机组的飞行运行要求等。

——修订航空承运人运行中心（AOC）政策与标准。为了持续提高飞行安全水平，使承运人运行中心建设与机队、航线网络、运行规模的发展保持同步，优化管理要素，提高运行控制品质和驾驭风险的能力，民航局修订了《航空公司运行中心（AOC）的政策与标准》。详细规定了运行中心体系、人员要求、系统与设施、流程、设计、实施以及运行控制，为航空承运人运行中心的建设、运行与内部审计提供政策与指南，为民航局对航空承运人运行控制能力评估提供依据和指南。

——进一步加强对飞行签派工作的监督管理。改进飞行签派员资质能力是确保飞行运行持续安全重要工作内容之一，为加强对飞行签派工作的管理，民航局制定了航空承运人飞行签派员资质管理标准和签派资源管理训练大纲。详细规定了作为合格飞行签派员应当具备条件和标准，从飞行签派员养成、知识、技能和运行经历等多个方面作出了明确规定。为全面提升航空公司运行中心（AOC）能力和各岗位之间的共同协作，民航局提出了建立资源管理训练大纲的要求，详细规定了训练大纲的制定方法和训练要求，详细解释了 CCAR-121 部要求的合格签派员标准，为民航各级监管部门和航空公司提供了指导标准。

——加强对航材流通的管理。为了对 CCAR-121 规章条款进行进一步解释和说明，同时也为 CCAR-121 部航空运营人除湿租以外的航空器如何在使用和维修中确保航材的合法性、合格性提供相应的符合性方法和指导，民航局制定了相关咨询通告，详细规定航材的标识和文件、航材供应商的文件、航材采购合同的要求、航材的适航状况限制、可疑非经批准航材的识别和限制、航材租用和借用的要求、航材共享的要求以及航材分销商必须遵守的要求，并提供航材分销商评估大纲，为航材分销商的评估提供指导，以便航空运营人、有关机构或单位对航材分销商的评估和管理能够满足中国民航相关法规中关于航材适航性管理的要求。

——规范和完善维修工时管理。在民用航空器维修中，企业追求利益最大化和保障航空运行安全的矛盾使维修管理和维修人员面临越来越大的压力，而这种压力也是导致发生维修差错的诱因之一。过去 20 年的事故调查数据显示，维修差错导致的事故增加了 4 个百分点，而大部分维修差错都与维修工作时间不足和维修人员疲劳作业有关，因此维修工时管理和控制就成为了维修生产运行和控制中的一个重要组成部分。为此民航局研究制定了维修工时管理规定，对所有按照 CCAR-145 部批准的航空器和航空器部附件维修单位如何合理安排维修人员的工作时间和进行科学的维修工时管理提供具体要求和指导，以减少维修差错和保证维修工作质量，详细规定了维修人员的工作时间限制、标准工时的确定、维修过程控制以及维修工时资源的评估。

三、适航管理

——制定修改规章提高适航管理的法治化水平和管理能力。为保持我国适航标准与国际标准同步，防止国外不符合现行国际标准的发动机进入我国造成民用航空飞行隐患，配合国际民航组织安全审计和我国新支线飞机项目及大型商用飞机发动机项目的开展，民航局第二次修订《航空发动机适航规定》，新增加了发动机静承压件、发动机限寿件、发动机超扭试验、活塞发动机的涡轮增压器转子和获得早期 ETOPS 资格的设计和试验共 5 个条款内容；删除了第 33.14 条；更新了对发动机安装和使用说明手册、发动机额定值和使用限制、防火、耐用性、涡轮压气机风扇和涡轮增压器转子、发动机电气和电子控制系统、仪表连接、活塞发动机部件试验、燃油系统、润滑系统、持续转动、安全分析、吸鸟、持久试验、发动机超温试验、初次维修检查、涡轮发动机部件试验、分解检查和持续适航文件等条款的要求，共涉及 20 个条款。

为保持我国适航标准与国外适航标准在安全水平上的一致性，促进我国航空工业的健康发展，民航局对民用航空规章《运输类飞机适航标准》进行第四次修订，修订内容涵盖安装动力装置的防火要求、燃油箱系统设计评估，抑制可燃性，维修和检查的要求、起落架减震试验要求、液压系统适航标准、飞机运营限制规定和飞机飞行手册要求、驾驶舱设计的保安事项、刹车系统适航标准、1*g* 失速速度、空速指示系统要求、下层服务舱、隔热隔音材料的可燃性标准、材料强度性能和设计许用值要求等内容，涉及条款 154 条。

加强运输类飞机的持续适航和安全改进管理。长期以来，由于运营飞机在结构损伤、电气线路故障起火和燃油箱爆炸等方面存在的安全问题，国际民用航空业运营机队的持续适航安全受到了严重威胁。为保证我国民用航空运输安全，民航局提出适合我国国情的运输类飞机持续适航与安全改进措施，对电气线路互联系统、结构修理和改装的损伤容限资料以及燃油箱安全提出了强制要求，增加DAH对运输类飞机持续适航与安全改进的责任和作用，对保证运营机队在预防燃油箱爆炸、减少电气线路故障、保证结构完整性等方面起到重要作用。

——开展航空器型号合格审定、国籍登记管理、技术标准规定项目管理等适航管理工作。由于适航管理工作的深入发展，2002年第3次修订的《型号合格审定程序》的某些内容亟待修补以满足适航管理发展的需要，并与国际上主要的与民用航空产品型号合格审定相关的适航管理程序相协调。为了指导和规范民用航空器型号合格审定活动，民航局制定适用于民用航空器型号合格证、型号设计批准书的申请、颁发和管理的管理程序。

为规范航空器债权人向中国民用航空局申请注销民用航空器国籍的活动，民航局制定管理程序，规定了申请办理备案和注销的基本要求和限制条件、《不可撤销的注销登记和出口请求许可书》(简称《许可书》)的备案债务人申请对《许可书》进行备案的应当是在中华人民共和国登记注册的民用航空器、向适航审定司申请对《许可书》进行备案的程序以及依据《许可书》的注销登记程序。

针对目前较多中国民用航空技术标准规定(CTSO)项目在申请人提交申请时尚无对应CTSO标准的情况，民航局在《民用航空材料、零部件和机载设备的合格审定程序》基础上，对CTSO标准颁布及CTSO项目审定程序作出补充和修订。此外，为给欧洲航空安全局批准的欧洲技术标准规定项目批准书持有人申请CTSO项目批准书、以及给中国民用航空局批准的CTSO项目批准书授权持有者申请欧洲技术标准规定项目批准书提供指南，民航局还发布了《中国民用航空局和欧洲航空安全局就中国技术标准规定项目批准书和欧洲技术标准规定项目批准书的工作协调指南》(英文版)，明确了相关定义、审定程序和要求。

为保障国产飞机的验证试飞和大飞机型号合格审定，民航局发布管理文件，加强ARJ21-700飞机的审查组试飞队伍；同意将美国联邦航空局的咨询通告等文件作为C919型飞机型号合格审定可参考的审定技术指导文件。

为了给公众正确选择民用航空产品和零部件提供依据，民航局制定相关文件，公布了截至2010年12月31日所有获得民航局批准或认可的民用航空产品和零部件。

四、航空安全行业标准管理

——大力加强民用航空技术标准管理工作。中国民用航空技术标准规定(CTSO)是对用于民用航空器上的某些航空材料、零部件和机载设备接受适航审查时，必须遵守的规则。2011年民航局发布有关无线电设备的技术标准规定，包括工作范围117.975~137.000兆赫的VHF无线电通信收发设备、工作在75兆赫机载无线电信标接收设备为取得相应的CTSO标记所必须满足的最低性能标准。

发布机械类航空器零部件的技术标准规定，包括CCAR-23、27、29部航空器机轮、刹车和机轮刹车组件、救生船、运输类飞机机轮(无刹车)和由液压或电驱动的机轮刹车组件为获得批准和使用适用的CTSO标记进行标识所必须满足的最低性能标准。

发布电子电气类航空器零部件的技术标准规定，包括救生定位灯、记录器独立电源、978兆赫的通用访问收发机的广播式自动相关监视设备和/或UAT双工器、转弯侧滑仪、救倾斜俯仰仪、陀螺稳定型磁航向仪、非稳定型磁航向仪(磁罗盘)、自动驾驶仪、座舱音频记录器系统、航空器音频系统和设备、CTSO-C151b的A类、B类、C类地形提示和警告系统(TAWS)、飞行数据记录器系统设备为获得批准和使用适用的CTSO标记进行标识所必须满足的最低性能标准。

——全面强化民用航空行业标准建设。2011年，民航局从安全、飞行、维修、适航、空管、运输等领域加强行业标准工作。航空安全领域，民航局制定了民用航空器运输航空严重事故征候、运输航空一般事故征候、通用航空事故征候和航空器地面事故征候的确定依据。

飞行维修标准方面：明确了测试金属布氏硬度、维氏硬度、洛氏硬度、表面洛氏硬度、努氏硬度、肖氏硬度的方法、转换硬度值的表述和硬度标尺的转换表的使用；民用航空器维修用吊具的检测环境和检测设备、检测技术人员、检测机构、检测项目及程序、检测结果处理、复检时间间隔等吊具检测的要求；燃气涡轮发动机燃油喷嘴使用性能的基本测试条件、测试设备及测试的基本要求；民用航空器发动机状态监控地面站的运行需求、系统的基本功能和数据的输入、输出、存储要求等；民用航空器结构维修记录内容；民用航空器氧气系统维护和改装应注意的安全事项、设备安装和操作、接头力矩、氧气系统部件清洁的要求；推进系统中用保险钢索、保险丝、止动垫片和开口销给紧固件打保险的方法。

空中交通及管理标准方面：涉及民用航空运输机场配备的自动气象观测系统的电子数据输出格式；民用航空气象地面观测的记录内容和记录格式；航行通告系列划分及航行通告、雪情通告、火山通告的编写格式和拍发要求；民用航空航行通告代码及飞行类型、签发目的和影响范围代码的选择和使用；民用航空空中交通管理一、二次监视雷达的飞行校验科目、飞行校验程序和飞行校验报告的要求；民用航空空中交通管制自动化系统的飞行校验科目、飞行校验程序、校验数据分析和飞行校验报告的要求。

适航审定及其他标准：涵盖飞机维护用化学品对飞机结构铝合金搭接面（夹层）的腐蚀测试方法；飞机涡轮发动机清洗和维护用品对钛合金零件造成应力腐蚀倾向的试验方法；用红外热像法检测民用航空器复合材料构件近表面缺陷的要求及质量控制。

运输管理标准：发布了森林航空消防巡护预警、火场侦察、调度指挥、航空灭火等方面的技术方法和要求；民用航空运输过程中头等舱、公务舱旅客服务和设施设备配备的要求；民用航空地面服务代理协议主协议中服务提供，公平做法，分包代理服务，承运方代表，服务标准，付费，收费标准及结算，责任与赔偿，仲裁，有效期限、修改和终止等的基本要求；公共航空运输企业及其地面服务代理人提供旅客运输、行李运输、货物邮件运输、机坪保障等航空运输地面保障服务要求；国内航空运输过程中发生航班不正常时对旅客提供服务的要求；公共航空行李运输服务的基本要求、行李计费、行李声明价值、行李运输信息告知、行李的运输、行李不正常运输的处理及行李损失赔偿的要求；通用航空基本术语及定义；农用航空器喷施设备的喷施率和分布模式的测定条件、程序和方法。

五、机场安全管理

——制定防止机场地面车辆和人员跑道侵入管理规定。为确保机场安全，防止机场地面车辆和人员发生跑道侵入事件，民航局制定了防止机场地面车辆和人员跑道侵入管理规定。界定了航空器着陆，起飞地面保护区的范围，明确了机场管理机构的职能及其与空中交通管制机构之间的衔接与配合，并对相关人员，包括巡视检查人员和塔台管理人员的培训内容和要求作出了详细的规定。

——规范B747-8使用4E及其以下民用机场的技术标准和运行要求。在详细研习B747-8机型的特性和各相关技术参数，结合经济可行性论证分析的基础上，民航局颁布了供B747-8使用4E及其以下民用机场的技术标准和运行要求的咨询通告。该通告明确了主降场运行的最低技术要求以及在此情形下运行的配套设施技术要求，包括对机场救援车辆和设备所需的应急救援要求。

——进一步加强机场鸟害防治工作。为贯彻落实《民用机场运行安全管理规定》，规范航空器鸟击残留物的收集，保存和提交行为，民航局制定航空器鸟击残留物收集，保存和提交办法。办法中规范和统一了在上述各阶段处理鸟击残留物的技术要求和标准，并建立鸟击残留物重点实验室对残留物样品进行鉴定。此外，为指导民用机场拦鸟网的应用，规范拦鸟网的布设、选用及维护等行为，机场司还制定了《民用机场拦鸟网应用指南》，供相关单位参考使用。

——制定机场外来物管理规定。为提高我国机场外来物管理水平，更好地保障飞行安全，指导各机场有效开展外来物防范工作，民航局制定了《机场外来物管理规定》。该规定明确了机场外来物管理工作的内容和组织机构，并对机场外来物防范、巡查与发现、移除、信息管理以及防范评估与持续改进等方面工作提出了具体的要求。

——发布机场使用手册范本。为进一步落实《民用机场使用许可规定》、《民用机场运行安全管理规定》和《中国民用航空安全管理体系建设总体实施方案》的相关要求，民航局发布了《机场使用手册》（范本），该范本融入了机场安全管理体系（SMS）的理念和要素，为机场管理机构组织编写、修订“手册”提供了指导。

六、空中交通管理

——制定民用机场使用许可空管事项申请与审批规定。为规范民用机场使用许可空中交通管理事项的申请与审批，保障民用机场安全、正常运行，提高办理效率，民航局空管办、机场司共同制定了《民用机场使用许可空管事项申请与审批规定》。规定了民用机场在投入使用之前应具备的基本条件，包括空管专业人员应当具有的相应资质。推进了航空情报服务机构，机场气象服务机构使用统一配置的建设。完善了申请所需要提交的材料以及审查材料的标准。

——制定民航空中交通管理安全评估管理办法。为进一步完善空管安全管理体系，明确空管运行单位安全评估工作要求，民用航空局空管行业管理办公室制定《民航空中交通管理安全评估管理办法》。办法以客观性、针对性、技术可行性、经济合理性为原则，详细列明安全评估事项、内容、步骤、程序。规定了危险辨识、风险分析以及配套的风险控制措施。确定了安全评估结论应涵盖相应的应对措施和评估报告中需包含的内容。

——继续推进空管运行单位安全管理体系（SMS）的建设。为保证各空管运行单位运用系统方法管理安全，根据民航局推进空管 SMS 建设进度的要求，结合空管运行单位在 SMS 建设过程中遇到的热点，难点问题，空管办修订并颁发了《民航空管安全管理体系建设指导手册（第二版）》。对安全政策目标、安全风险管理、安全保证、安全促进逐一提出更加细化的要求。

——制定民航空管运行单位安全管理体系（SMS）审核管理办法。为规范民航空管运行单位安全管理体系，空管办依据《民用航空空中交通管理运行单位安全管理规则》，制定并发布了《民航空管安全管理体系审核管理办法》，规定了空管运行单位安全管理体系建设的审核程序由审核申请、现场审核、审核整改三个阶段组成。对于审核结果为不合格的空管运行单位应当对 SMS 进行改进和完善，并向地区管理局提出重新审核的申请。

——进一步规范民航空中交通管理行政检查工作。为及时发现民航空管运行和保障中存在的疏漏和不足，保证空管安全运行，空管局依据《民用航空行政检查工作规则》制定了《民航空管行政检查工作程序》和《民航空管行政检查大纲》。明确了民航局、地区管理局、监管局空管行业管理部门实施空管行政检查的职责、分工及主要工作内容，列明了检查大纲、方式、计划。空管行政检查可通过现场巡查，技术检查，文档检查，专项检查，综合检查等方式进行。检查情况报告采取月度、季度、年度、定期的报告制度。除月度定期报告制度外，就空管运行中的重大事项，地区管理局应当及时向民航局空管行业管理部门及时报告。

——规范民用航空无线电管理检查行为。为加强民航无线电管理，规范无线电管理行政检查工作，空管办制定了《民用航空无线电管理检查手册》。检查种类包括民用航空无线电台（站）检查和民用航空器电台（站）检查。手册中的民用航空器无线电管理检查单按照检查项目、检查内容、检查依据、检查方式、检查对象应提供的材料、检查结果、处理依据和处理意见共八个子项编写，具体包含了 24 项检查内容。

——规范民用航空空中交通通信导航监视设备使用许可管理工作。为规范民用航空空中交通通信导航监视设备使用许可管理工作，空管办制定《民用航空空中交通通信导航监视设备使用许可工作管理细则》。该细则主要适用于通信导航监视设备的购置、使用和监督管理。具体规定了通信导航监视设备合格的审定机构的资质与职责以及合格审定的管理程序。明确了临时使用许可证的申请与延期，使用许可证的申请与换发的条件和使用有效期。在监督管理中，民航局确认对生产厂家以欺骗，贿赂等不正当手段获得临时使用许可证或使用许可证的，应当予以撤销；且禁止该设备生产厂家在三年内申请任何通信导航监视设备的临时许可证或者使用许可证。同时也规定了撤销临时使用许可证或使用许可证的情形。

——制定变更管制方式安全评估指导材料。为指导空管运行单位开展变更管制方式情况下的安全评估工作，依据《民用航空空中交通管理运行单位安全管理规则》和《民航空中交通管理安全评估管理办法》，空管办颁发了《变更管制方式安全评估指导材料》。指导材料以 5M 模型理论为指导，介绍了变更管制方式情况下开展空管安全评估工作要从管制系统设备、管制运行环境、运行管理程序、管制工作及相关人员技能水平等多方面综合考虑，为管制运行工作风险的分析、控制、防范提供了指导。

七、空防安全

——加强队伍建设，制定民航空中警察队伍发展规划。为促进空警队伍健康发展，确保民航持续安全，更好地服务于民航强国战略，民航局依据《中国民用航空发展第十二个五年规划》、《中国民航安全生产“十二五”规划》以及局党组对空警队伍建设与发展的总体要求，编制并发布了《中国民航空中警察队伍建设与发展五年规划（2011—2015）》。规划坚持安全第一、预防为主方针，深入贯彻持续安全理念，紧紧围绕空防安全核心目标，从空警队伍管理、保障、勤务等方面着手，明确“十二五”期间空警队伍建设总体思路、发展目标和工作任务。规划要求到2015年，空警队伍建设与发展取得突破性进展，管理水平显著改进，执勤质量大幅提升，保障能力明显增强，达到管理制度完善、职责定位明确、队伍管理规范、保障措施得力、执勤效果明显的基本目标，实现队伍自身建设良性循环，为确保空中持续安全奠定坚实基础。

——加强公共航空运输企业安全保卫工作。航空安全保卫工作与人民生命财产安全、社会稳定、国家安全息息相关。为此民航局发布了《关于加强公共航空运输企业安全保卫工作的意见》，意见指出在加强航空安保组织领导和机构建设的同时，应当制定和完善切合实际的航空安全保卫工作方案和配套的工作制度。此外，加强在空防安全管理各个环节的安全保卫工作，明确企业内部安全防范工作制度的具体内容，特别要巩固预防措施和建立完备的责任追究体制。意见还积极推进情报信息系统的运作和管理。为应急处理和处置突发事件提供了指导。

——进一步规范民航空勤登机证管理工作。为保障民用航空正常运输秩序，维护民用航空安全，民航局修订了《中国民航空勤登记证管理规定》，规定了公共航空运输公司向民航局公安局提出空勤登记证书面申请的具体条件，明确了空勤人员和非空勤人员申办需要提供的材料和批准的程序。进一步为登机证的管理措施提供了指导。

——制定民航公务乘机通行证管理规定。为规范中国民航公务乘机证管理，确保民航安全和运输生产秩序，民航局制定了《中国民航公务乘机通行证管理规定》。明确了公共运输航空公司申请公务乘机通行证的条件及申办人员材料，规范了公务乘机通行证的管理和持证人员登机前后应当遵守的事项。民航公务乘机通行证的颁证机关为民航局公安局。

第四部分　经济管理

面对燃油价格大幅增长、国际航空业不景气局面，我国民航全行业经济效益稳中有升，业绩突出。航空公司联合重组效应显现，经营更加理性。根据快报数据，全行业完成营业收入5 001亿元，比上年增长21.2%；利润总额363亿元，比上年下降13.9%。积极争取和落实各类补贴、补助政策；通过航路截弯取直、使用临时航路，大力开展行业节能减排。航空延误治理取得明显成效，航班运行协调机制得到加强。

一、民航财经政策

——完善民航发展基金管理制度。为规范使用管理，提高资金使用效益，国务院批准机场管理建设费与民航基础设施建设基金合并为民航发展基金，使用范围扩大用于通用航空、货运航空、节能减排、民航科技创新、持续安全和适航审定能力建设等。为此民航局发布通知，决定从2011年1月1日至2015年12月31日，继续征收机场管理建设费。同时，为促进支线航空发展，旅客于2011年1月1日及以后购买支线飞机执飞的支线航班机票，免缴机场管理建设费。

——积极落实各项民航财经政策。2011年共安排民航企业各类补贴28亿元，包括：中小机场补贴9.2亿元；支线航空补贴4.4亿元；特殊远程国际航线补贴4.2亿元；民航基建项目给予贷款贴息6.9亿元；争取中央预算内资金3亿元用于民航节能减排。安排139亿元用于补助地方机场建设。协调财政部，建立西藏机场补贴长效机制。

——完善民航基础设施项目投资补助管理。为更好地履行行业管理职能，规范投资补助行为，充分发挥民航发展基金的宏观调控作用，支持和服务地方经济社会的发展，民航局制定了《民航基础设施项目投资补助管理暂行办法》。办法明确规定了民航发展基金投资补助主要用于空中交通管理、科技教育、行政能力等直属行政事业单位项目和机场（含通勤机场和通用机场）、航空公司安全、保障系统储备及灾备等非直属单位项目。同时规定申请民航发展基金投资补助的建设项目，应具备以下条件：①符合民航发展规划及各专项规划，机场建设项目符合民航局或民航地区管理局批准的机场总体规划；②符合民航行业标准、技术规范要求；③符合国家土地、环保和节能规定；④符合规定的审批程序；⑤地方政府或投资主管部门出具资金申请文件；⑥地方政府和项目其他投资方出具资金承诺函。

二、航空运输管理

——加强对新开独家航线的保护。为积极引导和支持航空公司开辟新的客运市场，2011 年民航局经公示后发布《2011 年夏秋航季新开独家航线（含航段）保护通告》，决定对川航和山航 2011 年夏秋航季开辟的 3 条涉及北京、广州的区际独飞航线（含航段）进行为期两年的市场培育期保护，两年内原则上不再批准其他航空公司进入受保护的独飞航线（含航段）经营，具体航线如下：A. 川航：①昆明—万州—北京（独家航段：昆明—万州，万州—北京）②攀枝花—成都—北京（独家航段：攀枝花—北京）B. 山航：广州—烟台—广州（独家航线）。

——继续完善国内航线经营许可和航班评审工作。根据《中国民用航空国内航线经营许可规定》，2011 年民航局发布关于 2011 年 10 月 30 日至 2012 年 3 月 24 日期间国内航线经营许可管理和航班评审的规则的管理文件，对国内航线经营许可和航班评审的基本原则和制定依据、核准和登记的具体事宜、调控措施、核准管理航线评审办法、登记航线管理办法、申请和评审程序、换季后航线经营许可和航班管理进行了规定。

——提高航空运输服务质量、加强航班延误治理。提高全行业航空运输的服务水平的同时必须提高对航空运输服务质量检查的水平。2011 年民航局发布指导性文件，为航空运输安全、正常、优质服务提供详细的检查指南，制定了检查的基本要求，列明了旅客运输、行李运输、航班正常和航班延误处置、货物运输、危险品运输等 6 大检查类，并将 6 大类内容细化为各检查项、小项。此外，还规定了各小项航空服务的质量要求及评定内容，从而为监察员开展对航空公司的服务检查提供详细的指南和标准。

为切实做好航班正常的保障工作，进一步提升民航应对大面积航班延误应急处置能力，满足广大消费者的需求，民航局组织开展航班延误整治工作，提出构建以民航局空管局运行管理中心、地区空管局运行管理中心和空管分局为主题的三级民航航班运行常设协调机构，建立三级航班运行协调指挥中心的要求；同时要健全航班延误信息发布、报告机制；全力做好航班延误后的旅客服务工作及大面积航班延误处置的安全保卫工作。并从提高思想认识、切实落实各项措施、创新工作思路、正确处理安全与正常工作关系角度对航班延误治理工作提出了要求。

三、通用航空发展

——拓宽通用航空服务领域试点，推动通用航空发展壮大。2011 年，民航局同意将内蒙古呼伦贝尔市根河林业机场作为拓宽通用航空服务领域试点，按照试点方案，民航华北地区管理局、内蒙古发改委及根河市政府组织通用航空企业，以根河林业机场为基地，使用通用飞机，开展根河至海拉尔的短途运输，于 2011 年 9 月 15 日成功开航。该试点工作在实现通用航空对公共航空运输的补充和支持等方面进行了有益尝试。此外，通过着力加强通用航空政策法规标准体系建设，开展通用航空专项整治、推进联合监管，加强通用航空信息统计，推动通用航空会展经济等工作，推动通用航空更好更快的发展。

四、节能减排

——明确思路，突出重点，加快推进行业节能减排工作。为全面贯彻落实科学发展观，实现民航强国战略的目标要求，民航局以保证民航持续安全发展为前提，以节约能源和减少二氧化碳排放为重点，以强化精细化管理和科学技术创新为支撑，努力提高全行业对节能减排工作的认识和投入的积极性。

民航节能减排的工作目标是通过技术与管理创新，实现全行业能耗和二氧化碳排放增速低于行业发展速度，到 2020 年我国民航单位产出能耗和排放（收入吨公里能耗和收入吨公里二氧化碳排放）比 2005 年下降 22%。目标分三阶段实现：第一阶段——夯实基础阶段（2011—2012 年）。完善行业节能减排组织架构和体制机制，着力从行业生产组织和运行全过程加强节能减排的管理，出台相关政策，加强理论与技术研究，鼓励产学研用结合，推广应用成熟技术，全面建立适应国际节能减排发展趋势的技术和管理体系。到 2012 年，实现收入吨公里能耗和收入吨公里二氧化碳排放均比 2005 年下降 11%；第二阶

China Civil Aviation Policy Report 2011
(Summary)

PART ONE REFORM AND OPENING-UP

I. Deepening Reform and Restructuring

In 2011, with the focus on the theme of scientific development and transformation of the development model, CAAC took effective measures to deepen reform and restructuring. The air transport industry achieved steady and sound development.

CAAC guided large airlines including Air China, China Eastern Airlines and China Southern Airlines as well as large airports including Beijing, Shanghai, Guangzhou and Chengdu to the energetic implementation of strategic transformation, expedition in building air hubs and improvment of the air route network. With China Eastern Airlines' reorganization of the former China Cargo Airlines, Shanghai Airlines Cargo and Great Wall Airlines into a new cargo carrier still named China Cargo Airlines and the establishment of a joint-venture – a new Air China Cargo - by Air China and Cathay Pacific Airways, CAAC actively pushed forward merger and reorganization. The fleet structure was improved and the numbers of aircraft types were reduced. With the asset structure improved, airlines saw gradual decline in the asset-liability ratio.

段——全面推进阶段（2013—2015 年）。在第一阶段基础上，从航空运输组织和运行的全过程推进节能减排关键技术的实施，明显提高节能减排技术、设备、产品国产化能力，全方位推进节能减排管理环境、制度环境和人文环境建设，大幅度缩小我国民航业节能减排水平与主要航空发达国家的差距。到 2015 年，实现收入吨公里能耗和收入吨公里二氧化碳排放均比 2005 年下降 15%；第三阶段——创新优化阶段（2016—2020 年）。积极推进航空替代燃料和新型发动机等换代性技术的应用研究和推广，通过自主核心技术和产品创新，进一步优化内部资源配置，努力降低节能减排成本，根据国际与国内形势适时采取市场措施减少二氧化碳排放，使我国民航节能减排水平接近主要航空发达国家。到 2020 年，实现收入吨公里能耗和收入吨公里二氧化碳排放均比 2005 年下降 22%。

——加强协调，促进合作，积极应对国际航空排放问题。2011 年，民航局建设性地参加和推动国际社会探讨控制和减少国际航空温室气体排放问题的国际磋商与合作。参加了国际民航组织第 195 届理事会，新德里非欧盟国家反对欧盟排放交易体系国际磋商会，签署了《中国民航局—俄罗斯联邦交通运输部关于就欧盟将航空纳入欧盟排放交易体系问题的共同声明》、《新德里宣言》等立场文件。

中国民航在国际航空减排和应对气候变化的总体立场是：《联合国气候变化框架公约》、《京都议定书》和“巴厘路线图”是处理国际航空温室气体排放问题的基本法律框架和前提。“共同但有区别的责任”原则不仅是公约的原则，更是国际航空温室气体排放谈判和合作的基本原则。中国民航高度重视节能减排工作，坚持维护国际航空运输可持续发展。在各种减排措施中，技术和运营是最直接、最有效的减排方法，各国国情不同，技术和运营措施在发展中国家中减排潜力巨大，是当前减排的主要工作和优选路径。中国民航反对采取单方面、不加区别的强制性基于市场的减排措施，反对欧盟将航空纳入欧盟排放交易体系的单边做法并保留反制的权力。中国民航坚持认为，国际航空减排应遵从《联合国气候变化框架公约》和《京都议定书》的基础法律框架，应通过多边协商共同商讨解决之道。■

Progress was made in the pilot reform of the management model of Yantai new Airport. The market management reform was deepened and the online management and disclosure of domestic traffic rights and flights were implemented. Pricing and charging reform was advanced, and studies were carried out and plans were developed for the domestic transport tariff reform, the air traffic management (ATM) charges reform and the airport charges integration. China exempted customs duty for aviation kerosene imports. China National Aviation Fuel completed its corporate system reform. CAAC and its subsidiary entities intensified the personnel system reform, extended competition-based selection and broadly promoted job rotation and temporary secondment at posts of lower levels.

II. Optimizing the Setting of Regulatory Bodies and Enhancing the Regulatory Force

To accommodate the continuous and rapid development of the civil aviation industry and strengthen the safety supervision of civil aviation, CAAC set up additional safety supervision and management bureaus in Wenzhou, Qingdao, Guilin, Sanya, Lijiang and Kashi with the approval of the State Commission Office for Public Sector Reform.

The jurisdictions of safety supervision and management bureaus of Wenzhou, Qingdao, Guilin and Sanya cover the civil aviation operations within the respective purview under the authorization by the CAAC East Regional Administration and the CAAC Central-South Regional Administration. The jurisdiction of Lijiang safety supervision and management bureau covers the civil aviation operations in Lijiang, Diqing and Dali under the authorization by the CAAC Southwest Regional Administration. The jurisdiction of Kashi safety supervision and management bureau covers the civil aviation operations in Kashi, Kizilsu Kirghiz and Hetian under the authorization by the CAAC Xinjiang Administration.

The six new safety supervision and management bureaus are resident agencies of and overseen by the relevant CAAC regional administrations. The relevant CAAC regional administrations may authorize local provincial safety supervision and management bureaus to carry out administration of safety supervision and management bureaus in Wenzhou, Qingdao, Guilin, Sanya and Lijiang.

PART TWO LEGAL SYSTEM BUILDING

In order to strengthen the work regarding civil aviation legislation, facilitate the implementation of rules and regulations by all the units and increase work efficiency, the Collection of China Civil Aviation Regulations (2009-2010 Volume) was issued. The collection includes all rules and regulations published by CAAC from 2009 to 2010 and filed with the Legislative Office of the State Council.

The collection consists of the Provisions on Management of the Civil Aviation Safety Information (CAAC Order No. 194), Regulations on Examination and Approval of Operational Qualification for Public Carrier of Large Aircraft (CAAC Order No. 195), Provisions on the Management of Civil Aviation Emergencies in China (CAAC Order No. 196), Regulations on the Management of Civil Flight Dispatchers Licensing (CAAC Order No. 197), Working Rules on Civil Aeronautical Information (CAAC Order No. 198), Regulations on Licenses Management of Information Personnel of Civil Aviation (CAAC Order No. 199), Regulations on the Management of Civil Aviation Telecommunication Personnel Licensing (CAAC Order No. 200), Regulations on the Management of Civil Air Traffic Controller Licensing (CAAC Order No. 201), Regulations on the Management of Civil Aviation Meteorological Personnel of (CAAC Order No. 202), Management Methods for Civil Aviation Meteorological Observation Environment (CAAC Order No. 203), Safety Management Regulations for Civil Air Traffic Management Operating Entities (CAAC Order No. 204), Supplementary Provisions (IV) to the Provisions on the Foreign Investment in Civil Aviation Industry (CAAC Order No. 205) and Supplementary Provisions (V) to the Provisions on Foreign Investment in Civil Aviation Industry (CAAC Order No. 206).

PART THREE SAFETY SUPERVISION

I. Strengthening Comprehensive Safety Management and Prioritized Supervision

—Urging the principal safety responsibility to be fulfilled. CAAC issued the Notice on Continuously Doing a Good Job in Signing Aviation Safety Responsibility Contracts, clarified the safety responsibility that the transport airlines should assume for their branches and subsidiaries, the principal safety responsibility, guided regional administrations in their continuous signing of the safety responsibility contracts and maintained ongoing supervision of safety responsibility implementation by entities within their jurisdictions. Safety responsibility and objectives were broken down and incorporated into all operating activities, making the safety evaluation system more sound and sophisticated, having the combinations of safety performance with operating results, process management with detail management and safety threats management with actual results and effectively facilitating the fulfillment of all safety work.

—Clarifying functions of pilots-in-command of transport aircraft. In order to further clarify relevant duties of captains and improve aviation safety, CAAC developed the Functions of Pilots-in-command in Civil Air Transport. A civil air transport pilot-in-command ("pilot-in-command") is a pilot who obtains the airline transport pilot license pursuant to the civil aviation regulations of China and is hired as a pilot-in-command by an air transport company. The pilot-in-command is responsible for management of the on-duty crew. All persons carried by a civil aircraft should abide by the orders issued by the pilot-in-command within his mandate. The captain should observe and urge the aircrew to observe laws, regulations, provisions and standards and the ratified or signed international conventions. If the pilot-in-command finds any crew member unsuitable for executing the flight task, he/she may request adjustments in order to ensure flight safety. The pilot-in-command may refuse to take off when discovering any non-compliance of the civil aircraft or airport weather conditions. The pilot-in-command shall have the right to take necessary and appropriate measures, on the basis of ensuring safety, against any in-flight activities that damage the civil aircraft, disturb the order in the civil aircraft, endanger the safety of people or property carried by the civil aircraft or otherwise undermine flight safety. The pilot-in-command shall have the right to take all necessary means and instruct crew members and others onboard the aircraft to take emergency steps when the aircraft is in distress. In the case of emergencies that necessitate evacuation from the civil aircraft, the pilot-in-command shall first evacuate passengers from the civil aircraft; crew members shouldn't leave the civil aircraft without the permission of the pilots-in-command or before the evacuation of all passengers; the pilots-in-command should be the last person to leave the aircraft.

—Regulating licensing for the flight crew. In order to standardize the licensing procedures, harmonize the criteria and clarify specific issues, CAAC revised the Clarification on Pilot License Issues (dated July 14, 2008) and the management document (MD-FS-2003-03), namely Notice on License Application by Students of Flight Schools in Their Schooling Period (dated December 26, 2003). Clarity was provided on alternative requirements for complex airplane training applicable to all holders of and applicants for China's civil aircraft pilot license, and the clarification added the explanations for remark codes on the license and identified the inspectors carrying out overseas aircraft type examination.

—Improving management of entrusted representatives for civil aviation. Pursuant to the Provisions on the Management of Entrusted Representatives and Entrusted Entity Representatives for Civil Aviation Flight Standards (CCAR Part 183FS), CAAC examined and entrusted representatives for medical examination of aviation personnel, requiring all entrusted representatives for medical examination of aviation personnel to strictly discharge their entrusted duties and strengthen clinic study and medical examination training. In addition, changes were made to information on two entrusted corporate representatives for medical examination, namely the Outpatient Department of the Civil Aviation Medicine Center, CAAC and the Civil Aviation Medical Center, CAAC Northwestern Regional Administration.

In 2011, CAAC approved 43 entrusted representatives for flight dispatcher inspection of the CAAC Southwest Regional Administration, requiring them to fulfill such duties as license examination, training and technical inspection of flight dispatchers pursuant to aviation rules and regulations under the supervision of CAAC aviation supervisors.

—Modifying restrictions on the English proficiency deviation of crew members. In accordance with the Regulations on Examination and Approval of Operational Qualification for Public Carriers of Large Aircraft (CCAR Part 121), as of

March 5, 2008, any persons whose license does not provide a certification of English Language Proficiency Level 4 or above shall not serve as a crew member for air routes that use communication in English. CAAC modified the Relevant Requirements on Communication in English and Restrictions on Deviation from CCAR Part 121.479 in line with China's current situations and relevant requirements of the International Civil Aviation Organization (ICAO). The new provisions require that each crew may only include up to one pilot who does not pass the English Language Proficiency Test Level 4; in the case of persons born before 1960, the crew shall include at least two members who have passed the English Language Proficiency Test Level 4 or above, including one pilot-in-command or senior co-pilot; in the case of persons born in or after 1960, all shall have passed the English Language Proficiency Test Level 3 and the crew shall include at least two members who have passed English Language Proficiency Test Level 4 or above, including one pilot-in-command or senior co-pilot.

—Modifying the industry standard-Quota of Civil Aviation Security Check Personnel (Trial). Given the rapid development of civil aviation and major changes in the civil aviation security check requirements and environment in recent years, the original standard-Quota of Civil Aviation Security Check Personnel became incompatible with security check realities. In order to further enhance scientific management of security check and ensure aviation security, CAAC modified, in 2011, the original standard. The new standard sets out requirements on the setting of security check posts (excluding managerial roles) and the basic staffing quota and qualifications: in order to meet the minimum staffing necessary for safe operation, all entities shall not install security check personnel below the foregoing minimum standard. The staff quota for passenger security check aisle shall meet the maximum standard on security assurance, and the hourly passenger traffic through a single aisle shall be strictly controlled pursuant to the said standard. CAAC will conduct supervisory inspection of standard implementation and punish violating entities pursuant to relevant regulations.

—Modifying the Standards of Civil Aircraft Incidents. In 2011, CAAC modified the Standards of Civil Aviation Aircraft Incidents under the principle of differentiation by level of severity and proportion. The modified standards were aligned with the 16 clauses set forth in the latest ICAO Annex 13 in respect of serious incidents. Clauses regarding general incidents of air transport were refined and standardized. Transport airlines were guided to enhance safety management and increase safety margin. Clauses on general aviation incidents were appropriately relaxed to facilitate general aviation development and flight training.

—Regulating supervised investigation, handling and rectification of major safety issues of civil aviation. In accordance with the Regulations on the Reporting, Investigation and Disposition of Work Safety Accidents (Order of the State Council No. 493) and the Measures for Supervised Investigation and Handling of Major Accidents issued by the State Council, CAAC developed the Interim Methods for Supervised Investigation, Handling and Rectification of Major Safety Issues in Civil Aviation. These measures mainly address major and extraordinary safety hazards. The so-called major civil aviation safety issues refer to civil aircraft accidents and major or extraordinary safety hazards. These measures require that CAAC be responsible for supervised investigation, handling and rectification of cross-regional, controversial or long-standing major and extraordinary safety hazards, and that CAAC regional administrations be responsible for supervised investigation, handling and rectification of major and extraordinary safety threats within their respective jurisdiction. In addition, CAAC also set forth the supervision and rectification procedures.

—Developing the CAAC Interim Methods for Administrative Summons on Safety Supervision. In accordance with relevant laws, regulations and the Circular of State Council Concerning Further Strengthening Work Safety of Enterprises, CAAC formulated the CAAC Interim Methods for Administrative Summons on Safety Supervision, setting forth four circumstances in which CAAC may conduct an administrative summon with civil aviation entities and its procedures, and also pointing out the following elements that should be at least included in it: (a) guiding the interviewee in correctly understanding the boundary between legal and illegal acts and fully recognizing the severity of relevant safety problems; (b) clarifying the hazards of irregular or illegal acts and possible legal liabilities; (c) putting forward rectification requirements; and (d) announcing the disposition decision as appropriate. In addition, these measures also include standard formats for the Notice of CAAC Administrative Summons (Sample) and the Notice of Rectification Concerning Issues of Administrative Summons (Sample).

II. Flight Standard Management

—Developing the certification procedures for flight dispatcher training agencies. In accordance with the Regulations on Examination and Approval of Operational Qualification for Public Carriers of Large Aircraft (CCAR Part 121) and the Training Manual (ICAO Doc 7192 Part D-3-Flight Operations Officers/Flight Dispatchers), CAAC developed the advisory circular-The Certification Procedures for Flight Dispatcher Training Agencies, including the functions of CAAC and its regional administrations in the certification of flight dispatcher training agencies, the requirements in the management manual, the requirements for training agencies and personnel, the training agency certification procedures, the requirements for the training syllabus, the facilities, equipment and personnel and record-keeping requirements, thereby providing guidance on certification of organizations providing flight dispatcher training services for CCAR Part 121 air carriers. Guidance was also provided to inspectors on operation approval and supervisory inspection.

—Developing requirements on the training of high-performance multi-engine airplanes. In order to prepare persons who had obtained the multi-engine pilot license for commercial flight and instrument registration and had finished theoretical training on airline transport pilot license for airlines' high-altitude, high-speed and multi-person crew modern commercial airplanes, enable them to operate equipment of large and medium sized airplanes and cope with safety threats, and adjust and improve pilots' way of thinking and behavior, CAAC issued relevant advisory circulars, specifying the access conditions on transitional training courses, training time requirements, requirements for flight instructors, aviation knowledge training, examination requirements, certification requirements, etc. and provided in detail the high-performance airplane training and examination standards for guiding examinations.

—Establishing health requirements for large public air transport airplanes. These requirements provided professional guidance on public health of large public air transport airplanes, specified duties and obligations of certificate holders, aviation doctors and crew members, and provided basic requirements in detail for certificate holders, aviation doctors and crew members, requirements on the development of aviation heath management manual, aviation health expertise training and healthcare instructions, health management and risk control of diseases, health management during duty performance of the crew members and requirements for the diet of crew members. Requirements were also set forth on the management of crew health files and medical records, information reporting, aircraft sanitation, aviation catering safety, aviation health support in external resident locations, response to public health emergencies, etc.

—Improving the onboard emergency medical capability for large public transport airplanes. In order to provide guidance to public air carriers of large airplanes or certificate holders and their agents with respect to supplying onboard emergency medical equipment and developing the procedures and training syllabus for crew to respond to in-flight medical emergencies and offer training on medical emergency response, CAAC set forth requirements on the supply of onboard emergency medical equipment for large public transport airplanes and relevant training, clarifying the requirements, management, use and government supervision of onboard emergency medical equipment, the training requirements on medical emergency response, etc. But certificate holders and their agents were not required to provide in-flight professional emergency medical services, and the medical emergency response training did not require that crew members' emergency medical measures replace or reach the emergency aid capability of certified medical professionals.

—Continuing to enhance the management of civil airport operation. In order to improve all-weather safety of civil aviation operation, standardize the establishment and implementation of the minimum standards for airport operation, align with generally established international standards, set minimum airport operation standards for the use of civil aircraft at civil airports and civil-military airports that had established visual or instrument flight procedures, and provide guidance for the development of minimum operation standards implementation rules for CCAR Part 91, Part 121 and Part 135 air carriers, CAAC published the Standards for Development and Implementation of the Minimum Standards for Civil Airport Operations, specifying the aircraft types, minimum requirements on visual operation, minimum takeoff standards, the minimum standards for Class I PA, APV and NPA, Class II PA and Class III PA and circling approach; the impact of airport equipment malfunctions or downgrading and the requirements for operators and crew flight operations.

—Modifying the policies and standards for airlines operational center (AOC). In order to continuously improve flight safety, align AOCs with the development of fleets, air route network and operation scale, optimize management elements, improve the control quality operation and controlling rein over risks, CAAC amended the Policies and Standards for Airlines Operational Centers (AOC), specifying in detail the AOC system, personnel requirements, systems and facilities, procedures, design, implementation and operational control, offering policies and guidance for the establishment, operation and internal audit of AOCs, and providing basis and guidance for CAAC to assess the operational control capability of air carriers.

—Further enhancing the supervision and management of flight dispatch. Improving the competency of flight dispatchers represented an important part of the work aiming at ensuring continuous flight safety. In order to enhance the management of flight dispatch, CAAC developed the qualification management standards for flight dispatchers of air carriers and the training syllabus for dispatch resources management, setting forth detailed requirements on the eligibility conditions for flight dispatchers, covering the fostering, knowledge, skills and work experience of flight dispatchers. In order to comprehensively enhance the capability of AOCs and synergy between posts, CAAC required establishment of the training syllabus for resource management, setting forth the detailed requirements for the development of training syllabus and training, the detailed explanations for the CCAR Part 121 eligibility standards for flight dispatchers and thus providing guidance for civil aviation regulatory agencies at various levels and airlines.

—Strengthening the management of aviation supplies circulation. In order to offer even more detailed explanation to CCAR Part 121 and provide relevant methods and guidance on ensuring the legality and compliance of aviation supplies in the use and maintenance of aircraft (excluding wet lease) operated by CCAR Part 121 air carriers, CAAC developed relevant advisory circulars that set forth requirements in detail on the labeling and documentation of aviation supplies, documentation of suppliers, requirements for aviation supplies purchase contracts, airworthiness restrictions on aviation supplies, identification and control of questionable and unapproved aviation supplies, requirements for leasing and borrowing of aviation supplies, requirements for sharing of aviation supplies and compliance requirement for aviation supply distributors. In addition, the outline for aviation supply distributor assessment was provided to enable the assessment and management of aviation supply distributors by air carriers and other relevant organizations to comply with China's civil aviation laws and regulations on airworthiness of aviation supplies.

—Regulating and improving the management of maintenance hours. In civil aircraft maintenance, the contradiction between pursuing the maximum profits and ensuring flight safety imposes increasing pressure on maintenance management and maintenance personnel. Such pressure is among the triggers of maintenance errors. According to an accident survey covering the past 20 years, maintenance-error-caused accidents rose by 4 percentage points, and most maintenance errors were related with insufficient maintenance hours and fatigue of maintenance personnel. Therefore, the management and control of maintenance hours constitute an important part of maintenance management. Hence, CAAC developed rules for maintenance work hours management, providing detailed requirements and guidance on how to reasonably arrange maintenance personnel and scientifically manage maintenance work hours by maintenance entities for aircraft and aircraft parts approved pursuant to CCAR Part 145, so as to reduce maintenance errors, ensure the quality of maintenance and specifying the working hour restrictions on maintenance personnel, definition of standard man-hour, maintenance process control and assessment of maintenance man-hour resources.

III. Airworthiness Management

—Developing and modifying rules and regulations to improve the legal and managerial capability in airworthiness management. In order to keep China's airworthiness standards in pace with international ones, to prevent any flight risks in China's civil aviation due to the use of any imported engines that do not conform to current international standards, and to support the ICAO safety audit and the implementation of new feeder line aircraft project and the large commercial aircraft engine project of China, CAAC amended the Airworthiness Provisions for Aircraft Engines a second time to add five additional clauses, namely the static pressure parts of engine, engine life-limited parts, engine over-torque test, turbocharger rotor of reciprocating aircraft engines and design and test requirements for early ETOPS eligibility; Clause 33.14 was deleted; the requirements in 20 clauses were updated, including the manual on engine installation and operational instruction, engine ratings and operating limitations, fire protection, durability, fans of turbine compressor and turbocharger rotor, engine electrical and electronic control systems, instrument connections, reciprocating engine component tests, fuel system, lubrication system, continuous rotation, safety analysis, bird ingestion, endurance test, engine over-temperature test, initial maintenance inspection, component tests of turbine aircraft engine, teardown inspection, documents for continued airworthiness, etc.

In order to maintain the consistency of safety level between Chinese and foreign airworthiness standards and promote healthy development of China's aviation manufacturing industry, CAAC amended the Airworthiness Standards for Transport Aircraft a fourth time, involving 154 clauses, covering the power plant fire protection requirements, assessment of fuel tank system design, inhibition of flammability, maintenance and inspection requirements, landing gear damping test, airworthiness standards for hydraulic systems, airplane operation limitations and airplane flight manual requirements, security factors of cockpit design, airworthiness standards for braking system, 1g stalling speed, airspeed indicating system requirements, lower deck service compartments, flammability standards for thermal/acoustic insulation materials, requirements for material strength performance and design allowable values, etc.

CAAC strengthened management of continued airworthiness and safety improvement of transport category airplanes. Due to long-standing safety problems of airplanes regarding structural damages, fire from electric circuit failure and fuel tank explosion, the safety of continued airworthiness of aircraft fleets operating in the international civil aviation industry are seriously endangered. In order to ensure safety of civil air transport in China, CAAC put forward continued airworthiness and safety improvement measures for transport airplanes in light of actual conditions in China, imposing mandatory requirements upon the electrical wiring interconnection systems, damage tolerance information for structural repair and modification and fuel tank safety, and adding the responsibility and role played by DAH in airworthiness and safety improvement of transport airplanes, which was critical in preventing fuel tank explosion, reducing electric circuit failures and ensuring structural intactness of the operating fleet.

—Carrying out airworthiness management of aircraft type certification, nationality registration management and technical standard management, etc. Given the in-depth development of airworthiness management, the Procedures for Aircraft Type Certification (as revised in 2002 for the third time) needs to be further modified to accommodate airworthiness management development and ensure compatibility with international airworthiness management procedures relating to civil aircraft type certification. In order to guide and regulate civil aircraft type certification activities, CAAC developed the procedures for the application, issuance and management of the civil airworthiness type certificate and the type design approval.

In order to regulate the aircraft creditors applying to CAAC for deregistration of civil aircraft nationality, CAAC developed regulatory procedures, specifying the basic requirements and restrictions on filing and deregistration that the subject aircraft in the Irrevocable De-Registration and

Export Request Authorization (the "Authorization") filed by the debtor shall be a civil aircraft registered in the People's Republic of China and in the procedures for filing for Authorization with the Department of Aircraft Airworthiness Certification and Authorization-based deregistration procedures.

To address the unavailability of applicable CTSO standards for proposed CTSO projects in China, CAAC made additions and revisions to the issuance of CTSO standards and the procedures for approval of CTSO projects based on the Certification Procedures for Aviation Supplies, Parts and Appliances on Board Civil Aircraft. In addition, in order to provide guidance to ESAS ETSOA holders applying for CTSOA certification and CTSOA holders applying for ETSOA certification, CAAC also issued the Guidance for Working Arrangement between CAAC and EASA on ETSOA and CTSOA Articles (English version), clarifying the relevant definitions, certification procedures and requirements.

In order to ensure flight inspection and testing of domestically made aircraft and large aircraft type certification, CAAC issued management documents to strengthen the flight test team of ARJ21-700 review group and agreed to use the FAA advisory circulars as references for C919 aircraft type certification.

In order to provide the public with a basis for selection of the right civil aviation products and components, CAAC issued relevant documents, announcing the civil aviation products and components approved or recognized by CAAC as of December 31, 2010.

IV. Management of Industry Standards for Aviation Safety

—Strengthening CTSO management for civil aviation. The Chinese Technical Standard Order (CTSO) for civil aviation represents rules that must be followed in airworthiness certification of supplies, parts and equipment on civil aircraft. In 2011, CAAC issued CTSO for radio equipment, including the minimum performance standards for CTSO labeling that must be met by the 117.975-137.000 MHz VHF radio transceiver equipment and the 75 MHz airborne radio beacon equipment.

CTSO documents were issued for mechanical aircraft parts and components, including the minimum performance standards that must be met for approval and use of applicable CTSO labeling of CCAR Part 23, Part 27 and Part 29 aircraft wheels, brakes and wheel brake components, lifeboats, transport aircraft wheels (without brake) and hydraulic or electrical wheel brake components.

CTSO documents were issued for electronic and electrical aircraft parts and components, including the minimum performance standards that must be met for approval and use applicable CTSO labeling of life-saving locator lights, independent power supply for recorders, UAT ADS-B function equipment operating at 978 MHz and/or UAT duplexers, turn and bank indicator, peg top horizon, gyro-based stable magnetic heading sensor, unstable magnetic heading sensor (magnetic compass), automatic pilot, cockpit voice recorder system, aircraft audio system and equipment, the Class A, Class B and Class C terrain awareness and warning systems (TAWSs) under CTSO-C151b, and the flight data recorder system equipment.

—Comprehensively strengthening the building of the civil aviation industry standards. In 2011, CAAC strengthened industry standards for safety, flight, maintenance, airworthiness, air traffic management and transport. In the aviation safety field, CAAC formulated the basis for ascertaining serious and generic incidents of civil aircraft in air transport, general aviation incidents and aircraft ground incidents.

With regard to aircraft maintenance standards: testing methods were laid down for Brinell hardness, Vickers hardness, Rockwell hardness, Rockwell surface hardness, Knoop hardness and Shore hardness of metals, the description of hardness value conversion and the use of the conversion table for hardness scales; testing requirements on slings for civil aircraft repair and maintenance, including testing environment and equipment, testing personnel, testing agency, tested items and procedures, processing of test results and test intervals; basic performance testing conditions, testing equipment and requirements for the fuel nozzles of gas turbine engines; operating requirements for the ground station for civil aircraft engine status monitoring, basic system features, requirements for data input, output and storage, etc.; structural maintenance record of civil aircraft; safety precautions for maintenance and modification of the civil aircraft oxygen system, equipment installation and operation, joint torque and cleaning of oxygen system parts; and methods of applying lock wires, safety fuse, tab washers and cotter pins to fasteners in the propulsion system.

Air traffic and management standards: electronic data output format for the automatic weather observation system of civil transport airports; content and format of ground-based civil aviation weather observation records; NOTAM series classification, and the compilation formats and delivery of NOTAM, SNOWTAM and ASHTAM; selection and use of civil aviation NOTAM code, flight type, dispatch purpose and scope; requirements for the flight inspection subjects, flight inspection procedures and flight inspection reports of the primary and secondary surveillance radars for air traffic management in civil aviation; the flight inspection subjects, flight inspection procedures, inspection data analysis and flight inspection reports of the automatic systems for air traffic control in civil aviation.

Airworthiness certification and other standards: testing methods for the corrosive effects of aircraft maintenance chemicals on the aluminum alloy overlap joint (interlayer) in the aircraft structure; the testing methods for stress corrosive trend of titanium alloy parts caused by aircraft turbine engine cleaning and maintenance products; and requirements and quality control regarding the application of the infrared thermography to the testing of the near-surface defects of composite material components of civil aircraft.

Transport management standards: CAAC issued technical methods and requirements for fire patrol and warning, fire reconnaissance, dispatching and commanding, and aerial firefighting in forestry aviation; requirements for services to first-class and business-class passengers and facilities and equipment during civil air transport; basic requirements for service provision, fair practices, subcontracting and agent services, carrier's representative, service standard, fee payment, fee rates and settlement, responsibility and indemnity, arbitration, validity term, modification and termination provisions among the others in the master agreement on agency ground services in civil aviation; requirements for ground services provided by public air transport companies and their ground service agents, including passenger transport, luggage transport, cargo and mail transport and apron support; requirements for passenger services during flight irregularities in domestic air transport; basic requirements, luggage charges, luggage value declaration, notification of luggage transport information, luggage transport, handling of luggage transport mistakes and compensation for luggage damage with respect to luggage services in public aviation; basic terms and definitions for general aviation; and conditions, procedures and methods for determining the application rate and distribution model of agricultural aircraft's aerial applicator.

V. Airport Safety Management

—Developing administrative measures for prevention of runway incursions by airport surface vehicles and persons. In order to ensure airport safety and prevent runway incursions by airport surface vehicles and persons, CAAC developed administrative regulations on prevention of runway incursions by airport surface vehicles and persons, defining the extent of protected areas for aircraft landing and takeoff, identifying the functions of the airport management entities, clarifying the interfacing and collaboration between the airport management entities and air traffic management entities and setting forth detailed provisions on the training content and requirements for relevant personnel, including patrolling inspectors and tower management staff.

—Regulating the technical standards and operation requirements for the use of 4E or lower-rate civil airports for B747-8. Based on thorough studies on features and relevant technical parameters of B747-8 and the financial feasibility study, CAAC issued the advisory circular on the technical standards and operation requirements for the use of 4E or lower-rate civil airports for B747-8. The circular sets forth the minimum technical requirements for the primary airport and the technical requirements on auxiliary facilities, including emergency rescue requirements for airport rescue vehicles and equipment.

—Further strengthening the prevention and control of airport bird hazards. In order to implement the Regulations on Operation Safety Management of the Civil Airports and regulate the collection, storage and submission of bird strike remains, CAAC formulated the methods for collection, storage and submission of bird strike remains, standardizing and consolidating the technical requirements and standards for the handling of bird strike remains at the above mentioned stages, and establishing a key lab dedicated to the study of bird strike remains to analyze the sample remains. In addition, in order to provide guidance to the application of the civil airport bird netting and regulate the setup, selection and maintenance of the bird netting, the Department of Airport formulated the Application Guidance on Civil Airport Bird Netting as a reference for relevant entities.

—Developing provisions for the management of airport foreign object debris (FOD). In order to improve the airport FOD management in China, provide stronger support for flight safety and guide airports in effectively preventing FOD, CAAC developed the Management Regulations on Foreign Object Debris at Airports specifying the scope and organizational structure of airport FOD management and laying down detailed requirements for FOD prevention, detection, removal, information management, prevention assessment and continuous improvement.

—Publishing the manual on airport use. In order to further implement the Provisions on Certification of Civil Airports, Provisions on Operation Safety Management of the Civil Airports and the Master Implementation Plan for the Building of Safety Management System for Civil Aviation of China, CAAC published the Manual for Airport Use (model), incorporating the concept of safety management system (SMS) and its elements, and providing guidance to airport management entities in the development and revision of the manual.

VI. Air Traffic Management

—Developing provisions for application and approval regarding the items of air traffic management in civil airport licensing. In order to standardize the application and approval regarding the items of air traffic management in civil airport licensing, ensure safety and proper functioning of air airports and increase the efficiency of application handling, the Office of Air Traffic Management and the Department of Airport of CAAC jointly developed the Provisions on Civil Airport ATM Items Applications and Approval, setting forth basic conditions that must be met before civil airports are put into service, including the qualifications of air traffic management professionals. CAAC also promoted the use of unified utilities and equipment of aeronautic information service agencies and airport weather service entities, and improved the standards for the application documents and review.

—Developing management methods for the safety assessment of air traffic management in civil aviation. In order to further improve the safety management system of air traffic management and clarify requirements for the safety assessment work of air traffic management entities, the Office of Air Traffic Management of CAAC formulated the Management Methods for the Safety Assessment of Civil Aviation ATM, specifying, in compliance of the principles of objectivity, directivity, technical feasibility and financial rationality, the safety assessment items, components, steps and procedures, providing for hazard identification, risks analysis and supporting risk control measures, requiring the inclusion of response measures in the safety assessment conclusion and specifying the components of the assessment report.

—Continuing to push forward the building of safety management system (SMS) in air traffic management entities. In order to ensure that systematic approaches were used by air traffic management entities in safety management, the Office of Air Traffic Management issued the Guidance Manual on the Building of Civil Aviation Safety Management System (SMS) (Version 2), providing more detailed requirements in terms of safety policy objectives, safety risk management, safety assurance and safety enhancement, in accordance with the CAAC requirements on pushing forward the SMS building in air traffic management entities, and in light of major issues and difficulties that the air traffic management entities encountered during the SMS building.

—Developing management methods for the verification of the safety management system (SMS) in air traffic management entities. In order to standardize the safety management system (SMS) in air traffic management entities,

the Office of Air Traffic Management developed and issued the Management Methods for Safety Management System Review of Civil Aviation ATM, which requires that the SMS verification process of air traffic management entities comprise three stages, namely verification request, onsite verification and post-verification rectification in accordance with the Management Regulations on the Safety of Management Operation Entities of Civil Aviation ATM. Air traffic management entities that fail to pass the verification should improve and refine the SMS, and file a re-verification request with the relevant regional administration of CAAC.

—Further regulating the administrative inspection of civil air traffic management. In order to detect defects and deficiencies in the civil air traffic management and ensure the safe operation of air traffic management, CAAC Air Traffic Management Bureau developed, in accordance with the Working Rules for Administrative Inspection in Civil Aviation, the Working Procedures for Administrative Inspection of Civil Air Traffic Management and the Outline of Administrative Inspection of Civil Air Traffic Management, setting forth the duties and responsibilities of the air traffic management units of CAAC, its regional administrations and safety supervision and management bureaus in respect of the administrative inspection of air traffic management, and providing the inspection syllabus, means and plan. The administrative inspection of air traffic management can be carried out through on-site inspection, technical inspection, document inspection, dedicated inspection or comprehensive inspection. The reporting on inspection adopts monthly, quarterly, annual and otherwise periodical reporting system. In addition to monthly reporting, the regional administrations should timely report significant matters in air traffic management to the air traffic management entities of CAAC.

—Regulating the inspection of civil aviation radio management. In order to strengthen civil aviation radio management and standardize the administrative inspection of radio management, the Office of Air Traffic Management developed the Inspection Manual on Civil Aviation Radio Management. The inspection comprises civil aviation radio (stations) inspection and civil aircraft radio (stations) inspection. The checklist for civil aircraft radio management in the manual consists of eight elements, namely inspection items, content of inspection, basis for inspection, means of inspection, documents to be provided by the inspected entity, result of inspection, basis for disposition and disposition opinion. The eight elements are sub-divided into 24 items.

—Regulating the management of communication, navigation, and surveillance equipment license for air traffic management in civil aviation. In order to standardize the management of communication, navigation, and surveillance equipment licensing for air traffic management in civil aviation, the Office of Air Traffic Management developed the Working Rules for the User Permit Management of Civil Aviation CNS Equipment in Air Traffic, mainly applying to the purchase, use, supervision and management of communication, navigation, and surveillance equipment, and specifying the qualification and duty requirements for the certifying agencies for communication, navigation, and surveillance equipment and certification management procedures. Requirements are also set forth on the application and extension of temporary license, license application and re-issuance and the validity period of the licenses. If CAAC finds and confirms, in its supervision and management, that any manufacturer that obtains the license or temporary license by fraud, bribery or other illegal means, such licenses shall be revoked and prohibited from applying for the license or temporary license for communication, navigation, and surveillance equipment within three years. Circumstances that lead to revocation of license or temporary license are also specified.

—Formulating the guidance on safety evaluation under the changed control mode. In order to guide air traffic management entities through safety assessment under the changed control mode, the Office of Air Traffic Management developed, in accordance with the Safety Management Rules for Air Traffic Management Entities in Civil Aviation and the Management Methods for the Safety Assessment of Civil Aviation ATM, the Guidance on Safety Evaluation under Changed Control Mode, pointing out, based on the 5M model theory, that the safety assessment of air traffic management under the changed control mode should be conducted in a comprehensive way from the perspectives of control system equipment, environment of control operations, operations management procedures, control tasks and skills of relevant personnel so as to provide guidance on analysis, control and prevention of risks in control operations.

VII. Aviation Security

—Strengthening team building and developing the plan for air marshal team development. In order to promote healthy development of the air marshals, ensure sustained safety of civil aviation and better serve the strategy of building a country with a strong civil aviation industry, CAAC developed and issued, in accordance with the 12th Five-Year Plan for Civil Aviation Development of China, the 12th Five-Year Plan for Safe Operation in China's Civil Aviation and the CAAC Party Group's overall requirements for air marshal development, the Five-Year Plan for Development of the Air Marshals for Civil Aviation of China (2011-2015), insisting on the principle of safety first and prevention foremost, implementing in-depth the philosophy of sustained safety, focusing on the core objectives of aviation security and setting forth, in terms of air marshal management, support and operations, the overall roadmap, development objectives and tasks of air marshals development during the 12th Five-Year Plan period. The plan requires that, by 2015, the air marshals building should have made breakthroughs, significant improvement in management capability, great promotion in the quality of operations and pronounced uplift of supporting capacity, and should have fulfilled the basic objectives of refinement in management system, explicitness in functions and positioning, standardization in team management, efficiency in support measures and clear definition of duties, thus realizing the positive cycle of team development and assuring a solid foundation for sustained aviation safety.

—Strengthening the security work of public air transport companies. Air security work bears a close tie to the life and property safety of people, social stability and national security. For this, CAAC issued the Opinions on Strengthening the Security Work of Public Air Transport Enterprises, pointing out, besides strengthening air security leadership and institutional building, that pubic air transport enterprises shall develop and improve practical aviation security plans and support procedures. In addition, these enterprises should also strengthen security work in all areas of aviation safety management, clarify details of internal security safeguard policies and procedures and, in particular, fortify preventive measures and put in place a complete accountability process. The Opinions also encourages the operation and management of the information system and provides guidance on emergency response.

—Further regulating the management of civil airmen boarding passes. In order to ensure the normal transport order of civil aviation and maintain civil aviation safety, CAAC amended the Provisions for Airmen Boarding Pass Management in Civil Aviation of China, clarifying the specific conditions on public air transport companies applying to the Bureau of Aviation Security for flying crew aircraft boarding passes, specifying the documents to be submitted by aircrew and non-aircrew as well as the approval procedures and further providing guidance on pass management measures.

—Developing rules for the civil aviation business pass management in civil aviation. In order to regulate the civil aviation business pass management of China and ensure civil aviation safety and good transport order, CAAC formulated the Provisions for Civil Aviation Business Pass Management in China, clarifying the conditions on public air transport companies applying for the civil aviation affair staff pass and application documentation, and also standardizing the requirements that must be followed by pass holders before and after boarding airplanes. The civil aviation affair staff pass is issued by the Bureau of Aviation Security of CAAC.

PART FOUR ECONOMIC MANAGEMENT

China's civil aviation industry saw steady improvement in financial performance and remarkable operating results, despite fuel price hikes and international aviation weakness. The merger and reorganization of airlines began to pay off and operations became more reasonable. According to new bulletin data, the industry-wide operating income stood at 500.1 billion yuan, up 21.2% over that of the previous year; the total profit was 36.3 billion yuan, down 13.9% over that of the previous year. Subsidies were implemented and subsidizing policies were applied for actively. Energy conservation and emission reduction were strengthened via straightening

air routes and using temporary routes. The rectification of airline flight delays delivered good results and the flight coordination mechanism was enhanced.

I. Financial Policies of Civil Aviation

—Improving the management system of Civil Aviation Development Fund. In order to standardize the management of the fund and increase its use efficiency, the State Council approved the establishment of the Civil Aviation Development Fund by merging the airport management and construction fee and the civil aviation infrastructure construction fund, its scale expanding to cover generation aviation, cargo aviation, energy conservation and emission reduction, innovation in civil aviation science and technology, sustained safety and capacity building for airworthiness assessment. Thus, CAAC issued a circular of its decision to continue to collect the airport management and construction fee from January 1, 2011 to December 31, 2015. In addition, for the purpose of promoting the development of feeder line aviation, passengers who buy tickets of feeder line flight using the feeder line aircraft are exempted from the airport management and construction fee, effective as of January 1, 2011.

—Actively implementing financial and economic policies for civil aviation. In 2011, 2.8 billion yuan subsidies of various sorts were granted to civil aviation companies, including 920 million yuan to small and medium sized airports; 440 million yuan to feeder line aviation; 420 million yuan to special long-distance international routes; and 690 million yuan of loan with discounted interests to civil aviation infrastructure projects. The central government budget allocated 300 million yuan to energy conservation and emission reduction in the civil aviation industry. 13.9 billion yuan was granted to local airport construction. After coordination with the Ministry of Finance, a long-standing subsidy mechanism was established for the airports in Tibet.

—Improving the management of civil aviation infrastructure investment subsidies. In order to better discharge the industry management functions, standardize investment subsidies, give full play to the role of macro-control by the Civil Aviation Development Fund and support and serve local eco-social development, CAAC developed the Provisional Methods for the Management of Civil Aviation Infrastructure Investment Subsidies, requiring that the Civil Aviation Development Fund be mainly used to support projects of administrative entities directly under CAAC, including air traffic management, scientific and technological education and administrative capacity and projects of entities not directly under CAAC, including airports (including commuting airports and general aviation airports) the safety of airlines, supporting system reserves and disaster recovery, and setting forth, in addition, the eligibility requirements for applicants for Civil Aviation Development Fund subsidies: a) conforming to the civil aviation development plan and other specialized plans, and the airport construction projects that shall conform to the overall airport plan approved by CAAC or its regional administrations; b) conforming to civil aviation industry standards and technical specifications; c) conforming to regulations of the State on land, environment and energy conservation; d) conforming to established approval procedures; e) the local government or investment authority submitting the fund application document; and f) the local government and other project investors submitting the letter of funding commitment.

II. Air Transport Management

—Strengthening protection of newly opened exclusive routes. In order to guide and support airlines in tapping into new passenger market, CAAC issued, in 2011, the Notice on Protection of Newly Opened Exclusive Routes (Segments) in Summer Season 2011 and decided to provide two-year protection for the three exclusive regional routes (including segments) including Beijing and Guangzhou opened by Sichuan Airlines and Shandong Airlines during summer season, and in the two-year period of protection, other airlines would not be approved to operate the protected exclusive routes (including segments), namely: A. Sichuan Airlines: a) Kunming-Wanzhou-Beijing (exclusive segments: Kunming-Wanzhou, Wanzhou-Beijing); and b) Panzhihua-Chengdu-Beijing (exclusive segment: Panzhihua-Beijing). B. Shandong Airlines: Guangzhou-Yantai-Guangzhou (exclusive route).

—Continuing to improve domestic air route licensing and flight evaluation. Pursuant to the Regulations on Licensing the Operation of Domestic Air Routes of Civil Aviation of

China, CAAC issued an administrative document in 2011, setting forth rules for domestic air route licensing and flight evaluation between October 30, 2011 and March 24, 2012, providing for the basic principles of domestic air route licensing and flight evaluation and the basis for development, approval and registration procedures, regulatory measures, the evaluation methods for the regulated route approval, the management methods for route register, application and evaluation procedures and post-season air route licensing and flight management.

—Improving the quality of air transport services and strengthening rectification of flight delays. In conjunction with the improvement of the industry-wide aviation transport service capability, the level of the improvement in quality inspection of air transport services must be raised to a new high. In 2011, CAAC issued guidance documents, providing detailed guidance on the inspection of safety, regularity and high service quality of air transport, developing the basic inspection requirements, clarifying six categories of inspection activities, i.e. passenger transport, luggage transport, flight regularity, the handling of flight delays, cargo transport and the transport of dangerous goods and further breaking them down into specific and small items of inspections. In addition, the quality requirements and evaluation elements were set forth for individual items of air services, so as to provide detailed guidance and standards for inspectors to inspect services rendered by airlines.

In order to effectively assure flight regularity, further improve the capability of emergency response to massive flight delays and meet the needs of consumers, CAAC launched the rectification of flight delays and required the establishment of a three-tiered permanent body for civil flight coordination that comprised the Operations Management Center of ATMB of CAAC, operations management centers of regional ATMBs and ATMB sub-bureaus and the establishment of a three-tiered coordination center for flight operations. In the meantime, CAAC also required the improvement in the disclosure and reporting mechanisms for flight delays, satisfactory passenger services for delayed flights and the excellent security work during massive flight delays. It also set forth requirements on flight delay rectification from the perspectives of awareness enhancement, implementation of measures, innovation in work approaches and balance between safety and normal work.

III. General Aviation Development

— Expanding the pilot program for general aviation service scope and promoting general aviation development. In 2011, CAAC approved the Genhe Forestry Airport in Hulunbeier, Inner Mongolia as the pilot airport for expanding general aviation service scope. According to the pilot plan, CAAC North Regional Administration, Development and Reform Commission of Inner Mongolia and the Genhe Municipal Government organized general aviation companies, taking Genhe Forestry as the base, to provide short-distance transport services between Genhe and Hailar with general aviation aircraft. This air route was officially opened on September 15, 2011. The pilot program represented a good trial in supplementing and supporting public air transport with general aviation. In addition, policies, regulations and standards on general aviation were developed or improved, special rectifications in general aviation and joint supervision were carried out, general aviation statistics were enhanced and the general aviation exhibition economy was developed, which promoted the better and faster development of general aviation.

IV. Energy Conservation and Emission Reduction

—Defining the way forward, identifying priorities and accelerating the energy conservation and emission reduction work. In order to fully implement the scientific outlook on development and achieve the strategy of building China with a strong civil aviation industry, and by ensuring sustained safety of civil aviation as precondition, saving energy and cutting carbon dioxide emission as priority, and strengthening detail-oriented management and technological innovation as backing, CAAC endeavored to increase the awareness of energy conservation and emission reduction and the investment in it across the industry.

Energy conservation and emission reduction in the civil aviation industry are aimed at achieving a slower-than-industry-growth rate of increase in energy consumption and carbon dioxide emissions by means of technological and managerial innovation. By 2020, both China's energy consumption and emission per unit output (energy consumption per revenue tonne-km and carbon dioxide per revenue tonne-km) should have dropped by 22% from that of 2005 in civil aviation industry. This goal is divided into three stages: The first stage is fortifying foundation (2011-2012), in which the organizational structure, systems and mechanisms of energy conservation and emission reduction will be improved, the management of energy conservation and emission reduction in the course of business operation will be strengthened, relevant policies will be introduced, theoretical and technical studies will be enhanced, industry-university-research cooperation will be encouraged, the application of proven technologies will be promoted and full technology and management systems that align with the international trends of energy conservation and emission reduction will be established. By 2012, both China's energy consumption per revenue tonne-km and carbon dioxide per revenue tonne-km should have dropped by 11% from that of 2005. The second stage is full-scale implementation (2013-2015), in which the key technologies for energy conservation and emission reduction in the entire process of air transport organization and operation will be, based on the first stage, pushed ahead, the capability of domestic production of energy conservation and emission reduction technologies, equipment and products will be noticeably improved, full-scale of managerial, regulatory and cultural environment for energy conservation and emission reduction will be pressed ahead and the gap between China and main developed countries in energy conservation and emission reduction in the civil aviation industry will be significantly narrowed. By 2015, both the energy consumption per revenue tonne-km and carbon dioxide emissions per revenue tonne-km will have dropped 15% from that of 2005. The third stage is innovation and optimization (2016-2020), in which the applied research and promotion of alterative aviation fuels, new-generation engines and other new-generation technologies will be actively pushed forward, internal resource allocation will be further optimized and the cost of energy conservation and emission reduction will be reduced by means of applying proprietary core technologies and developing innovative product and appropriate market measures will be taken to cut down carbon dioxide emissions in light of domestic and international situations and achieve a level of energy conservation and emission reduction close to that of the main developed countries. By 2020, both energy consumption per revenue tonne-km and carbon dioxide per revenue tonne-km will have dropped by 22% from that of 2005.

—Strengthening coordination, promoting cooperation and actively dealing with emission issues in the international aviation sector. In 2011, CAAC constructively participated in and facilitated international consultations and cooperation in controlling and reducing greenhouse gas emission from international aviation. CAAC participated in the 195th session of the ICAO Council, attended the New Delhi international consultative meeting against the European Union Emissions Trading Scheme (EU-ETS) and signed the Joint Statement of CAAC and Russian Federation's Ministry of Transport on the Inclusion of Aviation in the EU-ETS, the New Delhi Declaration and other position papers.

The general position of CAAC in emission reduction and climate change response in the international aviation community is as follows: The United Nations Framework Convention on Climate Change and its Kyoto Protocol and Bali Roadmap constitute the basic legal framework and precondition for addressing greenhouse gas emission from international aviation. The principle of "common but differentiated responsibility" is not only a principle of the convention, but also a cornerstone of negotiations and cooperation concerning greenhouse gas emission from international aviation. CAAC attaches great importance to energy conservation and emission reduction and persistently support sustainable development of international air transport. Of all emission reductions, technology and operation are the most immediate and effective approach to emission reduction. Depending on national conditions, technological and operational measures have a huge potential in emission reduction among developing countries, representing the main tasks and optimal approach to emission reduction at present. CAAC opposes any unilateral, undifferentiated mandatory market-based emission reduction measures, opposes the unilateral means adopted by UN to the inclusion of aviation in the EU-ETS and reserves the right to take countermeasures. CAAC maintains that the international aviation emission reduction should conform to the basic legal framework outlined by the United Nations Framework Convention on Climate Change and its Kyoto Protocol and be addressed through multilateral consultations and discussions. ■

2011年度
中国民用航空安全报告
（摘要）

2011 年全行业实现运输飞行 556.1 万小时、253.5 万架次，同比分别增长 8.88%、6.03%。全年未发生运输飞行事故和空防事故。实现通用航空飞行 46.5 万小时、85.5 万架次，同比分别增长 15.61%、32.75%。截至 12 月 20 日，发生运输航空严重事故征候 9 起，同比下降 50%；发生通用航空一般飞行事故 4 起，通用航空事故征候万架次率同比下降 50%。厦航、川航、山航、春秋航等 34 家运输航空公司未发生人为责任事故征候，南航、国航、东航获得飞行安全“五星”奖后，向更高安全目标迈进，分别连续安全飞行 898 万、672 万和 544 万小时，海航获得飞行安全“三星”奖，飞行学院获得飞行训练安全“四星”奖。空管、机场、油料等系统事故征候万架次率均低于安全指标，中国航油实现安全供油 1 800 多万吨。“8・24”事故以来，全行业连续运输安全飞行 730 万小时。

2011 年，全行业根据国务院安委会关于“安全生产年”的统一部署，认真落实年初安全工作思路，在“三个深化”和“四个强化”上下功夫，取得了明显的成效。

一、主体责任落实进一步深化

落实安全生产主体责任，是做好安全工作、保持安全运行形势平稳的关键。2011 年，民航局进一步加强指导督促安全主体责任落实，明确航空公司对其分、子公司所承担的主体和监管责任，以及子公司的安全主体责任，防止安全责任虚泛化、管理链条脱节。强化安全监管措施，综合运用法律、行政、经济等多种监管手段，规范企业生产经营行为。各地区管理局继续做好安全责任书签订，持续监督辖区生产运行单位安全责任落实情况。各机场、航空公司、空管和服务保障单位进一步细化、分解安全生产指标，将主体责任落实到各级安全管理岗位和各个安全生产岗位，落实到生产运行的各个环节。健全完善安全考核评价体系，做到安全绩效与经营绩效相结合、过程管理与细节管理相结合、隐患治理与实际效果相结合，有力地推动了各项安全工作落实。进一步认真履行空防安全主体责任，确保各项空防安全工作得以有效落实。

二、资质能力排查进一步深化

全行业认真落实民航局关于专业人员资质能力排查的部署，采取专项检查与综合评估相结合的方式，扎实开展以运输航空机长为重点的专业人员资质能力排查工作。各地区管理局、各运输航空公司以职责落实、理论实践能力和非精密进近飞行技术为重点，排查运输机长 10 092 人次，合格率 98.2%。制定飞行员流动管理规定，加强对流动飞行员资质、训练、执照、档案管理。继续加强飞行人员专业技术职称评选，在飞行领域内首次开展对飞行专业技术正高级职称的审定工作，为飞行专业人员职业通道建设打开了空间。下发了《关于加强外籍飞行人员管理的通知》，对外籍飞行人员和湿租机组的准入、持续资质检查及安全培训进行规范。制定《航空公司签派员资质标准》，启动航空公司签派员资质排查工作。开展机务维修人员资质自查和抽查，暂停不符合要求的维修人员相关授权。建立空管专业人员执照管理系统，加强管制、情报、通导、气象等专业人员资质能力管理。开展安检人员、航空安全员资质管理及认证工作，安检单位持有中级以上国家职业资格证书的安检人员比例稳步上升。资质能力排查工作，促进了专业人员能力素质的普遍提高，为全面加强专业人员队伍建设积累了宝贵经验。

三、行业安全监管进一步深化

一是加强对重点单位重点环节的安全监管。强化对新公司、重组公司、发生问题多的公司，无精密进近能力的机场、高高原机场、军民合用机场，以及重要时期、重要节点和重大运输任务的安全监管。二是开展安全专项治理和挂牌督办。针对安全生产中存在的安全突出问题，组织开展了客舱安全、控制区证件、危险品运输、机场不停航施工、鸟击及外来物防范、跑道侵入、空管设备运行保障、地面保障车辆运行、航空货邮运输安保以及通航安全等专项治理。特别是“7・23”甬温特大铁路交通事故发生后，全行业按照国务院安委会要求，深入排查治理安全隐患，切实改进安全管理，共实施检查 33 583 次，查出各类安全隐患 6 930 个，其中重大隐患 42 个，都得到了扎实有效的整改。各地区管理局挂牌督办重大安全事项 20 项，重大安全隐患得到整治。三是严格安全问责和责任追究。针对生产运行中存在的重大问题，民航局及各地区管理局相继行政约见事发单位，严肃进行问责和责任追究。民航局先后约见了东航、国航、首都机场集团、新疆机场集团等单位，各地区管理局约见了 24 个单位。针对东航“3・20”严重事故征候，给予责任机长终身不得从事商业运行的行政处罚；针对吉祥航“8・13”拒让事件，给予韩籍机长吊销中国民航航线运输驾驶员执照的行政处罚。按照国务院“8・24”事故调查组要求，完成技术组调查报告并上报国务院事故调查组。

四、运行总量调控进一步强化

制定发布民航安全生产“十二五”规划和十年发展纲要，加强对行业安全发展的宏观掌控和引领。按照民航局党组“三个力戒、三个防止”的要求，认真落实行业安全工作“21 条”措施和安全监管工作“27 条”措施，实施适度从严的总量调控措施，牢牢把握安全发展的主动权。适当调节减缓飞机引进速度，全年推迟引进飞机共 60 架，为行业安全保障能力建设赢得时间和空间。加强对安全发展的宏观掌控，对发展速度过快、保障能力不足，以及安全形势严重滑坡的航空公司，实施行政干预措施，削减其飞行总量、暂停其航线航班和设立分（子）公司的申请。通过总量调控措施，各项生产指标增长得到理性控制的同时，经济效益得到较快增长。

五、科技支撑作用进一步强化

（1）航行技术应用步伐加快 民航局安排 6 亿多元资金，为 23 个支线机场配备仪表着陆、助航灯光系统和气象设施。实现新建、改建、扩建机场“基于性能的导航（PBN）”程序同步设计、费用同步审批，完成 23 个机场 PBN 飞行程序设计，目前有 40 个机场具备 PBN 飞行条件，其中首都、广州、浦东、虹桥、深圳等五大机场全面实现“区域导航（RNAV）”运行。日喀则机场实施了“要求授权的所需导航性能（RNP AR）”飞行程序，伊春、温州等机场实施了“所需导航性能—进近（RNP APCH）”程序。飞机平视显示器技术（HUD）应用试点工作取得成功，山航获得使用 HUD 实施 II 类和低于 I 类的运行资格。广播式自动相关监视（ADS-B）应用工作初见成效，国航、东航、南航、海航在国外正式运行 ADS-B。

（2）机场科技保障能力提高 全国旅客吞吐量 100 万以上的机场绝大部分具备了双向盲降功能。推进外来物监控技术、围界报警及监视技术的应用，推广航空器慢速除冰和定点除冰技术。

（3）安全科技研发取得新成果 完成跑道端拦阻系统（EMAS）全尺寸真机验证，我国成为第二个掌握此项技术的国家。人为因素、鸟击预防、疲劳管理等安全基础理论和安全科技项目研究应用不断深入。紧紧围绕提升安全防范和应急处突等核心功能，航空安保综合信息化建设取得初步成果。

六、基础安全工作进一步强化

（1）规章标准进一步完善 制定、修订《民用运输机场突发应急救援管理规则》等 4 部规章和《民用航空器事故征候标准》、《运输类飞机适航标准》等 51 个标准，出台了《民用航空运输机长职责》、《民用航空重大安全事项挂牌督办及整改工作暂行办法》、《防止机场地面车辆和人员跑道侵入管理规定》等一系列规范性文件。生产运行单位落实规章标准，进一步完善运行规范和手册。

（2）安全体系建设不断深入 完成所有在运行的 37 家运输航空公司 SMS 和 CCAR121-R4 补充合格审定，完成 179 家机场 SMS 要素整合到机场使用手册的审核工作，完成 29 家空管单位的 SMS 审核，及 4 家机务维修部门的 SMS 补充审定。航空安保管理体系（SeMS）建设在系统总结试点工作的基础上逐步

Report on China's Civil Aviation Safety 2011
(Summary)

In the year 2011, the entire industry recorded 5.561 million flight hours, 2.535 million aircraft movements, representing year-on-year increases of 8.88% and 6.03% respectively. There was no transport flight accident or aviation security accident. General Aviation recorded 465 000 flight hours and 855 000 aircraft movements, increasing by 15.61% and 32.75% over those of the previous year. By December 20, 2011, 9 severe incidents had happened, a year on year decrease of 50%. 4 generic accidents in general aviation had occurred and the incident rate per 10 000 GA aircraft movements had decreased by 50% over that of the previous year. 34 transport aviation companies including Xiamen

---

展开，顺利完成厦航航空安保审计试点工作。圆满完成 SMS 审核试点工作，为更好地促进 SMS 效能发挥做了有益的尝试。

（3）安全培训力度持续加大 围绕资质能力建设和监管能力建设，加大对生产运行单位负责人、安全管理人员和行政管理部门各类别监察员的培训力度。开展多人制机组驾驶员执照（MPL）培训，满足航空公司对飞行人才的需求。全年举办 30 期安全管理人员培训班，培训 1 700 余人次；开展 4 期安全监管局局长培训和 15 期监察员初训复训，培训 980 余人次。

（4）适航审定能力稳步提升 积极推进 ARJ21 飞机影子审定，针对影子审定工作中出现的问题，及时制订应对措施。稳步推进 Z15 直升机等在审项目的型号合格审定及 C919 大型客机型号合格审定。圆满完成国家“863”计划星基 LASS 导航系统的校验飞行和民航多个管制区域 ADS-B 监控系统的校验工作。

七、重大任务安全保障工作进一步强化

进一步完善安全保障机制和应急管理机制，重大航空运输任务安全保障能力稳步提升。圆满完成党和国家领导人专、包机保障任务，出色完成埃及、利比亚、日本大规模撤离我国公民紧急运输任务，以及深圳大运会、西藏和平解放 60 周年大庆等重大航空运输任务的安全保障工作。特别是在中国—亚欧博览会期间，新疆机场执行一级空防安全响应，涉疆航线执行一级空中勤务派遣，在异常复杂严峻的空防安全形势下，圆满完成了博览会航空运输保障和安全保卫任务，尤其是新疆乌鲁木齐机场安检、公安部门成功挫败“8·7”恐怖团伙蓄谋破坏事件，为新疆的社会稳定和全国反恐工作做出了重大贡献。油料、航信、航材等服务保障单位围绕飞行运行安全，提高服务保障能力，为行业持续安全作出了积极的贡献。

在看到成绩的同时，我们更要看到安全工作存在的问题。截至到 2012 年 12 月 20 日，全行业发生事故征候 224 起，其中一些严重不安全事件已经接近事故的边缘，暴露出的问题不容忽视。

分析这些问题的原因，主要表现在四个方面。一是安全保障能力不足的问题依然比较突出。可用空域、人力资源、设施设备等安全生产的关键资源依然短缺。部分地区机场、空管单位安全保障能力难以满足快速增长的航空运输需求。二是安全主体责任落实还不到位。一些单位安全管理链条过长，一些业务或外包、或代理，存在安全责任主体不明确，安全管理不到位，安全责任没有实现全覆盖的情况。一些单位偏重物质激励，忽视专业技术人员职业精神培养。一些单位存在“等、靠、要”思想，用于技术改进和隐患治理的投入严重不足。三是安全监管能力亟待提高。监察员队伍数量和质量有待提高，尤其是通用航空类监察员严重缺乏；监管手段创新不足，监管平台建设进展缓慢。四是个别专业技术人员诚信缺失、操守失范，遵章守纪意识淡薄。■

Airlines, Sichuan Airlines, Shandong Airlines, Spring Airlines, etc. did not see human factors-related incident, and after receiving the Five Star Prize for Flight Safety, China Southern Airlines, Air China and China Eastern Airlines headed towards higher safety targets and successively flew safely for 8.98 million hours, 6.72 million hours and 5.44 million hours respectively. Hainan Airlines received Three Star Prize for Flight Safety and the Civil Aviation Flight University of China received Four Star Prize for Flight Training. Incident rates per 10 000 aircraft movements of air traffic management, airports, fuel supply departments, etc. were lower than safety indicators. China National Aviation Fuel Group Corporation supplied over 18 million tons of fuel safely. Since August 24, 2010 accident, the industry witnessed 7.3 million hours of safe flight.

In 2011, in accordance with the unified arrangement of the Work Safety Year made by the Work Safety Committee of the State Council, the whole industry conscientiously implemented the thinking of safety work defined at the beginning of the year, made efforts in the Three Deepenings and Four Strenghenings, and made notable progress consequently.

I. Implementing in an In-depth Manner the Principal Responsibilities

Discharging the principal safe production responsibilities is the key to good safety work and maintaining stability in the momentum of safe operations. In 2011, in order to ensure that safety responsibilities be concrete and specific and prevent the delinking of the management chain, CAAC further increased its guidance, supervised and urged the discharge of principal safety responsibilities, and clarified the principle supervision responsibilities that should be shouldered by airlines to their branches and subsidiaries as well as the principal safety responsibilities of their subsidiaries. The safety supervision measures were reinforced and diversified supervision means of legality, administration, economy, etc. were employed to regulate business operations. Regional administrations continued to push for the signing of safety responsibility contracts and supervise the performance of safety responsibilities at operations within their jurisdictions. Airports, airlines, ATM bureaus and service support entities further defined and broke down work safety indicators, and assigned principal safety responsibilities to every safety management post at various levels, every safety work post and every link in the operation. The safety review and evaluation system was improved to combine safety performance and operational performance, process management and micro-management, and hazards rectification and actual effect, pushing ahead strongly with the implementation of all safety work. The principal aviation security responsibility was earnestly carried out, ensuring the effective execution of all aviation security work.

II. Deepening the Capability of Qualification Examination

The whole industry seriously implemented the CAAC arrangement on qualification examination of professionals, took the measure of combining dedicated examination and comprehensive evaluation and solidly carried out qualification examination of professionals with the focus on pilots-in-command of transport aircraft. Regional administrations and transport airlines examined 10 092 pilots-in-command with the focus on discharge of duties, theoretical application capabilities and flight techniques of non-precision approach, and 98.2% of the examined were qualified. The provisions on pilot turnover were developed to reinforce the qualification, training, license and archive management. Efforts were made to continuously strengthen the pilot professional and technical title appraisal, and the senior title appraisal for professional pilots was started for the first time, which paved the way for the career development of professional pilots. The Notice on Strengthening the Management of Foreign Airmen was issued, standardizing the access of foreign flight personnel and wet lease crew, continuous qualification examination and safety training. The Standards of Airline Dispatcher Qualification was developed, initiating the qualification examination of airline dispatchers. Self-examination and random examination of aircraft maintenance personnel were launched and authorization of unqualified maintenance personnel was suspended. The license management system for ATM professionals was established, strengthening the qualification management of professionals in fields of air traffic control, information, communication and navigation and meteorology. Qualification management and certification of security check personnel and aviation security officers were carried out; as a result, the ratio of security check personnel holding the national professional qualification certificate at the intermediate level and above in security check units increased steadily. Qualification examination contributed to the general improvement of professional proficiency and accumulated invaluable experiences in strengthening in an all-around way the professional capacity building.

III. Strengthening in-depth Industrial Safety Supervision

First, safety supervision of the key entities and key links was strengthened. Safety supervisions were strengthened over new companies, re-organized companies and companies with frequent problems, airports without precision approach capability, high plateau airports and civil-military airports as well as the safety supervisions in critical periods, at important junctures and when carrying out major transport tasks. Second, dedicated safety rectification was conducted with the establishment of supervises investigation and handling supervisory entities. In response to outstanding safety issues, the industry conducted dedicated rectifications of passenger cabin safety, certificate to access controlled areas, transport of dangerous goods, engineering constructions without suspension of airport operation, bird strike and foreign object prevention, runway incursions, support of air traffic management equipment operation, operation of ground support vehicles, air cargo and mail transport security and safety of flight services. It was noteworthy that after the railway accident on the Ningbo-Wenzhou line on July 23, the whole industry carried out in-depth safety hazards screening and rectification in accordance with the requirements of the Safety Committee of the State Council to effectively improve safety management. It launched 33 583 inspections, and spotted 6 930 hidden hazards of various kinds including 42 critical ones, which were all effectively rectified. Third, safety responsibility and accountability were tightened. In light of major problems in production and operations, CAAC and its regional administrations initiated administrative summons of the entities concerned successively and investigated the responsibilities of the people concerned. CAAC summoned China Eastern Airlines, Air China, Capital Airports Holding Company, Xinjiang Airport Group, etc., and CAAC regional administrations summoned 24 entities. In response to the severe incident of China Eastern Airlines that occurred on March 20, the administrative penalty of life-time ban on commercial operations for the pilot-in-command was meted out. In light of the severe incident of refusal of Juneyao Airlines to let go of the emergency MAYDAY call on August 13, the administrative penalty was given, revoking the Chinese civil aviation transport pilot license of the Korean pilot-in-command. In accordance with the requirements of the Investigation Committee of the State Council on August 24 Air Crash in 2010, the technical investigation report was developed and submitted to the Committee.

IV. Reinforcing In-depth the Overall Operations Volume Control

The 12th Five-Year Plan for civil aviation safety and the 10-year development outline were developed and published, enhancing the macro-regulation and guidance for the safe development of the industry. In accordance with the requirements of Three Prohibitions and Three Preventions, 21 industrial safety measures and 27 safety supervision measures were earnestly implemented, and moderately tight macro-regulatory measures on the overall capacity were adopted, tightly holding the initiative of safe development. With the import of 60 aircraft being postponed in the year, the speed of aircraft introduction was moderated, earning the time and space needed for the building of safety support capacity. The macro-regulation of safe development was reinforced. In response to airlines that had developed excessively fast, lacked support capability and operated with safety situation seriously corroded, administrative interference such as cutting their overall flight business volume, suspending their route and flight operations and their applications for setting up subsidiaries was carried out. Through overall business volume control measures, the economic profits, with the growth of various business indicators under reasonable control, increased at a relatively fast speed.

V. Enhancing in-depth the Supporting Roles of Science and Technology

1. The pace of application of navigation technologies was speeded up. CAAC set aside 600 million yuan to install instrument landing system (ILS), nav-aid lighting system and meteorological system in 23 feeder line airports. With the synchronized designing and expenditure approval of performance-based navigation (PBN) implemented in the newly built, renovated or expanded airports, 23 airports completed their PBN flight procedure design. Now there are 40 airports with PBN flight conditions, among which, the 5 major airports, namely Beijing Capital International Airport, Guangzhou Airport, Pudong Airport, Hongqiao Airport and Shenzhen Airport have wholly switched to RNAV operations. The flight procedure of RNP AR was implemented in Rikaze Airport. The RNP approach (RNP APCH) procedure was implemented in airports of Yichun and Wenzhou. The pilot work of head up display (HUD) in aircraft was successful, and Shandong Airlines acquired the qualification of using HUD to conduct category II operations or operations lower than category I. ADS-B application showed initial success and Air China, China Eastern Airlines and China Southern Airlines officially operated ADS-B overseas.

2. The scientific and technologic support capabilities of airports were improved. The overwhelming majority of the airports with passenger traffic over 1 million were capable of two-way blind landing. The application of foreign objects monitoring technology, perimeter alarm and surveillance technology, and aircraft slow deicing and fixed-place de-icing technologies were promoted.

3. Fresh progress was made in safety-related R&D. The full-size real-machine experiment of engineered material arresting system (EMAS) was completed, making China the second country that had kept abreast of this technology. Application of safety rudiments, such as human factors, bird strike and fatigue management as well as the research and application of safety science and technology projects continued to go deeper. Comprehensive aviation security IT development, with the focus on boosting core functions, such as safety protection and emergency response, made preliminary progress.

VI. Strengthening in-depth Basic Safety Work

1. Rules and standards were further perfected. 4 regulations such as Management Regulations of Emergency Response and Rescue in Case of Sudden Outbreak of Events at Civil Transport Airports, and 51 standards such as Standards of Civil Aircraft Incidents and Airworthiness Standards for Transport Category Aircraft were developed and revised. A series of regulatory documents were issued, including Functions of Pilots-in-command in Civil Air Transport, Interim Methods for Supervised Investigation, Handling and Rectification of Major Safety Issues in Civil Aviation and Management Regulations on the Prevention of Ground Vehicle and Personnel's Intrusion into Runways, etc. The production and operation entities implemented the regulations and standards and further perfected the operation standards and manual.

2. The building of safety management system was continuously deepened. The supplemental SMS and CCAR Part 121 R4 certifications of all 37 operating transport airlines, the review of integrating 179 airports' SMS elements into the airport utilization manual, SMS review of 29 air traffic management entities and supplemental SMS certification of 4 aircraft maintenance entities were completed. The SeMS building was gradually rolled out on the basis of summarizing pilot work experiences and the pilot aviation security audit of Xiamen Airlines was successfully accomplished. The impeccable fulfillment of the pilot SMS audit made useful contribution to the better enhancing of SMS' efficiency.

3. Safety training was constantly intensified. By focusing on professional capacity building and supervisory capacity building, CAAC intensified training for people in charge and safety management personnel in production and operation entities, and for supervisors and inspectors of various sorts in administrative departments. Multi-crew pilot license (MPL) training was provided to meet airlines' demand for flight personnel. 30 training sessions for safety management personnel were held with over 1 700 persons trained. 4 trainings for directors of safety supervision and management bureaus and 15 initial and recurrent trainings for supervisory officers were organized with over 980 persons trained.

4. Airworthiness certification capacity was steadily enhanced. Active efforts were made in the shadow certification of ARJ21, and coping measures were developed timely in response to the problems identified during the shadow certification. The type certification of projects under review, such as Z15 helicopter as well as large passenger aircraft C919, progressed steadily. The trial flight for the satellite-based LASS navigation system, a project of the national 863 Hi-Tech R&D Program, and the trial of ADS-B surveillance system in several control areas were successfully completed.

VII. Reinforcing in-depth the Safety Support for Major Transport Tasks

Safety support mechanism and emergency response and management mechanism were further reinforced so that the safety support capacity for major transport tasks was steadily boosted. The tasks of supporting special and charter flights for leaders of the Party and the State were successfully fulfilled. The emergency transport tasks of large-scale evacuation of Chinese compatriots from Egypt, Libya and Japan, and the safety support for major air transport tasks such as Universiade 2011 Shenzhen and celebration of the 60th anniversary of the peaceful liberation of Tibet were all superbly carried out, especially the air transport support and security task successfully accomplished under extremely complex and grave aviation security situation during the China-Eurasian Expo. when level-1 aviation security response was activated at airports in Xijiang and level-1 dispatch of in-flight security officers was executed to flights to and from Xinjiang, and the security check unit and public security bureau at the Urumqi airport, in particular, successfully thwarted the "8·7" terrorist plot, contributing greatly to the social stability and national anti-terrorist program. By focusing on flight operations safety, all supporting entities such as China National Aviation Fuel Group Corporation, TravelSky, China Aviation Supplies Holding Company, etc. improved their service support capacity, making positive contribution to the sustained safety of the industry.

We should keep a sober mind of the problems in safety work while celebrating the achievements. By December 20, 2011, 224 incidents had occurred in the industry, and some of the severe incidents were on the verge of accidents, and the exposed problems were too serious to neglect.

The analysis of these problems shows four main reasons. First, weak safety support capacity remains prominent. There is lack of critical resources for safety, such as airspace available, human resources, facilities and equipment, etc. In some airports and air traffic management entities, safety support capacity cannot meet the rapidly increasing demand for air transport. Second, the implementation of the principal safety responsibilities is not quite in place. Some entities have an excessively long safety management chain. For some businesses like outsourcing and agency, there are problems such as unclear principals of safety responsibility, flawed safety management and safety responsibility loopholes. Some entities prefer material incentives to the cultivation of work ethics in technical professionals. In some entities, there is a mentality of waiting for, relying on and asking for external support, thus there has been severely inadequate investment in technological improvement and hazard rectifications. Third, safety supervision capacity should be enhanced urgently. The number and capacity of supervisory personnel have yet to be enhanced. In particular, there is a serious shortage in GA supervisors. There is insufficient innovation of the supervision means and little progress in the building of supervision platform. Fourth, a few technicians have poor credit, misconduct and poor awareness of regulatory compliance.

2011年度航空公司主要生产指标完成情况统计表

单位 Company	飞行小时 Flight Hours	运输总周转量（万吨公里）Total Air Traffic('0000 tonne-km)		
		2011年	2010年	增加(%) Increased(%)
总计 Total	5 594 901	5 774 427.40	5 384 489.70	7.2
国内航线 Domestic Routes	4 740 457	3 806 074.99	3 454 800.56	10.2
其中：港澳台地区航线 Hong Kong, Macao & Taiwan Regional Routes	146 710	126 425.12	115 895.37	9.1
国际航线 International Routes	854 444	1 968 352.41	1 929 689.14	2.0
长安航空有限责任公司 Chang'an Airlines Co., Ltd.	34 170	30 867.93	34 227.90	－9.8
四川航空股份有限公司 Sichuan Airlines Co., Ltd.	223 567	198 696.08	163 755.40	21.3
云南祥鹏航空有限责任公司 Yunnan Lucky Air Co., Ltd.	52 323	40 446.79	34 069.39	18.7
春秋航空有限公司 Spring Airlines Co., Ltd.	96 557	96 617.79	76 735.43	25.9
奥凯航空有限公司 Okay Airways Co., Ltd.	35 754	28 992.45	14 563.94	99.1
中国国际航空股份有限公司 Air China Company Limited	965 449	1 058 918.49	994 225.19	6.5
中国国际货运航空有限公司 Air China Cargo Co., Ltd.	33 325	214 822.12	229 622.56	－6.4
新华航空控股有限公司 Grand China Air Co., Ltd.	10 853	9 681.64	9 372.09	3.3
中国南方航空股份有限公司 China Southern Airlines Company Limited	1 153 442	1 174 703.34	1 069 087.43	9.9
贵州航空有限公司 Guizhou Airlines Co., Ltd.	31 925	25 914.32	23 337.77	11.0
厦门航空有限公司 Xiamen Airlines Co., Ltd.	241 055	191 199.49	165 328.71	15.6
南航（集团）汕头航空有限公司 Southern Airlines Shantou Airlines Company Limited	35 132	22 423.82	21 904.89	2.4
珠海航空有限公司 Zhuhai Airlines Co., Ltd.	18 924	14 958.19	14 971.34	－0.1
成都航空有限公司 Chengdu Airlines Co., Ltd.	34 309	24 584.84	18 498.07	32.9
上海国际货运航空有限公司 Shanghai Airlines Cargo Int'l Co., Ltd.	5 327	15 731.13	73 683.36	－78.7
上海航空股份有限公司 Shanghai Airlines Co., Ltd.	205 360	160 119.89	168 946.62	－5.2
华夏航空有限公司 China Express Air Co., Ltd.	17 378	3 073.23	2 472.93	24.3
银河国际货运航空有限公司 Grandstar Cargo International Airlines Co., Ltd.	3 639	30 654.57	33 623.91	－8.8
天津航空有限公司 Tianjin Airlines Co., Ltd.	115 075	39 925.72	32 507.12	22.8
上海吉祥航空有限公司 Juneyao Airlines Co., Ltd.	73 078	65 024.84	50 983.64	27.5

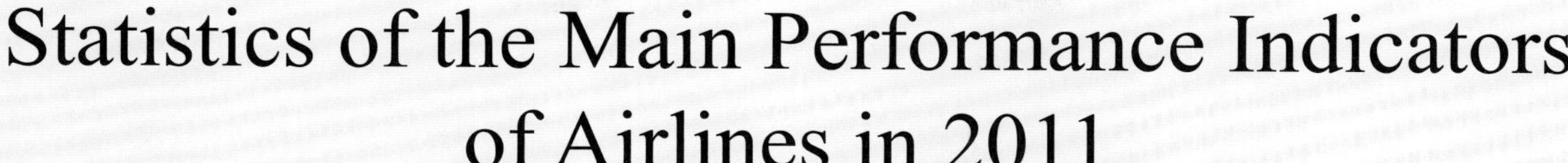

旅客运输量（人次）Passengers Carried			货邮运输量（吨）Cargo & Mail Carried(tonne)		
2011年	2010年	增加(%) Increased(%)	2011年	2010年	增加(%) Increased(%)
293 166 582	267 691 437	9.5	5 574 778.9	5 630 370.5	– 1.0
271 986 055	248 377 134	9.5	3 794 352.2	3 704 055.6	2.4
7 601 877	6 723 740	13.1	210 027.6	216 603.0	– 3.0
21 180 527	19 314 303	9.7	1 780 426.7	1 926 314.9	– 7.6
1 937 443	2 153 714	– 10.0	21 384.6	26 337.3	– 18.8
12 948 760	10 667 547	21.4	170 349.1	169 932.4	0.2
3 144 568	2 712 100	15.9	27 690.6	24 712.0	12.1
7 150 814	5 859 697	22.0	38 653.1	34 931.1	10.7
2 008 773	1 006 536	99.6	20 589.4	10 147.7	102.9
48 672 216	46 245 017	5.2	757 547.0	762 965.6	– 0.7
			391 307.5	385 193.2	1.6
729 642	703 702	3.7	8 645.0	84 79.5	2.0
58 504 693	56 636 882	3.3	907 753.2	902 135.0	0.6
1 846 473	1 653 608	11.7	20 178.1	17 508.4	15.2
15 316 509	13 561 359	12.9	166 520.6	158 074.9	5.3
2 317 413	2 207 183	5.0	14 523.2	16 007.8	– 9.3
1 053 025	945 799	11.3	12 244.7	10 284.4	19.1
1 995 616	1 409 868	41.5	15 369.4	13 282.2	15.7
			48 108.7	116 116.8	– 58.6
11 656 207	11 903 970	– 2.1	124 336.7	158 848.5	– 21.7
377 395	340 525	10.8	730.6	779.5	– 6.3
			48 060.6	46 973.4	2.3
4 520 996	3 861 036	17.1	12 694.8	10 203.0	24.4
4 346 469	3 588 227	21.1	41 636.6	34 776.1	19.7

单 位 Company	飞行小时 Flight Hours	运输总周转量（万吨公里） Total Air Traffic('0000 tonne-km)		
		2011年	2010年	增加(%) Increased(%)
海南航空股份有限公司 Hainan Airlines Group Co., Ltd.	249 857	275 934.72	239 464.00	15.2
长城航空有限公司 Great Wall Airlines Co., Ltd.	4 156	32 892.85	100 395.46	- 67.2
东海航空有限公司 Donghai Airlines Co., Ltd.	14 878	10 391.00	9 038.30	15.0
首都航空有限公司 HNA Capital Airlines Co., Ltd.	79 917	66 022.09	40 023.38	65.0
翡翠国际货运航空有限公司 Jade Cargo International Co., Ltd.	24 602	134 035.19	175 906.55	- 23.8
幸福航空公司 Joy Air Co., Ltd.	9 831	1 008.48	628.02	60.6
中国联合航空有限公司 China United Airlines Co., Ltd.	41 177	31 946.42	27 357.86	16.8
昆明航空公司 Kunming Airlines Co., Ltd.	23 635	15 559.98	14 591.00	6.6
中国东方航空股份有限公司 China Eastern Airlines Co., Ltd.	822 158	742 789.92	689 008.29	7.8
中国货运航空有限公司 China Cargo Airlines Co., Ltd.	48 286	288 764.82	204 553.08	41.2
中国东方航空江苏有限公司 China Eastern Airlines Jiangsu Ltd.	105 431	71 552.02	62 041.95	15.3
中国东方航空武汉有限责任公司 China Eastern Airlines Wuhan Co., Ltd.	59 476	31 955.69	33 638.28	- 5.0
河北航空有限责任公司 Hebei Airlines Co., Ltd.	17 392	10 024.28	3 190.32	214.2
顺丰航空有限公司 S.F. Airlines Co., Ltd.	6 590	8 483.99	3 611.70	134.9
重庆航空有限公司 Chongqing Airlines Co., Ltd.	26 864	17 992.29	15 679.75	14.7
西部航空有限责任公司 China West Air Co., Ltd.	26 136	21 136.10	18 045.37	17.1
中国货运邮政航空有限责任公司 China Postal Airlines Co., Ltd.	25 372	15 431.37	13 792.31	11.9
山东航空股份有限公司 Shandong Airlines Co., Ltd.	172 775	120 721.84	95 373.52	26.6
西藏航空公司 Tibet Airlines	3 490	1 872.68	—	
友和道通航空有限公司 Uni - top Airlines	828	1 426.03	—	
河南航空有限责任公司 Henan Airlines Co., Ltd.	—	0	3 643.53	- 100.0
中国新华航空有限责任公司 China Xinhuan Airlines Co., Ltd.	84 584	82 508.43	80 427.95	2.6
扬子江快运航空有限公司 Yangtze River Express Co., Ltd.	32 094	70 551.80	82 778.65	- 14.8
深圳航空有限责任公司 Shenzhen Airlines Co., Ltd.	328 730	274 068.74	239 382.74	14.5

旅客运输量（人次） Passengers Carried			货邮运输量（吨） Cargo & Mail Carried(tonne)		
2011年	2010年	增加(%) Increased(%)	2011年	2010年	增加(%) Increased(%)
13 780 307	11 508 391	19.7	216 351.6	195 763.2	10.5
			60 615.6	185 495.0	－67.3
			76 165.2	64 269.0	18.5
4 825 476	3 032 922	59.1	23 362.1	14 065.5	66.1
			241 088.2	331 749.0	－27.3
238 570	150 428	58.6			
2 645 180	2 186 473	21.0	23 845.2	17 618.7	35.3
1 356 731	1 078 891	25.8	9 860.2	8 307.8	18.7
45 704 878	43 063 011	6.1	549 726.1	574 969.8	－4.4
			602 395.1	513 364.4	17.3
5 553 157	4 759 046	16.7	60 752.4	54 598.8	11.3
3 103 091	3 010 700	3.1	26 755.6	27 131.9	－1.4
714 102	307 635	132.1	6 885.3	1 014.6	578.6
			64 012.7	28 951.1	121.1
1 632 826	1 451 512	12.5	13 470.0	13 350.3	0.9
1 973 130	1 694 899	16.4	15 264.8	14 473.4	5.5
			155 818.8	137 053.2	13.7
9 887 030	8 071 913	22.5	97 484.6	82 433.7	18.3
134 912	—		602.1	—	
			5 044.2	—	
	465 262	－100.0	0	1 587.9	－100.0
4 809 375	4 966 081	－3.2	55 394.5	60 377.4	－8.3
			172 095.2	167 439.9	2.8
18 280 805	16 487 503	10.88	249 465.9	228 667.1	9.1

2011年度民航各运输机场吞吐量和飞机起降架次统计表

机场 Airport	旅客吞吐量（人次） Passengers Handled			
	名次 Ranking	2011年	2010年	增加(%) Increased(%)
合计 Total		620 536 534	564 309 654	10.0
北京 / 首都 Beijing / Capital	1	78 674 513	73 948 114	6.4
广州 / 白云 Guangzhou / Baiyun	2	45 040 340	40 975 673	9.9
上海 / 浦东 Shanghai / Pudong	3	41 447 730	40 578 621	2.1
上海 / 虹桥 Shanghai / Hongqiao	4	33 112 442	31 298 812	5.8
成都 / 双流 Chengdu / Shuangliu	5	29 073 719	25 805 815	12.7
深圳 / 宝安 Shenzhen / Bao'an	6	28 245 738	26 713 610	5.7
昆明 / 巫家坝 Kunming / Wujiaba	7	22 270 130	20 192 243	10.3
西安 / 咸阳 Xi'an / Xianyang	8	21 163 130	18 010 405	17.5
重庆 / 江北 Chongqing / Jiangbei	9	19 052 706	15 802 334	20.6
杭州 / 萧山 Hangzhou / Xiaoshan	10	17 512 224	17 068 585	2.6
厦门 / 高崎 Xiamen / Gaoqi	11	15 757 049	13 206 217	19.3
长沙 / 黄花 Changsha / Huanghua	12	13 684 731	12 621 333	8.4
南京 / 禄口 Nanjing / Lukou	13	13 074 097	12 530 515	4.3
武汉 / 天河 Wuhan / Tianhe	14	12 462 016	11 646 789	7.0
大连 / 周水子 Dalian / Zhoushuizi	15	12 012 094	10 703 640	12.2
青岛 / 流亭 Qingdao / Liuting	16	11 716 361	11 101 176	5.5
乌鲁木齐 / 地窝堡 Urumqi / Diwopu	17	11 078 597	9 148 329	21.1
三亚 / 凤凰 Sanya / Fenghuang	18	10 361 821	9 293 959	11.5
沈阳 / 桃仙 Shenyang / Taoxian	19	10 231 185	8 619 897	18.7
海口 / 美兰 Haikou / Meilan	20	10 167 818	8 773 771	15.9
郑州 / 新郑 Zhengzhou / Xinzheng	21	10 150 075	8 707 873	16.6

Statistics of the Turnover and Aircraft Movements of Civil Airports in 2011

货邮吞吐量（吨）Cargo & Mail Handled (tonne)				起降架次 Aircraft Movements			
名次 Ranking	2011年	2010年	增加(%) Increased(%)	名次 Ranking	2011年	2010年	增加(%) Increased(%)
	11 577 677.2	11 289 870.7	2.5		5 979 664	5 530 558	8.1
2	1 640 231.8	1 551 471.6	5.7	1	533 166	517 585	3.0
3	1 179 967.7	1 144 455.7	3.1	2	349 259	329 214	6.1
1	3 085 267.7	3 228 080.8	-4.4	3	344 086	332 126	3.6
6	454 069.4	480 438.1	-5.5	4	229 846	218 985	5.0
5	477 695.2	432 153.2	10.5	6	222 421	205 537	8.2
4	828 375.5	809 125.4	2.4	5	224 329	216 897	3.4
8	272 465.4	273 651.2	-0.4	9	191 744	181 466	5.7
13	172 567.4	158 054.0	9.2	10	185 079	164 430	12.6
11	237 572.5	195 686.6	21.4	11	166 763	145 705	14.5
7	306 242.6	283 426.9	8.0	12	149 480	146 289	2.2
9	260 575.1	245 644.0	6.1	13	135 618	116 659	16.3
18	114 831.1	108 635.2	5.7	16	116 727	115 635	0.9
10	246 572.2	234 359.0	5.2	14	120 534	116 087	3.8
17	122 762.4	110 190.8	11.4	15	117 010	112 521	4.0
15	137 859.1	140 554.3	-1.9	19	94 344	91 628	3.0
14	166 533.1	163 748.7	1.7	17	105 835	103 975	1.8
19	107 580.5	95 124.2	13.1	18	97 801	86 491	13.1
31	48 290.8	45 255.6	6.7	25	74 392	70 575	5.4
16	133 903.5	123 816.4	8.1	23	77 866	70 786	10.0
21	97 826.9	91 667.3	6.7	22	83 057	73 824	12.5
20	102 802.4	85 798.1	19.8	20	93 014	84 180	10.5

机 场 Airport	旅客吞吐量（人次） Passengers Handled			
	名 次 Ranking	2011年	2010年	增加(%) Increased(%)
济南 / 遥墙　Ji'nan / Yaoqiang	22	7 879 707	6 898 936	14.2
哈尔滨 / 太平　Harbin / Taiping	23	7 841 521	7 259 498	8.0
天津 / 滨海　Tianjin / Binhai	24	7 554 172	7 277 106	3.8
贵阳 / 龙洞堡　Guiyang / Longdongbao	25	7 339 228	6 271 701	17.0
福州 / 长乐　Fuzhou / Changle	26	7 196 800	6 476 773	11.1
南宁 / 吴圩　Nanning / Wuxu	27	6 464 428	5 632 933	14.8
太原 / 武宿　Taiyuan / Wusu	28	5 876 005	5 252 783	11.9
温州 / 永强　Wenzhou / Yongqiang	29	5 598 674	5 326 802	5.1
桂林 / 两江　Guilin / Liangjiang	30	5 489 481	5 259 260	4.4
南昌 / 昌北　Nanchang / Changbei	31	5 347 853	4 748 980	12.6
宁波 / 栎社　Ningbo / Lishe	32	5 014 002	4 517 070	11.0
长春 / 龙嘉　Changchun / Longjia	33	4 971 667	4 749 471	4.7
合肥 / 骆岗　Hefei / Luogang	34	4 398 739	3 817 051	15.2
呼和浩特 / 白塔　Hohhot / Baita	35	4 331 529	3 663 383	18.2
石家庄 / 正定　Shijiazhuang / Zhengding	36	4 021 167	2 723 596	47.6
兰州 / 中川　Lanzhou / Zhongchuan	37	3 809 023	3 603 512	5.7
银川 / 河东　Yinchuan / Hedong	38	3 376 964	2 939 822	14.9
无锡 / 硕放　Wuxi / Shuofang	39	2 940 122	2 535 277	16.0
北京 / 南苑　Beijing / Nanyuan	40	2 644 598	2 140 474	23.6
烟台 / 莱山　Yantai / Laishan	41	2 547 499	2 496 318	2.1
丽江 / 三义　Lijiang / Sanyi	42	2 183 597	2 217 824	－1.5
西宁 / 曹家堡　Xining / Caojiabao	43	2 030 378	1 664 823	22.0
泉州 / 晋江　Quanzhou / Jinjiang	44	1 975 836	1 997 126	－1.1
西双版纳 / 嘎洒　Xishuangbanna / Gasa	45	1 918 825	1 887 362	1.7
揭阳 / 潮汕　Jieyang / Chaoshan	46	1 901 856	1 727 934	10.1
珠海 / 三灶　Zhuhai / Sanzao	47	1 797 306	1 819 051	－1.2
九寨 / 黄龙　Jiuzhai / Huanglong	48	1 717 603	1 740 728	－1.3

货邮吞吐量（吨）Cargo & Mail Handled (tonne)				起降架次 Aircraft Movements			
名次 Ranking	2011年	2010年	增加(%) Increased(%)	名次 Ranking	2011年	2010年	增加(%) Increased(%)
23	77 623.9	70 175.3	10.6	24	77 856	69 145	12.6
24	76 490.6	71 265.2	7.3	29	62 520	61 002	2.5
12	182 856.7	202 484.1	－9.7	21	84 831	85 034	－0.2
25	69 130.3	61 653.0	12.1	27	67 759	61 231	10.7
22	87 573.8	79 350.2	10.4	26	67 866	62 108	9.3
26	67 633.5	55 633.5	21.6	31	59 181	52 396	12.9
33	39 702.7	41 227.3	－3.7	28	62 746	57 525	9.1
30	48 997.2	50 024.2	－2.1	34	49 995	49 854	0.3
36	33 613.7	32 543.2	3.3	38	47 431	48 103	－1.4
35	34 330.5	32 417.8	5.9	33	50 177	51 820	－3.2
29	58 763.0	55 966.6	5.0	40	44 083	39 289	12.2
28	62 255.8	61 672.4	0.9	41	41 364	42 199	－2.0
34	38 425.3	31 883.0	20.5	37	48 001	46 452	3.3
40	25 218.2	20 675.3	22.0	35	48 870	43 331	12.8
37	33 229.1	25 709.8	29.2	32	54 903	51 929	5.7
38	32 033.3	30 742.6	4.2	43	34 510	33 700	2.4
41	23 742.5	20 343.2	16.7	45	29 889	26 334	13.5
27	66 208.0	57 070.7	16.0	49	26 040	21 978	18.5
42	23 557.3	17 476.3	34.8	51	21 642	16 507	31.1
32	40 331.6	41 514.2	－2.8	47	26 573	27 932	－4.9
59	4 370.2	3 058.7	42.9	52	20 138	21 085	－4.5
45	11 882.3	12 265.9	－3.1	54	18 176	15 645	16.2
39	31 226.6	22 931.9	36.2	53	19 992	20 123	－0.7
56	4 814.8	7 400.9	－34.9	56	17 729	17 772	－0.2
47	10 160.9	10 842.5	－6.3	55	17 903	16 761	6.8
44	16 768.3	17 578.8	－4.6	36	48 059	37 651	27.6
165				58	14 946	15 126	－1.2

机场 Airport	旅客吞吐量（人次） Passengers Handled			
	名次 Ranking	2011年	2010年	增加(%) Increased(%)
拉萨 / 贡嘎　Lhasa / Gongga	49	1 581 538	1 296 328	22.0
包头 / 二里半　Baotou / Erliban	50	1 345 598	1 332 132	1.0
鄂尔多斯 / 伊金霍洛　Erdos / Yijinhuoluo	51	1 301 806	816 737	59.4
张家界 / 荷花　Zhangjiajie / Hehua	52	1 148 396	1 126 361	2.0
延吉 / 朝阳川　Yanji / Chaoyangchuan	53	1 016 274	943 336	7.7
威海 / 大水泊　Weihai / Dashuibo	54	935 450	824 938	13.4
常州 / 奔牛　Changzhou / Benniu	55	933 663	658 033	41.9
喀什　Kashi	56	912 591	792 681	15.1
榆林 / 榆阳　Yulin / Yuyang	57	910 424	905 161	0.6
徐州 / 观音　Xuzhou / Guanyin	58	846 267	658 395	28.5
宜昌 / 三峡　Yichang / Sanxia	59	778 004	724 121	7.4
义乌　Yiwu	60	761 938	695 148	9.6
运城 / 张孝　Yuncheng / Zhangxiao	61	749 924	618 463	21.3
海拉尔 / 东山　Hailaer / Dongshan	62	713 037	608 804	17.1
北海 / 福成　Beihai / Fucheng	63	699 148	694 177	0.7
临沂 / 沭埠岭　Linyi / Mufuling	64	666 024	542 759	22.7
台州 / 路桥　Taizhou / Luqiao	65	628 268	616 861	1.8
绵阳 / 南郊　Mianyang / Nanjiao	66	622 816	577 236	7.9
柳州 / 白莲　Liuzhou / Bailian	67	600 856	321 610	86.8
武夷山　Wuyishan	68	594 562	589 554	0.8
西昌 / 青山　Xichang / Qingshan	69	522 093	445 329	17.2
腾冲 / 驼峰　Tengchong / Tuofeng	70	517 838	465 778	11.2
赣州 / 黄金　Ganzhou / Huangjin	71	515 068	315 246	63.4
德宏 / 芒市　Dehong / Mangshi	72	506 452	443 843	14.1
湛江　Zhanjiang	73	488 835	484 499	0.9
伊宁　Yining	74	483 967	455 584	6.2
黄山 / 屯溪　Huangshan / Tunxi	75	465 336	343 033	35.7

货邮吞吐量（吨） Cargo & Mail Handled (tonne)				起降架次 Aircraft Movements			
名次 Ranking	2011年	2010年	增加(%) Increased(%)	名次 Ranking	2011年	2010年	增加(%) Increased(%)
46	11 347.1	13 827.3	－17.9	61	13 932	11 720	18.9
49	7 491.7	6 075.1	23.3	65	11 261	11 502	－2.1
52	5 992.9	3 074.1	95.0	60	14 118	8 862	59.3
76	2 075.7	1 272.3	63.1	70	9 381	9 363	0.2
55	4 915.6	4 192.1	17.3	74	7 884	7 962	－1.0
57	4 570.4	3 751.5	21.8	62	12 006	10 579	13.5
48	8 362.7	6 720.0	24.4	68	10 160	6 765	50.2
63	3 705.7	3 207.2	15.5	69	9 880	6 189	59.6
87	1 312.5	639.0	105.4	67	10 304	9 774	5.4
54	4 930.0	3 772.3	30.7	64	11 523	8 951	28.7
62	3 769.3	3 184.7	18.4	39	45 492	8 204	454.5
64	3 414.0	3 802.1	－10.2	77	6 746	6 148	9.7
73	2 192.6	1 677.8	30.7	73	8 132	6 820	19.2
67	2 986.9	2 130.4	40.2	75	7 632	6 202	23.1
60	4 027.9	2 849.2	41.4	50	24 931	10 553	136.2
66	3 200.4	2 016.6	58.7	76	7 181	6 979	2.9
51	6 179.1	5 483.4	12.7	79	6 212	6 278	－1.1
58	4 491.5	4 833.8	－7.1	7	207 140	189 906	9.1
53	5 035.3	3 844.4	31.0	71	9 136	3 949	131.3
98	839.6	1 047.9	－19.9	87	5 249	5 740	－8.6
65	3 366.6	2 550.8	32.0	88	5 156	4 702	9.7
95	981.2	538.6	82.2	86	5 258	5 228	0.6
68	2 948.1	2 205.5	33.7	81	6 106	5 066	20.5
61	3 929.9	3 654.1	7.5	91	4 927	4 528	8.8
75	2 104.2	1 969.6	6.8	72	9 065	8 993	0.8
102	712.7	556.0	28.2	78	6 562	6 201	5.8
84	1 429.5	1 499.8	－4.7	90	5 024	3 752	33.9

机 场 Airport	旅客吞吐量（人次） Passengers Handled			
	名 次 Ranking	2011年	2010年	增加(%) Increased(%)
连云港 / 白塔埠 Lianyungang / Baitabu	76	460 784	423 031	8.9
库尔勒 Korlar	77	415 277	359 137	15.6
长治 / 王村 Changzhi / Wangcun	78	412 167	390 379	5.6
阿克苏 Akesu	79	412 085	225 393	82.8
大庆 / 萨尔图 Daqing / Sa'ertu	80	404 083	363 404	11.2
舟山 / 普陀山 Zhoushan / Putuoshan	81	384 859	356 869	7.8
迪庆 / 香格里拉 Diqing / Shangrila	82	374 710	263 323	42.3
和田 Hetian	83	359 040	260 396	37.9
景德镇 / 罗家 Jingdezhen / Luojia	84	355 930	307 889	15.6
洛阳 / 北郊 Luoyang / Beijiao	85	354 677	285 774	24.1
宜宾 / 菜坝 Yibin / Caiba	86	325 560	289 541	12.4
牡丹江 / 海浪 Mudanjiang / Hailang	87	313 333	288 742	8.5
常德 / 桃花源 Changde / Taohuayuan	88	308 559	268 789	14.8
赤峰 / 玉龙 Chifeng / Yulong	89	304 642	270 709	12.5
井冈山 Jinggangshan	90	302 406	182 412	65.8
泸州 / 蓝田 Luzhou / Lantian	91	284 886	246 357	15.6
大理 Dali	92	274 486	227 072	20.9
锡林浩特 Xilinhaote	93	258 918	201 251	28.7
万州 / 五桥 Wanzhou / Wuqiao	94	251 169	244 045	2.9
南通 / 兴东 Nantong / Xingdong	95	249 494	271 440	－8.1
敦煌 Dunhuang	96	248 805	204 242	21.8
普洱 / 思茅 Pu'er / Simao	97	238 486	219 689	8.6
盐城 / 南洋 Yancheng / Nanyang	98	232 315	191 336	21.4
淮安 / 涟水 Huaian / Lianshui	99	230 462	39 174	488.3
南阳 / 姜营 Nanyang / Jiangying	100	227 056	190 072	19.5
乌海 Wuhai	101	227 021	180 883	25.5
满洲里 / 西郊 Manzhouli / Xijiao	102	226 891	174 187	30.3

货邮吞吐量（吨） Cargo & Mail Handled (tonne)				起降架次 Aircraft Movements			
名次 Ranking	2011年	2010年	增加(%) Increased(%)	名次 Ranking	2011年	2010年	增加(%) Increased(%)
86	1 374.4	1 148.7	19.6	84	5 408	5 548	− 2.5
74	2 116.2	1 131.4	87.0	80	6 160	6 360	− 3.1
81	1 641.3	769.7	113.2	82	5 555	4 982	11.5
99	833.6	454.2	83.5	83	5 460	5 168	5.7
79	1 939.5	1 307.7	48.3	99	3 645	3 577	1.9
120	286.6	377.2	− 24.0	66	10 314	7 644	34.9
111	512.5	871.9	− 41.2	93	4 167	3 440	21.1
88	1 270.4	899.5	41.2	105	3 236	2 326	39.1
106	678.5	466.9	45.3	109	3 104	2 666	16.4
92	1 158.3	1 170.1	− 1.0	8	198 086	212 738	− 6.9
69	2 737.6	2 205.1	24.2	95	3 859	3 429	12.5
85	1 387.2	979.1	41.7	106	3 202	3 126	2.4
127	159.7	251.1	− 36.4	30	60 399	16 717	261.3
112	509.3	333.9	52.5	92	4 757	4 553	4.5
93	1 121.5	769.8	45.7	102	3 502	2 614	34.0
70	2 425.6	1 791.5	35.4	101	3 518	2 974	18.3
96	952.9	465.4	104.8	100	3 559	2 764	28.8
115	445.7	214.6	107.7	94	4 133	3 568	15.8
77	2 000.6	2 078.1	− 3.7	96	3 846	4 471	− 14.0
50	6 496.7	4 654.2	39.6	46	27 538	28 435	− 3.2
128	137.3	162.5	− 15.5	97	3 796	3 312	14.6
101	734.4	508.0	44.5	117	2 572	2 628	− 2.1
71	2 323.3	1 615.2	43.8	118	2 558	2 092	22.3
82	1 556.8	1.4	111 982.3	89	5 060	642	688.2
107	677.4	721.2	− 6.1	57	16 256	39 850	− 59.2
103	711.5	129.2	450.8	114	2 778	2 115	31.3
83	1 528.0	1 217.8	25.5	107	3 173	2 323	36.6

机场 Airport	旅客吞吐量（人次） Passengers Handled			
	名次 Ranking	2011年	2010年	增加(%) Increased(%)
嘉峪关　Jiayuguan	103	222 134	133 513	66.4
大同 / 倍加皂　Datong / Beijiazao	104	217 027	166 420	30.4
达州 / 河市　Dazhou / Heshi	105	215 948	164 435	31.3
佳木斯 / 东郊　Jiamusi / Dongjiao	106	212 904	191 592	11.1
襄樊 / 刘集　Xiangfan / Liuji	107	203 722	161 645	26.0
秦皇岛 / 山海关　Qinhuangdao / Shanhaiguan	108	191 378	200 976	– 4.8
济宁 / 曲阜　Jining / Qufu	109	189 365	243 684	– 22.3
阿勒泰　Altay	110	183 280	164 004	11.8
通辽　Tongliao	111	178 006	118 316	50.4
阜阳　Fuyang	112	172 107	108 630	58.4
南充 / 高坪　Nanchong / Gaoping	113	170 908	124 570	37.2
恩施 / 许家坪　Enshi / Xujiaping	114	170 845	295 660	– 42.2
邯郸　Handan	115	154 176	126 464	21.9
保山 / 云瑞　Baoshan / Yunrui	116	153 616	154 372	– 0.5
唐山 / 三女河　Tangshan / Sannühe	117	151 051	32 793	360.6
齐齐哈尔 / 三家子　Qiqihar / Sanjiazi	118	149 995	123 218	21.7
衢州　Quzhou	119	148 907	133 498	11.5
林芝 / 米林　Linzhi / Milin	120	143 793	148 796	– 3.4
佛山 / 沙堤　Foshan / Shadi	121	142 337	118 192	20.4
乌兰浩特 / 义勒利特　Ulanhot / Yilelite	122	140 643	98 204	43.2
潍坊　Weifang	123	139 559	141 129	– 1.1
丹东 / 浪头　Dandong / Langtou	124	132 362	99 822	32.6
布尔津 / 喀纳斯　Bu'erjin / Kanasi	125	130 743	82 530	58.4
白山 / 长白山　Baishan / Changbaishan	126	127 531	103 359	23.4
临沧　Lincang	127	119 067	126 636	– 6.0
延安 / 二十里铺　Yan'an / Ershilipu	128	112 098	120 121	– 6.7

货邮吞吐量（吨） Cargo & Mail Handled (tonne)				起降架次 Aircraft Movements			
名次 Ranking	2011年	2010年	增加(%) Increased(%)	名次 Ranking	2011年	2010年	增加(%) Increased(%)
108	615.9	201.1	206.2	120	2 521	1 650	52.8
80	1 799.3	1 193.5	50.8	103	3 428	2 305	48.7
78	1 993.3	1 691.3	17.9	122	2 462	1 986	24.0
100	758.5	1 053.4	– 28.0	123	2 230	2 038	9.4
109	611.9	473.9	29.1	42	40 434	39 388	2.7
116	349.2	256.9	36.0	110	3 046	2 900	5.0
123	258.6	881.8	– 70.7	115	2 712	3 284	– 17.4
134	56.3	19.8	184.4	112	2 814	2 481	13.4
91	1 186.7	477.4	148.6	104	3 351	2 217	51.2
149	8.8	5.3	66.5	121	2 518	2 512	0.2
104	695.4	306.1	127.2	44	33 690	39 188	– 14.0
89	1 215.4	840.2	44.7	129	1 677	2 962	– 43.4
148	10.6	31.1	– 65.8	111	2 879	2 497	15.3
117	306.6	361.9	– 15.3	127	1 740	1 704	2.1
94	1 004.8	86.1	1 067.4	119	2 537	832	204.9
105	685.0	507.1	35.1	137	1 354	1 230	10.1
121	263.8	180.2	46.4	133	1 474	1 716	– 14.1
114	477.3	544.3	– 12.3	136	1 362	1 296	5.1
72	2 200.0	420.5	423.2	149	1 016	1 075	– 5.5
124	224.7	120.5	86.5	108	3 137	1 980	58.4
43	18 688.8	18 608.8	0.4	98	3 699	3 376	9.6
97	864.4	634.1	36.3	143	1 160	972	19.3
159	1.5	1.5	– 0.5	132	1 484	808	83.7
144	26.4	33.0	– 20.1	125	2 052	1 623	26.4
113	500.6	589.0	– 15.0	139	1 304	1 412	– 7.6
140	38.8	42.9	– 9.4	116	2 614	2 860	– 8.6

机 场 Airport	旅客吞吐量（人次） Passengers Handled			
	名 次 Ranking	2011年	2010年	增加(%) Increased(%)
锦州 / 小岭子 Jinzhou / Xiaolingzi	129	102 801	96 355	6.7
黑河 Heihe	130	90 568	94 878	－4.5
鸡西 / 兴凯湖 Jixi / Xingkaihu	131	89 567	80 955	10.6
中卫 / 香山 Zhongwei / Xiangshan	132	88 569	67 466	31.3
怀化 / 芷江 Huaihua / Zhijiang	133	88 268	133 109	－33.7
九江 / 庐山 Jiujiang / Lushan	134	85 429	81 555	4.8
广元 / 盘龙 Guangyuan / Panlong	135	85 277	48 540	75.7
昌都 / 邦达 Changdu / Bangda	136	85 213	88 842	－4.1
文山 / 普者黑 Wenshan / Puzhehei	137	84 336	56 771	48.6
二连浩特 / 赛乌苏 Erlianhot / Saiwusu	138	79 725	47 005	69.6
漠河 / 古莲 Mohe / Gulian	139	79 115	65 729	20.4
安庆 Anqing	140	76 241	76 330	－0.1
玉树 / 巴塘 Yushu / Batang	141	75 838	81 131	－6.5
哈密 Hami	142	72 647	49 538	46.6
格尔木 Germu	143	70 502	41 979	67.9
东营 Dongying	144	67 994	66 545	2.2
兴义 Xingyi	145	62 176	31 882	95.0
梅县 / 长岗岌 Meixian / Changgangji	146	61 539	49 372	24.6
攀枝花 / 保安营 Panzhihua / Bao'anying	147	58 974	162 796	－63.8
昭通 Zhaotong	148	55 431	37 372	48.3
库车 / 龟兹 Kuche / Qiuci	149	54 462	49 669	9.6
连城 / 冠豸山 Liancheng / Guanzhaishan	150	47 691	41 931	13.7
克拉玛依 Kelamayi	151	45 765	34 051	34.4
伊春 / 林都 Yichun / Lindu	152	44 507	43 903	1.4
铜仁 / 凤凰 Tongren / Fenghuang	153	43 430	42 249	2.8
梧州 / 长洲岛 Wuzhou / Changzhoudao	154	32 569	42 218	－22.9

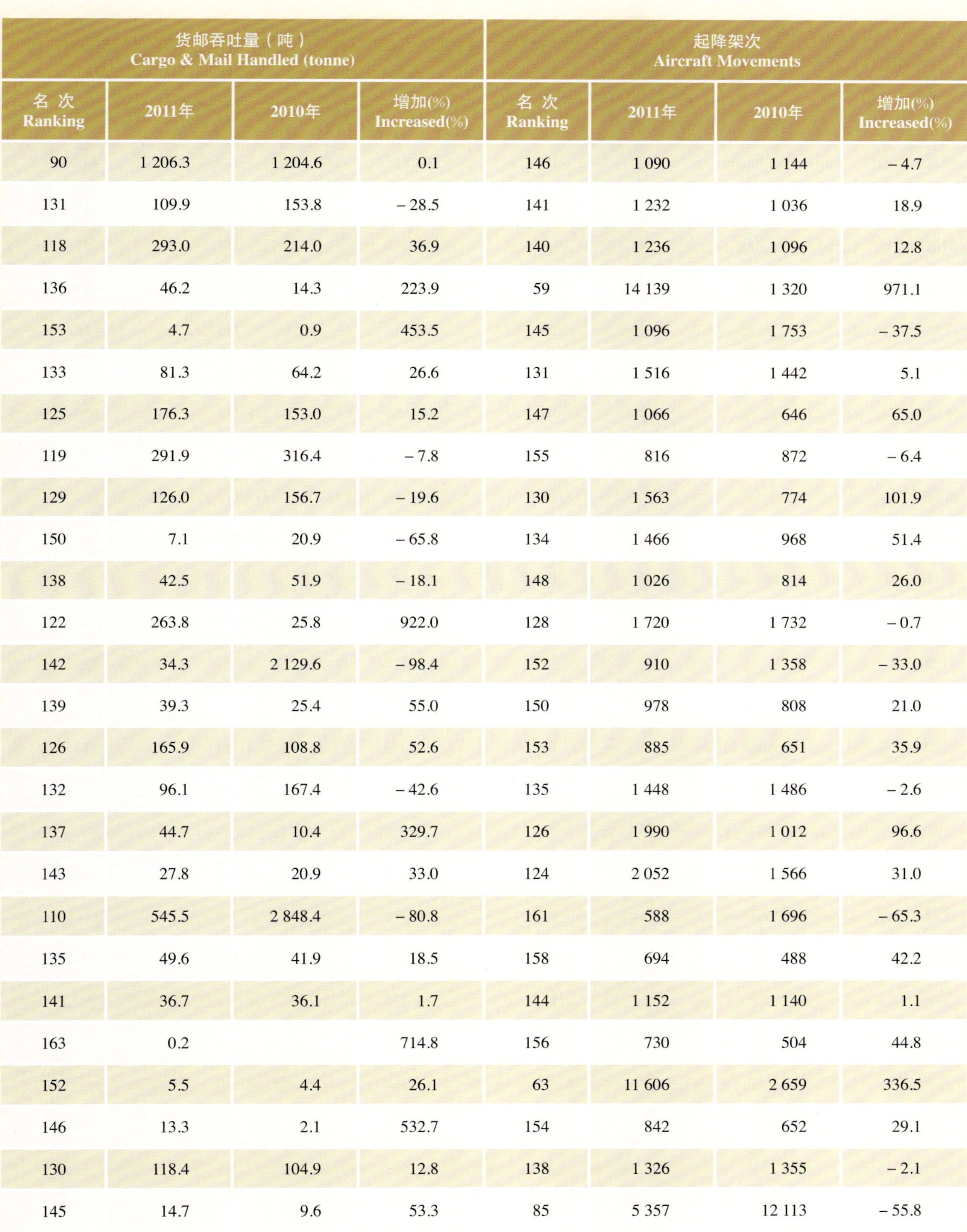

货邮吞吐量（吨） Cargo & Mail Handled (tonne)				起降架次 Aircraft Movements			
名次 Ranking	2011年	2010年	增加(%) Increased(%)	名次 Ranking	2011年	2010年	增加(%) Increased(%)
90	1 206.3	1 204.6	0.1	146	1 090	1 144	– 4.7
131	109.9	153.8	– 28.5	141	1 232	1 036	18.9
118	293.0	214.0	36.9	140	1 236	1 096	12.8
136	46.2	14.3	223.9	59	14 139	1 320	971.1
153	4.7	0.9	453.5	145	1 096	1 753	– 37.5
133	81.3	64.2	26.6	131	1 516	1 442	5.1
125	176.3	153.0	15.2	147	1 066	646	65.0
119	291.9	316.4	– 7.8	155	816	872	– 6.4
129	126.0	156.7	– 19.6	130	1 563	774	101.9
150	7.1	20.9	– 65.8	134	1 466	968	51.4
138	42.5	51.9	– 18.1	148	1 026	814	26.0
122	263.8	25.8	922.0	128	1 720	1 732	– 0.7
142	34.3	2 129.6	– 98.4	152	910	1 358	– 33.0
139	39.3	25.4	55.0	150	978	808	21.0
126	165.9	108.8	52.6	153	885	651	35.9
132	96.1	167.4	– 42.6	135	1 448	1 486	– 2.6
137	44.7	10.4	329.7	126	1 990	1 012	96.6
143	27.8	20.9	33.0	124	2 052	1 566	31.0
110	545.5	2 848.4	– 80.8	161	588	1 696	– 65.3
135	49.6	41.9	18.5	158	694	488	42.2
141	36.7	36.1	1.7	144	1 152	1 140	1.1
163	0.2		714.8	156	730	504	44.8
152	5.5	4.4	26.1	63	11 606	2 659	336.5
146	13.3	2.1	532.7	154	842	652	29.1
130	118.4	104.9	12.8	138	1 326	1 355	– 2.1
145	14.7	9.6	53.3	85	5 357	12 113	– 55.8

机 场 Airport	旅客吞吐量（人次） Passengers Handled			
	名 次 Ranking	2011年	2010年	增加(%) Increased(%)
固原 / 六盘山 Guyuan / Liupanshan	155	28 828	5 283	445.7
永州 / 零陵 Yongzhou / Lingling	156	28 131	33 216	− 15.3
甘孜 / 康定 Ganzi / Kangding	157	27 616	21 687	27.3
百色 / 田阳 Baise / Tianyang	158	26 421	60 310	− 56.2
那拉提 Nalati	159	25 818	30 275	− 14.7
塔城 Tacheng	160	25 460	25 896	− 1.7
黔江 / 舟白 Qianjiang / Zhoubai	161	21 686	1 258	1 623.8
博乐 Bole	162	18 397	11 798	55.9
朝阳 Chaoyang	163	15 380	16 113	− 4.5
黎平 Liping	164	14 466	25 784	− 43.9
日喀则 / 和平 Rikaze / Heping	165	11 463	0	
阿里 / 昆莎 Ali / Kunsha	166	9 350	6 434	45.3
吐鲁番 Turpan	167	8 424	1 224	588.2
金昌 / 金川 Jinchang / Jinchuan	168	5 671	0	
黔南州 / 荔波 Qiannanzhou / Libo	169	5 013	4 387	14.3
天水 / 麦积山 Tianshui / Maijishan	170	4 966	6 768	− 26.6
安顺 / 黄果树 Anshun / Huangguoshu	171	4 251	219	1 841.1
长海 / 大长山岛 Changhai / Dachangshandao	172	3 516	4 645	− 24.3
张掖 / 甘州 Zhangye / Ganzhou	173	2 630	0	
且末 Qiemo	174	2 269	8 361	− 72.9
汉中 Hanzhong	175	1 436	11 651	− 87.7
阿尔山 / 伊尔施 Aershan / Yiershi	176	1 083	0	
巴彦淖尔 / 天吉泰 Bayannur / Tianjitai	177	434	0	
鞍山 / 腾鳌 Anshan / Tengao	178	319	24 607	− 98.7

货邮吞吐量（吨） Cargo & Mail Handled (tonne)				起降架次 Aircraft Movements			
名 次 Ranking	2011年	2010年	增加(%) Increased(%)	名 次 Ranking	2011年	2010年	增加(%) Increased(%)
165				151	940	162	480.2
151	6.2	32.5	－81.0	159	632	678	－6.8
165				163	542	445	21.8
165				142	1 167	1 400	－16.6
158	1.8	23.0	－92.1	167	310	422	－26.5
156	2.1	1.9	10.4	157	696	749	－7.1
165				160	614	36	1 605.6
160	1.0	0.2	317.2	162	560	310	80.6
165	0	0.5	－100.0	48	26 094	296	8 715.5
157	2.0	2.4	－18.4	164	522	624	－16.3
154	3.7	0		171	148	0	
147	11.7	1.7	571.9	169	214	110	94.5
165	0	0.1	－100.0	168	240	72	233.3
164				172	142	0	
161	0.3	0.1	476.4	166	348	175	98.9
155	2.2	9.1	－75.5	170	190	344	－44.8
165		0		113	2 790	2 077	34.3
165		0		165	450	520	－13.5
165		0		175	70	0	
162	0.3	5.6	－95.0	173	82	258	－68.2
165		30.8	－100.0	174	74	480	－84.6
165		0		176	16	0	
165		0		177	8	0	
165		0		178	6	418	－98.6

2011年度通用航空作业统计表

单 位 Company	通用航空作业小时合计 General Aviation Operation Hours: Total		
	2011年	2010年	增加(%) Increased(%)
总计 Total	502 731	391 135	28.5
安阳通用航空有限责任公司 Anyang General Aviation Co., Ltd.	3 448	1 726	99.8
白城通用航空有限责任公司 Baicheng General Aviation Co., Ltd.	306	651	– 53.1
北大荒通用航空有限公司 Beidahuang General Aviation Co., Ltd.	8 957	7 756	15.5
北京泛亚通用航空有限公司 Beijing PanAisa General Aviation Co., Ltd.			
北京飞人动力体育器材有限公司昌平技术培训中心 Changping Trainning Center of Beijing Flying – man Aviation Sports Equipment Co., Ltd.	361	454	– 20.5
北京航空有限责任公司 Beijing Aviation Co., Ltd.	1 558	—	
北京市航空运动学校 Beijing Aviation Sports School	40	—	
北京首都航空有限公司 Beijing Capital Airlines Co., Ltd.	12 505	—	
北京首航直升机通用航空服务有限公司 HNA Capital Helicoper	411	—	
北京泰格尔航空飞行俱乐部有限公司 Beijing Taiger Aviation Club	1 031	1 130	– 8.8
北京天行创美航空俱乐部有限公司 Beijing Tianxing Chuangmei Aviation Club	177	161	9.7
北京天行航空运动发展有限公司 Beijing Tianxing Aviation Sports Co., Ltd.	43	30	42.3
北京天鑫爱航空俱乐部有限公司 Beijing Tianxin'ai Aviation Club			
北京中恒飞行俱乐部有限公司 Beijing Zhongheng Flying Club	80	80	0.0
常州江南通用航空有限公司 Changzhou Jiangnan General Aviation Co., Ltd.	1 666	2 019	– 17.5
大庆通用航空有限公司 Daqing General Aviation Co., Ltd.	999	1 157	– 13.6
东北通用航空有限公司 East General Aviation Co., Ltd.	2 712	2 111	28.5
东方公务航空服务有限公司 China Eastern Airlines Executive Air	756	—	
东方通用航空有限责任公司 Eastern General Aviation Corporation Co., Ltd.	4 340	4 539	– 4.4
东海公务机有限公司 Donghai Jet Company	1 047	45	2 226.1
甘肃敦煌飞天通用航空有限责任公司 Gansu Dunhuang Flying Apsara General Aviation Co., Ltd.	139	1 267	– 89.0

Statistics of General Aviation Operations in 2011

工业航空作业小时 Industrial Aviation Operation Hours			农业航空作业小时 Agricultural Aviation Operation Hours			其他通用航空作业小时 Other General Aviation Operation Hours		
2011年	2010年	增加(%) Increased(%)	2011年	2010年	增加(%) Increased(%)	2011年	2010年	增加(%) Increased(%)
56 682	65 430	-13.4	33 158	29 619	11.9	412 892	296 086	39.4
18	229	-92.1	91	69	31.2	3 340	1 428	133.9
0	266	-100.0		49	-100.0	306	336	-9.0
135	315	-57.2	6 323	6 029	4.9	2 500	1 412	77.0
	23	-100.0				361	431	-16.2
						1 558	—	
						40	—	
						12 505	—	
282						129	—	
0	50	-100.0	945	460	105.4	86	620	-86.1
0	64	-100.0		16	-100.0	177	81	118.0
						43	30	42.3
						80	80	0.0
1 390	1 960	-29.1	259			17	59	-70.6
			999	837	19.4	0	320	-100.0
			2 712	2 111	28.5			
						756	—	
3 740	4 445	-15.9	0	94	-100.0	600	—	
						1 047	45	2 226.1
0	1	-100.0				139	1 266	-89.0

单 位 Company	通用航空作业小时合计 General Aviation Operation Hours: Total		
	2011年	2010年	增加(%) Increased(%)
甘肃敦煌福来德航空俱乐部 Gansu Dunhuang Fulaide Aviation Club	1 759	1 100	59.9
广东省通用航空有限公司 Guangdong General Aviation Co., Ltd.	147	—	
广州穗联直升机通用航空有限公司 Guangzhou Suilian Helicoper General Aviation Co., Ltd.	2 402	1 257	91.1
国网通用航空有限公司 State Grid General Aviation Co., Ltd.	2 440	1 718	42.1
海南航空学校有限责任公司 Hainan Aviation Academy Co., Ltd.	13 101	2 960	342.6
海南亚太通用航空有限责任公司 Hainan Asia – Pacific General Aviation Co., Ltd.	787	910	– 13.5
和静汗戈尔迪草原航空俱乐部有限公司 Hejing Hangeerdi Prairie Aviation Club	138	—	
河北金鹏航空俱乐部有限公司 Hebei Jinpeng Aviation Club Co., Ltd.	1 094	1 200	– 8.8
河南蓝翔通用航空公司 Henan Lanxiang General Aviaiton Co., Ltd.	761	380	100.2
黑龙江凯达通用航空有限公司 Heilongjiang Kaida General Aviaiton Co., Ltd.	732	877	– 16.6
呼伦贝尔通用航空有限责任公司 Hulunbeier General Aviation Co., Ltd.	772	484	59.4
湖北楚天通用航空有限公司 Hubei Chutian General Aviation Co., Ltd.	1 803	1 355	33.0
湖北蔚蓝国际航空学校有限公司 Hubei Sky – Blue International Aviation Academy Co., Ltd.	71 593	23 991	198.4
湖北银燕通用航空有限公司 Hubei Yinyan General Aviation Co., Ltd.	171	—	
湖南衡阳通用航空有限公司 Hunan Hengyang General Aviation Co., Ltd.	946	708	33.6
吉林省通用航空有限公司 Jilin General Aviation Co., Ltd.	249	380	– 34.4
江苏华宇通用航空有限公司 Jiangsu Huayu General Aviation Co., Ltd.	609	840	– 27.5
江苏省徐州农用航空站 Jiangsu Xuzhou Agricultrue Aviation	366	—	
荆门通用航空公司 Jinmen General Aviation Co., Ltd.	1 540	1 245	23.7
荆州同诚通用航空公司 Jingzhou Tongcheng General Aviation Co., Ltd.	5 182	2 919	77.5
精功（北京）通用航空有限责任公司 Jinggong(Beijing) General Aviation Co., Ltd.	375	407	– 7.9
南山公务机有限公司 Nanshan Jet Co., Ltd.	104	—	
鄂尔多斯通用航空有限责任公司 Erdos General Aviation Co., Ltd.	2 166	3 714	– 41.7
齐齐哈尔鹤翔通用航空有限责任公司 Qiqihar Hexiang General Aviation Co., Ltd.	1 790	582	207.5
青岛九天 — 斯巴腾国际飞行学院有限公司 Qingdao Jiutian International Flight Academy	8 864	7 062	25.5
青岛直升机航空有限公司 Qingdao Helicoper Company	1 112	1 030	7.9

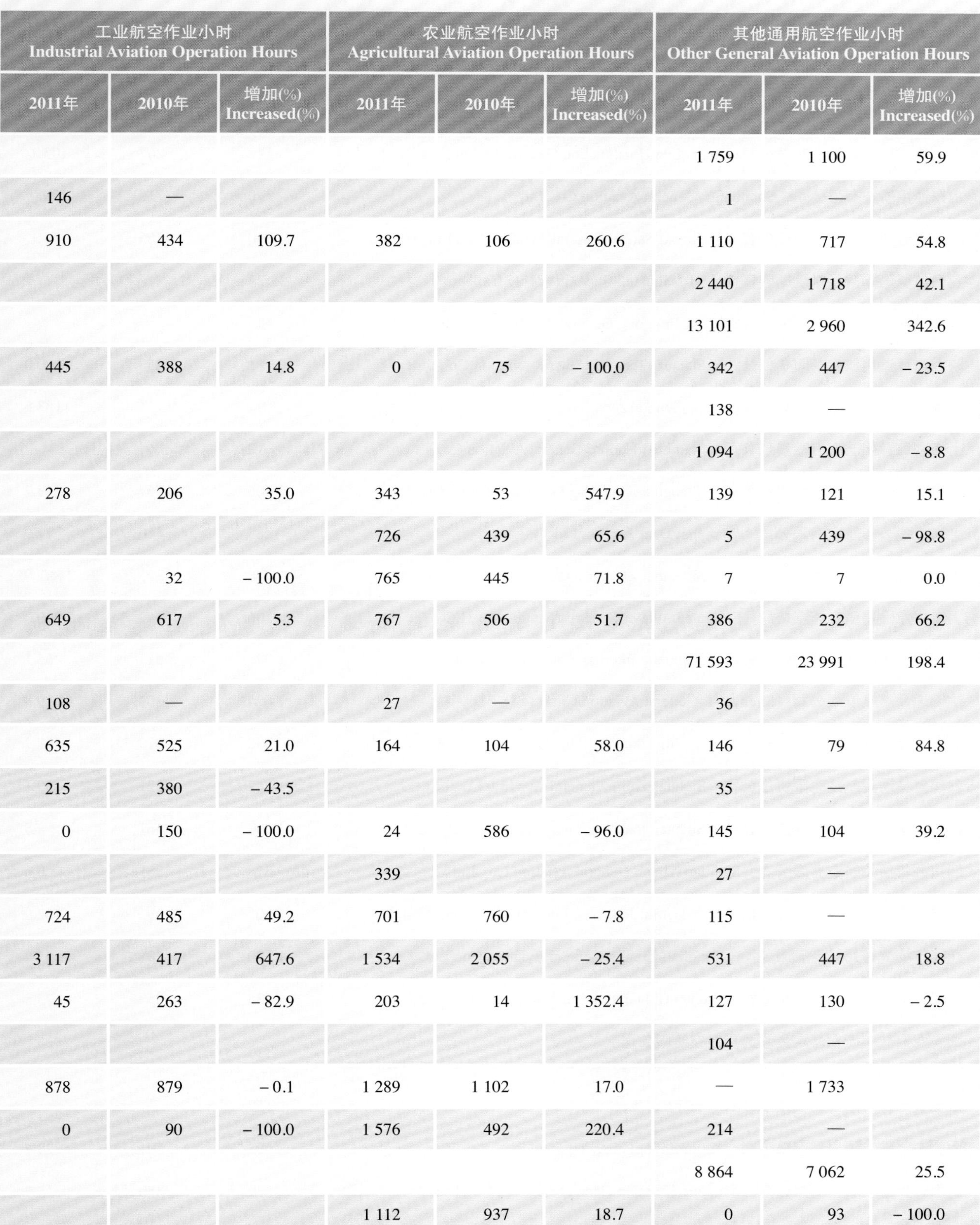

工业航空作业小时 Industrial Aviation Operation Hours			农业航空作业小时 Agricultural Aviation Operation Hours			其他通用航空作业小时 Other General Aviation Operation Hours		
2011年	2010年	增加(%) Increased(%)	2011年	2010年	增加(%) Increased(%)	2011年	2010年	增加(%) Increased(%)
						1 759	1 100	59.9
146	—					1	—	
910	434	109.7	382	106	260.6	1 110	717	54.8
						2 440	1 718	42.1
						13 101	2 960	342.6
445	388	14.8	0	75	- 100.0	342	447	- 23.5
						138	—	
						1 094	1 200	- 8.8
278	206	35.0	343	53	547.9	139	121	15.1
			726	439	65.6	5	439	- 98.8
	32	- 100.0	765	445	71.8	7	7	0.0
649	617	5.3	767	506	51.7	386	232	66.2
						71 593	23 991	198.4
108	—		27	—		36	—	
635	525	21.0	164	104	58.0	146	79	84.8
215	380	- 43.5				35	—	
0	150	- 100.0	24	586	- 96.0	145	104	39.2
			339			27	—	
724	485	49.2	701	760	- 7.8	115	—	
3 117	417	647.6	1 534	2 055	- 25.4	531	447	18.8
45	263	- 82.9	203	14	1 352.4	127	130	- 2.5
						104	—	
878	879	- 0.1	1 289	1 102	17.0	—	1 733	
0	90	- 100.0	1 576	492	220.4	214	—	
						8 864	7 062	25.5
			1 112	937	18.7	0	93	- 100.0

单 位 Company	通用航空作业小时合计 General Aviation Operation Hours: Total		
	2011年	2010年	增加(%) Increased(%)
山东黄河口通用航空有限公司 Shandong Huanghekou General Aviation Co., Ltd.	542	267	103.1
山东通用航空有限公司 Shandong General Aviation Co., Ltd.	0	713	– 100.0
山西三晋通用航空有限责任公司 Shanxi Sanjin General Aviation Co., Ltd.	810	1 765	– 54.1
陕西凤凰国际飞行学院有限责任公司 Shaanxi Phoenix Flying College	24	—	
陕西精功通用航空有限公司 Shaanxi Jinggong General Aviation Co., Ltd.	125	—	
陕西腾飞通用航空有限责任公司 Shaanxi Tengfei General Aviation Co., Ltd.		250	– 100.0
上海东方通用航空有限公司 Eastern General Aviation Corporation Co., Ltd.	11	4	183.5
上海豪海通用航空有限责任公司 Shanghai Haohai General Aviation Co., Ltd.	12	—	
上海金汇通用航空有限责任公司 Shanghai Kingwing General Aviation Co., Ltd.	2 406	767	213.7
上海金鹿公务航空有限公司 Shanghai Deer Jet Co., Ltd.	783	440	77.9
上海中瑞通用航空有限责任公司 Shanghai Zhongrui General Aviation Co., Ltd.	748	25	2 892.0
上海中意通用航空有限公司 Shanghai Avieye General Aviation Co., Ltd.	106	2	5 200.0
深圳鲲鹏国际飞行学校 Shenzhen Kunpeng Internantional Flight Academy	1 925	5 519	– 65.1
沈阳通用航空有限公司 Shenyang General Aviation Co., Ltd.	1 624	1 362	19.3
石家庄冀华通用航空有限责任公司 Shijiazhuang Jihua General Aviation Co., Ltd.	888	1 079	– 17.7
四川奥林通用航空有限责任公司 Sichuan Aolin General Aviation Co., Ltd.	782	521	50.1
四川三星通用航空有限责任公司 Sichuan Sanxing General Aviation Co., Ltd.	609	561	8.5
四川西华通用航空有限公司 Sichuan Xihua General Aviation Co., Ltd.	378	355	6.6
天津杰普逊国际飞行学院有限公司 Tianjin Jeppesen International Flight College	6 502	1 293	402.9
通辽市神鹰通用航空有限公司 Tongliao Gening General Aviation Co., Ltd.	1 370	701	95.4
武汉直升机通用航空有限公司 Wuhan Helicopters General Aviation Co., Ltd.	635	853	– 25.5
西安阎良航空产业基地金胜通用航空有限公司 Jinsheng General Aviation Co., Ltd. (Xi’an Yanliang National Aviation Hi – tech Industrial Base)	110	—	
西安直升机有限公司 Xi’an Helicopter Co., Ltd.	157	—	
西安中飞航空俱乐部有限公司 Xi’an ZhongFei Aviation Club	625	501	24.7
新疆开元通用航空有限公司 Xinjiang Kaiyuan General Aviation Co., Ltd.	379	450	– 15.9
新疆水电设计院疆海测绘院航测飞行中心 Jianghai Flying Suveying and Mapping Center of Xinjiang Hydro & Power Design Institute	131	0	

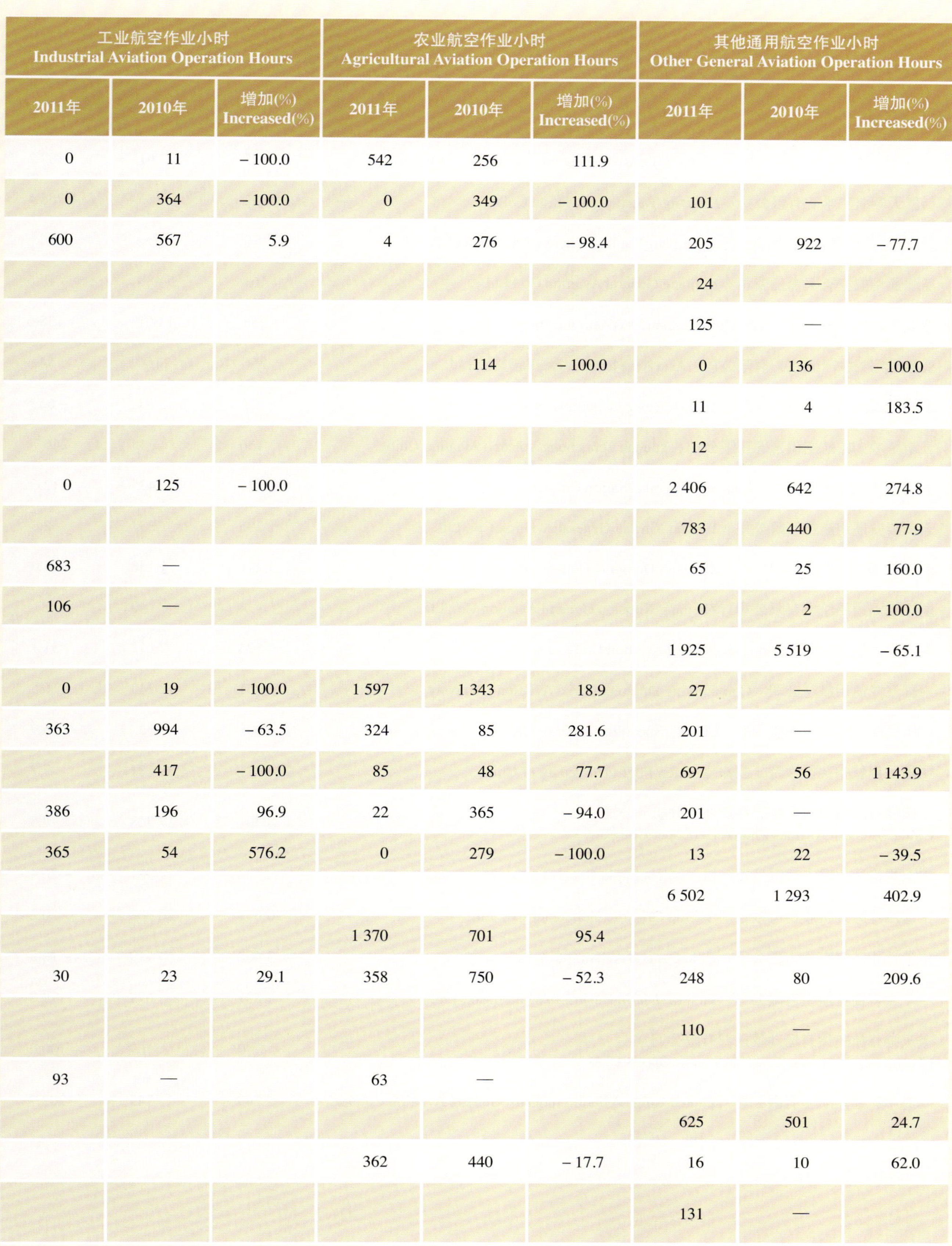

工业航空作业小时 Industrial Aviation Operation Hours			农业航空作业小时 Agricultural Aviation Operation Hours			其他通用航空作业小时 Other General Aviation Operation Hours		
2011年	2010年	增加(%) Increased(%)	2011年	2010年	增加(%) Increased(%)	2011年	2010年	增加(%) Increased(%)
0	11	－100.0	542	256	111.9			
0	364	－100.0	0	349	－100.0	101	—	
600	567	5.9	4	276	－98.4	205	922	－77.7
						24	—	
						125	—	
				114	－100.0	0	136	－100.0
						11	4	183.5
						12	—	
0	125	－100.0				2 406	642	274.8
						783	440	77.9
683	—					65	25	160.0
106	—					0	2	－100.0
						1 925	5 519	－65.1
0	19	－100.0	1 597	1 343	18.9	27	—	
363	994	－63.5	324	85	281.6	201	—	
	417	－100.0	85	48	77.7	697	56	1 143.9
386	196	96.9	22	365	－94.0	201	—	
365	54	576.2	0	279	－100.0	13	22	－39.5
						6 502	1 293	402.9
			1 370	701	95.4			
30	23	29.1	358	750	－52.3	248	80	209.6
						110	—	
93	—		63	—				
						625	501	24.7
			362	440	－17.7	16	10	62.0
						131	—	

单 位 Company	通用航空作业小时合计 General Aviation Operation Hours: Total		
	2011年	2010年	增加(%) Increased(%)
新疆天山通用航空有限公司 Xinjiang Tianshan General Aviation Co., Ltd.	175	61	187.2
新疆天翔航空学院有限公司 Xinjiang Tianxiang Aviation College	2 832	153	1 756.4
新疆天翼直升机航空有限公司 Xinjiang Tianyi Helicopter Aviation Co., Ltd.	70	—	
新疆通用航空有限责任公司 Xinjiang General Aviation Co., Ltd.	4 461	5 483	– 18.6
亚联公务机有限公司 Asia United Business Aviation Limited	3 963	1 661	138.6
亚盛医疗救护（北京）有限公司 Asia Air Medical (Beijing) Co., Ltd.	256	166	54.3
云南和谐通用航空有限公司 Yunnan Hexie General Aviation Co., Ltd.	28	81	– 65.6
云南腾冲火山航空俱乐部有限公司 Yunnan Tengchong Volcano Aviation Club	156	45	246.7
云南通用航空有限公司 Yunnan General Aviation Co., Ltd.	925	435	112.6
云南英安通用航空有限公司 Yunnan Ying'an General Aviation Co., Ltd.	1 205	1 237	– 2.6
浙江东华通用航空有限公司 Zhejiang Donghua General Aviation Co., Ltd.	1 111	1 158	– 4.0
浙江新洲通用航空有限公司 Zhejiang Xinzhou General Aviation Co., Ltd.	4	0	
中飞通用航空公司 Zhongfei General Aviation Co., Ltd.	1 524	2 212	– 31.1
中国飞龙通用航空公司 China Flying Dragon Special Aviation Company	13 041	12 243	6.5
中国民用航空飞行校验中心 Flight Inspection Center of CAAC	6 905	6 522	5.9
中国民用航空飞行学院 Civil Aviation Flight University of China	246 311	228 681	7.7
中国南方航空股份有限公司珠海直升机分公司 China Southern Airlines Zhuhai Helicoper Company	8 304	7 728	7.5
中山雄鹰通用航空有限公司 Zhongshan Eagle General Aviation Co., Ltd.	722	981	– 26.4
中信海洋直升机股份有限公司 Citic Offshore Helicopter Co., Ltd.	20 647	20 608	0.2
中信通用航空有限责任公司 Citic General Aviation Co., Ltd.	3 602	4 419	– 18.5
中一太客商务航空有限公司 First Mandarin Business Aviation Co., Ltd.	1 221	679	79.8
重庆神州航空体育运动俱乐部有限公司 Chongqing Shenzhou Aviation Athletic Sports Club	0	167	– 100.0
珠海中航通用航空有限公司 Zhuhai China Aviation Industry General Aviation Co., Ltd.	2 249	743	202.7

工业航空作业小时 Industrial Aviation Operation Hours			农业航空作业小时 Agricultural Aviation Operation Hours			其他通用航空作业小时 Other General Aviation Operation Hours		
2011年	2010年	增加(%) Increased(%)	2011年	2010年	增加(%) Increased(%)	2011年	2010年	增加(%) Increased(%)
0	50	-100.0	175	—		0	11	-100.0
						2 832	153	1 756.4
						70	—	
757	1 814	-58.3	2 952	3 669	-19.5	752	—	
						3 963	1 661	138.6
						256	166	54.3
						28	81	-65.6
						156	45	246.7
	363	-100.0				925	72	1 184.4
1 043	1 154	-9.6	57	83	-31.8	105	—	
928	1 010	-8.1	43			140	148	-5.3
						4	—	
1 274	2 212	-42.4				250	—	
2 136	6 636	-67.8	3 275	2 695	21.5	7 731	2 912	165.5
5 188	6 522	-20.5				1 717	—	
						246 311	228 681	7.7
7 406	7 728	-4.2				899	—	
268	144	85.8	0	263	-100.0	454	574	-20.9
19 712	20 054	-1.7				935	554	68.8
	2 360	-100.0	465	385	20.8	3 137	1 674	87.4
						1 221	679	79.8
						0	167	-100.0
1 627	394	313.0	182	180	0.9	441	169	160.7

2011年度我国（不含港澳台）航空公司新开辟及恢复国际航线表

序号 No.	公司(简称) Comapmy Name	航线 Route	机型 Aircraft Type	班次 Number of Flights	开航日期 Date of Launching	备注 Notes
1	国航 Air China	北京 — 杜塞尔多夫 v.v. Beijing-Düsseldorf v.v.	A330	3	2011 – 3 – 27	客运 Passenger Transport
2		北京 — 米兰 v.v. Beijing-Milan v.v.	A330	3	2011 – 6 – 15	
3		北京 — 普吉 v.v. Beijing-Phuket v.v.	B757	4	2011 – 11 – 20	
4		北京 — 慕尼黑 — 雅典 v.v. Beijing-Munich-Athens v.v.	A330	2	2011 – 5 – 11	
5	东航 China Eastern Airlines	北京 — 暹粒 v.v. Beijing-Siem Reap v.v.	A320 / B738	7	2011 – 11 – 3	客运 Passenger Transport
6		昆明 — 南宁 — 新加坡 v.v. Kunming - Nanning - Singapore v.v.	B737	2	2011 – 3 – 28	
7		昆明 — 南宁 — 吉隆坡 v.v. Kunming - Nanning - Kuala Lumpur v.v.	B737	2	2011 – 1 – 27	
8		上海浦东 — 河内 v.v. Shanghai Pudong - Hanoi v.v.	B737	7	2011 – 7 – 12	
9		上海浦东 — 胡志明 v.v. Shanghai Pudong - Ho Chi Minh v.v.	B737	7	2011 – 7 – 11	
10		上海浦东 — 夏威夷 v.v. Shanghai Pudong - Hawaii v.v.	A343	2	2011 – 8 – 7	
11		成都 — 上海浦东 — 广岛 v.v. Chengdu - Shanghai Pudong - Hiroshima v.v.	A320	7	2011 – 7 – 22	
12		上海浦东 — 法兰克福 — 汉堡 v.v. Shanghai Pudong - Frankfurt - Hamburg v.v.	A332	2	2011 – 8 – 30	
13		上海浦东 — 昆明 — 迪拜 v.v. Shanghai Pudong - Kunming - Dubai v.v.	B763	2	2011 – 7 – 5	
14		上海浦东 — 罗马 v.v. Shanghai Pudong - Rome v.v.	A343	7	2011 – 3 – 29	
15	南航 China Southern Airlines	北京 — 广州 — 布里斯班 v.v. Beijing - Guangzhou - Brisbane v.v.	B772	4	2011 – 10 – 30	客运 Passenger Transport
16		广州 — 阿姆斯特丹 v.v. Guangzhou - Amsterdam v.v.	A332	3	2011 – 6 – 7	

Newly Launched and Resumed International Routes by Domestic Airlines (Hong Kong, Macao & Taiwan not Included) in 2011

序号 No.	公司(简称) Comapmy Name	航线 Route	机型 Aircraft Type	班次 Number of Flights	开航日期 Date of Launching	备注 Notes
17	南航 China Southern Airlines	广州 — 温哥华 v.v. Guangzhou - Vancouver v.v.	B772	3	2011 – 6 – 15	客运 Passenger Transport
18		北京 — 广州 — 珀斯 v.v. Beijing - Guangzhou - Perth v.v.	A333	3	2011 – 11 – 8	
19		北京 — 乌鲁木齐 — 伊斯坦布尔 v.v. Beijing - Urumqi - Istanbul v.v.	B752	3	2011 – 11 – 22	
20		广州 — 奥克兰 v.v. Guangzhou - Auckland v.v.	A332	3	2011 – 4 – 8	
21		乌鲁木齐 — 第比利斯 v.v. Urumqi-T'bilisi v.v.	B73G	3	2011 – 9 – 1	
22	海航 Hainan Airlines	杭州 — 深圳 — 悉尼 v.v. Hangzhou - Shenzhen - Sydney v.v.	A330	3	2011 – 1 – 19	客运 Passenger Transport
23		北京 — 苏黎世 v.v. Beijing - Zurich v.v.	A330	5	2011 – 5 – 31	
24		满洲里 — 赤塔 v.v. Manchuria - Chita v.v.	B738	2	2011 – 6 – 30	
25		满洲里 — 伊尔库茨克 v.v. Manchuria - Irkutsk v.v.	B763	2	2011 – 7 – 11	
26		北京 — 釜山 v.v. Beijing - Busan v.v.	B738	7	2011 – 6 – 29	
27		北京 — 冲绳 v.v. Beijing - Okinawa v.v.	B738	3	2011 – 7 – 28	
28		海口 — 新加坡 v.v. Haikou - Singapore v.v.	B738	4	2011 – 9 – 25	
29		深圳 — 加尔各答 Shenzhen - Kolkata	B738	3	2011 – 10 – 1	
30		北京 — 马累 v.v. Beijing - Male v.v.	A330	2	2011 – 11 – 1	
31		杭州 — 普吉 Hangzhou - Phuket	B738	2	2011 – 4 – 23	
32	厦航 Xiamen Airlines	郑州 — 厦门 — 新加坡 v.v. Zhengzhou - Xiamen - Singapore v.v.	B738	7	2011 – 3 – 27	客运 Passenger Transport

序号 No.	公司(简称) Comapmy Name	航线 Route	机型 Aircraft Type	班次 Number of Flights	开航日期 Date of Launching	备注 Notes
33	川航 Sichuan Airlines	成都 — 上海浦东 — 塞班 v.v. Chengdu - Shanghai Pudong - Saipan v.v.	A330	2	2011－5－8	客运 Passenger Transport
34		成都 — 广州 — 塞班 v.v. Chengdu - Guangzhou - Saipan v.v.	A330	2	2011－5－9	
35		成都 — 南宁 — 胡志明 v.v. Chengdu - Nanning - Ho Chi Minh v.v.	A320	2	2011－9－15	
36		重庆 — 河内 v.v. Chongqing - Hanoi v.v.	A320	2	2011－3－6	
37		南宁 — 雅加达 v.v. Nanning - Jakarta v.v.	A320	2	2011－6－17	
38		重庆 — 普吉 v.v. Chongqing - Phuket v.v.	A321	3	2012－3－16	
39	春秋航 Spring Airlines	上海浦东 — 日本香川 v.v. Shanghai Shanghai Pudong - Japan, Kagawa v.v.	A320	4	2011－3－27	客运 Passenger Transport
40	国货航 Air China Cargo	上海浦东 — 安克雷奇 — 达拉斯 — 芝加哥 — 安克雷奇 — 上海浦东 Shanghai Pudong - Anchorage - Dallas - Chicago - Anchorage - Shanghai Pudong	B74Y	3	2011－8－26	货运 Freight Transport
41		上海浦东 — 安克雷奇 — 洛杉矶 — 芝加哥 — 安克雷奇 — 上海浦东 Shanghai Pudong - Anchorage - Los Angeles - Chicago - Anchorage - Shanghai Pudong	B77F / M1F	6	2011－6－1	
42		上海浦东 — 安克雷奇 — 亚特兰大 — 芝加哥 — 安克雷奇 — 上海浦东 Shanghai Pudong - Anchorage - Atlanta - Chicago - Anchorage - Shanghai Pudong	B74F / M1F	6	2011－6－1	
43		上海浦东 — 阿姆斯特丹 v.v. Shanghai Pudong - Amsterdam v.v.	B77F	5	2011－7－16	
44		上海浦东 — 阿姆斯特丹 — 天津 — 上海浦东 v.v. Shanghai Pudong - Amsterdam - Tianjin - Shanghai Pudong v.v.	B77F	3	2011－6－1	
45		上海浦东 — 南宁 — 达卡 v.v. Shanghai Pudong - Nanning - Dhaka v.v.	ABF	2	2011－10－20	
46		上海浦东 — 安克雷奇 — 圣路易斯 v.v. Shanghai Pudong - Anchorage - St. Louis v.v	B74F	1	2011－10－18	
47	银河航 Grandstar Cargo International Airlines	天津 — 首尔仁川 v.v. Tianjin-Seoul Incheon v.v.	B74Y	2	2011－4－14	货运 Freight Transport
48	邮航 China Postal Airlines	天津 — 大连 — 大阪 v.v. Tianjin - Dalian - Osaka v.v.	B73F	5	2012－3－29	货运 Freight Transport

序号 No.	公司(简称) Comapmy Name	航线 Route	机型 Aircraft Type	班次 Number of Flights	开航日期 Date of Launching	备注 Notes
49	扬子江快运 Yangtze River Express	上海浦东 — 安克雷奇 — 芝加哥 v.v. Shanghai Shanghai Pudong - Anchorage - Chicago v.v.	B74F	3	2011 – 6 – 17	货运 Freight Transport
50		上海浦东 — 郑州 — 卢森堡 — 布拉格 — 上海浦东 Shanghai Pudong - Zhengzhou - Luxembourg - Prague - Shanghai Pudong	B74F	2	2011 – 7 – 30	
51		青岛 — 首尔 — 天津 — 首尔 Qingdao - Seoul - Tianjin - Seoul	B73F	4	2011 – 8 – 17	
52		上海浦东 — 莫斯科 — 卢森堡 — 成都 — 上海浦东 Shanghai Pudong - Moscow - Luxembourg - Chengdu - Shanghai Pudong	B74F	1	2011 – 11 – 2	
	总计			179		

注：“v.v.”为往返航班
Notes: v.v. means round-trip flight

2011年度航空公司新开辟港澳台航线表

序号 No.	公司(简称) Company Name	航线 Route	机型 Aircraft Type	每周班次 Number of Weekly Flights	开航日期 Date of Launching	备注 Notes
1	国航 Air China	天津—台北松山 Tianjin - Taipei Songshan	B737	4	2011-10-30	客运 Passenger Transport
2		天津—台中 Tianjin - Taichung	B737	2	2011-10-30	
3	东航 China Eastern Airlines	无锡—桃园 Wuxi-Taoyuan	A320 / A321	12	2011-4-25	客运 Passenger Transport
4		盐城—桃园 Yancheng - Taoyuan	A320 / A321	2	2011-9-7	
5		南京—台中 Nanjing - Taichung	A320 / A321	2	2011-10-30	
6		无锡—香港 Wuxi - Hong Kong	A321 / A320	28	2011-3-27	
7		太原—西安—香港 Taiyuan - Xi'an - Hong Kong	B737 / B738	14	2011-5-18	
8	南航 China Southern Airlines	长春—台中 Changchun - Taichung	A319 / A320	2	2011-10-30	客运 Passenger Transport
9		海口—桃园 Haikou - Taoyuan	B733	4	2011-10-30	
10	海航 Hainan Airlines	三亚—桃园 Sanya - Taoyuan	B738	6	2011-12-28	客运 Passenger Transport
11		兰州—桃园 Lanzhou - Taoyuan	B738	2	2011-12-28	
12	上航 Shanghai Airlines	徐州—桃园 Xuzhou - Taoyuan	B738	4	2011-3-27	客运 Passenger Transport
13		徐州—香港 Xuzhou - Hong Kong	B738 / A320	6	2011-3-27	
14	深航 Shenzhen Airlines	无锡—桃园 Wuxi - Taoyuan	B738 / A320	12	2011-4-15	客运 Passenger Transport
15		南宁—桃园 Nanning - Taoyuan	B738 / A320	2	2011-12-1	
16		泉州—香港 Quanzhou - Hong Kong	B738 / A320	28	2011-12-1	
17		无锡—澳门 Wuxi - Macao	B738 / A320	8	2011-12-1	
18	川航 Sichuan Airlines	成都—台中 Chengdu - Taichung	A321	2	2011-11-3	客运 Passenger Transport
19		宜昌—香港 Yichang - Hong Kong	A320	4	2011-7-16	

Newly Launched Routes to Hong Kong, Macao & Taiwan by Airlines in 2011

序号 No.	公司(简称) Company Name	航线 Route	机型 Aircraft Type	每周班次 Number of Weekly Flights	开航日期 Date of Launching	备注 Notes
20	山航 Shandong Airlines	济南 — 台中 Ji'nan - Taichung	B737 / B738	2	2011 – 10 – 30	客运 Passenger Transport
21	厦航 Xiamen Airlines	泉州 — 桃园 Quanzhou - Taoyuan	B737	6	2012 – 1 – 6	客运 Passenger Transport
22		泉州 — 香港 Quanzhou - Hong Kong	B738	14	2012 – 1 – 15	
23		泉州 — 澳门 Quanzhou - Macao	B737	6	2011 – 12 – 1	
24	天津航 Tianjin Airlines	天津 — 香港 Tianjin - Hong Kong	E190	14	2011 – 7 – 1	客运 Passenger Transport
25	吉祥航 Junyao Airlines	上海浦东 — 澳门 Shanghai Pudong - Macao	A319 / A320	14	2011 – 3 – 27	客运 Passenger Transport
26	春秋航 Spring Airlines	上海浦东 — 澳门 Shanghai Pudong - Macao	A320	14	2011 – 3 – 27	客运 Passenger Transport
27	国货航 Air China Cargo	上海浦东 — 香港 Shanghai Pudong - Hong Kong	B747-400F	14	2011 – 7 – 15	货运 Freight Transport
28	中货航 China Cargo Airlines	厦门 — 桃园 Xiamen - Taoyuan	B757F / AB6F / B777F / B747F	4	2011 – 3 – 27	货运 Freight Transport
29	扬子江快运 Yangtze River Express	重庆 — 桃园 Chongqing - Taoyuan	B747F / B737F	4	2011 – 3 – 27	货运 Freight Transport
30		广州 — 桃园 Guangzhou - Taoyuan	B737F	14	2011 – 10 – 30	
31		上海浦东 — 无锡 — 香港 Shanghai Pudong - Wuxi - Hong Kong	B747-400F	6	2011 – 5 – 15	
32		成都 — 香港 Chengdu - Hong Kong	B737F	14	2011 – 12 – 1	
33		厦门 — 香港 Xiamen - Hong Kong	B737F	14	2011 – 12 – 15	
34		郑州 — 香港 Zhengzhou - Hong Kong	B737F	14	2011 – 12 – 15	

序号 No.	公司(简称) Company Name	航线 Route	机型 Aircraft Type	每周班次 Number of Weekly Flights	开航日期 Date of Launching	备注 Notes
35	华航 China Airlines	桃园 — 武汉 Taoyuan - Wuhan	B744 / A333 / A343 / B738	4	2011 – 1 – 26	客运 Passenger Transport
36		桃园 — 三亚 Taoyuan - Sanya	B744 / A333 / A343 / B738	4	2011 – 9 – 6	
37		高雄 — 北京 Gaoxiong - Beijing	B738 / A333	2	2011 – 9 – 9	
38		桃园 — 海口 Taoyuan - Haikou	B738 / A333 / A343 / B744	6	2011 – 10 – 30	
39		桃园 — 南昌 Taoyuan - Nanchang	B738 / A333 / A343 / B744	4	2011 – 10 – 30	
40		高雄 — 重庆 Gaoxiong - Chongqing	B738 / A333 / B744	4	2011 – 10 – 30	
41		桃园 — 大连 Taoyuan - Dalian	A333 / B744 / B738 / A343	2	2011 – 10 – 30	
42		台中 — 南昌 Taichung - Nanchang	E90	2	2011 – 10 – 30	
43		台中 — 重庆 Taichung - Chongqing	E90	4	2011 – 10 – 30	
44	复兴 TransAisa Airways	台北松山 — 重庆 Taipei Songshan - Chongqing	A321 / A320	4	2011 – 3 – 3	客运 Passenger Transport
45		桃园 — 上海浦东 Taoyuan - Shanghai Pudong	A321 / A320	2	2011 – 8 – 5	
46		高雄 — 长沙 Gaoxiong - Changsha	A321 / A320	2	2011 – 8 – 14	
47		桃园 — 徐州 Taoyuan - Xuzhou	A321 / A320	6	2011 – 11 – 1	
48		高雄 — 合肥 Gaoxiong - Hefei	A321 / A320	2	2011 – 11 – 2	
49		高雄 — 南宁 Gaoxiong - Nanning	A321 / A320	2	2011 – 11 – 5	

序号 No.	公司(简称) Company Name	航线 Route	机型 Aircraft Type	每周班次 Number of Weekly Flights	开航日期 Date of Launching	备注 Notes
50	复兴 TransAisa Airways	花莲 — 杭州 Hualian - Hangzhou	A321 / A320	2	2011 – 11 – 3	客运 Passenger Transport
51		花莲 — 武汉 Hualian - Wuhan	A321 / A320	2	2011 – 11 – 7	
52	长荣 EVA Airways	桃园 — 成都 Taoyuan - Chengdu	A332 / B744 / B773 / MD90	4	2011 – 3 – 27	客运 Passenger Transport
53		桃园 — 哈尔滨 Taoyuan - Harbin	A330 / B777 / B747 / MD90	6	2011 – 10 – 31	
54		桃园 — 黄山 Taoyuan - Huangshan	MD90	6	2011 – 10 – 31	
55		桃园 — 海口 Taoyuan - Haikou	MD90 / A330 / B747 / B777	4	2011 – 10 – 31	
56		高雄 — 天津 Gaoxiong - Tianjin	MD90 / A330	2	2011 – 10 – 31	
57		高雄 — 郑州 Gaoxiong - Zhengzhou	MD90 / A330	4	2011 – 10 – 31	
58		高雄 — 桂林 Gaoxiong - Guilin	MD90 / A330	6	2011 – 10 – 31	
59	立荣 Uni Airways	台中 — 南京 Taichung - Nanjing	MD90	2	2011 – 4 – 1	客运 Passenger Transport
60		桃园 — 盐城 Taoyuan - Yancheng	MD90	2	2011 – 9 – 6	
61		台东 — 南京 Taidong - Nanjing	MD90	2	2011 – 11 – 2	
62		高雄 — 昆明 Gaoxiong - Kunming	MD90 / A330	4	2011 – 11 – 2	
63		桃园 — 西安 Taoyuan - Xi'an	MD90 / A330 / B747 / B777	4	2011 – 11 – 2	
64		桃园 — 沈阳 Taoyuan - Shenyang	MD90 / A330 / B747 / B777	6	2011 – 11 – 2	

序号 No.	公司(简称) Company Name	航线 Route	机型 Aircraft Type	每周班次 Number of Weekly Flights	开航日期 Date of Launching	备注 Notes
65	华信 Mandarin Airlines	桃园 — 盐城 Taoyuan - Yancheng	B738	4	2011 – 9 – 7	客运 Passenger Transport
66		台中 — 郑州 Taichung - Zhengzhou	E90	2	2011 – 10 – 30	
67		台中 — 武汉 Taichung - Wuhan	E90	2	2011 – 10 – 30	
68		高雄 — 长沙 Gaoxiong - Changsha	A333 / B744 / B738	2	2011 – 10 – 30	
69	远东 Far Eastern Air Transport	台北松山 — 太原 Taipei Songshan - Taiyuan	MD83 / MD82	6	2011 – 10 – 31	客运 Passenger Transport
70		台北松山 — 南宁 Taipei Songshan - Nanning	MD83 / MD82	2	2011 – 11 – 1	
71		桃园 — 石家庄 Taoyuan - Shijiazhuang	MD83 / MD82	6	2011 – 10 – 31	
72		桃园 — 贵阳 Taoyuan - Guiyang	MD83 / MD82	4	2011 – 11 – 1	
73		桃园 — 三亚 Taoyuan - Sanya	MD83 / MD82	10	2011 – 10 – 28	
74		高雄 — 成都 Gaoxiong - Chengdu	MD83 / MD82	4	2011 – 10 – 31	
75		高雄 — 合肥 Gaoxiong - Hefei	MD83 / MD82	4	2011 – 11 – 1	
76		高雄 — 南宁 Gaoxiong - Nanning	MD83 / MD82	2	2011 – 11 – 3	
77		高雄 — 海口 Gaoxiong - Haikou	MD83 / MD82	4	2011 – 10 – 30	
78	香港快运 Hong Kong Express Airways	香港 — 长春 — 哈尔滨 Hong Kong - Changchun - Harbin	B738	14	2011 – 4 – 4	客运 Passenger Transport

序号 No.	公司(简称) Company Name	航线 Route	机型 Aircraft Type	每周班次 Number of Weekly Flights	开航日期 Date of Launching	备注 Notes
79	国泰 Cathay Pacific Airways	香港 — 成都 — 上海浦东 Hong Kong - Chengdu - Shanghai Pudong	B747F / A330 / A340	4	2011 – 8 – 1	货运 Freight Transport
80		香港 — 成都 Hong Kong - Chengdu	B747F / A330 / A340	6	2011 – 8 – 1	
81		香港 — 重庆 Hong Kong - Chongqing	B747F / A330 / A340	4	2011 – 7 – 18	
82		香港 — 重庆 — 上海浦东 Hong Kong - Chongqing - ShanghaiPudong	B747F / A330 / A340	4	2011 – 11 – 2	
83	香港航空 Hong Kong Airlines	香港 — 厦门 — 上海浦东 Hong Kong - Xiamen - Shanghai Pudong	A330-200F	14	2011 – 10 – 1	货运 Freight Transport
84		香港 — 郑州 Hong Kong - Zhengzhou	A330-200F / B737-300F	14	2011 – 10 – 30	
85		香港 — 石家庄 — 天津 Hong Kong - Shijiazhuang - Tianjin	A330-200F / B737-300F	14	2011 – 12 – 1	
86		香港 — 天津 Hong Kong - Tianjin	A330-200F / B737-300F	14	2011 – 12 – 1	
87	澳航 Air Macau	澳门 — 太原 Macau - Taiyuan	A319 / A320 / A321	4	2011 – 7 – 16	客运 Passenger Transport
88		澳门 — 重庆 Macau - Chongqing	A319 / A320 / A321	6	2011 – 7 – 16	

2011年度外国航空公司新开辟我国航线表

序号 No.	航空公司 Airlines	航线 Route	机型 Aircraft Type	班次 Number of Flights	开航日期 Date of Launching	备注 Notes
1	泰国亚洲航空公司 Thai Air Asia	曼谷—杭州 v.v. Bangkok - Hangzhou v.v.	A320	7	2011-1-31	客运 Passenger Transport
2	泰国曼谷航空公司 Bangkok Airways	曼谷—桂林 v.v. Bangkok - Guilin v.v.	A319	2	2011-2-1	客运 Passenger Transport
3	菲律宾飞龙航空公司 Zest Airways Inc.	卡利博—上海 v.v. Kali Bo - Shanghai v.v.	A320	2	2011-1-24	客运 Passenger Transport
4		宿务—上海 v.v. Cebu - Shanghai v.v.	A320	2	2011-7-2	
5	俄罗斯西伯利亚航空公司 Siberia Airlines	叶卡捷琳堡—北京 v.v. Yekaterinburg - Beijing v.v.	A319	4	2011-10-2	客运 Passenger Transport
6		哈巴罗夫斯克—北京 v.v. Khabarovsk - Beijing v.v.	A319	5	2011-6-8	
7	俄罗斯“乌拉尔航空公司”开放式股份公司 Joint Stock Company “Ural Airlines”	克拉斯诺亚尔斯克—哈尔滨 v.v. Krasnoyarsk - Harbin v.v.	A320	2	2011-5-25	客运 Passenger Transport
8	俄罗斯洲际航空公司 Transaero Airlines	圣彼得堡—北京 v.v. St. Petersburg - Beijing v.v.	B777	2	2011-3-27	客运 Passenger Transport
9	俄罗斯空桥货运航空公司 Air Bridge Cargo Airlines	莫斯科—郑州 v.v. Moscow - Zhengzhou v.v.	B74F	3	2011-8-19	货运 Freight Transport
10	土耳其航空公司 Turkish Airlines	伊斯坦布尔—广州 v.v. Istanbul - Guangzhou v.v.	A330	3	2011-1-30	客运 Passenger Transport
11	新加坡捷星亚洲航空公司 Jetstar Asia Airways	新加坡—杭州 v.v. Singapore - Hangzhou v.v.	A320	3	2011-3-22	客运 Passenger Transport
12		新加坡—宁波 v.v. Singapore - Ningbo v.v.	A320	3	2011-9-9	
13		墨尔本—新加坡—北京 v.v. Melbourne - Singapore - Beijing v.v.	A330	7	2011-11-24	
14	缅甸国际航空有限公司 Myanmar Airways International	仰光—广州 v.v. Yangon - Guangzhou v.v.	A320	2	2011-3-3	客运 Passenger Transport

Newly Launched International Routes to China by Foreign Airlines in 2011

序号 No.	航空公司 Airlines	航线 Route	机型 Aircraft Type	班次 Number of Flights	开航日期 Date of Launching	备注 Notes
15	斯里兰卡航空公司 SriLankan Airlines	科伦坡 — 曼谷 — 广州 v.v. Colombo - Bangkok - Guangzhou v.v.	A330	3	2011 – 1 – 28	客运 Passenger Transport
16	大韩航空 Korean Air	成都货机 Chengdu Freighter	B74F	2	2011 – 9 – 22	货运 Freight Transport
17		首尔 — 浦东 — 清州 Seoul - Pudong - Cheongju	B74F	3	2011 – 9 – 23	
18		清州 — 杭州 v.v. Cheongju - Hangzhou v.v.	A333	3	2011 – 6 – 30	客运 Passenger Transport
19		首尔 — 黄山 v.v. Seoul - Huangshan v.v.	B738	4	2011 – 7 – 28	
20	韩亚航空 Asiana Airlines	首尔 — 黄山 v.v. Seoul - Huangshan v.v.	A321	3	2011 – 7 – 30	客运 Passenger Transport
21	比什凯克航空公司 Air Bishkek	比什凯克 — 乌鲁木齐 v.v. Bishkek - Urumqi v.v.	A320	1	2011 – 6 – 2	客运 Passenger Transport
22	意大利航空公司 Alitalia	罗马 — 北京 v.v. Rome - Beijing v.v.	A332	4	2011 – 6 – 2	客运 Passenger Transport
23	埃塞俄比亚航空公司 Ethiopian Airlines	亚的斯亚贝巴 — 德里 — 杭州 v.v. Addis ababa - Delhi - Hangzhou v.v.	B763	5	2011 – 5 – 5	客运 Passenger Transport
24	荷兰皇家航空公司 KLM Dutch Royal Airline	阿姆斯特丹 — 厦门 v.v. Amsterdam - Xiamen v.v.	B772	3	2011 – 3 – 27	客运 Passenger Transport
25	美国长青国际航空公司 Evergreen International Airlines	成都货机 Chengdu Freighter	B74F	2	2011 – 3 – 27	货运 Freight Transport
26	美国南方航空公司 Southern Air Inc.	上海货机 Shanghai Freighter	B74F	3	2011 – 3 – 27	货运 Freight Transport
27	美国航空公司 American Airlines	洛杉矶 — 上海 v.v. Los Angeles - Shanghai v.v.	B772	7	2011 – 4 – 6	客运 Passenger Transport
28	沙特阿拉伯航空公司 Saudi Arabian Airlines	吉达 — 利雅得 — 广州 v.v. Jeddah - Riyadh - Guangzhou v.v.	A332	3	2011 – 3 – 27	客运 Passenger Transport

序号 No.	航空公司 Airlines	航线 Route	机型 Aircraft Type	班次 Number of Flights	开航日期 Date of Launching	备注 Notes
29	德国汉莎货运航空公司 Lufthansa Cargo	深圳货机 Shenzhen Freighter	M1F	3	2011－3－27	货运 Freight Transport
30	土耳其麦纳古货运航空公司 MNG Airlines	上海货机 Shanghai Freighter	ABY	3	2011－3－27	货运 Freight Transport
31	美国UPS联合包裹航空公司 United Parcel Service Co.	成都货机 Chengdu Freighter	M1F	5	2011－8－15	货运 Freight Transport
32	美佳环球航空（马尔代夫）有限公司 MEGA Global Air Services (Maldives) Pvt. Ltd	马累 — 北京 v.v. Male - Beijing v.v.	B763	7	2011－7－22	客运 Passenger Transport
33		马累 — 上海 v.v. Male - Shanghai v.v.	B763	7	2011－7－16	
34		马累 — 重庆 v.v. Male - Chongqing v.v.	B763	7	2011－11－24	
35	全日空 ANA	东京 — 成都 v.v. Tokyo - Chengdu v.v.	B737	7	2011－6－19	客运 Passenger Transport
36	韩国真航空股份有限公司 Jin Air	济州 — 上海 v.v. Cheju - Shanghai v.v.	B738	7	2011－6－28	客运 Passenger Transport
37	美国世界航空公司 World Airways	上海货机 Shanghai Freighter	MD11F	2	2011－6－10	货运 Freight Transport
38	越南航空公司 Vietnam Airlines	岘港 — 广州 v.v. Danang - Guangzhou v.v.	A320	2	2011－7－4	客运 Passenger Transport
39	毛里求斯航空公司 Air Mauritius	毛里求斯 — 吉隆坡 — 上海 v.v. Mauritius - Kuala Lumpur - Shanghai v.v.	A319	1	2011－7－4	客运 Passenger Transport
40	符拉迪沃斯托克航空公司 Vladivostok Air	哈巴罗夫斯克 — 大连 v.v. Khabarovsk - Dalian v.v.	A320	1	2011－7－8	客运 Passenger Transport
41	吉尔吉斯特拉菲克航空有限公司 Aria Traffic Company	奥什 — 乌鲁木齐 v.v. Osh - Urumqi v.v.	B462	2	2011－8－1	客运 Passenger Transport
42	伊朗马汉航空公司 Mahan Air	德黑兰 — 上海 v.v. Tehran - Shanghai v.v.	B743	2	2011－9－2	客运 Passenger Transport
43	俄罗斯飞行航空公司 Russian Polet Airlines	新西伯利亚 — 北京 v.v. New Siberia - Beijing v.v.	IL96	3	2011－8－28	货运 Freight Transport
44	新加坡货运航空公司 Singapore Airlines Cargo	新加坡 — 重庆 — 上海 v.v. Singapore - Chongqing - Shanghai v.v.	B74Y	2	2011－10－30	货运 Freight Transport

序号 No.	航空公司 Airlines	航线 Route	机型 Aircraft Type	班次 Number of Flights	开航日期 Date of Launching	备注 Notes
45	新加坡胜安航空公司 Silk Air	新加坡 — 长沙 v.v. Singapore - Changsha v.v.	A319	3	2011 – 10 – 31	客运 Passenger Transport
46	美国联邦快递 Federal Express	成都货机 Chengdu Freighter	M1F	5	2011 – 11 – 1	货运 Freight Transport
47	卡塔尔航空公司 Qatar Airways	多哈 — 重庆 v.v. Doha - Chongqing v.v.	A330	3	2011 – 11 – 28	客运 Passenger Transport
48	阿提哈德航空公司 Etihad Airways	阿布扎比 — 成都 v.v. Abu Dhabi - Chengdu v.v.	A332	4	2011 – 12 – 15	客运 Passenger Transport
	总计 Total			173		

注：“v.v.”为往返航班
Notes: v.v. means round-trip flight

2011年度我国（不含港澳台）航空公司新开辟国内航线表

序号 No.	公司（简称）Company Name	航线 Route	批准班次 Entitlement	经营许可审定结果 Operating Permit Approved	开航期间 Date of Launching	机型 Aircraft Type
1	海航 Hainan Airlines	阿克苏—乌鲁木齐—上海(合计) Aksu - Urumqi - Shanghai (total)	14	独家航段 同意新进航线 核准 分段航线 exclusive flight segments, newly approved routes, approved, segmented routes	2011年夏秋航季 Summer Season in 2011	B737-800
2	海航 Hainan Airlines	库尔勒—乌鲁木齐—上海(合计) Korla - Urumqi - Shanghai (total)	14	独家航段 同意新进航线 核准 分段航线 exclusive flight segments, newly approved routes,approved and segmented routes	2011年夏秋航季 Summer Season in 2011	B737-800
3	海航 Hainan Airlines	乌鲁木齐—西宁—合肥(合计) Urumqi - Xining - Hefei (total)	14	独家航段 同意新进航线 exclusive flight segments, newly approved routes	2011年夏秋航季 Summer Season in 2011	B737-800
4	海航 Hainan Airlines	三亚—福州—连云港(合计) Sanya - Fuzhou - Lianyungang (total)	6	独家航段 同意新进航线 exclusive flight segments, newly approved routes	2011年冬春航季 Winter Season in 2011	
5	海航 Hainan Airlines	三亚—桂林—兰州(合计) Sanya - Guilin - Lanzhou (total)	6	独家航段 同意新进航线 分段航线 exclusive flight segments, newly approved routes, segmented routes	2011年冬春航季 Winter Season in 2011	B737-800
6	海航 Hainan Airlines	三亚—榆林—哈尔滨(合计) Sanya - Yulin - Harbin (total)	6	独家航段 同意新进航线 exclusive flight segments, newly approved routes	2011年冬春航季 Winter Season in 2011	
7	南航 China Southern	白山—长春—北京(合计) Baishan-Changchun-Beijing (total)	14	独家航段 同意新进航线 核准 exclusive flight segments, newly approved routes, approved segment	2011年夏秋航季 Summer Season in 2011	A319
8	南航 China Southern	白山—长春—上海(合计) Baishan-Changchun-Beijing (total)	14	独家航段 同意新进航线 核准 exclusive flight segments, newly approved routes, approved segment	2011年夏秋航季 Summer Season in 2011	A321
9	南航 China Southern	揭阳潮汕—义乌—郑州(合计) JieyangChaoshan-Yiwu-Zhengzhou (total)	6	独家航段 同意新进航线 exclusive flight segments, newly approved routes	2011年冬春航季 Winter Season in 2011	B737-300
10	南航 China Southern	九寨沟—重庆—广州(合计) Jiuzhaigou - Chongqing - Guangzhou (total)	14	独家航段 同意新进航线 exclusive flight segments, newly approved routes	2011年冬春航季 Winter Season in 2011	A319
11	南航 China Southern	乌鲁木齐—兰州—海口(合计) Urumqi - Lanzhou - Haikou (total)	14	独家航段 同意新进航线 exclusive flight segments, newly approved routes	2011年冬春航季 Winter Season in 2011	B737-700
12	天津航 Tianjin Airlines	包头—西安—南宁(合计) Baotou - Xi'an - Nanning (total)	28	独家航段 同意新进航线 exclusive flight segments, newly approved routes	2011年夏秋航季 Summer Season in 2011	EMB
13	天津航 Tianjin Airlines	鄂尔多斯—呼和浩特—二连浩特(合计) Erdos - Hohhot - Erenhot (total)	2	独家航段 同意新进航线 分段航线 exclusive flight segments, newly approved routes,segmented routes	2011年冬春航季 Winter Season in 2011	EMB
14	天津航 Tianjin Airlines	鄂尔多斯—呼和浩特—满洲里(合计) Erdos-Hohhot-Manzhouli (total)	6	独家航段 同意新进航线 exclusive flight segments, newly approved routes	2011年冬春航季 Winter Season in 2011	ERJ145

Newly Launched Domestic Routes by Domestic Airlines (Hong Kong, Macao & Taiwan not Included) in 2011

序号 No.	公司（简称） Company Name	航线 Route	批准班次 Entitlement	经营许可审定结果 Operating Permit Approved	开航期间 Date of Launching	机型 Aircraft Type
15	天津航 Tianjin Airlines	天津 — 鄂尔多斯 — 乌鲁木齐(合计) Tianjin - Erdos - Urumqi (total)	14	独家航段 同意新进航线 exclusive flight segments, newly approved routes	2011年冬春航季 Winter Season in 2011	
16		天津 — 西安 — 嘉峪关(合计) Tianjin - Xi'an - Jiayuguan (total)	14	独家航段 同意新进航线 exclusive flight segments, newly approved routes	2011年冬春航季 Winter Season in 2011	EMB
17		天津 — 郑州 — 南昌(合计) Tianjin - Zhengzhou - Nanchang (total)	14	独家航段 同意新进航线 exclusive flight segments, newly approved routes	2011年冬春航季 Winter Season in 2011	ERJ145
18		乌海 — 呼和浩特 — 锡林浩特(合计) Wuhai - Hohhot - Xilinhot (total)	14	独家航段 同意新进航线 exclusive flight segments, newly approved routes	2011年冬春航季 Winter Season in 2011	ERJ145
19		西安 — 兰州 — 张掖(合计) Xi'an - Lanzhou - Zhangye (total)	6	独家航段 同意新进航线 exclusive flight segments, newly approved routes	2011年冬春航季 Winter Season in 2011	ERJ145
20	川航 Sichuan Airlines	常州 — 珠海 — 三亚(合计) Changzhou - Zhuhai - Sanya(total)	14	独家航段 同意新进航线 exclusive flight segments, newly approved routes	2011年夏秋航季 Summer Season in 2011	
21		成都 — 兰州 — 嘉峪关(合计) Chengdu - Lanzhou - Jiayuguan (total)	28	独家航段 同意新进航线 分段航线 exclusive flight segments, newly approved routes, segmented routes	2011年夏秋航季 Summer Season in 2011	
22		成都 — 临沂(合计) Chengdu - Linyi (total)	16	独家航段 同意新进航线 分段航线 exclusive flight segments, newly approved routes, segmented routes	2011年夏秋航季 Summer Season in 2011	A320
23		成都 — 乌鲁木齐 — 喀什(合计) Chengdu - Urumqi - Kashi (total)	7	独家航段 同意新进航线 分段航线 exclusive flight segments, newly approved routes, segmented routes	2011年夏秋航季 Summer Season in 2011	A319
24		成都 — 乌鲁木齐 — 伊宁(合计) Chengdu - Urumqi - Yining (total)	7	独家航段 同意新进航线 分段航线 exclusive flight segments, newly approved routes, segmented routes	2011年夏秋航季 Summer Season in 2011	
25		哈尔滨 — 太原 — 桂林(合计) Harbin - Taiyuan - Guilin (total)	14	独家航段 同意新进航线 exclusive flight segments, newly approved routes	2011年夏秋航季 Summer Season in 2011	
26		攀枝花 — 成都 — 北京(合计) Panzhihua - Chengdu - Beijing (total)	14	独家航段 同意新进航线 核准 exclusive flight segments, newly approved routes,approved	2011年夏秋航季 Summer Season in 2011	A319
27		西安 — 中卫 — 北京(合计) Xi'an - Zhongwei- Beijing (total)	14	同意新进航线 独家航段 newly approved routes,approved,exclusive flight segments	2011年夏秋航季 Summer Season in 2011	A320
28		常州 — 南宁 — 海口(合计) Changzhou - Nanning - Haikou (total)	14	独家航段 同意新进航线 exclusive flight segments, newly approved routes	2011年冬春航季 Winter Season in 2011	A320

序号 No.	公司（简称） Company Name	航线 Route	批准班次 Entitlement	经营许可审定结果 Operating Permit Approved	开航期间 Date of Launching	机型 Aircraft Type
29	川航 Sichuan Airlines	常州—珠海—海口(合计) Changzhou - Zhuhai - Haikou (total)	14	独家航段 同意新进航线 exclusive flight segments, newly approved routes	2011年冬春航季 Winter Season in 2011	A320
30		成都—九江—上海(合计) Chengdu - Jiujiang - Shanghai (total)	14	独家航段 同意新进航线 核准 分段航线 exclusive flight segments, newly approved routes,approved and segmented routes	2011年冬春航季 Winter Season in 2011	A320
31		成都—西安—临沂(合计) Chengdu - Xi'an - Linyi (total)	14	独家航段 同意新进航线 分段航线 exclusive flight segments, newly approved routes,segmented routes	2011年冬春航季 Winter Season in 2011	A320
32		哈尔滨—徐州—贵阳(合计) Harbin - Xuzhou - Guiyang (total)	6	独家航段 同意新进航线 exclusive flight segments, newly approved routes	2011年冬春航季 Winter Season in 2011	ERJ145
33		三亚—绵阳—西宁(合计) Sanya - Mianyang - Xining (total)	14	独家航段 同意新进航线 分段航线 exclusive flight segments, newly approved routes, segmented routes	2011年冬春航季 Winter Season in 2011	A320
34	厦航 Xiamen Airlines	福州—成都—拉萨(合计) Fuzhou - Chengdu - Lhasa (total)	14	独家航段 同意新进航线 exclusive flight segments, newly approved routes	2011年夏秋航季 Summer Season in 2011	B737
35		厦门—西安—西宁(合计) Xiamen - Xi'an - Xining (total)	8	独家航段 同意新进航线 exclusive flight segments, newly approved routes	2011年夏秋航季 Summer Season in 2011	
36		济南—武汉—泉州(合计) Jinan - Wuhan - Quanzhou (total)	14	独家航段 同意新进航线 exclusive flight segments, newly approved routes	2011年冬春航季 Winter Season in 2011	B737-700
37		泉州—长沙—贵阳(合计) Quanzhou - Changsha - Guiyang (total)	14	独家航段 同意新进航线 exclusive flight segments, newly approved routes	2011年冬春航季 Winter Season in 2011	B737-700
38	华夏航 China Express	贵阳—北海—桂林(合计) Guiyang -Beihai - Guilin (total)	28	独家航段 同意新进航线 exclusive flight segments, newly approved routes	2011年夏秋航季 Summer Season in 2011	CRJ-200
39		贵阳—南宁—梧州(合计) Guiyang - Nanning - Wuzhou (total)	14	独家航段 同意新进航线 exclusive flight segments, newly approved routes	2011年夏秋航季 Summer Season in 2011	CRJ-200
40		贵阳—太原—大同(合计) Guiyang - Taiyuan - Datong (total)	6	独家航段 同意新进航线 exclusive flight segments, newly approved routes	2011年夏秋航季 Summer Season in 2011	CRJ-200
41		重庆—鄂尔多斯—通辽(合计) Chongqing - Erdos - Tongliao (total)	16	独家航段 同意新进航线 exclusive flight segments, newly approved routes	2011年夏秋航季 Summer Season in 2011	CRJ-200
42		重庆—南宁—梧州(合计) Chongqing - Nanning - Wuzhou (total)	6	独家航段 同意新进航线 exclusive flight segments, newly approved routes	2011年夏秋航季 Summer Season in 2011	CRJ-200
43		重庆—南通(合计) Chongqing - Nantong (total)	8	独家航段 同意新进航线 exclusive flight segments, newly approved routes	2011年夏秋航季 Summer Season in 2011	CRJ-200
44		重庆—太原—大同(合计) Chongqing - Taiyuan - Datong (total)	14	独家航段 同意新进航线 exclusive flight segments, newly approved routes	2011年夏秋航季 Summer Season in 2011	CRJ-200
45		重庆—潍坊—大连(合计) Chongqing - Weifang - Dalian (total)	12	独家航段 同意新进航线 exclusive flight segments, newly approved routes	2011年夏秋航季 Summer Season in 2011	CRJ-200

序号 No.	公司（简称）Company Name	航线 Route	批准班次 Entitlement	经营许可审定结果 Operating Permit Approved	开航期间 Date of Launching	机型 Aircraft Type
46	国航 Air China	海拉尔 — 呼和浩特 — 武汉(合计) Hailaer - Hohhot - Wuhan (total)	14	独家航段 同意新进航线 exclusive flight segments, newly approved routes	2011年夏秋航季 Summer Season in 2011	A320
47	东航 China Eastern	邯郸 — 厦门(合计) Handan - Xiamen (total)	14	独家航段 同意新进航线 exclusive flight segments, newly approved routes	2011年夏秋航季 Summer Season in 2011	
48		杭州 — 柳州 — 昆明(合计) Hangzhou - Liuzhou - Kunming (total)	14	独家航段 同意新进航线 exclusive flight segments, newly approved routes	2011年夏秋航季 Summer Season in 2011	B737-700
49		昆明 — 百色 — 桂林(合计) Kunming - Baise - Guilin (total)	14	独家航段 同意新进航线 exclusive flight segments, newly approved routes	2011年夏秋航季 Summer Season in 2011	
50		昆明 — 长沙 — 南通(合计) Kunming - Changsha - Nantong (total)	28	独家航段 同意新进航线 exclusive flight segments, newly approved routes	2011年夏秋航季 Summer Season in 2011	B737-700
51		临沂 — 长沙 — 丽江(合计) Linyi - Changsha - Lijiang (total)	14	独家航段 同意新进航线 exclusive flight segments, newly approved routes	2011年夏秋航季 Summer Season in 2011	B737-700
52		柳州 — 三亚(合计) Liuzhou - Sanya (total)	14	独家航段 同意新进航线 分段航线 exclusive flight segments, newly approved routes, segmented routes	2011年夏秋航季 Summer Season in 2011	ERJ145 B737-300
53		南京 — 揭阳潮汕 — 湛江(合计) Nanjing - Jieyang Chaoshan - Zhanjiang (total)	8	独家航段 同意新进航线 exclusive flight segments, newly approved routes	2011年夏秋航季 Summer Season in 2011	
54		南京 — 太原 — 鄂尔多斯(合计) Nanjing - Taiyuan - Erdos (total)	14	独家航段 同意新进航线 exclusive flight segments, newly approved routes	2011年夏秋航季 Summer Season in 2011	
55		伊春 — 大连 — 上海(合计) Yichun - Dalian - Shanghai (total)	14	独家航段 同意新进航线 exclusive flight segments, newly approved routes	2011年夏秋航季 Summer Season in 2011	A320
56		杭州 — 乌鲁木齐 — 阿克苏(合计) Hangzhou - Urumqi - Aksu (total)	6	独家航段 同意新进航线 exclusive flight segments, newly approved routes	2011年冬春航季 Winter Season in 2011	A320
57		合肥 — 乌鲁木齐 — 和田(合计) Hefei - Urumqi - Hetian (total)	4	独家航段 同意新进航线 exclusive flight segments, newly approved routes	2011年冬春航季 Winter Season in 2011	A320
58		昆明 — 济宁 — 北京(合计) Kunming - Jining - Beijing (total)	14	独家航段 同意新进航线 核准 exclusive flight segments, newly approved routes,approved segments	2011年冬春航季 Winter Season in 2011	A320
59		南京 — 郑州 — 西宁(合计) Nanjing - Zhengzhou - Xining (total)	14	独家航段 同意新进航线 分段航线 exclusive flight segments, newly approved routes,segmented routes	2011年冬春航季 Winter Season in 2011	A320
60		宁波 — 淮安(合计) Ningbo - Huai'an (total)	14	独家航段 同意新进航线 exclusive flight segments, newly approved routes	2011年冬春航季 Winter Season in 2011	ERJ145
61		青岛 — 临沂 — 深圳(合计) Qingdao - Linyi - Shenzhen (total)	14	独家航段 同意新进航线 exclusive flight segments, newly approved routes	2011年冬春航季 Winter Season in 2011	
62		青岛 — 武汉 — 柳州(合计) Qingdao - Wuhan - Liuzhou (total)	14	独家航段 同意新进航线 exclusive flight segments, newly approved routes	2011年冬春航季 Winter Season in 2011	B737-300

序号 No.	公司（简称） Company Name	航线 Route	批准班次 Entitlement	经营许可审定结果 Operating Permit Approved	开航期间 Date of Launching	机型 Aircraft Type
63	东航 China Eastern	上海 — 昆明 — 德宏(合计) Shanghai - Kunming - Dehong (total)	14	独家航段 同意新进航线 exclusive flight segments, newly approved routes	2011年冬春航季 Winter Season in 2011	B737-300
64		上海 — 西安 — 延安(合计) Shanghai - Xi'an - Yan'an (total)	14	独家航段 同意新进航线 exclusive flight segments, newly approved routes	2011年冬春航季 Winter Season in 2011	
65		厦门 — 淮安(合计) Xiamen - Huai'an (total)	14	独家航段 同意新进航线 exclusive flight segments, newly approved routes	2011年冬春航季 Winter Season in 2011	ERJ145
66		宜昌 — 南京(合计) Yichang - Nanjing (total)	14	独家航段 同意新进航线 exclusive flight segments, newly approved routes	2011年冬春航季 Winter Season in 2011	ERJ145
67		张家界 — 海口(合计) Zhangjiajie - Haikou (total)	14	独家航段 同意新进航线 exclusive flight segments, newly approved routes	2011年冬春航季 Winter Season in 2011	B737-300
68	山航 Shandong Airlines	济南 — 温州 — 北海(合计) Ji'nan - Wenzhou - Beihai (total)	14	独家航段 同意新进航线 exclusive flight segments, newly approved routes	2011年夏秋航季 Summer Season in 2011	CRJ-200
69		济南 — 郑州 — 绵阳(合计) Ji'nan - Zhengzhou - Mianyang (total)	28	独家航段 同意新进航线 exclusive flight segments, newly approved routes	2011年夏秋航季 Summer Season in 2011	CRJ-200
70		赣州 — 南昌 — 济南(合计) Ganzhou - Nanchang - Ji'nan (total)	14	独家航段 同意新进航线 exclusive flight segments, newly approved routes	2011年冬春航季 Winter Season in 2011	CRJ-200
71		济南 — 杭州 — 珠海(合计) Jinan - Hangzhou - Zhuhai (total)	6	独家航段 同意新进航线 exclusive flight segments, newly approved routes	2011年冬春航季 Winter Season in 2011	CRJ-200、B737
72		济南 — 南昌 — 北海(合计) Ji'nan - Nanchang - Beihai (total)	8	独家航段 同意新进航线 exclusive flight segments, newly approved routes	2011年冬春航季 Winter Season in 2011	CRJ-200
73		济南 — 宁波 — 揭阳潮汕(合计) Ji'nan - Ningbo - Jieyang, Chaoshan (total)	14	独家航段 同意新进航线 exclusive flight segments, newly approved routes	2011年冬春航季 Winter Season in 2011	CRJ-200
74		武夷山 — 济南 — 北京(合计) Wuyishan - Ji'nan - Beijing (total)	14	独家航段 同意新进航线 核准 exclusive flight segments, newly approved routes,approved	2011年冬春航季 Winter Season in 2011	B737-800
75		厦门 — 景德镇 — 成都(合计) Xiamen - Jingdezhen - Chengdu (total)	14	独家航段 同意新进航线 exclusive flight segments, newly approved routes	2011年冬春航季 Winter Season in 2011	B737-800
76		烟台 — 济南 — 成都(合计) Yantai - Ji'nan - Chengdu (total)	14	独家航段 同意新进航线 exclusive flight segments, newly approved routes	2011年冬春航季 Winter Season in 2011	B737-800
77		烟台 — 太原 — 西安(合计) Yantai - Taiyuan - Xi'an (total)	14	独家航段 同意新进航线 exclusive flight segments, newly approved routes	2011年冬春航季 Winter Season in 2011	B737
78	昆明航 Kunming Airlines	昆明 — 重庆 — 义乌(合计) Kunming - Chongqing - Yiwu (total)	28	独家航段 同意新进航线 分段航线 exclusive flight segments, newly approved routes,segmented routes	2011年夏秋航季 Summer Season in 2011	B737-700
79	深航 Shenzhen Airlines	上海 — 景德镇 — 深圳(合计) Shanghai - Jingdezhen - Shenzhen (total)	14	独家航段 同意新进航线 核准 exclusive flight segments, newly approved routes, approved	2011年夏秋航季 Summer Season in 2011	B737-800

序号 No.	公司（简称） Company Name	航线 Route	批准班次 Entitlement	经营许可审定结果 Operating Permit Approved	开航期间 Date of Launching	机型 Aircraft Type
80	春秋 Spring Airlines	上海—黔江—昆明(合计) Shanghai - Qianjiang - Kunming (total)	14	独家航段 同意新进航线 分段航线 exclusive flight segments, newly approved routes, segmented routes	2011年夏秋航季 Summer Season in 2011	A320
81	河北航 Hebei Airlines	石家庄—重庆—南宁(合计) Shijiazhuang - Chongqing - Nanning (total)	28	独家航段 同意新进航线 exclusive flight segments, newly approved routes	2011年夏秋航季 Summer Season in 2011	B737-700
82		石家庄—鄂尔多斯—兰州(合计) Shijiazhuang - Erdos - Lanzhou (total)	8	独家航段 同意新进航线 exclusive flight segments, newly approved routes	2011年冬春航季 Winter Season in 2011	ERJ145
83	首都航 Capital Airlines	西安—呼和浩特—海拉尔(合计) Xi'an - Hohhot - Hailar (total)	14	独家航段 同意新进航线 exclusive flight segments, newly approved routes	2011年夏秋航季 Summer Season in 2011	EMB190
84		西安—黄山—厦门(合计) Xi'an - Huangshan - Xiamen (total)	14	独家航段 同意新进航线 exclusive flight segments, newly approved routes	2011年夏秋航季 Summer Season in 2011	A319
85		恩施—武汉—海口(合计) Enshi - Wuhan - Haikou (total)	14	独家航段 同意新进航线 exclusive flight segments, newly approved routes	2011年冬春航季 Winter Season in 2011	A319
86	奥凯航 Okay Airways	哈尔滨—黑河—漠河(合计) Harbin - Heihe - Mohe (total)	14	独家航段 同意新进航线 exclusive flight segments, newly approved routes	2011年冬春航季 Winter Season in 2011	MA60
87	成都航 Chengdu Airlines	景德镇—武汉—恩施(合计) Jingdezhen - Wuhan - Enshi (total)	14	独家航段 同意新进航线 分段航线 交回 exclusive flight segments, newly approved routes,segmented routes, returned routes	2011年冬春航季 Winter Season in 2011	A319
88	中联航 China United Airlines	上海—佛山(合计) Shanghai - Foshan (total)	14	独家航段 同意新进航线 exclusive flight segments, newly approved routes	2011年冬春航季 Winter Season in 2011	

2011年9月17日，民航局局长李家祥在天津会见了法国交通运输部部长蒂埃里·马里亚尼，双方就中法两国间航空运输、飞机引进、通用航空发展等事宜深入交换了意见

On September 17, 2011, Li Jiaxiang, Administrator of CAAC, Meets with Thierry Mariani, French Secretary of State for Transport in Tianjin. Both Sides Discuss about Bilateral Air Transport, Introduction of Aircraft and the Development of General Aviation etc

2011年11月22日，民航局李军副局长出席“2011民航强国论坛”，并为全国民航文明单位颁牌

On November 22, 2011, Li Jun, Deputy Administrator of CAAC, Attends the 2011 Civil Aviation Power Forum and Presents Awards to National Role Model Civil Aviation Entities

2011年6月14日，民航局李健副局长率团出席2011年欧美国际航空安全年会

On June 14, 2011, Li Jian, Deputy Administrator of CAAC, Heads a Delegation to Attend the 2011 Europe/US International Aviation Safety Conference

2011年4月18日，民航局夏兴华副局长会见美国贸易发展署署长李·扎克女士，并签署中美航空合作项目第七期赠款协议

On April 18, 2011, Xia Xinghua, Deputy Administrator of CAAC, Meets with Leocadia I. Zak, Director of US TDA, and Signs the 7th Grant Agreement under the ACP

2011年7月27日，民航局党组纪检组组长梁宁生出席海航北京至冲绳航线开航仪式

On July 27, 2011, Liang Ningsheng, Group Head of Discipline Inspection of the Party Group, Attends the Launching Ceremony of Beijing-Okinawa Route by Hainan Airlines

中国民用航空局行政机构组织机构图

中国民用航空局

- 综合司 Department of General Affairs
- 航空安全办公室 Office of Aviation Safety
- 政策法规司 Department of Policy, Law and Regulation
- 发展计划司 Department of Development Planning
- 财务司 Department of Finance
- 人事科教司 Department of Personnel, Science & Technology and Education
- 国际司 Department of International Affairs
- 运输司 Department of Transport
- 飞行标准司 Department of Flight Standard

Administrative Organizational Structure of CAAC

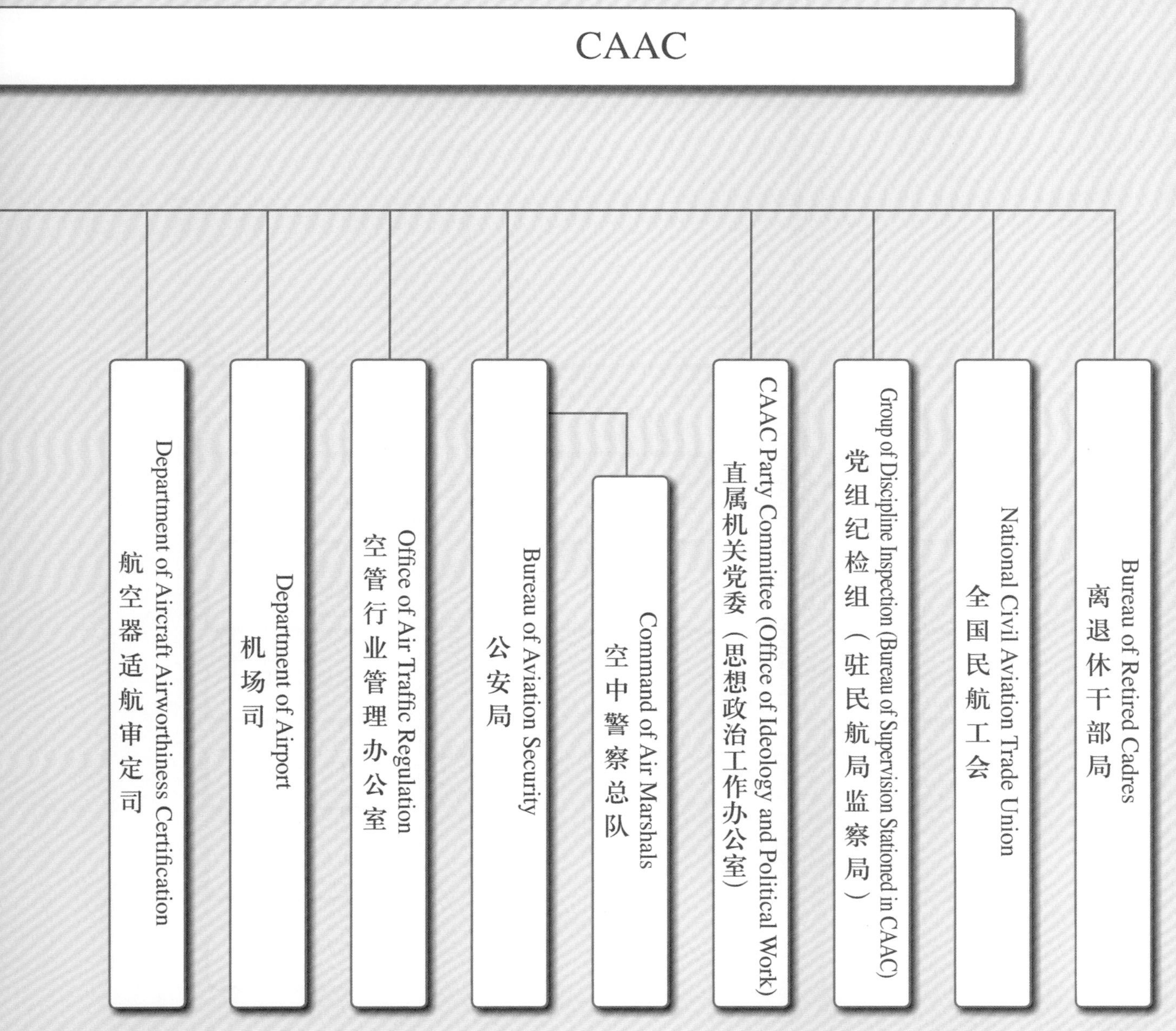

中国民用航空地区行政机构组织机构图

中国民用航空局

- 华北地区管理局 CAAC North Regional Administration
  - 北京监管局 Beijing SSMB
  - 天津监管局 Tianjin SSMB
  - 河北监管局 Hebei SSMB
  - 山西监管局 Shanxi SSMB
  - 内蒙古监管局 Inner Mongolia SSMB
  - 天津滨海国际机场公安分局 Tianjin Airport Sub-bureau of Aviation Security
- 东北地区管理局 CAAC Northeast Regional Administration
  - 辽宁监管局 Liaoning SSMB
  - 吉林监管局 Jilin SSMB
  - 黑龙江监管局 Heilongjiang SSMB
  - 大连监管局 Dalian SSMB
- 华东地区管理局 CAAC East Regional Administration
  - 上海监管局 Shanghai SSMB
  - 江苏监管局 Jiangsu SSMB
  - 浙江监管局 Zhejiang SSMB
  - 安徽监管局 Anhui SSMB
  - 福建监管局 Fujian SSMB
  - 江西监管局 Jiangxi SSMB
  - 山东监管局 Shandong SSMB
  - 温州监管局 Wenzhou SSMB
  - 厦门监管局 Xiamen SSMB
  - 青岛监管局 Qingdao SSMB

Regional Administrative Organizational Structure of CAAC

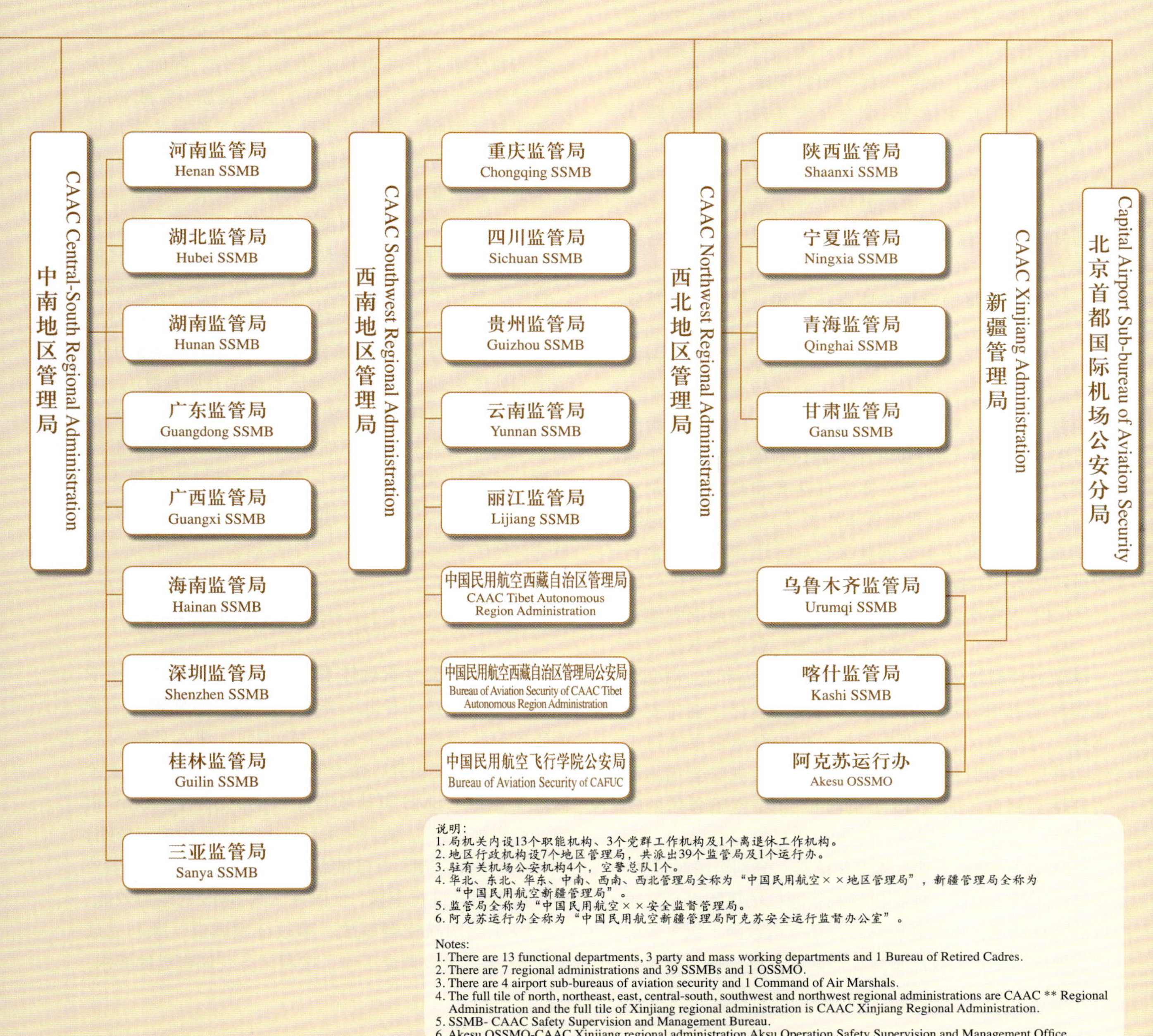

说明:
1. 局机关内设13个职能机构、3个党群工作机构及1个离退休工作机构。
2. 地区行政机构设7个地区管理局，共派出39个监管局及1个运行办。
3. 驻有关机场公安机构4个，空警总队1个。
4. 华北、东北、华东、中南、西南、西北管理局全称为“中国民用航空××地区管理局”，新疆管理局全称为“中国民用航空新疆管理局”。
5. 监管局全称为“中国民用航空××安全监督管理局。
6. 阿克苏运行办全称为“中国民用航空新疆管理局阿克苏安全运行监督办公室”。

Notes:
1. There are 13 functional departments, 3 party and mass working departments and 1 Bureau of Retired Cadres.
2. There are 7 regional administrations and 39 SSMBs and 1 OSSMO.
3. There are 4 airport sub-bureaus of aviation security and 1 Command of Air Marshals.
4. The full tile of north, northeast, east, central-south, southwest and northwest regional administrations are CAAC ** Regional Administration and the full tile of Xinjiang regional administration is CAAC Xinjiang Regional Administration.
5. SSMB- CAAC Safety Supervision and Management Bureau.
6. Akesu OSSMO-CAAC Xinjiang regional administration Aksu Operation Safety Supervision and Management Office.

航空安全办公室

一、加强督导督查，落实主体责任

（1）深化资质能力排查，深化主体责任落实 充分发挥航安办督导和协调的作用，狠抓专业技术人员资质能力排查工作。一是督促各航空公司把落实主体责任和资质能力建设结合起来，通过基层宣讲、轮训等多种手段，狠抓《民用航空运输机长职责》等重要文件的执行和落实。二是针对外籍飞行员职业操守和违规违章等问题，会同飞标司研究制定了外籍飞行员选聘和监管的安全措施，联合下发《关于加强外籍飞行人员管理的通知》，对确保外籍飞行员按章运行提出具体要求。三是在飞行人员资质排查基础上，会同飞标司研究下发《关于继续做好专业人员技术排查工作的通知》，将排查范围扩大到机务、签派、空管等各类重要专业岗位，推动技术排查常态化。

（2）以监督检查促主体责任落实 根据国务院安委会总体部署，先后组织多次民航系统安全检查和督察。特别是"7·23"特大铁路事故发生后，航安办立即按局领导指示，下发电报传达国务院常务会议和民航电视电话会议精神，部署安全大检查，查出各类隐患 6 930 个，重大隐患 42 个，通过对隐患整改的跟踪监察，推动了安全生产主体责任落实和隐患治理常态化与规范化。国务院批复调查组关于"7·23"甬温线特别重大铁路交通事故调查报告后，迅速组织向全行业进行传达，并提出工作要求。

（3）以安全考核促主体责任落实 按照局党组提出"安全责任全覆盖"的指示精神，航安办下发《关于继续做好航空安全责任书签订工作的通知》，指导各管理局明确母公司对分、子公司安全责任，细化安全指标，完成与民航各生产运行单位安全责任书签订工作，并以持续监督和量化考核的方式促进安全措施和责任落实到位。完成 35 个机场和 11 个空管单位的安全审计。

（4）以行政约见促主体责任落实 分别组织对国航、东航、川航、上航、首都机场及新疆机场集团等 6 家单位的行政约见，除诫勉谈话外，还采取致函上级主管部门、提出对主要领导问责建议等配套措施，强化行政约见的力度，促进主体责任落实和安全问题整改。

二、重视顶层设计，突出政策引导

（1）制定行业安全发展纲要 组织编写下发《中国民航安全生产"十二五"规划》和《中国民用航空安全规划纲要》，明确未来一段时期的安全目标、主要任务和重大项目，并组织规划宣讲工作。同时，还完成了国家"十二五"安全规划的意见反馈。完成 2011 年初民航"两会"局领导讲话及安全工作报告重点任务分解，并定期跟踪进展情况，推动"十二五"开局之年各项安全重点工作的细化和落实。

（2）完善安全监管制度 编写下发《民用航空重大安全事项挂牌督办及整改工作暂行办法》和《民航局安全监管行政约见暂行办法》，完成《安全监管局安全绩效考核办法》修改草案。编写下发《民用航空其他不安全事件样例》，明确其他不安全事件信息的上报范围和处理原则，并督察各地区管理局开展宣贯。

（3）修订《民用航空器事故征候标准》 本着严格运输航空、适当放宽通用航空的宗旨，对《民用航空器事故征候标准》进行修订，使征候标准更科学更具有操作性，进一步引导运输航空公司进一步强化安全管理、提高安全裕度。

三、狠抓基础建设，提高监管能力

（1）开展安全管理体系（SMS）审核试点 组织航科院相关人员在华北、华东、中南、西南等地区挑选多家有代表性的航空公司进行调研，深入了解 SMS 实施情况，反复研究，修改制定了符合 ICAO 最新安全管理举措的"SMS 审核检查单"，并完善了"SMS 审核试点实施方案"，协调相关部门和管理局组成审核组，按期完成厦航 SMS 审核试点工作。目前，多家企事业单位请求对其进行审核，全面评估其 SMS 的运行效能。

（2）组织航空器事故、事故征候调查 顺利完成了"8·24"事故调查工作，按照国务院调查组的要求，

Office of Aviation Safety

I. Strengthening Supervision and Oversight to Implement the Principal Responsibilities

1. Carrying out in-depth the qualification examinations and the implementation of the principal responsibilities. The Office of Aviation Safety brought into full play its coordination and supervision roles and made great efforts in the qualification examinations of the professional technicians. First, the airlines were urged to combine the implementation of the principal responsibilities and the qualification capacity building. Through multiple means such as grass root publicity and training, it paid a great deal of attention to the implementation of important documents such as the Functions of Pilots-in-command in Civil Air Transport, etc. Second, in light of the foreign pilots' occupational ethics and their breaches of the regulations, the office worked together with the Department of Aircraft Airworthiness Certification to develop and adopt safety related measures on the selection and supervision of foreign pilots, jointly issued the Notice on Strengthening the Management of Foreign Airmen, and raised specific requirements to ensure the foreign pilots operating according to regulations. Third, on the basis of qualification examination of pilots, the office and the Department of Flight Standards jointly issued the Notice on Continuously Doing a Good Job in Examinations of the Professional Technicians, extending the examinations to the important professional posts like mechanics, dispatchers and air traffic controllers, and pushing forward their normalization.

2. Facilitating the implementation of the principal

按时高质量地完成了技术组调查报告的提交，受到调查组领导的充分肯定。完成“11·28”浦东津巴布韦货机冲出跑道事故调查，赴印尼参加鸽航“5·7”MA60坠海事故调查；完成“6·19”东航A319空中失火严重事故征候调查工作。此外，还对“3·20”严重事故征候、“3·29”赛斯纳失踪和“12·4”低油量备降等不安全事件的调查进行了督察。

（3）加强安全信息共享，改进安全信息工作 推进局方和企事业单位安全信息共享机制试点建设开展调研，起草信息共享协议，完善安全信息网功能，增加安全信息透明度和共享度，全年安全信息收集量达到9 300条，比上年增长86%。根据安全信息网收集的不安全事件信息和国际安全信息，定期编发《民航不安全事件月度统计分析报告》和《世界民航事故调查跟踪》等。

（4）开展国际安全交流与合作 组织召开中国—新加坡航空安全研讨会，双方就安全管理组织机构、国家航空安全纲要（SSP）、SMS等情况进行了介绍和交流，并就加强双方在航空安全沟通、航空安全培训机构、事故征候/事故调查与预防、安全信息管理、航空安全项目研究、安全系统建设等六个方面达成了一致的合作意向。加强与法国调查机构交流，法国航空事故调查局与航安办、综合司共同探讨事故调查中媒体应对及家庭援助的事宜，并通报法航447事故调查工作的进展情况。积极响应国际民航组织第37届大会发表声明，与霍尼韦尔集团在京联合举办跑道安全论坛，探讨解决跑道安全问题的新技术和新方法。此外，通过参加会议、联合演练等形式，加强与台湾及国外事故调查机构的交流合作。

（5）组织实施安全培训和宣传 贯彻落实三部委安全培训要求，围绕提高安全管理人员资质能力开展安全培训工作。全年组织民航企事业单位负责人和运输航空公司高层安全管理人员等安全培训班27期，共1 659人接受培训，超过此前三年受训人数总和。大力宣传全国民航航空安全会议精神，部署开展“安全生产月”活动。依托《航空安全》杂志，积极宣传行业安全发展政策和安全管理理念，推广航空安全技术。组织召开《航空安全》杂志首届理事会会议。■

responsibilities by supervision and examination. In accordance with the overall deployment of the Work Safety Committee of the State Council, the office organized safety inspections and supervisions in the civil aviation industry for many times. Especially after the high speed railway crash on July 23, 2011, the office, in accordance with the instructions of administrators of CAAC, immediately sent out telegraphs disseminating the guiding principles of the Executive Conference of the State Council and the telephone and television conference of CAAC. Overall safety examinations were arranged, screening out 6 930 hidden hazards of various kinds and 42 major hazards, and through the follow-up supervision of the hazards rectified, promoting the implementation of principal safety responsibilities and the normalization and standardization of hazards rectification. After the State Council's approval of the accident investigation report on the high speed railway crash of Ningbo to Wenzhou line on July 23, 2011, the office immediately communicated the report to the whole industry and put forward the work requirements.

3. Facilitating the implementation of the principal responsibilities by safety assessment. In accordance with the guiding principles of "Making Safety Responsibilities Cover All Sectors" proposed by the Leading Party Group of CAAC, the Office of Aviation Safety issued the Notice on Continuously Doing a Good Job in Signing Aviation Safety Contracts, guiding regional administrations in defining the safety responsibilities shouldered by the mother companies for their subsidiaries and branches and the breakdown of safety indicators, completed the signing of the safety responsibility contracts with the production and operation entities in civil aviation industry, and promoted the implementation of the safety measures and responsibilities by continuous supervision and quantitative evaluation. It also accomplished 35 airports and 11 air traffic control entities' safety audits.

4. Reinforcing the implementation of the principal responsibilities by administrative summons. Administrative summons for 6 entities such as Air China, China Eastern Airlines, Sichuan Airlines, Shanghai Airlines, Capital Airport and Xinjiang Airport Group were organized. Besides dissuasive talks, the implementation of the principal responsibilities and the rectification of safety problems were reinforced by strengthening the administrative summons with supporting measures such as addressing letters to superiors in charge and proposing recommendations accountable to the key leaders.

II. Prioritizing Top Level Design and Giving Prominence to Policy Guidance

1. Developing the outline of the safe development of the industry. The 12th Five-Year Plan for Civil Aviation Work Safety and the Outline of Safety Plan for China Civil Aviation were developed and issued, clarifying and organizing the publicity of the safety targets, major tasks and important projects for the future time to come. Meanwhile, the feedbacks were proposed to the state safety plan for the 12th Five-Year Plan period. The office accomplished the breaking down of the key tasks proposed in the speeches made by the administrators of CAAC during the civil aviation work and civil aviation safety work conferences held at the beginning of 2011, and in the safety work report, and followed up regularly their progress, propelling the refinement and implementation of all key safety work at the beginning year of the 12th Five-Year Plan period.

2. Perfecting the safety supervision system. Interim Methods for Supervised Invistigation, Handling and Rectification of Major Safety Issues in Civil Aviation and the CAAC Interim Methods for Administrative Summons on Safety Supervision were developed and issued. The amended draft of Methods for Safety Performance Evaluation of the Safety Supervision and Management Bureaus was completed. Exemplary Cases of Other Unsafe Incidents in Civil Aviation was developed and issued, in which the reporting scope and disposing principles for other unsafe incidents were identified, and the all regional administrations were urged to carry out its publicity and implementation.

3. Amending the Standards of Civil Aircraft Incidents. In accordance with the principle of tightening transport aviation and moderately easing general aviation, the office amended the Standards of Civil Aircraft Incidents, making the incident standards more scientific and operational, and further guiding transport airlines in furthering safety management and increasing safety margin.

III. Making Great Efforts in Fundamental Construction to Improve Supervision Capacity

1. Carrying out SMS pilot review. Personnel from China Academy of Civil Aviation Science and Technology were organized to survey in the representative airlines selected in north China, east China, central and south China, and southwest regions. The office studied the implementation of SMS, made repeated researches, amended and developed SMS review checklist that was in compliance with the latest initiatives adopted by ICAO. It also refined the Pilot SMS Review Implementation Program, coordinated relevant departments and regional administrations to set up a review group and fulfilled the pilot SMS review in Xiamen Airlines. Currently many enterprises and institutional entities have filed requests for verification to comprehensively evaluate their SMS operational efficiency.

2. Organizing the investigation on aircraft accidents and incidents. The office successfully completed the investigation of the air crash auident on August 24, 2010 and in accordance with the requirements of the State Council Investigation Group, timely and excellently completed the submission of investigation report by the technical group, which was well received by the leaders of the Investigation Group. It completed the accident investigation on Zimbabwe freighter overshooting the runway on November 29, 2009 and participated in the investigation of MA60 maritime crash of Merpati Nusantara Airlines on May 7, 2011. It also completed the severe incident investigation of the A319 air fire of China Eastern Airlines on June 19 and supervised the investigations of the severe incident on March 20, the disappearance of Cessna aircraft on March 29 and the unsafe incident of aircraft low fuel volume on December 4.

3. Strengthening safety information sharing to improve information safety work. The office carried out the survey of the pilot safety information sharing mechanism building between CAAC and enterprises and institutional entities, drafted information sharing agreements, improved the functions of the safety information network and enhanced the transparency and sharing of safety information, thus collecting 9 300 pieces of safety information in the whole year, increasing by 86% over that of the previous year. In accordance with the unsafe incidents information and the international safety information collected by safety information network, the office regularly developed and issued Monthly Statistical Analysis Report of Unsafe Incidents in Civil Aviation, and Accident Investigation and Follow-up of the World Civil Aviation, etc.

4. Carrying out international safety exchange and cooperation. The China-Singapore Aviation Safety Symposium was held, introducing and discussing the safety management organizational structures, state safety program (SSP) and SMS, and reaching consensus, by both sides, on strengthening the cooperation in 6 fields, including aviation safety communication, aviation safety training organizations, incident/accident investigation and prevention, safety information management, aviation safety research projects, and the safety system building. The office strengthened communications with French investigation institutions, BEA, the office and the Department of General Affairs of CAAC discussed media response and aids to the victim families during an accident investigation, and circulated the notice of the progress of Air France Flight 447 accident investigation in 2009. It also responded actively to the declaration of the 37th Assembly of ICAO and held a runway safety forum in Beijing with Honeywell, discussing new technologies and new methods in handling runway safety problems. In addition, the office intensified, through participation in meetings, joint rehearsals, etc., the exchange and cooperation with Taiwan and foreign accident investigation institutions.

5. Organizing safety training and publicity. The office implemented the requirements on safety training by the three ministry level departments and carried out safety trainings with focus on improving the qualification of safety management personnel. In 2011, 27 safety training sessions were organized for the responsible persons of the civil aviation enterprises and institutional entities, and for senior executives of the airlines, and the number of persons received training reached 1 659, exceeding the total number of the previous three year. It vigorously publicized the national civil aviation safety work conference, arranged the activity of Work Safety Month and actively publicized, based on the magazine-Aviation Safety, the policy of safe development in the industry and the concept of safety management, and promoted safety technology. The office also organized and convened the first council member meeting of the Aviation Safety magazine. ■

政策法规司

一、全面推进立法工作

2011 年，对 32 部规章送审稿进行了审查，其中已发布 4 部。公布了我局现行有效规章、规范性文件目录。制定并印发了《中国民用航空局规章立法后评估规定》。做好行政审批第六轮集中清理工作。

二、加强行政执法

举办监察员初始法律培训和综合执法类监察员初始业务培训，共计 89 人。指导地区管理局的监察员持续法律培训工作。继续做好监察员证件核发管理工作，开展民航监察员管理制度研究。举办了民航中青年政策法规干部研修班及公职律师业务培训。

撰写了《2010 年度行政执法统计分析报告》。对民航行政系统行政执法问题提出执法建议，指导民航企事业单位法律工作。草拟了《民航优秀监察员评选办法》。2011 年共处理行政复议申请 9 件（其中已办结 7 件，2 件正在办理）。代表我局参加 1 起诉讼。

三、做好体制改革和社团管理

参与研究云南省民航管理机构、甘肃机场集团和贵州机场集团管理体制及烟台新机场运营管理模式等改革试点工作。提出有关完善民航局管理体制的意见和建议。配合国家发改委等部门完成支线机场发展改革调研，牵头起草《支线机场管理体制情况调研报告》。

与民政部相关部门协调民航社团管理问题。组织协调完成民航局业务主管社团组织 2010 年年检初审工作。指导完成有关协会换届更名等工作。依法受理民航企业机场联合重组改制申请 7 件。

四、推进政策研究

围绕调结构、转方式开展政策研究。对涉及民航企业经营者集中、航空公司联营协议反垄断豁免等案件与问题，做好民航局与相关部委产业政策的协调工作。编写发布《2010 年民航政策白皮书》，编辑出版 5 期《政策法规参考资料》。做好《欧盟民航业法律法规手册》出版工作。

对 2011 年接受世贸审议的成员国组织提出审议问题单，就 WTO 对华第四次贸易政策审议解释阐明我民航业相关政策。组织研究、稳妥应对 WTO 对我国最后一次过渡性审议涉及民航的问题。对已开展的中国与瑞士、澳大利亚、新加坡等自贸区以及 CEPA、ECFA 组织做好出要价方案和谈判工作。2011 年共办理航空器国内权利登记 846 项，国际利益登记授权代码核发 547 项。■

(Continued from 109)

Civil Aviation Industry.

We provided a list of questions for review to the Member States which were reviewed by WTO in 2011 and explained and clarified policies related to China civil aviation industry in connection with the fourth WTO trade policy review of China. The civil aviation issues involved in the last WTO transitional review of China were studied and appropriately dealt with. With regard to the free trade zones between China and Switzerland, Australia and Singapore etc., as well as to CEPA and ECFA, the work of putting forward request schemes and making preparation for negotiations was well organized. In 2011, we handled a total of 846 aircraft domestic right registrations, and approved and issued a total of 547 authorized codes for international interest registrations. ■

Department of Policy, Law and Regulation

I. Pushing Forward Legislative Work in an All-Round Way

In 2011, we reviewed a total of 32 sets of regulations submitted for approval or revision, 4 of which were issued. A table of content for the currently effective regulations and regulatory documents was published. The Provisions on Assessment of CAAC Regulations after Their Enactment was formulated and distributed. The 6th round of centralized review of the administrative examinations and approvals was well implemented.

II. Strengthening Administrative Law Enforcement

We organized initial law trainings for general supervisors and initial business training for the comprehensive law enforcement supervisors, and a total of 89 supervisors participated in the trainings. We guided the regional civil aviation administrations to carry out continuous law trainings for supervisors. Continuous efforts were made to do a good job in approving and issuing supervisors' certificates, and research work on the system of supervisor management was implemented. Seminars were held for the young and middle-aged cadres responsible for implementation of policies, laws and regulations, and professional trainings were organized for public lawyers.

We compiled the Statistical Analysis Report on the Administrative Law Enforcement for the Year 2010, and put forward law enforcement suggestions with regard to the problems arising from the administrative law enforcement by the civil aviation administrative system, in order to provide guidance to the civil aviation enterprises and institutional organizations in the field of laws. The Methods for Norminating Outstanding Civil Aviation Supervisors was drafted. In 2011, we dealt with 9 applications for administrative reconsiderations (7 of which were closed, and 2 of which were being processed), and participated in one lawsuit on behalf of CAAC.

III. Promoting System Reform and Management of Associations

We participated in the study on trial reforms of the Yunnan provincial civil aviation administrative organs, the management systems of the Gansu Airport Group, the Guizhou Airport Group and the operation management pattern of the new airport of Yantai etc. Opinions and suggestions with regard to the improvement of CAAC management system were put forward. We cooperated with the National Development and Reform Commission in completing the reform research on the development of regional airports, and took the lead in drafting the Research Report on the Management System of Feeder Airports.

We coordinated with relative departments of the Ministry of Civil Affairs in dealing with the issues of the management of civil aviation associations, and also coordinated in the completion of the preliminary review for the 2010 annual inspection of the associations whose business was within the jurisdiction of CAAC. We guided the name changes of the relative associations upon expiration of their office terms. 7 applications for the combination, reorganization and restructuring of civil aviation enterprises and airports were handled according to laws.

IV. Stepping up Policy Research

Policy research was performed on the structural adjustment and mode transformation. Coordination was well implemented between the industrial policies of CAAC and those of the relative ministries and commissions with regard to the cases or issues of merger of civil aviation enterprise operators and exemption from anti-monopoly enjoyed by the parties to joint financing agreements between airlines. We developed and issued the White Paper on China Civil Aviation Policies of 2010, and compiled and published five issues of the Reference Materials for Policies, Law and Regulations. A good job was done in publishing the Manual for the Laws and Regulations of EU on

财务司

一、发挥财税政策综合导向作用，促进行业持续健康发展

联合国家财政、税务等部门召开民航财税政策协调会，深入沟通交流，建立民航财税政策协调长效机制，争取民航运输业增值税转型等几项重点财税政策。协调财政部，建立西藏地区机场补贴长效机制。高等教育经费、公益性科研单位和科技项目投入等经费增长获重大突破，公益性科研单位基本支出同比大幅增长，科技类项目支出同比增长近1倍。会同财政部研究制定《民航发展基金征收使用管理办法》，使用范围扩大至通用航空、货运航空、节能减排、民航科技研发和新技术应用、持续安全能力和适航审定能力建设等。汇总分析地方政府给予民航企业财税优惠政策情况，研究建立中央与地方政策协调配合机制。

二、推动预算管理规范化，确保安全保障投入

组织完成2011年民航部门预算。组织完成民航发展基金等非税收入的收缴工作。探索更加合理的预算安排模式，召开财务与业务司局座谈会，确定资金支持重点。规范直属单位重大活动专项经费预算申报。制订并实施空管集中折旧资金预算管理办法。开展部门预算支出绩效考评，研究建立民航支出定额标准体系。推进预算信息公开，在相关媒体上公布2011年部门预算和“三公经费”信息。完成2010年空管系统年终资金清算及2009年企业工效挂钩工资清算。采取多种措施，加快预算执行，全年财政资金预算执行率达到95%。调整和优化资金使用方向，确保安全管理和建设专项资金需求。安排民航政府性基金用于对全国机场新增候机楼入口防爆检测设备补助。完成24家航空公司2010年和2011年上半年安全保障财务考核，通报考核情况，表彰先进单位，并跟踪催促考核欠佳单位及时落实整改要求。

三、加强制度建设，提升管控能力

全年制订下发11项办法规定。对航科院、民航报社等单位财务管理体制和专项补贴机制，调整思路，变输血为造血，发挥政策引导作用。协调有关部门调整民航五项行政事业性收费标准，并将收费全部用于安全项目。完善资产管理系统，实时监控资产情况。加强对首都机场集团等重点企业的管控，制订《关于进一步理顺首都机场集团公司资产财务管理关系的通知》，提出非主业资产处置和整合思路，协调解决资产重组、对外投资等重大事项审批，处置并回笼大量资金。细化政府采购预算编制，组织开展政府采购培训，完成2011年度民航GPA（世贸组织政府采购协议）研究报告。制订下发关于建设民航统一清算体系的指导意见。组织32家航空公司和157家机场签订清算协议。2011年7月，统一清算系统正式建成运行。

四、发挥信息系统优势，提高审计监督效能

利用实时监控平台，及时发现并纠正问题，提高系统使用效率。建立监控日志制度。针对系统建设和运行提出8类44项整改建议。完成系统三期建设筹备工作，明确项目需求和建设内容。组织开展财经政策审计调查及评价工作，涉及民航260家单位。掌握政策落实情况、实施效果，并对存在问题提出修改意见。组织开展各级津补贴规范，及时纠正违规问题。完成32个建设项目的竣工决算批复，组织实施空管局6个建设项目竣工决算评审。完成6个单位负责人任期和离任审计。■

Department of Finance

I. Playing a Comprehensive Guiding Role of the Financial and Taxation Policies to Promote Sustainable and Healthy Development of the Industry

We held a coordinating meeting on the civil aviation financial and taxation policies in conjunction with the State's financial and taxation departments to communicate and exchange ideas fully and set up a long-term mechanism of coordination for civil aviation financial and taxation policies. Several key financial and taxation policies, such as VAT transformation for the civil aviation transport industry, were strived for. A long-term mechanism was set up for the Tibet regional airport subsidies in coordination with the Ministry of Finance. Funds for the higher education and investment in the non-profit R&D organizations and in science technology projects gained a big breakthrough. The basic expenditure of the non-profit R&D organizations was greatly increased year on year. The expenditure of the science and technology projects nearly doubled year on year. Together with the Ministry of Finance, we discussed and formulated the Management Methods for the Collection and Use of Civil Aviation Development Fund and the applicability of the method was extended to general aviation, freight aviation, energy conservation and emission reduction, research and development of civil aviation science and technology, application of new technology, building of sustainable safety capabilities and airworthiness certification capabilities, etc. The financial and taxation preferential policies provided by the local governments to the civil aviation enterprises were collected and analyzed, and a mechanism to coordinate the central and local policies was established after discussion.

II. Pushing forward the Standardization of the Budget Management to Ensure Safety Assurance Investments

The industry budget for 2011 was finalized. The non-tax revenue collections of the industry, such as collection of the civil aviation development funds, were completed. A pattern for the more rational budget arrangement was explored. We held a forum with the functional departments and bureaus of CAAC to determine the focal points of the financial support. Standard procedures were formulated for the directly affiliated organizations to apply for the special expenditure budgets for the major events. A budget management method for the centrally depreciated fund of the air traffic control was formulated and implemented. We carried out performance assessment of the industry's budget expenditure, and established a system for the industry's expenditure quota standards. The budget information disclosure was promoted, and the industry's budget and "three public expenditures" of 2011 were made public on the relative media. The air traffic control system's year-end funds liquidation of 2010 and the liquidation of the enterprises' performance-linked salaries of 2009 were completed. We took various measures to expedite the budget execution, and the execution rate of the all-year financial fund budgets reached 95%. We also adjusted and optimized the use of funds to ensure that special fund requirements for safety management and construction were met. The industry's governmental fund was arranged to subsidize explosive detection equipment for the entrances to the newly-built terminals throughout the country. The safety assurance financial assessments on 24 airlines for 2010 and the first half of 2011 were completed; the results of the assessments were circulated; the advanced organizations were awarded; and the substandard organizations were urged to take immediate corrective action as required.

III. Strengthening System Construction to Uplift the Management and Control Capabilities

We formulated and distributed 11 methods and regulations throughout the year. The way of thinking was adjusted for the financial management system and special subsidy mechanism of such organizations as China Academy of Civil Aviation Science and Technology and CAAC News, to make a change from "blood transfusion" to "blood creation", so as to bring

into full play the role of policy guiding. The industry's five charging standards for administrative and institutional fees were adjusted in coordination with relevant organizations, and the fees collected were all used in safety-related projects. We improved the assets management system and realized real-time monitoring of the assets. Control on the Capital Airport Group and other key enterprises was strengthened; the Notice on Further Streamlining of the Assets and Financial Management for the Capital Airport Group Companies was formulated; train of thoughts for handling and integrating non-main business assets was put forward; examinations and approvals on such major issues as assets reorganization and overseas investments were coordinated and completed; and a large amount of funds were processed and withdrawn from circulation. We refined the development of the government procurement budget, organized government procurement trainings, and completed the industry's GPA research report of 2011. We also formulated and distributed guidelines for setting up a unified liquidation system, and made arrangements for 32 airlines and 157 airports to sign liquidation agreements. In July, 2011, a unified liquidation system was set up and put into operation.

IV. Taking Advantage of the Information System to Improve the Audit Monitoring Efficiency

We made use of the real-time monitoring platform to discover and rectify problem in time and to improve the system operational efficiency, and established a monitoring logbook system. 44 rectification proposals in 8 categories were put forward with regard to the system construction and operation. The preparatory work for the system construction (Phase III) was completed, and the project requirements and the construction items were defined. We organized audit investigations and assessments on financial policies, which involved 260 organizations of the industry. Implementation of the policies and their effect were supervised, and rectification measures were put forward for the problems discovered. Allowances and subsidies at all levels were regulated, and any violations were corrected in time. The final accounts of 32 completed projects were given official, written replies; reviews on the final accounts of 6 completed projects of the Air Traffic Management Bureau of CAAC were organized. Tenurial audits and audits on the departure for 6 leading officials of relevant organizations were completed.

国　际　司

2011 年，国际司在外事管理、发展双边和多边国际民航关系等方面积极稳妥地开展工作，各项工作进展顺利。

一、外事管理

严格按照中央和有关部委的要求，在因公出国（境）审批、证照管理、外国人员因公来访审批以及外航常设机构和人员管理等方面加强了规范化管理。按照中办、国办要求，从严审批各项因公出国（境）任务。在 2010 年因公出国（境）情况及 2011 年计划的基础上，要求各单位各部门科学、合理安排本年度因公出国（境）任务，保证重点项目，严肃外事纪律。

积极与有关部门协调，解决多家外航因《外国企业常驻代表机构登记管理条例》实施带来的在华常驻机构代表人数问题。

二、双边民航关系

国际司坚持以科学发展观为指导，按照统筹三种利益（国家利益、行业利益和公众利益）、稳妥发展关系的思路，根据不同双边航空运输市场的特点积极稳妥地发展双边航空运输关系。

2011 年，与澳大利亚、牙买加、欧盟、英国、墨西哥、乌兹别克斯坦、法国、俄罗斯、美国、南非、东盟、乌克兰、伊朗、日本、加拿大、智利、韩国等 17 个国家 / 地区举行了 18 次双边航空谈判，适度扩大了中外航权安排，以满足中外空运企业近中期的航权需求；与牙买加草签了中牙航空运输协定，与瑞士重新签署了两国航空运输协定，与喀麦隆和格鲁吉亚正式签署了航空运输协定，为发展与上述国家的民航关系奠定了法律基础。

在民航技术合作方面，与美方成功举办了第六次中美航空峰会，并积极开展了中美、中欧民航技术合作与交流项目。新一期中欧民航合作项目已于 2010 年 10 月正式进入实施阶段。项目的总体工作计划及第一年年度工作计划已获批准，第一年开展二十余项活动，内容涉及法规、适航、飞标、空管、机场等方面，目前项目实施状况总体良好。

三、多边工作

在积极发展中国与国际民航组织等政府间国际组织和非政府间国际组织关系的同时，协调促成了民用空中航行服务组织（CANSO）、亚太航空运输协会（AAPA）和国际航空货运协会（TIACA）等国际组织成为国际民航组织观察员事项，稳步推进了中国民航与这些组织的关系。

四、2011 年民航局领导出席的重大外事活动

1. 1 月 17 日，夏兴华副局长会见日本冲绳县知事仲井真弘多，双方就开通北京至冲绳航线事交换意见。

2. 1 月 20 日至 21 日，李家祥局长访问了美国德保罗大学法学院。对方授予李家祥局长荣誉客座教授及杰出国际学者称号。

3. 1 月 24 日，李健副局长会见巴西航空工业公司总裁兼首席执行官弗雷德里克·科拉多（Frederico Curado）。

4. 2 月 13 日至 19 日，李健副局长访问了巴西，与巴西民航局签署了《中国民用航空局与巴西民用航空局关于促进民航安全谅解备忘录》，并参观了巴西航空工业公司。

5. 2 月 14 日，夏兴华副局长会见塞斯纳飞机公司董事会主席、总裁兼首席执行官杰克·佩尔顿（Jack Pelton），双方就推动中国通用航空事业发展和合作事宜交换了意见。

6. 2 月 21 日，夏兴华副局长会见国际航空运输协会理事长比西尼亚尼（Giovanni Bisignani），双方就国际航空 2050 愿景的最新进展情况进行了交流。

7. 2月22日，李家祥局长会见即将上任的国际航空运输协会理事长及行政总裁汤彦麟（Tony Tyler)。

8. 2月28日，李家祥局长会见星空联盟总裁杨安博（Jaan Albrecht），双方就星空联盟中国业务的发展进行了交流。

9. 3月1日，李家祥局长与瑞士联邦驻华大使顾博礼（Blaise Godet）分别代表两国政府在北京重签《中华人民共和国政府和瑞士联邦委员会航空运输协定》。

10. 4月12日，夏兴华副局长会见世界旅游业理事会总裁大卫·斯克斯尔（David Scowsill）。

11. 4月18日，夏兴华副局长会见美国贸易发展署署长李·扎克女士，并签署中美航空合作项目第七期赠款协议。

12. 4月20日，李家祥局长与喀麦隆交通国务部长马伊加里在北京分别代表两国政府正式签署《中华人民共和国政府和喀麦隆共和国政府关于在两国领土之间及其以远地区建立定期航班的航班协定》。

13. 4月28日，夏兴华副局长会见阿联酋航空公司首席执行官马克拖姆殿下，就阿联酋航空公司在华运营交换意见。

14. 5月6日，李家祥局长会见德国汉莎航空集团公司新任董事长兼首席执行官傅朗斯（Dr. Christoph Franz)。

15. 5月10日和11日，李家祥局长和夏兴华副局长分别会见来京参加中国民航发展论坛的国际民航组织秘书长邦雅曼。

16. 5月10日，夏兴华副局长宴请来京参加中国民航发展论坛的美国联邦航空局副局长胡尔塔。

17. 5月11日，夏兴华副局长会见并宴请来京参加中国民航发展论坛的美国运输部助理部长苏珊·科兰德，并与对方签署了高官对话机制备忘录。

18. 5月11日，李健副局长会见来京参加中国民航发展论坛的国际飞行安全基金会总裁威廉·沃斯。

19. 5月11日，夏兴华副局长会见来京参加中国民航发展论坛的新加坡民航局局长叶旺兴。

20. 5月11日，夏兴华副局长会见日本富山县知事石井隆一。

21. 5月16日，夏兴华副局长会见日本国土交通省审议官大口清一。

22. 5月17日至25日，夏兴华副局长参加国航北京—雅典航线复航仪式并访问芬兰、瑞典。

23. 5月27日，李家祥局长会见波音公司董事长、总裁兼首席执行官詹姆斯·迈克纳尼（W.James McNerney），双方就人员培训、高原飞机性能、飞机技术更新及中国大型客机的研发等交换了意见。

24. 6月7日，李家祥局长会见日本航空公司董事长稻盛和夫。

25. 6月8日，夏兴华副局长会见美国航空公司总裁 Horton。

26. 6月9日至14日，夏兴华副局长访问新加坡、越南，分别参加了中国—新加坡民航高官委员会第八次会议及第三次中越民航高官会。

27. 6月19日至28日，原副局长王昌顺参加第49届巴黎航展并访问匈牙利、俄罗斯。

28. 7月6日至15日，夏兴华副局长率团访问了英国和法国。

29. 7月8日，李家祥局长会见日本广岛县知事汤崎英彦。

30. 7月8日，李家祥局长会见日本冈山县知事石井正弘。

31. 9月6日，李家祥局长会见韩国驻华大使李揆亨，双方就加强双边民用航空关系等事宜交换了意见。

32. 9月19日，李家祥局长会见日本国民新党干事长、众议院议员下地干郎，以及冲绳中国友好协会理事长山口芳弘等一行3人，双方就加强双边民用航空关系等事宜交换意见。

33. 9月21日至29日，夏兴华副局长率中国民航代表团赴华盛顿参加第六次中美航空论坛。

34. 10月14日，李家祥局长会见日本航空公司董事长稻盛和夫。

35. 10月17日，原副局长王昌顺会见欧洲委员会气候行动总司总司长 Jos Delbeke。

36. 10月24日至30日，李健副局长赴澳大利亚参加第三届中澳航空保安研讨会。

37. 10月25日，夏兴华副局长会见密苏里州州长杰伊·尼克松（Jay Nixon)。

38. 10月27日，李家祥局长会见新加坡交通部部长兼外交部第二部长吕德耀（Lui Tuck Yew）。

39. 11月17日，夏兴华副局长会见荷兰基础设施和环境国务秘书约普·阿斯玛（Joop Atsma）。

40. 12月2日，夏兴华副局长会见法航新任总裁朱尼克（Alexandre de Juniac）。

41. 12月5日，夏兴华副局长会见苏格兰政府首席部长（正部长级）亚历克斯·萨蒙德（Alex Salmond），双方就开通中国与苏格兰直航交换意见。

Department of International Affairs

In 2011, Department of International Affairs actively and prudently carried out it work in the fields of foreign affairs management and the development of bilateral and multilateral international relations in civil aviation, and various aspects of the internal affairs work proceeded smoothly.

I. Foreign Affairs Management

In strict accordance with the requirements of the CPC Central Committee and relevant ministries, the department enforced standardized management of public officials overseas travel review, management of certification and licensing, review of official visits by foreigners and management of resident offices and personnel of foreign airlines. In accordance with requirements of the General Affairs Office of CPC Central Committee and the General Affairs Office of the State Council, it tightened the review of official overseas travels of various sorts. On the basis of the 2010 conditions and the 2011 plan for official overseas travels, the department required that all the entities and departments work out scientific and reasonable arrangements for their official overseas travels with key projects supported and foreign affairs disciplines strictly followed.

The department actively made coordination with relevant departments to solve the problem related to the number of representatives of several foreign airlines' resident offices in China, which was caused by the implementation of Regulations on the Registration of Resident Offices of Foreign Enterprises in China.

II. Bilateral Ties

The Department of International Affairs persisted the guidance of Scientific Outlook on Development, followed the thought of balancing the three types of interests (national, industrial and public interests) and prudently developing external ties, and actively and solidly developed bilateral air transport relations in light of characteristics of different bilateral air transport markets.

In 2011, the department held 18 bilateral air service talks with 17 countries/regions, i.e. Australia, Jamaica, European Union, the United Kingdom, Mexico, Uzbekistan, France, Russia, the United States, South Africa, ASEAN, Ukraine, Iran, Japan, Canada, Chile and Republic of Korea, and moderately expanded the air traffic rights arrangements between China and foreign countries to meet the short/medium term needs for air traffic rights of Chinese and foreign air transport enterprises. The department initialed air service agreement with Jamaica, re-signed the agreement with Switzerland, and officially signed the agreement with Cameroon and Georgia, which laid a legal foundation for developing civil aviation relations with the afore mentioned countries.

In the field of civil aviation technical cooperation, the 6th China-U.S. Aviation Summit was successfully held, and the civil aviation technical cooperation and exchange programs with U.S. and Europe were actively carried out. The new China-Europe Civil Aviation Cooperation Program officially entered the implementation phase in October 2010. The overall work plan for the program and its annual work plan for the first year were approved, over 20 activities covering regulations, airworthiness, flight standards, air traffic control, airports, etc., were conducted in the first year, and the project went on smoothly so far.

III. Multilateral Relations

While actively developing the relationship between China and international intergovernmental organizations like ICAO as well as non-governmental international organizations, the department made coordinated efforts to facilitate the Civil Air Navigation Services Organization (CANSO), Asia Pacific Air Transport Association (AAPA) and the International Air Cargo Association (TIACA) becoming ICAO observers and steadily promoted the China civil aviation's relations with these organizations.

IV. Major Foreign Events Attended by CAAC Leaders in 2011

1. On January 17, Xia Xinghua, Deputy Administrator of CAAC, met with Nakaima Hirokazu, Governor of Okinawa Prefecture of Japan and exchanged views on the opening of Beijing-Okinawa air routes.

2. From January 20 to 21, Li Jiaxiang, Administrator of CAAC, visited the College of Law, DePaul University. The university conferred on Administrator Li Jiaxiang the title of Honorary Visiting Professor and Distinguished International Scholar.

3. On January 24, Li Jian, Deputy Administrator of CAAC, met with Frederico Curado, President and CEO of Embraer.

4. From February 13 to 19, Li Jian, Deputy Administrator of CAAC, paid a visit to Brazil, signed the Memorandum of Understanding between CAAC and National Civil Aviation Agency of Brazil on Promotion of Civil Aviation Safety, and visited Embraer.

5. On February 14, Xia Xinghua, Deputy Administrator of CAAC, met with Jack Pelton, Chairman of the Board, President and CEO of Cessna Aircraft Company, and exchanged views on the promotion of China general aviation and co-operation.

6. On February 21, Xia Xinghua, Deputy Administrator of CAAC, met with Giovanni Bisignani, Director General of IATA, and exchanged views on the latest progress of the vision of the international aviation 2050.

7. On February 22, Li Jiaxiang, Administrator of CAAC, met with Tony Tyler, the Director General elected and CEO of IATA.

8. On February 28, Li Jiaxiang, Administrator of CAAC, met with Jaan Albrecht, CEO of Star Alliance, and exchanged views on business development of Star Alliance in China.

9. On March 1, Li Jiaxiang, Administrator of CAAC, and Blaise Godet, Swiss Ambassador to China, re-signed the Air Service Agreement between the Government of the People's Republic of China and the Swiss Federal Council on behalf of the two governments in Beijing.

10. On April 12, Xia Xinghua, Deputy Administrator of CAAC, met with David Scowsill, President of the World Travel & Tourism Council.

11. On April 18, Xia Xinghua, Deputy Administrator of CAAC, met with Ms. Leocadia I, Zach, Director of U.S. Trade and Development Agency, and signed the Grant Agreement of the 7th Phase under the China-U.S. Aviation Cooperation Program.

12. On April 20, Li Jiaxiang, Administrator of CAAC, and Bello Bouba Maigari, Minister of State for Transport of Cameroon, officially signed the Air Service Agreement between the Government of the People's Republic of China and the Government of the Republic of Cameroon on the Establishment of Scheduled Flights between and beyond the Territories of the Two Countries on behalf of the two governments in Beijing.

13. On April 28, Xia Xinghua, Deputy Administrator of CAAC, met with Ahmed bin Saeed Al Maktoum, CEO of Emirates Airlines, and exchanged views on Emirates operations in China.

14. On May 6, Li Jiaxiang, Administrator of CAAC, met with Dr. Christoph Franz, the new chairman and CEO of the Lufthansa Group.

15. On May 10 and 11, Li Jiaxiang, Administrator of CAAC and Xia Xinghua, Deputy Administrator of CAAC met respectively with Raymond Benjamin, Secretary General of ICAO, who came to China to attend China Civil Aviation Development Forum.

16. On May 10, Xia Xinghua, Deputy Administrator of CAAC, held a banquet for Michael P. Huerta, Deputy Secretary of U.S. Federal Aviation Administration, who came to Beijing to attend China Civil Aviation Development Forum.

17. On May 11, Xia Xinghua, Deputy Administrator of CAAC, met with and hosted a banquet for Susan Kurland, Assistant Secretary of U.S. Department of Transportation, who came to Beijing to attend China Civil Aviation Development Forum, and signed the memorandum of the dialogue mechanism for senior officials.

18. On May 11, Li Jian, Deputy Administrator of CAAC, met with William Voss, President of Flight Safety Foundation, who came to Beijing to attend China Civil Aviation Development Forum.

19. On May 11, Xia Xinghua, Deputy Administrator of CAAC, met with Yap Ong Heng, Director General of the Civil Aviation Authority of Singapore, who came to Beijing to attend China Civil Aviation Development Forum.

20. On May 11, Xia Xinghua, Deputy Administrator of CAAC, met with Takakazu Ishii, Governor of Japan Toyama Prefecture.

21. On May 16, Xia Xinghua, Deputy Administrator of CAAC, met with Oguchi Shinichi, Review Officer of Japan Ministry of Land, Infrastructure, Transport and Tourism.

22. From May 17 to 25, Xia Xinghua, Deputy Administrator of CAAC, attended the ceremony for Air China's re-open of services on the Beijing-Athens route, and visited Finland and Sweden.

23. On May 27, Li Jiaxiang, Administrator of CAAC, met with W. James McNerney, Chairman, President and CEO of Boeing, and exchanged views on staff training, high-altitude aircraft performance, aircraft technology updates and China's R&D of large passenger aircraft.

24. On June 7, Li Jiaxiang, Administrator of CAAC, met with Kazuo Inamori, Chairman of Japan Airlines.

25. On June 8, Xia Xinghua, Deputy Administrator of CAAC, met with Thomas W. Horton, President of American Airlines.

26. From June 9 to 14, Xia Xinghua, Deputy Administrator of CAAC, paid visits to Singapore and Vietnam, and attended the 8th meeting of China-Singapore Civil Aviation Senior Officials Committee and the 3rd China-Vietnam Civil Aviation Senior Officials Meeting.

27. From June 19 to 28, Wang Changshun, former Deputy Administrator of CAAC, attended in the 49th Paris Air Show and visited Hungary and Russia.

28. From July 6 to 15, Xia Xinghua, Deputy Administrator of CAAC, led a delegation and visited the United Kingdom and France.

29. On July 8, Li Jiaxiang, Administrator of CAAC, met with Hidehiko Yuzaki, Governor of Japan Hiroshima Prefecture.

30. On July 8, Li Jiaxiang, Administrator of CAAC, met with Masahiro Ishii, Governor of Japan Okayama Prefecture.

31. On September 6, Li Jiaxiang, Administrator of CAAC, met with Lee Kyu-hyung, ROK ambassador to China, and exchanged views on strengthening bilateral civil aviation relations.

32. On September 19, Li Jiaxiang, Administrator of CAAC, met with Mikio Shimoji, President of Japan People's New Party, also a member of House of Representatives, and Yamaguchi Yoshihiro, Director of Okinawa-China Friendship Association. The two sides exchanged views on strengthening bilateral civil aviation relations.

33. From September 21 to 29, Xia Xinghua, Deputy Administrator of CAAC, headed a China civil aviation delegation to Washington and participated the 6th China-U.S. Aviation Forum.

34. On October 14, Li Jiaxiang, Administrator of CAAC, met with Kazuo Inamori, Chairman of Japan Airline.

35. On October 17, Wang Changshun, former Deputy Administrator of CAAC, met with Jos Delbeke, the Director General for Climate Action of European Commission.

36. From October 24 to 30, Li Jian, Deputy Administrator of CAAC, paid a visit to Australia for the 3rd China Australia Aviation Security Seminar.

37. On October 25, Xia Xinghua, Deputy Administrator of CAAC, met with Jay Nixon, Governor of Missouri State.

38. On October 27, Li Jiaxiang, Administrator of CAAC, met with Lui Tuck Yew, Transport Minister and the 2rd Minister for Foreign Affairs of Singapore.

39. On November 17, Xia Xinghua, Deputy Administrator of CAAC, met with Joop Atsma, State Secretary for Infrastructure and the Environment of the Netherlands.

40. On December 2, Xia Xinghua, Deputy Administrator of CAAC, met with Alexandre de Juniac, the new President of Air France.

41. On December 5, Xia Xinghua, Deputy Administrator of CAAC, met with Alex Salmond, First Minister of Scotland. The two sides exchanged views on the opening of direct flights between China and Scotland.

港澳台事务办公室

2011 年是两岸民航稳步推进、全面发展、承上启下的重要一年。民航局认真贯彻中央对台大政方针，牢牢把握两岸和平发展主题，采取切实措施，有力推动了两岸民航大交流、大合作。与此同时，民航局认真执行中央支持香港、澳门保持经济社会繁荣发展的方针政策，积极落实内地与香港 / 澳门“关于建立更紧密经贸关系的安排（CEPA）”相关内容，进一步巩固深化内地与港澳民航交流合作，取得了新的进展。

一、积极协调，推动两岸直航稳健发展

发挥海峡两岸航空运输交流委员会与台北市航空运输商业同业公会的联系作用，组织、协调、落实两岸航空运输主管部门的工作沟通与协商的重要谈判，达成共识，做出了惠及两岸民航企业与两岸民众的安排。

航班航点方面。两岸定期客运航班从每周 370 班增至 558 班，增幅超过 50%；货运航班增加为双方每周各 48 班。增班后，在大陆一些热点地区，如华北地区每周将达 44 班，长江三角洲地区将达 165 班，珠江三角洲地区将达 48 班。同时，新增加兰州、盐城、温州和黄山机场 4 个对台空中通航点，扩容增效，形成了一线城市有增班，二、三线城市增班更多的空运优势。使两岸航空运输运力得到充分保障。

特别是开通泉州晋江、温州对台空中通航点，具体落实了国务院批准的《海峡西岸经济区发展规划》中开通对台空中通航点的相关要求，为发挥海峡西岸经济区对台先行先试起到了积极推动作用。

航空运输方面。2011 年两岸 15 家航空公司共飞行超过 4 万多个班次，提供座位总数超过 920 万个。共运送旅客 717.5 万人，平均载客率 76.8%。其中，台湾航空公司载客 421.5 万人，占 58.7%；大陆航空公司载客 296 万人，占 41.3%。运送旅客人数比 2010 年增长 25.1%。货运两岸双方合计运载货物 15.7 万吨。

2011年5月16日，民航局局长李家祥接见台湾民航负责人尹承蓬

On May 16, 2011, Li Jiaxiang, Administrator of CAAC, Meets with Yin Cheng-pong, Director General of Civil Aviation Authority of Taiwan

二、加大力度，促进交流合作更加深化

（1）强化航空安全交流合作 推动实现对台湾航空运输企业的安全审定与技术考察，按照 CCAR-60 部要求，重点

对其飞行模拟器与飞行训练中心进行合格审定与鉴定，并在航空安全、飞行技术、飞行训练与管理，以及对飞机维修单位进行民用航空器维修许可的实施审查等多方面进行了专业技术研讨和交流。推动实现航空保安就建立航空安保标准机制的交流与研讨，顺利参加“2011年海峡两岸航空保安座谈会”，主要就航空安检作业规则及业务执行情况、特殊突发状况处理程序等双方共同关切的航空保安议题进行沟通协调，交流经验。还就建立两岸航空保安训练交流机制等问题进行了深入探讨，达成了进一步加强航空保安教员培训协作的共识，提出了下一步加强交流合作的初步意向，取得了很好的收效。

（2）力促空管交流获新进展 在开通航路、保障安全、交流互访等各个方面取得了积极的成果。推动实现了两岸空中管理高层访问交流，成功举办了2011年海峡两岸民航空管交流座谈会，主要就海峡两岸现有航路的运营与管理、容量和时刻的分配、空域结构和管制工作的优化等进行沟通探讨和深入研究并取得共识，为两岸空管未来交流发展搭建了一个更高的平台。

（3）搭建新的交流合作平台 推动首次组织首都机场公安分局单独组团应邀赴台，就建立航空保安标准机制与台湾相关机场和企业交流与考察。为落实《海峡两岸经济合作框架协议》（ECFA）对台湾航空维修作出开放承诺的要求，促成实现民航适航高层管理人员应邀赴台，就适航审定事务、民用航空产品审定与维修等适航管理业务等沟通交流。协调办理了首都机场集团负责人带团应邀赴台，加强与台湾民航机场间的交流合作，提高两岸机场运行和服务标准，深入研究强化双方合作的措施，更好地保障两岸直航。

（4）继续巩固民航教育交流 做大两岸民航校际、校企交流合作平台，实现民航院校充分利用教育资源特有优势，结合发展实际，深化与台湾航空公司校企间研习合作，范围涵盖了两岸民航教育、教学和师资培训交流、两岸两校学分互认、两岸直航法律问题与实践、民航管理、机务维修管理、航空安全管理、证照培训和航空安全的管理信息和成果的交流等学科领域，并取得了新进展、新成效、新提高，进一步优化了两岸民航的教育、科研水平。

（5）着力办好重点研讨会议 促成两岸共同举办第八届海峡两岸飞行安全暨飞行技术研讨会和第六届海峡两岸航空气象与飞行安全研讨会。继续强化两岸飞行安全方面交流合作，以及两岸航空气象服务与保障的交流沟通。

2011年共办理两岸民航双向交流48批，360人次。其中接待台湾民航界来访27批，187人次；民航机关、直属企事业单位赴台交流21批，173人次。

三、强化服务，努力做好相关各项保障

一是协调、指导有关部门和航空公司，继续做好两岸空中急救飞行，并不断完善空中绿色通道的政策管理环境与条件。全年共受理23班两岸医疗救助包机紧急飞行，抢运台胞危重患者、病人家属和医护人员251人。审核并协调空管部门完成了190班非商业公务包机的飞行保障任务，运送台湾企业家和相关人员850人，配合相关部门、地方政府做好台商工作，为各地扩大吸引台资，发展两岸经贸交流合作，发挥了积极作用。

二是做好台港澳在大陆（内地）常设机构及人员的行政审批工作，细化驻点企业申办程序，全年审核办理台港澳企业在大陆（内地）人员替换/增加等相关手续130件，机构延期手续93件，办理新增机构手续22件。

四、密切联系，扩大内地与港澳的交流

协调并做好内地与香港、澳门航空运输有关部门之间交流、沟通的安排。在指定承运人、内地通航点、客货运航班运力安排及代码共享等多方面都有明显提升。澳门新增无锡、泉州、徐州、满洲里、西宁和盐城为定期通航点。继续贯彻落实CEPA相关内容，落实中央政府2011年8月颁布的36条支持香港发展的政策措施，推动两地民航交流合作取得阶段性成果。新辟一条连接香港与内地的航线并于2011年12月15日正式启用，扩大了空中交通容量。

继续加强内地与港澳民航的联系与协调，全年共办理接待香港、澳门民航界，以及民航机关、直属企事业单位进行与香港、澳门双向交流16批/77人次。其中，来访10批/45人次，往访6批/32人次。■

Office of Hong Kong, Macao and Taiwan Affairs

2011 was an important transitional year for the steady and overall development of cross-Straits civil aviation. CAAC conscientiously implemented the major policies and guidelines of the Central Committee of CPC towards Taiwan, firmly focused the theme of cross-Straits peaceful development, and took effective measures to strongly push forward cross-Straits large scale exchanges and cooperation in civil aviation. At the same time, CAAC earnestly implemented the guideline and policy of the Central Committee of CPC to support sustained economic and social prosperity and development in Hong Kong and Macao, actively implemented items contained in Closer Economic Partnership Arrangement (CEPA) between Mainland and Hong Kong/ Macao, further consolidated and deepened the exchanges and cooperation between Mainland and Hong Kong and Macao in civil aviation, and as a result made fresh progress.

2011年12月20日，民航局副局长夏兴华（右）会见台湾复兴航空公司董事长林明升

On December 20, 2011, Xia Xinghua (right), Deputy Administrator of CAAC, Meets with Vincent Lin, Chairman of Taiwan TransAsia Airways

I. Promoting the Steady Development of Cross-Straits Direct Flights through Active Coordination

The office called into play the liaison between Cross-Straits Aviation Transport Exchanges Council and the Taipei Airlines Association, arranging, coordinating and carrying out the working communication and consultation between air transport authorities across the Straits, which reached consensus and made arrangements beneficial to civil aviation enterprises and the general public on both sides.

Flights and destinations. The weekly number of scheduled cross-Straits passenger flights rose from 370 to 558, an increase over 50%, and the weekly number of cargo flights increased to 48 from each side. After the flight frequency increase, in some hot spots on the mainland, such as North China, the weekly number of flights would reach 44; the number for the Yangtze River Delta Region would reach 165 and 48 for Pearl River Delta Region. Meanwhile, 4 service points in the mainland providing air service to and from Taiwan were newly added, i.e. Lanzhou, Yancheng, Wenzhou and Huangshan airports, in order to boost transport capacity and efficiency, building an air transport advantage featuring additional flights in big metropolitans and more additional flights in small and medium sized cities, which fully guaranteed the cross-Straits air transport capacity.

Especially, the opening of the air service points of Quanzhou Jinjiang and Wenzhou to Taiwan was the fulfillment of the specific requirements set in the Development Plan for the Economic Zone on the Western Side of Taiwan Straits approved by the State Council, which significantly contributed to the pilot cooperation between the western side of the Taiwan Straits and Taiwan.

Air transport. In 2011, the 15 airlines on the two sides of the Straits operated more than 40 000 flights, providing over 9.2 million seats and transporting 7.175 million passengers with an average passenger load factor of 76.8%, among which, airlines of Taiwan carried 4.215 million passengers, accounting for 58.7%; airlines of the mainland carried 2.96 million passengers, accounting for 41.3%. The number of passengers carried rose by 25.1% from the 2010 level and airlines on both sides transported a combined total of 157 000 tons of cargo.

II. Intensifying Efforts to Strive for Deepened Exchanges and Cooperation

1. The exchanges and cooperation in aviation safety were strengthened. The office worked to facilitate the safety certification and technical inspection of air transport enterprises of Taiwan. In accordance with the requirements of CCAR Part 60, it gave priority to the review and certification of their flight simulators and flight training centers, and had technical discussions and communication on aviation safety, flying skills, flight training and management as well as the examination of the civil aircraft maintenance license at aircraft maintenance units. The office facilitated the communication and discussion of the development of aviation security standards body and attended the 2011 Cross-Straits Aviation Security Symposium to communicate, coordinate and share experiences on aviation security issues of common interest to both sides, such as rules governing aviation security operations and their compliance status as well as the coping procedure for unusual emergencies. It's also had in-depth discussions on the creation of a cross-Straits aviation security training and communication mechanism, reached the agreement on further increasing collaboration on training for aviation security instructors and expressed the initial intent for further increasing communication and cooperation, which proved very fruitful.

2. New progress in ATM exchanges was made. The office achieved positive results in opening air routes, ensuring safety and exchanging visits and realized cross-Straits high level ATM visits and exchanges. It held 2011 Cross-Straits Civil Aviation ATM Symposium where consensus was reached through communication, discussion and in-depth research mainly on the operations and management of existing cross-Straits routes, allocation of entitlement and slots and optimization of the airspace structure and ATM operations etc., which built a better platform for future cross-Straits ATM development and exchanges.

3. New platforms for exchanges and cooperation were built. The office facilitated the first invited visit of the Aviation Security Sub-Bureau of Beijing Capital International Airport to Taiwan for communication with and inspection of relevant airports and enterprises on the establishment of an aviation security standards body. In order to meet the commitment made in the Economic Cooperation Framework Agreement (ECFA) to open up aviation maintenance to Taiwanese businesses, the office facilitated the invited visit of senior airworthiness managerial staff to Taiwan for communication on airworthiness management issues, such as airworthiness certification, civil aviation product certification and maintenance. The office supported the delegation led by Beijing Capital Airport's executives to Taiwan at its invitation to strengthen exchanges and cooperation with civil airports in Taiwan, improve the cross-Straits standards for airport operations and services, deepen the study of measures to strengthen bilateral cooperation and better support cross-Straits direct flights.

4. Exchanges on civil aviation education were continuously consolidated. The office broadened the platform for cross-Straits exchanges and cooperation between civil aviation colleges and between colleges and enterprises. It helped civil aviation colleges take the unique advantage of educational

resources and deepen the cooperation in research and study with airlines of Taiwan, where necessary, covering civil aviation education, exchange on teaching and teacher training, mutual recognition of academic credits, legal issues and practices in cross-Straits direct flights, civil aviation management, aircraft maintenance management, aviation safety management, certificate and license training and the exchanges of aviation safety management information and achievements and so on, where new progress, new achievements and new improvement were made and civil aviation education and scientific research on both sides of the Straits were further optimized.

5. Efforts were made in holding key seminars and conferences. The office contributed to co-hosting the 8th Cross-Straits Flight Safety and Flying Technology Seminar and the 6th Cross-Straits Aviation Meteorology and Flight Safety Seminar. It further boosted cross-Straits exchanges and cooperation on flight safety and communication on aviation meteorological services and support.

In 2011, the office supported 48 cross-Straits civil aviation visits involving 360 people, among which, it received 27 delegations of 187 people from Taiwan and sent 21 delegations of 173 people from various CAAC departments and affiliated enterprises and institutional entities to Taiwan.

III. Improving Services and Making Efforts to Do a Good Job in Various Jobs of Support

Firstly, the office coordinated and guided relevant departments and airlines concerned to continue operating cross-Straits rescue flights and improving the environment and conditions for policy management of the green corridor air travel. In the whole year, a total of 23 cross-Straits emergency medical charter flights were handled, carrying 251 critical patients, their family members and medical staff. It reviewed and coordinated with the ATM department in supporting 190 non-commercial business charter flights, transporting 850 Taiwanese entrepreneurs and other relevant people. The office also cooperated with relevant departments and local governments to deal with work concerning Taiwan businessmen and played an active role in attracting investments from Taiwan and increasing cross-Straits economic and trade exchanges and cooperation.

Secondly, the office well conducted administrative review of resident offices of Taiwan, Hong Kong and Macao in the mainland and their personnel and specified the application procedures for setting up mainland-based businesses. Through the whole year, the office reviewed and handled 130 personnel reshuffles/additions for businesses from Taiwan, Hong Kong and Macao enterprises, 93 extensions for their resident offices and 22 new resident offices.

IV. Maintaining Close Ties and Expanding Exchanges with Hong Kong and Macao

The office made good coordination and arrangements for the communication and exchanges with relevant air transport authorities in Hong Kong/Macao. Significant improvements were made in designated carriers, air service points in the Mainland, passenger and cargo flight entitlement arrangement and code sharing. Macao added scheduled air service points in Wuxi, Quanzhou, Xuzhou, Manchuria, Xining and Yancheng. The office continued to implement CEPA and the 36 policies and measures issued by the Central Government in August 2011 in an effort to support the development of Hong Kong, making periodic achievement in promoting the exchanges and cooperation in civil aviation between the mainland and Hong Kong. A new air route connecting Hong Kong and the mainland was opened and officially came into service on December 15, 2011, which expanded the air traffic capacity.

Liaison and coordination between the mainland and Hong Kong/Macao civil aviation authorities continued to be strengthened. During the whole year, the office supported a total of 16 two way visits involving 77 people, including those from Hong Kong and Macao and from CAAC departments and affiliated enterprises and institutional entities to Hong Kong and Macao, among which, it received 10 delegations with a total of 45 people and sent 6 delegations with a total of 32 people.

一、贯彻国内航线航班管理制度的改革，积极支持新疆航空运输发展

贯彻落实《关于进一步做好航权航班和时刻管理工作的通知》要求，除货运航线和重大、紧急和特殊航空运输及春运、暑运和国家法定节假日外，不再批复航空公司的加班和包机申请。增加航线航班经营许可透明度，航线经营许可和航班计划的申请、审核和公示及信息发布均已在“中国民航航班管理信息（监测）系统”上进行。加强航班执行情况监管，按月公布航空公司国内客运航线正班执行率数据，撤销、注销航空公司不符合规定的航线经营许可 63 条。

重点支持新疆自治区航空运输发展。乌鲁木齐已经与国内 46 个城市的 48 个机场通航，2011 年至 2012 年冬春航季与上一个冬春航季相比，航线由 71 条增至 82 条，增长 17.1%；航班由 1 768 班增至 2 044 班，增长 15.6%。乌鲁木齐机场旅客吞吐量突破了 1 000 万人次大关。

二、海峡两岸航空运输得到突破性发展

完成了与台湾民航主管部门的第 5、6 次沟通会议，达成了新增航点、班次和春节加班等多项共识。2011 年大陆通航台湾的航点增至 41 个，每周定期往返航班增至 558 个。目前，大陆 9 家航空公司开通 39 个航点至台湾桃园、台北松山、高雄和台中 4 个航点的定期航班，台湾 6 家航空公司开通台湾桃园、台北松山、高雄、台中、花莲、台东 6 个航点至大陆 36 个航点的定期航班，每天约有 100 个往返航班（含定期航班和不定期旅游包机）。

三、实施“走出去”战略，航空公司开辟一批中远程国际航线

加强与海关总署沟通协调，加快“大通关”步伐，提高了国际航空货运通关效率。简化旅客中转联程手续，在三大机场开展国内转国际航班旅客行李直挂和通程登机业务。研究推动非洲、欧洲及北美航空运输发展战略，积极配合国家外交、经贸开辟国际航线。国内公司新开 34 条国际客运航线，9 条货运航线。包括国航开辟北京—杜塞尔多夫航线，恢复北京—慕尼黑—雅典航线；东航开辟上海浦东—罗马航线；南航开辟广州—奥克兰航线；海航开通上海浦东—圣路易斯定期货运航班；翡翠航开辟上海浦东—深圳—河内—迪拜—阿姆斯特丹货运航线。国内航空公司在中澳客运航线上运力增加 70%。

四、以完善立法为龙头，加强航空运输市场的管理工作

《公共航空运输企业经营许可规定》、《民用航空运输销售代理管理办法》两部规章已完成审定。《民用航空市场管理条例》、《民用机场地面服务业务暂行管理办法》正在抓紧修改和完善。跟踪筹建及新设航空公司的进展和运营情况。督促长龙、英安航空抓紧筹建。到部分新设航空公司进行调研，全面了解公司运营情况。加强对分公司的管理，要求航空公司对不符合要求的分公司进行整改，对不能完成整改的分公司进行处理，注销了国航西藏、深航郑州、华夏赣州分公司。

五、扎实推进通用航空的发展

推进内蒙古拓展通用航空服务领域试点工作，根河林业机场拓宽通用航空服务领域试点已于 2011 年 9 月开航。配合有关部门开展第一次通用航空普查，为决策提供依据。开办“民航中青年通用航空管理干部研修班”，加大通用航空队伍建设力度。组织举办了中国国际通用航空大会，为通用航空有关企业搭建了展示和交流的平台。

六、对大面积航班延误应急处置专项整治工作，取得了比较明显的效果

为贯彻民航局《航班延误整治专题会议纪要》的

Department of Air Transport

I. Implementing Domestic Routes and Flights Management System Reform and Providing Active Support for the Air Transport Development in Xinjiang

The department implemented the requirements contained in the Notification on Further Strengthening Management of Traffic Rights, Flights and Slots and no longer made approval of airlines' application for operating extra flights and charter flights, except for the application for cargo transport, emergency or specialized air transport, or the transport during the Spring Festival, summer holidays and statutory holidays. The increase of the transparency of the routes and flight operating permits and all the activities related to the applications, review & approval, and public disclosure of the route operating permits and flight schedules were carried out via the website of China Civil Aviation Flights Management Information (Monitoring) System. It strengthened the supervision and management of the flights operation, published on monthly basis airlines domestic passenger flights regularity rate and canceled or revoked the operating permits for 63 non-compliant air routes.

Priority was given to support the development of air transport in Xinjiang Autonomous Region. Urumqi was connected with 48 airports in 46 cities. A comparison between the

---

精神，运输司印发了相关工作规定，对航班延误专项整治作出部署，明确了任务分工。建立了民航局、地区管理局、监管局三级航班运行协调指挥中心，作为本辖区航班延误运行协调的最高指挥机构。明确了航空公司的航班放行主体责任，空管部门及时向航空公司通报管制信息和气象预报，航空公司根据天气、运力等情况，合理安排旅客登机时间，避免旅客在机舱长时间等待。加强信息平台建设，在大面积航班延误情况下，各机场公司充分利用各种媒体、多种途径主动及时将航班延误信息、处置情况在第一时间向旅客和社会公布。建立了航班延误信息报告制度，使得民航局能够及时掌握延误情况作出应急反应。

七、切实加强危险品航空运输的管理工作

加强危险品运输管理。由运输司牵头成立了民航局危险品航空运输协调领导小组，建立了提供技术支持的专家组工作机制。下发了《危险品培训大纲锂电池知识部分修订指导意见》，填补了这方面的空白。

2011 年 4 月至 11 月份，开展了危险品违规运输专项治理工作。重点开展了对旅客行李中锂电池运输管理的专项治理工作，旅客行李中锂电池运输管理规定的信息告知与宣传、人员培训、旅客问询和安全检查得到加强，明确了旅客携带大电池的批准程序，强化了政府监管，取得了较好的效果。

八、出色完成了重大紧急航空运输保障任务和国防动员工作

圆满完成组织航空公司赴埃及、利比亚、日本撤侨任务。尤其在历时 10 天的利比亚撤侨任务中，共紧急部署国航、东航、南航、海航执行撤离包机 91 班，实际接回 26 240 人，得到了中央领导的高度评价和社会各界的广泛赞誉。圆满完成两会、庆祝西藏和平解放 60 周年大会、中央经济工作会议、深圳大运会、西安世园会、大连夏季达沃斯、中国—亚欧博览会等大型会议、遣返犯罪嫌疑人及朝觐包机等航空运输保障工作。建立重大紧急航空运输的保障长效机制。向国务院呈报民航执行国家紧急航空运输任务工作报告，对完善重大紧急航空运输工作协调机制提出了建议。为了整合力量，加强协调，提出了增设重大紧急航空专门管理机构的相关设想，已经局党组会讨论通过。

IATA winter season 2010/2011 and 2011/2012 showed an increase of routes from 71 to 82 (an increase of 17.1%) and an increase of flights from 1 768 to 2 044 (an increase of 15.6%). The passenger traffic handled at Urumqi Airport exceeded 10 million.

II. Making Breakthroughs in Cross Straits Air Transport

The fifth and sixth communication meetings with Taiwan appropriate civil aviation authority were held, and several common understandings were reached with regard to adding new points, increasing frequency and operating extra flights during the Spring Festival. In 2011, the number of points connecting Mainland and Taiwan increased to 41, and the number of weekly scheduled flights to and from Taiwan increased to 558. Currently, 9 Mainland airlines launched scheduled flights connecting 39 domestic points to the 4 points in Taoyuan, Taipei Songshan, Gaoxiong and Taichung, 6 Taiwan airlines launched scheduled flights connecting 6 points in Taoyuan, Taipei Songshan, Gaoxiong, Taichung, Hualian and Taidong to 36 domestic points, and there were about 100 round-trip flights (including scheduled flights and unscheduled tourist charter flights) every day.

III. Launching by Airlines a Number of Medium and Long-haul International Routes by Implementing "Going Out" Strategy

Coordination with the General Administration of Customs was reinforced, thus accelerating the implementation of One-stop Custom Clearance and increasing the international air cargo clearance efficiency. Luggage and passenger "through check-in" services were provided, by facilitating procedures for processing passengers taking transfer and connecting flights, at three hub airports for passengers connecting from domestic to international flights. Efforts were made to examine the strategies to be implemented in promoting air transport cooperation with Africa, Europe and North America, and to launch international flights by following China's foreign policies. Domestic airlines newly launched 34 international passenger routes and 9 cargo routes, including the launching by Air China of an air route connecting Beijing with Dusseldorf and the restoration by Air China of an air route connecting Beijing-Munich-Athens; the launching by China Eastern Airlines of an air route connecting Pudong with Rome; the launching by China Southern Airlines of an air route connecting Guangzhou with Auckland; the launching by Shanghai Airlines of a scheduled cargo air route connecting Shanghai with St. Louis; and the launching by Jade Airlines of a cargo air route connecting Shanghai Pudong-Shenzhen-Hanoi-Dubai-Amsterdam. The capacity of the domestic passenger airlines operating on the routes between China and Australia was increased by 70%.

IV. Strengthening Air Transport Market Management by Focusing on the Improvement of Legislation

The review of Provisions on the Operation Licensing of Public Air Transportation Enterprises, and Methods for the Administration of the Civil Air Transport Sales Agents was finished. The amendment and refinement of the Regulations on the Administration of Civil Aviation Market, and the Interim Administration Methods for Ground Service Provision at Civil Airports were under way. Progress made in the establishment of new airlines and operations of newly-established airlines was closely monitored. CDI Cargo Airlines and Ying'an Airlines were urged to speed up their establishment. The department made field trips to some newly-established airlines to get an in-depth understanding of their operation, required airlines to strengthen their management of their subsidiaries by carrying out rectifications in those non-compliant subsidiaries and taking measures against those that could not satisfactorily conduct rectification activities. As a result, Tibet subsidiary of Air China, Zhengzhou Subsidiary of Shenzhen Airlines, and Ganzhou Subsidiary of China Express Air were de-registered.

V. Steadily Promoting General Aviation Development

As part of the efforts to promote the trial provision of general aviation service in Inner Mongolia, Genhe Airport started providing trial general aviation service on September 2011. The department cooperated with relevant departments in conducting the first general aviation comprehensive survey which served as the basis for decision making. It launched Executive Management Development Training in General Aviation to reinforce the

team building in general aviation industry, organized and held China International General Aviation Convention, setting up an exhibition and communication platform for general aviation enterprises.

VI. Scoring Notable Achievements in Special Rectification of Massive Flight Delays

As part of its efforts to follow the guiding principles of Minutes of the Thematic Conference on the Rectification of Flight Delays, the department printed and issued relevant provisions, making arrangement for the special rectification of flight delays and assigning tasks to different entities. A three-level flight operation coordination and commanding center was established, namely at the level of CAAC,the regional administrations and the supervision and management authorities, to serve as the highest commanding organ for the operational coordination of delayed flights within their respective jurisdictions. It was clarified that airlines should be mainly responsible for issuing flight clearance, ATC departments should timely notify airlines of the ATC information and meteorological data and airlines should, in accordance with weather and traffic conditions, make arrangement for passengers embarkment and avoid their long time waiting in the cabin. Efforts were made to strengthen the establishment of an information platform, which will be used by various resident companies at airport to make the earliest possible announcement to passengers and the general public the information related to flight delays and measures taken in this regard. A flight delay information reporting system was established, enabling CAAC to have a timely knowledge of the delays and deliver emergency response.

VII. Earnestly Strengthening the Management of Dangerous Goods Transport

Efforts were made to strengthen the management of dangerous good transport. The department took the lead in establishing a CAAC Steering Group to coordinate the air transport of dangerous goods and a working mechanism for the expert panel providing technical support. The Guidance on the Amendment of the Provisions for Lithium Battery in the Dangerous Goods Training Program was issued, which filled the gap in this regard.

From April to November 2011, specialized rectification activities were carried out to address violations in dangerous goods transport. The specialized rectification was directed toward the transport of lithium batteries in the luggage of the passengers. With respect to the transport in passenger luggage of lithium batteries, efforts in this regard were reinforced to make the public informed of relevant provisions, and to hold training, answer passenger inquiry and conduct security checks. The procedures for approving the carriage by passengers of large-sized batteries were clarified, and the regulatory control by the government was strengthened. As a result, notable achievements were scored.

VIII. Brilliantly Accomplishing Major and Emergency Air Transport Support Tasks and National Defense Mobilization

The tasks of sending airlines to evacuate Chinese compatriots from Egypt, Libya and Japan were successfully accomplished, especially during the 10 days withdrawal of Chinese compatriots from Libya, in which a total of 91 charter flights from Air China, China Eastern Airlines, China Southern Airlines and Hainan Airlines were deployed to evacuate 26 240 persons, which was highly appraised by the CPC Central Committee leaders and widely acclaimed by the general public. The tasks of providing air transport support for the NPC and CPPCC, the celebration of 60th anniversary of the peaceful liberation of Tibet, the Economic Conference of CPC Central Committee, the Universiade in Shenzhen, Xi'an World Horticultural Expo., Summer Davos Forum in Dalian and China–Eurasia Expo. were successfully accomplished. Also, charter flights were sent to carry pilgrims and deported suspects. A mechanism of providing long term support for major and emergency air transport was established. A work report on execution by civil aviation industry of emergency air transport tasks was submitted to the State Council, in which a proposal was made on improving the coordination mechanism for major and emergency air transport. In order to integrate the efforts and strengthen coordination, the department also delivered a proposal to set up an agency dedicated to the management of major and emergency air transport, which was adopted at the meeting of the Party Group of CAAC. ■

飞行标准司

2011年，飞行标准司紧紧围绕民航局落实“持续安全”的总体要求，坚持系统建设与日常监管并重，在规章体系及安全监管能力建设、专业人员资质管理、航行新技术应用等方面取得了较大进展。

一、规章标准体系及安全监管能力建设

截至2011年年底，已经颁布中国民航飞行标准规章20余部，其内容涵盖了航空人员管理、航空公司运行、驾驶员学校及维修单位等合格审定、委任代表管理等涉及航空安全管理等诸多方面，基本形成较为完善的飞行标准规章体系，为实现依法管理奠定良好基础。

不断推动航空运营人安全管理达到世界先进水平，2011年是《大型飞机公共航空运输承运人运行合格审定规则》（CCAR-121部）第四次修订实施关键年，2011年年底前所有121部航空运营人必须完成符合121部第四次修订的补充运行合格审定。在指导地区管理局结合本地区具体情况制订补充审定计划并完成审定的同时，我司及时组织对飞行品质监控、延程运行、非精密进近、五边实施持续稳定下降、航空器使用困难报告和调查、航空卫生工作要求等方面下发咨询通告进行政策指导，确保了2011年年底前所有相关航空运营人均完成补充审定。同时，着手对多部规章进行修订，组织起草《民用航空卫生工作管理规则》，制定及修订近30部咨询通告等指导文件，对行业提供政策指导。

飞行标准监督管理系统（FSOP）建设正在有序开展，使用困难报告（SDR）、电子化运行规范等多个子系统均已开发完成；核心模块审定监察子系统实现网上运行，并依此进行了航空公司初始运行合格审定。

加强飞行标准各级管理人员专业培训，建立了较完备的飞行标准培训体系，实施从飞行标准管理人员到一线监察员的法规、管理和专业知识水平培训，2011年度累计受训飞标监察人员达到450余人次。

二、专业人员资质管理

2011年我司强化对运行关键人员的管理力度，并将飞行人员资质管理作为加强运行关键人员管理的核心，通过细化管理规定、加强日常监督和组织专项检查相结合的方式，共计评估运输航空公司机长10 092人次，评估合格率为98.2%。这项工作的实施在安全管理上效果显著，有效提高了飞行安全水平。

针对外籍驾驶员参加我国飞行运行过程中出现的问题，进一步规范了外籍驾驶员的执照管理，增加了执照的有效期要求、明确外籍驾驶员体检合格证及体

2011年7月5日，民航飞行标准会议在广州举行
On July 5, 2011, Civil Aviation Flight Standards Meeting Is Held in Guangzhou

2011年7月14日，中国民用航空局与空中客车公司高层安全指导委员会会议在三亚举行
On July 14, 2011, CAAC/Airbus Safety Steering Committee Meeting Is Held in Sanya

检鉴定要求、以及航空公司如何加强对外籍驾驶员管理等要求，进一步规范了外籍飞行员资源利用。

在全国范围内开展航空公司维修系统人力资源状况的检查和调研工作，督促航空公司配备足够的航线维修人员。加强航空公司签派人员资质管理，开展航空公司飞行签派员资质能力的评估检查，纠正航空公司签派员训练不规范和教学质量不高的行为。

三、航行新技术应用

基于性能的导航（PBN）在全国全面推广应用，2011年共完成23个机场的PBN飞行程序设计和试飞，全国排名前五位的繁忙国际机场全部实施了区域导航，占全国终端区域运行量的30%。推动广播式自动相关监视（ADS-B）应用初见成效，国航、东航、南航和海航四大航空公司都已在国外开始ADS-B正式运行，推动航空公司将ADS-B用于飞行动态监控。协调东北局完成ADS-B 1090ES试验试点，为低空空域开放后解决通用航空监视问题奠定基础。推进北斗卫星的应用，协调完成北斗在民航的首次测试飞行。完成飞机平视显示器技术应用试点工作，制定发展路线图。

四、加强空中停车预防措施研究

为及时解决机队运营中存在的重大安全技术问题，通过与飞机、发动机生产厂家交流研讨，研究预防空停的有效措施，加强机务人员与机组的沟通、强化原设备制造商OEM对航空公司的技术支援，总结故障原因，监控故障趋势。研究飞机实时监控故障软件的性能，编写航空公司实时故障监控系统调研报告。推动维修行业发动机孔探技术大比武和防空停大会，采取切实措施提高维修人员防空停整体水平。

五、航空卫生管理工作

研究编制民用航空卫生工作“十二五”规划，确定民用航空卫生工作发展方向和未来五年民用航空卫生工作主要内容。组织对飞标司委任体检机构调研，确定体检鉴定机构三级管理的思路及体检医师复训和重新认可的工作计划，确定中国民航体检鉴定工作的管理模式和发展目标。通过对民用航空医学学科特点、研究内容、服务领域的研究，提出民用航空医学的研究重点是解决民用航空活动中航空人员和旅客出现的各种医学问题，由此重新明确了民用航空医学的定义和内涵。建立中国民航民用运输机场应急救护能力信息库，配合机场司完成机场安全审计工作。

六、积极进行对外交流与联络

我司作为民航局中美合作项目（ACP）、波音、空客、国际民航组织北亚地区运行安全及持续适航合作项目（COSCAP-NA）的联络单位，在2011年圆满完成了对外交流与联络工作，创造了良好的外部环境：协调组织ACP框架下的合作项目，与波音、空客等机构和国外航空企业之间保持平稳而紧密的合作关系，为我国的政府和企业充分获取技术及人力资源的支持；保障COSCAP北亚组织及其办公室工作的顺利开展，参与并主持在蒙古举办的第十二次指导委员会会议。同时与美国飞行标准部门保持密切的合作联系，组织第15次中美飞标年会，中美飞行标准方面的合作逐渐进入到双方共同研究前沿课题的新高度。■

Department of Flight Standard

In 2011, the Department of Flight Standard focused its efforts on the general requirement of Sustained Safety of CAAC, attached equal importance to system building and daily supervision, and made fair progress in the building of regulatory system and safety supervision capability, the management of qualifications of professionals and the applications of new navigation technologies.

I. Building of Regulation and Standard System and Safety Supervision Capability

By the end of 2011, the department had published over 20 documents of regulations in relation to civil aviation flight standards of China, covering many aspects of aviation safety management such as aviation personnel management, operation of airlines, certification of pilot schools and maintenance entities, and management of agents, forming on the whole a relatively complete regulatory system of flight standards and, paving the way for the management according to law.

Efforts were continuously made to press ahead with the safety management of air operators to the world top level. 2011 marked a critical year for the implementation of the Fourth Amendment to the Regulations on Examination and Approval of Operational Qualification for Public Carrier of Large Aircraft (CCAR Part 121) and by the end of 2011, all air operators under CCAR Part 121 must complete supplementary certification for the operational qualifications consistent with the Fourth Amendment to CCAR Part 121. In addition to the guidance to regional administrations in developing supplementary certification plans according to their specific conditions and completing the certification, the department provided policy guidance by issuing advisory circulars on issues like monitoring of flight quality, extended range operation, non-precision approach, continuous stable descending in the implementation of final approach, reporting and investigation of difficulties in aircraft use, aviation hygiene, etc., ensuring the completion of the supplementary certification before the end of 2011by all air operators concerned. Besides, the department made revision to quite a few regulatory documents, organized the drafting of the Management Rules for Civil Aviation Hygiene Work, developed and revised guidance documents of nearly 30 advisory circulars to provide policy guidance for the industry.

The building of FSOP was systematically carried out and the development of its several sub-systems such as SDR and e-operation specifications was completed. The core module of FSOP i.e. the certification and supervision sub-system was put online with which the initial operational certification of airlines was carried out.

The department reinforced the professional training for flight standards management personnel, established a relatively complete training system of flight standards, and implemented trainings on regulations, management and professional knowledge for flight standards management personnel and supervisors in work with over 450 flight standards supervisors being trained throughout 2011.

II. Management of Qualifications of Professionals

In 2011, the department strengthened, with a focus on the qualification management of flight personnel, its management of personnel critical to operation and through a combination of developing detailed management provisions, strengthening daily oversight and organizing special inspections, it evaluated 10 092 pilots-in-command with a pass rate of 98.2%. The implementation of this work resulted in notable progress in safety management and effective improvement in flight safety.

In light of the problems that occurred in the flight operations of foreign pilots, the department further standardized the license management of foreign pilots, added requirements on the term of validity, clarified the requirements on physical examination certificates and physical examination appraisals and on how to reinforce foreign pilot management by airlines, further standardizing the utilization of foreign pilots.

The department carried out nationwide inspections and surveys of airlines' maintenance human resource conditions, urging the airlines to install sufficient maintenance personnel. It also reinforced, by launching evaluations of the qualifications of airlines' flight dispatchers and correcting the irregularities and poor teaching behaviors in their dispatcher training, the qualification management of dispatchers in airlines.

III. Applications of New Navigation Technologies

The application of performance-based navigation (PBN) was pushed ahead throughout the country, with 23 airports completing the designing and test flights for PBN procedures, and all of the national top 5 busy airports implemented area navigation, accounting for 30% of the terminal area operations in China. Initial results were achieved in the application of automatic dependent surveillance-broadcast (ADS-B), with the four major airlines of Air China, China Eastern Airlines, China Southern Airlines and Hainan Airlines starting their official application of ADS-B in foreign countries. ADS-B was promoted as the means for dynamic surveillance of flights. Coordination was provided to the Northeast Regional Administration in implementing the ADS-B 1090ES pilot program, laying foundation for the surveillance of general aviation after the opening of lower airspace. The application of Compass Satellite Navigation System was facilitated, and the first test flight using the Compass system was coordinated and completed. The pilot program for the application of head up display technology was finished and the development roadmap was developed.

IV. Reinforcing Studies on Preventive Measures against In-flight Shutdowns

In order to solve in time the major technological problems affecting safety in fleet operations, the department conducted communications and discussions with aircraft and engine manufacturers to study effective preventive measures against in-flight shutdowns, strengthened the communication between ground crew and flight crew, improved the technical support of original equipment manufacturers (OEM) to airlines, summarized failure reasons and monitored failure trends. The performances of aircraft's real time failure monitoring software were studied, and a study report for the use of real time failure monitoring systems in airlines was developed. A contest of engine borescope inspection technology for the aircraft maintenance sector and a meeting for in-flight shutdowns were organized, and effective measures were taken to improve the overall capability of maintenance personnel in prevention of in-flight shutdowns.

V. Management of Aviation Hygiene

The department studied and compiled the 12th Five-Year Plan for the civil aviation hygiene work, made clear of its development orientation and its major aspects for the future five years. It carried out a survey for the physical examination institutions entrusted by the department, identified the concept of three-level management for the physical examination institutions and the work plan for recurrent trainings for and re-recognition of physical examiners, and determined the management mode and development objectives of physical examination in the civil aviation sector. Through the studies of the characteristics, content and service fields of civil aviation medicine, the department proposed that the focus of civil aviation medicine was to address the various medical problems of aviation personnel and passengers engaged in aviation activities, and thereby redefined the definition and connotation of civil aviation medicine. It also established the information database for emergency rescue capabilities of China civil transport airports, and cooperated with the department of Airport in completing airport safety audit.

VI. Actively Carrying Out International Exchange and Liaison

As the point of contact for the China-U.S. aviation cooperation program (ACP), Boeing, Airbus and ICAO COSCAP-NA, the department successfully fulfilled its mission of international exchanges and liaison in 2011 and created a good external environment. It coordinated and organized the cooperative projects under ACP, maintained stable and tight ties with foreign organizations such as Boeing and Airbus and foreign airlines to provide support for the Chinese government and enterprises in securing technologies and human resources. It offered support to the COSCAP-NA and its office to ensure that they were in smooth operation and participated as a host in the 12th steering committee meeting held in Mongolia. The department also maintained close relations with the flight standard department of the U.S., and organized the 15th China-U.S. annual meeting on flight standards. The cooperation of flight standards between China and the U.S. was ushered into the new level of joint study of topnotch subjects.

航空器适航审定司

一、加强适航审定能力的建设及审定人员的培训

落实航空器生产审定监督职责，积极促进在航空器主机厂所在地设立生产监督办公室。

编制适航监察员年度培训工作计划；开展对培训机构的资质评估；组织培训机构开展多期适航审定相关专题培训班；组织对《航空器型号合格审定程序》、《生产批准和监督程序》和《依据〈不可撤销的注销登记和出口请求许可书〉的民用航空器国籍注销登记管理程序》等新颁布程序的宣传贯彻。

利用国外资源为审定人员和航空工业部门提供培训，包括 EASA21 部、FAA21 部、地面共振试验、型号检查核准书、复合材料等多项培训。

二、不断修订完善规章程序

修订《运输类飞机适航标准》、《运输类飞机的持续适航和安全改进》和《航空发动机适航规定》等民用航空规章；制定颁发《基于 978 兆赫通用访问收发机的广播式自动相关监视（ADS-B）设备》等 14 份中国民用航空技术标准规定；制定颁发《航空器型号合格审定程序》、《〈CAAC 与 EASA 关于 CTSO 及 ETSO 项目工作安排〉实施指南》、《已获批准的民用航空产品和零部件目录》、《关于对技术标准规定项目管理的补充要求》、航空发动机适航参考资料（第一期）和《民用航空器适航检查文件汇编》等文件。

三、继续加强各项适航的审定工作

（1）加强航空产品型号的合格审定 继续加强 ARJ21-700 飞机型号合格审定工作。加强项目计划管理，形成每月一周现场办公工作制度；增加试飞员和试飞工程师进入审定队伍；向国务院和有关部门报送 ARJ21 信息专报，通报项目审定工作进展，对项目审定工作中遇到的问题提出解决建议。

2011年10月28日，适航司张红鹰司长（左）代表民航局在中国可持续生物燃料首次验证试飞仪式上向国航颁发特许飞行证

On October 28, 2011, Zhang Hongying(left), Director General of the Department of Aircraft Airworthiness Certification, on Behalf of CAAC, Issues a Special Flight Permit to Air China for the First Demonstration Flight Using China-made Sustainable Bio-fuel

召开 C919 型飞机型号合格审定委员会首次和第一次中间会议，初步确定审定基础，正式启动项目审查工作。与中航商发公司建立日常沟通机制，多次召开专题研讨会，为国产大型客机发动机的研制和适航取证工作奠定基础。

完成国产直 8F-100（AC313）直升机型号合格审定工作并为其颁发型号合格证。组织开展 Y12F、初教 7、直 15、直 11、AC310、N5B 和海鸥 300 等航空器和 WZ8F、WZ16、HS-9、涡轴 8C/8J、CA9C/CA9D 和 HS6K1 发动机及 JL-5 和 JL-1 螺旋桨型号合格审定。

开展引进航空产品型号和补充型号认可。共受理 200 项、组织审查 174 项、批准 163 项。颁发了包括 A330 货机、G150 和皮拉图斯公司 PC-6 等产品在内的航空产品型号认可证，保证了有关航空产品的正常引进和初始安全。

（2）加强航空器生产许可的审定 开展生产批准证件清理整顿工作，加强对持证人监督和管理，促使

其更好落实规章和程序要求。以百慕高科技生产制造质量体系为例，开展零部件制造人批准书持有人全国联合检查，加强适航审定系统各地区间生产监督工作的经验交流。完成德国飞行设计公司 CTLS 轻型运动飞机生产许可证复查。

（3）贯彻执行航空器的国籍登记及适航检查 2011 年新注册航空器 392 架，颁发各类适航证件 784 份（适航证 428 份，特许飞行证 290 份，出口适航证 62 份，适航认可声明 4 份）。执行开普敦公约，组织修订了《依据〈不可撤销的注销登记和出口请求许可书〉的民用航空器国籍注销登记管理程序》。将公务机适航检查工作作为重点，有效解决公务机适航检查及交付中遇到的问题。

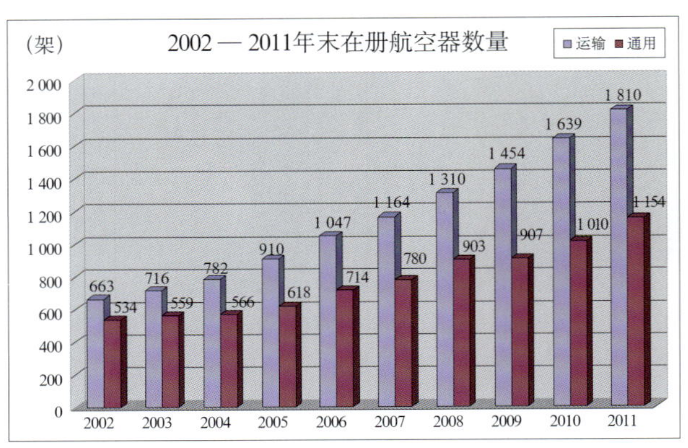

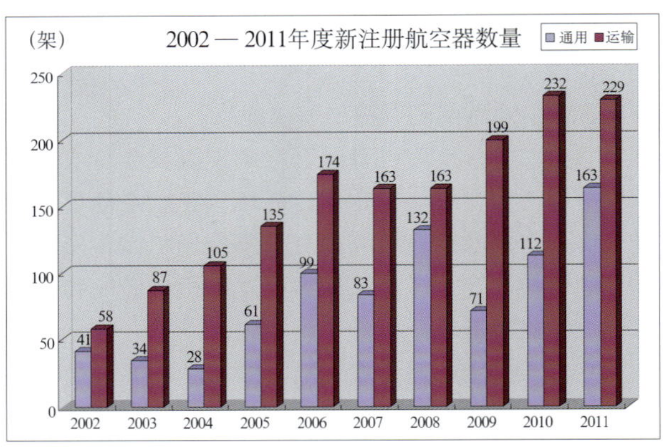

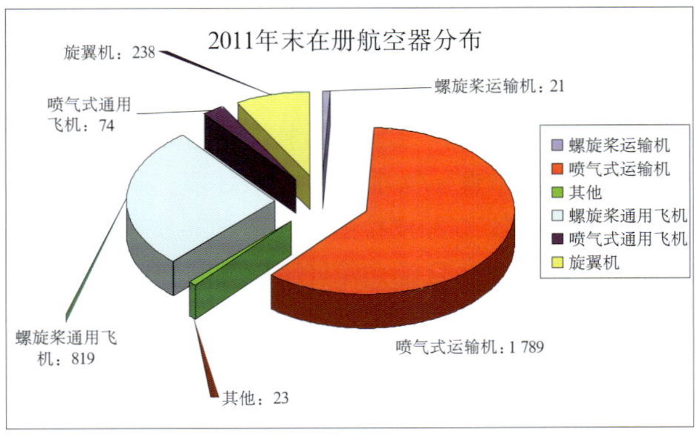

2011年4月14日，张红鹰司长代表民航局为安华农业保险公司无人机颁发特许飞行证

On April 14, 2011, Zhang Hongying, Director General of the Department of Aircraft Airworthiness Certification, Grants Special Flight Permit to the Unmanned Aircraft of Anhua Agricultural Insurance Co., Ltd.

（4）开展航油航化的适航审定及标准计量 开展生物燃油适航审定工作，通过明确适航审定标准、监督航油生产过程并完成适航检查，保证生物燃油首次试飞取得成功。

将航油中小企业纳入适航审定范畴，从而支持民营航油企业和解决 100 号航油短缺问题；完成对多家航空燃油、润滑油、特种油供应企业适航换证工作和对航油检测单位能力验证工作；向中航油华北油品质量检验中心和华南蓝天油品应用研究中心颁发委任单位代表证书；完成对中航油物流板块换证复查并开展对中航油陆地石油公司航油供应板块适航审查，全面推进航油全供应链各环节适航管理工作；推进民用航空润滑油国产化进程，国产润滑油已送专业实验室试验并取得初步结果；完成航化产品适航审查，规范航化产品适航审查程序。

规范民航标准制定和审批程序，组织完成民航行业标准立项报批。组织完成《飞机除防冰液》等 4 项国家标准和《民用航空燃料码头管理及操作程序》等 38 项行业标准的审查工作。成立民航计量检测委员会并召开第一届委员会会议。

（5）开展节能环保工作 研究“航空生物替代燃料”适航审定相关技术要求；参加国际民航组织航空

2011年3月21日，适航司殷时军副司长（前排右）代表适航司与加拿大民航局适航部门签署庞巴迪C系列飞机同步审查技术安排

On March 21, 2011, Yin Shijun (right in the first row), Deputy Director General of the Department of Aircraft Airworthiness Certification Signs the Technical Arrangement for the Simultaneous Certification of Bombardier Aerospace C-Series Aircraft with TCCA

环保委员会会议，研究国际环保新要求；为应对国际民航组织取消使用哈龙灭火剂的提议，对我国哈龙灭火剂使用情况进行调研。

四、持续跟踪及改进航空产品的安全工作

全年共颁发 254 份各机型适航指令。

与空客公司召开使用困难报告设计问题专题研讨会，促进空客飞机在我国运营的持续安全。根据民航局对 A319 飞机货舱失火事故征候调查结论，督促欧洲航空安全局（EASA）要求空客公司进行设计更改，空客公司已着手制订系统改装方案。对 A321 飞机主轮胎面脱层分离事故征候，要求 EASA 提供进一步分析说明。

完成飞行学院 PA-44-180 飞机发动机配重组件失效时间最终调查；调查 CFM56-7B 发动机停车事件及 A380 所装罗罗发动机重大非包容事件技术成因，督促制造商尽快出台整改措施；对可能造成漏油引起火灾的航油芳香烃低问题进行调查；跟踪国泰 CPA780 航班航油受污致双发空停事件调查情况，对全国所有机场油料过滤系统进行普查。

组织召开预防飞机外来物经验交流会。

五、加强国际交流及适航双边拓展工作

与美国联邦航空局加强交流合作，努力拓展中美适航双边。在美国对我国运输类飞机审定认可方面，积极推进美国联邦航空局（FAA）对 ARJ21 飞机影子审查；在美国对我国设计更改审定能力认可方面，双方达成可实现路径并启动相关工作；在美国对我国机载零部件审查认可方面，通过促成航宇公司航空座椅获取 FAA 技术标准规定设计批准函，相应扩展了认可范围。

积极促进国产航空产品和零部件走向国际市场。指导国内机载设备厂家向 FAA 申请技术标准规定设计批准函；促成菲律宾民航局修订相应法律，取消对我国航空产品出口限制；协助 Y12E 飞机取得委内瑞拉民航局型号认可证；组织协调 Y12F 型飞机申请 FAA 型号合格证等工作。

与香港、澳门开展零部件制造人批准书关键件互认、设计更改和修理设计批准互认以及适航证互认等工作，为内地及港澳航空产品和零部件转移使用创造了条件。派员参加首届两岸民用航空产品适航审定业务交流研讨会，创建了海峡两岸民用航空适航审定业务交流平台。

继续保持与美国联邦航空局、欧洲航空安全局、加拿大民航局等国外适航当局及与波音、空客、安博威、湾流等国外航空产品制造厂家的定期沟通和年会制度。■

Department of Aircraft Airworthiness Certification

I. Strengthening Capacity Building in Aircraft Airworthiness Certification and Training of Certification Personnel

The department discharged its function of overseeing aircraft manufacturing certification, and pushed for the establishment of manufacturing supervision offices at aircraft engine manufacturing facilities.

The department developed the annual training work plan for airworthiness supervisors, launched the assessment of the qualifications of training organizations, directed training organizations to hold several workshops dedicated to airworthiness certification and organized the publicity activities for the implementation of the newly promulgated procedures such as the Procedures for Aircraft Type Certification, the Procedures for the Production Approval and Supervision, and the Administrative Procedure for Civil Aircraft Nationality Registration per "Irrevocable De-registration and Export Request Authorization".

2011年5月6日，适航司张红鹰司长（左）代表民航局向航宇公司航空座椅颁发FAA-TSO设计批准函

On May 6, 2011, Zhang Hongying (left), Director General of the Department of Aircraft Airworthiness Certification Issues FAA-TSO Design Approval for Passenger Seats to Aerospace Life-Support Industries Ltd. on Behalf of CAAC

The department utilized overseas resources to provide training for airworthiness certifying personnel and aeronautical manufacturing sector, including the training in EASA Part 21, FAA Part 21, ground co-vibrating experiment, letter of approval of type checks, compound materials, etc.

II. Continuously Amending and Refining Regulations and Procedures

The department amended civil aviation regulations such as Airworthiness Standards for Transport Aircraft, Continuous Airworthiness and Safety Improvement for Transport Aircraft, and Airworthiness Provisions for Aircraft Engines, developed and promulgated 14 technical standards and provisions for China's civil aviation such as ADS-B Equipment based on 978 MHz Universal Access Transceivers and documents such as the Procedure for Aircraft Type Certification, Guidance on the Implementation of CAAC and EASA's Work Plan for CTSO and ETSO Projects, Catalog of the Approved Civil Aviation Products and Parts, Supplemental Requirements for the Project Management of Technical Standards and Provisions, Reference Material for Aircraft Engine Airworthiness (first issue), and the Collection of Aircraft Airworthiness Check Documents, etc.

III. Continuously Strengthening Various Airworthiness Certifications

1. Strengthening the type certification of aeronautical

products. The department strengthened aircraft type certification of ARJ21-700. It reinforced the project planning and management and instituted a mechanism of one-week on-site working every month. It added test pilots and flight test engineers to the certification team. It submitted to the State Council and relevant departments information circulars of ARJ21, notifying certification progress of the project and the making suggestions on the solution of problems encountered during the project certification.

The department held the preliminary C919 type certification board (TCB) meeting and one interim TCB meeting, which initially determined the certification basis and officially started the project certification. The department also established a daily communication mechanism with AVIC Commercial Aircraft Engine Co., Ltd. and held many ad hoc workshops, laying the foundation for the development of engines for China-made large-sized passenger aircraft and evidence collection for aircraft airworthiness certification.

The type certification for the 8F-100 (AC313) helicopter was completed and its type certificate was granted. The department organized and carried out the airworthiness certification of aircraft such as Y12F, L7, Z15, Z11, AC310, N5B and Seagull 300, i.e. WZ8F, WZ16, HS-9, turboshafts i.e. 8C/8J, CA9C/CA9D and HS6K1 engine as well as propellers i.e. JL-5 and JL-1.

The department conducted the recognition of the types of imported aeronautical products and supplemental types. It processed a total of 200 applications, with 174 reviewed and 163 approved. It has granted type recognition certificates for aeronautical products like A330 freighter, Gulfstream G150, PC-6 from Pilatus, etc., ensuring the smooth introduction of relevant aeronautical products and their initial safety.

2. Reinforcing the certification of the aircraft production license. The department reviewed and sorted out production licensing documents to enhance the supervision and management of license holders and urge their better compliance with relevant regulations and procedures. Referenced by the production and manufacturing quality system of Baimtec Material Co., Ltd., the department conducted the nation-wide joint inspection of the certificate holders among component part manufacturers and increased experience sharing on production oversight among different regions in the airworthiness certification community. The department completed the re-examination of the light sports airplane production permit of CTLS, which is a German flight design company.

3. Carrying out aircraft nationality registration and airworthiness inspection. In 2011, there were 392 new aircraft registered, and 784 airworthiness certificates of various kinds issued, including 428 aircraft airworthiness certificates, 290 chartered flight permits, 62 export airworthiness certificates and 4 airworthiness recognition statements. The department enforced Cape Town Convention, organized the amendment of the Administrative Procedures of Civil Aircraft Nationality De-registration per "Irrevocable De-Registration and Export Request Authorization". It gave priority to inspection of business aircraft and effectively solved the problems encountered during the airworthiness inspection and delivery of business aircraft.

4. Carrying out airworthiness certification of aviation fuel and aeronautical chemicals and developing relevant metrics. The department conducted airworthiness

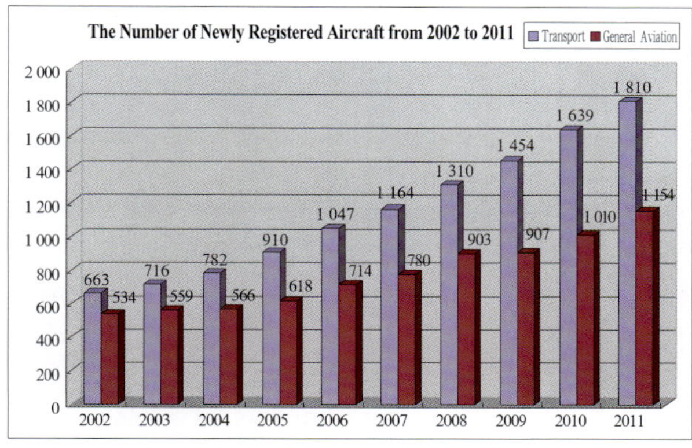

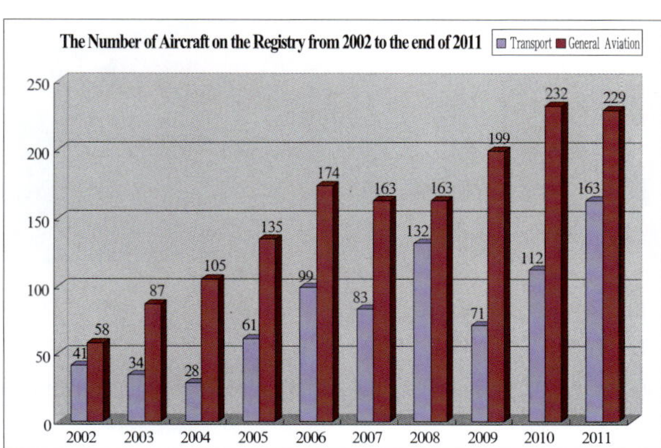

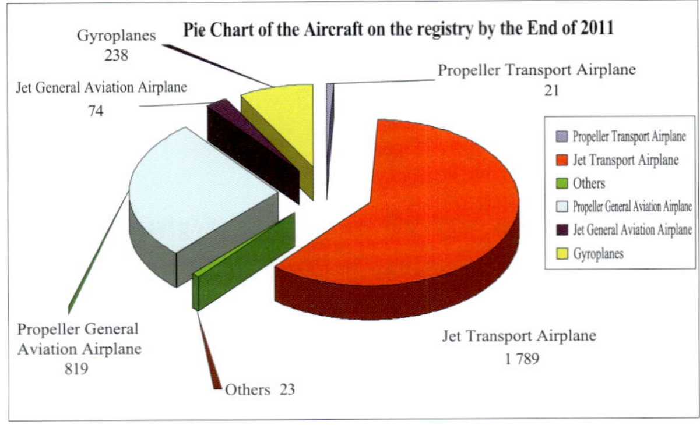

certification of bio-fuel and made it a success of the first trial flight on bio-fuel by clarifying airworthiness certification standards, overseeing the fuel production process and completing airworthiness inspections.

The department included the small and medium-sized aviation fuel enterprises into the airworthiness certification scope to support privately owned enterprises and address the problem of No.100 fuel shortage. It carried out and completed the renewal of airworthiness certificates for suppliers of aviation fuel, lubricants and special fuel and the capability verification of aviation fuel testing entities. It issued entrusting letters to North China Fuel Quality Testing Center and South China Blue Sky Fuel Applications Research Center of China National Aviation Fuel. The department completed the re-examination for the renewal of the logistics certificate of China National Aviation Fuel, carried out airworthiness review of the aviation fuel supply business of the Land Oil Company of China National Aviation Fuel and pushed ahead the airworthiness certification management of all linkage points on the entire fuel supply chain. Besides, the department facilitated the localization of civil aviation lubricant production, and homemade lubricants were already sent to specialized labs for test, whose initial results already came out. The department completed the airworthiness review of aviation chemical products and standardized the airworthiness review procedures for aviation chemical products.

The department standardized the development and approval procedures for civil aviation standards, and fulfilled the filing of the standards for approval. It led the review of 4 national standards such as the Aircraft De-icing and Anti-icing Liquids and 38 industrial standards such as the Management and Operation Procedures for Civil Aviation Fuel Ports. It established Civil Aviation Measurement and Testing Committee and held the first committee meeting.

2011年4月18日，国产C919大型客机首次型号合格审定委员会会议在上海召开

On April 18, 2011, the First Type Certification Board Meeting for China-Made C919 Aircraft Opens in Shanghai

5. Pursuing energy conservation and environmental protection. The department studied relevant technical requirements for airworthiness certification of alternative aviation bio-fuel, attended the Environmental Protection Committee meetings of ICAO and made research on new international requirements for environmental protection. In response to ICAO's proposal to stop the use of the Halon extinguishing agent, the department surveyed Halon's use in China.

IV. Continuously Monitoring and Improving the Safety of Aviation Products

In 2011, 254 airworthiness directives for various aircraft types were issued.

An ad hoc workshop on design problems in the report on use difficulties was held together with Airbus, which contributed to the sustained operation safety of Airbus aircraft in China. In accordance with the findings of CAAC's investigation into the fire incident in A319 aircraft cargo hold, the department urged EASA to direct Airbus to make design modifications, and Airbus has started to develop its system modification plan. In light of the incident of A321's main tire surface delamination, the department requested EASA to provide further analytic explanation.

The department completed the final investigation into the expiration of PA-44-180 aircraft engine counter weight assembly of Civil Aviation Flight University of China. It's also investigated the CFM56-7B engine shutdown and technical reasons for major incompatibility incidents of Rolls Royce engine installed on A380 and urged the manufacturer to develop rectification measures. It carried out the investigation of the low aromatic hydrocarbon density in aviation fuel which would cause fuel leaks and fires. It followed the investigation of the fuel contamination on the Cathy Pacific CPA780 flight which caused in-flight shutdown of both engines and inspected fuel filtering systems at all airports.

The department also held a meeting to share experiences on prevention of foreign objects to aircraft.

V. Intensifying International Exchange and Airworthiness Bilateral Cooperation

The department enhanced its cooperation and exchange with FAA to open new grounds for China-U.S. airworthiness cooperation. In terms of certification and recognition of China's transport aircraft, the department promoted FAA's shadowing certification of ARJ 21; in terms of recognition by U.S. of China's capability for certification of design modifications, both sides agreed on the achievable path and initiated relevant work; in terms of certification and recognition of China's airborne parts, the recognition scope was expanded by assisting Aerospace Life-Support Industries Ltd. in obtaining FAA-TSO design approval for its aeronautical seats.

Active efforts were made to promote the international marketing of China's aeronautical products and component parts. Guidance was provided to domestic equipment manufactures for applications for FAA-TSO design approval. The department contributed to the Civil Aviation Authority of the Philippines' amendment of relevant laws to cancel restrictions on Chinese aviation products. The department helped Y12E aircraft obtain the type recognition certificate from National Institute of Civil Aeronautics of Venezuela and coordinated in Y12F aircraft's application for FAA type certificate.

The department coordinated with relevant authorities in Hong Kong and Macao for mutual recognition of key parts of certificates of component parts manufacturers, mutual recognition of design modifications and repair design approval and mutual recognition of airworthiness certificates, creating the conditions for the transferred use of aeronautical products and component parts made in the mainland, Hong Kong and Macao. It sent a delegation to the Cross-Straits Civil Aviation Products Airworthiness Certification Workshop and set up a platform for cross-Straits exchange on civil aviation airworthiness certification.

The department maintained the regular communication and annual meeting mechanism with foreign airworthiness certification authorities such as FAA, EASA and TCCA and foreign aeronautical products manufacturers such as Boeing, Airbus, Embraer and Gulfstream.

机　场　司

一、机场使用许可证颁发及运输机场概况

截至 2011 年底，全国（未包括港澳台地区）颁证的运输机场共计 180 个，比去年增加 5 个；颁证的通用航空机场（未包括临时机场及起降点）计 44 个。新增颁证运输机场全部是支线机场，分别位于西南、西北及华北地区，它们是：日喀则和平、阿尔山伊尔施、金昌金川、张掖甘州、巴彦淖尔天吉泰机场，机场飞行区指标均为 4C。另外，2 个迁建机场为库车龟兹、揭阳潮汕机场，分别替代了老库车机场和汕头外砂机场，现已投入运营。在 180 个运输机场中，按飞行区指标分类：4F 机场 4 个，4E 机场 29 个，4D 机场 43 个，4C 机场 94 个，3C 机场 9 个，1B 机场 1 个。

2011 年，北京首都国际机场年旅客吞吐量达 7 867 万人次，位居国际机场协会（ACI）世界排名第 2 位；上海浦东国际机场年货邮吞吐量达 308 万吨，位居国际机场协会（ACI）世界排名第 3 位。2011 年，年旅客吞吐量 1 000 万人次以上的机场新增了 5 个，分别是：乌鲁木齐地窝堡、沈阳桃仙、三亚凤凰、海口美兰、郑州新郑机场；全国年旅客吞吐量超过 1 000 万人次的机场达到 21 个。

二、机场建设与管理法规规章及技术标准

2011 年，继续深入贯彻国务院《民用机场管理条例》，按照条例的相关规定和要求，组织完成了规章《民用运输机场突发事件应急救援规则（修订版）》（民航局 208 号令）（CCAR-139-Ⅱ-R1），并下发实施。

完成并下发了规范性文件：《航空器鸟击残留物收集、保存和提交办法》管理程序（AP-140-CA-2011-1）、《机场外来物管理规定》管理程序（AP-140-CA-2011-2）、《防止机场地面车辆和人员跑道侵入管理规定》管理程序（AP-140-CA-2011-3）、《供 B747-8 使用的 4E 及其以下民用机场的技术标准及运行要求》咨询通告（AC-139-CA-2011-01）、《民用机场栏鸟网应用指南》咨询通告（AC-140-CA-2011-02）。

完成并下发了行业标准《民用机场勘测规范》（MH/T 5025—2011），组织修订并下发了《民航空管专业工程概、预算编制办法及费用定额（2011 年试行版）》。民航局与国家发改委等九部委局联合下发了《简明标准施工招标文件》（发改法规〔2011〕3018 号）和《标准设计施工总承包招标文件》；民航局组织修编并与住房与城乡建设部、国土资源部联合审定发布了《民用航空运输机场工程项目建设用地指标（修订版）》（建标〔2011〕157 号）。

三、机场安全管理

认真落实持续安全理念，确保机场安全运行管理扎实有效。一是大力推进鸟击防范工作。组织召开中国民航鸟击防范委员会第一次会议暨鸟击防范新技术、新产品研讨会；组织协调航科院与南京师范大学联合成立了中国民航鸟击残留物鉴定重点实验室，为各机场验证鸟击物种信息提供帮助。二是努力推进机场飞机活动区防止外来物（FOD）损伤航空器轮胎的工作，推广上海浦东、杭州萧山等机场的先进做法，并会同飞标司发布了《机场外来物管理规定》（管理程序），形成长效机制。三是通过加强机场安全审计，下发《机场使用手册范本》，深入推进机场 SMS 建设工作；除新建机场外，全国各运输机场第一轮安全审计工作全面完成。四是加强应急救援管理工作，宣贯了《民用运输机场突发事件应急救援规则（修订版）》（民航局 208 号令），全国各机场均至少进行了一次单项或综合应急救援演练。五是积极推动机场除冰雪管理工作，推进飞机除冰资源整合试点，配合飞标司推动飞机怠速除冰工作。全国机场 2011 年未发生因机场保障原因造成的航空地面事故，实现了民航局制定的 2011 年安全目标。

四、机场及配套设施建设

2011 年，积极推进 25 个重点建设项目实施进度。其中，4 个计划竣工项目中，南昌昌北机场扩建和长

Department of Airport

I. Overview of Airport Certification and Transport Airports

By the end of 2011, there had been a total of 180 certificated transport airports nationwide (excluding those in Hong Kong, Macao and Taiwan), with an addition of 5 to 2010's number; and there had been 44 certificated general aviation airports (excluding makeshift airports and landing points). All of the newly certificated airports were feeder airports, located in the southwest, northwest and north regions of China respectively, i.e. Rikaze Peace Airport, Arxan Yiershi Airport, Jinchang Jinchuan Airport, Zhangye Ganzhou Airport and Bayannur Tianjitai Airport, whose movement area standards were all classified as 4C. Besides, the 2 relocated airports, i.e. Kuqa Qiuci Airport and Jieyang Chaoshan Airport, were put into operation to replace the previous Kuche Airport and Shantou Waisha Airport. Among the 180 transport airports, there were, according to the classification of the movement area

---

沙黄花机场扩建工程通过行业验收并投入使用；昆明新机场、东部和西部航路雷达工程将推至 2012 年竣工验收。10 个续建项目进展顺利，预计 2012 年完成 8 个，分别是：合肥新机场、杭州萧山机场扩建、拉萨贡嘎机场扩建、贵阳龙洞堡机场扩建、成都双流机场扩建、西安咸阳机场扩建、成都区域管制中心、西安区域管制中心等工程。计划新开工的 11 个项目中已开工沈阳桃仙机场扩建、上海浦东机场飞行区扩建、南京禄口机场扩建 3 个项目，其余 8 个项目包括北京新机场工程在内，正在推进前期工作。

在全面调研全国支线机场配置仪表着陆系统（ILS）和 I 类助航灯光系统情况的基础上，根据“确保安全、严格标准、分步实施、加快推进”的原则，确定了两批 25 个支线机场实施 I 类助航灯光设施改造工程。其中，在 23 个已批可研报告的项目中，18 个项目初步设计已批复。截至 2011 年底，2 个项目已完工，7 个正在施工，9 个准备开工。此项工作将进一步提高支线机场的运行保障能力。另外，组织完成了新疆塔中等 8 个机场场址审查并出具了行业审查意见；审查批准了厦门高崎等 7 个机场的总体规划；审查批复了贵阳龙洞堡机场扩建等 40 个工程的初步设计及概算；组织了 4 个建设项目的行业验收。

五、推动机场管理模式改革和特许经营试点

继续积极协调推动烟台新机场管理模式改革试点，组织召开了第二次领导小组及领导小组办公室会议，研究确定了“烟台新机场运营管理模式改革试点总体方案”。继续推动北京、上海、厦门和深圳机场的特许经营试点工作。

六、科研课题与对外交流

推广新技术、新产品研究与应用，提升机场建设与安全管理水平，组织成立了民航局跑道“特性材料拦阻系统”行业审查领导小组，开展审查工作；探讨引进跑道外来物监控技术、激光驱鸟技术、雷达驱鸟技术、围界警报及视频监控技术，以及场道和航空器除冰防冰新技术的研发与应用。继续深化“绿色机场”研究，逐步确定节能减排及环境保护等相关指标和措施，推进昆明新机场建设“绿色机场”的相关工作。

参与国际民航组织关于机场标准修订的工作；积极开展中英、中新机场管理年度交流工作；组织召开了“航站楼规划与设计研讨会”，以进一步提升我国机场航站楼规划设计和建设水平。

七、其他资质审查等工作

完成了住房与城乡建设部委托的共计 15 家施工、监理企业申报民航专业工程资质的行业审核工作；审核颁发民用机场专用设备审定合格证 95 项。组织完成了 2010 年度民航机场工程专业高级技术职务评审工作。■

standards, 4 4F airports, 29 4E airports, 43 4D airports, 94 4C airports, 9 3C airports and 1 1B airport.

In 2011, the annual passenger turnover at Beijing Capital International Airport reached 78.67 million, ranking No.2 in the world rankings by Airports Council International (ACI); the annual cargo and mail turnover at Shanghai Pudong International Airport hit 3.08 million tons, ranking No.3 in the world rankings by ACI. In 2011, there were 5 more airports whose annual passenger turnover reached over 10 million, namely, Urumqi Diwopu Airport, Shenyang Taoxian Airport, Sanya Fenghuang Airport, Haikou Meilan Airport and Zhengzhou Xinzheng Airport, bringing the total number of airports with passenger turnover exceeding 10 million to 21.

II. Laws, Regulations and Technical Standards for Airport Construction and Management

In 2011, the department continued to earnestly act upon the Regulation on the Management of Civil Airports by the State Council and, in accordance with relevant provisions and requirements thereof, completed the development of Management Regulations of Emergency Response and Rescue on Sudden Outbreak of Events at Civil Transport Airports (Revised) (CAAC Order No.208) (CCAR Part 139-II-R1) and put it into effect.

The department developed and issued other regulatory documents as follows: the management procedures for the Methods of the Collection, Storage and Submission of Remnants of Bird Strike against Aircraft (AP-140-CA-2011-1), the management procedure for the Management Regulations on Foreign Object Debris at Airports (AP-140-CA-2011-2), the management procedures for the Management Regulations on the Prevention of Ground Vehicle and Personnel's Intrusion into Runways (AP-140-CA-2011-3), the Advisory Circular on Technical Standards and Operational Requirements for Airports at 4E and below Used by B747-8 (AC-139-CA-2011-01), and the Advisory Circular on the Application Guidance for Airport Bird Netting (AC-140-CA-2011-02).

The department also developed and issued the industry standard of Survey Rules for Civil Airports (MH/T 5025-2011), and coordinated the revision and issuance of the Methodology for the Financial Estimate and Budgeting of Civil Aviation ATM Projects and Expenditure Rating (2011 Trial Edition). CAAC worked in conjunction with 9 ministries and administrations such as the National Development and Reform Commission in the issuance of the Brief Bidding Document for Standard Constructions (NDRC Regulation 2011 No. 3018) and the General Contract Bidding Document for Standard Design and Constructions; CAAC coordinated the development of Standards on Construction-use Land for Civil Aviation Transport Airports' Construction Projects (Revised) (Ministry of Housing and Urban-Rural Development Standard 2011 No. 157), and worked with the Ministry of Housing and Urban-Rural Development and the Ministry of Land and Resources in its examination and issuance.

III. Airport Safety Management

The department earnestly implemented the concept of sustained safety to ensure that safe operation management at airports be solid and effective. First, the department vigorously promoted bird strike prevention. It held the First Meeting of the China Civil Aviation Bird Strike Prevention Committee and Workshop on New Technologies and New Products, and also coordinated between China Academy of Civil Aviation Science and Technology and Nanjing Normal University for their joint establishment of the Chinese Civil Aviation Key Laboratory for Bird Strike Remnants Examination, assisting airports in verifying bird breed information. Second, the department aggressively pushed ahead with the prevention of foreign object debris (FOD) from damaging aircraft tires in airport movement areas by popularizing advanced practices at airports like Shanghai Pudong Airport and Hangzhou Xiaoshan Airport, and pairing up with the Department of Flight Standard in issuing Management Regulations on Foreign Object Debris at Airports (Management Procedure) to make it a long-term mechanism. Third, the department advanced in-depth SMS construction at airports by strengthening airport safety audit and issuing the Airport Use Manual Template, and completed the first round of safety audit at all transport airports nationwide except those newly-built ones. Fourth, the department strengthened emergency response and rescue management by issuing and implementing Management Regulations of Emergency Response and Rescue on Sudden Outbreak of Events at Civil Transport Airports (Revised) (CAAC Order No.208) whereby all airports in China performed at least 1 specific or comprehensive emergency response and rescue drill. Fifth, the department actively pressed ahead with airport deicing management, promoted the pilot consolidation of aircraft deicing resources and coordinated with the Department of Flight Standard in advancing aircraft idling deicing. In 2011, there was no support-induced aviation ground accident at airports in China, realizing the safety targets set by CAAC at the beginning of 2001.

IV. Construction of Airports and Supporting Facilities

In 2011, the department energetically pushed ahead with the construction progress of 25 key projects, among which in the 4 projects planned to be completed, the expansion projects at Nanchang Changbei Airport and Changsha Huanghua Airport passed the industry check and acceptance and began operation, while the projects of the Kunming New Airport and the radar installation on the eastern and western routes were planned to postpone till 2012. The 10 extension projects preceded smoothly, 8 of which were expected to be completed in 2012, namely, Hefei new Airport, the expansion projects at Hangzhou Xiaoshan Airport, Lhasa Gongga Airport, Guiyang Longdongbao Airport, Chengdu Shuangliu Airport, Xi'an Xianyang Airport, and the regional ATC centers in Chengdu and in Xi'an. Of all the 11 new projects planned to be launched, 3 were already started, namely, expansion projects at Shenyang Taoxian Airport, Shanghai Pudong Airport movement area and Nanjing Lukou Airport, and for the remaining 8 projects, including the construction of Beijing New Airport, their preparatory work was being pushed forward.

The department identified, on the basis of a comprehensive study of the use of ILS and Class I airfield lighting system at feeder airports nationwide, 2 batches of a total of 25 feeder airports for their renovation of Class I airfield lighting system in accordance with the principle of "ensuring safety, rigorously enforcing standards, executing by stages and accelerating speed". Of the 23 projects whose feasibility study reports had been approved, 18 had received approval for their preliminary designs. By the end of 2011, 2 projects had been completed, 7 still ongoing and 9 about to start their construction, the above of which would further boost the operational support of the feeder line airports' capacity. Besides, the department also completed the siting review of 8 airports such as Xinjiang Tazhong Airport and made industry review comments; it reviewed and approved the overall plans of 7 airports such as Xiamen Gaoqi Airport, the preliminary designs and financial estimates of 40 projects such as the expansion project at Guiyang Longdongbao Airport; and conducted industry check and acceptance of 4 construction projects.

V. Promotion of Airport Management Model Reform and Pilot Franchising

The department continued to actively coordinate and promote the pilot reform of airport management model at Yantai New Airport and organized the second meeting of the leadership group and leadership group office, at which it decided, after study, on the Overall Plan for the Pilot Reform of Operation Management Model at Yantai New Airport. It continued to push forward pilot franchising at airports in Beijing, Shanghai, Xiamen and Shenzhen.

VI. Academic Researches and Foreign Exchanges

The department promoted the research and application of new technologies and new products to accelerate airport construction and improve safety management, set up a CAAC industry review leadership group on Special Material Blockage and Resistance System for runways to conduct reviews, and held discussions on the introduction of runway FOD monitoring technology, laser bird expulsion technology, radar bird expulsion technology, fence alarm and video monitoring technology as well as the research and application of new technologies in deicing and ice prevention for runways and aircraft. The department continued to deepen researches into green airports, gradually established indicators and measures related to energy saving, emissions reduction and environmental protection and pushed forward the green airports project at Kunming New Airport.

The department took part in ICAO's revision of airport-related standards, took an active part in annual exchange on airport management with the U.K. and Singapore, and organized Terminal Plan and Design Seminar to further promote the level of China's airport terminal plan, design and construction.

VII. Other Qualification Reviews

Entrusted by the Ministry of Housing and Urban-Rural Development, the department completed the industry reviews on 15 construction and construction supervision businesses' applications for specialized civil aviation construction qualifications, reviewed and issued 95 certificates for specialized civil airport equipment, and organized and completed 2010 appraisals of senior technical professionals in civil airport engineering.

空管行业管理办公室

一、加强政策规划研究制定，引导空管行业健康发展

2011 年，空管行业管理办公室在深入调研的基础上，提出了解决中小机场空管问题的政策措施和建议。结合中小机场建设需求，组织开展了《中国民航气象观测技术应用政策》研究制定工作，配合阿拉善盟通勤机场试点，制定了《通勤机场空管建设与运行试点工作的指导意见》。为全面推动广播式自动监视器（ADS-B）在我国的应用，组织行业专家进行深入研讨，明确了下一阶段 ADS-B 实施的技术政策和技术路线。组织民航数据通信网建设规划和实施方案的论证，明确了全国民航数据通信网建设规划和总体方案。为做好传统导航与卫星导航的衔接过渡，组织开展了中国民航导航技术应用政策研究。继续推进法规工作，完成了 7 部规章的修改和送审工作。修订、发布了 9 部规范性文件和 4 部行业标准。

2011年发布的规范性文件及空管行业标准

规范性文件	1	《民航空中交通管理安全评估管理办法》
	2	《民航空管安全管理体系审核管理办法》
	3	《民航空管行政监察工作程序》
	4	《民用机场使用许可空管事项申请与审批规定》
	5	《民用航空通信导航监视设备使用许可管理工作细则》
	6	《民航空中交通管理安全管理体系建设指导手册》
	7	《民用航空无线电管理检查手册》
	8	《民用机场电磁环境保护区划定规范与保护要求》
	9	《民用机场电磁环境测试规范》
行业标准	1	《民用航空气象观测系统数据输出格式》
	2	《民用航空气象地面观测记录》
	3	《民用航空航行通告编发规范》
	4	《民用航空航行通告代码选择规范》

二、加强空管行业人才队伍建设，逐步规范人员资质管理工作

组织制定了 6 部空管行业培训大纲及规范，初步建立起空管专业人员执照网上申请和管理平台，组织各地区管理局开展了四类空管专业人员执照信息的入库、补录和清理工作，全面掌握了空管专业人员资质的相关情况，共退回和要求补充材料 1 200 多人次，清理无效执照人员 42 人。指导各地区管理局做好空管专业人员执照的考试、考核、审查、上报工作，全年新颁发管制员执照 862 人次，情报员执照 41 人次，电信人员执照 707 人次，气象人员执照 105 人次。下发管制员英语等级签注 567 人次。在全行业组织开展了一线管制员资质检查清理工作，取得了良好效果。

2011年发布的空管行业培训大纲及规范

1	《民用航空空中交通管制基础培训大纲》
2	《民用航空情报基础培训大纲》
3	《民用航空空中交通管制员执照理论考试大纲》
4	《民用航空情报员执照理论考试大纲》
5	《民航通信导航人员培训大纲》
6	《机场塔台管制培训模拟设备技术规范》

全年共组织一期民航空管类航空监察员初始业务培训班，一期监管局空管处长培训班，四期中小机场导航人员技术培训班，二期中小机场气象预报人员培训班，三期中小机场气象观测人员培训班，二期无线电管理与业务知识培训班，五期中小机场空管安全管理培训班和一期航班时刻协调员业务培训班，受训人员共计 1 000 多人次。这些培训面向一线，突出安全主题，贴近技术操作，受到了各中小机场的高度评价。

三、加强空管设备与无线电管理，把好安全关口

为切实加强空管监督管理，前移安全关口，制定下发了《民用机场使用许可空管事项申请与审批规定》，规范了机场开放运行许可中空管管理的内容和审批要求，明确了机场运行应当具备的空管设施、设备、人员、制度等方面要求和审查程序，进一步完善了机场管制单位运行的资格审查制度。

2011年8月25日，空管办在成都召开民航ADS-B应用专家研讨会空管办主任苏兰根（前排左五）、空管办副主任李其国（前排左四）参加会议

On August 25, 2011, the Office of Air Traffic Regulation Holds an Expert Symposium in Chengdu on ADS-B Application in Civil Aviation Director General Su Lan'gen (fifth from the left in the front row) and Deputy Director General Li Qiguo (fourth from the left in the front row) Attend the Symposium

为确保设备运行安全可靠，制定颁布了《民用航空空中交通通信导航监视设备使用许可管理工作细则》，初步建立起设备使用合格审定与设备测试机制。全年共受理22个型号通信导航监视设备申请，颁发18个型号通信导航监视设备使用许可，把住了安全入口关。完成1 126套通信导航监视设备开放的批复，17个机场气象观测、探测设备的选址和开放审批，组织解决了连云港机场仪表着陆系统安装调试的技术难题，使该机场达到一类精密进近标准。全年核发航空器电台执照共计1 411本，指配无线电通信频率102个，导航频率133个，航空器选呼号码217个。

为进一步保护民用机场电磁环境，编制下发了《民用航空无线电管理检查工作手册》、《民用机场电磁环境保护区划定规范与保护要求》和《民用机场电磁环境测试规范》。为保障中国民航未来能够拥有稳定和充足的无线电频谱资源，组织协调相关部委、空军、院校共同研究并跟踪2012年世界无线电通信大会（WRC-12）有关的航空议题，确定了中国民航所持观点立场。

四、推进空管安全管理体系和审核工作，有效发挥政府监管职能

就空管行业落实安全主体责任、强化人员资质管理、加强设备运行保障、防止航空器相撞、加强安全监管等5个方面，提出10条具体措施要求。通过符合性检查，明确了航行情报资料上报的渠道，确立了机场与情报部门原始资料提供与收集的责任与有关机制。组织完成了对空管系统的11个空管运行单位及35个机场空管运行部门的安全审计工作。为提高我国民航突发事件处置能力，进一步加强民航国际间协调合作，起草了《交通运输部关于签署中俄民用航空器搜寻援救协议的请示》报请国务院审批并已获批。会同局有关单位与俄罗斯民航当局举行了中俄民航空管工作组会谈，商谈搜寻救援协议、新开中俄之间航路及入出境点等事宜。

五、加强机场容量和航班时刻资源管理工作，提高资源使用效率

研究确定了21个航班时刻协调机场及其容量，从而进一步规范了机场容量的调整和使用原则，为航班时刻的管理和分配提供了更加科学的依据。在容量评估的基础上，对北京、重庆、大连、乌鲁木齐、南京等机场的航班时刻容量标准进行了调整，21个繁忙机场共增加了2 700余个可用时刻资源。启动了深圳、大连、青岛、西安、杭州、昆明等机场的航班时刻容量评估工作。组织2012冬春航班时刻换季协调与分配集中办公。

Office of Air Traffic Regulation

I. Strengthening Policy Planning, Research and Development to Guide the Sound Development of the ATM Industry

In 2011, the Office of Air Traffic Regulation, on the basis of in-depth survey, proposed policy measures and suggestions to address the air traffic control problems in feeder airports. In light of their specific needs, the office organized and carried out the development of studies on the Policy on Applications of Meteorological Observation Technologies in the Civil Aviation Industry of China, and in cooperation with the pilot implemented at the commuter airport in Alxa League Prefecture, it developed the Guidelines on the Air Traffic Management and Pilot Implementation at Commuting Airports. In order to promote large scale application of automatic dependent surveillance-broadcast (ADS-B) in China, it invited industrial experts to discuss and identify the technical policy and technical roadmap for the next phase implementation of ADS-B. It held a case study for and determined the construction planning and the overall implementation program for a civil aviation data communication network in China. In order to make a smooth transition from traditional navigation to satellite based navigation, the office organized and carried out a study on the policy related to the application of navigation technologies in China civil aviation industry. It continued pressing ahead with the legislative work and finished amending 7 regulations and their submission for review. The office also amended and published 9 regulatory documents and 4 industrial standards.

Regulatory Documents and Air Traffic Management Standards Published in 2011

Standardized Documents	1	Management Methods for the Safety Assessment of Civil Aviation ATM
	2	Management Methods for Safety Management System Review of Civil Aviation ATM
	3	Administrative Supervision Work Procedures for Civil Aviation ATM
	4	Provisions on Civil Airport ATM Items Applications and Approval
	5	Working Rules for the Certificate Management of Civil Aviation CNS Equipment
	6	Guidance Manual for the Establishment of a Safety Management System for Civil Aviation ATM
	7	Inspection Manual for Civil Aviation Radio Management
	8	Delimitation Specifications and Protection Requirements for the Civil Airport Magnetic Protection Area
	9	Testing Specifications on the Civil Airport Magnetic Environment
Industrial Standards	1	Data Output Format of Civil Aviation Meteorological Observation System
	2	Ground Observation Records of Civil Aviation Meteorological Data
	3	Specification for the Development and Distribution of Civil Aviation NOTAM
	4	Specification for Civil Aviation NOTAM Code Selection

II. Strengthening the Cultivation of ATM Professionals to Gradually Standardize Personnel Qualification Management

The office developed 6 civil aviation training programs and specifications, initially established online licenses application and management platform for ATM professionals, guided regional administrations in inputting, adding and nullifying the license information of four types of ATM professionals, had an overall picture of the licenses held by ATM professionals, rejected more than 1 200 license applications for the lack of sufficient materials, and nullified the invalid licenses held by 42 persons. The office offered guidance to regional administrations in organizing examination, evaluation, review and reporting for ATM professionals licensing. In 2011, 862 new licenses were granted to the controllers, 41 to the information professionals, 707 to telecommunication professionals and 105 to meteorological professionals. Underwriting for English language level of controllers was issued for 567 person-times. It organized licenses review for the controllers in work across the industry and achieved good effect in this respect.

ATM Industrial Training Programs and Specifications Published in 2011

1	Basic Training Program for Civil Aviation ATC
2	Basic Training Program for Civil Aviation Information
3	Theory Examination Program for Civil Aviation Air Traffic Controllers Licensing
4	Theory Examination Program for Civil Aviation Information Personnel Licensing
5	Training Program for Civil Aviation Communication and Navigation Professionals
6	Technical Specifications for Airport Tower Control Training Simulators

In 2011, the office organized 1 initial training session for the civil aeronautic supervisors in the field of ATM, 1 training session for the ATM directors from supervision and management bureaus, 4 technical training sessions for the navigation personnel in feeder airports, 2 and 3 training sessions respectively for weather forecasting professionals and weather observers in small and medium sized airports, 2 training sessions on the radio management and business knowledge, 5 training sessions on ATM safety management for small and medium sized airports and 1 training session for flight slot coordinators, with a total of over 1 000 persons trained. These training sessions were oriented toward the personnel in work, focused on technical operation skills and closely connected with technical operation, and as a result, were highly acclaimed by various small and medium sized airports.

III. Strengthening ATM Equipment and Radio Management to Guarantee Safety Control

In order to efficiently strengthen the ATM supervision and management and move ahead safety control, the office developed Provisions on Civil Airport ATM Items Application and Approval, standardized the ATM information to be included in the airport operation permit and their review and approval requirements, identified the requirements and review procedures for the ATM facilities, equipment, personnel and system necessary for airport operation, further improving the examination system of the operational licenses held by control units at airports.

In order to ensure operational safety and reliability, the office developed the Working Rules for the User Permit Management of Civil Aviation CNS Equipment, preliminarily establishing an equipment certification and testing mechanism. In 2011, applications for 22 types of CNS equipment were accepted and processed, user permits were issued for 18 types of CNS equipment, excellently guaranteeing the safety control. It made approval for the open use of over 1 126 sets of CNS equipment, and for the location selection and operation plan for the meteorological observation and detection equipment in 17 airports, organized the solution of the technical difficulties encountered during the installation and commissioning of ILS at Lianyungang Airport, enabling it to meet the standards for CAT I precision approach. In 2011, 1 411 aircraft radio licenses were issued, and 102 radio communication frequencies, 133 navigation frequencies and 217 selective call codes were designated.

In order to further protect the magnetic environment of airports, the office developed and issued Inspection Manual for Civil Aviation Radio Management, Delimitation Specification and Protection Requirements for the Civil Airport Magnetic Area and Testing Specifications of the Civil Airport Magnetic Environment. In order to ensure stable and sufficient radio spectrum resources for China civil aviation, the office invited relevant departments at ministerial level, air force and educational institutions to study and follow aeronautic agenda items of World Radio Communication Conference (WRC-12) and identified the positions of CAAC for those agenda items.

2011年11月16日，空管办主任苏兰根（左）在南京为14所颁发我国第一部国产二次雷达使用许可证

On November 16, 2011, Director General Su Lan'gen (left) Issues Certificate for the First China Made SSR to the 14th Research Institute in Nanjing

IV. Pressing Ahead with the Implementation and Review of ATM Safety Management System to Give a Better Play to the Regulatory Role of the Government

The office proposed 10 specific measures with regard to 5 aspects, namely the implementation of principal safety responsibilities in the ATM industry, the reinforcement of qualification management of the personnel, the enhancement of operational support of equipment, aircraft collision avoidance and strengthening of safety supervision. Through compliance checks, it identified the channels through which the aeronautic information could be submitted and determined the responsibilities and relevant mechanism of the provision and collection of source material by the airports and information department. It conducted safety audits for 11 ATM operating entities and 35 airport ATM operating departments. In order to improve emergency handling capabilities of civil aviation in China and strengthen international coordination and cooperation in civil aviation, the office drafted Ministry of Transport Requests for Instructions on Signing China-Russia Agreement on Civil Aircraft Search and Rescue and submitted it to the State Council for its approval. The office, in conjunction with relevant departments under CAAC, held Sino-Russia civil aviation ATM working group talks with competent Russian civil aviation authority to discuss such matters as signing search and rescue agreement, opening new routes and designating entry and exit points.

V. Strengthening the Resources Management for Airport Capacity and Flight Slots to Improve Resources Utilization Efficiency

The office identified, through careful evaluation, 21 airports which needed flight slot coordination and their capacity, and further standardized the principles to be followed in the adjustment and use of airport capacity, laying a more scientific basis for the flight slot management and allocation. On the basis of capacity evaluation, the office adjusted flight slots and capacity for airports in Beijing, Chongqing, Dalian, Urumqi and Nanjing, and added more than 2 700 available flight slots in 21 busy airports. Flight slots and capacity evaluation was initiated for the airports in Shenzhen, Dalian, Qingdao, Xi'an, Hangzhou, Kunming, etc. The office also organized centralized handling of official business for the reshuffle of IATA winter season flight slots.

公 安 局

2011 年，民航局公安局着力加强规章建设，强化行政监管，加强空防安全和公安保卫各项基础工作，实现了行业空防安全的总体平稳，确保了良好的机场治安秩序。

一、突出重点，切实加强我国重大活动的安全保障保卫工作

圆满完成了党和国家领导人出访专机保障任务，并顺利完成全国“两会”、深圳大运会、金砖国家领导人第三次正式会晤、博鳌亚洲论坛年会、庆祝西藏和平解放 60 周年、新疆首届中国—亚欧博览会、大连达沃斯论坛、青海玉树地震一周年纪念等重大活动中的民航安保任务。

大运会期间，确保各国贵宾、政要、大运会参赛运动员和参加博览会人员、物品抵离机场的绝对安全。安检部门出色完成涉大航班 1 669 架次、涉大人员 1 万人次运输安保任务；完成警卫任务 27 批、专机监护 17 架次、保障大运物资 26 批次和运动枪支 329 支、子弹 19.4 万发。实现了“安全、正常、优质、高效”的总体目标。

在新疆首届中国—亚欧博览会的安全保卫工作中，民航局公安局进一步部署各单位全面加强各项安全防范措施和督导检查工作，调整空防安全威胁预警等级，并派出检查组实地检查新疆空防安全工作，切实筑起首届亚欧博览会期间的民航安保防线，确保了亚欧博览会各项活动安全顺利，确保了与会中外警卫对象绝对安全。

二、固本强基，建立牢固的安检保障系统

围绕资质审查，全面强化安检系统质量控制。一是重点加强对安检机构成立、安检日常勤务等的规范，增加法律责任的追究条款；对用于民航安全检查工作的设备从鉴定、使用许可、使用验收技术检测和在用设备定检管理等环节进行系统规范；对航空货物收运、安全检查、航空货运区、航空货物装运等进行系统规范。

二是继续大力推进在用旅客安检设备定检工作，全面启动在用货物安检设备定检工作。制定发布相关标准，强化对货运 X 射线安检设备和痕量爆炸物安全检查设备的入口关和持续有效运行把控。同时，继续强化安检设备认证、鉴定和许可工作，对不符合规章要求的安检设备坚决不予批准行政许可延期。

三是开展航空货邮运输安保专项整治行动。进一步明确航空货邮运输主体的安保责任，规范货邮运输安保流程，使航空货邮运输环境得到明显改善。

三、立足地面，打造和巩固“平安机场”工程

以《民用机场公共区域治安防控规定》和《机场公安机关治安防控工作实施细则》等规范性文件的贯彻落实为抓手，进一步加强机场公共区域治安防控工作力度，深入开展治安秩序专项整治。一年来全系统未发生造成社会影响、危及空防安全的重大治安案件、事件。按照公安部统一部署，民航局公安局在民航公安系统组织开展“清网行动”，在查获枪支弹药、查处违法犯罪案件、抓获网上在逃人员工作方面成绩显著。

四、开拓创新，扎实推进和实施航空保安管理体系（SeMS）

民航局公安局深入研究中国民航空防安全特点，提出 SeMS 在运行管理中实现“落地”的“四个体系”建设要求，使 SeMS 真正起到改进提高安保管理水平、效能的作用。下发《关于全面开展航空保安管理体系（SeMS）建设工作的通知》，就 SeMS

Bureau of Aviation Security

In 2011, Bureau of Aviation Security of CAAC maintained overall stability of aviation security and ensured good security order at airports by strengthening regulatory building, intensifying administrative supervision and stepping up efforts in basic work in aviation security and public security.

I. Strengthening Security Support and Security Safeguard for Major Events in China with Emphasis on the Key Work

The bureau successfully accomplished support for charter flights carrying party and government leaders on foreign visits, and also provided civil aviation security for the NPC

建设的范围、基本内容、实施步骤、组织实施等方面进行全面部署。举办SeMS建设培训班，前往西南、新疆等地区指导检查SeMS建设进展情况。研究制定航空公司安保审计项目，指导厦门航空公司开展安保审计试点工作。

五、全面部署，未雨绸缪，积极开展反恐反劫机工作

2011年面临严峻的国际国内反恐形势，民航局公安局有针对性地加强防范和处置；部署空防安全工作。对全国通用航空公司、飞行员培训机构、飞行员俱乐部基本情况进行初步调研，会同飞标司有关处室，就在飞行员训练课程中增加空防安全形势教育有关事宜进行研究。

集中部署内蒙古机场、黑龙江哈尔滨机场、湖北武汉机场、中国国际航空公司、东方航空公司、南方航空公司新疆分公司等六个单位反劫机应急处置演练工作，并赴黑龙江哈尔滨、内蒙古呼和浩特观摩反劫机演练。

六、强化监管，确保空防安全的持续性

继续完善并大力推行以挂牌监管为重点的空防安全监管通报制度，研究制定《民航空防安全重大事项挂牌督办工作暂行规定》，指导各地区管理局加强挂牌督办工作。

部署开展控制区证件专项整治工作，研究制定《中国民航公务乘机通行证管理规定》和《中国民航空勤登机证管理规定》，组织人员就空勤登机证换发和制作技术规范进行讨论。

七、提升素养，进一步加强队伍管理和培训工作

深入开展人员队伍的资质建设和能力建设。组织民航公安、空防、空警队伍基本级执法资格等级考试，切实提高人员队伍执法工作水平。参加考试共计4 341人。

继续加强安检人员资质管理工作，会同人教司、航科院完成《民航安检员岗位定员定额》标准的修改、发布和宣贯。规范安检专家管理，充分发挥安检专家作用。

举办航空安全员教员培训班，拟定航空安全员日常训练试点工作方案，开展为期5个月的航空安全员执照管理及人员资质专项整治，促进空警（安全员）队伍管理水平和业务素质的不断提高。

会同国际司（港澳台办）下发了《关于规范境内航空公司招聘台湾空勤人员背景调查表的通知》，对台湾空勤人员背景情况进行规范。

and CPPCC sessions, Universiade Shenzhen 2011, the Third BRICS Leaders Meeting, the Boao Forum for Asia Annual Conference, the celebration on the 60th anniversary of Tibet's peaceful liberation, the first China-Eurasia Expo held in Xinjiang, Dalian Summer Davos Forum, the mourning for the first anniversary of Qinghai Yushu earthquake and other major events.

During the Universiade Shenzhen 2011, the bureau assured absolute security of VIPs, political leaders, athletes, expo participants and articles arriving at and departing from airports. The security check department provided excellent security support services for 1 669 flights and 10 000 passengers relating to the Universiade Shenzhen 2011. The bureau also fulfilled 27 batches of guard missions and safeguarded 17 charter flights and 26 shipments of supplies, 329 sport guns and 194 000 bullets for the Universiade Shenzhen 2011. The overall goal of "Safety, Regularity, Quality and Efficiency" was achieved.

During the first China-Eurasia Expo held in Xinjiang, the bureau made further arrangements for fully heightening security measures and supervisory inspection, adjusted the early alerting level for aviation security threats, dispatched a team to conduct a field inspection of aviation security in Xinjiang and built a strong civil aviation security firewall for the first China-Eurasia Expo, thus ensuring the success of all China-Eurasia Expo activities and absolute security of domestic and foreign participants in the event.

II. Establishing a Robust Security Check Support System by Cementing the Foundation and Bases

The bureau fully enhanced quality control over the security check system based on qualification examination. First, priority was placed on strengthening the regulation of security check body setup and routine security check operations and introducing additional provisions legal liabilities prosecution. Security check equipment for civil aviation were systematically regulated in terms of appraisal, licensing, technical testing for acceptance and regular inspection of equipment in service. Air cargo was systematically regulated in terms of collection, transportation, security check, air cargo area and air cargo loading.

Second, the bureau continued to conduct regular inspection of passenger security check equipment in service and extensively launched the cargo security check equipment in service. Relevant standards were developed and issued to strengthen the access control and ongoing operation control over X-ray security check equipment and trace explosive detection equipment. In addition, the certification, appraisal and licensing of security check equipment were enhanced. Equipment that did not comply with security check regulations were denied any approval for renewal of administrative permission.

Third, the rectification campaign for cargo and mail transport security was launched. The bureau further clarified the security responsibility of air cargo carriers, standardized air cargo security procedures, which significantly improved the environment for air cargo transportation.

III. Building and Reconsolidating "Secure Airports" Project Based on Ground Efforts

By implementing the Provisions on Security Prevention and Control in Public Areas at Civil Airports and the Rules for the Implementation of Security Prevention and Control by Airport Aviation Security Agencies, the bureau further stepped up preventive and control efforts for public area security at airports and carried out the security campaign in an in-depth manner. During the year, no major security cases or incidents that had a social impact or endangered aviation security took place across the system. Pursuant to overall arrangements of the Ministry of Public Security, the bureau launched the "hunting convicts online initiative" in the civil aviation security sector with remarkable achievements delivered in seizing guns and ammunition, investigating criminal cases and hunting criminals wanted online.

IV. Promoting and Implementing the Development of Aviation Security Management System (SeMS) through Innovation

The bureau conducted in-depth studies on the characteristics of China's civil aviation security, put forward the "Four Systems" building requirements on incorporating SeMS into management activities, so that SeMS could play the role

of improving the capability, effectiveness and efficiency of security management. The Notice on Fully Launching SeMS Building was issued, providing comprehensive arrangements for the scope, items, steps and implementation of SeMS development. SeMS development training was provided and on-site examination of the SeMS progress was conducted in the Southwest China and Tibet. The bureau developed the airlines security audit program and guided Xiamen Airlines to carry out the pilot security audit program.

V. Actively Carrying Out Anti-terrorism and Anti-hijack Work Based on Comprehensive Arrangements and Preemptive Efforts

In the face of the severe anti-terrorism situation at home and abroad in 2011, the bureau put in place well-targeted preventive and coping measures and made arrangements for aviation security. Preliminary inspections were conducted on general aviation companies, pilot training organizations and pilot clubs in the country. Studies were made in combination with the Department of Flight Standard of CAAC with respect to addition of the education of aviation security situation to the curriculum.

Unified arrangements were made for anti-hijack emergency drills at the Inner Mongolia Airport, the Heilongjiang Harbin Airport, the Hubei Wuhan Airport, Air China, China Eastern Airlines and the Xinjiang Branch of China Southern Airlines. The Bureau also observed the anti-hijack drills in Harbin, Heilongjiang and Huhhot, Inner Mongolia.

VI. Ensuring Continuity of Aviation Security Based on Enhanced Supervision

The bureau continued to improve and promote the aviation security regulatory bulletin system focused on major case supervision. Interim Provisions for Supervised Investigation, Handling and Rectification of Major Aviation Security Issuses was developed to provide regional administrations with guidance on strengthening major case ad-hoc supervision.

The bureau launched the credentials rectifications for controlled areas, developed the Provisions for Civil Aviation Business Pass Management in China and the Provisions on Airmen Boarding Pass Management in Civil Aviation of China and organized discussions on renewal and printing techniques for the flying crew passes.

VII. Further Strengthening Team Management and Training to Improve Competency

The bureau stepped up efforts in qualification and capacity building. Basic-level law enforcement qualification examinations for public security, aviation security and air marshal force were organized to effectively improve the law enforcement capability of team members. A total of 4 341 persons attended the examination.

The bureau continued to strengthen the qualification management of security check personnel. The Quota of Civil Aviation Security Check Personnel was amended, released and promoted in combination with the Department of Personnel Science & Technology and Education and the China Academy of Civil Aviation Science and Technology. Management of security check experts was standardized to give full play to role of the security check experts.

Training for aviation security officer instructors was provided. The pilot program for routine training of aviation security officers was developed. A five-month program on aviation security officer license management and qualification review was carried out to seek continuous improvements in the management capability and functional skills of air marshals (and security officers).

The Notice on Standardizing the Background Check Sheet for Taiwanese Flight Crew Hired by Mainland Airlines was issued in collaboration with the Department of International Affairs (Office of Hong Kong, Macao and Taiwan Affairs) to regulate the background check of flight crew members from Taiwan. ■

低空空域改革和通用航空发展

一、通用航空的概念

按照《国际民航组织公约》附件的定义，民用航空运行分为：商业航空运输运行、空中作业运行和通用航空运行。其中，商业航空运输运行是航空器为取酬或者收费而从事旅客、货物或邮件运输的运行；空中作业运行是使用航空器进行专业服务的航空器运行，如农业、建筑、摄影、测量观察与巡逻、搜寻与援救、空中广告等；通用航空运行是指除商业航空运输运行或者空中作业运行以外的航空器运行。美国将民用航空分为两类，一类是定期航班和定期航空货运，其余的民用航空活动统称为通用航空。

在我国，1995 年颁布的《中华人民共和国民用航空法》中对通用航空的定义是：使用民用航空器从事公共航空运输以外的民用航空活动，包括从事工业、农业、林业、渔业和建筑业的作业飞行以及医疗卫生、抢险救灾、气象探测、海洋监测、科学实验、教育训练、文化体育等方面的飞行活动。2003 年颁布的《通用航空飞行管制条例》中对通用航空的概念与《中华人民共和国民用航空法》一致，对具体列举项目有个别调整。

从定义上看，我国通用航空的范围与美国的概念接近，比国际民航组织概念范围更为广泛，不但包括了国际民航组织规定的通用航空，同时包括了其规定的空中作业，以及部分取酬非公共航空运输（如公务飞行）的范畴。

二、低空空域管理改革对通用航空的影响

国务院、中央军委高度重视通用航空对改善人民生活和促进经济发展的作用，于 2010 年 8 月 19 日下发了《国务院、中央军委关于深化我国低空空域管理改革的意见》。国家空管委根据国务院中央军委的要求，制定了贯彻落实的具体措施。低空空域管理改革任务和措施主要包括以下九个方面：一是分类划设低空空域；二是加快推进低空空域管理改革试点；三是构建低空空域法规标准体系；四是建立高效便捷安全的运行管理机制；五是加强低空空域管理配套设施建设；六是完善通用航空服务保障体系；七是建立健全飞行人员培训机制；八是加强低空空域飞行安全监控和管理；九是建立低空空域管理评估监督机制。2011 年，国家空管委正在组织低空空域管理改革的扩大试点工作，扩大试点范围包括：沈阳、广州飞行管制区和唐山、西安、青岛、杭州、宁波、昆明飞行管制分区。

低空空域管理改革的核心是对低空空域进行分类管理，通过划设管制空域、监视空域和报告空域，根据航空活动的特点，简化审批环节，提供差异化的空中交通服务。今后，监视空域和报告空域将不再提供管制服务。对于监视空域内飞行活动，航空用户只需报备飞行计划，空管单位监视飞行动态，提供飞行情报和告警服务；对于报告空域，航空用户报告飞行计划，向空管单位通告起飞和降落时刻，自行组织实施飞行，空管单位根据用户需要提供航空情报服务。实施低空空域分类后，通用航空的飞行活动将变得便捷、灵活，更加适应其发展特点。

三、公务飞行的特殊性

公务飞行是近些年来兴起的一类通用航空活动。随着我国经济的发展和人们对生活水平要求的提高，公务飞行需求日益旺盛。与其他传统通用航空活动相比，公务飞行除不提供客票服务外，其航空器性能、使用空域和航线、起降地点、保障服务等与公共航空运输更为相似。为此，公务航空活动的空中交通服务也与航班相同。目前低空空域管理改革的重点是垂直范围真高 1 000 米以下，这类空域对固定区域内的低高度飞行的通用航空活动，特别是作业飞行的促进更为明显，而公务飞行的高度远远超出了低空空域的范围。根据公务飞行的特点，未来应当主要做好简化公务飞行任务计划审批手续和提高服务便利程度等方面的工作。

Low-altitude Airspace Reform and Development of General Aviation

I. Concept of General Aviation

In accordance with definitions contained in the annex to the Convention on International Civil Aviation, civil aviation is classified into commercial air transport, aerial work and general aviation. Commercial air transport refers to an aircraft operation involving the transport of passengers, cargo or mail for remuneration or hire. Aerial work refers to an aircraft operation in which an aircraft is used for specialized services such as agriculture, construction, photography, surveying, observation and patrol, search and rescue, aerial advertisement, etc. General aviation refers to an aircraft operation other than a commercial air transport operation or an aerial work operation. In the United States, civil aviation is classified into two categories, namely scheduled flights and scheduled cargo flights, and the rest is called general aviation.

In China, the definition for general aviation enshrined in the Civil Aviation Law of the People's Republic of China enacted in 1995 is as follows: civil aviation operations other than public air transport with civil aircraft, including aerial work in the fields of industry, agriculture, forestry, fishery and building industry, and flight operations in the field of medical and health work, emergency and disaster relief, meteorological service, ocean monitoring, scientific experiment, education and training, culture and sports. While in the Regulations on the Control of General Aviation Flight published in 2003, the definition of general aviation in the Civil Aviation Law of the People's Republic of China was borrowed, except for some minor adjustments to certain enumerations.

A comparison of the definitions shows that the definition of general aviation adopted by China is similar to that in the United States, and is more inclusive than that of ICAO. It includes not only GA operations defined by ICAO, but also aerial work and some for-remuneration non-public air transport operations (e.g. business flight).

II. Impact of Low-altitude Airspace Management Reform on General Aviation

The State Council and the Central Military Commission of CPC attached great importance to general aviation's contributions to improving people's life and driving economic development, and issued Opinion of the State Council and the Central Military Commission of CPC on Deepening the Low-altitude Airspace Management Reform in China on August 19, 2010. The State Air Traffic Management Commission developed concrete implementation measures in accordance with the requirements of the State Council and the Central Military Commission of CPC. The reform tasks and measures consist of nine aspects: first, zone up and divide low-altitude airspace into different categories; second, expedite pilot reform of low-altitude airspace management; third, build the legal and standards system for low-altitude airspace; fourth, establish an efficient, convenient and safe operation management mechanism; fifth, accelerate the development of supporting facilities for low-altitude airspace management; sixth, improve the service support system for general aviation; seventh, establish and improve the pilot training mechanism; eighth, reinforce the monitoring and management of flight safety in low-altitude airspace; and ninth, put in place the evaluation and supervision mechanism for low-altitude airspace management. In 2011, the State Air Traffic Management Commission was expanding pilot reform to flight control areas in Shenyang and Guangzhou as well as flight control sub-areas in Tangshan, Xi'an, Qingdao, Hangzhou, Ningbo and Kunming.

The centerpiece of low-altitude airspace management reform is classified management of low-altitude airspace, which is aimed at simplifying the approval process and providing differentiated air traffic service through setting up controlled airspace, monitored airspace and report airspace in light of the characteristics of aviation activities. In the future, control service will not be provided in monitored airspace or report airspace. As for flight activities in the monitored airspace, aviation users only need to report their flight plans, and the air traffic control entities will take the flight under surveillance and provide flight information and alerting services. As for report airspace, the aviation users are supposed to report their flight plans, advise the ATC entity of the take-off and landing time and operate the flight by themselves, and the air traffic control entities will provide aeronautic information at the request of the users. The classification of the low-altitude airspace would make flight activities of general aviation more convenient and flexible, and better accommodate its development.

III. Uniqueness of Business Flight

Business flight is a general aviation operation that's burgeoned of late. With the development of China's economy and people's higher demand for living conditions, the demand for business flight is on the rise. Relative to traditional general aviation operations, business flight is similar to public air transport in aircraft performance, airspace and routes used, take-off and landing locations and support services, except for customer ticket services. As such, air traffic services for business flight are the same as those for scheduled flights. Presently, the priority of low-altitude airspace management reform is put on the airspace below QFE 1 000 m, which is more relevant to the development of general aviation activities in the low-altitude airspace of a certain area, especially aerial work flight, whereas business flight altitudes go much beyond the scope of low-altitude airspace. Based on the characteristics of business flight, attention should be paid to approval process facilitation for its flight plans and more convenience of its services, etc.

中华人民共和国常驻国际民航组织理事会代表处

（1）2011 年 3 月 16 日，中国民航选派的 11 名借调人员抵达国际民航组织开始工作。根据 2010 年中国民航与国际民航组织签署的合作协议，中国民航将自 2011 年起，5 年内，每年向国际民航组织派遣 10 名业务骨干进行短期借调工作，为我国培养国际型人才，同时解决国际民航组织工作人员紧缺的问题。

（2）2011 年 5 月，国际民航组织秘书长邦雅曼访华并出席了中国民航发展论坛。

（3）2011 年 10 月 5 日，国际民航组织理事会邀请我国北斗卫星导航系统专家与美国、欧盟和俄罗斯的专家一道，在国际民航组织总部做全球卫星导航系统介绍，并回答了兼容与互操作等相关问题，为我国北斗卫星导航系统融入国际民航组织全球卫星导航系统，启动了良好的开端。

（4）2011 年 10 月 24 日，拉美地区民航委员会主席罗德里格斯访华，并与中国民航局签署了关于加强中国与拉美地区民航委员会合作的谅解备忘录。

（5）2011 年 10 月，白建军少将率国家空管委员会航空立法考察团到国际民航组织进行考察与交流全球空管体制及模式，为修订我国航空法进行前期调研活动。

中国常驻国际民航组织理事会代表处马涛代表（左六）与借调人员合影

Ma Tao (sixth from the left), the Representative of the Permanent Mission of the People's Republic of China to ICAO Poses for a Photo with the Staff Seconded from China

（6）2011 年，我国继续积极参与国际民航组织关于国际航空与气候变化工作。2011 年 11 月 2 日，第 194 届理事会第 2 次会议审议并通过了由包括中国在内的 26 个理事国联合签署的工作文件，敦促欧盟停止将国际航空纳入其排放交易体系的单边行动。

（7）2011 年 11 月 14 日，国际民航组织第 194 届理事会批准在亚太地区设立分办事处。作为亚太地区办事处（曼谷）的分支机构，分办事处将以项目为主导，侧重于改进空域组织和管理，通过便利空域准入的空域组织与管理以及需求与容量平衡的行动，高效管理亚太地区空域和空中交通流量，以期实现亚太地区空中交通管理的绩效最大化。分办事处作为国际民航组织经常工作方案的一部分，统一由国际民航组织管理，办公场所由东道国赞助，运作资金由各国自愿捐助，分办事处主任由国际民航组织总部委派，向曼谷办事处主任负责，其工资和差旅费用由国际民航组织承担，其余人员向亚太各国免费借调，人员编制依据各国需要和所提供的捐助灵活确定。国际民航组织计划 2012 年 5 月确定东道国，亚太地区分办事处于 2013 年 1 月开始运作。

（8）2011 年 11 月和 12 月，中国民航飞行学院和中国民航大学相继与国际民航组织签署协议，为国际民航组织提供开发相关程序和数据库等服务。

（9）中国常驻国际民航组织理事会代表处参加了国际民航组织理事会第 192 届、193 届、194 届理事会会议，航行委员会第 186 届、187 届和 188 届会议，参加了国际民航组织理事会运输委员会、非法干扰委员会、财务委员会、人力资源委员会和技术合作委员会等，以及非洲航空安全全面实施地区计划、国际航空安全财务机制、机读旅行证件等专题会议。

Permanent Mission of the People's Republic of China to ICAO

1) On March 16, 2011, the 11 staff seconded from CAAC arrived at ICAO. In accordance with the cooperation agreement signed in 2010 between CAAC and ICAO, as part of the efforts to nurture international talents for China and address the issue of ICAO staff shortage, it's agreed that in 5 years starting from 2011, CAAC will dispatch, on temporary basis, each year 10 backbone professionals to assist ICAO's work.

2) In May of 2011, Raymond Benjamin, Secretary General of ICAO, paid a visit to China and attended China Civil Aviation Development Forum.

3) On October 5, 2011, China's experts on Compass Satellite Navigation System were invited, along with the experts from the US, EU and Russia, to make introduction of global navigation satellite system (GNSS) at ICAO headquarters and answer questions associated with compatibility and interoperability, which made a good start for the future integration of China's Compass Satellite Navigation System into ICAO's GNSS.

4) On October 24, 2011, Luis Paulino Rodriguez ARIZA, President of Latin American Civil Aviation Commission (LACAC), paid a visit to China and signed with CAAC a memorandum of understanding on strengthening the cooperation between China and LACAC.

5) In October of 2011, as part of the efforts to conduct preliminary investigation and research activities to enact China's aviation law, Major General Bai Jianjun headed an aeronautic legislation delegation under China State Air Traffic Management Commission to conduct an inspection and exchanges at ICAO headquarters on the global air traffic management systems and patterns.

6) In 2011, China continued to be actively involved in ICAO's work related to international aviation and climate change. The council, at the second meeting of its 194th session held on November 2, 2011, considered and adopted the working paper jointly signed by 26 council member states including China, urging EU to cease the unilateral action to incorporate emissions from international aviation into its emissions trading scheme.

7) On November 14, 2011, the Council endorsed the establishment of sub-regional offices for Asia-Pacific region at its 194th session. As the subsidiaries to the ICAO Asia and Pacific Regional Office in Bangkok, the sub-regional offices will be dominated by programs, focus on improving airspace organization and management, and conduct efficient management of the airspace and the air traffic flow through airspace organization and management which facilitates airspace access and demand and capacity balancing, with the objective of achieving the maximum performance in air traffic management for Asia-Pacific region. As part of ICAO's regular program, the sub-regional offices are under the integrated management by ICAO, with their office sites provided by the host states and their operating fund contributed from member states on voluntary basis. The director of the sub-regional offices will be appointed by ICAO headquarters, who will report to Bangkok regional office director and whose salaries and travel expenses will be covered by ICAO, while the other staff members will be seconded free of charge from Asia-Pacific countries. The size of the personnel force will be determined flexibly based on member states' needs and the amount of contributions provided. ICAO plans to determine the host states in May of 2012, and the sub-regional offices for Asia-Pacific region will start their operation in January of 2013.

8) In November and December of 2011, Civil Aviation Flight University of China and Civil Aviation University of China respectively signed with ICAO agreements concerning the provision to ICAO of services covering the development of relevant programs and database.

9) The Permanent Mission of China to ICAO attended the 192nd, 193rd and 194th sessions of the ICAO Council; the 186th, 187th and 188th sessions of Air Navigation Commission; meetings hosted by Air Transport Committee, Unlawful Interference Committee, Finance Committee, Human Resources Committee and Technical Cooperation Committee of the ICAO Council; as well as thematic meetings related to AFI Plan, IFFAS and MRTD.

2011年公布的国际民航组织国际公约、规章文件简介

（1）第192届理事会于2011年3月4日审议通过了对《国际民用航空公约》附件1《人员执照的颁发》的第170次修订，2011年7月17日生效，2011年11月17日开始适用。修订内容对经批准的培训的定义及现行要求做了澄清，增加了飞行机组和空中交通管制员在经批准的培训机构进行培训的要求，增加了航空器维修人员进行经批准的以能力为基础的培训要求，对航空器维修人员完成以能力为基础的培训大纲之后遵守附件1执照的经验要求引入了替代做法。

（2）第192届理事会于2011年3月7日审议通过了对附件9《简化手续》的第22次修订，2011年7月17日生效，2011年11月17日开始适用。修订内容涉及国家对于传染病国际爆发的准备、国际商定的预报旅客资料（API）系统的实施和协助因不可抗力而使航班中断的航空旅行者的措施等。

（3）第192届理事会于2011年3月4日审议通过了对附件10《航空电信》第I卷《无线电通信设施》的第86次修订，2011年7月17日生效，2011年11月17日开始适用。本次修订反映了在初步实施全球导航卫星系统（GNSS）的地基增强系统（GBAS）方面获得的经验，同时虑及与现行系统的向后兼容性。对地基增强系统的标准和建议措施提出了若干修改。

（4）第192届理事会于2011年3月4日审议通过了对附件16《环境保护》第I卷《航空器噪声》的第10次修订以及第II卷《航空器发动机的排放》的第7次修订，2011年7月17日生效，2011年11月17日开始适用。本次修订处理源自于在应用示范机制和相关的航空器噪声合格审定指南方面所出现的技术问题，主要包括修改了适用性规定，以便消除案文中不必要的复杂、重复和累赘现象，同时提高清晰度，保持各个章节间的一致。对于噪声合格审定起飞参考速度引入了进一步规定。将关于倾转旋翼的噪声合格审定程序的措词，与第8章和第11章中已经采用的直升机有关措词，进行协调一致。完善了关于合格审定测试条件和程序的一些技术事项，并做了少量编辑修改。对附件16第II卷《航空器发动机的排放》的修订，是更新关于排放标准严格度的规定，并处理源自在应用示范机制和相关的航空器发动机排放合格审定指南方面所出现的技术问题。修订主要包括提高氮氧化物（NO_x）排放标准的严格度，并更新停产日期的规定。引入了“等效程序”一词，以改进附件16第II卷内及其与Doc 9501号文件——《环境技术手册》第II卷——《航空器发动机的排放》的一致性和协调性。将某些段落移至更恰当的地方，并纠正了某些编辑问题，从而提高了可读性和条理性。

（5）第192届理事会于2011年3月4日审议通过了对附件18《危险品的安全航空运输》的第10次修订，2011年7月17日生效，2011年11月17日开始适用。本次修订内容主要出现在第1章“定义”、第2章“适用范围”以及第8章“经营人的责任”部分，新增并澄清了有关定义和要求。

（6）第193届理事会于2011年6月13日审议通过了对附件6《航空器的运行》第I部分《国际商业航空运输——飞机》的第35次修订、附件6第II部分《国际通用航空——飞机》第30次修订、附件6第III部分《国际运行——直升机》第16次修订。本次修订涉及救援和消防服务、疲劳风险管理制度以及哈龙替代品。附件6第I、II、III部分的修订于2011年10月31日生效，2011年12月15日开始适用，但盥洗室灭火器哈龙替代品和手提灭火瓶规定的预设日期分别为2011年12月31日和2016年12月31日。

（7）第193届理事会于2011年6月13日审议通过了对附件8《航空器适航性》第103次修订。附件8修订后的新标准，要求航空器发动机、辅助动力装置和盥洗室的灭火或灭火系统的设计和制造，必须使用替代哈龙的灭火剂。附件8的修订于2011年10月31日生效，这项标准适用于2014年12月31日或其后向设计国申请型号合格证的航空器型号。

（8）第194届理事会于2011年10月31日审议通过了对国际民用航空指导材料《国际民航组织关于机场和空中航行服务收费的政策》（Doc 9082号文件）的修订。

Brief Introduction to International Conventions and Regulations Published by ICAO in 2011

1. Amendment 170 to Personnel Licensing (Annex 1 to the Convention on International Civil Aviation) was adopted by the Council at its 192nd Session on 4 March 2011. It was resolved that the amendment would become effective on 17 July 2011 and applicable on 17 November 2011. The amendment clarified the definitions and existing requirements related to approved training; introduced the requirements that approved training for flight crews and air traffic controllers shall be conducted within an approved training organization and that competency-based approved training shall be provided for aircraft maintenance personnel; and introduced an alternative means of compliance with the Annex 1 experience requirements for aircraft maintenance personnel licences, after completion of a competency-based training programme.

2. Amendment 22 to Facilitation (Annex 9 to the Convention on International Civil Aviation) was adopted by the Council at its 192nd Session on 7 March 2011. It's resolved that the amendment would become effective on 17 July 2011 and applicable on 17 November 2011. The amendment included States' preparations for international outbreaks of communicable diseases; the implementation of internationally agreed advance passenger information (API) systems; and measures to assist air travellers whose flights are disrupted as a result of force majeure.

3. Amendment 86 to Annex 10-Aeronautical Telecommunications, Volume I (Radio Navigation Aids) was adopted by the Council at its 192nd Session on 4 March 2011. It's resolved that the amendment would become effective on 17 July 2011 and applicable on 17 November 2011. The amendment reflected the initial experience gained with the ongoing technical implementations of GBAS for Category I operations with the introduction of forward compatibility requirements. A number of changes to the GBAS SARPs were also proposed.

4. Amendment 10 to Annex 16-Environmental Protection, Volume I (Aircraft Noise) and amendment 7 to Volume II (Aircraft Engine Emissions) were adopted by the Council at its 192nd Session on 4 March 2011. It's resolved that the amendment would become effective on 17 July 2011 and applicable on 17 November 2011. The purpose of the amendment of the SARPs in Annex 16, Volume I was to address technical issues arising from the application of demonstration schemes and related guidance for aircraft noise certification. The amendment to Annex 16, Volume I included changes to the applicability provisions in order to remove unnecessary complexity, repetition and redundancy in the text while improving clarity and harmonization amongst different chapters. Further specification was introduced of the noise certification take-off reference speed. The language for noise certification procedures of tilt-rotors has been harmonized with that of helicopters already adopted in Chapters 8 and 11. Several technical issues concerning the certification test conditions and procedures have been refined in addition to minor editorial changes. The purpose of the amendment of the SARPs in Annex 16, Volume II was to update the provisions regarding the stringency of emissions Standards and to address technical issues arising from the application of demonstration schemes and related guidance for aircraft engine emissions certification. The amendment to Annex 16, Volume II includes an increase in stringency of NO_x emissions Standards and an update to the production cut-off provisions. The terminology of "equivalent procedures" has been introduced in order to improve consistency and harmonization within Annex 16, Volume II and with the Environmental Technical Manual (Doc 9501), Volume II-Procedures for the Emissions Certification of Aircraft Engines. Readability and organization were improved by moving some paragraphs to more appropriate places and correcting some editorial issues.

5. Amendment 10 to the Safe Transport of Dangerous Goods by Air (Annex 18 to the Convention on International Civil Aviation) was adopted by the Council at its 192nd Session

on 4 March 2011. It's resolved that the amendment would become effective on 17 July 2011 and applicable on 17 November 2011. The amendment mainly included the clarification of the related definition and requirements in Chapter 1 DEFINITIONS, Chapter 2 APPLICABILITY, and Chapter 8 OPERATOR'S RESPONSIBILITIES.

6. Amendment 35 to Annex 6-Operation of Aircraft, Part I (International Commercial Air Transport-Aeroplanes), amendment 30 to Part II (International General Aviation-Aeroplanes), and amendment 16 to Part III (International Operations-Helicopters) were adopted by the Council at its 193rd Session on 13 June 2011. The amendment included requirements related to the availability of rescue and fire fighting services (RFFS), the Fatigue Risk Management systems, and Halon replacement. It's resolved that the amendment would become effective on 31 October 2011 and applicable on 15 December 2011. The embedded dates for the provisions on halon replacement in lavatory fire extinguishers will be 31 December 2011 and 31 December 2016 for handheld fire extinguishers.

7. Amendment 103 to the International Standards and Recommended Practices, Airworthiness of Aircraft (Annex 8 to the Convention on International Civil Aviation) was adopted by the Council at the meeting of its 193rd Session on 13 June 2011. The amendment included adding a new Standard which would require the design and manufacture of an aircraft's fire extinguishing and/or suppression systems for engines, APUs and lavatories to use alternative fire extinguishing agents to halon. The Council prescribed 31 October 2011 as the date on which it will become effective. The amendment would be applicable to an aircraft type for which an application for a type certificate is submitted to the State of Design on or after 31 December 2014.

8. The amendment proposed to ICAO's Policies on Charges for Airports and Air Navigation Services (Doc 9082) was adopted by the Council at the meeting of its 194th Session on 31 October 2011.

中国民用航空局空中交通管理局

2011年6月29日，民航局李家祥局长出席中国国际航空股份有限公司、民航局空管局、首都机场集团公司组织的“飞行员、管制员、指挥协调员”交流合作项目启动仪式

On June 29, 2011, Li Jiaxiang, Administrator of CAAC, Attends the Launching Ceremony for the Project on the Exchange and Cooperation of “Pilots, Controllers and Command Coordinators” Organized by Air China, CAAC ATM Bureau and Capital Airports Holding Company

2011 年，空管系统牢固树立持续安全理念，提升空域资源配置和使用效率，努力减少航班延误，确保了全年运行安全平稳。全年事故征候万架次率为 0.002，大大低于民航局规定的万架次率 0.1 的安全目标，共保障各类起降飞行655万架次，同比增长8.15%，服务保障能力稳步增强。

一、严控风险，安全管理扎实有效

一是开展专项整治，解决一批突出问题。大力开展“军民航严防相撞宣传教育月”、“安全生产月”、“错忘漏治理”等专项整治活动，强化管制人员的安全意识，有效防范了不安全事件的发生。二是加强管制人员资质管理。制定了《2010—2011 年管制人员资质能力建设纲要》，明确管制员的培训教育、放单考核、淘汰机制等各个环节要求，完成管制员的技术等级评定和职务聘任，利用网络管理平台对 3 706 名管制员资质进行跟踪管理，开展管制专业教学改革，切实把好养成训练质量关。三是增强安全风险防范能力。科学管控安全风险，重视“过程管理”的理念，围绕“军民航严防相撞、跑道侵入和管制错忘漏”三大风险源，及时发现隐患和薄弱环节，在安全风险管理和安全绩效管理两方面花大气力，促使不安全风险得到有效管控。四是全面推进质量安全管理体系建设工作。进一步完善了规章标准，全面完成空管系统推进质量安全管理体系建设的前期准备工作。五是重视安全管理手段的研究。探索无后果违章管理制度，推广空管运行风险快速检测系统，开发空管运行风险实时监测系统和风险评估系统，开发了民航气象业务运行能力评估系统。六是班组资源管理取得新突破。初步形成了以管理规程为基础、以核心队伍建设为重点、以电子工具开发与应用为平台、以测试与评估为抓手、以班组及系统联动为创新的长效工作机制。

二、合力攻关，运行保障服务能力稳步增强

一是重大保障任务圆满完成。圆满完成世界园艺博览会、深圳大运会、亚欧博览会、达沃斯论坛、亚洲博鳌论坛、“金砖国家”领导人会晤等重大航空运输空管保障任务，顺利保障埃及、利比亚、日本强震灾区撤侨包机等紧急运输任务。二是排堵保畅取得效果。开展京沪、京广航路排堵保畅专项整治活动，对西安、郑州、大连、重庆、成都等繁忙地区实施重点协调和疏通，规范长时间延误航班处置，明确流控措施发布权限，切实加强与航空公司、机场的运行协调。治理后京沪航路航班正常率达到 73%，京广航路航班正常率达到 66%，分别提高了 30 和 11 个百分点。三是流量管理水平得到提升。有力推进全国飞行流量管理工作，全国民航航班放行正常率达到 77.15%，比上年同期增长 2.2%。正式实施了 24 小时流量监控的运行模式，完成对雷达信号、飞行数据、动态报文等飞行信息的引接，准确掌握航班运行动态，及时疏导

繁忙地区的飞行流量，全面提升飞行流量管理能力。四是设备运行管理机制得到创新。建立重要设备故障技术管理通告制度，推广设备运行保障工作交叉检查机制，完善设备运行保障季度讲评机制和案例分析制度，落实完善设备巡检大修制度、推进电子值班系统和零备件管理信息系统建设。全年系统设备正常率达到 99.97%，设备完好率达到 99.923%。五是气象服务品质得到提高。开展“尽职尽责保安全”的气象安全教育月活动，强化风险意识，努力提高复杂天气的临近预报准确率，对趋势预报准确率进行业务化质量评定，降低观测错情率。六是航行情报提供准确。制定《民用航空图编绘规范》等 3 个规范性文件，推进《民用机场原始资料上报系统》的实施，完成 AIM 建设项目的预可研；启动航空情报最新资料讲解服务机制，有效保障日常航行资料的准确及时。

三、注重配合，空域管理水平全面提升

一是推进二线繁忙机场的进离场航线分离和全国骨干航路航线网络规划。在郑州、青岛、重庆、天津、太原、呼和浩特、石家庄等 7 个飞行繁忙机场实施了进离场航线分离工作，降低了运行风险，增加了空域容量；研究拟订了“五轴九纵十六横”的全国骨干航路网络规划建议方案，总距离 94 000 公里，航路航线非直线系数由目前的 1.11 下降至 1.05；完成 14 个试点扇区的容量评估工作。二是首次在全国范围内实现了跨地区高空管制移交指挥。济南 7 800 米（不含）以上高空管制空域空管指挥权正式移交华北空管。北京、上海高空管制区域管制下限统一调整至 7 800 米（不含）。华北高空管制指挥区域由原来的 75 万平方公里扩大到 87 万平方公里，有效缓解了天津等机场延误状况，增加了首都等机场的运行容量。三是扎实推进节能减排。全年新辟 26 条临时航线，全国共计有 117 条临时航线，总距离 3.4 万多公里，约占航路航线总距离 19.8%。全年共有 36 万架次航班使用临时航线，节省空中飞行距离 1 296 多万公里，累计节省燃油 7.0 万吨，减少二氧化碳排放 22 万吨。四是组织全国 WGS-84 坐标实施过渡。组织测量了全国 165 个机场，4 900 多个重要地理位置的 WGS-84 坐标，分五批公布和实施了全国所有飞行情报区、管制区、航路航线、民用机场的 WGS-84 坐标过渡。完成了航行情报系统软件升级改造，对全国 75 套空管自动化系统进行了数据适配和过渡转换。

四、改进模式，基本建设步伐加快

一是深化“十二五”规划编制，加强规划执行。完成民航空管“十二五”发展规划，对规划项目进行认真梳理，合理安排项目启动，细化空管项目分类和规划建设内容，完善空管项目储备机制，加快推进项目的前期工作。二是优化规划建设程序。协调国家发改委、空管委办公室等六部委进行空管工程前期工作和建设管理调研，在土地、环评、项目审批等方面争取更多有利于空管发展建设的政策。三是推进了一批重点工程。加快东部地区及西部主要航路雷达管制工程，空管设备保障与测试基地工程，成都、西安区管工程以及潮汕、深圳、昆明等地机场配套空管工程的建设进度；完成八个空管生产用房项目的评估；博物馆工程建设项目通过行业验收；推进值班宿舍工程立项，深入基层开展调研，组织专家多次论证，统一各地建设标准，该项目可行性研究报告已通过评估。

五、统筹规划，推进新技术应用及实施

一是推进广播式自动相关监视（ADS-B）工作。组织完成了《ADS-B 实施路线图》的上报工作，编写完成了《ADS-B 地面站建设方案》和“十二五”专项规划。根据不同的依托条件和建设环境，梳理地面站对基础设施的建设要求，为空管行业提供 ADS-B 建设和运行指导。二是推进基于性能的导航（PBN）工作。完成全国支持 PBN 运行的 DME/DME 地面台站建设规划初稿。制定了区域导航航路划设和运行指导材料。编制了《民航空管系统飞行程序设计管理暂行规定》，拟从组织关系、项目管理、资源分配和质量保障等方面对飞行程序设计管理工作予以规范。三是加强系统科技管理。召开民航空管新技术应用研讨会，明确了空管新技术应用工作规划；推进国家科技支撑计划项目，完成课题实施方案评审；做好卫星导航专项工作；“北斗”卫星导航系统在国际民航领域的技术标准研究取得了实质性突破。四是气象科技工作取得新局面。通过了《关于加强民航气象科技工作若干意见》；完成了中国新一代航空气象系统框架研究；成立了民用航空气象研究中心，开展了机场终端区以及高原机场气象服务技术的研究；推广使用民航空管科技信息系统。■

CAAC Air Traffic Management Bureau

2011年12月16日，民航局空管局王利亚局长（二排中）在新疆空管局检查指导工作

On December 16, 2011, Wang Liya, Director General of CAAC ATM Bureau (middle in the second row) Inspects Xinjiang ATM Bureau and Gives Instructions

In 2011, the ATM system firmly established the concept of sustained safety, improved the allocation of airspace resources and utilization efficiency, tried to reduce flight delays and ensured year-round safe and stable operations. The annual incident rate per 10 000 movements stood at 0.002, significantly lower than the 0.1 safety target set by CAAC. It supported 6.55 million aircraft movements of various sorts in total, increasing by 8.15% over that of the previous year, steadily strengthening its service support capacity.

I. Tightening Risk Control with Solid and Effective Safety Management

First, the bureau conducted dedicated rectification and solved a series of outstanding problems. It made vigorous efforts to conduct the activities like Awareness-Raising Campaign Month on the Prevention of Military and Civil Aircraft Collision, Month of Work Safety, Rectification of Errors, Negligence and Lapses, improving the safety awareness of controllers and effectively preventing unsafe incidents. Second, the bureau strengthened the management of controllers' qualifications. It developed the Outline Program of Controller Qualifications Improvement and Capacity Building for 2010-2011, clarifying the requirements of the mechanism in every link such as training and education, examination and elimination of controllers, etc. It completed the skill level appraisal and post appointment of controllers, carried out follow-up management of 3 706 controllers' qualifications by way of web-based management platform and conducted teaching reform of the ATM discipline to hold a good pass of training quality. Third, the bureau improved the capability for safety risk prevention. It scientifically controlled safety risk, emphasized the concept of "process management", timely spotted hazards and weak links by focusing on 3 major risk sources, namely "military-civil aircraft collision, runway intrusion and control errors, negligence and lapses", and paid equal attention to safety risk management and safety performance management, which enabled effective control of safety risks. Fourth, the bureau comprehensively pushed forward the institutional development for quality safety management. It further bettered the rules and standards and comprehensively completed the preparatory work for the institutional development for quality safety management. Fifth, the bureau attached importance to the study of means of safety management. It explored the no-consequence violation management system, promoted the rapid detection system for ATM operational risks, and developed the real-time monitoring system for ATM operational risks, risk evaluation system and the capacity evaluation system for civil aviation meteorological service operations. Sixth, the bureau made new breakthroughs in work shift resources management. It tentatively built a long-term work mechanism with management rules as the bedrock, development of core teams as the focus, development and application of electronic tools as the platform, tests and evaluations as the grip and interactive operation of work shifts and system as the innovations.

II. Tackling Hard Problems with Joint Efforts to Steadily Improve Service Capacity for Operational Support

First, the bureau impeccably completed its major support tasks. It successfully performed significant air transport

ATM support tasks, such as International Horticulture Expo, Universiade Shenzhen, Eurasia Expo, Summer Davos Forum, Boao Forum for Asia and BRICS Leaders Meeting, etc. It successfully provided support for emergency transport tasks, such as charter flights to evacuate compatriots in Egypt, Libya and earthquake-stricken areas in Japan, etc. Second, the bureau made good achievement in congestion mitigation and traffic smoothness. It conducted dedicated congestion mitigation and smooth traffic rectification on Beijing-Shanghai and Beijing-Guangzhou routes. It conducted, with priorities, coordination to smoothen traffic in busy cities like Xi'an, Zhengzhou, Dalian, Chongqing and Chengdu, standardized the handling of flights with long delays, clarified the authority in issuing air traffic control measures and effectively strengthened the operational coordination with airlines and airports. The rectification campaigned increased the flight regularity on Beijing-Shanghai route to 73% and that on Beijing-Guangzhou route to 66%, up by 30 and 11 percentage points respectively. Third, the bureau boosted its traffic flow management level. It vigorously pushed forward the flight traffic management nationwide. The national civil aviation flight clearance regularity stood at 77.15%, an up of 2.2% over that of the previous year. It officially instituted the operational model of 24 hours traffic monitoring and gained access to among other flight information, radar signals, flight data and dynamic messages, helping it get accurate flight operations information, timely adjust flight traffic in busy areas and comprehensively enhance the capacity for flight traffic management. Fourth, the bureau made innovations in the management mechanism for equipment operations. It established the notification mechanism on technical management of significant equipment failure, promoted the cross-check mechanism on equipment operations support, bettered the quarterly reward and ranking mechanism on equipment operations support and case study system, implemented and improved the mechanism on equipment inspection tour and overhaul and promoted the development of the electronic on-duty system and zero-backup management information system. As a result, the annual operational normality ratio of systems and equipment hit 99.97%, and the equipment integrity ratio reached 99.923%. Fifth, the bureau improved its meteorological services. It conducted the awareness campaign of meteorological safety month for Conscientious Safety Guarantee to strengthen the risk awareness and improve the short-term forecast accuracy ratio for complicated weather conditions. It conducted quality evaluation of trend forecast accuracy to reduce observation error ratio. Sixth, the bureau provided accurate aeronautical information. It made 3 regulatory documents including the Standards on the Making of Civil Aviation Maps, promoted the institution of the Report System for Original Civil Airports Information and completed the preliminary feasibility study of AIM construction project. It also launched the explanation service mechanism for the latest aeronautical information to effectively guarantee the accuracy and timeliness of daily aeronautical information.

III. Emphasizing Coordination to Comprehensively Improve Airspace Management

First, the bureau pushed forward the separation of inbound and outbound routes at busy tier-2 airports and the planning of the national trunk line network. It implemented the separation of inbound and outbound routes at 7 airports with heavy traffic, including those in Zhengzhou, Qingdao, Chongqing, Tianjin, Taiyuan, Hohhot and Shijiazhuang, reducing the operational risks and increasing the airspace capacity; it drafted a proposal for the planning of a national trunk line network characterized by "5 hubs, 9 vertical lines and 16 horizontal ones", with a total distance of 94 000 km, lowering the non-linear coefficient of routes from the current 1.11 to 1.05; it also completed the capacity evaluation for 14 pilot sectors. Second, the bureau delivered first the relay of high-altitude ATC command nationwide. The ATC command of high-altitude controlled airspace with altitudes above 7 800 meters (not including the altitude at 7 800 meters) was officially relayed to the north regional ATM management bureau. The ATC floor for high-altitude controlled airspace in Beijing and Shanghai was uniformly adjusted to 7 800 meters (not including 7 800 meters). The area under the north regional ATC command increased from 750 000 km^2 to 870 000 km^2, effectively easing the delays at airports such as in Tianjin and increasing the operational capacity at airports such as in Beijing. Third, the bureau solidly pushed forward energy efficiency and emissions reduction. Through the whole year, it opened 26 interim routes, bringing the total of interim routes in China to 117 with a total distance of more than 34 000 km, accounting for 19.8% of the total distance of flight routes. There were a total of 360 000 flights that had used the interim routes, saving the flight distance of over 12.96 million km, conserving 70 000 tons of fuel and cutting 220 000 tons of CO_2 emissions. Fourth, the bureau carried out the WGS-84 Coordinate transition. It organized the measurement of WGS-84 coordinates at over 4 900 important geographical positions at 165 airports nationwide and announced and implemented the WGS-84 coordinate transition in flight information zones, controlled zones, flight routes and civil airports. It completed the software upgrading and transformation of aeronautic information systems and carried out data adaptation and transitional transformation of 75 ATM automation systems in the country.

IV. Improving the Model to Accelerate the Infrastructural Development

First, the bureau deepened the development of the 12th Five-Year Plan and strengthened its execution. It completed the 12th Five-Year development plan for civil aviation ATM, carefully sorted out the projects on the plan, arranged the proper launch of the projects, specified the categorization of ATM projects and the development plan, improved the backlog mechanism for ATM projects and expedited the preparation work for such projects. Second, the bureau optimized the plan development process. It coordinated with 6 departments at ministerial level, including National Development and Reform Commission and the Office of State ATM Commission, in making preparations for ATM projects and conducting study of construction management. It also tried to gain more favorable policies to ATM development in areas like land use, environmental impact evaluation and project review and approval, etc. Third, the bureau pushed forward a series of key projects. It accelerated the radar control project on major routes in the east and west regions, ATM equipment support and testing base project, the regional ATM project in Chengdu and Xi'an and supportive ATM projects at airports such as in Chaoshan, Shenzhen and Kunming. It completed the evaluation of 8 ATM production-use property projects; the museum engineering construction project passed the industry checks and acceptance; it also pushed ahead with the approval of the project for dormitory construction for on-duty workers, conducted grass-roots study, organized multiple expert proving and unified the construction standards in various regions, and the feasibility study report for the project has already passed the evaluation.

V. Planning in a Balanced Way to Promote the Applications and Experiments of New Technologies

First, the bureau pushed ahead with the ADS-B project. It completed the submission of the ADS-B Implementation Roadmap, developed the ADS-B Ground Station Construction Plan and the project-specific 12th Five-Year Plan. Based on the support conditions and construction

北京区域管制中心管制员正在为华北和青岛地区空域结构调整作认真准备

Controllers in Beijing Area ATC Center Are Busy Making Preparations for Adjustment of Airspace Structure in the North China Region and Qingdao Region

environment, it sorted out ground stations' requirements for infrastructure development to provide guidance on ADS-B development and the operation of ATM system. Second, the bureau pushed forward PBN project. It completed the draft plan for the nationwide construction of DME/DME ground stations that support PBN operations, developed the guidance document on allocation and identification of RNAV routes and their operations, and developed the Interim Provisions on Management of Flight Procedure Designs within the Civil Aviation ATM System, aiming at standardizing the management of flight procedure designs in organization relations, project management, allocation of resources and quality assurance, etc. Third, the bureau reinforced its sci-tech management. It held Civil Aviation ATM New Technology Application Workshop and identified the plan for application of new ATM technologies; it pushed forward the National Sci-tech Support Plan projects and completed the evaluation and review of project implementation plan; it carried out the dedicated project of satellite navigation and the technical standards research for the Compass Satellite Navigation System and made substantial breakthroughs in the international civil aviation community. Fourth, the bureau opened a new chapter for the meteorology-related sci-tech work. It adopted the Suggestions on Strengthening Work Related to Civil Aviation Meteorological Science and Technology, completed the research into China's new-generation aviation meteorological system framework, built up Civil Aviation Meteorological Research Center and carried out researches into meteorological service technologies for airport terminal areas and plateau airports. In addition, the bureau promoted the use of Civil Aviation ATM Sci-tech Information System.

民航华北地区管理局

2011年，民航华北地区管理局深化落实持续安全理念和建设民航强国战略，统筹做好各项工作，圆满完成各项任务，实现了“十二五”的良好开局，行业发展呈现新局面。

一、安全形势持续平稳，运输生产稳步增长

2011年，民航华北地区管理局从源头控制不安全风险，督促企事业单位落实安全主体责任，安全形势保持平稳。华北民航全年安全运行109万飞行小时，未发生辖区责任运输飞行事故或空防事故，较好地实现了年度安全目标。

全年华北地区各机场共完成旅客吞吐量10 974万人次，完成货邮吞吐量196.5万吨，飞机起降88.7万架次，三项指标同比分别增长9%、4.7%和6.1%。其中，河北、内蒙古旅客吞吐量分别同比增长46.5%、21.3%，增速排名全国第一和第五；货邮吞吐量内蒙古、河北分别同比增长34.3%、32.6%，增速排名全国第一和第二。

二、切实加强安全监管，确保华北民航安全发展

始终保持高度安全意识，围绕安全责任落实，逐步形成“做好常态、突出重点、抓好长远”相结合的安全管理工作新机制。紧紧抓住重点单位、重点人员、重点设施设备、重点机型、重点环节、重点环境“六个重点”，进行有效的监督管理，初步形成了安全管理“抓重点、重点抓”局面。

前移安全关口，严格许可审批。重点强化对建设工程行业验收的管理、新成立公司的初始运行合格审定及新引进机型的审定。积极开展危险品运输专项整治和锂电池专项治理，整顿危险品运输市场。开展防跑道入侵、刮蹭航空器整治，强化不停航施工监管，维护机场安全运行秩序。重点组织区内机场设备设施和人员配备的专项调研，督促企业改进保障设施，提高运行保障能力。深入开展各专业人员技术排查，切实加强人员资质管理，组织辖区内所有航空公司共4 149名飞行员进行《民用航空运输机长职责》、非精密进近程序等理论考试以及非精密进近技术检查。完成辖区内10家运输航空公司的CCAR-121-R4的补充运行合格审定。完成Ameco的安全管理体系（SMS）审定，成为中国民航首家通过SMS审定的维修单位。完成区内外5家机场安全审计，完成区内华北空管局、区外广西空管分局的空管安全审计。完成5个机场的航空保安后续审计工作。

三、继续深化制度建设，夯实安全管理基础

着力完善安全监管制度，加强安全基础建设。从

北京监管局对首都机场进出港航班进行机长职责检查

Beijing SSMB Inspects Pilot-in-Command Responsibilities of Arriving and Departing Flights at Capital Airport

“学、用、审、改”四方面狠抓《安全管理手册》的贯彻落实。建立季度安全形势分析制度，分析研判区内安全状况，系统查找安全监管存在的问题和不足，明确不同阶段工作重点，检查监管措施的落实，进行基于安全风险排序的监管资源配置，实现有针对性的重点监管。加入隐患风险评估、隐患升级机制、督促整改手段、挂牌督办和公布公示制度等内容，实施重大隐患行政约见，扩展充实了隐患排查治理的内容和手段，为隐患排查治理工作的深入开展进一步奠定制度基础。加大航权航班时刻管理力度，完善行政审批事项监督机制，出台《航权航班时刻管理工作手册》和《航权航班时刻管理风险防控手册》，清理权力事项，全面规范航权航班时刻管理程序和标准，基本形成公开、透明的航权航班时刻审批协调分配机制。

完善细化《航空企事业单位安全责任制考核评分办法》，对相对人安全责任制落实进行分级量化考评。同时制定《安全监管绩效管理办法》、《安全监管绩效考核细则和评分标准》和《航空安全监管问责制度》，初步建立起安全监管测评指标体系和考评方法，把安全监管绩效考核作为年度考核的重要依据，严格责任追究，着力解决行政不作为或作为不充分问题，有效避免监管不力和监管缺失，确保监管责任落到实处。建立区内重点飞行人员档案，进一步将排查工作扩展到维修、签派、管制等关键岗位技术人员和地面人员与运输服务人员。加强应急管理工作的属地管理，修订完善各项应急工作制度。

四、研究落实各项工作，主动服务行业发展

（1）加强“十二五”规划宣贯和落实 完善出台《华北地区民航发展“十二五”规划及2030年远景规划》，对民航“十二五”总体规划、支线航空发展、机队规划、航空快运发展等专项规划进行宣贯解读。

（2）努力推进空域调整优化 重点协调对北京、天津、石家庄、太原、呼和浩特、鄂尔多斯、大同等7个飞行流量较大和空域环境复杂的机场进行集中空域调整，对进离场航线优化开展评审工作并批复优化方案，新增和优化调整39条进离场飞行航线，调整35条班机航线走向，修改了44张进离场航线图。空域调整和飞行程序优化大幅度提高了机场进离场运行效率，为缓解华北地区空域紧张状况，打破瓶颈制约，提升飞行安全管理水平，实现飞行流量的进一步增加创造了条件。

（3）科学增加机场航班容量 在科学评估的基础上，积极推进首都机场增容工作，首都机场高峰小时航班时刻容量进一步提高；同时组织对南苑、天津、太原机场的航班时刻容量标准进行调整，部分缓解了时刻资源制约矛盾，为今后华北民航可持续发展奠定基础。

（4）大力提高服务管理水平 积极主动协调自治区政府，出台支持措施，大力推进内蒙古民航又好又快发展。落实民航局、河北省政府《关于加快推进河北民航发展的会谈纪要》精神，积极支持河北民航跨越式发展。按照重点突出国际—国内集散功能，承担干线运输，兼顾华北区域枢纽功能的定位结合始发航班航向，梳理分析首都机场航班时刻时段、数量与地面综合保障能力的匹配关系，均匀单位时段航班分布，优化首都机场航班时刻布局。大力推进枢纽建设，积极引导航空公司实施差异化发展战略，鼓励基地航空公司加强航班波建设和拓展国际航线，在公共政策、时刻分配上予以大力支持，增强其核心竞争力。完成运输飞机引进保障能力评估项目15个、引进进口通用航空飞机初审项目35个。

（5）积极推进通用航空发展 编制完成《华北地区通用航空机场布局规划的意见》。制定出台《民航华北地区通用航空市场管理办法》。积极协调推进阿拉善盟通勤航空试点，根河利用林业机场拓宽通用航空服务领域试点建设，推动通勤、通用航空发展。

（6）大力开展航班延误整治 首先从时刻编排上全面优化首都、天津、太原和南苑机场5分钟时刻容量，从源头提高航班正常保障水平。二是在首都机场建立始发航班正常通报奖惩制度。三是制定并下发《首都机场航班延误原因判定办法》，从统计指标体系、统计口径、统计方法、数据来源等方面查找分析原因，督促各单位实现统计数据的统一。四是协调天津、太原、石家庄、呼和浩特机场建立大面积航班延误联动指挥机制，编写大面积航班延误应急处置手册。五是继续发挥首都机场大面积航班延误联动指挥机制作用，开展空地统一放行和协调处置，持续改善航班不正常情况下的服务。六是组织开展华北地区机场备降保障能力调研，着力解决航班备降与机场保障能力存在的不协调问题。■

CAAC North Regional Administration

In 2011, CAAC North Regional Administration deepened the implementation of the concept of sustained safety and the strategy of building a country with a strong civil aviation industry, well balanced and coordinated various jobs, impeccably completed various tasks and made a good start for the 12th Five-Year Plan period, opening a new chapter for the development of the industry.

I. Continuous Stableness in Safety Situation and Solid Increment of Transport Production

In 2011, CAAC North Regional Administration addressed the safety risks from their sources and urged businesses and public service entities to implement their safety responsibilities and therefore maintained a stable safety situation. The civil aviation industry in the north China safely operated 1.09 million flight hours without any transport flight accidents or aviation security accidents within the jurisdiction of the administration, successfully realizing their annual safety objectives.

Throughout the year, all the airports in the region recorded a passenger traffic of 109.74 million people, cargo and mail turnover of 1.965 million tons and 887 000 aircraft movements, year-on-year increases of 9%, 4.7% and 6.1% respectively. Within the region, the passenger traffic in Hebei Province and Inner Mongolia Autonomous Region had year-on-year increases of 46.5% and 21.3% respectively, being the fastest and 5th fastest pace in China, and the cargo turnover in Inner Mongolia and Hebei grew by 34.3% and 32.6% respectively over that of the previous year, being the fastest and the 2nd fastest nationwide.

II. Effective Enhancement in Safety Oversight to Ensure Safe Development of Civil Aviation in North China

The administration has always been keen on the alert for safety and gradually formed a new safety management work mechanism combining Well Handling Daily Safety, Highlighting Key Issues and Addressing Long-term Safety. It conducted effective supervision and management through addressing "6 keys", i.e. key units, key personnel, key facilities and equipment, key aircraft types, key links and key environments, leading to an initial safety management situation of Addressing the Prioritized Issues and Making Prioritized Efforts to Address Some Issues.

The administration advanced safety checkpoints and tightened approval review. It gave priority to strengthening the management of industrial checks and acceptance of construction projects, the certification of initial operations of start-up companies and the certification of newly introduced aircraft types. It actively conducted dedicated rectification of transport of dangerous goods and lithium batteries to straighten up the dangerous goods transport market. It conducted campaigns to prevent runway incursion and rectify aircraft scrapes, and strengthened construction supervision without suspending flight services and maintained the order of safe operations at airports. It also gave priority to organizing special study of equipment, facilities and staffing at airports within its jurisdiction and urging enterprises to improve the support facilities and boost their capacity for operational

2011年民航华北局积极推进内蒙古根河通用航空拓宽服务领域试点工作

In 2011, CAAC North Regional Administration Actively Pushes Forward with the Pilot Work of Expanding General Aviation Service Fields in Genhe, Inner Mongolia

support. It deepened the screening for professionals' skills to concretely strengthen the management of personnel qualifications. It held theoretical tests for a total of 4 149 pilots regarding Functions of Pilots-in-Command in Civil Air Transport and non-precision approach procedure and conducted technical inspection of non-precision approach. It completed CCAR Part 121-R4 supplemental operational certification of 10 transport airlines and the certification of SMS in Ameco, making it the first maintenance entity that passed SMS certification in China's civil aviation industry. It also completed safety audit of 5 airports inside and outside the region, ATM safety audit of the North China Regional ATM Bureau inside the region and Guangxi ATM Sub-bureau outside the region, and the follow-up aviation security audit of 5 airports.

III. Continuous Reinforcement of Institutional Building to Cement the Groundwork for Safety Management

The administration focused on improving its safety oversight system and fortifying its safety groundwork. It emphasized the implementation of Safety Management Manual from 4 respects, namely, "studying, using, auditing and rectifying". It established a quarterly safety situation analysis system to analyze and assess the safety situation within the region, systemically pinpoint problems and deficiencies in safety oversight, identify work priorities for different stages, inspect the implementation of oversight measures, conduct oversight resources distribution based on prioritization of safety risks and carry out targeted and prioritized oversight. It introduced hazards and risks evaluation, hazard upgrading mechanism, means of urging for rectification, supervised investigation and handling, public notification system, etc., implemented administrative summons for major hazards, expanded and enriched means of hazards screening and rectification which all laid an institutional foundation for the in-depth implementation of hazards screening and rectification. It redoubled efforts in management of traffic rights and flight slots, improved the supervisory mechanism for administrative review matters, issued the Manual for Management of Traffic Rights and Flight Slots and the Manual on the Management and Risks Prevention of Traffic Rights and Flight Slots, sorted out authority issues and comprehensively standardized the management procedure and standards for the management of traffic rights and flight slots, thereby forming on the whole an open and transparent mechanism for review, coordination and allocation of traffic rights and flight slots.

The administration improved and specified the Methods for Safety Responsibility Evaluation and Rating of Aviation Enterprises and Institutions to conduct graded quantitative evaluation of safety responsibility performance for the people concerned. In the meantime, it built up, by developing the Management Methods of Safety Oversight Performance, the Specifications on Evaluation of Safety Oversight Performance and its Rating Standards and the Accountability System for Aviation Safety Oversight, a nascent indicator system and examination methods for evaluation of safety oversight, including the performance evaluation of safety oversight into the annual evaluation as an important basis, tightening the accountability investigation, paying attention to the problems such as administrative inaction or lack of action, effectively preventing lack or absence of oversight and ensuring oversight responsibilities put concretely in place. It built up the archives for key flight personnel within the region and further expanded the screening to technicians in key positions, such as maintenance, dispatch, ATC as well as ground personnel and transport service personnel. In addition, it strengthened the home-place management in emergency response management and amended and refined various work systems of emergency response.

IV. Study and Implementation of All Kinds of Work to Help the Development of the Industry

1. The administration strengthened the publicity and implementation of the 12th Five-Year Plan. It issued and polished up the 12th Five-year Plan and Long-term Plan till 2030 for the Development of Civil Aviation in North China, publicized, implemented and expounded some major dedicated plans such as the civil aviation's master 12th Five-Year Plan, feeder line aviation development, fleet plan and aviation express transport development.

2. The administration tried to push forward the adjustment and optimization of airspace. It gave priority to coordinating airspace adjustment of 7 airports with heavy flight traffic and complicated airspace environments in Beijing, Tianjin, Shijiazhuang, Taiyuan, Hohhot, Ordos and Datong, conducted review of the optimization of inbound and outbound routes and approved the optimization plan, whereby 39 inbound and outbound flight routes were newly added, optimized and adjusted; 35 flight routes were adjusted and

44 inbound and outbound flight charts were revised. Airspace adjustment and flight procedure optimization significantly improved the operational efficiency of airport arrivals and departures and paved the way for easing the airspace stress, breaking bottlenecks, boosting the management of flight safety and further increasing flight traffic.

3. The administration rationally increased airports' flight frequencies. On the basis of scientific assessment, it vigorously pushed forward capacity increase at Beijing Capital International Airport, further increasing the peak-hour flight frequency at the airport; in the meantime, it coordinated for the adjustment of flight frequency standards for Nanyuan, Tianjin and Taiyuan airports, partially easing the stress in the timeslot resources, laying a good foundation for the future sustainable development of civil aviation in north China.

4. The administration vigorously improved service management. It actively coordinated with the local autonomous regional government to adopt supportive measures and vigorously promoted sound and rapid development of civil aviation in Inner Mongolia. The regional government acted upon CAAC and Hebei provincial government's Minutes of Talks Concerning Expediting the Development of Civil Aviation in Hebei Province and lent strong support for quantum-leap development of the industry in Hebei. According to the principle of prioritization, it undertook trunk line transport with an emphasis on the function as an international-domestic hub and based on the combination of considering the north region's positioning as a hub and the destinations of routes of original flights, analyzed the matchup of flight slot periods, frequencies and overall ground support capacity, smoothened out the unit slots distribution and optimized the flight slots distribution at Beijing Capital International Airport. It strongly pushed forward the hub building, actively guided airlines in implementing the strategy of differentiated development, encouraged resident airlines to accelerate the flight-wave development and expand international routes, and gave strong support in the form of public policies and slots distribution to boost their core competitiveness. It also completed 15 evaluations of support capacity for introduced aircraft and 35 initial reviews of introduced and imported general aviation aircraft.

5. The administration actively pushed forward general aviation development. It developed the Opinions on the Layout Plan for General Aviation Airports in North China, developed and issued the Methods for General Aviation Market Management in the Region of North China. It actively coordinated for the promotion of pilot commuting aviation in Alxa Prefecture and the pilot project of expanding general aviation service with forestry airports in Genhe to push forward the development of commuting and general aviation.

6. The administration vigorously conducted flight delay rectification. First, it improved the flight regularity support capacity from the root sources by comprehensively optimizing the 5-minute slot capacity at Beijing Capital International Airport, Tianjin Airport, Taiyuan Airport and Nanyuan Airport. Second, it established an incentive and punitive mechanism for flight regularity at the Capital Airport. Third, it developed and issued the Methods for the Ascertaining of Flight Delay Causes at Beijing Capital International Airport to examine the causes from perspectives of statistic indicator system, statistic standards, statistics method and data sources in order to urge all entities to realize their statistical consistency. Fourth, it coordinated with airports in Tianjin, Taiyuan, Shijiazhuang and Hohhot in establishing a joint-interactive command mechanism for massive flight delays and developing the Manual on Emergency Response during Massive Flight Delays. Fifth, it continued to capitalize on the interactive command mechanism for massive flight delays at the Capital Airport and conducted coordinated air-ground clearance and coordinated disposition to consistently improve services during flight irregularities. Sixth, it organized the inspection and study of the support capacity for alternate landing at airports in north China to address the mismatch between alternate landing and support capacity at airports.

天津监管局监察员对空客飞机进行监察

The Supervisor in Tianjin SSMB Monitors Airbus Aircraft

民航东北地区管理局

2011年，民航东北地区管理局以科学发展观为指导，按照民航局部署，紧密结合自身实际，积极推进各项工作，圆满完成了年度任务，实现了“十二五”良好开局。

一、安全态势持续平稳

辖区单位杜绝了飞行事故、航空地面事故、航空维修事故和空防安全事故，各项安全指标均控制在民航局规定的范围内。运输航空公司克服机型置换带来的不利因素，连续31个月未发生人为原因运输航空事故征候，连续36个月无发动机空中停车事件；通用航空扭转了不利趋势；空管局连续实现了15个安全年；中国航油东北公司没有发生油料原因不安全事件。

管理局根据安全综合保障能力，合理控制了发展速度。持续推进安全体系建设。大连航空公司、飞龙公司、朝阳飞行学院、中一太客公司通过运行合格审定和补充运行合格审定；南航北方分公司、深航沈阳分公司、南航沈阳维修基地通过安全管理体系（SMS）符合性认证；东北空管局通过SMS审核；黑龙江空管分局、朝阳、长白山、漠河机场通过安全审计。管理局全面开展飞行、机务、运控、空管行业重点人员检查、专项技术排查，坚持局方监察员实施机长航线检查和转升级训练，专业技术人员资质能力建设初见成效。

2011年12月6日，民航局李家祥局长（左）与黑龙江省人民政府代表在哈尔滨签署了《关于进一步加快黑龙江省民航事业发展会谈纪要》

On December 6, 2011, Li Jiaxiang (left), Administrator of CAAC, and the Representative of Heilongjiang Provincial Government in Harbin, Signs the Minutes of Talks on Further Promoting Civil Aviation Development in Heilongjiang Province

切实维护空防安全，及时有效处置非法干扰事件。哈尔滨、延吉、漠河、丹东机场组织了反劫机综合演练，大庆机场通过航空保安审计。

认真开展安全大检查、安全督察，强化日常安全监察，支线机场应急救援能力不足、机场净空和电磁环境遭破坏等一批重大安全隐患得到治理。全年批复安全项目44项，总投资3.5亿元，安排民航发展基金补助2.3亿元，有力改善了支线机场、空管系统基础设施条件和安全保障能力。

二、生产运营持续增长

全区运输机场完成旅客吞吐量3 783.8万人次，货邮吞吐量42.3万吨，运输飞机起降30万架次，同比分别增长11.7%、3.8%和3.9%。“千万级机场”战略取得新进展，沈阳机场旅客吞吐量顺利突破1 000万人次，大连机场达到1 200万人次。航线网络继续延伸，全区新开和恢复航线31条，其中新开通国际航线2条。支线航空稳步发展，支线机场旅客吞吐量278万人次，增长9%。通用航空增势强劲，区内通航单位作业飞行3.5万小时，起降6.7万架次，分别增长28.8%和47.1%，净增通用航空器31架。

三、运行品质不断提升

坚决贯彻民航局航班延误整治要求，狠抓大面积航班延误治理工作。各航空公司、机场、空管、油料等单位，落实责任，完善制度，加强值班。成立了航班运行协调指挥机构，各单位明确分工，协调配合，全区航班平均正常率78.1%，机场放行率94.9%，较上年均有所提高。

CAAC Northeast Regional Administration

Guided by Scientific Outlook on Development and based on CAAC deployment and the regional realities, the administration actively carried out all its work, successfully completing its 2011 tasks and making a good beginning of the 12th Five-Year Plan.

I. Sustained Stability in Safety Situation

There were no flight accidents, ground accidents, aircraft maintenance accidents or aviation security accidents within the jurisdiction, and all safety indicators were controlled within CAAC's specified range. Transport airlines overcame the adverse impact of aircraft replacement and kept zero transport incident rate for 31 consecutive months and zero in-flight engine shutdown for 36 consecutive months. General aviation turned the corner. The Air Traffic Management Bureau had maintained aviation safety for 15 consecutive years. There had been no fuel-related safety incidents at Northeast Branch of China National Aviation Fuel.

Based on the overall safety support capacity, the administration maintained reasonable control over the development speed and continuously stepped up the SMS building. Dalian Airlines, China Flying Dragon Special Aviation Company, Chaoyang Flight College of CAUC and First Mandarin Business Aviation Co., Ltd. passed the operational certification and supplementary operational certification; the North Branch of China Southern Airlines, Shenyang Branch of Shenzhen Airlines and Shenyang Maintenance Base of China Southern Airlines passed the SMS compliance certification, and Northeast Air Traffic Management Bureau passed SMS examination.

积极推动航行新技术应用，完成伊春、加格达奇机场的基于性能的导航（PBN）项目，完成朝阳飞行学院ADS-B试点工作。空域、航路结构不断优化，完成沈阳空中禁区调整、优化航路走向、缩小雷达管制间隔等工作，空域运行效率提升较快。量化空域和机场资源，完成沈阳机场容量评估，小时高峰容量由20架次增加至23架次，启动长春、大连机场容量评估，全区行业运行品质得到较快提升。

四、基础建设稳步推进

机场建设全面启动。沈阳机场站坪扩建、长春机场航站区设施扩建、极地航路雷达管制工程等12个项目通过行业验收并投入运行；哈尔滨航管楼顺利启用；沈阳机场航站区扩建、大连机场航站区扩建、新建通化机场等工程项目开工建设；抚远、加格达奇、五大连池、建三江、绥芬河、白城、松原、营口等新建机场项目以及大连新机场、延吉、锦州迁建机场项目前期工作进展顺利；沈阳机场二跑道项目、哈尔滨、长春、丹东机场改扩建工程等前期工作稳步推进。航空公司加大基础设施投入，南航沈阳维修基地新机库等项目正在建设中。

五、行业管理不断深化

2011年全局共开展行政检查4 200余次，发现问题1 400余个，下发《行政检查整改通知书》和《行政检查整改建议书》420份，实施行政处罚10宗11起，行政约见相对人13次，有效整改违法违章问题980项。严肃查处违章行为。对部分严重违章案件，采取行政约见、限制运行等措施，取得成效。强化监管能力建设，努力探索监察员队伍的管理和培训工作，不断提升监察员业务素质和执法能力。航空器适航审定工作扎实推进，适航审定基础建设进一步加强。坚持监管与服务并重。及时协调辖区各单位发展中遇到的问题，为东北民航创造良好的发展环境。

Heilongjiang Air Traffic Management Bureau and airports in Chaoyang, Changbaishan and Mohe passed safety audit. The administration carried out comprehensive inspection of key personnel and screening of specialized technologies in flight, engineering maintenance, operation control and air traffic management, and insisted that CAAC inspectors carry out inspection of pilot-in-command and routes and offer training in the case of aircraft replacement as well as upgrading training, leading to initial progress in the capacity building for technical personnel.

The administration conscientiously maintained its aviation security and timely and effectively handled illegal interferences. Comprehensive anti-hijack drills were conducted at airports in Harbin, Yanji, Mohe and Dandong. Daqing Airport passed the aviation security audit.

The administration earnestly carried out safety overhaul and safety supervision. It enhanced regular safety supervision and inspection, thus some major safety hazards such as weakness in emergency rescue and relief at feeder airports and damage to airport net clearances and electromagnetic environment were rectified. In the whole year, 44 safety projects with a total investment of 350 million yuan were approved and 230 million worth of civil aviation development fund subsidies were provided, significantly improving the infrastructure conditions and safety support capacity of feeder airports and the air traffic management system.

II. Steady Growth in Transport Operations

The regional passenger turnover was 37.838 million; cargo and mail turnover was 423 000 tons, and transport aircraft movements were 300 000, year-on-year increases of 11.7%, 3.8% and 3.9% respectively. With passenger turnover at Shenyang Airport topping 10 million and that in Dalian Airport reaching 12 million, new progress was made in the strategy of building airports with passenger turnover at ten-million. The route network continued to extend, with 31 routes newly opened and restored in the whole region, 2 of which were newly opened international routes. Feeder aviation developed steadily, with passenger turnover at feeder airports reaching 2.78 million, increasing by 9%. General aviation in the region developed vibrantly, with 35 000 hours of general aviation flights and 67 000 aircraft movements, increasing by 28.8% and 47.1% respectively, and with a net increase of 31 general aviation aircraft.

III. Continuous Improvement in Operation Quality

Focusing on large-scale flight delay rectification, the administration firmly implemented CAAC's flight delay rectification requirements. Airlines, airports, air traffic management bureaus and fuel companies fulfilled their responsibilities, improved their institutions and strengthened their shift arrangement. The administration established a flight operation coordination and command unit, clearly assigned various tasks and made good coordination among all work units, thus making a 78.1% average flight regularity rate and 94.9% airport clearance rate, higher than those in the last year.

The administration actively promoted the application of new navigation technologies and accomplished the PBN projects in Yichun and Jiagedaqi airports, and the ADS-B pilot program at Chaoyang Flight College of CAUC. It continued to optimize airspace and air route structure, completed the adjustment to off-limits zone in Shenyang, optimized the route heading and reduced radar control separation minimum, rapidly improving the airspace operation efficiency. The administration quantified airspace and airport resources, completed the capacity assessment of Shenyang Airport, whose number of peak-hour aircraft movements increased from 20 to 23, and initiated the capacity assessment of Changchun and Dalian airports, resulting in rapid improvement of operation quality of the industry through out the region.

IV. Steady Progress in Infrastructure Development

The airport construction was initiated on a full scale. 12 projects, such as the expansion of Shenyang Airport aprons and the expansion of Changchun Airport terminal area facilities and the polar-region route radar control project, received the industry acceptance inspection and were put into operation. The air traffic management building of Harbin Airport was successfully put into service. The expansion of terminal areas at Shenyang and Dalian airports and the construction of new Tonghua Airport were started.

Preparatory work for new constructions like airports in Fuyuan, Jiagedaqi, Wudalianchi, Jiansanjiang, Suifenhe, Baicheng, Songyuan and Yingkou and for relocated constructions like new Dalian Airport and airports in Yanji and Jinzhou was carried out smoothly. Preparatory work for the second runway construction at Shenyang Airport and revamp and expansion projects at airports in Harbin, Changchun and Dandong proceeded steadily. Airlines increased their infrastructure input and projects such as new hangars at Shenyang maintenance base of China Southern were under construction.

V. Constant Deepening of Industry Management

In 2011, the administration carried out 4 200 administrative inspections in the region, detected 1 400 problems, issued 420 Notices on Rectification after Administrative Inspection and Proposals on Rectification after Administrative Inspection, made 11 administrative penalties for 10 cases, made 13 administrative summons and effectively rectified 980 infractions. The administration seriously investigated and dealt with such infractions and adopted measures such as administrative summons and operation restraints on some serious cases, thus achieving positive results. It enhanced the supervision capacity building, tried to explore management and training of inspectors and constantly improved their professional expertise and law enforcement capability. It steadily pushed ahead with aircraft airworthiness certification and further stepped up its foundation building. The administration attached equal importance to supervision and service and timely coordinated with all units under its jurisdiction for problems that they met in their development, thus creating a good environment for the development of civil aviation in the northeast region.

民航华东地区管理局

2011年，华东地区39个运营机场共完成旅客吞吐量18 500.93万人次，同比增长7.25%；货邮吞吐量507.21万吨，同比减少1.25%；运输起降157.45万架次，同比增长6.03%。安全飞行约156.5万小时，同比增长14%。发生在华东地区的责任原因运输航空事故征候7起，同比减少2起。全年未发生飞行事故和航空器地面事故。

一、安全管理

（1）加强安全体系建设，创新安全运行管理方式和手段 与华东地区66家企事业单位签订了2011年航空安全责任书；修订《民航华东地区航空安全考核与奖励实施办法》，完成辖区内63家企事业单位2010年度航空安全工作的考评以及对9个监管局的安全监管绩效考核。按计划完成安全管理体系（SMS）审定及培训工作，推进机场、空管、维修单位SMS建设，制定华东地区航空安保管理体系（SeMS）建设方案。

拟定《民航华东地区“十二五”期间PBN实施计划》，正式实施上海两场区域导航（RNAV）飞行程序运行，完成温州、厦门等机场所需导航性能—进近（RNP APCH）飞行程序设计及验证试飞。启动与东航关于使用困难报告（SDR）合作项目。制定下发了华东地区机场跑道侵入事件调查处置程序、专职模拟机教员管理实施办法、主任运行监察员效能评优实施办法等。组织修订了不明物体非法升空调查处置暂行办法、华东地区飞行员流动管理办法等。

2011年5月23日，民航华东局沈泽江局长（左一）出席在葡萄牙里斯本举办的民用机场管理培训班开班仪式

On May 23, 2011, Shen Zejiang (first from the left), Director General of CAAC East Regional Administration, Attends the Launching Ceremony for Civil Aviation Airport Management Training Held in Lisbon, Portugal

（2）强化深度持续监管，加大技术专项检查力度 将东航、上航（以下简称东上）重组后的运行及新中货航合并重组等作为监管重点，制定了《关于对东航专项飞行技术训练和检查进行重点监察的计划》；针对部分公司安全管理方面存在的问题，采取专项调研、督察监察、行政约见、发警示函、削减运行总量及依法处理等措施，督促整改；加大航空安保监管力度，开展华东地区安全大检查；开展违规运输危险品专项治理；开展飞行技术专项检查、非精密进近补充训练和技术检查、模拟机训练暗查、开展对外籍飞行员专项检查，航空公司维修人员资质能力检查，运输航空公司运行控制岗位上值勤的飞行签派员技术检查，一线管制员的技术排查等。

（3）开展机场飞行区保障能力核查 协调地方政府加大对机场的安全投入。对辖区39个运输机场的飞行区场地、供电、助航灯光系统和残损航空器搬移等进行飞行区保障能力的核查和综合评估，对机场安全急需项目采取特事特办的方式予以解决，提高机场飞行区保障能力。

（4）认真做好各项审定和审计工作 完成东航等8家运输航空公司的CCAR-121-R4部补充审定、东方公务航等公司的CCAR-91部审定和补充审定、22家外航的CCAR-129部初始审定和补充审定、东上维修系统重组审定等；对山东滨奥DA40飞机生产线开展常态化适航监管；按时间节点牵头组织完成ARJ21-700 等国家重点项目专项适航审定；完成10个机场的安全审计，辖区39个机场第一轮安全审计2011年全部完成；完成对5个机场的航空安保审计和6个机场的后续审计，以及厦航航空安保审计试点工作。

CAAC East Regional Administration

In 2011, the 39 operating airports in East China handled a total passenger of 185.0093 million, cargo and mail of 5.0721 million tons, 1.5745 million aircraft movements and about 1.565 million hours of safe flights, year-on-year increases of 7.25%, -1.25%, 6.03% and 14% respectively over that of the previous year. There were 7 transport aviation incidents that occurred in this region, 2 incidents less than that of the previous year. There were no flight accidents or aircraft ground accidents the whole year.

I. Safety Management

1. Strengthening safety system building and innovating the modes and measures of safe operation management. In

（5）规范不安全事件调查处置和信息管理，加强行政执法工作 制定《民航华东地区管理局不安全事件调查处置管理细则》；加强航空安全信息规章制度的宣贯和培训，查处未按规定程序报送重要不安全事件信息的情况。

二、航空运输管理

（1）加强航线航班管理，扎实推进航班延误整治工作 协调解决上海与重点城市间的航班密度，构建通达顺畅的航线网络；切实做好航线航班行政许可工作，加大航班时刻执行的清查力度；编写完成华东局航线航班时刻管理工作手册；成立上海地区航班运行协调指挥中心，制定上海机场大面积航班延误、航班预计离港时刻协同决策工作程序，修订完善上海地区航班大面积延误应急处置预案。

（2）做好重大航空运输保障和消费者事务工作 圆满完成第14届国际泳联世界锦标赛、春运、国庆、两会代表运输、国际国内会议、中外要客航班及利比亚撤侨等重大、紧急、特殊航空运输保障的组织协调工作；完成东南沿海交通保障计划编制工作，修订完成自然灾害应急预案等；定期公布辖区各航空公司、机场旅客投诉率等数据，督促企业改进服务工作；组织辖区机场开展消费者权益保护日宣传活动。

（3）加强通用航空市场监管 2011年共批复申请甲类通用航空企业4家、筹建15家、变更10家、经营许可换证2家；注销通用航空企业1家。协助开展通航相关立法调研，做好辖区18家通航年度财经信息分析上报工作。

三、基础设施建设与机场运行管理

（1）加快推进民航基础设施建设 全年华东地区各机场完成固定资产投资共计89亿元；实施改扩建和新建、迁建的机场32个，处于前期启动阶段的新建、迁建机场4个，前期论证阶段的新建、迁建机场7个；批复各类小型基础建设项目43个（含助航灯光更新改造），总投资估算1.3亿元；全年共审查机场场址6个，批复扬州江都机场等9个机场总体规划和上海虹桥机场跑道大修等51个项目初步设计，组织对南昌机场扩建等31个项目行业验收；完成改扩建通用机场1个，2个直升机场通过了行业验收，处于建设前期论证阶段的通用机场7个、在建1个。

（2）规范机场运行管理，加强超净空事先防范工作 审核变更6个运输机场和1个通用机场使用许可证，换发1个运输机场和2个通用机场使用许可证，颁发通用机场使用许可证1个，暂停1个通用机场的开放使用，批复命名通用机场2个；开展机场标志标识专项整治，辖区各机场共投入约9 000余万元，对跑道滑行道和机坪的标志标识系统进行全面整改；加强不停航施工管理，加大现场监管力度；全年完成35个拟建净空项目的101个单体的净空审核，处理5起超净空事件；做好机场净空保护区图审批工作。

（3）做好民航专业工程质量监督和招投标管理工作 全年共完成民航专业工程质监项目34个；加强民航专业工程招投标管理，受理102个民航专业工程及货物招投标备案手续，其中86个工程项目已办结。

2011, the administration signed aviation safety responsibility contracts with 66 enterprises and institutions, revised the Implementation Methods for Evaluation and Reward of Aviation Safety in East China Regional Administration of CAAC, completed the assessments of 2010 aviation safety work at 63 enterprises and institutions within its jurisdiction and the evaluations of safety supervision performance at 9 supervision bureaus. The administration also completed, according to the plan, the SMS certification and training, pushed forward SMS development at airports, ATM and maintenance units and formulated the development plan for SeMS in the region of East China.

The administration drafted the PBN Implementation Plan for the 12th Five-Year Plan Period in East China Regional Civil Aviation, officially put into operation the RNAV flight procedure at 2 airports in Shanghai and completed the design and trial flight of RNP APCH flight procedure at airports in Wenzhou, Xiamen, etc. It initiated the SDR cooperation project with China Eastern Airlines and formulated and issued the Investigation and Handling Procedure for Runway Intrusion Incidents at Airports in the Region of East China, the Implementation Method for Professional Simulation Machine Trainers Management, the Implementation Method for Performance Evaluation of Director-level Operation Supervisors, etc. It also organized the revision of the Interim Method for Investigation and Handling of Illegal Flight of Unidentified Objects, the Management Method for the Turnover of Pilots in the Region of East China, etc.

2. Enhancing in-depth sustained oversight and redoubling efforts in ad-hoc technical inspection. The administration took the supervision over the post-reorganization operation of China Eastern Airlines and Shanghai Airlines and the consolidation and reorganization of the new China Cargo Airlines as focus. It also formulated the Plan for Taking Supervisions over Ad-hoc Flight Technical Training and Inspection at Eastern Airlines as Focus. In response to problems in safety management at some companies, the Administration took measures, e.g. ad-hoc investigation and research, supervision and inspection, administrative summons, issuing cautionary letters, curtailing total operations, adopting treatment according to law, etc. to encourage transformation. It redoubled efforts in aviation security supervision, conducted a wide-scale safety inspection in the region of East China and launched ad-hoc rectifications on the illegal transport of dangerous goods. It also conducted ad-hoc flight technical inspections, supplementary training and technical inspections of non-precision approach, hidden inspections of simulator training, dedicated inspections of foreign pilots, qualification and capacity inspections of maintenance personnel at airlines, technical inspections of flight dispatchers working in operations control positions at transport airlines, technical screening of frontline controllers, etc.

3. Conducting examination and verification of support capacity at airports' movement areas. The administration coordinated with local governments in increasing safety input at airports. It conducted verification and comprehensive evaluation of support capacity for movement areas, power supply, lighting system and removal of damaged aircraft at 39 transport airports within its jurisdiction and took extraordinary measures to deal with urgent safety projects, thus improving the support capacity at airport movement areas.

4. Implementing earnestly all certifications and audits. The administration completed CCAR Part 121-R4 supplementary certification of 8 transport airlines including China Eastern Airlines, CCAR Part 91 certification, supplementary certification of China Eastern Airlines Executive Air, etc., CCAR Part 129 initial and supplementary certifications of 22 foreign airlines, certification of the reorganization of China Eastern Airlines' and Shanghai Airlines' maintenance systems. It also conducted regular airworthiness supervision over Shandong Bin'ao's DA40 aircraft production line, led and organized, according to schedule, the dedicated airworthiness certification of key national projects such as ARJ21-700, and completed safety audit of 10 airports and the first round of safety audit of all the 39 airports within its jurisdiction in 2011. Besides, it also completed the aviation security audit of 5 airports, the follow-up audit of 6 airports and the pilot aviation security audit of Xiamen Airlines.

5. Regulating the investigation, handling and information management of unsafe incidents and strengthening the administrative enforcement. The administration developed the Detailed Managerial Rules on Investigation and Handling of Unsafe Incidents in East China Regional Administration of CAAC, strengthened the promotion, execution and training on the rules and regulations for aviation safety information and cracked down upon failures to report important unsafe incidents that were according to the set procedures.

II. Air Transport Management

1. Reinforcing management of routes and flights and

solidly pushing forward rectification of flight delays. The administration tried, through coordination, to address the frequency of flights between Shanghai and other major cities to build a smooth and orderly network. It earnestly dealt with the administrative licensing of routes and flights, strengthened screening of compliance with flight schedules, and completed the preparation of the CAAC East Regional Administration's Handbook on Management of Routes and Flight Schedules. Besides, the Administration set up the Coordination and Command Center for Flight Operations in Shanghai Region, formulated the work procedure for joint decision-making on expected departure times during massive flight delays at Shanghai airports and modified the contingency plan for massive flight delays in Shanghai Region.

2. Providing good air transport support for major events and good service for consumers. The administration successfully organized and coordinated the significant, urgent and special air transport tasks such as the air transport support for the 14th FINA World Championships, the Spring Festival, National Day, the National People's Congress and the Chinese People's Political Consultative Conference, other international and domestic conferences, flights for Chinese and foreign VIPs, the evacuation of Chinese nationals from Libya, etc. It completed the development of the Transport Support Plan for Coastal Areas in the South and East and revised the Contingency Plan for Natural Disasters. Besides, the administration published data of passenger complaint rates of airlines and airports within its jurisdiction on a regular basis to encourage its businesses to improve their service, and organized the airports within its jurisdiction to carry out the Awareness Campaign Day on Protection of Consumers' Rights and Interests.

3. Strengthening supervision over general aviation market. In 2011, the administration approved 4 applications for Class-I GA enterprises, 15 applications for preliminary preparations, 10 for alteration and 2 for license renewal and 1 GA enterprise deregistration. It assisted in the study for GA related legislation and successfully finished the analysis and reporting of annual financial information of 18 GA businesses within its jurisdiction.

III. Infrastructure Construction and Airport Operation Management

1. Accelerating civil aviation infrastructure construction. Throughout the year, all airports in the east region made a fixed-asset investment totaling 8.9 billion yuan. The region conducted 32 airport renovation, expansion, new construction and relocation projects, among which, 4 new construction and relocation projects were in the initial starting stage, while the other 7 were in the stage of preliminary feasibility study. In the year, the administration approved 43 small-scale infrastructure construction projects of various sorts (including revamp of navaid lighting system) with an expected investment of 130 million yuan, inspected 6 airports sites and approved the overall plan for 9 airports including Yangzhou Jiangdu Airport and preliminary designs for 51 projects, such as runway overhaul at Shanghai Hongqiao Airport, and organized check and acceptance inspection of 31 projects including Nanchang Airport expansion project. One GA airport was renovated and expanded, and 2 heliports gained industry acceptance. There were 7 GA airport projects in the stage of pre-construction feasibility study and there was 1 under construction.

2. Standardizing airport operation management and strengthening advance prevention against airport clearance breaches. The administration carried out reviews, altering certificates for 6 transport airports and 1 GA airport, renewing certificates for 1 transport airport and 2 GA airports, issuing certificate for 1 GA airport, suspending the public service of 1 GA airport, and approving the nomination for 2 GA airports. It conducted dedicated rectification of signs at airports and with approximately 90 million yuan invested in the airports within its jurisdiction, and conducted a comprehensive rectification of the sign systems on runways, taxiways and aprons. It also strengthened its management of construction without flight suspension and redoubled its efforts in on-spot supervision. In 2011, the administration completed the clearance review of 101 entities of 35 planned clearance projects and dealt with 5 clearance breaches. It also properly reviewed the clearance zone maps of airports.

3. Doing a good job in quality supervision over civil aviation engineering projects and in bidding management. In 2011, the administration conducted quality supervision over 34 civil aviation engineering projects and strengthened bidding management of civil aviation engineering projects. It handled the bidding documentation of 102 civil aviation engineering and cargo projects, 86 of which were completed.

民航中南地区管理局

2011年，民航中南地区管理局提出“科学监管促安全，通联协作领发展，规范管理重民生，齐抓共管铸合力”的方针，通过一年来扎实有效的工作，确保了中南地区航空安全态势的总体平稳。

一、突出重点，力求实效，辖区安全形势总体平稳

中南地区各航空公司全年实现运输飞行205万小时，约占全行业37%；各机场保障运输起降124万架次，旅客吞吐量1.5亿人次，货邮吞吐量264万吨，同比分别增长5.2%、9.4%和4.5%。全年没有发生运输航空事故、空防事故、重大航空地面事故和特大航空器维修事故。运输航空责任事故征候万时率为0.02，同比下降67%，其中人为原因事故征候万时率为0.01，同比下降75%。

（1）积极落实安全责任　与辖区49家企事业单位和7个监管局签订责任书，明确企事业单位的安全生产责任和局方的安全监管责任。制订年度安全监察计划，实施行业监察8 600多次，安全隐患整改率达到94%。深入开展机场标志标识、空管设备运行风险、地面保障车辆运行以及航空货邮运输安保、违规运输危险品等专项整治行动。强化安全防范指导，针对空中颠簸、跑道入侵等突出事件，及时发布系列安全指令、安全警示和安全提示。严厉查处违规违章行为，注销不符合规章要求的外航9家。督促辖区企事业单位积极落实安全主体责任，南航、海航、中南空管局、深圳机场等43家单位没有发生责任事故征候及以上事件，华南蓝天油料公司等12家单位被管理局评为安全责任考核优胜单位。

（2）加大专业人员资质排查力度　完成辖区全部飞行人员非精密进近理论普查，对飞行训练中心进行专项监察，对飞行人员开展技术抽查，累计检查飞行人员2 146人，对不合格人员采取降低技术等级、增加训练时间等措施。组织辖区内维修单位开展维修人员资质排查，重点检查南航、海航、深航等10家单位7 490名维修人员，对不符合要求的人员，予以取消资格或补充培训。组织开展管制和签派人员资质排查。

（3）进一步提升安全运行品质　深化安全管理体系（SMS）建设，广州飞机维修公司、深航机务工程部等试点维修单位通过SMS审定，宜昌、张家界机场空管单位通过SMS审计。组织引导航空公司开展运行控制中心（AOC）评审，强化航空公司运控体系建设。全年完成对7个机场、8个空管单位的安全审计，对5个机场和两个空管单位进行了复查，各单位的安全运行水平进一步提高。积极推进新技术应用，持续推进基于性能的导航（PBN）技术的应用；开展航空公司电子飞行包（EFB）和数据链通信（CPDLC）补充审定，平视显示器（HUD）、广播式自动相关监视（ADS-B）推广工作进展顺利。

（4）全力以赴确保空防安全　进一步健全反劫反恐机制，果断处置恐怖威胁信息事件，开展反劫处突、飞机灭火等综合演练。加强安检工作，把大量的空防安全隐患堵截在地面。积极开展空防安全事件调查，对白云机场、长沙机场、南航、海航等单位进行行政约见。开展货邮安保、控制区证件、空防大排查大整治等专项整治活动，杜绝劫炸机等严重空防事件的发生，实现第16个空防安全年。

二、抓住契机，加强引领，推动行业持续健康发展

（1）组织完成第26届世界大学生夏季运动会等重大保障任务　组织安全保障涉及大运会航班1 790架次，大运客人13 496 人次，重要旅客1 864人次，航空运输保障实现零事故、零差错、零投诉、零责任延误，航空安保取得十项“零”指标,实现了“安全、正常、优质、高效”的总体目标，为大运盛会的成功举办作出了重要贡献，向社会展示了民航的综合实力，树立了良好的行业形象。圆满保障博鳌亚洲论坛年会、中国—东盟“两会一节”等重要活动，参与

CAAC Central-South Regional Administration

In 2011, CAAC Central-South Regional Administration proposed the guideline of promoting safety by scientific oversight, steering development by coordination and synergy, prioritizing people's livelihood by standardized management and making joint efforts in comprehensive management and endeavors. Thanks to solid and effective work during the whole year, the administration maintained an overall stable safety situation.

I. Giving Prominence to Key Work and Striving for Tangible Effects to Maintain Overall Stability in the Safety Situation

Airlines in the central and south China recorded 2.05 million transport flight hours, approximately accounting for 37% of the whole industry figure. Airports under its jurisdiction supported 1.24 million aircraft movements, 150 million passenger traffic and 2.64 million tons of cargo and mail, up by 5.2%, 9.4% and 4.5% respectively over those of the previous year. In addition, there was no transport aviation accident, aviation security accident, major aviation related ground accident or serious aircraft maintenance accident through the whole year. The transport aviation incident rate per 10 000 flight hours was 0.02, a year-on-year decrease of 67%, in which human performance-induced incident rate per10 000 flight hours was 0.01, a year-on-year decrease of 75%.

组织利比亚撤侨等紧急航空运输任务。

（2）深入落实省部合作协议 与中南各省（区）及广州、深圳、珠海、株洲四地进行会谈，细化落实各省(区）与民航局合作协议的具体措施。初步形成管理局、监管局与各省（区）政府及其工作部门之间的多层次信息沟通和业务协作机制。联手军地各方，努力改善中南民航发展环境，推动广东、湖南、海南“两区一岛”低空空域管理改革试点。

（3）积极推进机场建设和发展 揭阳潮汕机场顺利建成并转场，黄花机场T2航站楼和深圳机场第二跑道启用，支持广西河池、湖北神农架机场建设工程，配合海南博鳌等10个机场建设项目的前期工作，到位机场建设管理费、基建项目贷款贴息、中小机场补贴等资金18.2亿元。积极开展辖区内空域容量优化，探索实施珠三角机场统一放行，构建京广线空中绿色通道，组织开展繁忙机场容量评估，支持区内区域性枢纽机场发展。白云机场年旅客吞吐量突破4 500万人次，深圳、长沙、武汉机场吞吐量再创新高，三亚、海口、郑州机场旅客吞吐量首次突破千万人次大关，在全国21个年旅客吞吐量超千万人次的机场中，中南地区占了7个。

（4）不断加强航空市场管理 不断完善航线航权集体审批制度，坚持经营许可审批与安全运行和航班正常情况联动管理，全年对95条客运航线采取“强制取消”、“自动取消”等强制措施，对29条客运航线进行“交回”、“置换”等处理，对离港正常率排名后20位且低于50%的航班公开通报，对连续被通报的航空公司采取暂停受理航线申请等行政措施。继续做好航班时刻管理工作，坚持公正透明，统筹分配航班时刻，对未按计划执行航班和虚占时刻的航空公司，收回和调减时刻，确保时刻资源有效使用。

（5）深入开展航班延误专项整治 切实加大专项整治力度，建立管理局和监管局领导现场值班制度，启动各地航班运行协调指挥中心，建立完善驻场单位每周协调会、大面积航班延误处置情况报告制度，督促建立统一的信息发布工作机制，落实航班放行主体责任，建立优先放行程序，提高地面运行和空管放行效率。2011年以来，广州等区内重要机场受天气影响，多次启动大面积航班延误预案，由于领导靠前指挥，后续处理工作及时到位，虽然多次出现航班延误、旅客滞留事件，但均得到妥善处置，未造成不良社会影响。

1. Actively delivering on safety responsibilities. The administration signed safety responsibility contracts with 49 public service entities and enterprises and 7 safety supervision and management bureaus under its jurisdiction, clarifying work safety responsibilities of the public service entities and enterprises and safety oversight responsibilities of the administration. It developed its annual safety supervision plan, carried out 8 600 industrial supervisions and realized a 94% hazard rectification rate. The administration launched the following dedicated rectifications: airport signage system, ATM equipment operational risks, operation of ground support vehicles, aviation security of cargo and mail and illegal transport of dangerous goods. It also reinforced the guidance on safety protection and timely released, in light of air turbulence and runway incursions safety directives, safety alerts and safety precautions, etc. Breach of rules and regulations was seriously dealt with, and 9 incompliant foreign airlines were deregistered. The administration urged the enterprises and public service entities under its jurisdiction to actively discharge the principal safety responsibilities. There were no responsibility incidents or incidents aforementioned at 43 entities such as China Southern Airlines, Hainan Airlines, Central-South Air Traffic Management Bureau and Shenzhen Airport, and 12 entities such as South China Bluesky Aviation Oil Co., Ltd. were ranked as outstanding units in safety responsibility performance by the administration.

2. Intensifying efforts to screen the qualifications of professionals. The Administration completed the general survey of all pilots on their theoretical knowledge of non-precision approach. It conducted special supervision over flight training centers and made spot checks on pilots' techniques and skills, with a total number of 2 146 pilots examined. And for those who were unqualified, the administration took such measures as downgrading their technical status and requesting extra training time. It also organized the screening of qualifications of maintenance personnel, focusing on 7 490 maintenance personnel in 10 entities such as China Southern Airlines, Hainan Airlines, Shenzhen Airlines, etc., and took measures of revoking the certificates or licenses or requiring supplementary training for the unqualified. It organized the screening of the qualifications of controllers and dispatchers as well.

3. Further improving the operational safety. With the deepening of the safety management system (SMS) building, pilot maintenance entities like GAMECO and mechanic engineering department of Shenzhen Airlines passed SMS certification. ATM entities at airports in Yichang and Zhangjiajie passed SMS audit. The administration guided airlines' AOC examination to step up the development of airlines' operation control system. In 2011, the administration completed safety audit of 7 airports and 8 ATM units, conducted re-audit of 5 airports and 2 ATM units, further improving the operation safety of all units. It made vigorous efforts to promote the application of new technologies, constantly pushed ahead with the performance based navigation (PBN) application, carried out the supplemental certification of electronic flight bag (EFB) and controller-pilot data-link communication (CPDLC). Popularization of head up display (HUD) and automatic dependent surveillance-broadcasting (ADS-B) proceeded smoothly.

4. Going all out to ensure aviation security. The administration further refined its anti-hijack and anti-terrorism mechanism, resolutely dealt with terrorist threat information, and conducted integrated drills on anti-hijack, emergency response and aircraft fire fighting, etc. It put more weight on security check to limit most of the aviation security hazards on the ground. It carried out active investigation into aviation security events and made administrative summons with Baiyun Airport, Changsha Airport, China Southern Airlines, and Hainan Airlines, etc. The administration also launched special rectification on cargo and mail security, certificate use in the controlled areas and massive aviation security screening, etc., to prevent severe aviation accidents like aircraft hijack and bombing, thereby realizing the 16th year of aviation safety.

II. Seizing Opportunities and Enhancing Guidance to Promote Sustained Safe Development of the Industry

1. Organizing and accomplishing major support tasks such as the 26th Universiade in Shenzhen. The administration provided safety support for 1 790 Universaide related flights, 13 496 passengers and 1 864 VIPs with zero accident, zero error, zero complaint and zero attributable delays. Aviation security scored 10 "zero" indicators and met the overall objectives of "safety, normality, quality and efficiency", making important contributions to the success of Universiade, revealing to the society the civil aviation's comprehensive strength and establishing a good industry image. It also successfully supported major events such as the annual Bo'ao Forum for Asia conference, China-ASEAN Expo., China-ASEAN Business and Investment Summit and Nanning International Folk Song Arts Festival, and contributed to emergency aviation transport tasks, such as the evacuation of Chinese compatriots from Libya.

2. Implementing in depth cooperation agreements with provincial governments and other departments. The administration had talks with provinces in the central and south region, and also with cities like Guangzhou, Shenzhen, Zhuhai, and Zhuzhou, detailing measures to implement the agreement signed between CAAC and provincial governments, initially establishing a multi-layered information communication and business coordination mechanism between the administration, supervision and management bureaus, provincial governments and other departments. The military and local government departments were invited to make joint efforts to improve the civil aviation development environment in the central and south region and to promote pilot reform of lower airspace management in the two regions of Guangdong and Hunan provinces and Hainan international tourism island.

3. Pressing ahead airport construction and development. Chaoshan Airport of Jieyang was successfully built and took over operations from the old one. Terminal 2 of Huanghua Airport and the second runway of Shenzhen Airport were put into operation. Support was rendered to airport construction in Hechi of Guangxi Province and Shenlongjia of Hubei Province, and coordination was made for the preliminary work for 10 airport construction projects including Bo'ao Airport of Hainan Province. With the help of the administration, 1.82 billion yuan for airport construction management, interest subsidies for infrastructure development loans, subsidies for small and medium sized airports, etc. was allocated. The administration made active efforts to optimize the airspace capacity under its jurisdiction, carried out trial work to seek unified flight clearance in the Pear River Delta region, constructed the green air corridor between Beijing and Guangzhou, organized the capacity evaluation of busy airports and supported the development of regional airport hubs under its jurisdiction. The passenger turnover at Baiyun Airport exceeded 45 million, and the turnover at airports of Shenzhen, Changsha and Wuhan made new highs. Airports of Sanya, Haikou and Zhengzhou saw their passenger turnover for the first time over 10 million threshold. Among 21 domestic airports whose annual passenger turnover exceeded 10 million, 7 were in the central and south region.

4. Reinforcing constantly the air transport market management. The administration continuously improved the collective route and traffic right review system, stuck to the joint management of business licensing, operation safety and flight regularity. In the year of 2011, mandatory measures like "mandatory canceling" and "automatic canceling" were imposed on 95 passenger routes, and measures like "returning" or "exchanging" were implemented on 29 passenger routes. Flights whose departure regularity ratio ranked among the bottom 20 and was under 50% were made public. For those airlines that had been repeatedly revealed, the administration took administrative measures such as temporary suspension of route use applications. The administration continued to well deal with flight slots management and their coordinated allocation in the spirit of fairness and transparency. For the airlines that did not execute flights in accordance with the schedule or those that occupied slots but did not use them, the administration took back or cut down their slots to ensure efficient use of the slot resources.

5. Carrying out in-depth special rectification on flight delays. The administration earnestly intensified special rectification, established on-site duty system for the leaders of the administration and supervision and management bureaus, initiated the flight operation, coordination and command centers in different areas, and established and improved the mechanism of weekly coordination meeting for resident entities and the reporting on the disposition of massive flight delays. It also urged the establishment of a unified information publication mechanism, discharge of principal clearance responsibilities, establishment of clearance prioritization procedures and improvement of ground operations and ATM clearance efficiency. In 2011, due to bad weather conditions at important airports such as Guangzhou Airport, emergency plans for massive flight delays were activated many times. Because the leaders were working at the frontline and follow-up coping actions were timely taken. Though flight delays and passenger holdups occurred several times, they were all handled properly without negative social impact.

民航西南地区管理局

2011年，民航西南地区共安全完成各类飞行116.5万小时、87.4万架次，同比分别增长10.3%和5.4%。各运输机场完成旅客吞吐量9 042万人次，保障起降78万架次，分别比上年增长13.2%和9%。圆满完成了西藏和平解放60周年航空运输保障及春运、两会、世界园艺博览会等航空运输保障任务。

一、安全运行态势保持平稳有序

2011年，管理局全面贯彻持续安全理念。年初与管理局签订安全责任书的单位均实现了安全目标，区内平稳安全态势得到了保证。

（1）着力实施总量调控，确保安全裕度 通过安全保障能力评估，对部分航空公司运行总量和飞机日利用率进行了调减，严格控制了繁忙机场和高原特殊机场日起降架次及高峰小时架次。

（2）狠抓资质能力建设 对区内6 253名飞行人员、维修人员和一线空管人员进行了资质能力评估和技术排查。

（3）不断完善安全管理体系（SMS） 除3家新建机场外，完成了区内所有机场的安全审计；区内所有运输航空公司和4个主要维修基地全部通过了SMS补充运行合格审定；西南空管局及3个分局、19个机场通过了局方组织的空管SMS审核。

（4）安全基础设施得到进一步加强 成都、重庆等干线机场相继实现双跑道运行，综合保障能力显著提高；林芝、迪庆等支线机场助航灯光、仪表着陆系统（ILS）等设施设备明显改善。基于性能的导航（PBN）、广播式自动相关监视（ADS-B）等新技术在高高原机场和复杂航线得到更广泛的应用。

（5）风险控制能力明显增强 对防超时飞行和疲劳作业、加强高高原机场安全运行都采取了行之有效的监管措施，对外来物（FOD）扎伤轮胎、繁忙机场跑道道面巡查不足等问题进行了专项治理。

（6）行业管理不断深化 编制下发了高原机场运行指南；出台了航线航班经营许可评审与监管实施办法；制订了飞行人员流动管理暂行办法、管制员执照管理实施细则、航空情报员执照管理实施细则等规范性文件。

（7）空防安保工作不断加强 全面推进了航空保安管理体系（SeMS）建设，航空保安审计和货运安保专项整治工作取得了明显成效。

二、航空运输市场发展形势良好

管理局积极协调多方单位，多措并举，着力解决空域瓶颈和空管保障问题，有力促进了西南地区运输生产持续快速增长。其中，成都双流机场完成旅客吞吐量2 904万人次，排名上升到全国第5位；重庆江北机场、昆明巫家坝机场旅客吞吐量分别超过了1 900万人次和2 200万人次，排名均位于全国前10位；贵阳龙洞堡机场、拉萨贡嘎机场保持了两位数增长，分别达到734万人次和158万人次。西昌、绵阳等二线城市机场旅客吞吐量均突破50万人次，实现了质的飞跃。

与此同时，航线网络布局不断完善。区内目前已有564条航线，其中港澳台和国际航线82条，较上年增加101条；每周班次为13 151班，较上年增加636班。7月，西藏航空公司正式运行，西藏民航事业有了新的发展。

三、基础设施建设有序推进

全区共完成基础设施建设投资116亿元。区内在建工程项目48个，新建项目21个，竣工验收项目27个。其中，昆明新机场建设工程总投资230亿元，是全国民航第一个按照绿色、环保标准设计的机场，现已基本竣工，即将转场投入试运行；重庆机场第三跑道和东航站区工程奠基，该工程总投资达260亿元，重庆机场将拥有3条跑道，70万平方米航站楼，具有保障年旅客吞吐量4 500万人次的能力。

四、航班大面积延误处置工作取得成效

进一步加强对航班不正常服务工作的监管和指导，积极协调各企事业单位完善制度，落实责任，制定下发了《民航西南地区大面积航班延误应急处置预案》，编制完成了《民航西南地区大面积航班延误应急处置手册》。对大面积航班延误的信息报送、应急值守制度进行了专题培训；建立健全了航班大面积延误新闻发布机制。成都、昆明、贵阳、重庆和拉萨5个大面积航班延误应急处置中心相继建立。针对航班延误后旅客的安置问题，采取与市场准入相挂钩的方式，制订了相应管理办法，督促航空公司认真做好航班延误后的旅客安置工作。此外，还建立了西南地区投诉报告长效制度，各监管局定期上报辖区消费者投诉处置情况及统计数据，共受理旅客投诉122起，均作了妥善处理。

五、应急管理工作扎实推进

2011年，管理局从网络信息安全、航空器事故、航班大面积延误以及反恐、劫炸机空防安全和自然灾害等方面重点强化了应急演练工作，分别在拉萨机场、贵阳机场举办了3次专项应急演练。重新调整了应急工作领导小组成员单位并修订了相关职责，首次将应急管理工作全面系统地纳入到航空安全大检查工作中，大力提升了应急管理水平。

2011年4月25日，民航西南管理局周毅洲局长（左一）陪同四川省政府领导调研成都机场第二跑道运行情况

On April 25, 2011, Zhou Yizhou (first from the left), Director General of CAAC Southwest Regional Administration, Accompany the Leaders of Sichuan Provincial Government to Inspect the Operation of the Second Runway at Chengdu Airport

CAAC Southwest Regional Administration

In 2011, the civil aviation industry in China Southwest region registered a total of 1.165 million hours of safe flights, 874 000 aircraft movements, passenger traffic volume of 90.42 million at all of the transport airports in the region and 780 000 aircraft movements of taking-off and landing, year-on-year increases of 10.3%, 5.4%, 13.2% and 9% respectively. It successful accomplished the air transport support tasks for the celebration of the 60th anniversary of Tibet's peaceful liberation, the Spring Festival, NPC & CPPCC, Xi'an World Horticultural Expo., etc.

I. Stableness in Safe Operation Momentum

In 2011, the administration fully followed the concept of sustained safety and the units which signed safety responsibility contracts with the administration at the beginning of the year all achieved their safety objectives, maintaining a stable and safe operation momentum of the region.

1. Reinforcing control over the total traffic volume to ensure safety margin. Based on evaluation of safe operation capabilities, it adjusted downward the total traffic and aircraft daily utilization rate of some airlines and strictly controlled the daily and peak-hour aircraft movements at busy airports and special plateau airports.

2. Paying close attention to strengthening qualifications and capabilities building. It carried out qualification and technical skills assessments for 6 253 pilots, maintenance staff and air traffic controllers in work.

3. Refining continuously the safety management system (SMS). It completed the safety audits for all the airports in the region, except for the three newly built ones and all the transport airlines and the 4 main maintenance bases within the region passed the SMS supplemental operations certification. The ATM Bureau Southwest and its 3 branches, and 19 airports passed the ATC SMS certification organized by CAAC.

4. Further enhancing the safety infrastructure. Trunk airports including the ones in Chengdu and Chongqing successively introduced dual parallel runway operation, significantly improving the overall traffic support capability. The facilities and equipment at Linzhi, Diqing and other feeder airports, such as flight support lights and instrument landing system (ILS), witnessed significant improvement. New technologies such as performance-based navigation (PBN) and automatic dependent surveillance-broadcast (ADS-B) were widely used at high-altitude plateau airports and on complex air routes.

5. Significant enhancement in risk control capability. The Administration executed effective regulatory measures to avoid overtime flying and fatigue operations, and strengthen the safe operations at high-altitude plateau airports, and carried out special rectifications of the problems such as the puncture of tires by foreign objects debris (FOD), insufficient patrolling on runway pavements at busy airports, etc.

6. In-depth enhancement in industry regulation. The administration developed and issued the Operation Guidance for Plateau Airports, put into use of the Measures on Evaluation and Supervision of Air Routes and Flights Operating Permits, developed several regulatory documents,, including the Interim Measures for Flight Crew Flow Management, the Detailed Rules on the Implementation of ATC Controller License Management and the Detailed Rules on the Implementation of Aeronautical Information Personnel License Management.

7. Continuous consolidation in aviation security. The administration carried out, in full swing, the construction of aviation security management system (SeMS) and made obvious achievements in aviation security audit and specialized rectifications of cargo security.

II. Excellent Development Situation in Air Transport Market

The administration, through positive coordination with various entities and adoption of appropriate measures, strived to deal with the issues in airspace bottleneck and ATC support, effectively promoting the sustained and rapid growth of air transport industry in the southwest. For example, Chengdu Shuangliu Airport handled 29.04 million passengers, ranking No.5 among all the airports nationwide; Chongqing Jiangbei Airport and Kunming Wujiaba Airport handled more than 19 and 22 million passengers respectively, both ranking among the top 10 of all the airports in the country; Guiyang Longdongbao Airport and Lhasa Gonggar Airport both maintained a double-digit growth, handling 7.34 and 1.58 million passengers respectively; passengers handled at airports in second-tier cities such as Xichang and Mianyang all exceeded 500 000, making a big qualitative leap.

At the same time, the route network layout witnessed constant improvement. There are currently 564 air routes in the region, including 82 routes connecting Hong Kong, Macao, Taiwan and overseas cities, an increase of 101 over the previous year. The weekly flights were 13 151, a year-on-year increase of 636. In July, Tibet Airlines officially started its operation, marking a new development in Tibet civil aviation industry.

III. Systematical Progress in Infrastructure Construction

A total of 11.6 billion yuan was invested into infrastructure construction in the whole Southwest region. Within the Region, there were 48 projects under construction, 21 newly constructed and 27 that passed the check and acceptance. A new airport in Kunming, the first environmental friendly airport in China, was invested with a total of 23 billion yuan in its construction and was basically completed and would soon be ferried to put to trial operation. With a total investment of 26 billion yuan, the first stone was laid for the construction projects of the third runway and east terminal area at Chongqing Airport, and upon their completion, Chongqing Airport would have three runways, a terminal building of 700 000 square meters, and the ability to handle 45 million passengers per year.

IV. Achievements in Dealing with Massive Flight Delays

The administration further strengthened its supervision and guidance in handling irregular flights, made actively coordination with various enterprises and institutions to improve their relevant systems and responsibilities implementation, developed and issued the "Contingency Plans for Managing Massive Flight Delays in Southwest Region", and compiled and completed the "Emergency Manual for Managing Massive Flight Delays in Southwest Region". It held thematic trainings on the rules to be followed in message reporting and duty keeping in case of massive flight delays, and established and improved a mechanism for press release in case of massive flight delays. Five massive flight delay emergency response centers were successively set up in Chengdu, Kunming, Guiyang, Chongqing and Lhasa. With respect to the issues of how to take care of passengers affected by flights delays, the administration developed appropriate management approaches and, by way of connection to market entry, urged the airlines to take good care of the passengers affected by flight delays. In addition, it set up in southwest region a long term effective mechanism for complaint reports, requiring supervision and management authorities at various levels to regularly report the actions taken within their jurisdictions according to consumer complaints and relevant statistical data. In 2011, a total of 122 passenger complaints were received and all of them were properly handled.

V. Solid Progress in Emergency Management

In 2011, the administration placed special emphasis on emergency response drills in network and information security, dealing with aircraft accidents, massive flight delays and counter terrorism, aircraft hijacking or bombing, and natural disasters. It held three specialized emergency response drills in Lhasa Airport and Guiyang Airport. The administration also made re-adjustment to the member units of the emergency response leading group and amended their relevant duties, and comprehensively and systematically integrated for the first time the emergency management into the general inspection on aviation safety, promoting greatly the level of emergency management.

民航西藏区局

2011年是建党90周年和西藏和平解放60周年，是民航实施行业“十二五”规划的起步之年，西藏区局深入贯彻落实两级民航工作会议精神，按照年初工作部署，各项工作稳步推进。

西藏和平解放60周年大庆期间，民航局李家祥局长亲临西藏具体指挥专机保障工作

During the Celebration of the 60th Anniversary of Peaceful Liberation of Tibet, Li Jiaxiang, Administrator of CAAC, Visits Tibet in Person to Give Instructions for Supporting Special Flights

一、安全态势总体平稳

深入落实安全责任制，积极开展安全隐患排查治理，认真组织实施“应急演练周”活动，组织完成邦达机场安全审计和阿里机场保安审计工作，扎实推进安全管理系统（SMS）建设，认真开展反思整顿，深入开展安全大检查，查找和消除安全隐患，适时提高响应等级，严格安全检查，加强风险控制，推动持续安全，实现连续保障飞行安全46周年。

二、运输生产快速增长

以加大航空公司引进力度，完善西藏航线网络和机场布局为重点，不断提高民航服务西藏的能力和水平。2011年7月8日，日喀则机场正式通航，区内所有地市均有通航机场的目标初步实现；全年保障航班安全起降16 429架次，完成旅客吞吐量183.1万人次，同比分别增长17.6%、18.9%，旅客吞吐量再创历史新高。

三、服务质量进一步提高

严格落实《民航西藏区局服务质量检查管理办法》，监督检查工作全面开展；深入探讨研究、解决旅客投诉和反映的焦点问题，服务质量管理由事后处理向事前控制转变，旅客认同度进一步提高；航班延误专项整治工作全面开展，大面积航班延误处置工作水平稳步提高，后续服务保障工作进一步加强。2011年，区局航班正常率为85%，无旅客有效投诉。

四、基础设施建设稳步推进

拉萨贡嘎机场飞行区改造，配套工程子项目中的飞行区跑道盖被、站坪扩建、助航灯光改造等项目，拉萨贡嘎机场贵宾室、大门、道路等改扩建工程均已按时完成；昌都、林芝、阿里助航灯光工程，拉萨贡嘎机场航站楼UPS改造，西藏航油配送中心等工程稳步实施；那曲新建机场、拉萨贡嘎机场航管楼迁建等项目的前期工作正在扎实开展。区内机场基础设施更加完善，保障能力进一步增强。

CAAC Tibet Autonomous Region Administration

2011 marks the 90th anniversary of the founding of CPC and the 60th anniversary of the peaceful liberation of Tibet, and is also the first year for the civil aviation industry to carry out the 12th Five-Year Plan. Tibet administration implemented the spirit of CAAC working meetings at the regional and national levels in an in-depth manner, and made smooth progress in all work according to the plan drawn up at the beginning of the year.

I. Overall Safety Situation Kept Stable

The safety responsibility system was executed; hidden safety hazards were investigated and handled actively, and the Week of Emergency Drills was organized and conducted earnestly. The safety audit for Bangda Airport and the security audit for Ali Airport were organized and completed, and the solid construction of the safety management system (SMS) was promoted. Reflections and rectifications were made conscientiously; general safety inspections were earnestly carried out to look for and eliminate the hidden safety hazards. The response level was heightened when needed; security checks were made strictly, and risk control was tightened for sustained safety, and flight safety was supported for the 46th consecutive year.

II. Transportation Growing Rapidly

In order to continuously improve the civil aviation's ability to provide quality services for Tibet, emphasis was placed on redoubling the efforts to introduce airlines and better Tibet route network and the airport layout. On July 8th 2011, Rikaze Airport was officially inaugurated, and the goal that all the cities in Tibet have airports was initially realized. For the whole year, 16 429 aircraft movements were supported with a passenger turnover of 1.831 million, year-on-year increases of 17.6% and 18.9% respectively, and the passenger turnover made a record high.

III. Service Quality Further Improved

The Inspection and Management Approaches of CAAC Tibet Administration for Service Quality was strictly implemented, and oversight and inspections were carried out in an all-round way. In-depth discussions were made to address the main problems that the passengers complained about and pointed out. Service quality management was changed from post-response to pre-control and the passenger satisfaction was further improved. The special rectification for flight delays was fully carried out, with the capacity to handle massive flight delays steadily improved. Follow-up services and support were further enhanced. In 2011, the rate of flight regularity was 85%, and no effective passenger complaints were ever lodged.

IV. Infrastructure Construction Progressing Steadily

The project of the renovation of Lhasa Gonggar Airport movement area and its auxiliary projects, such as the runway pavement, the aircraft apron expansion, and the airfield lighting renovation, and the reconstruction and expansion of Lhasa Gonggar Airport VIP lounge, the gates and the roads were completed as scheduled. Projects of airfield lighting at Changdu, Linzhi and Ali, Airports, the UPS reconstruction at Lhasa Gonggar Airport terminal building, and Tibet aviation fuel distribution center were progressing steadily. The preliminary work of the projects of Naqu new Airport, and the relocation of Lhasa Gonggar Airport ATC building proceeded steadily. Infrastructure at airports in Tibet was better improved, with their support capacity further enhanced.

民航西北地区管理局

2011年，西北地区各机场共保障运输飞行28.7万架次，完成旅客吞吐量3 215.1万人次，货邮吞吐量24.3万吨，同比分别增长11.38%、15.58%、7.91%。西安咸阳机场旅客吞吐量突破2 000万人次，银川机场突破300万人次，西宁机场突破200万人次。截止到2011年底，西北民航持续保证安全210个月，为推动民航强国战略的实施奠定了牢固基础。

一、以落实主体责任为核心，实现行业持续安全

（1）强化体系建设，安全管理进一步规范 管理局结合实际制定《关于加强西北民航安全管理工作的若干措施》，针对突出问题实施行政约见，严格执行安全监管问责、执法交叉检查、手册内审制度。完成固原、玉树、贵州荔波、山东济宁机场以及甘肃、湖北空管分局安全审计。

各单位积极推进安全管理体系（SMS）建设。西北空管局SMS建设取得阶段性成果。西部机场集团建立了安全监察体系，整治突出问题，严格落实领导责任。幸福航空公司通过CCAR-121补充运行合格审定，12家机场使用手册通过SMS审核，东航西安维修基地获得SMS运行批准。

（2）强化资质管理，从业人员能力进一步提高 管理局加强专业人员资质监管，严格按标准核发各类证照，开展飞行、空管、运控、机务等重点岗位人员资质能力专项检查和培训，加强体检合格证管理和职业技能鉴定，开展专业技术人员资质动态管理和新建机场重点岗位人员资质备案。

（3）强化风险管理，安全运行水平进一步提升 努力从源头上防控安全隐患，提高安全管理的针对性和实效性。强化新机场、新公司、新机型、新机长管理，开展机场安全运行、老旧设施设备、危险品运输以及通用航空等专项整治，全面加强不停航施工管理，对新舟60飞机重复性多发故障进行风险分析和系统整改。截至11月底，管理局共实施行政许可3 563项，各类检查3 276次，发现安全问题406项，到期完成整改392项，整改完成率96.55%。

西北空管局在飞行流量持续处于高位、安全压力加大的情况下，及时开展安全整顿，加强现场运行管理和班组资源管理。陕西监管局建立安全提示机制，推动咸阳机场开展地面交通专项整治；甘肃监管局对中川机场飞行区供电问题进行专项督查；宁夏监管局探索飞行培训机构监管工作；青海监管局制订措施，全力确保西宁机场新跑道施工安全和顺利启用。这些工作的开展，提升了安全保障能力，有效地保证了运行安全。

加大空防安全工作力度，加强机场控制区证件、安检人员配备执勤、安保设施配置、货邮安检等环节管理。推进航空安保管理体系建设，对玉树机场实施了国家航空安保审计。加强应急管理工作，修订完善了各类预案，开展航空器搬移、应对大雾天气、中断起飞应急撤离、离港系统以及航油消防等各类专项和综合演练。

（4）强化科技保障，运行环境进一步改善 深化新技术推广应用。全面规划西北地区基于性能的导航（PBN）推广工作，完成西宁、张掖、金昌、格尔木、敦煌机场所需导航性能（RNP）项目验证，辖区具备PBN飞行条件的机场达到7个。引进空客公司等专业力量为咸阳机场设计RNAV程序。西宁—玉树、西宁—格尔木航路9个广播式自动相关监视（ADS-B）设备地面站基本建成。

管制运行环境得到优化。兰州管制区域雷达覆盖范围内的航路、航线全面实施了雷达管制。银川进近管制区正式启用，西安、兰州管制扇区进一步优化，完成WGS-84坐标系转换工作。与地方协商形成联动机制，加强净空保护，建立机场电磁环境保护区，协调解决西安、兰州区域无线电干扰通讯问题，排查自由气球干扰飞行事件。

二、以落实规划为抓手，不断夯实发展基础

（1）完善协调机制，增强发展动力 陕西省成立了民航发展协调工作领导小组；青海省成立了铁路和机场建设协调小组，出台《青海民航运输发展专项资金使用办法》；宁夏自治区出台了《关于加快推进宁夏民航事业发展的若干意见》；甘肃省采取有力措施，加快了机场建设进度。

（2）强化协调部署，枢纽建设初见成效 成立枢纽建设和空域协调领导小组，启动《西安咸阳机场枢纽建设大纲》编制工作，全力推进枢纽建设进程。机场二期工程、油料工程、空管工程同步实施，东航开工建设枢纽配套基础设施。加强空域协调和试飞验证工作，空域协调取得了实质性成果，A380试飞工作圆满完成。机场与航空公司深化战略合作，进一步构建航线航班网络和中转服务体系。

（3）加大工作力度，基本建设稳步推进 2011年完成机场建设投资28亿元，截至11月底到位民航发展基金补贴9.56亿元；争取项目总投资1.45亿元，其中民航发展基金1.43亿元。金昌、张掖机场建成通航，辖区机场增至18个。咸阳机场二期扩建工程、西安区域管制中心工程、西部航路工程进入收尾阶段。西宁机场二期扩建工程新建跑道正式投运。银川机场三期扩建工程奠基，榆林机场扩建工程获总体规划批复，安康机场迁建工程进入立项批复阶段，花土沟机场进入立项评审阶段，汉中城固机场军民合用改扩建工程立项已获批复，府谷机场项目列入民航“十二五”发展规划。完成天水机场迁建以及新建府谷、果洛机场选址评审工作。积极推进延安机场迁建工程，德令哈、陇南、庆阳、兰州机场改扩建工程前期工作。

（4）加强监督引导，通用航空发展迅速 坚持“以点带面、重点突破、稳步发展”的方针，扶持通用航空规范发展。辖区通用航空企业达到11家，通用航空筹建企业达到10家。截至11月底，辖区完成通用航空飞行1.98万架次，同比增长103%，通用航空飞行时间约4 744小时，同比增长34%。

（5）加强适航管理，航空制造、维修业取得新成绩 严格实施新舟60/600飞机审定工作，积极参与ARJ21等国产民机审定，配合FAA对ARJ21进行影子审查；大力支持航空制造业发展，航空制造企业新增生产项目16项。维修单位加大基础设施投入，拓展业务范围，提高维修水平，产值和效益稳步提升。维修培训机构培训能力得到提高。

三、以世园会保障为契机，促进航空运输健康发展

（1）圆满完成世园会航空运输服务保障 管理局提前谋划筹备，统一部署世界园艺博览会运输服务保障工作；西北民航各单位制订专项服务保障方案、服务承诺和安全保障计划；辖区开展“优质服务创品牌，精心保障展风采”服务竞赛活动。通过各单位的共同努力，西北民航为世界园艺博览会提供了优质的航空运输服务，取得了零差错、零投诉、零事故的优异成绩。

（2）航空服务品质得到改善 加大航班大面积延误整治力度，成立了西北地区航班运行协调指挥中心，定期召开航班延误联席会议。制订了航班延误应急处置十条措施和咸阳机场航班放行排序规则。落实领导值班制度，组织开展交叉检查，实行限时整改，提升服务质量和运行品质。西北空管局建立航班延误通报协调机制，机场、航空公司和服务保障单位细化完善了服务保障和应急处置措施。圆满完成了“两会”代表运输、春运、暑运、朝觐包机等重大运输保障任务。

（3）航空运输市场更加繁荣 完善审核许可机制，定期召开航空运输（通用航空）委员会会议，按照公正、公开、透明的原则，做好航线航班时刻管理工作。提高航班时刻资源利用率，对航班执行率低于50%的6家航空公司进行了通报，取消了7家航空公司的12条航线航班。新增通航点23个，新进、新开冬春航季航线24条，夏秋航季航线31条。争取民航局补贴，支持支线航空发展，截至11月底，到位支线航空补贴8 170万元，中小机场补贴1.07亿元。宁夏机场公司开通银川—昆明—迪拜航线，国际航线业务取得新突破。青海机场公司充分运用青海省民航运输发展专项资金，加大航线航班开辟力度。甘肃机场集团争取地方补贴，推进包机合作，生产经营取得新进步。

CAAC Northwest Regional Administration

In 2011, the airports under the jurisdiction of CAAC Northwest Regional Administration supported 287 thousand transport flights, witnessed a passenger traffic volume of 32.151 million person, and cargo and mail turnover of 243 thousand tons, representing year-on-year increases of 11.38%, 15.58% and 7.91%. The passenger traffic at Xi'an Xianyang International Airport exceeded 20 million, Yinchuan Airport 3 million and Xining Airport 2 million. By the end of 2011, the safety of civil aviation industry at the northwest region had maintained for 210 consecutive months, laying a solid foundation for building China into a country with a strong civil aviation industry.

I. Focusing on the Implementation of Principal Responsibilities to Achieve Sustained Safety of the Industry

1. Strengthening system building and further standardizing the safety management. The administration developed, in light of reality, the Measures on Strengthening the Aviation Safety Management in the Northwest Region of China, instituted administrative summoning for prominent problems, strictly carried out safety supervision accountability, cross law enforcement and internal auditing system of safety manuals. It fulfilled safety audit for Guyuan,

2011年5月24日，民航局与宁夏回族自治区人民政府签署了《加快推进宁夏民航发展会谈纪要》

On May 24, 2011, CAAC and the Government of Ningxia Hui Autonomous Region Sign Minutes of Talks on Spurring Civil Aviation Development in Ningxia

Yushu, Guizhou Libo and Shandong Jining Airports and air traffic management sub-bureaus in Gansu and Hubei provinces.

Entities under its jurisdiction actively pressed ahead with the building of Safety management system (SMS). Periodic progress was made in SMS building by the sub-bureau of air traffic management of northwest region. China West Airport Group established safety supervision system to rectify prominent problems and strictly put into effect the responsibilities. Joy Air passed the supplemental operation certification of CCAR Part 121, operation manuals of 12 airports passed SMS review and Xi'an maintenance base of China Eastern Airlines received SMS operation approval.

2. Strengthening qualification management and further improving the capabilities of the staff. The administration reinforced the supervision and management of the qualifications of professionals, strictly issued various certificates in accordance with standards, launched special inspections and training on the qualifications and capabilities of personnel at key posts of flight, air traffic management, operation control and maintenance, enhanced the certificate management for physical examination and professional skill appraisal, carried out a dynamic management of professional technicians and the personnel qualification archiving for the key positions in the newly- built airports.

3. Strengthening risks management and further promoting safe operation level. Efforts were made at the sources to prevent and control hidden safety hazards and to make safety management more targeted and more practical. The administration reinforced the management of the new airports, new companies, new aircraft types and pilots-in-command, carried out special rectifications of airport operational safety, old and obsolete equipment, transport of dangerous goods, general aviation, etc., reinforced in an all-round way the management for engineering works without suspension of flights, and carried out risks analysis and system rectification for repeating and frequency failures of MA60. By the end of November, the administration had implemented 3 563 administrative permits and 3 276 various checks, and detected 406 problems, having 392 rectified, with a rectification rate of 96.55%.

Under the backdrop of high-level air traffic volume and increased pressure on safety, the northwest sub-bureau of air traffic management timely carried out safety rectification to enhance on-site operation management and work teams and shifts management; Shaanxi Safety Supervision and Management Bureau established an alerting mechanism for safety and urged Xianyang Airport to carry out airport ground traffic rectification; Gansu Safety Supervision and Management Bureau exercised special supervisions over movement area supply power problems at Zhongchuan Airport; Ningxia Safety Supervision and Management Bureau explored the ways of carrying out supervision work over flight training institutions; and Qinghai Safety Supervision and Management Bureau laid down measures to fully ensure the construction safety and smooth operation of the newly-built runway at Xining Airport. The implementation of all that uplifted the safety support capabilities and effectively ensured the operation safety.

The administration also intensified its aviation security work by enhancing the management of certificates of the controlled areas, the placement of security check personnel, the allocation of security check facilities and the security checks of cargo and mails. It pressed ahead with the aviation security management system building and carried out national aviation security audit at Yushu Airport. The administration strengthened the emergency response management, amended and refined various reserve plans, conducted special and comprehensive drills and rehearsals of aircraft relocation, responses to thick fog weather conditions, aborted take-off emergent evacuation, departure system and fire-fighting of the aviation fuel.

4. Strengthening scientific and technological support and further improving the operation environment. The administration deepened the applications of new technology. It planned in an all-round way the promotion of the performance-based navigation (PBN) in the northwest region of China and completed the PBN projects validations in Xining, Zhangye, Jinchang, Geermu and Dunhuang airports, having the number of airports under its jurisdiction capable of PBN reach to 7. Professional enterprises such as Airbus were introduced to design RNAV procedures for Xianyang Airport. 9 ADS-B ground stations on Xining-Yushu and Xining-Geermu routes were basically built.

The administration optimized its air traffic control operational environment. Radar control was comprehensively implemented on the routes within the coverage of radar in Lanzhou control area, the approach air traffic control area in Yinchuan was put into effect officially, the control sectors in Xi'an and Lanzhou were further optimized, and the transition to the WGS-84 coordinates was completed. The joint reaction mechanism of consultation with the local authorities was formed to reinforce the clearance protection. The electromagnetic protection areas in the airports were established and the radio communication interferences in Xi'an and Lanzhou areas were addressed through coordinating. The administration also made investigations on the interferences of flights by free balloons.

II. Holding Tight to the Grip of Plan Implementation to Constantly Reconsolidate the Bases of Development

1. Improving coordination mechanism to spur development. Shaanxi Province established the steering group for the coordinated development of civil aviation. Qinghai Province established the coordination group for the railway and airport construction and established the Methods for the Use of Special Fund of Civil Aviation Development in Qinghai. Ningxia Autonomous Region made the Suggestions on Accelerating Civil Aviation Development in Ningxia. Gansu Province took forceful measures to speed up airport construction.

2. Strengthening coordinated deployment with the effects of hub building gradually revealing. The leading group for hub building and airspace coordination was established, and the development of the Outline for the Hub Building of Xi'an Xianyang Airport was initiated to fully press ahead with the hub building. The second phase project of the airport, fuel facility project and air traffic control project were executed simultaneously, and China Eastern Airlines started the construction of supporting facilities of the hub. Airspace coordination and test flight verification were reinforced, making tangible progress in airspace coordination and a complete success in the test flight of A380. Airports deepened their cooperation with airlines, further building the routes and flights network and transit service system.

3. Making more efforts to steadily promote infrastructural construction. In 2011, a total investment of 2.8 billion yuan was accomplished, and by the end of November, 956 million yuan coming from the civil aviation fund had been appropriated as the subsidy. The investment for its garnered projects had reached 145 million yuan in which 143 million yuan was from civil aviation development fund. Jinchang and Zhangye airports had been built up and opened to air service, having the number of airports under its jurisdiction reach to 18. The second phase expansion project of Xianyang Airport, the project of area control center of Xi'an and air route projects in the west had been ushered into the concluding phase. The newly built runway in the second phase expansion project of Xining Airport had become officially operational. The foundations had been laid for the third phase expansion project of Yinchuan Airport and the expansion project plan for Yulin Airport had been approved. The relocation of Ankang Airport had been in the project filing and approval phase and Huatugou Airport had been in the project filing and assessment phase. The filing of civil-military reconstruction project of Chenggu Airport in Hanzhong had been approved and Fugu Airport project had been incorporated into the 12th Five-Year Plan for civil aviation development. The assessment of the relocation of Tianshui Airport and the locations selection of newly-built Fugu and Guoluo airports had been completed. Active efforts were made in the removal and construction project of Yan'an Airport, and in the reconstruction and expansion projects in Delingha, Longnan, Qingyang and Lanzhou airports.

4. Strengthening supervision and guidance to promote rapid development of general aviation. Persisting in the guideline of "taking individual points as the examples to promote the overall development, making breakthroughs in key points and pursuing steady development", the administration supported the general aviation to develop in a standardized way. There were 11 general aviation enterprises altogether under its jurisdiction and those under preparation for establishment reached 10. By the end of November, there had been 19.8 thousand aircraft movements for general aviation under its jurisdiction, increasing by 103% over that of the previous year and the flight hours stood at 4 744, increasing by 34% over that of the previous year.

5. Strengthening airworthiness management and making fresh progress in aeronautic manufacturing and maintenance sectors. The administration implemented strictly the examination and approval of MA60/600 aircraft, actively engaged in the examination and approval work of China-made civil aircraft such as ARJ21 and coordinated with FAA to conduct the shadow examination of ARJ21. It rendered strong support for the development of the aeronautic manufacturing industry, having 16 new production projects added to the manufacturing enterprises. The maintenance entities reinforced their infrastructural input, having their service scope expanded, maintenance level enhanced and the production value and profits steadily increased. The training capabilities of the maintenance training entities were also enhanced.

III. Taking the Opportunity of Xi'an International Horticultural Expo. to Promote Sound Development of the Air Transport Industry

1. Successfully accomplishing the tasks of air transport for the International Horticultural Expo. The administration made early plans and preparations to unitarily arrange the air transport support for the International Horticultural Expo. The civil aviation entities in the northwest region developed thematic support programs, service promises and security supporting plans. Within the jurisdiction of the administration, a service competition of "establishing the brand by high quality services and showing the image by detailed support" was carried out. Thanks to the joint efforts, the civil aviation in the northwest region provided, with no errors, no complaints and no accidents, high-quality air transport services for the International Horticultural Expo. and made outstanding progress.

2. Having air service quality improved. The administration made vigorous efforts to tackle large scale flight delays and established flight operation coordination and commanding center to regularly convene joint meetings to address flight delays. It established 10 emergency handling measures on addressing flight delays and the release and reordering rules of flights for Xianyang Airport. It implemented the leaders-on-duty system, organized cross inspections and conducted time-limit rectification, thus improving the service and operation quality. The sub-bureaus of air traffic management in the northwest region instituted a notification and coordination mechanism for flight delays, and airports, airlines and service supporting entities refined and improved their service support and emergency handling measures. The administration made complete success in the major transport support tasks for the NPC and CPPCC sessions, the Spring Festival, summer holidays and pilgrims.

3. The air transport market becoming more prosperous. The administration improved its review and approval mechanism, regularly convened the air transport (general aviation) committee meetings and, in accordance with the principle of being fair, open and transparent, did a good job with regard to flight and slot management. It improved the utilization rate of flight slots, gave warning notifications to 6 airlines whose execution of the flight slots allocated were below 50% and canceled 12 flight routes of 7 airlines. 23 new points started air services, 24 winter and spring seasons routes and 31 summer and autumn seasons routes were added. It made efforts to obtain the subsidy from CAAC to develop its feeder aviation and by the end of November, 81.70 million yuan had been appropriated to feeder line flights and 107 million yuan to small and medium sized airports. Ningxia Airport Company launched flight of Yinchuan-Kunming-Dubai, making a breakthrough in launching international flights. Qinghai Airport Company made full use of the special fund for civil aviation development and endeavored to open new routes. Gansu Airport Group tried to obtain local government subsidy to promote charter flight cooperation, thus making new progress in its operation.

民航新疆管理局

2011年是《关于加快推进新疆民航跨越式发展的会谈纪要》（简称《会谈纪要》）在新疆民航的落实年。管理局全力推进新疆民航持续安全、跨越发展，各方面工作取得了新的成绩，作出了新的贡献。

一、加强安全管理，保持安全态势平稳

2011年，新疆民航各单位积极实施“持续安全”战略，大力推进安全管理体系（SMS）建设，努力提升安全运行品质，全年未发生人为原因的运输航空事故征候，实现了运输飞行和空防安全57周年。安全基础工作进一步加强，安全普查数据系统基本建立。完成ATR72飞机退役和E190飞机的引进。哈密、鄯善雷达等一批空管设施陆续投入使用，乌鲁木齐进近实施了雷达管制。完成辖区首次所需导航性能（RNP）飞行程序实地试飞工作，南航股份新疆分公司B737-NG系列机型通过所需导航性能—进近（RNP APCH）补充运行合格审定演示验证。

空防安全工作抓紧抓实。根据周边地区社会形势，及时、相应地调整空防安全预警。2011年6月29日起，全疆机场启动并常态化实施候机楼入口处防爆检查措施，机场安检工作得到了中央领导和相关部委的高度评价。确保了博览会期间空防安全和治安形势总体平稳。完成和田、喀什等5个支线机场安防设施改造项目。深入开展“大排查、大整治”、航空货运安保、打击托运行李和货物盗窃等专项行动。航空安保管理体系（SeMS）建设扎实推进，《新疆民航航空安全保卫工作“十二五”规划》编制完成。安全监管工作扎实有效。

阿克苏运行办挂牌运行，喀什监管局筹划成立。出台了重大安全隐患挂牌督办、行政约见等制度规范。综合运用行政检查、安全督察、专项整治、保障能力评估、行政约见、限制运行等多种手段和措施，增强安全监管效能。

二、抓机遇谋发展，推进《会谈纪要》落实

领导小组成功召开第一次会议，协调落实《会谈

2011年10月25日，新疆局局长许浩赴阿克苏机场调研

On October 25, 2011, Xu Hao, Director General of CAAC Xinjiang Administration, Makes a Field Trip to Akesu Airport

纪要》。自治区、民航局共商新疆民航发展大计，在各个方面给予积极支持，提供有利条件，共同支持和引导新疆民航科学发展，推动《会谈纪要》落实。

民航助力地方发展达成共识。管理局赴伊犁、乌鲁木齐、哈密、阿克苏、喀什、和田等地调研，加强与各地（州）的沟通联系，形成发展合力；伊犁州加大伊宁机场改扩建工程建设投入力度，哈密地区加快筹建“临空产业园区”，阿克苏、和田地区投资建设机场周边相关市政配套设施，喀什地区依托空港优势建设辐射周边的商贸物流基地。

新疆民航各单位积极推进项目落实。行业文化试点初见成效，辖区文化建设呈现出多层次、多样性繁荣发展的局面；南航股份新疆分公司、海航股份新疆分公司以开辟国际航线为重点，强化乌鲁木齐枢纽建设；《新疆空管跨越式发展建设项目预可行性研究报告》通过论证；南疆航油应急保障储运工程建设有序开展，并签署了《关于国家战略物资新疆喀什储备基地合作建设会议纪要》。

三、加快项目进程，完善基础设施建设

基础设施建设取得新进展。完成固定资产投资约2.7亿元。机场、空管、管理局等各类续建项目15项，新开工项目10项。“十二五”规划和《会谈纪要》重点工程项目稳步推进。乌鲁木齐国际机场四期改扩建等疆内重点项目进入前期阶段。库车机场完成行业验收，飞行区投入使用。民航新疆应急指挥中心项目施工进展顺利，完成主体建设。乌鲁木齐空管自动化测试平台、乌鲁木齐进近管制区配套工程等项目启动。乌鲁木齐管制区VHF遥控通信系统工程等项目竣工验收。上报富蕴、且末机场预可研初审意见和民航新疆行业文化交流中心、空防安保训练基地立项（代可研）报告。会同自治区发改委初审了哈密机场改扩建、轮台塔中机场工程项目。完成了2010年中小机场运营资金补贴454万元，支线航空补贴9 130万元，基本建设贷款贴息112万元。

四、积极营造发展环境，航空市场增长强劲

全疆机场完成旅客吞吐量1 422万人次、货邮吞吐量11.6万吨、运输起降14.9万架次，同比分别增长21.6%、14.7%、21.7%。乌鲁木齐国际机场旅客吞吐量突破1 000万人次大关，迈入全国千万级大型机场行列。

乌鲁木齐国际机场西部门户枢纽机场已具雏形。通过开展专题调研，并向自治区、民航局上报调研报告以及开放第五航权的请示，开通国际航班旅客快速过站区，有效减少过站旅客的通关时间等方式，逐步增强乌鲁木齐机场各项服务保障功能。

以乌鲁木齐区域性枢纽机场为核心的航线网络布局日益完善形成。新开北京—乌鲁木齐—伊斯坦布尔等3条国际航线和南京—乌鲁木齐—伊宁等4条对口援疆直达航线；在新疆航空市场运营定期航班的航空公司达到29家，其中，国内16家、国际13家，运营支线公司达到9家；乌鲁木齐国际机场实际运营航线141条，其中，国内航线105条（含疆内17条）、国际航线36条，开通直达援疆航线10条；有21个国家、31个国际城市和52个国内城市与乌鲁木齐通航。

加强航班正常和服务保障工作。修订了《新疆民航乌鲁木齐机场航班延误应急处置工作手册》，完善航班运行管理，加强领导现场值班，在辖区各单位的共同努力下，较为妥善地做好了乌鲁木齐国际机场大面积航班延误的应急处置工作。

航班时刻管理更加科学。修订了《新疆民航航班时刻管理细则》，制定了《民航新疆管理局航权和航班时刻资源分配会签制度》，清理了5 881个航班时刻，对5 280个航班时刻给予警告，确保了资源分配的公开透明和有效使用。

做好重大航空运输保障工作。圆满完成了首届中国—亚欧博览会、从利比亚撤离我国公民、朝觐、第二届新疆国际民族舞蹈节等重大保障任务。

通用航空稳步发展。通用航空完成生产作业飞行7 267小时，起飞10 447架次（其中教学训练2 755小时，起飞7 848架次），同比分别增长29.4%、185%，保持了较快增长。成立了新疆天翼直升机航空有限公司、新疆水电设计研究院疆海测绘院航测飞行中心、和静汗戈尔迪航空草原俱乐部。通航企业经营范围不断拓展，运行品质不断提升，经济社会效益进一步提高。

CAAC Xinjiang Administration

2011 was the year for Xinjiang civil aviation industry to implement the Minutes of Talks on Accelerating the Leaps-forward Development of Xinjiang Civil Aviation (hereinafter referred to as the Minutes). The administration made new contributions to fully promoting sustained safety and leaps-forward development for Xinjiang civil aviation, and made new achievements in all aspects of work.

I. Strengthening Safety Management to Maintain the Stableness of Safe Operation

In 2011, all the units in Xinjiang civil aviation industry actively implemented the strategy of "sustained safety" and vigorously promoted the construction of safety management system (SMS) in an effort to enhance the quality of safe operations. There occurred no human-factor-induced air transport incidents the whole year, thus laying a solid foundation for ensuring air transport safety and aviation security for 57 years. The administration further strengthened its basic safety-related work and established its safety comprehensive survey data system on the whole. Tasks related to the retirement of ATR72 aircraft and the introduction of E190 aircraft were completed. A series of ATC facilities like radars were successively put into operation at airports in such cities as Hami and Shanshan, and radar approach control system was introduced at Urumqi Airport. The first field test within the administration's jurisdiction for required navigation performance (RNP) flight procedures was completed and B737-NG series aircraft owned by Xinjiang Branch of China Southern Airlines successfully conducted demonstration flights for the required navigation performance-approach (RNP APCH) supplemental operation certification.

Intensive efforts were made in ensuring aviation security. In light of the situation in the surrounding areas, relevant adjustment was made to the early aviation security warning system in a timely manner. From June 29 2011, all the airports in Xinjiang put into effect explosives inspection measures at the entrance of the terminal buildings, while the work done in airport security checks was highly praised by leaders of the State and relevant ministries. Aviation security and stable social order were ensured during the Exposition. The reconstruction projects of the aviation security facilities at the 5 feeder line airports including the ones in Hetian and Kashi were completed. Specialized rectifications were carried out to conduct "large-scale investigation and rectification", ensure air cargo transport security, and crack down on checked baggage and cargo theft. The establishment of an aviation security management system (SeMS) was pushed forward solidly, and the 12th Five-Year Plan for Ensuring Civil Aviation Security in Xinjiang was developed. Safety supervision was solid and effective.

The Aksu Operation Control Office started its operation, and a plan was made to set up a regulatory authority in Kashi. Regulatory documents were issued, dealing with the supervision of the handling of the significant safety hidden hazards and with administrative appointments. To increase safety supervision effectiveness, efforts were made in the comprehensive application of various means and measures such as administrative inspections, safety supervisions, specialized rectifications, support capacity assessments, administrative appointments and operation restrictions.

II. Seizing Development Opportunities and Pushing Ahead with the Implementation of the "Minutes"

The leading group successfully held its first meeting to coordinate the implementation of the Minutes. To promote the implementation of the Minutes, the autonomous region government and CAAC jointly discussed development strategies for Xinjiang civil aviation, actively furnished all-round support and provided favorable conditions to jointly support and guide the scientific development of Xinjiang civil aviation.

A consensus was reached that civil aviation industry would

boost local development. The administration conducted field trips in such cities as Yili, Urumqi, Hami, Akesu, Kashi and Hetain in an effort to strengthen communication and contacts with the different regions (prefectures) and make joint efforts for future development. Yili Prefecture increased its investment into the renovation and expansion construction project of Yining Airport, Hami accelerated the preparatory work for the Airport Industrial Park construction, Akesu and Hetian invested into the construction of the relevant municipal supporting facilities around the airports, and Kashi built a trade and logistics base by taking full advantage of its proximity to the airport.

All the units in Xinjiang Civil Aviation industry made energetic efforts to push forward projects implementation. Initial results were shown in the trial efforts to shape up an industry culture, and the cultural construction within the jurisdiction showed a promising scenario featuring multi-leveled and diversified development. Xinjiang Branch of China Southern Airlines and Xinjiang Branch of Hainan Airlines reinforced, by focusing on opening up international routes, the construction of Urumqi Airport into a hub airport. The Pre-feasibility Study on the ATC Infrastructure Construction Projects to Meet Leaps-forward Aviation Development was approved, the construction project of the storage and transportation facilities used for providing emergency aviation fuel support in South Xinjiang was systematically executed, and the Minutes of Talks on the Cooperative Construction of a National Strategic Materials Reserve Base in Xinjiang Kashi was signed.

III. Accelerating Infrastructure Construction Projects Execution

New progress was made in infrastructure construction. About 270 million yuan was invested in fixed assets. There were 15 ongoing projects and 10 new projects owned by such entities as airports, ATM bureaus and the administration. The key construction projects listed in the 12th Five-Year Plan and the Minutes witnessed steady progress, and the key projects within Xinjiang such as the 4th phase of the Urumqi International Airport renovation and expansion project also started. Kuche Airport passed acceptance inspection and its movement area was put into use. With the main body already completed, the construction project of Xinjiang civil aviation emergency command center progressed smoothly. Projects such as the construction of Urumqi Airport ATC automatic system test platform and of supporting facilities in Urumqi approach control area started. Projects such as the construction of a remote VHF communication system in Urumqi ATC area were completed and passed acceptance inspection. The preliminary reports based on the review of the pre-feasibility study on construction of Airports in Fuyun and Qiemo and the project feasibility reports on the construction of a cultural exchange center for Xinjiang Civil Aviation industry and of an aviation security training base were submitted. Preliminary examinations were conducted, in conjunction with the Autonomous Regional Development and Reform Commission, on the renovation and expansion project of Hami Airport and the construction project of Luntai Tazhong Airport. In 2010, a total of 4.54 million yuan was allocated as capital subsidies to small and medium-sized airports, 91.3 million yuan to the feeder line aviation and 1.12 million yuan of discount-interest loans to the infrastructure construction.

IV. Actively Creating Development Environment and Aviation Market Growing Strongly

Airports in Xinjiang handled a total of 14.22 million passengers, 116 000 tons of cargo and mail, and 149 000 aircraft movements, with a year-on-year increase of 21.6%, 14.7% and 21.7% respectively. The number of passengers handled at Urumqi International Airport exceeded 10 million, becoming one of the domestic large-scale airports with annual handling capacity of ten million passengers.

Urumqi International Airport as a hub airport in Western China was taking shape. By means of carrying out special investigations, submitting investigation report to the Autonomous Regional Government and CAAC, applying for the grant of the fifth traffic rights, opening express transit areas for international passengers, and effectively cutting the time for customs clearance of transit passengers, Urumqi Airport's service support capabilities were gradually strengthened.

An air route network centered on Urumqi Airport, a regional hub, was gradually formed. 3 international routes including

Beijing-Urumqi-Istanbul, and 4 direct routes serving the purpose of delivering support to Xinjiang including Nanjing-Urumqi-Yining were newly opened. The number of airlines operating scheduled flights in Xinjiang aviation market reached 29, 16 of which were domestic airlines and 13 were international ones, and 9 were feeder line airlines. There were currently 141 routes connecting Urumqi International Airport, 105 of which were domestic ones (including 17 operating within Xinjiang), 36 were international ones, and 10 were direct routes delivering support to Xinjiang. There were 21 countries, 31 international cities and 52 domestic cities providing air service to Urumqi.

The administration reinforced its flight regularity rate and service support work. It amended the Working Manual on Emergency Handling of Flight Delays at Urumqi Airport, improved its flight operation management, enhanced the policy of requiring leaders to carry out field duties and with the joint efforts of all the units within the its jurisdiction, did an excellent job in dealing with the massive flight delays at Urumqi International Airport.

More scientific management was realized on flight schedule. It amended the Detailed Rules on Xinjiang Civil Aviation Flight Slots Management, developed Countersigning System Concerning the Allocation by CAAC Xinjiang Administration of Air Traffic Rights and Flight Slots Resources and cancelled 5 881 flight slots and sent warnings to 5 280 flight slots, ensuring the openness, transparency and efficiency of the resource allocation.

A good job was done in air transport support. It successfully accomplished a series of significant air transport support tasks such as the first China-Eurasia Expo, evacuating Chinese compatriots from Libya, making pilgrimage tours, and the 2nd Xinjiang International Folk Dance Festival.

Steady development was made in general aviation industry, the general aviation in Xinjiang witnessed a completion of 7 267 hours of flight operations and 10 447 take-offs (including 2 755 hours and 7 848 take-offs for instruction and training), rapid year-on-year increases of 29.4% and 185% respectively. Xinjiang Tianyi Helicopter Aviation Co., Ltd., Aerial Survey Flights Center of Xinjiang Surveying and Mapping Institute under Xinjiang Water Resources and Hydropower Survey and Design Institute, and Hejing Khan Geerdi Aviation Prairie Club were set up. General aviation enterprises continued to expand their business scope and upgrade their operating quality, further improving the economic and social benefits.

撤侨——归国同胞们兴奋之情溢于言表

Evacuation of Overseas Chinese Compatriots-the Happy Fellow Countrymen

中国民航大学

一、贯彻落实学校“十二五”规划，成功举办建校60周年庆典

2011年，中国民航大学（以下简称学校）依据民航局和天津市“十二五”规划，在广泛征求意见基础上，制定完成了学校“十二五”事业发展规划，并召开多次专题会议，对规划的实施进行部署。2011年9月17日，学校举行建校60周年庆典，中共中央政治局委员、国务院副总理张德江亲临大会并发表重要讲话，对学校60年的办学成就给予充分肯定，并对学校发展提出了殷切的期望，使学校的社会影响力、知名度和美誉度得到进一步提升。

二、推进人才培养模式改革加强特色专业建设

国家教育部批准学校为第二批“卓越工程师教育培养计划”试点院校。中欧航空工程师学院以及飞行器动力工程、交通运输、飞行技术、电子信息工程专业列入试点。学校在民航局组织下开展了大工程观理念下的教学改革。与华北空管局开展提高管制学员工程实践能力改革试点工作。根据市场需要，增设了民航空中安全保卫专业。加强飞行训练基地建设，朝阳飞行学院获得CCAR-141部正式运行审定合格证书，新接收钻石系列单双发训练飞机16架，机队规模达到28架，完成飞行训练教学8 088小时，安全起飞

2011年9月17日，中国民航大学建校60周年庆祝大会隆重举行

On September 17, 2011, CAUC Held Its 60th Anniversary Celebration

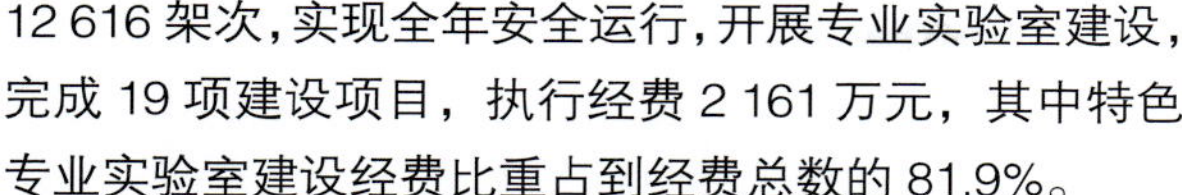
12 616 架次，实现全年安全运行，开展专业实验室建设，完成 19 项建设项目，执行经费 2 161 万元，其中特色专业实验室建设经费比重占到经费总数的 81.9%。

三、加大重点领域科技创新力度，提高科技产业化能力

学校增强对接行业发展战略意识，科技立项与科研成果显著，获批各类纵向科研项目 67 项，其中，国家级各类科研项目获批 27 项、省部级获批 40 项，全年度科研项目到款总经费 6 600 万元，获得天津市科学技术二等奖 1 项、三等奖 1 项、中国民航科技奖 8 项，申请专利 70 项、软件登记 1 项、授权专利 34 项，完成民航机务工程研究基地、地面特种设备研究基地、空中交通管理研究基地、经济运输与管理研究基地验收工作，成立了“民航空管研究院”，参与国家“大飞机”重大项目和“十二五”民航空管支撑计划指南及“北斗二代在民航空管的应用”指南的编写工作。成立了“节能减排研究推广中心”，承担民航局节能减排多项具体工作和气候对外谈判技术支持工作。组织召开了第 13 届中国科协年会第 22 分会场“中国通用航空发展研讨会”，民航科技产业化基地获批为天津市第一批科技企业孵化器。

四、加大人才引进与培养力度，师资队伍整体水平进一步提升

学校广泛宣传，引进教师 73 人，其中海外留学归国人员 1 名，教授 1 名，博士 38 人，学校选派 97 人次教师赴国外大学、科研机构、民航企事业单位进行学术交流或培训考察，筹集 150 万元用于机务、空管、飞行、机场等特色教师的培养。充分利用工程训练中心等校内培训机构加大对民航特色专业教师的培训，53 名教师到民航企业事业单位进行实践，有 119 名民航特有专业教师参加了各项专题培训。通过制度建设、专题培训、干部互相挂职交流，提升学生工作干部整体水平和工作能力，有 58 人次学生工作干部参加各项专题培训，有 17 人参与挂职锻炼。

五、推进国际化、开放式办学，加强与国内外行业组织的合作与交流

学校中欧航空工程师学院的办学模式受到民航局领导高度评价。目前，学院已进入工程师教育阶段，成功召开第四次中欧航空工程师学院执行委员会，依托中欧航空工程师学院项目，积极争取国外优质资源，提升重点领域综合实力。经过积极努力，学校与法方合作成功申报了飞行员培养、空管与机场两个欧盟援华项目，将使我校飞行和空管专业的人才培养水平得到很大提升。加强与国内民航业和航空工业单位的合作，与云南机场集团共建云南民航工程技术中心，与东航武汉公司签署全面战略合作框架协议，与中国商飞公司签订战略合作协议，共同建设“民用航空器适航技术研究基地”和“民用飞机客户服务支持与技术研究中心”，推动与中航工业共同实施的每年 1 000 万元产学研项目的申报和落实。

六、深化内部管理体制改革，管理效能和公共服务体系建设不断加强

学校稳步推进内部管理体制和人事制度改革，简政放权，重心下移，提高管理效率，完成新一轮人事分配制度改革方案的制订，并已顺利推行。完成学校定编和事业单位岗位设置改革工作，组织开展新一聘期的全校教职员工的聘任工作，规范财务制度，出台《中国民航大学会计委派实施细则》。航大中天科技发展有限公司和天津杰普逊国际飞行学院有限公司已派入会计主管并开始相应工作。推进学校“三期工程”项目建设进度，北院 24 号学生公寓、朝阳飞行学院 1 号学生宿舍楼、中欧航空工程师学院楼、乘务飞行楼、北院浴室、游泳馆建成并投入使用，图书馆印刷与电子出版物总量达到 150 万册（件），电子图书达到 143 万册，数据库达到 70 个，完成校园网核心设备升级万兆项目规划，完成后勤公司独立法人的改制工作。

七、推进大学生全面发展，学生综合能力和整体素质不断提升

通过开展以“立德树人”为核心的思想政治教育，培养学生的责任感和使命感，树立大学生勇于担当、乐于奉献的时代精神。学校创建学工微博，利用“微教育”平台，交流研讨职业生涯规划、重大事件和时政热点等话题，实施大学生素质拓展计划，开展丰富多彩的校园文化活动，全面提升学生的综合素质；通过开展科技立项工程、波音创新基金项目，加强科技创新能力的培养，在第十一届“挑战杯”中，荣获特等奖 1 项，一等奖 3 项，二等奖 6 项。

Civil Aviation University of China

I. Implementing the 12th Five-Year Plan of the University and Successfully Holding Its 60th Anniversary Celebration

In 2011, according to the 12th Five-Year Plans of CAAC and Tianjin Municipality and basing on extensive suggestion solicitations, Civil Aviation University of China (shortened as the university) formulated its own 12th Five-Year Plan for development. It held many thematic seminars to make arrangements for implementation of its plan. On September 17, 2011, the university held its 60th anniversary celebration. Zhang Dejiang, member of the Political Bureau of the CPC Central Committee and Vice Premier of the State Council, attended the celebration and made an important speech. He fully confirmed achievements made by the university over the past 60 years and expressed his sincere hope for development of the university. His attendance uplifted the University's social influence, prestige and reputation.

II. Stepping Up the Reform of Talents Training Pattern and Strengthening the Building of Featured Specialties

The university was selected as the pilot university in the second batch of Outstanding Engineers Education and Cultivation Plan by the Ministry of Education. Sino-European Institute of Aviation Engineers and specialties such as spacecraft power engineering, traffic/transport, flight technologies, electronic and information engineering were selected as pilot projects. Under the organization of CAAC, the university launched teaching reform with mega engineering concept. The university worked in tandem with ATMB North China in carrying out the reform pilot work to improve practical engineering capabilities of controller students. In light of market needs, specialty of civil aviation airborne security was added. Efforts were made to reinforce flight training base building. Chaoyang Flight Institute received qualification certificate for formal operation under CCAR Part 141 and bought 16 Diamond series single engine and double engine training aircraft, with its fleet scale up to 28 aircraft. The university completed 8 088 hours of flight training with safe movements of 12 616 flights, having safe operation for the whole year. It carried out specialized lab building and completed 19 building projects with a spending of 21.61 million yuan, among which 81.9% was on featured specialty labs.

III. Making More Efforts in Scientific and Technological Innovation in Key Fields and Enhancing Industrialization of Science and Technology

The university enhanced its strategic awareness of butt-joint industry development and made notable progress in scientific and technological project approval and scientific research outcome, having 67 vertical research projects of all kinds approved, among which 27 were approved at the state level and 40 at the provincial and ministerial levels. Scientific research fund in place annually totaled 66 million yuan. The university garnered 1 second prize and 1 third prize of Tianjin Municipal Scientific and Technological Progress Award, and 8 prizes of CAAC Scientific and Technological Progress Award. It had 70 patent applications, 1 software filing and 34 granted patents. The acceptance inspections for research base of civil aviation mechanic engineering, research base of ground special equipment, research base of air traffic management, and research base of economy, transportation and management were completed. The university established Civil Aviation ATM Research Institute and participated in compiling guidance for civil aviation ATM support plan for national "large aircraft" project, for the 12th Five-Year Plan and guidance for the Application of the Second Generation of Compass System in Civil Aviation ATM. It established a Center for Energy Conservation and Emission Reduction Research and Promotion, undertook many specific items of energy conservation and emission reduction work of CAAC and provided technical support for international climate negotiations. It organized and held the 22nd Subgroup

Seminar on the Development of China's General Aviation during the 13th Annual Meeting of China Association for Science and Technology. Its industrial base of civil aviation science and technology was approved to be among the first batch of incubators for scientific and technological enterprises in Tianjin.

IV. Intensifying Efforts to Introduce and Cultivate Talents and Further Promoting Faculty's Overall Level

After its extensive publicity, the university introduced 73 teachers, including 1 back from abroad, 1 professor and 38 doctors. It also selected and sent 97 person-times to foreign universities, research institutes and civil aviation enterprises and institutional units for academic exchange, training or inspection. 1.5 million yuan was raised for cultivation of featured faculty staff in mechanics, ATM, flight and airport. The university made good use of training institutions on its campus such as Engineering Training Center to improve training for featured specialty teachers. 53 teachers were sent to learn practical knowledge and accumulate experiences in civil aviation enterprises and institutional units and 119 featured specialty teachers participated in various thematic training. Through system building, thematic training and cadres' mutual job exchange of serving temporary position, the overall level and working ability of student-work cadres were uplifted, and 58 of them attended various thematic training and 17 participated in serving temporary position tempering.

V. Promoting International Exchange, Opening of the University and Reinforcing Cooperation and Exchange with Domestic and International Industrial Organizations

The Sino-European Institute of Aviation Engineers run by the university received high applause from leaders of CAAC. Now, the institute has entered into its engineering education phase and successfully held its 4th executive committee meeting. Relying on the project of Sino-European institute of Aviation Engineers, the university actively strived for foreign high quality resources so as to improve its comprehensive strength in key fields. Thanks to efforts made so far, it worked together with the École Nationale de l'Aviation Civile (ENAC), successfully applied for EU's aid to China in two projects: pilot cultivation, and ATM & airport, including two domestically demanding projects for engineering masters and cultivation of large number of teachers: newly-established air-ground coordination and satellite communication navigation, which would greatly uplift our University's talents cultivation level in flight and ATC majors. The university strengthened its cooperation with domestic civil aviation and aeronautic industrial units, jointly established Yunnan Civil Engineering Center with Yunnan Airport Group, signed comprehensive strategic framework cooperation agreement with Wuhan Company of China Eastern Airlines, and signed strategic framework cooperation agreement with COMAC to jointly build Airworthiness Technology Research Base for Civil Aircraft, and Customer Service Support and Technology Research Center for Civil Aircraft. It promoted joint application and implementation of annual 10 million yuan projects of industrialization, education and research with AVIC.

VI. Deepening Internal Management System Reform and Constantly Reinforcing Management Efficiency and Public Service System Building

The university steadily pressed ahead with reform in internal management system and human resources management system, simplified and delegated its administrative management, shifted its focus of management to lower levels, promoted management efficiency, finished the development of reform plans for new rounds of human resources management and allocations systems and had those plans smoothly implemented. It finished delimiting the university's organizational structure and reform work of position setting for its faculty and management personnel, organized engagement of all faculty staff for a new engagement term, standardized its financial system and established the Rules for Implementation of Entrusting and Assigning Accountants in Civil Aviation University of China. CAUC Zhongtian (Tianjin China) Science & Technology Co., Ltd. and Tianjin Jeppesen International Flight College Co., Ltd. already assigned chief accountants to the university and started corresponding work. The construction of Third Phase Project of the University was accelerated. No.24 dormitory building on the north campus, No.1 dormitory building of the Chaoyang Flight College, the building for Sino-European Institute of Aviation

Engineers, flight attendants building, public bathroom on the north campus and indoor swimming pool were built and put into use. The total amount of printed books and electronic publications of the library reached 1.5 million copies (or pieces), the e-books reached 1.43 million copies and its databases reached 70. The university completed its project plan for system upgrading of campus network core equipment to 10Gb. It completed system reforming of university logistics to independent legal person system.

VII. Pushing Ahead All-round with Development of Students, and Overall Capabilities and Quality of Students Constantly Improved

Through ideological and political education with focus on "cultivating virtues and morale of man", students were cultivated to have sense of responsibility and sense of mission and to set up spirit of the times as to be responsible and ready to devote. The university established a social network (micro-blog) for the students and faculty staff, and use "education on micro-blog" platform as a place to discuss career planning, major events, political hot spot issues, etc. Outdoor bound plans for quality of students were implemented and colorful cultural activities were launched on campus, overall improving comprehensive quality of students. By carrying out scientific and technological project approval program and the project of Boeing foundation for innovation, the university enhanced cultivation of scientific and technologic innovation capabilities among the students. As a result, the University garnered 1 special prize, 3 first prizes and 6 second prizes in the 11th Challenge Cup Competition.

中国民用航空飞行学院

2011 年，中国民用航空飞行学院（以下简称学院）坚持“以飞为主，协调发展”方针，开展“创先争优”活动，注重内涵发展，各项工作均取得新的进展。

一、训练能力稳中有升，安全态势持续稳定

2011 年，学院实现飞行训练 24.63 万小时，起落 435 731 架次，模拟机 / 训练器训练 87 836 小时，训练时数稳中有升，安全态势持续保持稳定。

通过拓展航线资源、完善训练网络、引进新机型、加大飞机利用率等多种途径，深挖潜力，提高运行效率，努力提升训练能力。加强新教师培训，规范初始带飞标准，统一各机型标准操纵程序和飞行程序；坚持飞行讲评和教学法研讨活动，加大对教学训练过程的监控和调整；贯彻执行新大纲和民航局第 139 号令，打造“学生质管监控平台”，建立合理的淘汰机制，进一步夯实安全基础。认真落实航空安全主体责任，开展了安全主体责任专项检查。深入推进安全管理体系（SMS）建设，搭建和完善 SMS 框架。机务维修攻克多项技术难题，提升了机务系统保障能力。开展“质量强化年”活动，召开安全运行形势分析会、飞行教学经验交流研讨会，努力提高安全管理水平。

二、教学质量有效提高，学生工作成绩斐然

2011 年，全院完成 22.3 万教学学时，教学质量稳步提高。圆满完成年度招生任务，招收全日制本专科学生 3 461 名（飞行技术专业全日制学生 1 271 名），录取研究生 52 名。学生就业形势良好，顺利毕业学生 2 839 人，就业率达到 91%。全年共发放各类奖助学金 1 258 万元，资助强度更大，覆盖范围更广。

开展全院性的教学检查工作，坚持教学例会、教学督导、教学检查以及学生座谈会等制度。完成年度培养方案修订，新增安全工程和飞行器动力工程两个专业培养方案。实施“卓越工程师”计划、飞行英语强化培训和英语教学一体化改革。6 个项目获得四川省 2011 年高等教育质量工程立项。学院通用航空维修培训考试中心顺利揭牌，扩大行业影响力。组织英语教师加拿大培训，提升英语教学水平。成立飞行教育客户服务部，加强与航空公司的沟通和协调。在学生工作中突出“严字当头，德育为先”的育人理念，着力推动准军事化管理和学风培育创新，强化纪律与作风养成。校园科技文化艺术活动丰富多彩，提高了学生综合素质。

三、人才建设有序发力，科研工作重大突破

积极推进人事制度改革，加强人力资源开发与管理，加强人才队伍建设。高层次人才建设取得明显成绩，郑孝雍院长、丁援朝同志当选中国民航首批特级飞行员；陈布科副院长荣获国务院政府特殊津贴。专业技术人员职称结构进一步优化，教师学历结构进一步改善。实施招聘制度改革，提高了招聘公正性与人员质量。深化多元化用工改革，在内部合同工方面建立成长激励机制，在劳务派遣方面扩大用工范围，在退休返聘方面出台规范制度，进一步增强用工的灵活性，降低办学的人力成本。

实施科研创新团队计划，建立科研团队管理机制，学院科研基金的孵化作用逐渐显现。继续实施高原飞

2011年11月29日，"人民日报"号飞机命名仪式在飞行学院举行
On November 29, 2011, the Naming Ceremony of the "People's Daily" Airplane Is Held in the University

行安全综合技术研究、新一代航空无线宽带通信技术开发、广播式自动相关监视（ADS-B）研发和测试等重大科研项目。积极参与国家、省部级重大项目申报工作，加大科研产业化推进力度，学院科研经费突破2 000万元。成功研制民航地空宽带通信系统，引领航空互联网新时代。

深化对外合作交流，继续开展"空客日"、"波音日"活动，拓展与塞斯纳公司、美国塞拉等飞行学校的合作。加强与国际民航高校交流，数批学生分别赴美国克帕技术学院、新加坡理工学院、美国绿河公共学院学习。顺利签署与国际民航组织的合作备忘录，开辟学院国际科研合作新渠道。签订学院与四川机场集团、重庆直升机产业投资有限公司战略合作协议，致力扩大教育培训。

四、基本建设稳步推进，后勤保障成效显著

2011年，学院完成自筹（含固定资产）投资计划，新增设备家具类固定资产2 085万元，政府集中采购1 100万元，二级学院实验室建设完成总投资预算金额约6 700万元。完成学院机场设施设备购置经费立项及评审、机场《使用许可证》换证工作，协助完成阆中机场续建工程可行性研究报告编制工作。认真抓好学院灾后重建工程，完成了教学行政楼、教学楼主体工程。公安业务楼、考试培训中心、空管实验楼工程验收投入使用，完成部分教师宿舍、实验室和学生宿舍改造工程。完成渝汉钢厂征地搬迁及后续工作，在建学生宿舍施工进展顺利。全年接收航油合计16 267吨，保证了飞行训练的正常进行。

Civil Aviation Flight University of China

In 2011, persisting in the strategy of "taking the flight as the principal business and seeking coordinated development" and carrying out "Pursue Excellence" campaign, the Civil Aviation Flight University of China (the university) emphasized in-depth development and made fresh progress in all respects.

I. Training Capacity Improved Steadily and Safety Situation Remained Continuously Stable

In 2011, the university fulfilled 246 300 hours of flight training, 435 731 aircraft movements and 87 836 hours of simulator/trainer training, training hours increased steadily and the safety situation remained continuously stable.

By expanding air route resources, improving training network, introducing new aircraft types and increasing the utilization of airplanes, the university tapped the potentials in an in-depth manner, increased its operating efficiency and improved its training capacity. It enhanced training for new instructors, standardized the initial instruction norms, unified the standard operating procedures and flight procedures; persisted in flight commenting and instructing and the study of teaching methodology, and strengthened the monitoring and adjustment of instruction and training processes. By implementing the new curriculum and CAAC Order No. 139, the university built up the Student Quality Monitoring Platform, established a reasonable elimination mechanism and further fortified the foundation of safety. It earnestly implemented principal aviation safety responsibilities, made special inspections of the responsibilities, further pushed forward the building of safety management system (SMS), and had its framework created and improved. Many technical difficulties in aircraft maintenance were tackled, enhancing the maintenance support capacity. The university launched the Year of Quality Enhancement activity and organized the safety situation analysis meetings and flight instruction experience sharing workshops, and made efforts to promote its safety management.

II. Teaching Quality Effectively Improved and Student Work Scored Remarkable Results

In 2011, the university completed 223 000 teaching hours and steadily improved its teaching quality. With 3 461 full-time undergraduate students (including 1 271 full-time students in flight technology) and 52 graduate students recruited, the university successfully accomplished its annual student recruitment goal. With 2 839 students successfully graduated and the employment rate reaching 91%, the situation of students employment showed good prospects. 12.58 million yuan of scholarship were offered in the year, and the financial support became stronger and the coverage more wide.

The university conducted school-wide teaching inspections, regularly carried out routine teaching meetings, instruction supervisions, teaching inspections and student talks. With two disciplines added, i.e. safety engineering and aircraft power engineering, it accomplished the amendment to the annual education plan. The Excellent Engineer Program, the aviation English enhancement training and the integrated English instruction reform were carried out. Six projects were approved as the 2011 higher education quality projects of Sichuan Province. The successful inauguration of the Center for Maintenance Training and Examination of General Aviation added credit for university in the industry. English teachers were trained in Canada to improve the quality of English instruction. The flight education customer service division was created to enhance communication and coordination with airlines. The university highlighted, in student work, the education philosophy of Strictness First in Terms of Management and Ethics First in Terms of Teaching, started to make efforts in quasi-military management and innovations in study morale fostering, strengthening the building up of discipline awareness and style of work. With a wide array of colorful scientific, technologic, cultural and artistic activities, the students' comprehensive competence was improved.

III. Talents Construction Stepped Up and Major Breakthroughs Made in Research

The university actively implemented the personnel system reform, strengthened development and management of human resources and enhanced talent team building, making noticeable achievements in high-level talents production: Zheng Xiaoyong, president of the university, and Ding Yuanchao being elected among first special-grade pilots in China's civil aviation sector, and Chen Buke, vice president of the university, being granted the State Council's special subsidy. The qualification structure of technician was further optimized and the instructors' academic background was further improved. The university made reform in recruitment system and improved fairness of recruitment and the quality of the staff. With the establishment of incentive mechanism in internal contract workers, the expansion of scope for temporary staffing services and the adoption of standardized system in retiree re-engagement policy, the university deepened its reform in diversified staff employment, further increasing the flexibility of employment and reducing the labor cost.

The university implemented the scheme of innovating team in scientific research, created the research team management mechanism and gradually unleashed the incubating role of its research fund. It continued to conduct integrated technology research on high plateau flight safety, and R&D and testing of major scientific and technological projects such as the new-generation aviation wireless wideband communication technology development, the automatic dependent surveillance-broadcast (ADS-B), etc. With its research fund breaking the record of 20 million yuan, it also actively applied for national and provincial major projects, making more efforts in commercialization of research findings. The university successfully developed the civil aviation wideband ground-air communication system, thus ushering in a new era of the aviation Internet.

The university deepened its international cooperation and exchange, continued the Airbus Day and Boeing Day activities, and expanded the cooperation with Cessna, Sierra among other flight schools. Communication was enhanced with international civil aviation colleges. Batches of students were sent overseas to study at the Clover Park Technical College, Singapore Polytechnic and the Green River Community College. The university signed a memorandum on cooperation with the International Civil Aviation Organization (ICAO), opening a new channel for international scientific research cooperation. It also entered into strategic cooperation agreements with Sichuan Airport Group and Chongqing Helicopter Investment Company to expand its education and training.

IV. Infrastructure Construction Advanced Steadily and Remarkable Achievements Made in Logistics Supports

In 2011, the university completed the self-funded (including fixed asset) investment plan, adding 20.85 million yuan in new equipment and furniture and 11 million yuan in centralized government procurement. About 67 million yuan of investment budget was completed for lab construction of the secondary colleges. The University completed the project filing and review for the funding of airport facility and equipment procurement, had the Airport Use Permit reissued and assisted Langzhong Airport in preparing the project feasibility study report on its continued construction. It also effectively carried out its post-disaster reconstruction, having the main structures of the teaching/administrative complex and the teaching building completed, the public security service building, the center for training and examination and the air traffic control lab building inspected and accepted, and put into use, and part of the faculty dormitories, labs and student dormitories reconstructed. The land requisition and relocation of Yuhan Steelworks and subsequent work were completed and the student dormitory construction works went on smoothly. It received in total 16 267 tons of aviation fuel, ensuring the normal flight training.

中国民航管理干部学院

2011 年，学院致力于建设“民航中高级管理人才培养基地”、“民航改革与发展思想库”、“民航实用型人才培养的摇篮”，紧紧围绕教学、科研中心工作，抓质量、创品牌、促发展，开创了“十二五”发展新局面。

一、教学培训再创佳绩

积极建设“民航中高级管理人才培养基地”，拓展培训领域，提升培训水平。坚持以创新思维拓展民航中高级管理培训，举办民航新疆地区中高级管理人员培训班、民航行业政策研究干部培训班等，进一步丰富、完善民航中青年管理干部培训体系。坚持以监察员培训为重点，大力开展安全管理类培训，加强安全专业类和专题类知识的培训，做好民航企事业单位安全从业人员的培训。加强培训建设，开展“情景模拟”研究，推动教学方法改革；建设“中国民航在线学习平台”，推进远程教育网络建设，解决民航职工工学矛盾。

2011 年，学院共完成培训班次 416 个，培训人次 17 269 人，标准人次 15 565 人，同比增长分别为 9.2%、10.8% 和 24%，取得良好的经济效益和社会效益。

二、科研发展迈上新台阶

大力推进“民航改革与发展思想库”建设，继续加强科研质量管理，积极推动科研学术交流与合作，加大科研市场开发力度和科研人才培养力度，不断拓展科研发展空间和项目渠道，深入开展民航应用技术和软科学研究，不断增强科研能力。一年来，学院积极组织申报高新技术发展及产业化领域 2012 年度国家科技计划预备项目、科技部“十二五”国家科技计划社会发展科技领域项目、北京市自然科学基金项目等，积极开发科普基金项目，学院的科研领域不断扩展，科研规模不断增大，科研水平不断提升，科研条件不断改善。

2011 年，全年在研项目 208 项，新立项目 76 项，同比增长 11.4%，其中纵向项目 42 项，横向项目 34 项，基本实现了横纵向项目平衡发展的格局。

民航局李家祥局长参观“民航强国之路展”中的管理干部学院展台

Li Jiaxiang, Administrator of CAAC, Visits CAMIC's Exhibit Booth at the “Road to Civil Aviation Power Exhibition”

三、学历教育稳中求进

积极建设“民航实用型人才培养的摇篮”。不断探索学历教育发展新方向，积极筹办中国民航管理工程学院，

拓展学历教育发展的新空间。坚持“以市场为导向，以能力为中心、以就业为目标，以应知应会为标准”的技能培训，坚持以培养出适应民航强国建设的高素质一线实用型人才为导向，切实加强专业建设，注重提高学生技术应用能力和综合职业素质，办出特色，办出质量；坚持“专业评定以质量为本、教学主体以学为本、教学效果以问题解决为本”的“三本”原则，深化教学改革，调整专业发展方向，加大实操性课程比重，不断夯实学历教育的基础地位，增强高等学历教育的竞争力。

通过努力，2011 年学院招生 1 638 人，毕业 1 743 人，就业 1 418 人，就业率高达 81.4%。

四、国际交流成果丰硕

努力打造亚太地区航空领域具有影响力的培训和研究机构，积极开拓国际市场。赴境外培训项目大幅增长，完成境外培训项目 50 个，培训 1 107 人次；援外培训项目渐成品牌，并成功举办荷兰皇家航空公司高层管理人员管理研修班、对发展中国家航空安保培训，境外来华培训项目获得突破；对外合作伙伴关系日益巩固，与国际民航组织、国际航空运输协会、休斯顿机场、慕尼黑机场、瑞典北欧空管学院等机构建立了良好合作关系，为学院涉外培训、科研持续发展奠定了坚实基础。

与此同时，积极引进和储备国际优质师资，不断充实学院师资库。并借助 2011 中国民航发展论坛的成功举办，提升学院国际竞争力和国际影响力。

五、发展基础日益夯实

人才配置稳步规范。积极引进高素质师资，合理培养现有职工，适当聘用编外员工，大力借用行业内外专家，全面整合学院内外人力资源，逐步形成一支规模适度、素质优良、结构合理、充满活力的员工队伍。

基础建设稳步推进。学院二期工程进展顺利，已完成结构封顶；昆明基地一、二期工程基本结束，三期工程立项工作启动；“十二五”学院重点建设项目推进步伐加快。

2011 年学院培训分类情况

培训类别	培训班次	培训人次	标准人次
管理培训	124	4 536	5 257.80
安全培训	236	10 341	6 329.55
代理人培训	49	2 280	1 944.40
外语培训	7	112	1 933.40
合　计	416	17 269	15 465.15

注：1标准人次=10人天

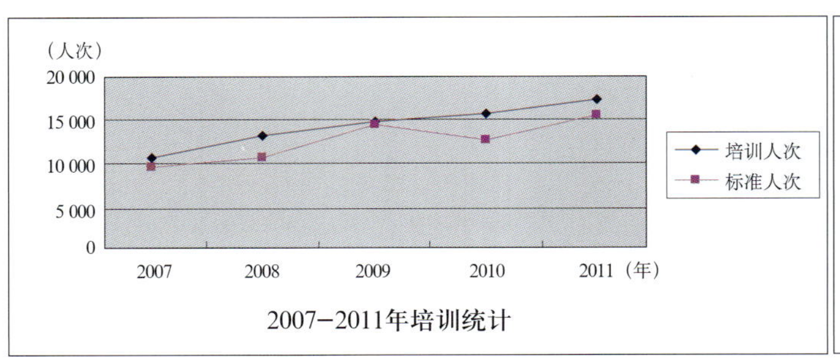

2007—2011年培训统计

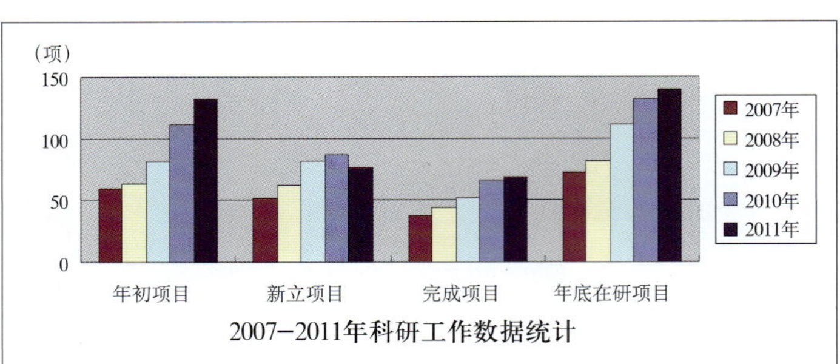

2007—2011年科研工作数据统计

Civil Aviation Management Institute of China

In 2011, the Civil Aviation Management Institute of China (the institute) was devoted to building a Civil Aviation Medium and Senior Management Training Base, a Think Tank for Civil Aviation Reform and Development and a Cradle for Practical Talent in Civil Aviation. Centered on teaching and scientific research activities, the Institute worked hard to improve quality, create brand and promote development, and opened a new prospect in implementing its 12th Five-Year Plan for development.

I. Good Results in Teaching and Training

The institute actively built the Civil Aviation Medium and Senior Management Training Base to expand its fields of training and improve its training level. Persisting in innovative thinking to expand training on medium and senior management in civil aviation, the Institute held civil aviation medium and senior management training courses in Xinjiang region and officer training courses on civil aviation industry policy research, further enriching and perfecting itself with training system for young management staff. Emphasizing consistently on inspector training, it paid more attention to security management training, strengthened trainings on security and other expertise, and did a good job in training security personnel of enterprises and institutions in the civil aviation sector. The institute pushed ahead with teaching method reform by enhancing training building and carrying out "scenario simulation" research. It eliminated contradiction between work and study of employees in civil aviation industry by developing China Civil Aviation Online Study Platform and promoting distance education network.

In 2011, the institute completed 416 training sessions that covered 17 269 trainees and 15 565 standard person-times, representing year-on-year increases of 9.2%, 10.8% and 24% respectively, achieving a good financial and social benefit.

II. Research Development Up to a Higher Level

The institute vigorously pressed forward with building of a Think Tank for Civil Aviation Reform and Development, continued to strengthen scientific research quality management and actively promoted academic exchange and cooperation. It stepped up developing research markets and fostering scientific research talent, continuously expanding room for scientific research development and project channels. It conducted in-depth research in civil aviation application technologies and soft science, continuously boosting scientific research capability. In the past year, by actively organizing applications for the 2012 National S&T Program preparatory projects in high-tech development and commercialization field, the social development S&T field projects under the 12th Five-Year National S&T Program of the Ministry of Science and Technology and Beijing Natural Science Foundation projects, and vigorously developing science popularization foundation projects, the institute saw continuous expansion in scientific research areas, continuous increase in research size, continuous uplift in research capacity and constant improvement in research conditions.

In 2011, the institute had 208 ongoing research projects and 76 newly-approved projects, increasing by 11.4% over that of the previous year, among which 42 were vertical projects and 34 were horizontal ones, with a basically balanced development pattern of horizontal and vertical projects.

III. Education of Academic Credentials in Stable Advancement

The institute energetically wove the Cradle for Practical Talent in Civil Aviation. It uninterruptedly explored new directions of academic credential education, actively carried out preparatory work for the Civil Aviation Management Engineering Institute of China and expanded new room for academic credential education development. Insisting on skill training of being "market-oriented, competency-centered, employment-targeted and up to the standard of being able to know and do" and persisting in the direction of fostering high quality front-line practical talent suited to building a country with strong civil aviation, the institute earnestly strengthened its specialty construction, paid great attention to improving students' ability in application and overall professional competency, trying to run the institute with features and qualities. It adhered to three principles of "quality-oriented specialty assessment, study-oriented teaching activities and problem-solving-oriented teaching results", deepened teaching reform, adjusted specialty development direction, gave higher weight to hands-on courses, continuously fortified the fundamental standing of academic credential education and sharpened the competitive edge of higher academic credential education.

In 2011, the institute recruited 1 638 students and 1 743 students graduated. 1 418 students were employed, with a high employment rate of 81.4%.

IV. Fruitful Results in International Exchange

The institute endeavored to establish it as a training and research organization influential in aviation field across Asian and Pacific region and actively tapped into international markets. Overseas training projects increased markedly. 50 overseas training projects with 1 107 trainees were completed. Aiding foreigner training project brand was taking shape. The KLM Royal Dutch Airlines senior management seminar and aviation security training of developing countries were successfully held, marking breakthroughs in foreigner training projects. International partnerships were cemented. It built good and cooperative relationship with the International Civil Aviation Organization (ICAO), the International Air Transport Association (IATA), Huston Airport, Munich Airport, Sweden-based EPN, etc., laying a solid foundation for the institute's foreign-related training and sustainable development of scientific research.

Meanwhile, the institute attracted and retained excellent international instructors to expand its instructor base. Relying on successful holding of China Civil Aviation Development Forum 2011, the institute increased its international competitiveness and influence.

V. Increasing Consolidation of Development Foundation

The institute steadily standardized its staffing deployment, eagerly introduced competent instructors, reasonably fostered its existing staff and appropriately hired temporary workers. It made efforts to borrow experts inside and outside of the industry and comprehensively integrated human resources inside and outside the institute, gradually forming a staff team with appropriate size, good quality, reasonable structure and strong robustness.

Infrastructure construction was steadily carried out. The institute's phase II project went smoothly and its main structure completed with its top cement sealing. Phases I and II projects of the Kunming base were substantially completed and process of Phase III for approval was launched. The institute accelerated its key construction projects in the 12th Five-Year Plan period.

Training Classification of the Institute in 2011

Type of Training	Training Classes	Number of Trainees	Standard Person-times
Management Training	124	4 536	5 257.80
Security Training	236	10 341	6 329.55
Agent Training	49	2 280	1 944.40
Foreign Language Training	7	112	1 933.40
Total	416	17 269	15 465.15

Note: 1 standard person-time = 10 person-day

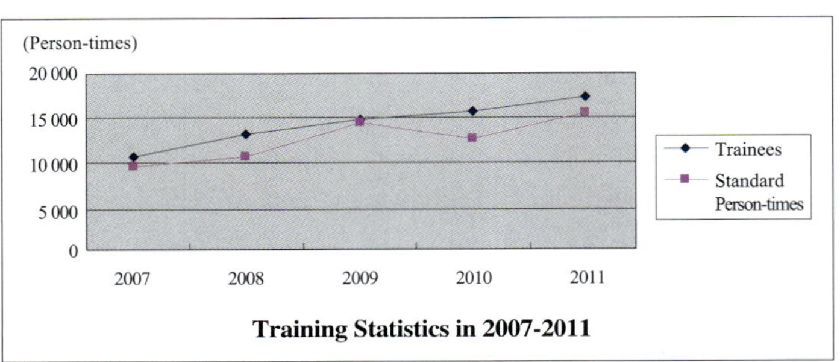

Training Statistics in 2007-2011

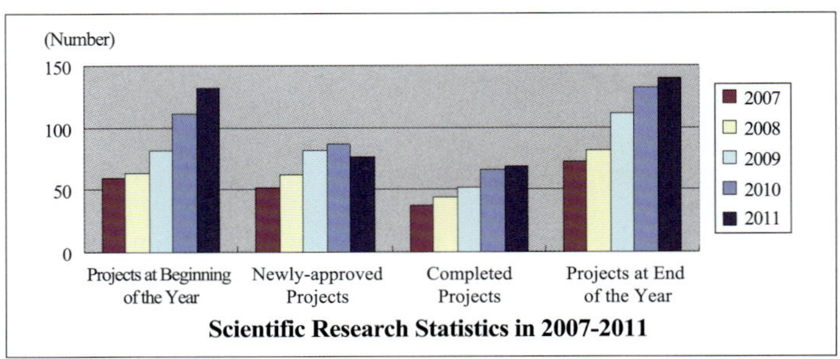

Scientific Research Statistics in 2007-2011

中国民航科学技术研究院

2011年是“十二五”开局之年，也是中国民航科学技术研究院（以下简称航科院）挂牌后正式运行的第一年。一年来，我们创新体制机制、转变发展方式、优化内部资源、强化核心能力，科研工作实现重点突破，技术支持工作的质量和科技含量稳步提高，科技服务市场进一步拓展，实现了航科院科学发展的良好开局。

一、进一步深化体制机制改革

完成组织机构调整，实现了内部资源优化整合 航科院按照新的三定方案，根据现代科研院所运行的特点，围绕内部资源优化整合这一主题，以“院一所一室”的模式重新构建了管理体系。

二、科研工作实现重点突破

抓好跑道拦阻系统（EMAS）研发工作 按照民航局领导的指示要求，航科院紧紧锁定EMAS这一具有发展前景的科研项目，组建了由8个小组数十名科研骨干参加的研发团队，经过不懈努力掌握了核心技术并实施了5次真机验证试验。数据表明，系

2011年1月10日，中国民航科学技术研究院成立大会在北京人民大会堂隆重举行

On January 10, 2011, the Inaugural Meeting of China Academy of Civil Aviation Science and Technology (CACAST) Is Held in the Great Hall of the People in Beijing

统的模型、设计方法、主体材料均达到了设计要求，验证未来投入使用后，能够明显减少因为飞机冲出跑道而造成的重大事故，从而进一步提高未来我国机场安全保障能力。

科研项目有序推进 2011年航科院各类在研科技项目达312项，包括新立项目161项。其中141项科技项目完成了研究任务，9项成果获航科院科技成果奖，“驾驶舱话音记录器背景声识别技术研究”获民航协会科技奖二等奖，“基于性能的导航（PBN）程序设计与验证系统”获软件著作权1项、申请发明专利3项，“爆炸物自动探测系统鉴定技术的研究”获实用新型专利1项。全年共发表各类论文111篇。

重大科技项目申请取得新突破 2011年，航科院成功申报的“机场跑道端飞机拦阻系统的关键技术研究与验证”入选2012年民航联合基金重点项目和2012年国家科技支撑计划项目重点项目；成功申报的“中国航空排放交易体系的制度建构研究”入选国家软科学研究计划项目并获科技部立项批准；以航科院为主申报的“民机运行故障事故数据库设计与开发”项目，以及航科院参与申报的“航空发动机适航条款符合性技术研究”、“民用大涵道比涡扇发动机总体设计技术研究”、“民用飞机模拟机D级数据包规范与开发技术研究”、“飞行训练品质分析与评估技术研究”等4个项目列入工信部国产民机重大专项并获立项批准。

科研条件平台建设取得新进展 2011年，航科院顺利通过了民航局组织的民航安全技术分析与鉴定实验室、民航经济运行实验室和民航数字图书馆的竣工验收。完成了民航安检技术试验室（痕量爆炸物检测部分）的建设；固定资产投资项目“PBN飞行程序运行支持平台”工程初步设计方案和“飞行记录器译码能力基础建设”立项获民航局批准。

三、技术支持工作稳步推进

2011年，航科院继续按照业务对口原则，积极推动专项任务的申请和研究。完成多部行业标准和规范性文件的编辑及修订工作。

完成中国民航维修系统工程能力评估、国内外维修单位管理工作；完成民航人力资源统计、培训、管理和职业技能鉴定工作；全年共鉴定境内外397台次飞行模拟设备，参与航空器评审组（AEG）对10个型号航空器的评审和30个型号的国内外航空器审定和认可审查，受理各类投诉1 750件；开展中欧民用航空机构能力建设项目。

四、科技服务工作有序开展

创新发展理念，转变发展方式 航科院实现了由服务政府为主，转向服务政府和服务行业同步发展；由服务航空运输业为主，转向服务航空运输业和航空制造业同步发展的转型，自我生存和发展能力得到了进一步的巩固和加强。

科技发展公司逐步进入正轨 积极开拓北斗导航在民航领域的应用、合同能源管理等具有较好发展前景的业务领域。承接跑道拦阻系统真机验证试验服务保障、产业化运作准备等工作，产研联动平台的作用初步显现，在科技成果形成产品并走市场的衔接作用方面进行了有益的探索。

科技服务领域进一步拓展 模拟机鉴定、飞行品质监控、一发失效应急程序设计、记录器译码和失效分析、安检设备鉴定、服务质量评估等传统优势领域得到稳步加强；适航审定、维修工程、航空器评审、运行技术进入航空制造和军方应用领域的工作取得了有效突破，与航空制造业合作的项目有10项；规划咨询和PBN程序设计等业务在公开招标中取得了较好的成绩。在科技服务方面，全年共签订各类合同或合作协议98项。

资质能力建设取得新进展 通过了ISO 9001质量管理体系认证，修订并发布了《质量手册》及相关文件，组织建立起院内ISO 9001质量管理内审员队伍，为持续改进和提高航科院科研项目质量提供了人才和制度保障。

China Academy of Civil Aviation Science and Technology

2011 marked the first year of the 12th Five-Year Plan, and also the first year of operation of the newly established China Academy of Civil Aviation Science and Technology (hereinafter referred to as CACAST). In the year, CACAST innovated systems and mechanisms, transformed development modes, optimized internal resources and enhanced core competencies, making major breakthroughs in sci-tech research, steady improvement in the quality and technological standard of technical supports and further expansion of sci-tech service market, and achieving a good start in its scientific development.

2011年12月13日，机场EMAS第三次真机试验在天津滨海国际机场进行

On December 13, 2011, the Third Airport EMAS Prototype Test Is Conducted at Tianjin Binhai International Airport

I. Further Enhancement in System and Mechanism Reforms

Fulfilling the organizational restructuring and realizing the optimization and integration of internal resources. In accordance with the new plan on the three predeterminations, the functioning characteristics of modern sci-tech research organizations and centering on the theme of optimizing and integrating internal resources, CACAST restructured, the management system into an Academy-Institute-Office mode.

II. Major Breakthroughs in Sci-Tech Research

Excellently carrying out research and development of engineered materials arresting systems (EMAS). As instructed by officials from CAAC, CACAST fixed a firm grip on the prosperous EMAS research project and assembled an R&D team comprising eight groups of tens of competent researchers who, through tireless efforts, acquired the key technologies of EMAS and conducted five prototype verification tests. Data showed that the system model, design methods and main materials all met design requirements, and it was verified that the systems could markedly reduce major accidents caused by aircraft running out of runways and thereby could further improve China's airport safety assurance capability in the future.

Methodically pushing ahead with sci-tech research projects. In 2011, CACAST had 312 sci-tech projects under research, including 161 new ones. 141 projects were completed in the year, with 9 being awarded the CACAST Sci-Tech Achievement Award. The Cockpit Voice Recorder (CVR) Sound Information Identification Technology Research won the second prize of CATA Sci-Tech Awards, the performance-based navigation (PBN) Procedure Design and Verification System was granted one software copyright and three invention patents, and the Research on Identification Technology for the Automatic Detection System for Explosives was granted one utility model patent. 111 papers of all kinds were published in the year.

New breakthroughs in major sci-tech projects applications. In 2011, the Key Technology Research and Verification for Engineered Materials Arresting Systems proposed by CACAST was successfully included in the list of major projects supported by the Joint Fund of Civil Aviation

Research and the list of major projects under the National Sci-Tech Support Program of China in 2012. The proposed China Aviation Emission Trading System Structuring Research was included in the National Soft Science Research Program and approved for initiation by the Ministry of Science and Technology; the Civil Aircraft Fault and Accident Database Design and Development project in which CACAST was the lead applicant as well as the Aero-Engine Airworthiness Clauses Conformity Research, the Research on Overall Design of Civil High Bypass Ratio Turbofan Engine, the Civil Aircraft Simulator D-level Data Package Specifications and Development Research and the Research on Flight Training Quality Analysis and Assessment Techniques in which CACAST was a participating applicant were included in the Major Program of China-Made Civil Aircraft of the Ministry of Industry and Information and got approved for initiation.

New progress in sci-tech research platforms building. In 2011, CACAST successfully passed CAAC's acceptance inspections of the Analysis & Appraisal Lab of Civil Aviation Safety Technologies, the Civil Aviation Economic Operation Lab and the Civil Aviation Digital Library. It also completed the building of the Civil Aviation Security Check Technology Lab (for trace explosive detection). The projects of the preliminary design of PBN Flight Procedure Operation Support Platform and the project of Flight Recorder Decoding Capacity Building of the fixed asset investment were filed with CAAC and obtained its approval.

III. Steady Promotion in Technical Supports

In 2011, CACAST continued to promote applications for and researches on specialized tasks under the principle of business matching. A series of industry standards and normative documents were compiled or revised.

CACAST accomplished engineering capacity assessment of the civil aviation maintenance systems of China and the management of domestic and foreign maintenance service providers; completed statistical compilation, training, management and professional skill appraisal of civil aviation human resources; approved 397 domestic and overseas flight simulators; participated in review of 10 aircraft types conducted by the aircraft evaluation group (AEG) as well as certification and review of 30 domestic and foreign aircraft types; handled 1 750 complaints; and launched the China-EU civil aviation organizations capacity building program.

IV. Systematical Development of Sci-Tech Services

With development philosophy innovated and development mode transformed. CACAST shifted itself from serving the government principally to serving government and industry equally, and from serving the air transport sector primarily to serving air transport and aviation manufacturing equally, thus further cementing and enhancing its capacity of self-sustaining survival and development.

The sci-tech development company gradually onto the right track. It energetically stepped up civil aviation applications of Compass Satellite Navigation System, energy performance contracting and other areas of business with a bright future, and undertook the EMAS verification test service supports and commercialization preparations, initially showing the effect of the research-industry collaboration platform and making productive explorations in commercialization of research findings.

Further expansion in sci-tech service areas. Traditional strength areas were steadily enhanced, including simulator evaluation, flight quality monitoring, design of one-engine-out emergency procedures, recorder decoding and failure analysis, security check equipment evaluation and service quality assessment. Breakthroughs were made in airworthiness certification, maintenance engineering, aircraft evaluation and examination, and application of operation technologies in aviation manufacturing and the military, and there were 10 projects launched in cooperation with aviation manufacturers. The business such as planning advisory services and PBN procedure design made good achievement in competitive bidding. There were a total of 98 contracts or cooperation agreements concerning sci-tech services signed in the year.

New progress in qualification capacity building. CACAST passed the ISO 9001 quality management system certification, modified and issued the Quality Manual and related documents and assembled an internal auditor team for ISO 9001 quality management, providing staffing and institutional supports for continuously improving the quality of CACAST sci-tech research projects.

广州民航职

2011年，广州民航职业技术学院（以下简称学院）全面推进落实各项工作，将学院下设机构由系调整为五个二级学院，实现了学院发展再上新台阶，办学声誉和影响力进一步扩大。2011年被中国民用航空局精神文明建设指导委员会授予“全国民航文明单位”称号。

基于行业标准的内涵建设走向深入，人才培养质量进一步提升

示范办学进一步提高了高职人才的培养水平。2011年，学院有毕业生2 754名，毕业生就业率达到99%以上。其中，飞机结构修理、航空物流、会计、航空乘务与旅游管理、机场运行管理、民航运输、信息管理7个专业的就业率达到100%，民航类专业对口率达到80%。此外应征入伍服义务兵役6人，直招士官27人，被地方政府授予“征兵工作全优单位”荣誉称号。

实施国家质量工程提升项目，进一步提高办学水平。高等学校继续教育示范基地建设和高职教育实训基地、广东省教育综合改革试点等项目，是国家、广东省继“国家示范高职院校”项目后的又一系列质量工程提升项目。学院紧抓这一发展机遇，积极申报并成功立项。其中，有两个专业成功申报了“2011年中央财政支持高职教育实训基地项目”；参与了由清华大学牵头实施的“高等学校继续教育示范基地建设”项目，成为50所先期启动该项目建设单位之一；成功申报了国家“网络教育数字化学习资源中心”项目，成为申报该项目首批职业学校分中心之一。学院提出的《广东省教育综合改革试点项目依托行业办学模式综合改革实施方案》进入了实施阶段。实施系列重大质量工程提升项目将有利于提高学院办学质量和办学水平，对学院发展产生深远影响，为学院未来发展赢得新起点。

业 技 术 学 院

两大基础建设项目稳步推进，为满足“十二五”规划硬件指标要求提供条件

2011 年，经过学院领导和项目工作领导小组长期不懈的努力，新机场实训基地的行政办公楼、教学楼及图书馆信息中心等项目建设顺利进行。该建设项目的顺利进行，将进一步改善学院的办学条件和环境，为下一步开展的人才培养水平评估提供了根本保障，也意味着“十二五”规划提出的三个校区（校本部、新机场校区、花都校区）的构架初步成形。

不断深化产学合作办学，提升社会服务能力

学院作为行业高技能人才培养基地，积极发挥人才支撑作用和资源集成、共享效应。以“双赢”的发展原则与行业企业合作结出了累累硕果。

校企共建共享实训基地：从行业调拨 32 架飞机、140 多台飞机发动机，目前生均教学设备居全国同类院校前列。

产学合作打造双师队伍。企业技术人员等兼职教师的课时占专业总课时的 50%。

培训机制灵活服务企业。利用行业授权的岗位资格证书培训和考试资格，积极开展面向民航企事业单位的多种类型培训，年培训近 10 万人日。

实施教育服务输出，国际合作增强办学活力

国际合作项目取得了积极进展。2011 年，学院首次招收 8 名留学生开展学历教育，标志着学院在教育服务输出工作方面迈上了新台阶。

与国内外院校的合作进一步加强。学院先后与新疆职业大学、加拿大卡纳多学院、加拿大圣力嘉学院、韩国湖西大学、加拿大爱德华王子岛大学、美国 DUPAGE 学院、美国普惠发动机公司，美国贝尔直升机公司以及阿联酋航空公司等单位洽谈合作办学事宜。同时，接收了 39 名香港专业教育学院青衣分校学生来我院学习。

民航高职校园文化建设亮点纷呈

学院始终秉承“育人为本，德育为先”的教育理念，积极探索和培育航院精神，不断创新富有民航特色的校园文化品牌，为学院的长期稳定发展提供了有力保障。为营造良好的“职业化”校园文化环境，学院积极开展了职业技能比武活动，通过举办近 20 余项专业技能比赛，有效地提升了学生的综合职业素质和就业竞争力，为今后形成具有中国特色的民航高职素质教育体系打下了坚实基础。2011 年，学生活跃在各大赛场上并取得优异的成绩。其中，省级以上的大型比赛中，共有 87 人次获得 13 个国家级和 24 个省级奖励，以及 17 个团体奖项，为学院赢得了荣誉。■

Guangzhou Civil Aviation College

In 2011, Guangzhou Civil Aviation College (hereinafter referred to as the college) pushed forward and implemented various jobs in an all-round way, and adjusted its departments into five secondary colleges, thus pushing the development of the college to a new level and further expanding the college reputation and influence. In 2011, CAAC Steering Committee for Ethics Civilization Building awarded the college the title of National Role Model Entity in Civil Aviation.

Deepening Inherent Management Building Based on the Industrial Standards and Further Improving the Talent Production Quality

Demonstrative Teaching Further Improved the Training Level of the Higher Vocational Talents.In 2011, the college produced 2 754 undergraduates in all, and more than 99% of whom were employed upon graduation. For such 7 majors as aircraft structural maintenance, civil aviation logistics, accounting, air stewards, tourism management, airport operational management, civil aviation transport and information management, the employment rates of the undergraduates upon graduation were 100%; for civil aviation majors, 80% of its undergraduates were employed by civil aviation businesses or institutions related with their majors. In addition, 6 undergraduates joined the compulsory military service, and 27 undergraduates were directly enrolled as non-commissioned officers by the military. The college was awarded the honorary title of Excellent Organization in the Conscription Work by the local government.

Carrying out the National Quality Uplift Program and Further Improving Teaching Level. The programs such as construction of the continued education demonstrative bases of higher learning institutions, training bases of higher vocational education and the pilot project in Guangdong comprehensive educational reform etc. are series of quality uplift programs developed by the State and Guangdong Province after the program of the State Demonstrative Higher Vocational Learning Institutions. The college firmly seized this development opportunity to actively apply for the programs and successfully initiate projects. Of which, two majors successfully applied for the 2011 Higher Vocational Education Training Base Projects with Financial Support from the Central Government; the college also participated in the project of Construction of Demonstrative Bases of Continued Education in the Higher Learning Institutions led and implemented by Tsinghua University, becoming one of the fifty construction organizations which started the project in advance; successfully applied for the national project of Digital Learning Resources Center of Network Education, becoming one of the first sub-centers in vocational schools applied for the project. The Comprehensive Implementation Scheme of Reform of Industrial School-Running Pattern under the Pilot Project in Guangdong Comprehensive Educational Reform put forward by the college entered into the implementation phase. The implementation of series important quality uplift programs will be of great advantage to the improvement of the college teaching quality and teaching level, will exert far-reaching influence on the college development, and will bring a new start for the future development of college.

机务专业学生英姿

Military Training of the Students Majoring in Mechanics

Steadily Pushing Forward the Building of the Two Major Infrastructure Projects to Provide Conditions for Realization of the College's Hardware Requirements in the 12th Five-Year Plan

In 2011, with long and persisting efforts made by the college leadership and the project leading group, the administrative office building, the teaching building and the lab's information center in the new airport training base were being constructed smoothly. The smooth construction of the project would further improve teaching conditions and environment of the college, and provide fundamental support for the next stage assessment of talents cultivation level. This also means that structures of the three campuses (the college head office, the new airport campus and Huadu campus) proposed in the 12th Five-Year Plan have taken shape basically.

Continuously Deepening the Collaboration with the Enterprises to Upgrade Social Service Capabilities

As a high-tech personnel training base, the college actively played the role in supporting talents, integrating resources and sharing the resources with the enterprises. The college collaborated with the enterprises in line with "pattern" development principle, and had made fruitful achievements.

Jointly constructing and sharing the training base by the college and enterprises: 32 aircraft and over 140 aircraft engines were dispatched to the college from the enterprises. At the moment, the number of the teaching equipment per student in the college stood in the forefront in the league of similar colleges and universities in China.

The college collaborated with the enterprises and provided enabling conditions to become teachers with dual qualifications. Lecturing hours of the technical personnel from the enterprises as part-time teachers accounted for 50% of the total in terms of aviation subjects.

Training mechanism was flexibly used to serve the enterprises. The post qualification training and examination qualification authorized by the industry was used to energetically carry out various kinds of trainings for the civil aviation enterprises and public institutions with nearly 100 000 person-day training being provided every year.

Implementing Education Service Export and Enhancing School-Running Vitality through International Cooperation

New progress was made in international cooperation project. In 2011, the college, for the first time, enrolled 8 foreign students for diploma-oriented education. This marked the fact that the college has reached a new level in the field of education service export.

The cooperation with other colleges and universities both at home and abroad was further strengthened. The college held talks successively on the matters of how to jointly run the college with the Canadian Canadore College, Seneca College, Korea Hoseo University, the Canadian University of Prince Edward Island, the American DUPAGE College, Xinjiang Vocational University, the American Pratt & Whitney Engine Company, the American Bell Helicopter Company and Emirates. Meanwhile, the college also accepted 39 students from Hong Kong Institute of Vocational Education (Tsing Yi) to study in our college.

Flourishing Campus Culture in Higher Vocational Institutes in Civil Aviation Field

The college has always followed the educational concept of "people-orientation and ethics cultivation first", actively explored and cultivated the college morale, and constantly innovated the campus culture brand characterized by civil aviation to provide a strong support for the long and stable development of the college. In order to create a good "vocation-oriented" campus cultural environment, the college actively organized over 20 vocational skill contests, which effectively improved students' comprehensive competence and employment competitiveness and laid a solid foundation for shaping the competence-oriented higher vocational education system with characteristics of China civil aviation in the future. In 2011, the students actively participated in the various major competitions and had made excellent results. In the major competitions at the provincial-level or above, 87 persons won 13 state-level and 24 provincial-level awards, and 17 team awards which added credit for the college. ■

中国民用航空局清算中心
CAAC Settlement Center

中国民用航空局清算中心

2011年，清算中心（以下简称中心）累计完成清算航班898.82万架次，清算资金349.55亿元，同比分别增长19.4%、36.66%，实现了对国内航空公司“一金一费”征收“零”拖欠的目标。

——民航基金 开账航班253.1万架次，同比增长6.28%；开账金额58.63亿元，同比增长6.29%；调整额为0.18亿元，调整率为0.31%。收款率为100%。

——机场管理建设费 开账航班245.14万架次，同比增长5.63%；开账金额154.42亿元，同比增长9.37%，其中代征旅游发展基金6.57亿元；调整额为0.59亿元，调整率为0.38%。国内航空公司收款率为100%，外航收款率为98%。

——空管服务收费 开账航班306.22万架次，同比增长7.98%；开账金额67.17亿元，同比增长13%。收款率为96.63%。其中，外航航路费和进近指挥费开账航班50.42万架次，同比增长13.87%；开账金额46.95亿元，同比增长15.21%。收款率97.38%。国内航路费和进近指挥费开账航班255.8万架次，同比增长6.9%；开账金额20.22亿元，同比增长8.19%。收款率为94.89%。

——机场服务费 外航开账航班304架次，同比增长10.36%；开账金额616.9万元，同比增长9.84%。国内航空公司（2011年8—12月）开账航班94.33万架次，开账金额69.27亿元。收款率为100%。

2011年11月21日，民航局李军副局长视察民航博物馆清算中心展位

On November 21, 2011, Li Jun, Deputy Administrator of CAAC, Visits the Settlement Center's Booth at the Civil Aviation Museum

2011年，清算中心完成了以下工作。

一、全面落实中心“十二五”规划

（1）制定中心信息化发展的“十二五”规划 为保障中心“十二五”规划的实施，2011年编写制定了中心信息化建设的“十二五”规划。重点建设完善中心四大信息化能力体系，即基础环境体系、应用平台体系、数据资源体系和运营保障体系，明确技术主线和项目建设重点。

（2）推进电子商务，开展机票政府采购工作 启动了机票政府采购项目前期准备工作，利用中心自身资源优势，明确与国管局采购中心合作的工作机制及下一阶段工作内容，积极推进机票定点采购的调研、流程设计及项目的实施工作。

二、机场服务收费正式纳入统一清算体系，进一步扩大统一清算范围

根据民航局《关于建立统一清算指导意见》的要求，2011 年 7 月 1 日，清算中心与国航、东航、南航、海航、首都机场、上海机场、广州机场、招商银行在北京签署了《机场服务收费统一清算项目协议书》，成为继民航基础设施建设基金、机场建设费、空管收费之后第四个实施统一清算规则的民航资金项目。目前，已签约航空公司 32 家、机场 158 家，开展机场服务费统一清算业务培训，累计培训人员 455 人，涉及 32 家航空公司和 161 家机场。

三、完善资金征缴与清欠手段，确保民航政府性基金及各类资金按时足额征缴

中心不断完善征缴与清欠机制，提高资金收缴率。通过 BSP 这一方式，逐步引导航空公司按民航局相关规定主动付款。在政府性基金采用 BSP 模式缴款的基础上，逐步探索将其他资金清算纳入该模式。加强与国际航协的合作，做好加入清算所前期准备工作。为规范航空公司付款行为、缩短收款周期、减少坏账损失、保障资金安全，制订了应收账款管理制度。

四、加强系统与基础设施建设，不断提升运维管理水平

（1）推进财务三期开发建设工作，进一步完善资金管控制度 2011 年完成了项目工程初步设计、招投标及合同谈判、签订等工作，目前项目已进入工程建设期。该项目建成后，将进一步强化民航财务系统监控功能，扩大监控范围，优化公共财政一体化系统，以信息化手段健全和强化预算体系、预算编制管理、预算执行管理、财政监督等职能。

（2）通过中心自主建设的方式，机场服务费结算系统运行顺利 2011 年 7 月，机场服务费清算系统通过测试如期上线运行，为中心以及国内 158 家机场和 32 家航空公司提供服务。目前，该系统运行稳定，为中心统一清算体系的顺利实施提供了可靠的系统平台。

（3）建立信息发布系统 中心完成了各业务信息发布系统的整合，建立了以发布中心业务信息为主的信息发布系统，方便业务操作和公众了解清算中心。

（4）构建中心信息安全体系，加强信息安全管理 启动信息安全评测咨询工作，对中心五大信息系统进行安全评估定级，通过差距分析和评估，对系统和网络安全进行加固，建立数据同城灾备机制，逐步完善信息安全体系。

五、政府采购和 GPA 研究工作扎实推进，为民航系统政府采购相关工作提供指导和服务

2011 年，民航系统计划采购上报金额为 8 亿元。前三个季度实际采购累计金额 2.3 亿元，较上年同期 0.86 亿元增长了 167%。在集中机构采购方面，2011 年的采购金额为 1.1 亿元，同比增长 25.6%。在部门采购方面，民航系统共申报政府采购进口产品项目 68 个，涉及采购金额 13.7 亿元。政府采购培训举办了 10 次，培训人员达到 500 余人次，提高了民航各单位领导层对政府采购工作的重视程度。2011 年，结合财政部第三次出价任务，按财务司要求，圆满完成了 GPA 谈判年度研究工作。

六、严格管控电子客票行程单，确保相关工作落实到位

2011 年发放行程单 1.86 亿份，回收、缴销行程单 964 万份，配合公安机关鉴定行程单 37 批次，共 143 万份。对行程单的管理工作不断向精细化目标稳步迈进，在业务流程改进方面，实施了多项措施。编制了《航空运输电子客票行程单自助打印系统服务推广标准》，并完成国航首都机场 T3 航站楼自助行程单打印系统的验收工作。

七、国库集中支付和行政事业性收费工作稳步推进，积极辅助民航预算工作

2011 年一般预算资金请款 34 亿元，政府性基金请款 103 亿元。中心积极配合财务司做好民航预算执行工作，参与国库集中支付资金监督检查工作，对部分单位的支出情况进行了前期调查，并对预算执行情况进行监督。进一步加强行政事业性收费工作，截至 2011 年 11 月，中心各项费用累计上缴金额 1.51 亿元，已全额上缴财政部。

CAAC Settlement Center

In 2011, the Settlement Center (the center) conducted settlement business for a total of 8 988 200 flights accumulatively and settlement amount of 34.955 billion yuan, increasing by 19.4% and 36.66% over those of the previous year and achieving the goal of "zero" default in payment of "airport construction charges and civil aviation fund" by domestic airlines.

— **Civil Aviation Fund.** the number of flights billed was 2 531 000 and the amount billable was 5.863 billion yuan, increasing by 6.28% and 6.29% respectively over those of the previous year. The adjusted amount was 18 million yuan with an adjustment rate of 0.31%. The bill collection rate was 100%.

— **Airport Management and Construction Charges.** the number of flights billed was 2 451 400 and the amount billable was 15.442 billion yuan, increasing by 5.63% and 9.37% respectively over those of the previous year, including 657 million tourism development fund. The adjustment amount was 59 million yuan with an adjustment rate of 0.38%. The bill collection rate of all domestic airlines was 100% and that of foreign airlines was 98%.

— **ATM Service Charges.** the number of flights billed was 3 062 200 and the amount billed was 6.717 billion yuan, increasing by 7.98% and 13% respectively over those of the previous year, the bill collection rate was 96.63%, among which the number of foreign flights billed for en-route and approach command charges was 504 200 flights and the amount billed was 4.695 billion yuan, increasing by 13.87% and 15.21% respectively over those of the previous year. The bill collection rate was 97.38%. The number of domestic flights billed for en-route and approach command charges

2011年7月1日，民航统一清算签约仪式在北京举行
On July 1, 2011, the Signing Ceremony for the Centralized Settlement of Civil Aviation Is Held in Beijing

was 2 558 000 flights and the total amount billed was 2.022 billion yuan, increasing by 6.9% and 8.19% respectively over those of the previous year. The bill collection rate was 94.89%.

— **Airport Service Charges.** the number of foreign flights billed was 304 and the amount billed was 6.169 million yuan, increasing by10.36% and 9.84% respectively over those of the previous year. The number of domestic flights (from August to December 2011) billed was 943 300 and the amount billed was 6.927 billion yuan. The bill collection rate was 100%.

The center accomplished the following work in 2011.

I. The 12th Five-Year Plan of the Center Fully Implemented

1. The center formulated the 12th Five-Year Plan for IT development. In order to facilitate the implementation of the center's 12th Five-Year Plan, it developed its 12th Five-Year Plan for IT development and placed emphasis on the four IT capacity systems of the center, namely, the basic environment system, the application platform system, the data resource system and the operation support system, identifying the main technological road and priority areas of projects.

2. The center pushed forward E-commerce and carried out the program of government purchasing for the air tickets. It started the preparatory work for program of government purchasing for the air tickets and by making good use of its resources, clarified the working mechanism of cooperation with the purchasing center of the Government Offices Administration and defined detailed items of next-step work. It actively pressed ahead with the survey, procedure design and project implementation of government procurement of air tickets.

II. Airport Service Charges Formally Included in the Centralized Settlement System Further Expanding the Settlement Scope

As required by CAAC in the Guideline on the Establishment of Centralized Settlement, the center entered into the Agreement on Centralized Settlement of Airport Service Charges with Air China, China Eastern Airlines, China Southern Airlines, Hainan Airlines, Capital Airport, Shanghai Airport, Guangzhou Airport and China Merchants Bank in Beijing on July 1, 2011. The airport service charges became the fourth item of civil aviation capitals covered by centralized settlement rules after civil aviation infrastructure construction fund, airport construction charges and ATM services charges. At present, contracts were signed with 32 airlines and 158 airports. Trainings on central settlement of airport service charges were provided to 455 persons from 32 airlines and 161 airports.

III. Debt Collection and Recovery Techniques Improved to Ensure Full and Timely Collection of Civil Aviation Governmental Funds and Other Funds

The center made continuous improvement in the collection and recovery techniques to increase the debt collection rate. BSP was introduced to gradually guide airlines to a positive stance in making payments as required by CAAC. Based on the BSP mode for governmental funds, the center gradually explored to extend the mode to other funds. It strengthened the cooperation with the International Air Transport Association (IATA) and made preparations for joining the clearing house. The accounts receivable management policy was developed, with the aim of regulating payment behaviors of airlines, shortening payment cycle, reducing losses on bad debts and ensuring the safety of capital.

IV. System and Infrastructure Development Enhanced to Continuously Improve Operation and Maintenance Management Capability

1. The center pressed ahead with the third phase construction in finance to further improve the management and control system of the capital. In 2011, it accomplished the preliminary design, bidding and contract negotiation and signing work of the project. Now the project is in the construction stage. The project, when completed, would further enhance the monitoring functions of the civil aviation financial system, expand the scope of monitoring, optimize the integrated system for public finance and improve, with information technology, the budget system, budgeting management, budget execution management and public finance oversight functions.

2. Based on the self-construction mode of the center, the airport service charges settlement system ran well. In July 2011, the airport service charges clearing system was tested and put online as scheduled to provide services for the center, 158 airports and 32 airline companies nationwide. At present, the system is operating stably, providing a reliable platform for the center to successfully implement the centralized clearing system.

3. The center established an information disclosure system. It consolidated information disclosure systems of all business areas, established an information disclosure system that mainly released business information of the center and thereby facilitated business operations and helped the public have a better understanding of the center.

4. The center created an information security system to strengthen information security management. It launched the information security testing and consulting work, conducted security assessment and grading for the center's five major information systems and, through gap analysis and assessment, enhanced the system and network security, established the intra-city disaster backup mechanism, and gradually improved the information security system.

V. Government Procurement and GPA Research Pushed Forward Solidly to Provide Guidance and Service for Government Procurement in the Civil Aviation Sector

In 2011, the planned procurement in the civil aviation sector amounted to 800 million yuan. Completed procurement was 230 million yuan in the first three quarters, a 167% increase over 86 million in the same period of the previous year. The centralized institutional procurement stood at 110 million yuan in 2011, up 25.6% over that of the previous year. With regard to departmental procurement, there were 68 government procurement projects regarding imported products in the civil aviation sector, totaling 1.37 billion yuan. 10 government procurement training sessions were held to train over 500 people, increasing the emphasis on government procurement among leaderships of civil aviation entities. In 2011, in line with the third bidding task assigned by the Ministry of Finance, the center successfully completed the annual research on GPA negotiation as required by CAAC Department of Finance.

VI. E-ticket Itinerary Business Controlled Strictly to Ensure Fulfillment of Relevant Work

186 million E-ticket itineraries were issued in 2011, with 9.64 million being recovered and cancelled and 1.43 million being authenticated in 37 batches with the public security organs. The center steadily refined itineraries management and took a wide range of measures to improve the business processes. It formulated the Standards for Air Transport E-ticket Itineraries Self-Service Printing System and checked and accepted the Air China's self-service itineraries printing system in T3 of the Beijing Capital Airport.

VII. Work on Collective Payment by the State Treasury and Administrative Institutional Charges Steadily Carried Out to Assist the Civil Aviation Budget Work

In 2011, 3.4 billion yuan general budget funds and 10.3 billion yuan governmental funds were requested. The center actively assisted the Department of Finance in executing the civil aviation budget, participated in the supervisory inspection of the collective payment by the state treasury, conducted early investigation of disbursements of some selected entities and oversaw their budget execution. It further enhanced the work of administrative institutional charges and as of November 2011, the center had collected a total of 151 million yuan and had it all submitted to the Ministry of Finance.

中国民用航空飞行校验中心

2011年，中国民用航空飞行校验中心（以下简称校验中心）认真贯彻落实民航工作会议和航空安全会议精神，狠抓安全主体责任落实、人员资质能力建设、校验服务质量管理、科研工作和各项基础建设，各项工作呈现出了新面貌。

一、圆满完成飞行校验任务

全年累计飞行6 905小时，校验机场187个，校验设备1 254台/套，保持了平稳的安全态势，圆满完成各项飞行校验任务，包括北京、上海、广州、香港、澳门等枢纽机场，加格达奇、巴彦淖尔等6个新投产机场在内的全国所有民用、军民合用机场及航路传统科目，以及国家“863”计划星基LASS导航系统的校验飞行和民航多个管制区域的广播式自动相关监视（ADS-B）监控系统的飞行校验工作。

二、深入贯彻持续安全理念

完善了安全委员会，调整了飞行技术委员会，建立了校验技术委员会，通过完善机制强化安全责任；加快推进机务安全管理体系（SMS）建设，健全了运行手册体系，通过完善体系规范安全生产；制定了《航空安全奖惩规定》和《飞行校验中心机长职责》，协助空管办起草了《飞行校验技术要求》部分章节，通过健全规章保障安全运行；开展了机长非精密进近飞行能力专项检查和安全大检查，通过自查自纠排除安全隐患；修订了五种机型飞行训练大纲，制定了《模拟机训练部门协作流程》，通过理顺培训巩固安全基础。

三、大力提升生产运行质量

完成了国家检测和校准实验室《质量手册》和《程序文件》改版，顺利通过了年度评审；先后获批湾流450飞机的2A/2C维修能力及塞斯纳750飞机120个月维修能力；飞机维护系统和发动机监控系统建设

校验机组正在对西藏阿里机场进行大转弯校验飞行
The Flight Inspection Crew Maneuvers a Large Degree Turnaround in Their Inspection Flight at Ali Airport of Tibet

进展顺利；深入落实《外出执行任务机组管理规定》、《飞行机组飞行期间着装规定》，安全、优质、高效的校验服务得到了广大用户的肯定和称赞。

四、积极研发新设备新技术

依托航空飞行测试联合实验室，开展了国家科技支撑计划项目——“空地协同的飞行校验与验证系统”研发，拥有自主知识产权的国产校验系统研制工作取得重大进展；与航天部卫星工作委员会等密切配合，开展了北斗卫星导航在民航的示范验证工作；为规范科研管理，成立了科学技术委员会，制定了《校验中心科研项目管理办法（试行）》，并广泛征集科研课题，推动了科研管理工作的规范化、体系化和标准化；完成了3架奖状S校验飞机监造、验收及投产前的各项准备工作。截至2011年底，校验中心机队规模已达14架。

五、全面理顺内部管理

结合“十二五”发展规划，启动了人力资源改革工作；设置了校验技术处（质量体系管理办公室），进一步整合了校验技术力量；加快推进新基地迁建工作，基本完成各项建设。

Flight Inspection Center of CAAC

In 2011, the Flight Inspection Center of CAAC (hereinafter referred to as the center) earnestly acted upon the guiding principles of the Civil Aviation Working Conference and the Aviation Safety Conference, focused on the implementation of safety responsibilities, the building of personnel qualification and abilities, the service quality management of the inspection, scientific research and other various basic constructions, making a new look in all its work.

I. Successful Fulfillment of the Flight Inspection Tasks

The whole year witnessed 6 905 flight hours, inspections of 187 airports, and inspections of 1 254 pieces/sets of equipment, maintaining a stable safety situation and seeing successful fulfillment of various flight inspection tasks, including traditional items of flight inspection tasks for all the civil and civil-military airports and routes such as the hub-airports of Beijing, Shanghai, Guangzhou, Hong Kong and Macao, and 6 newly built airports in Jiagedaqi, Bayannur etc., and the inspection flight tasks for the satellite based LASS navigational system, a project of the 863 Hi-Tech R & D Program, and flight inspections for ADS-B surveillance systems in several traffic control areas.

II. Thorough Implementation of Sustainable Safety Concept

The center refined its safety committee, adjusted its flight technique committee, and established an inspection technique committee, and by improving mechanism, strengthened safety responsibilities; it expedited the building of maintenance safety management system (SMS) and refined the operation manual system, and by improving its systems, standardized its safe production; it formulated the Reward and Punishment Regulations for Aviation Safety and the Captain's Functions in the Flight Inspection Center, and assisted the Office of Air Traffic Regulation in drafting some chapters of the Technical Requirements for the Flight Inspections, and by amplifying regulations, ensured safe operation; it conducted special inspections on the non-precision approach flight capabilities of the captains and comprehensive inspections on safety, and by self-inspections and self-rectifications, eliminated hidden hazards in safety; it revised the flight training curriculums for five types of aircraft, and formulated the Coordination Flow for the Simulator Training

Department, and by streamlining training, reconsolidated its safety foundation.

III. Energetic Promotion of Productive Operation Quality

The center completed the revision of the Quality Manual and Procedural Document for the National Monitoring and Calibration Lab, and both were successfully passed their annual evaluation and examination. It obtained successively the approval of the maintenance capability 2A/2C of Gulfstream 450 aircraft and 120-month maintenance capability for Cessna 750 aircraft. The building of the aircraft maintenance system and the engine monitoring system was progressing smoothly. The center implemented in-depth the Provisions on the Management of Aircrew Doing their Duties on Assignment and the Dress Code for Flight Crew during Flight, and its safe, excellent and highly efficient inspection services won affirmation and applause from the users.

2011年3月，校验中心对全国第二海拔高高原机场——西藏阿里机场进行飞行校验

In March 2011, the Flight Inspection Center Carries Flight Inspection for the Second High Altitude Plateau Airport-Ali Airport of Tibet

IV. Energetical Research and Development in New Equipment and New Technology

Relying on the Joint Lab of Aeronautic Flight Testing, the center carried out research and development work for the project of Air-Ground Coordinated Flight Inspection and Verification System set forth in the national scientific and technological supporting program, and a major progress was made in the research work for the home-made inspection system with the independent intellectual property rights. The center carried out, in close cooperation with the Satellite Working Committee of the competent astronautics departments, the demonstration and verification work for Compass Satellite Navigation System for the use in the civil aviation. In order to standardize the scientific research management, it established the Science and Technology Committee, developed the document of Methods for the Management of Scientific Research Work of the Flight Inspection Center (trial), and solicited extensively scientific research subjects, thus pushing ahead with the scientific research management in a more normative, systematic and standardized way. It also completed the supervised manufacture, acceptance of and pre-operation preparatory work for 3 Citation S inspection aircraft. By the end of 2011, the center had had a fleet of 14 aircraft.

V. Comprehensive Refinement of Internal Management

According to the development program of the 12th Five-Year Plan, the center initiated its reform of the human resources and set up an Inspection Technical Division (Office for the Management of Quality System), further integrating the inspection technical capabilities. It also expedited the relocation of the new base and completed all its constructions on the whole.

中国民用航空局信息中心

中国民用航空局信息中心（以下简称信息中心）肩负着加快民航电子政务建设与发展的重要任务。自2007年成立以来，不断深化民航电子政务的应用与拓展、加强信息系统资源整合，以提升民航行政机关公共服务水平和行业监管能力，建立起适合民航电子政务建设与发展的管理办法和标准体系，使民航电子政务更加规范化、系统化和科学化。

一、民航电子政务行业标准体系逐步建立

信息中心制定了3部有关电子政务的民航行业标准：《民航电子政务IP地址规划和域名命名规则》、《民航电子政务机构信息交换规范》及《基于可扩展置标语言的电子公文格式规范》。随着对电子政务认识的不断深入，在未来的电子政务建设实践中信息中心将不断补充完善相关标准规范。

二、民航电子政务基础设施更加先进完备

（1）建成860平方米国家A级标准机房，机柜120个，装机容量1 600台。

（2）建成统一共用的民航电子政务内网和民航局外网，其中政务外网拥有3条互联网专线，带宽出口不断拓宽。

（3）建成统一的本地数据存储备份系统及政务内网异地灾备系统。

（4）建成统一的运行监控系统，实现了机房基础设施、服务器、网络安全和软件系统等软硬件的统一实时监控，具备统一管理、提前预警、及时报警、快速响应等功能，实现了运行维护管理关口前移。

三、三大信息系统应用体系初步形成

（1）**安全监管体系** 航安综合管理信息系统（一期）、奥运安保信息系统、飞行标准监督管理系统。

（2）**经济运行与市场管理体系** 数字民航生产统计系统、固定资产投资项目管理信息系统、综合统计信息系统（筹建）、行业人才资源统计报送系统。

（3）**行政办公与公共服务** 内网综合办公系统、内网视频会议系统、政府网站。

四、建成统一的信息安全防护体系

建成统一CA认证体系，审计管理平台，漏洞扫描系统，网络杀毒系统，SSLVPN数据安全访问通道以及健全的防渗透、抗DDOS攻击系统。

与此同时，信息中心还积极探索云计算、物联网等新一代信息技术在电子政务实践中的应用，向民航局申报了《基于物联网技术的机场安保可视化监管平台研究》科技项目，并正式批复立项。开展关键核心技术的研究攻关，加速高新技术的引进，积极推动服务器虚拟化等重大技术变革。加强预研工作，提高应用水平，编写了《民航电子政务外网服务器虚拟化技术改造试验平台建设方案（草案）》，积极开展了虚拟化技术实验平台的应用与研究。

Information Center of CAAC

The Information Center of Civil Aviation Administration of China (hereinafter referred to as the information center) undertakes the important mission to speed up the construction and development of civil aviation e-governance. Since its inception in 2007, the information center has constantly deepened the application and development of civil aviation e-governance and strengthened the integration of information system resources to elevate the public services of CAAC administrative agencies and enhance the capacity for industry regulation, and established the managerial methodology and standards system conducive to the construction and development of civil aviation e-governance, which made civil aviation e-governance more standardized, systematic and scientific.

I. Industry Standard System for Civil Aviation E-governance Building up Gradually

The information center developed three industry standards for civil aviation e-governance, i.e. IP Address Plan and Domain Naming Rules for Civil Aviation E-governance, Information Exchange Norms for Civil Aviation E-governance Agencies and Electronic Document Format Specification Based on Extensible Markup Language. With the deepening of the understanding of e-governance, the information center will continue to add and improve the relevant norms and standards in the future construction and practice of e-governance.

II. Civil Aviation E-governance Infrastructure Becoming More Advanced and Sophisticated

1. A national class-A server room of 860 m^2 was built with 120 computer cabinets and an installment capacity for 1 600 computers.

2. A unified and shared civil aviation e-governance intranet and CAAC internet were set up, including 3 lines dedicated to e-governance internet access, and the bandwidth has been consistently expanded.

3. A unified local data storage backup system and a remote backup system for e-governance intranet in case of disaster were set up.

4. A unified operation monitoring system was set up, realizing unified real-time monitoring of hardware and software such as computer lab infrastructure, servers, network security and software systems. The system had the functions of unified management, advance warning, instant alarm and rapid response, thus realizing proactive operation and maintenance management.

III. Three Information Application Systems Taken Shape Initially

1. Safety regulation systems: Information system for aviation safety management (phase1), Olympic security information system, supervision and management system for flight standards.

2. Economic operation and market management systems: Digital production statistics system for civil aviation, information system for fixed-asset investments management, integrated statistics information system (under construction) and reporting system for industry human resources statistics.

3. Administrative work and public service: General office work intranet system, video conferencing intranet system and government websites.

IV. Unified Information Safety Protection System Established

The integrated CA certification system, audit management platform, vulnerability scanning system, network antivirus system, safe SSLVPN data access and a sound system for anti-infiltration and anti-DDOS attacks were set up.

At the same time, the information center also actively explored cloud computing and internet of things, which was a new generation of IT application in the practice of e-governance. The application for the technology project of Airport Security Visual Monitoring Platform Based on the Internet of Things Technology was filed to CAAC and officially approved. The information center carried out the research on key technologies, accelerated the introduction of high-tech, and actively promoted the major technological change such as server virtualization. It strengthened pre-research work, improved applications, developed the Construction Plan of the Trial Platform for Civil Aviation E-governance Internet Server Virtualization Transformation (Draft), and actively carried out the application and research of the trial platform for virtualization technology.

上海民航职业技术学院

2012年5月9日，上海民航职业技术学院成立大会在世博中心大会堂隆重举行。中国民用航空局局长、党组书记李家祥和上海市人民政府副市长沈骏在会上讲话并共同为上海民航职业技术学院揭牌，上海市市长韩正为凝聚了民航局、民航华东地区管理局多年期盼和几代民航中专人共同努力的上海民航职业技术学院的正式成立发来贺信。

32年中专办学辉煌成就，奠定高职办学基础

上海民航职业技术学院是在整合民航上海中等专业学校现有教育资源的基础上建立的。1985年，民航上海中等专业学校在1980年民航上海管理局技工学校的基础上成立，随后依托位居上海的地理位置和行业办学的优势，乘着时代的东风迅速发展。32年来，在民航华东管理局的领导下，经过全体教职员工的共同努力，学校连续多年获得"上海市职业教育先进单位"的称号，1998年通过上海中等职业学校办学水平A级评估，2000年通过国家级重点中等专业学校水平评估、被评为上海市十所现代化标志性示范学校之一，2002年开始培养民航高职专业人才，2003年通过上海市"百校重点建设"评估，2004年通过国家重点中等职业学校认定评估。

于再院长致辞

32年来，学校坚持服务民航、强化办学特色，在重点建设民航安检、空中乘务专业的同时大力加强航空服务、民航运输等专业的建设，并努力将民航机电维修专业建设成为上海市重点专业。

32年来，学校坚持依托行业、注重校企联动，按照行业技术岗位要求、企业用人标准，积极推动"订单培养"模式，培养民航企业急需人才，实现了人才培养与市场需求的结合、教学与工作岗位的结合，使课程设置、教学内容不断贴近岗位实际。学校坚持面向市场、突出就业导向，一直保持着招生优势，拥有上海最好的中职生源，就业率平均水平始终保持在96%以上。已经培养1万多名毕业生，深受用人单位欢迎，为培养行业技能型人才做出了积极贡献。

上海民航职业技术学院基本情况及发展定位

成立上海民航职业技术学院是民航局党组根据我国民航业快速发展，对行业院校做出的总体规划和布局。民航局在2011年9月正式向教育部递交了《关于申办上海民航职业技术学院的函》。在民航局、上海市政府的大力支持和上海市教委的全力配合下，上海民航职业技术学院的建立走上快车道，2012年3月获得教育部批准备案。2012年4月李家祥局长题写校名并为学院题词"民航强国教育先行"。

上海民航职业技术学院是经上海市人民政府批准、教育部备案、隶属于中国民用航空局的独立设置的一所全日制普通高等院校。学院以民航上海中等专业学校为建校基础，致力于培养具有大专学历层次、较强实践能力，服务于民航和社会发展所需的一线高素质、高技能型人才。

学院占地面积181亩，有超过14万平方米建筑面积和价值近6 000万元的各类教学仪器设备；有14个专业实训室，馆藏图书及电子图书达20余万册，为全校师生提供了良好的学习、教育和科研资源。学院拥有上海市民航职业

技能鉴定所资质，是上海地区唯一同时取得民航局CCAR-147部和CCAR-66部考点资质的学院。

2012年学院首批招生将面向全国15个省、市、自治区，招收航空机电设备维修、民航商务、民航安全技术管理、飞机制造技术4个专业。根据行业发展和社会经济建设的需要，学院将不断优化专业结构，坚持走内涵强校之路。学院还将利用自身优势，积极参与民航行业职业资格培训工作，不断扩大培训规模，更好地为经济建设服务。

李家祥局长在成立大会上对学院提出了“清晰发展定位，坚持办学特色；明确发展目标，突出内涵建设；加强队伍建设，强化师资力量；坚持育人为本，培养合格人才”的具体要求。站在新的历史起点上，学院将坚持“立足华东，服务民航，特色鲜明，社会满意”的办学定位，按照“培育适应高等职业教育发展需要、体现行业特色的办学理念，致力于打造职业技术教育、在职继续教育和成人学历教育的国内一流的示范性高等职业技术学院”的发展目标，以高等职业技术教育为主体，以服务民航事业为己任，以行业岗位培训和成人学历教育为支撑，立足上

民航局局长李家祥和上海市副市长沈骏推动启动杆为学院揭牌

展目标，以高等职业技术教育为主体，以服务民航事业为己任，以行业岗位培训和成人学历教育为支撑，立足上海、面向华东、辐射全国，为民航强国战略培养更多、更适用的高素质、高技能人才！

中国航空集团公司

中航集团总裁王昌顺春节前慰问飞行总队飞行员

Wang Changshun, President of CNAC, Greets Pilots of the General Flight Fleet before the Spring Festival

2011年，中国航空集团公司努力践行科学发展观，坚持稳健经营和可持续发展指导方针，充分发挥政治、品牌双优势，在提升安全品质、保持生产平稳较快增长、强化内部管理、增强发展能力、完成重要专包机任务等方面都取得了新的成绩，实现了“十二五”的良好开局。

一、安全品质进一步提升

中航集团认真落实安全生产责任制，修订了《航空安全监督管理暂行规定》，完成了《中航集团安全管控模式》项目研究。针对国航系多品牌安全管理链条长、跨度大的特点，加强对重点部位和薄弱环节的安全监管。特别是加强了对深圳航空、澳门航空、国货航等控股企业的安全监管。深入开展安全检查和安全审计，提升安全品质成效明显。国航股份安全管理基础进一步夯实，运行组织能力得到增强，以风险管理为核心的全面安全管理体系进一步健全。飞行部门以规章落实为主线加强安全信息管理，积极应用QAR安全品质监控等先进科学手段，重点强调决断意识、复飞意识和稳定进近意识，扩大了安全裕度。机务维修部门优化维修管理资源，关注老旧飞机，加大发动机维修深度，提高了机队可靠性。深圳航空、国货航采取了有针对性的综合安全管理措施，安全趋势明显好转。

中航集团全年安全飞行132.5万小时，同比增长5.4%；事故征候万时率为0.022 6，同比下降52.7%。各专业公司生产经营的安全状况良好。

二、圆满完成重大航空运输任务

圆满完成了重要专包机任务。出色完成埃及、利比亚、日本紧急撤侨，应对智利火山爆发，保障中央代表团赴藏等重要任务，得到了党中央、国务院和国内外各方面的充分肯定和好评。

三、生产经营保持平稳较快增长

集团全年完成运输总周转量、旅客运输量、货邮运输量分别为155.2亿吨公里、6 714.6万人和140.2万吨，同比分别增长6.2%、7%和1.8%。实现收入963.8亿元，实现利润总额102.4亿元。财务状况进一步优化，资产负债率进一步降低，抗风险能力有所增强。

集团推进全面预算管理，加大预算执行监控力度；深化生产效益分析，完善了“周监控、月快报、月分析、季回顾”的监控、评价机制；在全集团范围内大力开展降本增效工作，自上而下严格控制各项费用。国航股份坚决执行枢纽战略，加大市场开拓力度，增强了在主要航线、干线市场上的竞争力。客运直销收入比例提高明显，特别是大客户、电子商务、两舱和国际联盟收入指标分别增长35.5%、53.2%和17.0%、6.9%。优化资源配置，科学组织航班环，生产效率和收益水平同步提高。全年投入增长5.6%，产出增长超过了6.2%；座公里水平0.569元，同比增加7.9%。加强与深航、山航、澳门航空的效益联动，协同营销效应突出。国货航拓展网络营销能力，产品、服务质量有所提升，腹舱收入保持了稳定。深圳航空市场开发得力，生产组织有序，收入199.6亿元，利润20.5亿元，创历史最好业绩。集团各专业公司增收能力进一步提高，效益明显改善。

四、发展能力持续增强

集团2011年完成投资211.65亿元，同比增加48亿元。其中，国航股份完成205.45亿元（包括飞机、发动机投资167.6亿元）；专业公司完成6.2亿元。

国货航完成合资，北京航空、大连航空进入实际运营，内蒙古航空已报审批，参股西藏航空进展顺利。机务整合继续推进。完成澳门航空股权二次重组，向澳门政府定向增发募资近7亿澳门元。促进深航加入星空联盟，推动深航理顺股权关系，协助深航开展河南航和翡翠航重组谈判。中航有限增资西安机场人民币2.94亿元。配合生产需要，稳步推进西南基地、飞训基地、广州过夜基地、重庆飞行人员生产用房、深圳航空三机位机库等建设项目，着手研究主业在首都第二机场的规划和需求。集团总部大厦项目实施代建管理进展顺利。

加快服务体系建设，国航股份9个服务攻坚项目逐步落实，服务管理体系（CSM）初步建成，全流程服务、两舱服务、常旅客服务、电子商务、客户关系维护进一步改善，在业内首家推出了无线局域网服务，取得了通过SKTYRAX“四星级”评审的阶段性进步。

五、内部管理不断深化

加强投资管理，严控非主业投资。规范人力资源的调配、管理，严格工资总额预算，实施了国航股份股票增值权计划，集团企业年金成功推进。强化财务管理制度落实，构建了“小金库”专项治理长效机制。完善全面风险管理工作机制，加强业绩考核与企业动态监管，全面推进经济增加值考核和全员业绩考核。提升法律事务管理水平，开展战略、财务、市场、运营和法律风险评估。与专业机构合作开展新一轮油料套期保值研究。继续加强合同、采购管理整改专项效能监察，积极推进内部审计机构和制度建设，组织开展重点工程建设项目全过程跟踪审计试点，完成内审59项，提出管理建议230条。进一步开展内部资源整合，妥善处理了西南航空旅游项目等历史遗留问题。有效开展节能减排，完善能耗数据监测体系，实施了国内首次生物燃油试飞。

China National Aviation Holding Company

IIn 2011, China National Aviation Holding Company (CNAC) made great efforts to implement the Scientific Outlook on Development, adhered to the guiding principle of prudent operation and sustainable development, fully utilized its political and brand strengths and made new achievements in improving its safety quality, maintaining its steady and rapid production growth, strengthening its internal management, enhancing its development ability, fulfilling its major charter services, etc. making a good start for the 12th Five-Year Plan period.

I. Safety Quality Further Improved

CNAC earnestly implemented the responsibility system for work safety, amended the Provisional Rules for Aviation Safety Supervision and Management and completed its project research on the CNAC Safety Management Modes. In light of the characteristics of the extended, long-ranging safety management chain of CNAC brands, it strengthened safety supervisions over major areas and weak links, especially over Shenzhen Airlines, Air Macau and Air China Cargo. CNAC conducted in-depth safety inspections and audits and made obvious improvement in safety quality. Air China further cemented the basis of safety management, enhanced the operation and organization capacity and further improved the comprehensive safety management system focused on risk management. The flight department strengthened its safety information management mainly by enforcing rules and regulations implementation, actively applied QAR safety quality monitoring and other advanced techniques, emphasized the sense of decisiveness, go-around and stable approach, expanding the safety margin. The maintenance department optimized its maintenance management resources, paid great attention to the old airplanes and increased the depth of engine maintenance, boosting the liability of fleet. Shenzhen Airlines and Air China Cargo took a complete set of well-targeted safety management measures, improving obviously their safety situation.

In the whole year, CNAC safely completed 1 325 000 flight hours, an increase of 5.4% over that of the previous year; incident rate per 10 000 hours was 0.022 6, a decrease of 52.7% on that of the previous year. All its specialized companies maintained a good safety situation in operation and management.

II. Major Air Transport Tasks Fulfilled Successfully

CNAC successfully accomplished its important charter tasks. Other fulfilled major tasks included urgent evacuation of nationals from Egypt, Libya and Japan, response to the Chilean volcanic eruption, the central government delegation's Tibet tour, etc. receiving full recognition and applause from the CPC Central Committee, the State Council and all domestic and foreign communities.

III. Production Operation Maintained Stable and Rapid Growth

In 2011, CNAC handled a total turnover about 15.52 billion ton-km, 67.146 million passengers and 1.402 million tons of mail and cargo, representing year-on-year increases of 6.2%, 7% and 1.8% respectively. Its income was 96.38 billion yuan and total profit 10.24 billion yuan. It further optimized its financial situation and further reduced its asset-liability ratio, enhancing to some extent its risk-resistance ability.

CNAC pushed forward the integrated budget management and stepped up the monitoring of budget execution; deepened the analysis of operating profit and perfected the monitoring and assessment mechanism of "weekly monitoring, monthly report, monthly analysis and quarterly review"; carried out the cost reduction and efficiency enhancement initiative group-wide and strictly controlled, from above to below, its expenses. Air China unswervingly enforced the hub strategy and stepped up the market expansion efforts, sharpening its competitive edge in major air routes and trunk-line markets. The revenue of passenger direct sales accounted for a much higher percentage; in particular, the income from large customers, e-commerce, two cabins and international alliances grew by 35.5%, 53.2%, 17.0% and 6.9%, respectively. With optimized allocation of resources and reasonably devised flight loops, its productivity and profitability were both increased. Input and output increased by 5.6% and 6.2% respectively in the year; and the revenue of seat kilometer was 0.569 yuan, up 7.9% from that of the previous year. CNAC strengthened collaboration with Shenzhen Airlines, Shandong Airlines and Air Macau, producing remarkable synergies. With the expansion of its network marketing ability, Air China Cargo made some improvement in its quality of products and services and maintained a stable bellyhold income. Attributable to its right methods and orderly organization of production activities, Shenzhen Airlines made an income of 19.96 billion yuan and profit of 2.05 billion yuan, gaining its record achievement. Its specialized companies further enhanced their income growth capacity and improved obviously their profitability.

IV. Development Capability Continued to Strengthen

CNAC invested 21.165 billion yuan in 2011, up 4.8 billion yuan over that of the previous year, in which Air China accomplished 20.545 billion yuan (including16.76 billion yuan in airplane and engine investment) and specialized companies completed 620 million yuan.

Air China Cargo brought joint venturing to success, Beijing Airlines and Dalian Airlines were put into services, Inner Mongolia Airlines was proposed for approval and the equity participation in Tibet Airlines proceeded smoothly. Maintenance consolidation continued. The second equity restructuring of Air Macau was finished, with nearly 700 million MOP patacas raised from Macau government through private placement. CNAC promoted Shenzhen Airlines' access to Star Alliance, streamlined equity structure of Shenzhen Airlines and assisted Shenzhen Airlines in negotiating the reorganization of He'nan Airlines and Jade Cargo International. China National Aviation Corporation (Group) Limited injected 294 million yuan of additional capital into Xi'an Airport. CNAC, in light of operation needs, pushed forward steadily a series of construction projects, including those of the Southwest base, flight training base, Guangzhou overnight base, Chongqing aircrew production premises and Shenzhen Airlines three-bay hangar, and studied the planning and demand of the principal business at the second capital airport. The head office building project of the group was executed on an agency construction basis and went on smoothly.

With gradual implementation of Air China's nine service breakthrough projects, the initial establishment of service management system (CSM) and further improvements in total-process service, two-cabin service, frequent flyer service, e-commerce, customer relationship maintenance and the launch of the wireless LAN service for the first time in the industry, CNAC accelerated its service system construction, making phasic progress in the SKTYRAX "four-star" evaluation.

V. Internal Management Deepened Continuously

CNAC strengthened its investment management and strictly controlled its non-aviation investment. It standardized its allocation and management of human resources, strictly controlled its total wage budget, executed Air China's Stock Appreciation Rights Plan and pushed forward successfully the CNAC enterprise annuity. It further enforced its financial management policies and procedures, making in place a long-term mechanism for Off-book Accounts control. CNAC also improved the working mechanism for comprehensive risk management, strengthened performance assessment and dynamic business supervision, fully carried forward the economic value added assessment and performance assessment of total staff. It enhanced its legal affairs management capacity and conducted the assessment of the strategic, financial, market, operational and legal risks. It conducted in cooperation with specialized agencies the new round of fuel hedging research, continued enhanced supervisions over the effectiveness and efficiency of contract and procurement management rectification. With internal audit bodies and system building, it piloted in major projects the total-process follow-up audit, completed 59 internal audits and made 230 management recommendations. It further consolidated its internal resources and properly solved Southwest Airlines' tourism project and other long-standing problems. CNAC carried out energy conservation and emission reduction effectively, improved its energy consumption data monitoring system and conducted the bio-fuel flight test, the first across the country. ■

中国东方航空集团公司

2011年8月25日，中国民用航空局授予东航“飞行安全五星奖”

On August 25, 2011, CAAC Grants Five-Star Award for Flight Safety to China Eastern Airlines

2011年，中国东方航空集团公司以科学发展为主题，以加快转变发展方式为主线，强化安全管理，提高经营效益，改进服务质量，提升基础管理，深化内部改革，开展创先争优，各项工作平稳有序推进，取得了较好成绩，实现了“十二五”良好开局。

一、安全态势平稳，经营成效显著

截至2011年底，东航集团拥有在册飞机391架（其中运输飞机376架，通用飞机15架）。在“安全第一、预防为主、综合治理”的安全生产方针指导下，全年完成飞行129.3万小时，62.1万架次，获得中国民用航空局“飞行安全五星奖”。

2011年，东航集团完成运输总周转量137.3亿吨公里，旅客运输量6 872.5万人次，货邮运输量150.4万吨，飞机日利用率9.8小时/天，客座率和载运率分别为78.9%、72.0%。全年实现营业收入896.9亿元，利润总额51.9亿元。在全面提升生产经营水平的同时，东航集团积极倡导绿色飞行，开展节能减排工作，全年万元收入能耗为0.65吨标准煤/万元，同比下降7%。

2011年，东航集团各业务板块的大多数公司实现盈利。航食板块全面提高了服务质量和保障能力，提升了客户满意度，经营水平稳健提升；传媒板块积极应对后世博时期传媒市场的冲击，主营业务收入和利润总额大幅增长；金融板块加强了资金管理，调整了经营策略，创新金融业务，努力提高盈利能力；进出口板块优先优质服务主业，探索业务转型，开展降本增效，经营形势稳中有升；上海东航投资有限公司注重对内外风险全面管理，持续提升存量地产项目的一体化运作和管理能力，超额完成全部利润指标；中免免税品有限公司寻找新的增长点，及时调整经营策略，持续盈利能力突出；东航旅业投资（集团）有限公司通过与主业航空资源的组合，丰富和提升主业产品链，推进了东航产品市场化营销网络平台的构建，稳步拓展了新业务；上海东航实业有限公司通过整合资源，突出产品优势，巩固、提升现有业务，实现企业稳健经营。

二、基础管理加强，战略推进提速

2011年是东航集团的基础管理提升年，通过进一步完善法人治理结构，积极建立起产权清晰、权责分明、管理科学的现代企业制度。增强了风险管控能力，有效规避了投资、经营和管理风险，促进了国有资产的保值增值，保护了利益相关方的合法权益，推动了企业的发展。

2011年，东航集团采取十二项主要举措，努力把东航建设成具有全球竞争力的世界一流航空运输企业。着力打造以上海为复合枢纽，西安、昆明为区域枢纽，北京为隐形枢纽的规模网络；顺利加入天合联盟，并产生出显著的网络合作效应。

三、品牌价值提升，央企形象彰显

东航以客户需求为导向，以“精准、精致、精细”理念为指引，以SKYTRAX四星服务国际标准为标杆，致力于一致性服务、全流程服务、个性化服务，制订全面服务提升计划，大幅增加资金投入，推动服务品质快速改善，显著提升了旅客的感知度和认知度，东航“世界品位，东方魅力”服务品牌形象赢得越来越多的认可。

2011年，东航被《财富》杂志评为中国最具创新力公司；被国外权威机构评为“中国最具价值品牌50强”；“东方航空”被中国工商总局正式认定为“中国驰名商标”；在中国社科院与中国经营报社联合发布的排名中，东航获评上市公司品牌竞争力第三，被中国证券市场年会授予“金凤凰奖”；获得“2011中国最具创新力”企业社会责任报告认证。

2011年，东航连续执行埃及、利比亚撤离中国公民和云南、日本地震后紧急运输保障任务。在利比亚撤离任务中，做到了组织领导到位、保障措施到位、资源投入到位、细节服务到位这“四到位”，圆满完成了中国有史以来最大规模的海外包机撤离运输任务。安全、优质、高效地完成历时178天的西安世界园艺博览会的服务保障工作，东航西北分公司荣获全国民航西安世界园艺博览会航空运输服务保障和安全保卫工作先进单位荣誉称号，再次向世人展示了公司良好的服务品牌。

China Eastern Airlines Corporation Limited

In 2011, China Eastern Airlines Corporation Limited (China Eastern) strengthened its safety management, improved its service quality, and increased its operation profits, taking scientific development as its main theme and accelerating development pattern transformation as its main line. It uplifted its basic management, deepened its internal reform and carried out activities of striving to be advanced and outstanding ones, promoting all its work steadily and orderly, making a better achievement and having a good start for its 12th Five-Year Plan.

I. Keeping Safety Momentum Stable and Operation Achievement Notable

By the end of 2011, China Eastern had had 391 aircraft registered (including 376 transport aircraft and 15 general aviation aircraft). Under the guidance of work safety policy of "safety first, prevention foremost and comprehensive improvement", China Eastern recorded 1.293 million flight hours and 621 000 flights for the whole year, winning CAAC's Five Star Award for Flight Safety.

In 2011, China Eastern accomplished 13.73 billion ton-km transport turnover, 68.725 million passenger traffic, 1.504 million cargo and mail turnover, had daily aircraft utilization rate of 9.8 hours, and passenger load factor and load factor of 78.9% and 72.0% respectively. The annual business revenue reached 89.69 billion yuan and its profits hit 5.19 billion yuan. While comprehensively improving its business and operation level, China Eastern actively advocated green flights, launched energy conservation and emission reduction work, and its annual energy consumption for 10 000 yuan income was 0.65 ton standard coal, 7% less than that of the previous year.

2011年2月21日至3月5日，东航圆满完成利比亚撤侨任务

From February 21 to March 5, 2011, China Eastern Successfully Fulfills the Task of Withdrawing Overseas Chinese Compatriots from Libya

In 2011, most companies of China Eastern's business modules became profitable. The aviation catering module comprehensively promoted service quality and support capability, and improved customer satisfaction with its operation level upgraded steadily. The publicity module actively responded to post-World Expo period impact on media market, and its principal business income and overall profits increased significantly. The financial module reinforced its fund management, adjusted its operational strategy and innovated its financial business in an effort to improve profit earning capability. The import and export module prioritized its high-quality principal businesses, explored its business transformation and carried out activities to lower cost and increase profit, having its operation situation increased steadily. China Eastern Investment Company attached importance to comprehensive management of internal and external risks, continued to improve its integrated operation and management capability in its stocked real estate projects, and over-fulfilled all its target profits. China Duty Free Group Co. looked for new points of growth, timely adjusted its operation strategy and highlighted its capability in continual profit-making. China Eastern Tourism Investment Group Co. enriched and enhanced its principal business product chain through combination with principal aviation resources. It propelled building network platform for marketing of China Eastern's products and steadily expanded new businesses. China Eastern Industrial Company protruded its products' advantages through integration of resources, reconsolidated and uplifted its current businesses, realizing steady operation of the enterprise.

II. Having Basic Management Reinforced and Implementation of Company Strategy Accelerated

2011 marked a year for improvement of China Eastern's basic management. By further refining its legal person governance structure, China Eastern actively established a modern corporate system with clear equity rights, explicit rights and responsibilities, and scientific management. It strengthened its controlling capability over risks, effectively avoided risks in investment, operation and management, facilitated guarantee and increase of state-owned assets values, protected stake holders' legal rights and pushed forward development of the enterprise.

In 2011, China Eastern adopted 12 major measures in efforts to build China Eastern into a first-rate air carrier in the world with global competitiveness. It tried to build a large-scale network with Shanghai as a composite hub, Xi'an and Kunming as regional hubs and Beijing as an invisible hub. It successfully joined the SkyTeam Alliance and produced notable effects in network cooperation.

III. Having Brand Value Improved and State-owned Key Enterprise Image Conspicuous

Led by client needs, guided by concept of "being accurate, delicate and detailed" and taking four star service standards of SKYTRAX as mark posts, China Eastern developed a comprehensive service improvement plan to devote itself to unanimous, whole process and individualized services. It increased investment by a large margin and propelled rapid improvement of service quality, notably enhancing passengers' awareness and recognition China Eastern's service brand image of world level and oriental elegance is gaining more and more recognition.

In 2011, China Eastern was nominated as one of the Most Innovative Companies in China by the Fortune magazine, and as one of the Top 50 Most Valuable Brands in China by foreign authoritative organization. China Eastern Airlines was authenticated the Renowned Brand in China by the State Administration of Industry and Commerce. In the billboard list jointly issued by Chinese Academy of Social Sciences and China Business Journal, China Eastern ranked No.3 in brand competitiveness among public listed companies. It was awarded the Golden Phoenix Prize by the Annual Meeting of Chinese Securities Market. It received an authentication of social responsibility report on 2011 Most Innovative Companies in China.

In 2011, China Eastern successively carried out tasks of withdrawing Chinese citizens from Egypt and Libya and emergent transport support missions after earthquakes in Yunnan Province and Japan. In carrying out the tasks of withdrawing Chinese citizens from Libya, China Eastern did well in four aspects, namely organizational leadership, support measures, resource inputs and detailed services, and successfully accomplished the ever largest transport of Chinese citizens from abroad in Chinese history by chartered aircraft. It also fulfilled service support tasks for 178 day-long Xi'an International Horticultural Expo in a safe, high-quality and efficient way. The Northwest Branch Company of China Eastern was awarded an honorable title of advanced unit in air transport service support and aviation security for Xi'an International Horticultural Expo by CAAC, once again showing its good service brand to the world.

上海航空

上海航空有限公司是中国东方航空股份有限公司最大的全资子公司，目前拥有飞机60多架，主力机型为新一代B737NG系列，机队中还包含B757-200、B767-300以及CRJ-200，目前经营170多条国内和国际（地区）航线，通航60多个大中城市，包括香港、东京、新加坡、首尔、曼谷、墨尔本等。

一、安全形势总体平稳

2011年，公司坚持“安全第一、预防为主，综合治理、持续改进”的方针，进一步把握重组整合背景下安全工作的新特点、新任务和新要求，紧密结合安全管理体系（SMS）建设，不断完善SMS，努力提高安全管理水平。2011年，公司完成安全飞行20.54万小时，执行航班89 948班次；事故征候万时率0.08（年度指标为0.14），比上年下降0.02；未发生人为原因的严重不安全事件；未发生雷击不安全事件；未发生地面安全有责事故。各项安全指标均在可控范围之内，实现了第26个运输安全年。

二、经营效益再创佳绩

2011年，公司引进了2架B737-800飞机，并向母公司东航湿租4架B767-300飞机，使机队结构与航线网络的匹配效应进一步增强。同时，公司还先后顺利执飞了上海至墨尔本、新加坡、迪

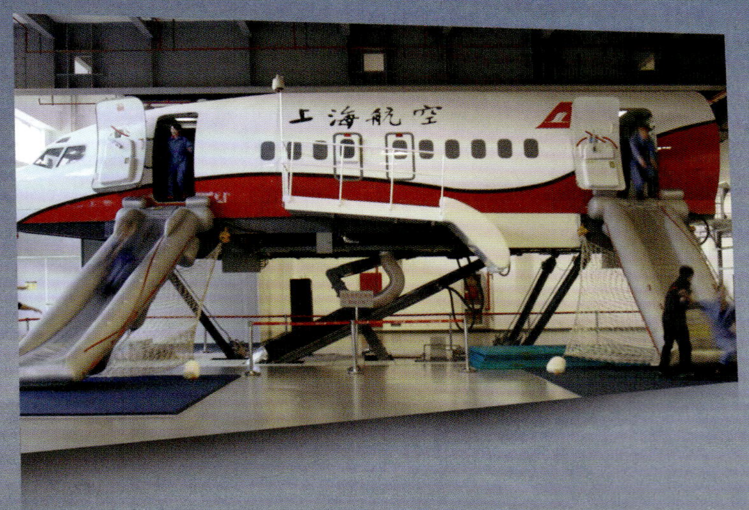

有 限 公 司

拜和莫斯科等国际中远程航线。2011年公司营业收入达到110.49亿元，运输总周转量16.01亿吨公里，客运量1 165.62万人次；客座率76.53%、载运率72.98%，比上年分别提高1.14和1.46个百分点；实现利润近10亿元，取得了良好的经营效益。

三、品牌形象得以提升

2011年，公司紧紧围绕“服务提升年”的目标，狠抓服务质量提升：一是SKYTRAX四星贯标，开展入盟对标和培训。二是完善服务改进制度。三是创新服务产品。持续推进客舱革命，完成了18架飞机客舱设施设备更新和5架飞机外部喷漆；对“两舱”的服务标准、服务内容等方面进行改进，推出了上航尊享服务、便携式机上娱乐设备（PMD）项目、“名店进客舱”等服务产品。2011年，上航顾客投诉率为1.83起/万人次、比上年下降25.3%。■

Shanghai Airlines Co., Ltd.

Shanghai Airlines Co., Ltd. ("Shanghai Airlines") is the largest wholly owned subsidiary of China Eastern Airlines Corporation Limited. Now Shanghai Airlines has over 60 airplanes in its fleet, mainly including the new-generation B737NG series supplemented by B757-200, B767-300 and CRJ-200. It currently operates over 170 domestic and international (regional) air routes connecting more than 60 large and medium-sized cities, including Hong Kong, Tokyo, Singapore, Seoul, Bangkok and Melbourne.

I. Security Situation in Overall Stability

In 2011, adhering to the principles of Safety First, Prevention Foremost, and Comprehensive Improvement, Shanghai Airlines further got hold of the new characteristics, tasks and requirements on security work against the backdrop of restructuring, made continuous improvements in the safety management system (SMS) in conjunction with its building and endeavored to boost its safety management capability. In 2011, it registered 205 400 hours of safe flights and operated 89 948 flights; the flight incident rate per 10 thousand hours was 0.08 (compared with the annual objective of 0.14), down 0.02 from the previous year. There were no serious human-factor-induced incidents, no lightning-related incidents and no ground security-related accidents. All safety indicators were within controllable range, marking 2011 as the 26th Year of Transport safety.

II. Excellent Achievements in Operating Efficiency

In 2011, Shanghai Airlines introduced two B737-800 airplanes and wet-rented four B767-300 airplanes from its parent company, China Eastern Airlines, making its fleet structure further compatible with the route network. In addition, it also successfully operated medium- and long-range international routes from Shanghai to Melbourne, Singapore, Dubai, Moscow, etc. In 2011, Shanghai Airlines recorded 11.049 billion yuan in operating income, 1.601 billion tons-km in cargo transport and passenger traffic of 11 656 200. The passenger load factor was 76.53% and cargo load factor 72.98%, 1.14 and 1.46 percentage points higher respectively than those of the previous year. It realized profit close to 1 billion yuan, making excellent achievements in operating efficiency.

III. Improvement in Brand Image

In 2011, Shanghai Airlines endeavored to improve its service quality by following the objectives set in the Year of Service Enhancement: the first was the four-star certification by SKYTRAX and its related work and training; the second was refinement of the service improvement system; the third was innovation in services and products. It pushed ahead with passenger cabin refurbishment, completing cabin facilities modification for 18 airplanes and exterior painting for five airplanes, improved service standards and service items for the Two Cabins, introduced a series of services and products, including Shanghai Airlines Exclusive Service, portable multimedia device (PMD) and Top Brands in Passenger Cabin. In 2011, the customer complaint rate of Shanghai Airlines was 1.83 per 10 thousand passengers, 25.3% lower than that of the previous year. ■

中国南方航空集团公司

2011年，中国南方航空集团公司（以下简称南航）在安全生产、经营管理、战略转型、品牌建设等方面取得了长足发展。

一、不断夯实发展基础

2011年，南航大力加强安全管理体系（SMS）建设，健全安全规章制度体系，严格落实安全生产责任制，牢固树立全员安全观念和意识，不断完善安全的绩效考核机制，全面提升安全管控力度，取得了历史上最好的安全业绩，全年安全飞行152.7万小时、73.2万架次。累计实现安全飞行898万小时，连续保证了146个月的飞行安全和211个月的空防安全，创造了“零”公司责任事故征候，“零”人为原因事故征候的“双零”佳绩，继续保持了中国航空公司最好的安全记录。

2011年，南航完成利比亚战乱、日本地震撤侨等应急保障任务146架次，运送受灾旅客1.2万多人次，捐赠“十分关爱基金”1 397万元，继续倡导绿色飞行，节能减排，节省燃油2.5万吨，减少碳排放8万吨，获得了多家机构颁发的社会责任奖，提升了企业美誉度，树立了企业形象，为发展奠定了坚实的社会基础。

二、不断探索发展方式

经过长期调研论证，南航把战略目标确定为建设国际化规模网络型航空公司。2011年10月，南航引进A380客机，成为全球第七家、国内首家运营A380的航空公司。南航把运营A380和战略目标紧密结合，推进枢纽建设，提升中转保障和中转销售能力。广州、北京、乌鲁木齐和重庆四大枢纽集中度已达到71.1%，全年中转收入达36.8亿元，同比增长47%，其中广州、北京的国际中转收入分别同比增长56.2%和17.3%；同时，加快国际航线网络建设，相继开通了6条国际航线，加密了6条国际航线，国际座公里投入比例已达到26.8%，比上年提高了3.5个百分点。每周有42个航班往返大洋洲，广州已成为中国通向大洋洲的第一门户，国际化航空公司的形

2011年4月13日，南航集团公司总经理司献民（右一）、股份公司总经理谭万庚（左一）拜会了新西兰总理约翰·基

On April 13, 2011, General Manager of China Southern Air Holding Company Si Xianmin (first from the right) and General Manager of China Southern Airlines Limited Tan Wangeng (first from the left) Meet with Prime Minister of New Zealand John Key

态初步形成。

进一步优化机队结构，淘汰老旧飞机22架，新进飞机52架，净增飞机30架，运力增长7.5%，进一步降低了安全风险和维修成本。招募了82名外籍空乘和14名外籍飞行员，解决了由于发展速度过快，带来人员培养滞后的矛盾，适应了国际化发展的新需要，开启了引进国际飞行人才的序幕。

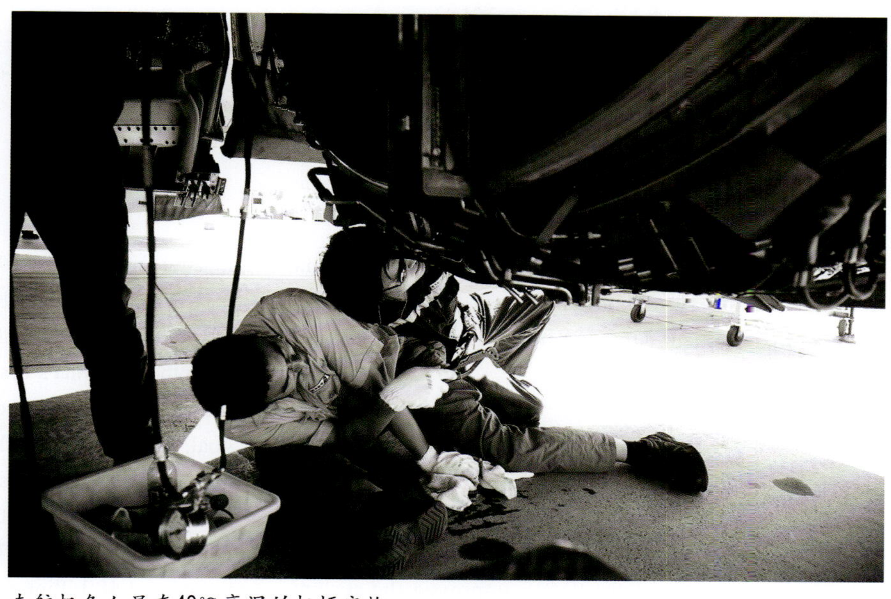

南航机务人员在40℃高温的机坪定检

Maintenance Staff of China Southern Airlines Conducts Regular Inspection at the Apron Where the Ground Temperature Hits 40℃

三、不断增强管理能力

作为大型骨干航空运输企业，南航17个分（子）公司分布在全国各主要省市。南航在发展中不断探索管理模式，调整组织结构，逐步形成了矩阵式管理的新模式，职能定位更加明确，决策科学性与风险管控水平有效提升。

2011年，南航以“为民服务创先争优”活动为契机，以打造“中国最好，亚洲一流”为服务品质的目标，以牢固树立“两一”为服务理念，开展“品牌服务创新年”活动。荣获SKYTRAX年度“全球最大进步航空公司奖”和“中国品牌百强第六名”。通过狠抓航班延误治理，让航班正常率得以有效提高。2011年航班正常率达到78.9%，同比提高2.45个百分点。

四、不断提高经营水平

2011年，共完成运输总周转量144亿吨公里，同比增长9.9%；旅客运输量8 067.7万人次，同比增长5.5%；货邮运输量113万吨，同比增长1.2%；座公里收入0.558元，同比提高0.056元。货运部在极为严峻的形势下，采取了积极推进改革，与外部有条件合作等有效措施，积极开拓市场，力抓收入，力减成本，为公司提高生产经营收益作出了重要的贡献。全集团实现营业收入932.5亿元，同比增长18.4%；实现利润总额67.8亿元，其中经营利润36.2亿元，实现EVA 18亿元，超额完成了全年的目标任务。A380机型的引进，提升了南航运营的机型实力、运营枢纽网络，以及公司品牌企业形象。

南航各专业公司积极拓展业务，整合资源，强化企业综合竞争力。文化传媒公司重点加强品牌建设，努力提升创新能力和管理水平，有效支持了主业发展；财务公司积极拓宽资金渠道，提高了资金集中度，稳健开展创新业务，超额完成了年度目标；贸易公司不断提升航材保障能力，圆满完成了A380通关验放工作，经营业绩获得新突破；客货代理公司有效拓展货运上下游业务，努力推进物流资源整合；建发公司积极实施“4+1”项目，总部大楼和三亚项目顺利开工，库尔勒、长春项目销售业绩良好，珠海项目取得了施工许可；天源证券公司克服市场持续低迷影响，积极开拓收入渠道，市场占有率企稳回升，有效遏制了亏损扩大；摩天宇公司狠抓维修质量，积极参与市场竞争，较好地完成了全年任务。各专业公司共实现营业收入8.3亿元，同比增长1[illegible]%，利润总额达2.1亿元。

2011年各项目标的圆满完成，为南航实现“十二五”规划打下了坚实基础。

China Southern Air Holding Company

In 2011, China Southern Air Holding Company (China Southern) made significant progress in work safety, business management, strategic transformation and brand development.

I. Fortifying the Foundation of Development Continuously

In 2011, China Southern stepped up efforts to build the safety management system (SMS), improved the system of safety policies and rules, strictly implemented the work safety responsibility system, firmly established the sense and mentality of safety among all employees, made continuous improvements in the safety performance assessment mechanism and enhanced safety management comprehensively, thus achieving the best safety performance in its history. The year witnessed 1.527 million safe flight hours of and 732 000 aircraft movements. China Southern realized 8.98 million cumulative hours of safe flight, 146 consecutive months of flight safety and 211 consecutive months of aviation security, and recorded zero liable incident and zero human factor caused incident, maintaining the best safety record among China's airlines.

In 2011, China Southern accomplished 146 emergency flights for evacuation of overseas Chinese during the Libyan turmoil and Japanese earthquake, carrying over 12 000 disaster-affected passengers and donating 13.97 million yuan to the Ten Cent Care Foundation. By continuing to advocate green flights, energy conservation and emission reduction, 25 000 tons of fuel was saved and 80 000 tons of carbon emissions were cut. China Southern won social responsibility awards from many agencies, which has boosted its credit, improved its corporate image and laid a solid foundation for its development.

II. Exploring the Development Mode Continuously

After long time surveys and studies, China Southern defined its strategic goal as building an airline with an international network of certain scale. In October 2011, China Southern introduced Airbus A380 in its fleet, becoming the world's seventh and China's first carrier to fly A380. China Southern closely integrated the operation of A380 with its strategic goal, pushed forward the hub construction and boosted the capability of transfer support and sales. The four hubs in Guangzhou, Beijing, Urumchi and Chongqing reached a concentration level of 71.1%, with annual transfer revenues reaching 3.68 billion yuan, increasing by 47% over a year ago. The international transfer revenue of Guangzhou and Beijing hubs grew by 56.2% and 17.3% year on year respectively. In addition, the international route network was expanded with 6 more major international routes opened and the flight frequency on 6 existing international routes increased. The proportion of kilometers to input of the available seat on international routes stood at 26.8%, up 3.5 percentage points over a year ago. With 42 flights to and from the Oceania a week, Guangzhou became the most important portal between China and the Oceania. The envisaged international carrier was taking shape.

The fleet was further optimized by cutting 22 old and aged aircraft and adding 52 new ones, representing a net increase of 30 airplanes and a 7.5% expansion of transport capacity, as a result the safety risk and maintenance costs were brought down. 82 foreign flight attendants and 14 foreign pilots were hired to solve the staffing insufficiency resulting from fast growth, to accommodate international development and open the door to recruiting international aviation talents.

III. Enhancing Management Capability Continuously

As a large air transport enterprise, China Southern operates from 17 branches and subsidiaries based in major provinces and cities across the country. It has gradually put in place the matrix management model after exerting uninterrupted efforts to explore management models and reengineer organizational structure. Roles and functions have been better defined, enabling the decision making more scientific and the capacity of risk control more effective.

In 2011, China Southern took the opportunity of the Serving the People & Pursuing Excellence initiative to launch the Year of Brand and Service Innovation program, aimed at rendering services that are Best in China and First-rate in Asia under the Double First service philosophy. China Southern was named by SKYTRAX as the World Most Improved Airline and ranked at No.6 among China's Top 100 Brands. The flight regularity rate was effectively increased after strong crackdown on flight delays. In 2011, the flight regularity rate reached 78.9%, 2.45 percentage points higher than that of the previous year.

IV. Improving Business Performance Continuously

In 2011, the total turnover was 14.4 billion ton-km, up 9.9% over a year ago; 80.677 million passengers and 1.13 million tons of cargo was carried, representing year-on-year increases of 5.5% and 1.2% respectively; the revenue per seat-km was 0.558 yuan, up 0.056 yuan over a year ago. In an extraordinarily tough situation, the cargo division made significant contributions to improving the company's operating profit by actively advancing reform, cooperating with external parties with string attached and took other effective measures to tap markets, increase revenues and cut costs. China Southern garnered 93.25 billion yuan in business revenue, up 18.4% over a year ago and 6.78 billion yuan in total profit, including 3.62 billion yuan worth of business profit, 1.8 billion yuan in EVA, beating the annual objectives. The inclusion of Airbus A380 has improved the fleet strength, hub network and brand image of China Southern.

Specialized subsidiaries of China Southern actively expanded their businesses, integrated resources and sharpened the overall competitive edge. The culture and media firm endeavored to improve the capability of innovation and management to effectively support the principal business, with an emphasis on brand building. The finance company actively diversified the funding sources, increased fund concentration and steadily carried out innovative business, managing to exceed annual objectives. The trade company continuously enhanced the capability of aviation supplies, fulfilled the A380 customs clearance and release and made new breakthroughs in financial results. The freight forwarding company effectively tapped into upstream and downstream businesses and pursued integration of logistic resources. The construction and development company actively executed the "4+1" project, with the construction of headquarters building and the Sanya project commenced successfully, the Korla and Changchun projects well sold and the Zhuhai project granted the construction permit. TeemRise Securities overcame the impact of continuous market downturn by expanding the income stream, steadily increasing its market share and effectively containing losses. MTU Maintenance Zhuhai was devoted to improving maintenance quality and actively participated in market competition, thereby fulfilling annual objectives. Specialized subsidiaries combined registered 830 million yuan in operating revenue, up 11% over a year ago, with 210 million yuan in profit.

Fulfillment of objectives set for 2011 lays a solid foundation for realization of China Southern's 12th Five-Year Plan.

静候验收的南航首架A380

The First A380 Assembled for China Southern Airlines Ready for Acceptance

厦门航空有限公司

2011年，厦门航空有限公司（以下简称厦航）紧紧围绕“十二五”发展战略目标，坚持以安全发展为主题，以提升科学管理水平为主线，实现了安全管理水平稳步提高，经营业绩稳步提升，在品牌建设、基础设施建设、信息化建设、企业文化建设等方面取得了显著的成效，成就了“十二五”的精彩开局。

一、安全形势总体平稳

2011年，厦航的安全形势总体平稳，实现了安全年。全年安全飞行25.83万小时、14.49万架次，同比分别增长18.1%、12.3%；已连续36个月未发生公司责任的事故征候及以上不安全事件。飞行严重差错万时率0.116，同比下降15.3%；机务直接原因造成的航班不正常千次率为2.63，同比下降20.78%。截止到2012年1月7日，公司已累计安全飞行200.15万小时，达到民航局设定的“飞行安全二星奖”标准。

深化安全责任落实，完善安全绩效考核办法，细化分解安全指标，进一步加大飞行、机务、运控等重要运行部门的安全责任绩效指标的权重。持续加大监督检查力度，加强过程监督和事前防范，对出现的安全问题，坚持按照“四不放过”原则调查处理。强化资质能力排查，严把飞行、机务、签派等关键岗位人员的准入关、养成训练质量关和实践能力关。提升风险防控能力，充分发挥安全管理体系在风险识别、风险防控、系统管理等方面的效用。提升规章执行力，全年共梳理了82册共计930多万字的管理手册，并开展手册管理复审，确保文文相符、文实相符。持续加大安全投入，充分发挥科学技术对提高安全裕度的支撑作用，在24家客运航空公司安全保障财务考核中以

2011年7月18日，民航华东地区管理局副局长唐伟斌（左三）向厦门航空总经理车尚轮（左二）颁发《航空承运人运行合格证》

On July 18, 2011, Tang Weibin (third from the left), Deputy Director General of CAAC East Regional Administration, Confers the Air Operator Certificate to Che Shanglun (second from the left), General Manager of Xiamen Airlines

9.5分荣获第一名。

公司积极推进空防安全体系建设，成为全民航首家通过CCAR-121-R4补充审定的航空公司，首家通过航空安保审计的航空公司，首家实行SMS审核试点工作的航空公司。

二、经营业绩大幅跃升

厦航坚持“高效精飞、以质为重”的经营思路，统筹安排好全年飞行资源，飞机日利用率达9.35小时，实现了月月盈利，利润再创新高，近两年的利润超过前25年的利润总和，成为全球少有、全国唯一连续25年盈利的航空公司。2011年，厦航共完成运输总周转量19.1亿吨公里，营业收入146.2亿元。实现年旅客运输量1 531.7万人次，货邮运输量16.7万吨，分别同比增长12.9%、5.3%。

时刻关注国内外经济形势，建立较为完善的市场监控和快速反应机制；每月定期召开生产经营分析会，及时总结营销工作的经验与不足；重点监控受市场影响严重的不保变航班和收益弱势航班，并及时采取措施提升低效航班收益。制定“向外飞、向西飞、向高飞”的市场发展策略，积极争取繁忙机场时刻，进一步巩固和完善了西部、高原以及国际航线网络。打造日常销售监控体系，通过在淡季、旺季期间实施差别定价获得了超越竞争对手的收益品质。

2011年11月17日，厦航与天合联盟签署了《入盟承诺协议》，全面启动入盟对标工作，并通过扩大代码共享合作范围逐步完善航线网络，为加快国际化进程迈出关键的一步。

三、服务品牌广获赞誉

厦航秉承“以诚为本、以客为尊”的服务理念，积极塑造“精、尊、细、美”的服务文化品牌。全年，公司未发生局方核定的旅客有效投诉和货主有效投诉，行李运输差错率万分之0.09，货物运输差错率万分之0.01。

严格治理航班不正常，完善内部各运行保障环节的工作流程，积极协调各地军方、局方、空管单位和机场。2011年，公司航班正常率为80.45%，位居全民航第一。积极推进服务品牌建设，改进旅客服务信息系统，构筑统一的客户服务平台；完善服务质量监控体系，加强对服务工作的全程监控。先后投入近6 000万元，用于4架B757和6架B737-700头等舱改造、飞机内饰美化以及头等舱休息室装修，客舱环境得到了全方位的改善。以高标准、高品质服务圆满完成了重要旅客的航班保障任务，赢得了社会各界的广泛赞誉。

四、发展战略扎实推进

成功引入河北航空投资集团的战略投资，总资产首次突破233亿元，净资产首次突破67亿元。提前落实了2012年12架新飞机的批文，签订了6架B787飞机的购买合同，推动“十二五”机队规划落地。厦门、杭州、福州等用地问题相继获批，突破了公司各基地发展的用地瓶颈，稳步推进战略实施。目前，厦航已形成了以厦门、福州为主基地，覆盖全国、辐射东南亚和东北亚、连接港澳台的航线网络，其中，国内航线190余条，国际及地区航线20余条，每周执行航班3 200多个。

五、科学管理水平稳步提升

持续完善财务管控模式，强化监控手段，连续实现了9个销售资金安全年。确立“人才强企”战略，建立并完善以“人座比”为核心的人员编制体系。实施空勤薪酬体系改革完善、地面人员增资与企业补充养老转制年金的制定工作；完善“关键绩效指标+基础指标”的绩效考核指标体系，加大了安全、服务和效益指标的考核权重。加强管理人员队伍建设，安排了近百名中高层管理人员分别前往国内外知名企业与学府进行中高层领导力发展项目培训，努力提升公司科学管理水平，助推企业健康发展。

六、信息化建设全面提速

公司已将信息化建设提高到公司“十二五”战略发展层面，从资金、组织和人力上加大了信息化建设的投入力度，带动信息化建设的全面提速。2011年，公司信息化建设投入达3 500余万元，完成了39个应用系统的开发。■

Xiamen Airlines Co., Ltd.

In 2011, by focusing on the strategic objectives of development in the 12th Five-Year Plan, adhering to the theme of safe development and giving high priority to improving its scientific management capacity, Xiamen Airlines Co., Ltd. (hereinafter referred to as Xiamen Airlines) witnessed steady improvement in safety management and operating performance and made noticeable progress in brand building, infrastructure construction, IT development and corporate culture building, accomplishing a great start for the 12th Five-Year Plan period.

I. Overall Safety Situation Remained Stable

In 2011, Xiamen Airlines maintained a stable situation in safety and completed another year of safe work. In the year, the company recorded 258 300 safe flight hours and 144 900 aircraft movements, up by 18.1% and 12.3% over the previous year respectively; no incidents or unsafe events above the incident level for which Xiamen Airlines was liable took place for 36 months in a row. The flight serious error rate per 10 thousand hours was 0.116, a decrease of 15.3% from one year ago; the irregularity rate per 1 000 flights caused directly by aircraft maintenance was 2.63, a decrease of 20.78% from the previous year. As of January 7, 2012, the company had accomplished 2 001 500 safe flight hours, a level eligible for the CAAC Two Star Award for Flight Safety.

In 2011, Xiamen Airlines deepened the implementation of safety responsibility system, improved the safety performance assessment procedures, broke down safety indicators and assigned higher weights to the safety performance indicators of flight, maintenance, operation control and other important functions. Supervisory inspection was stepped up to enhance process supervision and early prevention. Any safety problems were investigated and handled in accordance with the principle of Never Neglecting Four Things. Qualification screening was strengthened to strictly control the admission, quality of apprenticeship training

2011年11月17日，厦门航空加入天合联盟签字仪式在罗马举行

On November 17, 2011, the Signing Ceremony for Xiamen Airlines Joining the SkyTeam Alliance Is Held in Rome

and practical abilities of personnel in flight, maintenance, and dispatching positions and other key posts. The risk prevention and control capability was enhanced, and full play was given to the role of safety management system in risk identification, risk prevention, risk control and system management. Enforcement of regulations was strengthened, with 82 management manuals totaling over 9.3 million words being reviewed in the year to ensure consistency among the texts and pertinence of the texts to reality. Investment in safety was increased by maximizing the supporting function of technologies in improving safety margin. Among the 24 passenger airlines participating in the financial assessment of safety support capabilities, Xiamen Airlines ranked first with score of 9.5.

The company actively promoted the building of aviation security system, becoming the first airlines that passed the CCAR Part 121-R4 supplemental certification, the first airlines that passed the aviation security audit and the first airlines that launched the SMS audit pilot program in China's civil aviation industry.

II. Operating Performance Improved Remarkably

Xiamen Airlines deployed its aviation resources in the year under the operating philosophy of Highly Efficient and Detailed Flight, and Prioritizing Quality. The daily utilization rate of aircraft reached 9.35 hours, ensuring profitability of the company every month. Profits scaled new high, with the past two years recording more profits than the previous 25 years combined, making the company one of the world's few airlines and the only one in China that remained in profit for 25 consecutive years. In 2011, Xiamen Airlines completed a total turnover of 1.91 billion ton-km and garnered 14.62 billion yuan in operating income. 15 317 000 passengers and 167 000 tons of cargo and mail were handled in the year, representing year-on-year increases of 12.9% and 5.3% respectively.

Always keeping an eye on economic situations at the home and abroad, Xiamen Airlines has established a sound mechanism for market monitoring and quick response; operation analysis meetings were conducted monthly to review good practices and deficiencies in marketing; monitoring was focused on money losing flights vulnerable to market conditions and weaker-yield flights, with timely measures taken to improve the yield of less efficient flights. The market development strategy of Flying Overseas, Flying Westward and Flying to High Plateaus was defined and slots at busy airports were sought with vigor to further consolidate and improve the network of flights to West China, high plateaus and international destinations. A daily sales monitoring system was created, and pricing was differentiated between peak and low seasons to outperform competitors in profitability.

On November 17, 2011, Xiamen Airlines entered into the Accession Commitment Agreement with SkyTeam Alliance to launch, in an all-round way, the benchmark aligning work for the accession and gradually improve the air route network through expanded cooperation in code sharing, a critical step towards accelerated going global strategy

III. Service Brand Won Wide Recognition

Xiamen Airlines upheld the service philosophy of Being Integrity-based and Customer-oriented to build the service culture brand characterized by Delicacy, Respect, Detail and Beautifulness. Throughout the year, the company received no valid complaints from passengers or cargo owners confirmed by CAAC, the baggage handling error rate was 0.0009% and cargo handling error rate was 0.0001%.

Flight irregularity was strictly rectified. Workflows were improved in all the operation supporting links of the company and coordination was actively carried out with the militaries, CAAC regional administrations, air traffic control authorities and airports around China. In 2011, the company recorded a flight regularity rate of 80.45%, the highest across the civil aviation industry. Xiamen Airlines made active efforts to promote the service brand building, improve the passenger service information system and establish a uniform customer service platform. The service quality monitoring system was improved to intensify whole-process monitoring of services. A total of nearly 60 million yuan was invested in the modification of the first-class cabins and improving the interior decorations of four B757 and six B737-700 aircraft and in decorating first-class lounges, making all-sided improvements in passenger cabins. Transport service

温馨的机上服务

Warm In-flight Services

of high standards and high qualities were provided for VIP passengers to their satisfaction, winning the company broad recognition across all sectors of the society.

IV. Development Strategy Was Implemented Solidly

Xiamen Airlines successfully attracted a strategic investment from Hebei Aviation Investment Group, as a result of which, the company's total and net assets respectively rose above 23.3 billion yuan and 6.7 billion yuan for the first time. Approvals were obtained ahead of schedule for the 12 new aircraft to be introduced in 2012 and purchase contracts were signed for six B787 aircraft, a move getting the company closer to its fleet objectives set forth for the 12th Five-Year Plan period. Permits for land use in Xiamen, Hangzhou and Fuzhou were successively obtained, removing the bottlenecks in land use that had been hindering the company's development in its bases and steadily advancing the implementation of corporate strategy. At present, Xiamen Airlines operates a route network that serves the whole country (including Hong Kong, Macao and Taiwan) and Southeast and Northeast Asia, predominately from its main bases of Xiamen and Fuzhou. The network includes over 190 domestic routes and more than 20 international and regional routes, with over 3 200 flights every week.

V. Scientific Management Was Improved Steadily

In 2011, Xiamen Airlines continued to improve its financial management modes and strengthen its monitoring tools, which resulted in the 9th consecutive year for safety of sales capital. The strategy of boosting the enterprise by qualified personnel was established and the staffing system with person-to-seat ratio at its core was created and improved. The company implemented the air crew compensation reform, increased the salaries of ground crew and developed rules on enterprise supplementary pension insurance. The performance assessment indicator system comprising key performance indicators and basic indicators was improved, with higher weights assigned to the indicators of safety, service and profit. Managerial staff development was strengthened. Nearly 100 medium and senior executives were provided with medium and senior leadership training courses at well-known companies and schools in and beyond China to improve the company's scientific management and facilitate its healthy development.

VI. IT Development Gained Momentum in an All-round Way

The company upgraded IT development as an element of strategic development in its 12th Five-Year Plan period. Inputs into the IT field were increased in terms of money, organization and human resources to fully accelerate IT development. In 2011, the company invested over 35 million yuan in IT development and completed development of 39 application systems.

海南航空股份有限公司

2011年，海南航空股份有限公司积极推动安全体系建设，持续提升安全运营品质，巩固升级服务质量，强化国际航线开拓，着力推进品牌建设，加大节能减排工作力度，致力于绿色行业发展，企业保持了又好又快发展势头，为民航强国建设作出了应有的贡献。

一、勇担社会责任，展现良好形象

海南航空以国家和民族利益为重，圆满完成埃及、利比亚撤侨紧急运输任务。期间共执行38个航班，运送撤侨人员近5 000人、物资约40吨。荣获多项民航局授予的撤侨航班保障“先进集体”和“先进个人”荣誉称号。此外，顺利完成深圳第26届世界大学生夏季运动会、西安世界园艺博览会、两会、博鳌亚洲论坛等重要活动的保障任务，积极承担企业的社会责任，展现良好企业形象。

二、全面完成生产任务，生产经营稳步增长

2011年，海南航空实现总周转量389 064.8万吨公里，同比增长10.32%；旅客运输量2 049万人，同比增长9.98%；安全飞行36.85万小时，同比增长5.65%。

三、前置风险管控，推进安全体系建设

截至2011年底，海南航空累计安全飞行18年、326.93万小时，运送旅客超过2 000万人，平均客座率84.20%，在国内上市航空公司中居首位。荣获民航局授予的“安全飞行三星奖”称号。

海南航空安全工作以防范关口前移与人员资质建设为重点，通过大力加强全员前置性风险防范意识，开展关键风险管控，开发并上线运行“海航运行风险管控系统（HORCS）”；开展危险品违规运输项目治理，创新设立安全管理微博、设计制作《安全期刊》及宣传折页；积极制定并落实安全文化推进方案。安全管理水平得到进一步提高。

2011年6月22日，海南航空总裁陈明接受由SKYTRAX评选出的2011年度“中国最佳航空公司”及“中国地区卓越服务”两项大奖

On June 22, 2011, Chen Ming, President of Hainan Airlines, Receives Two Big Awards — Best Airlines of China in 2011 and Staff Service Excellence Award (China) Offered by SKYTRAX

四、提升服务品质，品牌建设实现重大跨越

海南航空提炼形成的USMILE服务理念，由服务愿景和U-SMILE服务准则构成。以“海南航空，改变期望”为服务愿景，通过满足旅客需求、超越客户期望，以“至诚、至善、至精、至美”的不懈追求，创造全新的旅行体验。U-SMILE服务准则主要内容为

Hainan Airlines Group Co., Ltd.

In 2011, Hainan Airlines Group Co., Ltd. (hereinafter referred to as Hainan Airlines) energetically promoted the construction of a safety management system, continuously uplifted its safe operation quality, cemented and upgraded its service quality, reinforced the expansion of international routes, earnestly promoted its brand building, exerted greater efforts in energy-saving and emission-reduction, devoted itself to the development of green civil aviation industry and maintained a good and fast development momentum, thus making its due contributions to turning China into a great country in civil aviation.

I. Shouldering Social Responsibility and Presenting a Fine Image

By giving priority to the national interests, Hainan

以客为亲、安全正点、东方优雅、创新激情、团队协作、平等仁爱。

采取系列措施提升服务品质：调整供餐模式，增加清醒服务，更新茶艺展示服务；统一A330旅客操作界面，改版《华翼——机上娱乐指南》，推进手持娱乐设备上机项目，提升头等舱旅客体验等机上娱乐设施，通过改版《云端》杂志，更换白瓷餐具等措施系统提升机供品质量；完成北京贵宾室动态区及海口贵宾室改扩建工程；开展行李专项整治，引进全球行李查询系统。

海南航空蝉联SKYTRAX“2011年中国最佳航空公司”及“中国地区卓越服务”两项大奖；荣获由美国著名高端商务杂志“GLOBAL TRAVELER”评选出的“2011年度中国最佳航空公司”称号，首次入选国际权威品牌咨询测评机构Millward Brown评定的“BRANDZ最具价值中国品牌50强”。实现了中国民航企业品牌的又一历史突破。

五、完善不正常航班应对机制，运行品质稳步提升

重点完善不正常航班处置和应对机制，建立相关值班制度及协调机制，降低管制因素对航班正常性的影响；通过建立考核制度、系统分解考核指标、开展运行质量审核、组织专项会议等措施，降低公司原因对航班正常率的影响，提高运行品质。

六、开展代码共享，大力拓展国际网络

2011年，海南航空新开国际、地区航线11条，涉及城市有苏黎世、伊斯坦布尔、悉尼、马累、普吉、釜山、冲绳、赤塔等。调整航线网络拓展思路，加密北京始发国际航线，提升首都机场国内与国际航线对接能力。与美国航空（American Airlines）正式签署关于开展代码共享合作的协议，双方将在代码共享、常旅客、时刻协调、优化中转服务等方面展开广泛合作，有效提升北美航线运营水平。

七、响应国家节能减排号召，助力打造绿色民航

按照民航局的具体部署，海南航空节能减排工作在巩固2010年成绩的基础上，重点推进公司已有节能减排项目的固化、提升。通过对主要项目的过程进行KPI控制，GPU替代APU的使用、二次放行、减少着陆阶段APU使用，三个项目较好地完成了年度及各月的控制指标。12个常态化管理的节能减排项目共实现节约燃油2.94万吨，节约运营成本约2.44亿元。

为贯彻海南省“十二五”期间的节能减排目标，海南航空通过大量数据分析，确定使用“修正吨公里耗油”作为公司单耗指标，最终通过审计组和省工信厅的核查，确定海南航空“十二五”期间节能减排的政府考核指标为“修正吨公里耗油同比2010年降低1.5%，绝对节能量15 000吨标煤”。■

2011年2月27日，海航第一班赴希腊接中国同胞航班机组返回北京

On February 27, 2011, the First Flight of Hainan Airlines to Receive Chinese Compatriots from Greece Returns to Beijing

Airlines successfully fulfilled the urgent transport tasks of withdrawing overseas Chinese from Egypt and Libya, with a total of 38 flights sent, carrying nearly 5 000 overseas Chinese and approximately 40 tons of materials. It won several honorable titles offered by CAAC such as Advanced Collective and Advanced Individual in terms of supporting overseas Chinese withdrawal. Besides, it smoothly fulfilled the support tasks for important activities such as Shenzhen 26th Summer Universiade, NPC, CPPCC and Boao Forum for Asia, actively shouldering its share of social responsibility and presenting a fine image to the general public.

II. Accomplishing Overall Production Task with Steady Increase in Business Operation

In 2011, Hainan Airlines registered a total traffic turnover of about 3 890.648 million ton-km, handled a passenger traffic volume of 20.49 million, and conducted 368 500 hours of safe flights, with year-on-year increases of 10.32%, 9.98% and 5.65% respectively.

III. Moving Risk Control Ahead and Promoting Safety System Building

By the end of 2011, Hainan Airlines had safely operated flights for an accumulative 18 years, 3.269 3 million hours, and transported more than 20 million passengers, with its passenger load factor averaging 84.20%, ranking the first among the domestic listed aviation companies. It won the Three-Star Flight Safety Award offered by CAAC.

By focusing its safety work on moving the prevention ahead, the building of personnel qualification and extensively enhancing all staff's awareness of risk prevention, Hainan Airlines carried out the key risk control, developed and put into operation the Hainan Airlines Operation Risk Control System (HORCS), conducted rectification of illegal transport of dangerous goods, creatively established safety management microblog, designed and produced the Periodical of Safety and some publicity folders, and earnestly developed and implemented a safety culture promotion plan, the above of which further improved its safety management level.

IV. Upgrading Service Quality with Big Leap in Brand Building

Hainan Airlines refined its service philosophy into USMILE, embracing a service target and core U-SMILE service standards. Service target implied the meaning of Hainan Airlines, Changing Expectation, i.e. creating entirely new travel experiences through meeting passengers' needs, surpassing passengers' expectations and by untiringly pursuing the objectives featuring honesty, benevolence, exquisiteness and excellence. The main body of the core U-SMILE service standards included sincerity to passengers, safety & regularity, manners & elegance, innovation & passion, leadership & teamwork and equality & love.

To upgrade its service quality, Hainan Airlines took a series of measures: a) adjusting catering supply mode, adding

refreshment service and updating tea-art exhibition service; b) unifying the A330 passenger operation interface, revising China Wings-Air Entertainment Guide, making handy entertainment device available on the aircraft, upgrading on-board passenger entertainment facilities especially in the first class cabin, and systematically uplifting the quality of on-board supplies by revising the magazine Over Cloud and using white porcelain tableware; c) completing the renovation and expansion projects of the dynamic area in Beijing VIP room and the Haikou VIP room; and d) carrying out special luggage rectification by importing global luggage inquiry system.

Hainan Airlines was for the second consecutive year named 2011 Best Airlines China and Staff Service Excellence China in the annual SKYTRAX awards. It was also acclaimed as the Best Airline in China in 2011 by American luxury travel magazine Global Traveller, and was listed for the first time in the BRANDZ Top 50 Most Valuable Chinese Brands, released by the international brand evaluation and consultancy firm Millward Brown, making another historical breakthrough in the consolidation of Chinese civil aviation brands.

V. Improving the Coping Mechanism for Irregular Flights with a Steady Enhancement in Operation Quality

By focusing on improving the mechanism to cope with irregular flights, Hainan Airlines established related shift system and coordinating mechanism to mitigate the influence of control factors on flight regularity. And by taking such measures as establishing an assessment system, systematically breaking down the assessment indicators, conducting operation quality reviews, organizing specialized conferences, etc. it lowered the company-induced influence on flight regularity and therefore enhanced the operation quality.

VI. Initiating Code-sharing and Making Great Efforts in Expanding International Network

In 2011, Hainan Airlines newly launched 11 international and regional routes, connecting cities such as Zurich, Istanbul, Sydney, Male, Phuket, Pusan, Okinawa, Chita, etc. By making adjustment to the conception of route network expansion, it increased the frequency of international flights originating from Beijing, uplifting the Capital Airport's capacity in connecting domestic routes with international ones. It formally signed a code-sharing cooperative agreement with American Airlines and the two sides would have extensive cooperation in areas such as code-sharing, frequent flyers program, slot coordination, transfer services optimization, etc. to effectively uplift its operational level on the routes connecting North American.

VII. Answering the State Call for Energy Saving and Emission Reduction and Striving to Shape a Green Civil Aviation Industry

By following the specific strategy arrangements made by CAAC and based on the consolidation of the achievements made in 2001 in energy-saving and emission-reduction, Hainan Airlines focused on facilitating the execution of the company's current energy-saving and emission-reduction projects. By using KPI for key projects management, Hainan Airlines replaced APU with GPU, implemented the second clearance approach and reduced the use of APU in landing stage, and with these three projects, the annual and monthly control targets were better fulfilled. The 12 energy-saving and emission-reduction projects under normal management saved a total of 29 400 tons of fuel and 244 million yuan in operation cost.

In order to fulfill energy-saving and emission-reduction target set by Hainan Province for the 12th Five-Year Plan, Hainan Airlines determined to use, through extensive data analysis, revised oil consumption per ton/km as the company's unit consumption target which was finally approved by the auditing group and the Provincial Industry and Information Department, and identified its official target in energy-saving and emission-reduction during the 12th Five-Year Plan period as 1.5% reduction in revised oil consumption per ton/km and an absolute energy-saving of 15 000 tons of standard coal in comparison with those of the previous year.

山东航空集团有限公司

2011年山东航空集团紧紧围绕“十二五”规划，在安全运行、综合效益、服务提升、创新发展等方面均有新的突破，取得了优异的业绩，实现了“十二五”良好开局。

一、落实安全管理体系，安全生产保持平稳

2011年共保障安全飞行20.39万小时、10.64万架次，同比分别增长12.3%、12.4%，未发生公司原因运输事故征候以上的不安全事件。整体形势持续平稳，实现了安全飞行17周年。一是加大安全管理体系（SMS）平台使用推进力度，全年共收到员工主动报告安全信息1 595条，同比增加943条，同比提高145%。加强对信息反馈的监控和考核力度，信息反馈率为96.4%。二是强化飞行训练管控，全年聘任责任机长38名，副驾驶93名。加强飞行品质监控，典型事件发生率2.4‰，三级事件发生率6.85%，同比分别下降17%、18.5%。三是完成了民航局CCAR-121-R4补充审定、第三次IOSA复审和国航湿租运行安全审计工作。

二、强化系统管理，运行品质持续改进

一是深入开展航班延误专项整治，加强运行基础保障，提升运控管理水平。2011年平均航班正点率为79.68%，列全民航第2位；4小时以上延误航班占总航班量的0.78%，同比下降0.69个百分

2011年12月26日山东航空公司实现安全飞行17周年

On December 26, 2011, SDAG Celebrates Its 17th Consecutive Year of Flight Safety

Shandong Aviation Group

In 2011, Shandong Aviation Group (SDAG) focused on the 12th Five-Year Plan and made new breakthroughs and outstanding progress in safe operations, overall efficiency, service improvement, innovations etc., achieving a good start to the 12th Five-Year Plan period.

I. Implementing Safety Management System and Maintaining Work Safety Stable

Throughout 2011, SDAG recorded 203.9 thousand hours of safe flight or 106.4 thousand aircraft movements, representing year-on-year increases of 12.3% and 12.4%

点；航班平均延误时间0.79小时，同比减少0.07小时。二是加强新技术应用，推进9个运行管控项目建设，完成“中断起飞”应急撤离演示验证和济南机场使用平视指引系统（HUD）实施特殊批准的I类运行验证飞行。三是加强应急体系建设，开展中高层管理人员应急管理培训和媒体应对知识培训；按计划推动应急演练，全年共实施综合演练4次，专业应急演练6次，完成家庭援助队伍培训13批323人次。

三、优化核心资源配置，效益实现历史最好水平

2011年，集团实现收入100.24亿元，同比增长31%；利润总额11.27亿元，同比增加1.89亿元；运输主业完成运输总周转量14.23亿吨公里，旅客运输量1 107万人次，货邮运输量11.29万吨，同比分别增长20.8%、18.5%和13.4%。一是科学调配组织生产，投产效率显著提高。全年执行计划停场696.5架日、非计划停场70.5架日，保障飞机可用率95.92%，同比提高0.21个百分点。二是统筹飞行资源与市场需求、对内保障与对外支援的关系，确保了旺季生产的运力投入。全年共引进B737-800飞机8架，机队规模达到54架。全年可用飞机日利用率为10.62小时/架日，安全飞行20.39万小时，同比增长12.3%。三是以精细化管理为中心，提升效益管理水平。全年座公里收入达0.505 2元，列全行业第二名；客座率为81.6%，同比增长0.7个百分点，在全民航保持较高水平。

四、建立健全服务管控体系，服务发展迈入正轨

服务品质持续改进，投诉率为1.17次/万人，同比下降0.4%。行李运输不正常率为0.66‰，优于公司考核指标。第三方旅客总体满意度86.88%，较2011年初目标提高6.8个百分点。一是完善服务管理体系，提高服务管控能力。引进第三方机构，系统规划服务发展。二是推进服务标准体系建设。改善旅客体验，打造全流程服务。三是推进品牌建设，丰富品牌内涵。以86.55亿元的品牌价值再次荣登“中国500最具价值品牌排行榜”，名列第147位，较上一届排名提升了3个位次，品牌增值26.17亿元。

五、全面启动软硬件基本建设，基础管理稳步提升

一是以促进理念转变、提升综合素质为重点，分层级、有重点地加大干部培训工作力度。二是推进人事、财务、投资等基本管控制度建设，推进内控机制优化，梳理、完善了涉及人事管理、财务管控、资产采购与管理、投资企业管控等相关管控制度82个。三是启动IT战略规划咨询，系统规划IT建设，计划投资2.9亿元；打造与业务协同的系统平台，推进IT项目50个。四是基建规划项目全面展开，实施基建工程20项，建筑面积约7万平方米，合同金额约7 400万元。■

respectively. No unsafe events above the incident level due to the reasons that can be attributed to the company occurred during the year. The overall situation remained stable, making the year the 17th consecutive year of safe flight. First, efforts were intensified to promote the use of the safety management system (SMS) platform, and a total of 1 595 messages regarding safety issues were received from employees throughout the year, increasing by 943 messages or 145% over the previous year. Monitoring and assessment of feedbacks were strengthened, with the feedback rate reaching 96.4%. Second, tightened control was imposed on flight training. In 2011, the company recruited 38 pilots-in-command and 93 first officers. Flight operational quality monitoring was strengthened, with the incidences of typical events and level-3 events standing at 0.24% and 6.85%, representing 17% and 18.5% decreases over those of the previous year respectively. Third, the Company successfully passed the CCAR Part 121-R4 supplemental certification conducted by CAAC and the third IOSA review, and completed operational safety audit on wet leases by Air China.

II. Reinforcing System Management and Improving Operational Quality Continuously

First, vigorous efforts were made to rectify flight delays so as to enhance basic support for operations and upgrade the control and management of operations. In 2011, the company's flight regularity rate was averaged at 79.68%, ranking the second in China's civil aviation industry. The flights delayed over 4 hours accounted for 0.78% of the total flights, 0.69 percentage points less compared to that of the previous year. The average delay time of all delayed flights was 0.79 hours, a reduction of 0.07 hour as compared to that of the previous year. Second, application of new technology was strengthened. Efforts were made to promote the construction of 9 operation control projects. The aborted takeoff emergency evacuation demonstration was carried out and validated and a test flight of the specifically approved type I with head-up display (HUD) by Jinan Airport was conducted. Third, the building of emergency response system was strengthened. Trainings on emergency management and on how to deal with the media were carried out for middle and senior executives. Emergency drills were launched as planned, with four comprehensive drills and six specialized emergency drills being completed during the whole year. Trainings were offered to 323 family support personnel in 13 batches.

III. Optimizing the Allocation of Core Assets and Making Record-high Benefits

In 2011, SDAG achieved a revenue of 10.024 billion yuan and the profits totaled 1.127 billion yuan, a year-on-year increase of 31% and 189 million yuan respectively; the principal business of transport completed a turnover of 1.423 billion ton-km, transporting 11.07 million passengers and 112.9 thousand tons of cargo and mail, increasing by 20.8%, 18.5% and 13.4% over those of the previous year respectively. First, resources were allocated in a scientific way, which resulted in a significant improvement in production efficiency. In 2011, the Company recorded 696.5 days of scheduled aircraft-on-ground and 70.5 days of unscheduled aircraft-on-ground. The availability rate of aircraft was maintained at 95.92%, 0.21 percentage points higher than that of the previous year. Second, efforts were made to coordinate and balance the relationship between flight resources and market demand and that between internal needs and external support, in order to ensure the transport capacity allocation in the peak season. The daily utilization rate of available aircraft during the whole year was 10.62 hours, and a total of 203.9 thousand hours of safe flight was recorded, a year-on-year increase of 12.3%. Third, refined management was centered on to improve the level of benefits management. In 2011, the revenue per seat-km reached 0.505 2 yuan, ranking the second in the industry. The passenger load factor stood at 81 6%, 0.7 percentage points higher than that of the previous year, which remained a relatively high level in the whole industry.

IV. Establishing and Improving Service Control System and Bringing Service Development onto the Right Track

Service quality was continuously improved, with customer complaints standing at 1.17 times per 10 000 passengers, decreasing by 0.4% as compared to that of the previous year. The irregularity rate in luggage transport was 0.066%, better than the indicators set for corporate evaluation. The overall passenger satisfaction rate from the third party evaluation was 86.88%, 6.8 percentage points higher than the target set forth at the beginning of 2011. First, the service management

system was improved to reinforce the company's service control capability. Third-party agencies were introduced to systematically plan the development of services. Second, efforts were made to promote the building of service standards system. Whole-process services were initiated to improve passengers' flying experience. Third, brand connotation was enriched by promoting brand construction. With a brand value of 8.655 billion yuan, SDAG was re-listed among China's 500 Most Valuable Brands, ranking the 147th, three places up than its position it got last time or increasing by 2.617 billion yuan in value.

V. Launching Software and Hardware Construction Projects and Improving the Basic Management Steadily

First, more efforts were made to train leaders in a hierarchical way and with a focus on facilitating the change of their thoughts and improving their overall qualities. Second, the building of basic control systems regarding personnel matters, finance and investment issues was promoted; internal control mechanism was further optimized; 82 control systems related to personnel management, finance management, asset procurement and management, investment companies control etc. were improved. Third, consultation on IT strategic planning was initiated to develop a systematic plan for IT construction with an estimated investment of 290 million yuan. System platforms consistent with business were built up and 50 IT projects were facilitated. Fourth, infrastructure planning was in full swing. 20 infrastructure projects were carried out, with a total construction area of approximately 70 000 square meters and a contract value of approximately 74 million yuan.

截至2012年2月底，山东航空公司机队规模达到57架

By February 2012, There Are 57 Aircraft in the Fleet of Shandong Airlines

北 京 航

北京航空有限责任公司简称北京航空公司，英文简称Beijing Airlines。2011年2月28日，北京航空有限责任公司注册成立，注册资本10亿元人民币。4月11日，北京航空公司获得中国民用航空局颁发的航空运营人运行合格证，进入正式运营阶段。北京航空公司由中国国际航空股份有限公司、北京控股集团有限公司、北京市国有资产经营有限责任公司、中达银瑞投资有限公司共同出资组建，出资比例分别为中国国航51%，北控集团18%，北京市国资公司18%，中达银瑞13%。

北京航空公司主要以国航公务机分公司原有业务为起点，以其整建制航空专业团队为技术力量基础，充分利用国航公务机分公司已具备的全球飞行运行能力、市场营销网络、适航维修能力

空有限责任公司

和全球机场保障能力等资源优势，以国内国际公务包机飞行、航空器代管、航空公司间业务代理为主营业务。目前，公司共拥有波音BBJ、空中客车318，湾流450、达索猎鹰7X以及庞巴迪环球快车、挑战者605等机型公务机十余架，中长程机型合理搭配，在很大程度上满足不同客户的行程需求。北京航空公司经过不断的积累和探索，已初步建立一定市场网络和客户群体，并赢得一定社会知名度和美誉度。

2011年，北京航空公司全面落实既定的工作任务和整体部署，提升安全管理水平，优化生产运行保障模式，准确把握市场机会和战略机遇，努力实现托管运力增长，积极拓展包机销售业务，经营效益持续向好，服务品质稳步提升。

中国民航信息集团公司

2011年，中国民航信息集团公司（简称中国航信）积极推进技术创新、管理创新、服务改善等工作，进一步夯实了公司可持续发展基础。在技术创新方面，公司先后与国内四大主流航空公司签署了新一代旅客服务系统战略合作协议，正式启动了新系统的研制工作，形成了“十二五”发展的良好开局。

中国航信荣获“2011中国软件和信息服务业最有价值品牌”奖及“2011年度中国IT项目管理卓越奖”，通过了“中国软件服务业企业信用评价AAA级（最高级）”复审。

一、安全生产持续稳定

中国航信始终坚持将安全生产作为各项工作的基础。2011年CRS、DCS主机系统及核心网络实现了零故障停机，ICS、接入网络及核心开放系统的可利用率超过了99.99%，结算系统运行平稳，未发生三级以上故障和重大信息系统安全事件。系统日处理旅客人数达到百万级。中国航信通过以下措施，保证了系统的安全稳定运行。

一是加强制度管理，注重应急演练。通过将应急演练与抽查测评相结合，将安全管理制度落实到各级岗位。全年各分支机构进行离港前端系统大规模应急演练次数68次，航班主动切转备份演练2 297次；总部生产部门进行各类应急演练288次。二是加强技术攻关，提升系统性能。完成了三大核心系统的4-HOST架构升级改造工作，解决了开放系统直读主机数据库、数据生命周期管理等技术难题。三是加强系统建设，提高反应速度。投产了跨平台作业计划和调度管理系统（TASK）、大型主机性能实时分析

2011年7月21日，中国民航信息网络股份有限公司与中国联合网络通信有限公司在京签署战略合作协议

On July 21, 2011, TravelSky Technology Limited and China Unicom Limited Sign a Strategic Cooperation Agreement in Beijing

China TravelSky Holding Company

In 2011, China TravelSky Holding Company (CTH) further fortified the foundation for sustainable development through technological innovation, managerial innovation and service improvement. With regard to technological innovation, CTH inked strategic cooperation agreements on the new-generation passenger service system with China's big four mainstream airlines successively, officially launched research and development of the new system and made a good start of the 12th Five-Year Plan period.

系统（OMAP）、主机集中式智能诊断及快速反应平台、统一测试平台等一大批自主研发的信息系统，提升了监控水平和响应速度，提高了工作效率。

二、经营业绩稳步提升

2011年，中国航信圆满完成年度目标任务和国资委业绩考核指标，主要业绩显著增长。从业务量上看，订座系统处理国内航空公司3.06 亿航段，外航1 283万航段，同比分别增长 8.94%和15.45%；离港系统处理旅客量 2.92 亿人次，同比增长 9.84%；酒店业务完成 185 万间夜，同比增长 21.7%；货运系统处理订单数 802.1 万张，同比增长 18.5%；结算系统处理交易量4.88亿张，同比增长12.43%； BSP数据处理2.32亿张，同比增长7.04%。

三、产品线建设不断完善

完成了新一代国际客运收入管理系统（IPRA）在三大航空公司的投产实施；承接国际航协（IATA）全球重点项目—— 新BSP数据处理系统，并完成了简化清算(SIS)系统的开发；推出了电子商务产品管理平台（EPM）和旅客服务引擎平台；无纸化通关服务平台在国内3家机场投产；投产了高速航班服务引擎，支持航空公司对销售动态进行实时监控和分析；“航空物流信息平台”被确定为民航局2011年科技项目；“航旅纵横”产品将系统服务延伸到移动终端；开发建设了游轮ICS/CRS系统产品，支持游轮产品的网上分销管理；完成国内EMD产品标准建设，成为全球第四家通过国际航协（IATA）认证的GDS，起草的《民航旅客运输登机牌二维条码格式和技术要求》被民航局采纳为中国民航行业标准。

四、新一代系统建设稳步推进

中国航信新一代旅客服务系统项目是自主创新提升核心技术能力的战略举措。项目建设的各项工作在2011年全面展开，成立了新系统项目管理办公室，建立了项目管理制度和总体流程框架，组建了以总部为主，包括北京、上海、广州、重庆在内的670人的研发队伍；与主要航空公司签署了新一代系统合作研发协议，开展了新一代系统整体开发规划工作，在客户最关注的前端航班控制系统、旅客服务系统等方面开始了产品设计和研发工作。

五、基础建设进展顺利

北京顺义高科技园区项目及嘉兴长三角共用信息（灾备）服务中心项目均已完成《建设用地规划许可证》和《国有土地使用证》的办理。顺义高科技园区项目节能、环评报告、项目设计方案等文件已获得相关部门批复，完成了地质勘察。长三角共用信息（灾备）服务中心项目顺利完成项目用地购置工作，项目整体规划通过了评审，完成了项目一期施工图设计审批及项目前期的场地准备和检测工作。

2011年4月27日，中国民航旅客服务系统单日销售旅客量突破100万发布会在北京华侨饭店举行

On April 27, 2011, a Press Conference Is Held at Prime Hotel Beijing, Announcing that China Civil Aviation Passenger Service System Breaks the Mark of 1 Million Tickets Sold in a Day

CTH received the award for China's Most Valuable Brand in the Software and Information Service Industry 2011 and the IT Project Management Excellence Award in China 2011. It also passed the re-examination for China Software Service Provider Credit Rating AAA (Highest) certification.

I. Continued Stability in Work Safety

CTH always regards work safety as the basis for all work. In 2011, CRS and DCS host systems and the core network recorded zero breakdown, the availability of ICS, access network and the core open system exceeded 99.99%, the settlement system maintained stable operation and no Grade 3 or severer faults or major information system security incidents took place. The daily passenger handling capacity of the systems reached the million level. CTH ensured system safety and stability by taking the following measures: First, system management was strengthened and emergency drill emphasized. Safety rules and procedures were implemented at various levels of individual job positions through a combination of emergency drill and selective examination. Branches and divisions conducted 68 large-scale emergency drills for the front-end departure system and 2 297 flight active switch-to-backup drills; the headquarters' production departments conducted 288 emergency drills of various sorts. Second, technical breakthroughs were enhanced to improve system performance. The 4-HOST architecture upgrading was completed for the three core systems, and some technical difficulties were solved, including open systems' direct access to host database and the data life cycle management. Third, system construction was accelerated and response speed built up. A large number of proprietary information systems were launched, including the cross-platform operation plan and the dispatch management system (TASK), the large host performance real-time analysis system (OMAP), the host centralized intelligent diagnosis and rapid response platform and the central testing platform, which improved monitoring and response speed and increased efficiency.

II. Steady Improvement in Operating Results

In 2011, CTH fulfilled its annual objectives and SASAC-defined performance targets, pulling off significant growth in major business indicators. By business volume, the seat reservation system processed 306 million segments for domestic airlines and 12.83 million segments for foreign airlines, up 8.94% and 15.45% over a year ago respectively. The departure system processed 292 million passengers, up 9.84% over a year ago. The hotel business reached 1.85 million room-nights, up 21.7% over a year ago. The freight system possessed 8.021 million orders, up 18.5% over a year ago. The settlement system processed 488 million tickets, up 12.43% over a year ago. The BSP data processing system processed 232 million tickets, up 7.04% over a year ago.

III. Continuous Improvement in Development of Product Lines

The new-generation international passenger revenue management system (IPRA) was lunched at three major airline companies. The new BSP data processing system project, a key global project of IATA, was awarded to CTH, and development of the simplified interline settlement (SIS) system was completed. The e-commerce product management (EPM) platform and the passenger service engine platform were introduced. The paperless customs clearance platform was launched at three domestic airlines. The high-speed flight service engine was brought on stream to facilitate airlines' real-time monitoring and analysis of sales. The Air Logistics Information Platform was named a sci-tech project of CAAC in 2011. Umetrip extended system services to mobile terminals. The cruise ICS/CRS system was developed to support online distribution management of cruise products. CTH developed standards for domestic EMD products, becoming the world's fourth IATA-certified GDS. The Two-dimensional Bar Codes of Boarding Passes for Civil Aviation Passenger Transport-Format and Technical Requirements drafted by CTH were adopted by CAAC as China's civil aviation industry standards.

IV. Steady Progress in New-generation System Development

The new-generation passenger service system project of CTH is a strategic move to improve the core technological capability through indigenous innovation. The project was fully carried out in 2011. The project management office was established, project management policies and procedures and the overall process framework were put in place and an R&D team was assembled, with its 670 members mainly from the headquarters and also from Beijing, Shanghai, Guangzhou and Chongqing. The new-generation system R&D cooperation agreement was signed with major airlines, the overall planning for development of the new-generation was carried out and the product design and R&D were started for the frontend flight control system and the passenger service system that attracts the most attention from clients.

V. Smooth Progress in Infrastructure Construction

The Planning Permit for Construction Land and the Certificate of State-owned Land Use Right were obtained for the Beijing Shunyi hi-tech park project and the Jiaxing-based Yangtze River Delta information sharing (disaster recovery) service center project. Approvals have been secured from relevant authorities for energy conservation, environmental impact report and project design proposal for the hi-tech park, and the geographical survey was completed. For the Yangtze River Delta information sharing (disaster recovery) service center project, project land procurement was completed, the overall project plan was approved and the working drawing design approval was obtained, and the project site preparation and testing were completed for phase I of the project.

中国航空油料集团公司

2011年，中国航空油料集团公司（以下简称集团公司）综合实力显著增强，集团公司首次进入世界500强企业、排名第431位，这是中国航油发展历程中具有里程碑意义的重大事件。在中国企业500强中排名第54位，荣获国资委经营业绩考评A级。在第十一届中国年度管理大会上被评为2011年中国最具价值管理榜样企业。这些都标志着集团公司进入了建设综合性世界一流航油公司、迈向跨国公司行列的新的历史发展时期。

一、经营业绩稳步提升，再创历史最好水平

全年中国航油共销售油化产品3 324万吨，同比增长15%。其中，销售航油1 403万吨，同比增长10%；其他成品油和化工产品909万吨，同比增长10.5%;国际油品和化工产品贸易量1 012万吨，同比增长29.5%。集团公司实现营业收入2 215亿元，同比增长45%；实现经济增加值16亿元，同比增长23%。主要经营指标都迈上了新台阶。

二、转变安全管理理念，安全生产实现“三零”目标

强化持续安全理念，安全管控由注重结果控制的“三零”目标，转向更加注重源头治理和过程控制的“零三违、零差错”。持续完善安全管理体系，制定和启动了安全生产约谈等制度，启动了危化品安全标准化体系建设，推行了“三到四确认”飞机加油标准化等作业指导书，梳理了生产作业类别，实现了各种指导书规范化、标准化。

三、全面推进战略合作，航油市场主导地位继续巩固

加大与石油石化企业沟通协调力度，加强一体化经营调度指挥，确保了全系统特别是西南、西北地区航油平稳供应，顺利完成了世园会、大运会、生物燃料验证飞行等重大航油供应保障任务。在发改委等部委的指导下，积极协调上下游企业，完成了国内航油价格与国际油价的顺利接轨。把握市场节奏，优化资源配置，强化库存管理，降低成本费用，全集团共挖潜增效1.35亿元。

积极推进国际业务重组，实现新加坡公司与香港、北美公司有效整合，以新加坡公司为核心的国际业务板块基本形成。与南航签订了海外战略合作协议，设立了集团中东办事处。新加坡公司航煤贸易量突破800万吨，成为亚太地区最大的航煤实货贸易商，经营业绩再创新高，连续三年获得新加坡证券投资者协会“最透明企业奖”。成功举办了北京国际航油大会暨展览会。

四、基础建设稳步推进，发展实力进一步夯实

全年基础建设及股权投资达到历史空前的53.6亿元，昆明、重庆、长沙、揭阳等机场航油工程，山西、新疆、福建成品油库增容项目等重点工程顺利竣工，宁波油库置换管线项目投入运营，平湖基地一期工程具备中交条件。集团公司储存能力提升44万立方米。海鑫万吨级船舶顺利启用，自有运力增长3.7万吨，达到17万吨，较上年增长27%.

五、持续强化内控管理，管理效率和效益不断提高

集团公司初步建立了以总法律顾问为核心的企业法律风险防范体系，巩固了重要风险业务的监控报告与风险提示机制，确立了新增业务风险评估与审核机制，有效防范了风险。建立规范的公司治理结构，启动了以董事会为核心的公司法人治理结构构建工作，为建立现代企业制度迈出了坚实的一步。

China National Aviation Fuel Group Corporation

In 2011, with its overall strength boosted markedly, China National Aviation Fuel Group Corporation (CNAF) made its debut on the Fortune Global 500 list, sitting at no. 431, which is a great milestone in its history. CNAF was ranked 54th among China's top 500 companies, its operating results being rated "A" by the State-owned Assets Supervision and Administration Commission (SASAC). CNAF was also honored as the Most Valuable Role-model Enterprise for Management in China 2011 at the 11th China Annual Management Conference. All these signify that CNAF has entered a new stage of development, aimed at growing into a world-class aviation fuel conglomerate and a multinational corporation.

中国航油物流公司专业化、一体化的油品配送体系

CNAF Logistics' Specialized and Integrated Oil Product Distribution System

I. Another Record High in Operating Results with Steady Growth

In 2011, CNAF sold a total of 33.24 million tons of petrochemical products, representing a year-on-year increase of 15%. Specifically, 14.03 million tons of jet fuel was sold, up 10% over a year ago; 9.09 million tons of other refined oil and chemical products were sold, up 10.5% over a year ago; 10.12 million tons of international oil products and chemical products were sold, up 29.5% over a year ago. CNAF recorded 221.5 billion yuan in business revenue and 1.6 billion yuan in economic value added, representing a year-on-year growth of 45% and 23% respectively. All main business indicators hit new highs.

II. Safety Management Concept Transformed to Achieve "Three Zeros" Objective in Work Safety

The Concept of Sustained Safety was underscored. The focus of safety management shifted from the result-oriented Three Zeros objective to the Zero Three Violations and Zero Error to source management and process control. CNAF improved safety management system continuously; created and launched the work safety interview system ; made efforts to build the system of hazardous chemicals safety standards, promoted the Three Attentions and Four Confirmations standard operating procedures for aircraft refueling and other working instructions documents reviewed classification of production activities and standardized all instructions documents.

III. Strategic Cooperation Furthered on All Sides, Cementing the Leading Position in Aviation Oil Market

CNAF ensured steady fuel supply industry-wide, in particular in the Southwest and the Northwest, and successfully accomplished aviation fuel supply for the World Horticultural Exposition, Universiade, biofuel validation flights and other major events by strengthening communication and coordination with petroleum and petrochemical companies and enhancing integrated

business dispatching. With the guidance provided by the National Development and Reform Commission and other authorities, CNAF actively coordinated upstream and downstream enterprises and successfully established linkage between domestic aviation fuel prices and international oil prices. CNAF followed market rhythms, optimized resource allocation, strengthened inventory management and reduced costs, thereby tapping potentials and increasing efficiency worth of 135 million yuan.

中国航油深入开展航油铁军活动

CNAF Carries out the Aviation Oil Iron Force Campaign in a Deep-going Manner

CNAF actively pushed forward international business restructuring, including consolidation of the Singapore branch with Hong Kong and North American companies, generally forming an international business structure with the Singapore Company as the core. An overseas strategic cooperation agreement was signed with China Southern Airlines and the Middle East representative office was established. The jet fuel trade volume of its Singapore operation exceeded 8 million tons, making it the largest jet fuel trader in the Asia Pacific and pushing its operating results to a new record high. The company won the Most Transparent Company award from the Securities Investors Association Singapore (SIAS). China International Aviation Fuel Conference and Exhibition was successfully hosted in Beijing.

圆满完成玉树抗震救灾运输保障工作

CNAF Completes Transport Support for Earthquake Relief in Yushu Successfully

IV. Steady Progress in Infrastructure Construction Further Underpinning Its Development Capacity

The infrastructure construction and equity investment reached an all-time high of 5.36 billion yuan. A number of key projects were completed, including airport aviation fuel projects in Kunming, Chongqing, Changsha and Jieyang as well as capacity expansion projects for refined oil depots in Shanxi, Xinjiang and Fujian. The alternative pipeline for Ningbo depot came on stream. The Pinghu base phase I project was ready for intermediate handover. CNAF increased its storage capacity to 440 000 m^3. The Haixin 10 000t ship was put into service, increasing its transport capacity by 37 000 tons to 170 000 tons, an increase of 27% over that of last year.

V. Ongoing Enhancement of Internal Control and Continuous Improvement in Effectiveness and Efficiency of Management

CNAF preliminarily established a corporate legal risk prevention system centered on a general counsel, cemented the monitoring reporting and warning mechanism for major risks and established the risk assessment and review mechanism for new businesses, which effectively prevented risks. A sound corporate structure was established and the corporate governance structuring centered on the board of directors was launched, representing a solid step towards the modern enterprise system.

中国航空器材集团公司

2011年，中国航材集团在连续七年盈利的基础上，经济效益继续保持良好增长态势，完成业绩利润总额比2010年增长显著，资产状况进一步改善，完成国资委下达的各项经营业绩考核指标，并全面落实民航“十二五”规划目标。

一、加强主业开拓，实现“十二五”良好开局

（1）贸易分销与物流板块取得重要进展 2011年1月和6月分别签署200架波音飞机和88架空客飞机的批量采购框架协议，经批量采购接收引进飞机133架，继续为降低航空公司采购成本、配合国家外交外贸政策发挥着特殊的积极作用。航材分销业务开拓取得重要进展，在做好深圳汉莎寄售、国航成都基地航材寄售、川航航材外包、Ameco航材外包、波音客户运营支援（COS）等重点项目的同时，与东航及多家维修企业、航空制造企业新客户建立良好的分销业务合作关系。民航大学、飞行学院、校飞中心等重点客户的通用航空相关业务稳步发展。2011年中航材有限公司成为第一家获得民航维修协会认可的合格航材供应商资质的企业。

（2）航空租赁业务板块成为最重要的利润来源，成功实现第一阶段发展目标 2011年，中国航材集团所属的奇龙航空租赁有限公司完成了4架A320-200飞机及2架B737-800飞机的交付、租赁。在两架波音飞机交付山东航空公司过程中，由奇龙航空租赁有限公司主导与民航局、波音公司等各方协调，完成了转换出口适航标准、实现中国飞机租赁史上首次空舱调机、开展交付后飞机座舱和设备改装等工作。至此，奇龙航空租赁有限公司共拥有17架飞机的机队规模，其不断提升的航空租赁业务关键能力和专业服务水平，正逐步成为超越资金实力强大的竞争对手的核心竞争能力，在国内外飞机租赁市场具有了一定的竞争力和影响力。

（3）航空维修与制造板块竞争力进一步增强 凯兰公司开发了G450型和GL605型等公务飞机刹车修理能力，通过安全管理体系（SMS）审查，完成了厂房改扩建，进一步增强了维修能力，拓展了包括地方航空公司、通用航空公司等刹车维修新的客户。B737-700/800机型BF. Goodrich国产刹车获得民航局零部件制造人批准件（PMA）认证，B737NG机型BF. Goodrich国产刹车在南航新疆公司顺利装机试飞，完成了A320国产刹车在四川航空公司装机试用的前期技术准备工作。进一步确立了以整体机轮综合保障服务为目标的商业运营模式，在以刹车销售和维修为核心的目标细分市场的竞争力和影响力逐步增强。

（4）地面设备与工程板块的市场优势地位继续巩固 重点开展西北、西南空管局区域管制中心、多地自动化备份系统等空管设备招标采购项目及成都、贵阳等多个机场扩建项目相关地面设备的招标采购工作。为中航信、中航油等民航保障企业提供设备及工程招标采购服务；为客户开展有针对性的专业知识培训，提升服务附加值。在新疆地区获得多个支线机场的地面设备与工程招标项目，物流输送和行李分拣项目进一步进入民航市场，成功中标北京首都机场、重庆机场海关快件项目。

二、航材共享和通用航空业务领域取得新突破

根据民航“十二五”规划提出的“打造航材共享平台，优化航空器材资源配置”的要求，集团公司制订了航材共享服务计划，积极推介航材共享业务合作模式。着力研究二手航材周转的技术标准、富余航材处置的价值标准等问题，取得阶段性成效。在通用航空领域中，加大参与力度，加强与业内单位的沟通合作。

三、优化管理模式，提升管理对业务的促进作用

一是加强战略管理，加大规划组织实施力度。二是加强投资及资源管理，大力提升管理效益。三是加强人力资源管理，完善激励约束机制。四是加强财务管理，整体提升财务管理水平。五是加强企业经营管理，加大子企业扶持和管理力度。六是加强信息化建设，明确信息化发展方向。七是加强内部控制，全面风险管理体系逐步健全。八是加强各项基础管理，为企业发展提供保障。■

China Aviation Supplies Holding Company

中国航材集团总经理李海在“2011中国民航发展论坛”上作航材共享主题演讲

Li Hai, General Manager of China Aviation Supplies Holding Company, Delivers a Speech Named Aviation Supplies Sharing in China Civil Aviation Development Forum 2011

In 2011, with its total business profit noticeably exceeding the 2010 level and further improvement of its assets condition, China Aviation Supplies Holding Company maintained a stable growth momentum in its financial performance after 7 successive years of profit-making, accomplishing every business performance evaluation indicator specified by the State-owned Assets Supervision and Administration Commission and implementing, the goals set in the 12th Five-Year Plan for civil aviation on a full scale.

I. Strengthening Principal Business Expansion and Making a Good Start for the 12th Five-Year Plan Period

1. Making significant progress in the areas of distribution and logistics. The company signed the framework agreements for batch purchases of 200 Boeing aircraft and 88 Airbus aircraft in January and June 2011 respectively. It received 133 imported aircraft through batch purchase, continually playing a special and active role in reducing airlines' purchasing costs and in coordinating with national policies in foreign affairs and foreign trade. In conjunction with handling key projects, such as Shenzhen-Lufthansa consignment, aviation supplies consignment at Air China's Chengdu base, aviation supplies outsourcing for Sichuan Airlines and Ameco and Boeing COS etc., the company established good cooperative relations in distribution with China Eastern Airlines and various maintenance business and aircraft manufacturers, thus making important progress in aviation supplies distribution service. Its general aviation-related business with key customers like Civil Aviation University of China, Civil Aviation Flight University of China and Flight Inspection Center of CAAC continued to expand steadily. In 2011, China Aviation Supplies Co., Ltd. became the first enterprise qualified for aviation supplies by Civil Aviation Maintenance Association.

2. Realizing the development objectives for phase 1 with aviation leasing being the most profitable business. In 2011, Dragon Aviation Leasing Company, a subsidiary of China Aviation Supplies Company, completed the delivery and leasing of 4 A320-200 aircraft and 2 B737-800 aircraft. In the delivery of 2 Boeing aircraft to Shandong Airlines, it, in coordination with CAAC, Boeing and various parties concerned, accomplished the conversion of airworthiness standards for export, realized for the first time in the history of China's aircraft leasing business the empty-cabin commissioning, and carried out the post-delivery modification of aircraft cabin seats and equipment, etc. With a fleet of 17 aircraft and its continual improvement in the core capacity of aviation leasing and professional services, Dragon Aviation Leasing Company gradually formed the core capacity in competitiveness that surpassed its opponents with strong finance and had, to some extent, the competitiveness and influence in the domestic and international aircraft leasing market.

3. Further enhancing the competiveness in aviation maintenance and manufacturing. Beijing Kailan Aviation Technology Company built up the brake maintenance capacity for commercial aircraft like G450 and GL605, passed the SMS review, completed its workshop renovation and expansion, further boosting the maintenance capabilities and acquiring new customers in local airlines and general aviation companies for its brake maintenance business. Home-made brake of B737-700/800 aircraft's BF. Goodrich gained the certification of CAAC PMA, the brake system of B737NG aircraft's BF. Goodrich was successfully installed and tested on a trial flight in Xinjiang Company of China Southern Airlines and the preliminary preparatory technical work for the home-made brake's installation on a trial basis in the aircraft of Sichuan Airlines was completed. These progresses further cemented, as the target, its business model of comprehensive support services for aircraft wheels, thus steadily strengthening its competitiveness and influence in its target market segment with brake sales and maintenance as the core.

4. Further reconsolidating the advantages in ground equipment and engineering markets. The company gave priority to conducting bidding and procurement of ATM equipment at northwest and southwest area control centers, such as multi-location automatic backup system, as well as bidding and procurement of relevant ground equipment at multiple airport expansion projects in Chengdu and Guiyang. It provided equipment and engineering bidding and procurement services for civil aviation support providers such as China TravelSky Holding Company and China National Aviation Fuel Group Corporation; in addition, the company provided targeted professional know-how training for customers to increase the added value of their service. It won the bid in ground equipment and engineering projects at several feeder airports in Xinjiang and its logistics and luggage selection projects entered further the civil aviation market. It also won the bid in customs express projects at Beijing Capital International Airport and Chongqing Airport.

II. Making New Breakthroughs in Aviation Supplies Sharing and General Aviation

In response to the requirement of the 12th Five-Year Plan for civil aviation to "forge the platform for aviation supplies sharing and optimize the allocation of aviation supplies resources", the company developed a service plan for the sharing of aviation supplies and actively promoted the cooperation model for aviation supplies. Besides, the company tried to develop the technical standards for the circulation of second-hand aviation supplies and the value standards for the disposition of redundant aviation supplies, making some preliminary progress. The company stepped up, in the field of general aviation, its participation and strengthened the communication and cooperation with other entities in the industry.

III. Optimizing the Management Model to Uplift Promotion Role of Management for Business

First, the company strengthened its strategic management and the implementation of planning and organization. Second, it enhanced its investment and resources management to increase management efficiency. Third, the company reinforced its human resources management to refine the incentive and constraint mechanism. Fourth, it heightened its financial management to improve the overall financial management capacity. Fifth, the company reinforced its corporate business management to better support and to manage subsidiaries. Sixth, it intensified its IT development to make clear the trend of IT development. Seventh, the company strengthened its internal control to gradually refine the comprehensive risk management system. Eighth, it enhanced all its fundamental management to provide support for business development.

2011年6月28日，中国航材集团与空客公司签署了购买88架A320系列飞机的框架协议

On June 28, 2011, China Aviation Supplies Holding Company and Airbus SAS Sign 88 A320 Aircraft Purchase Framework Agreement

▲ 北京 Beijing
▲ 南昌 Nanchang
▲ 天津 Tianjin
▲ 重庆 Chongqing
▲ 武汉 Wuhan
呼和浩特
▲ 呼和浩特 Hohhot
▲ 长春 Changchun

CAH
天地之道
大国之门
热烈庆祝
首都机场集团
成立
10
周年
▲ 哈尔滨 Harbin

首都机场集团公司

2011 年，首都机场集团公司所属机场旅客吞吐量、货邮吞吐量和运输起降架次分别实现 1.56 亿人次、249 万吨和 125 万架次，同比分别增长 9.5%、6.6% 和 6.2%，集团公司效益大幅提升，较好地实现了既定目标。

一、安全服务抓紧抓好

2011 年，集团公司深入贯彻落实持续安全理念，全年未发生责任原因造成的重大飞行、空防和航空地面事故，顺利完成了民航局下达的年度航空安全目标。

服务方面，牢牢抓住客户满意和航班正常两个核心要素。首都机场 ACI 旅客满意度跻身全球第三名，并成为国内首家获得 ASQA 服务质量认证的机场；重庆机场 ACI 旅客满意度在世界同量级机场中排名第二；成员机场平均航班放行正常率为 91.23%，高于全国主要机场平均水平 5.81 个百分点；成员机场没有发生重大旅客投诉事件。

二、重点项目进展顺利

集团公司坚持“三推行一跟踪”建设管理模式，机场建设管理得到切实加强。南昌机场改扩建工程顺利竣工，T2 实现安全转场。天津机场二期扩建完成航站楼桩基工程，贵阳机场二期扩建完成航站楼的地基和基础工程，神农架机场开工建设；首都机场 T3—T2 捷运联络线及汽车通道工程顺利推进。

积极落实机场建设“四个创新”，在争取政府支持方面取得了新的进展。武汉机场三期扩建可研阶段将资本金比例调增至 45%，重庆机场四期扩建资本金拟按 40% 约 100 亿元配置，神农架、恩施、通化、包头等支线机场新建、扩建工程均实现了民航及地方政府全额资本金投入。

北京新机场建设实现了独立法人运行，前期工作稳步推进。北京新机场建设“三方协议”正式签署。

2011年9月20日，由首都机场集团公司主办的“北京全球友好机场总裁论坛”隆重举行

On September 20, 2011, Beijing Global Friend Airports CEO Forum Hosted by Capital Airports Holding Company Is Held

Capital Airports Holding Company

In 2011, all the airports owned by Capital Airports Holding Company (the group) handled 156 million passengers, 2.49 million tons of cargo and mail and 1.25 million movements, representing year-on-year increases of 9.5%, 6.6% and 6.2% respectively. The group posted a spike in returns and successfully delivered on predefined objectives.

I. Good Performance in Security and Services

In 2011, the group carried out in depth the philosophy of sustainable security. No major human-factor-induced aviation security incidents or ground accidents took place in the year, signifying the fulfillment of the annual aviation security objectives set by CAAC.

With regard to services, Beijing Capital International Airport focused on the two core factors, namely the customer satisfaction and flight regularity, ranking the third worldwide in terms of ACI passenger satisfaction and becoming the first ASQA-certified airport in China. Chongqing Airport ranked

三、经营品质明显提升

集团公司在预算、实物资产等方面加大了管理力度。首都机场股份公司在业务量增长放缓的情况下，加大成本控制力度，实现了“成本费用的零增长”。重庆机场集团积极争取市政府加大航线开发支持力度，国际航空补贴增加到三年 10 亿元，国际货运量同比增长近 11 倍。湖北机场集团通过新增商业面积，每年实现增收 3 000 万元。天津机场积极拓展非航业务，专业化公司年增收达 1 000 万元。商贸公司、广告公司、餐饮公司、动力能源公司在年中新增任务指标后，积极行动，取得了良好的经营业绩，实现利润超过年初预算 1 亿元。资产管理公司回收资金 6.11 亿元，诉讼立案 4.95 亿元，资产处置工作成效显著。财务公司实现利润 1.68 亿元，同比增长 43%。旅业公司在新增大量资产的情况下，加大内部管控力度，减亏效果十分明显。

集团公司积极优化资本结构，降低负债率，化解财务风险。积极向国家申请注资；全面完成了民族证券和华闻传媒的股权转让工作；顺利完成了地面服务公司和配餐公司的股权多元化改革。

股份公司加大枢纽建设力度。首都机场枢纽建设合作机制进展显著。通过枢纽建设领导小组加强了与国航的合作和联动，就 T3D 启用、设置高端值机区等重要事项达成了共识；中转支持政策和过境免签工作获得重大进展；国际转国内行李直挂取得成效；推动民航局批复 2011 年冬春季航班时刻增容方案，已于 2011 年 12 月 15 日开始由每小时 83 架次增加至 88 架次。国际航线网络得到大幅拓展，增加了 9 家航空公司，复航了 3 家航空公司，新增了 10 个国际航点，加密了多个国际航点频次。

四、文化推进润物无声

以文化为引领，持续增强“中国服务”的影响力。举办了首届“中国服务”论坛。并持续推进品牌建设，将中国服务品牌具象化延伸，授予了 12 家成员企业“中国服务”品牌示范单位称号，进一步扩大了“中国服务”的影响。

首都机场国际影响力大幅提升。持续拓展国际友好机场间的合作关系，与洛杉矶机场、台湾桃园机场等 9 家机场建立了姊妹机场合作关系；圆满举办了首届北京全球友好机场总裁论坛，主导签署了《北京全球友好机场总裁论坛倡议书》，进一步提升了首都机场在国际航空业的话语权和影响力。

the second in terms of ACI passenger satisfaction among all the airports worldwide at the same level. Flight regularity rate of member airports averaged 91.23%, 5.81 percentage points higher than the national average. No major customer complaints were filed against any member airport.

II. Smooth Progress in Key Projects

The group effectively strengthened airport construction management by adhering to the Three Promotions and One Tracking mode applicable to construction management. The Nanchang Airport renovation and expansion project was successfully completed and all the aircraft were safely ferried to Terminal 2. The piling works of phase II expansion project for Tianjin Airport terminal and the foundation works of phase II expansion project for Guiyang Airport terminal were completed. The construction of Shennongjia Airport made its start and the T3-T2 APM and automobile passage project of Beijing Capital International Airport smoothly proceeded.

The group actively implemented the Four Innovations in airport construction and made new progress in seeking government supports. It increased the capital proportion to 45% during its conducting feasibility study on Wuhan Airport Phase III expansion and prescribed a capital ratio of 40% or 10 billion yuan for Chongqing Airport Phase IV expansion project. Capital contributions from civil aviation authority and local governments were all in place for new and expansion projects in regional airports including the ones in Shennongjia, Enshi, Tonghua, Baotou, etc.

With its preparatory work carried out steadily, the construction of the new airport in Beijing realized its independent legal entity operation. A tripartite agreement was officially signed on construction of Beijing's new airport.

III. Marked Improvement in Management Quality

The group strengthened its management of budget and physical assets. Despite the weakening business growth, Beijing Capital International Airport Co., Ltd. stepped up its cost control, achieving "zero-growth in costs". In its effort to seek stronger government support for air route development, Chongqing Airport Group garnered an increased three-year international aviation subsidy of 1 billion yuan and posted an 11-fold growth in international freight volume in the previous year. Hubei Airport Group allocated more space for commercial operation, generating annually 30 million yuan of additional income. Tianjin Airport actively expanded its non-aviation activities, recording an annual income growth of 10 million yuan from the specialized companies. The trade firm, the advertising company, the catering company and the power energy company under the group acted actively in response to the mid-year addition of business objectives, obtaining excellent operating results and exceeding the budgeted profit by 100 million yuan. The asset management company recovered 611 million yuan and the amount related to law suit was 495 million yuan, making remarkable achievements in asset disposal. The financial company made a profit of 168 million yuan, an up of 43% over that of the previous year. With its assets expanding steeply, the tourism company strengthened its internal controls and pronouncedly reduced its losses.

The group mitigated financial risk by actively optimizing its asset structure and reduced its liability ratio. It energetically applicated to the government for capital injection, successfully fulfilling the equity transfer of China Minzu Securities and Huawen Media Investment Corp. and smoothly carrying out the equity diversity reform of the ground service firm and the air catering firm.

The joint-stock company stepped up its hub construction efforts. The cooperation mechanism for building the Capital Airport into a hub made measurable progress. Cooperation and interaction with Air China were enhanced through the efforts made by the hub construction leadership group, with a consensus reached on the operation of T3D and setup of high-end check-in area. It made major progress in the development of transfer support policy and the implementation of "transit without visa" approach, and achieved good results in providing luggage through check-ins for passengers connecting from international to domestic flights. It also pushed ahead with the approval of CAAC for the flight schedule expansion of the IATA winter season 2011/2012, with hourly movements increased from 83 to 88 as of December 15, 2011. By adding 9 airlines, restoring 3 airlines, increasing 10 international flight way points and intensifying the frequency on quite a few international flight way points, the group greatly expanded its route network.

IV. Promotion of Corporate Culture

The group continuously strengthened the influence of China Services from the culture perspective. It held the first China Services forum and continuously promoted its brand building so as to embody and extend the brand of China Services. 12 member companies were recognized as the model performers for the China Services Brand, further expanding the influence of China Services.

The Capital Airport's international influence was boosted greatly. The group expanded its partnerships with international friend airports and established sister airport relationship with 9 airports, including Los Angeles Airport, Taiwan Taoyuan Airport, etc. It successfully held Beijing Global Friend Airports CEO Forum, at which the group took the lead in the signing of Beijing Global Friend Airports CEO Forum Initiative, further enabling the Capital Airport to have a bigger say and influence in the international aviation sector.

首都机场集团公司成功承办了中央电视台“心连心”艺术团赴民航慰问演出

Capital Airports Holding Company Successfully Sponsors the Performance Staged by CCTV “Heart to Heart” Art Ensemble for Civil Aviation Workers

 大连周水子国际机场集团公司

2011年，大连机场围绕“建设国内一流机场”的总目标，以持续安全、优质服务和科学管理“三大主题”入手，着眼于“近期”、“ 中期”、“远期”三大目标，抢抓机遇、拼搏奋进，圆满完成了各项任务，实现了“十二五”良好开局。

一、运输生产连续14年领跑东北各机场

2011年共完成旅客吞吐量1 201万人次，同比增长12.2%，增幅比全国平均水平高4个百分点，旅客吞吐量排名上升到全国第15位，其中国际旅客吞吐量连续9年位列全国第4位；完成航班起降9.3万架次，同比增长2.6%；完成货邮吞吐量13.8万吨，同比下降1.9%。三大运输生产指标连续14年保持在整个东北机场的领先地位。

二、初步形成大型机场运营保障新格局

大连机场以广泛开展“强化安全责任主体年”活动为主线，健全体系、落实责任、规范运行，构建了适应大型机场运行要求的大保障格局。

一是系统化落实安全责任，与所有保障单位签订了航空和消防安全责任状，进一步完善了机场安全责任网。二是常态化治理安全隐患，全年开展了8个专项整治行动，发布了4期风险预警，解决了消防安全、空防安全、供电保障、危险品运输、货邮运输、外来物（FOD）和标志标识等方面存在的问题和隐患。三是科学化推进安全管理，完成了安全管理体系（SMS）要素融入机场使用手册工作，编制了航空保安管理体系（SeMS）工作手册，组建现场运行指挥室，推进飞行区科学管理，深化安全品牌创建工作，落实民航局191号令。四是严格化执行安全规章，全年制定下发各类安全管理文件42个，安检查出违禁品2.1万件，证件不符96人次，机务排除较大故障151起，组织大规模综合演习1次，单项演练52次。五是开展全员安全培训，执行全年安全教育计划，分类、分层次地对员工进行安全培训，实现了安全培训的持续化、全员化、动态化。六是有效应对台风“梅花”袭击，按照省、市政府和各级民航管理机关要求，机场及时启动应急预案，上下努力、全场动员，果断采取六项措施应对台风“梅花”，确保了机场安全平稳运行。

2011年9月6日，大连机场举行航站楼三期扩建工程竣工庆典

On September 6, 2011, Dalian Airport Holds a Ceremony to Celebrate the Completion of the Third Phase Expansion Project of the Terminal

三、枢纽航线网络不断扩建完善

大连机场围绕“双枢纽”战略和“3+1+1”（即3家以上主航空基地、1个支线基地和1个货运基地）市场布局，增加运力、开拓航线、抢占市场，取得了四个方面

2011年12月22日，“中国大型机场航空市场发展联盟”成立大会在大连召开
On December 22, 2011, the Inaugural Meeting of China Large Airports Aviation Market Development Alliance s Held in Dalian

的新突破。

一是机场联盟运作取得新突破，主动发起了有北京、上海、广州等 14 家机场参加的全国大型机场联盟，召开支线机场联盟第四届年会，受邀出席第十届东亚机场联盟会议，与广州机场结为姊妹机场。二是“3+1+1”市场布局取得新突破，大连航空开航，与南航签署战略合作协议，海航新增 3 架运力，3 家主基地公司共同支持“双枢纽”战略的格局基本形成。三是航线开发取得新突破，开通东北首条国际货运航线（大连—法兰克福）。“烟大空中快线”达到每日 7 班，成功打造环渤海及东北地区首条空中支线快线品牌。富山、福冈、广岛航班延伸至北京、天津，恢复伊尔库茨克、海参崴、哈巴罗夫斯克夏季航班，大连通往日、韩、俄桥头堡地位不断巩固。新引入 5 家航空公司进入大连，新开通 6 条国内客运航线和 2 条国内货运航线，加密 3 个通航点。四是市场拓展取得新突破。与市旅游局签订了战略合作协议，与虎跃快客深化合作，丹东、大石桥和锦州城市候机楼正式营业，推出“易通卡”，发展会员 4.6 万人，市场开发成绩显著。

四、全方位促进一流机场建设

开展“服务提升年”活动，严格标准、解决短板、改善环境，服务水平和场区环境迈上了新台阶。全面启动一流机场创建工作。逐步完善服务质量控制体系。不断改进和完善机场大面积航班延误工作机制。建立了国内机场最先进的旅客航班气象信息服务系统，运用多种载体为广大旅客提供全方位的航空气象服务。成立了由 32 家单位参加的机场服务质量促进委员会，“大服务”格局初步形成。

五、航空运输保障能力大幅提升

大连机场按照远近结合、确保机场可持续发展的原则，大幅提升了机场基础设施水平，全年完成基本建设投资 16 亿元，同比增长 300%，机场建设发生了历史性的变化。三期航站楼按期投入使用后，航站楼面积由 6.5 万平方米增加到 13.6 万平方米，停机坪由 34 万平方米增加到 66 万平方米，登机桥由 10 个增加到 18 个，停车场面积达 23 万平方米，值机柜台 93 个，安检通道 36 条，基本保证了大连新机场建成前、周水子机场过渡期内航空业务快速发展的需要。为推动东北亚航空货运枢纽机场建设，大连机场还投资 10 亿元推进了新老货站建设。新建的国内货站占地面积 8.97 万平方米，全年货邮处理能力能够达到 14 万吨，同时将老货运区改造为国际货站，扩建海关监管库和新建保税库。建成后的货站，除了满足传统意义的航空货运需求外，还将提供现代化的快件、仓储、保税、物联网信息平台及航空物流综合配套服务功能，从而使机场由传统货运向现代物流转型。

Dalian Zhoushuizi International Airport Group Co., Ltd.

Centered on the general goal of building a first-rate airport in China in 2011, Dalian International Airport Group Co., Ltd. (hereinafter referred to as the group), focusing on the three big goals in the "near future", "mid-term" and "forward" periods, proceeding from sustained safety, quality service and scientific management, vigorously took opportunities, went all out in its work and successfully fulfilled all its tasks, making a good start for the 12th Five-Year Plan.

I. Taking the Lead in Transport of Northeast Airports for 14 Consecutive Years

In 2011, the group witnessed an annual traffic of 12.01 million passengers, with a year-on-year growth of 12.2% and growth margin being 4 percentage points higher than nationwide average level. Its annual traffic of passengers rose to the 15th in nationwide rank, of which its international passenger turnover ranked the 4th for 9 consecutive years. It handled a total of 93 000 movements and 138 000 tons of cargo and mail, a year-on-year growth of 2.6% and decrease of 1.9% respectively. Three transport targets had kept the lead for 14 consecutive years among the whole northeast airports.

II. Initially Forming a New Pattern for Operation Support of Large Airport

Taking activities of the Year of Reinforcing the Principal Safety Responsibility as a main line, the group improved its systems, implemented its responsibilities and normalized its operations, thus forming a big support pattern compatible with the requirements for large airport operations.

a) By systematically implementing safety responsibilities, the group signed safety responsibility contracts on aviation and fire control with all supporting units, further improving the safety responsibility network of the airport. b) By normalizing the rectification of hidden safety perils, conducting 8 special rectifying actions and releasing 4 issues of risk pre-warnings, it solved existing problems and hidden perils in aspects of fire control safety, aviation security, power supply guarantee, dangerous goods transport, cargo and mail transport, foreign object debris(FOD), signs and markers. c) By scientifically pushing forward with safety management, it completed the integration of safety management system (SMS) elements into its airport use manual, compiled aviation security management system work manual, established on-spot operation command office, pushed forward with scientific management in movement areas, deepened the creation work of safety brand and implemented CAAC Order No. 191. d) By strictly enforcing safety regulations, it formulated and released 42 safety management documents of all kinds throughout the year, detected at security checks 21 000 forbidden goods and 96 persons with unconformable documents, removed by aircraft engineers 151 relatively big faults and organized 1 large-scale comprehensive exercise and 52 separate drills. e) By carrying out all-staff safety training, implementing all-year safety education plan and having classified and tiered staff safety trainings, it realized consistent, all-staff involved and dynamic safety training. f) By effectively coping with attacks by typhoon Muifa, according to the requirements of the provincial & municipal governments and civil aviation administrative organs at all levels, it timely started the emergency plan and, with every body's hard working and all staff mobilized, resolutely took 6 measures to cope with typhoon Muifa, insuring the safe and smooth operations of the group.

III. Continuous Expansion and Refinement of the Hub Air Routes Network

Working around "double hubs" strategy and 3+1+1 market layout (namely, more than 3 main aviation bases, 1 feeder-line base and 1cargo transport base), the group increased its transport capacity, opened up new air routes and seized market, thus making new breakthroughs in the following 4 aspects.

a) With new breakthroughs made in operation of airports alliance, the group initiatively launched a Nationwide Large Airports Alliance involved by 14 airports from

Beijing, Shanghai, Guangzhou, etc. and held the 4th Annual Meeting of Feeder Airports Alliance. It was invited to participate in the 10th East Asia Airport Alliance Meeting and became a sister airport with Guangzhou Airport. b) With new breakthroughs made in 3+1+1 market layout, the group had its inaugural flight, signed strategic cooperation agreement with Southern Airlines, and Hainan Airlines newly increased 3 aircraft, basically forming the "double hubs" strategic mode that was jointly supported by the 3 main base companies. c) With new breakthroughs made in air route development, it opened its first international cargo transport route (Dalian to Frankfurt). Yantai to Dalian Air Express reached 7 flights per day, the first air feeder-line express brand successfully built. Flights to Toyama, Fukuokaken and Hiroshima were extended to Beijing and Tianjin. Summer flights to Irkutsk, Vladivostok and Khabarovsk were reopened. The bridgehead position of Dalian to Japan, Korea and Russia was constantly strengthened. There were 5 airlines ushered into Dalian, 6 internal passenger air routes and 2 international cargo transport air routes newly opened and 3 air services points added. d) With new breakthroughs made in market expansion, the group signed strategic cooperation agreement with Dalian Tourism Bureau and deepened the cooperation with Tiger-Leap Passenger Express. With terminals in cities of Dandong, Dashiqiao and Jinzhou starting their formal operations, the launch of Easy Pass Card and 46 000 members expanded, the group made great achievements in market development.

IV. Promoting First-Rate Airport Building in an All-around Way

By carrying out activities of the year of service improvement, the group made strict standards, solved shortages and improved environment, thus making its service level and airport environment up on a new stage. It started in full swing first-rate airport building and gradually perfected its service quality control system, constantly improved and refined its working mechanism of the airport for massive flight delays. It built the most advanced internal meteorological information service system for passenger flights, using multi-carriers to provide overall aviation meteorological service for the broad masses of passengers. It established Airport Quality Promotion Committee with participation of 32 units, preliminarily forming a "large-scale service" pattern.

2011年9月6日，大连机场举行航站楼三期扩建工程竣工庆典

On September 6, 2011, Dalian Airport Holds a Ceremony to Celebrate the Completion of the Third Phase Expansion Project of the Terminal

V. Uplifting Greatly Aviation Support Capability

According to the principle of far-near integration and insurance of sustainable development, the group greatly uplifted its infrastructure level, completing 1.6 billion annual infrastructure investments, 300% more than that of the previous year, bringing historical changes to the airport construction. After the third-phase project of terminal putting into use on schedule, its terminal area increased from 65 000 m^2 to 136 000 m^2, parking apron from 340 00 m^2 to 660 000 m^2 boarding bridges from 10 to 18, car parking area reaching to 230 000 m^2, duty counters totaling 93 and security check channels up to 36, basically guaranteeing the need for rapid development of aviation services before the completion of Dalian New Airport construction and during the transitional period of Zhoushuizi Airport. In order to promote the construction of aviation cargo transport hub airport in Northeast Asia, the group also invested 1 billion yuan in pushing forward with the construction of the old and new cargo stations. The newly-built domestic cargo stations occupied an area of 89 700 m^2, with an annual cargo-mail handling capacity of 140 000 tons. At the same time, the group transformed the old cargo transport area into an international cargo station, expanded the customs supervised warehouse and newly built the bonded warehouse. In addition to meeting traditional aviation cargo transport needs, the cargo stations when completed would provide functions of modern express mail service, warehouse storage, bonded service, information platform on internet and comprehensive aviation logistics supporting services, thus making the airport transform from traditional cargo transport to modern logistics.

上海机场（集团）有限公司

一、航空业务量持续增长，经营绩效超预期完成

2011 年上海虹桥、浦东两机场共完成飞机起降 57.4 万架次、实现旅客吞吐量 7 456 万人次、货邮吞吐量 354 万吨，同比分别增长 4.14%、3.73% 和 -4.56%。浦东机场货邮吞吐量在全球经济大背景下虽有回落，但仍连续第四年在全球机场中排名第三。

2011 年，受航空业务量增长和非航业务发展带动，集团公司收入增幅大于航空业务量增幅，投资收益增长突出，归属于母公司净利润实现年度预算翻番。单位客货运综合能耗控制在 12.21 吨 / 万人，综合能耗净增量为 -2 000 吨标准煤。

二、持续安全得到实现，安全管控能力进一步提高

全年未发生空防安全事故和因机场原因导致的运输航空重大事故、重大航空地面事故及安全事故征候。浦东、虹桥机场分别实现第 12 个、第 24 个安全年，圆满完成世界游泳锦标赛、利比亚撤侨等重要保障任务。安全管理体系（SMS）建设进一步强化，浦东机场航空安保管理体系（SeMS）建设试点工作得到落实，两机场均通过局方组织的适用性检查。浦东机场飞行区围界安防系统、虹桥机场飞行区运行安全监控系统建设与运行的经验和做法，得到民航局的肯定和推广。

三、服务质量稳中有进，文明服务持续领先

两场以 ACI 旅客满意度测评为抓手，持续改进服务，浦东机场测评得分保持前十，虹桥机场得分逐季提升。虹桥机场被 SKYTRAX 评为国内第三家“四星机场”。集团公司获得全国民航文明单位称号，股份公司被评为全国文明单位，航空港民航行业获上海市第六届文明行业称号，航空港窗口行业社会公众服务满意度测评持续保持“绿色”标识。集团公司主商标被认定为上海市著名商标。

四、硬件设施继续完善

浦东机场第四跑道建设完成了地基处理和排水工程，开始道面工程建设。第五跑道一阶段工程完成地基处理和排水工程，全面进入拖机道道面工程建设。DHL 北亚转运中心建设工程完成了主体结构施工。虹桥机场顺利完成东跑道不停航大修工程。

五、枢纽建设持续进步

浦东机场新增 7 家外航运营，新增 6 个国际定期客运航线通航点，其中毛里求斯航空公司通航浦东机场，填补了非洲客运航线空白。在浦东机场执行定期航班的中外航空公司达到 87 家，通航点达到 194 个。积极推进旅客中转业务，旅客中转率达到 7.72%。为增强枢纽机场辐射能力，协同基地航空公司开设了昆山城市航站楼，变等客上门为主动拓展，取得良好效果。

虹桥机场主动与局方、空管协同配合，清理虚占时刻，提高航班计划执行率和客座率。

六、信息化建设取得重要进展

完成了集团管理信息共享平台（iWS）一期建设和上线试运行。集团安全管理信息系统二期建设、飞行区运行安全监控系统一期建设，以及经营资源信息化管理试点基本完成，系统上线运行。启动了集团财务信息系统二期、人力资源管理信息系统一期建设。

七、调结构、促转型工作加快推进

抓住有利时机，扎实推进直接经营型向管理型转型，地服合资项目取得重要进展，完成合资谈判，具备了签约条件。部分投资企业重组、转型和股权优化工作抓紧开展。

Shanghai Airport Authority

I. Air Transport Continued to Grow and Operating Results Outperformed Expectations

In 2011, Hongqiao and Pudong airports in Shanghai together handled 574 000 aircraft movements, 74.56 million passengers and 3.54 million tons of cargo and mail, representing increases of 4.14%, 3.73% and -4.56% over those of previous year respectively. Despite its decline against the backdrop of weakening world economy, the cargo and mail turnover at Pudong Airport took the third place among global airports for the fourth consecutive year.

In 2011, due to air transport growth and non-aviation business expansion, the authority's income growth was greater than those coming from air transport and the return on investment saw outstanding increases. Net profit attributable to parent company doubled compared with the annual budget. The energy consumption per unit of passenger and freight transport was 12.21 tons/10 000 persons, which resulted in a net decrease of 2 000 tons of standard coal equivalent in overall energy consumption.

II. Achieving Sustained Safety and Further Enhancing Safety Management and Control Capability

In 2011, the authority recorded no aviation security accidents and no major air transport accidents, major ground accidents or incidents due to airport reasons. Pudong and Hongqiao

2011年4月29日，上海机场（集团）有限公司技术中心、技术咨询公司挂牌成立，这也是全国民航机场行业内成立的首家企业技术中心

On April 29, 2011, the Technology Center and the Technical Consulting Company of Shanghai Airport Authority Are Officially Established, with the Former Being the First Enterprise Technology Center in China's Civil Aviation Airport Industry

airports achieved their respective 12th and 24th year of safe operations, successfully accomplishing major safety support tasks for the FINA World Championships and evacuation of Chinese compatriots from Libya. The safety management system (SMS) was further enhanced. The pilot program of Pudong Airport security management system (SeMS) was implemented and both airports passed the applicability inspection conducted by CAAC. Good practices in the construction and operation of the airfield perimeter security system of Pudong Airport and the operational safety monitoring system for movement area at Hongqiao Airport were recognized and promoted by CAAC.

八、集团技术中心和教育培训体系建设稳妥起步

集团技术中心、教育培训学院按计划于二季度揭牌开业。技术中心取得了上海市企业技术中心资质认定。以技术中心为平台，走出了“跨出去”的第一步，开展了昆明新机场运营，义乌和郑州新郑机场扩建等对外技术咨询合作项目。

九、战略合作进一步增强

与上海海关签订了战略合作备忘录，促进了空港口岸客货通关效率的提升。加强与东航沟通，开展了浦东机场T1改造需求调研和协调工作，完成了改造方案的研究制订。支持并配合上海市综合保税区管理委员会工作，确保了浦东机场综合保税区的二期封关运行。

III. Improving Service Quality Steadily and Maintaining Leading Position with Outstanding Services

Both airports made continuous improvements in services based on ACI passenger satisfaction evaluations. Pudong Airport ranked among the top ten according to the evaluation results, while Hongqiao Airport improved its ratings quarter by quarter. Hongqiao Airport was rated by SKYTRAX as China's third Four-Star Airport. The authority was awarded the title of National Outstanding Air Aviation Entity, the joint stock company was recognized as the National Outstanding Entity, the airport civil aviation sector was listed among the Outstanding Sectors of Shanghai during the sixth appraisal and the airport service sector continued to win the Green mark in the public service satisfaction survey. The authority's main trademark was recognized as a Famous Trademark of Shanghai.

IV. Improving Infrastructure Continuously

The subgrade treatment and drainage works were completed and surface works commenced for the fourth runway of Pudong Airport. Subgrade treatment and drainage works were completed and the tractor surface works commenced for the first phase of the fifth runway. The DHL North Asia Hub completed the main structure construction. Hongqiao Airport successfully completed the east runway overhaul works without suspension of flight operations.

V. Making Progress Continuously in Hub Construction

Pudong Airport attracted seven additional foreign airlines, including Air Mauritius that filled the airport's blank of air services with Africa for passengers, and added six destinations for international scheduled passenger flights. 87 Chinese and foreign airlines operated scheduled flights between Pudong Airport and 194 destinations. The passenger transit business was actively promoted, with passenger transit rate reaching 7.72%. To increase the reach of hub airports, the Kunshan terminal was set up in collaboration with base airlines to turn from reactive to proactive stance in marketing, which delivered good results.

Hongqiao Airport cooperated with CAAC and the air traffic control bureaus to clear unused slots and increase the schedule execution rate and passenger load factor.

VI. Archieving Major Progress in IT Development

The authority completed the construction and trial on-line operation of the first phase of the management information sharing platform (iWS). The second phase of the authority's safety management information system, the first phase of the movement area operation safety monitoring system and the pilot program of IT-based operating resources management were basically completed and were put online. The authority also launched the second phase of the financial system and the first phase of the information system for human resource management.

VII. Speeding Up Restructuring and Transformation

The authority seized opportunities to shift from direct operation to management. Progress was made in the joint venture project of ground service, with negotiation being closed and ready for contract signing. Reorganization, transformation and equity optimization of some companies the authority invested in were expedited.

VIII. A Good Start in the Technology Center and the Education and Training System Building Made

The Technology Center and the Education and Training College of the authority were inaugurated as scheduled in the second quarter of 2011. The Technology Center was certified to be a Shanghai enterprise technology center. Based on the Technology Center, the authority took the first Step Out to launch technical consulting services for the operation of Kunming new airport, expansion of Yiwu and Zhengzhou airports, etc.

IX. Further Strengthening Strategic Cooperation

A memorandum of understanding on strategic cooperation was signed with Shanghai Customs to increase the customs clearance efficiency of passengers and cargo at airports. Communication was enhanced with China Eastern Airlines to carry out survey and coordination on the Pudong Airport T1 renovation needs and develop the revamping plan. Support and cooperation were provided to Shanghai Integrated Bonded Area Management Committee to ensure the successful completion of the construction and start of operation in the second phase of the integrated bonded area at Pudong Airport.

 杭州萧山国际机场有限公司

一、运输生产稳中有升

2011 年，杭州机场共保障航班起降 14.95 万架次，同比增长 2.2%；完成旅客吞吐量 1 751 万人次，同比增长 2.6%；完成货邮吞吐量 30.6 万吨，同比增长 8%。国内国际航线网络得到进一步完善，新开辟了杭州至悉尼、普吉、新德里、亚的斯亚贝巴、韩国清州及菲律宾卡里波等 7 条国际航线，强化了国内北京、广州、深圳、成都等骨干航线，国内外通航点达 104 个，通达亚洲、欧洲、非洲及大洋洲。国际业务得到较快发展，全年国际旅客吞吐量同比增长 28.8%，国际货邮吞吐量同比增长 18.3%，国内第四大航空口岸的地位得到了进一步稳固。

二、安全形势总体平稳

一年来，公司坚持“安全优先，持续安全”的指导思想，秉承“零容忍”的安全工作理念，按照“关口前移，重心下移”的安全工作思路，加强组织领导，强化教育培训，加大安全投入，建立健全长效机制，落实安全责任制和问责制，深化安全管理体系运行。全年组织各类安全培训 77 批 4 990 人次，细化、量化了 9 项安全控制指标和 28 条项考核标准，保障类设施设备投入达 5 000 余万元，组织了近 90 次各项应急演练，持续开展了五项专题整治活动，顺利通过了局方安保审计，强化了现场管理能力建设，不断夯实安全保障基础。全年安全形势总体平稳，实现了通航以来第 11 个安全年。

三、运营环境持续改善

通过整合资源、挖掘潜力等措施，增强了机场综合保障能力。大力推进杭州机场北航路进离场航线分流方案建设，并于 2012 年 1 月 12 日正式实施，大大改善了本场空域环境。完成机场终端区容量评估，高峰小时容量从 25 架次/小时提升到 31 架次/小时，拓宽了业务发展空间。建立多方信息沟通机制，加大虚占时刻的清查力度，提高了航班计划执行率和时刻利用率，目前杭州机场的航班计划执行率达到 90% 以上。

四、服务品质持续优化

公司加强组织领导，以“服务质量年”为载体，狠抓服务品质提升。全年机场 ASQ 旅客满意度得分为 4.34 分，同比提高约 2.1%，在全球同类机场排名第 3 位。杭州机场全年百万旅客投诉量与前一年同期相比下降 26.2%，服务质量明显改善。积极协调民航行业有关单位，建立“排堵保畅”机制，着力整治航班延误。目前，航班平均正常率维持在 72% 以上，有效提升了旅客满意度。圆满完成了“第八届全国残疾人运动会”保障工作。

五、非航业务发展良好

一年来，公司在努力加快发展航空业务的同时，继续加大非航项目的开发，充分挖掘非航业务盈利点，适时进行结构性调整，取得了明显成效。积极推行业务转型，将客、货运常规销售代理转向贵宾及其延伸服务和医药仓储业务，加快发展航站楼商业零售业务，较好地实施了广告业务外包。全年完成非航业务收入 7.22 亿元，同比增长 17%，占公司总营业收入的 47.8%，已成为公司营业收入的重要组成部分。

Hangzhou Xiaoshan International Airport Co., Ltd.

I. Increase in Stability of Traffic

In 2011, Hangzhou Airport handled 149 500 aircraft movements, 17.51 million passengers and 306 000 tons of cargo and mail, representing year-on-year increases of 2.2%, 2.6% and 8% respectively. The network of domestic and international routes was further improved, with seven new international routes opened to connect Hangzhou with Sydney, Phuket, New Delhi, Addis Ababa, Chungju and Kalibo and with the domestic trunk routes to Beijing, Guangzhou, Shenzhen and Chengdu enhanced, adding the number of domestic and international destinations to 104, covering Asia, Europe, Africa and Oceania. With year-on-year increases of 28.8% and 18.3% of its international passenger turnover and international cargo and mail turnover, Hangzhou Airport made rapid development in international business, further cementing its position as the fourth largest airport in China.

II. Overall Stability in Safety Situation

In 2011, adhering to the guiding principle of Taking Precedence in Safety and Making Safety Sustainable, upholding the security philosophy of Zero Tolerance and in accordance with the approach to security, i.e. Earlier Precaution & Shifting of Work Focus to Lower Levels, the company strengthened its leadership, intensified its training and education work, expanded its safety investment, established a sound and long-term efficient mechanism, implemented safety responsibility and accountability systems and deepened the operation of its safety management system. In the year, it held safety training sessions with 4 990 attendees in 77 groups, refined and quantified 9 safety control indictors and 28 items of assessment criteria and put in place over 50 million yuan of supporting facilities and equipment. It also organized nearly 90 emergency drills, carried out five special rectification campaigns and successfully passed the CAAC security audit, thus strengthening the building of on-spot management capability and fortifying continuously the foundation of safety assurance. Overall, the airports' safety situation was stable throughout the year, representing the 11th year of safe operations since its opening.

III. Continuous Improvement in Operational Environment

The company expanded the airport's overall service capacity through measures such as integrating resources and tapping the potential, vigorously promoted the building plan on approach and departure diversion for the northern route of the airport, and implemented the plan officially on January 12, 2012, making a significant improvement for the airport's airspace environment. With the capacity in peak hours expanding from 25 aircraft movements/hour to 31 aircraft movements/hour, it finished the terminal capacity assessment, widening its room for business growth. The company also created a multi-party communication mechanism, strengthening the checks on unused slots and increasing the flight schedule execution rate to the present rate of over 90% and also the slot utilization rate.

IV. Continuous Optimization in Service Quality

The company strengthened its leadership and endeavored to improve its service quality through the activities of the Year of Service Quality. In the year, the ASQ passenger satisfaction scored 4.34, an up of 2.1% from the previous year and ranking the 3rd among the comparable airports worldwide. Complaints filed against the airport per million passengers dropped by 26.2% from that of the previous year, showing marked improvements in service quality. The company actively coordinated relevant entities in the civil aviation sector to establish an Obstacle Elimination mechanism and rectification of flight delays. The current average flight regularity rate has maintained over 72%, effectively increasing the passenger satisfaction. In addition, it provided excellent supports for the 8th National Games for People with Disabilities of China.

V. Fine Development in Non-aviation Business

In 2011, while accelerating the aviation business, the company continued to strengthen the development of non-aviation projects and obtained obvious results by earnestly creating non-aviation profit-making points and appropriately making structural adjustment. It vigorously pushed ahead with business transformation, turning its conventional passenger and freight forwarding services to VIP and its extended services and pharmaceutical warehousing, accelerating the development of the terminal retail business and better outsourcing the advertising business. In the year, the company generated 722 million yuan in non-aviation income, an up of 17% from that of the previous year, making it an important part (47.8%) of its total operating income.

厦门国际航空港股份有限公司

2011 年，厦门空港共保障飞机安全起降约 13.6 万架次，同比增长 16.3%，其中运输起降约 13.3 万架次，同比增长 16.4%；完成旅客吞吐量 1 575.7 万人次，同比增长 19.3%；完成货邮吞吐量约 26.1 万吨，同比增长 6.1%。

一、首条洲际航线开通，拉近厦门与世界的距离

2011 年 3 月 28 日，厦门—阿姆斯特丹直达航线的开通，标志着厦门成为中国大陆继北京、上海、广州、杭州、成都、南京、深圳之后第八个开通越洋客运航线的机场，也是我国经济特区、海峡西岸经济区、副省级城市中首个开通欧洲客运航线的城市。此航线的开通进一步巩固了厦门空港作为海峡西岸经济区中心机场的地位，为周边前往欧洲的旅客提供集散作用，提升厦门空港的区域影响力，同时也进一步拉近了厦门与世界的距离。

2011 年，厦门空港共引进 3 家航空公司进驻，除了荷兰皇家航空公司之外，还有中国联合航空公司和天津航空，共增加 4 条新航线，每周增加 17 班。目前，厦门机场已通航 78 个境内外城市，其中国内 59 个，国际 13 个，地区 6 个；已开通 118 条境内外航线，其中国内 94 条，国际 17 条，地区 7 条。在厦门机场运营的航空公司有 38 家，其中，境内航空公司 20 家，境外航空公司 18 家。厦门机场目前日均运输航班 383 架次，其中国内航班日均 324 架次，国际航班日均 33 架次，港澳台地区航班日均 26 架次。随着厦门空港航线和旅客吞吐量的不断增长，现用 3 号候机楼已出现饱和状态。为了满足需求，2011 年，厦门空港启动了新候机楼建设和 2 号候机楼的重新装修工程。

二、持续风险管控，构筑安全文化

全面构建安全风险管控体系是厦门空港 2011 年安全工作的主线，也是固化和完善安全管理长效机制的有效途径。2011 年 6 月，厦门空港顺利通过了民航华东管理局航空保安审计专家组的航空保安后续审计，标志着厦门空港航空保安系统迈上了一个新台阶。

2011 年 11 月 3 日，随着一架进行测试的 B737-800 飞机在厦门机场平稳起降，厦门机场基于性能的导航（PBN）飞行程序顺利完成验证试飞。厦门机场新设计的 PBN 飞行航线中，在不需要任何地面导航设施投入的条件下，共计新增 8 条离场航线、11 条进场航线，整个程序南北纵深达 300 多公里。尤其是东南侧程序，良好地协调了厦门机场东南侧航线与金门空域的关系，解决了厦门机场开航 28 年来“一个机场，半个天空”的历史性难题。

厦门空港不断加强与局方的沟通，充分用好时刻资源，3 月初将厦门机场高峰小时容量从 25 架次提高到 26 架次，在夏秋航季更进一步提高到了 28 架次，夏秋航季日航班量提高到了 370 架次，冬春航季进一步提高到 380 架次。

三、竭诚服务旅客，携手奉献社会

2011 年，厦门空港着力打造服务软实力，创新提升服务品质，以软件补硬件，稳固、提升“厦空港”的服务品牌，为全面创建最佳服务机场打下坚实的基础。

从 2008 年至 2011 年，经过三年的努力，厦门空港在口岸核心能力建设、国际关注的突发公共卫生事件应对能力以及人员、机制、管理，设施、卫生、服务等方面基本达到了国际卫生机场的要求，取得显著的成效。

深化服务精品建设，积极开展“服务精品项目展示”活动。通过精品项目展示，检验服务品质成果，营造“倡导服务精细化，创新优质服务”的良好氛围。围绕公司经营管理、生产运作过程、顾客关注热点、难点和瓶颈问题开展专题攻关和 QC 活动，涌现了一批国优和省市优单位。

厦门空港积极推动文明创建工作，并将文明创建作为增强企业核心竞争力的主要手段常抓不懈。在文明创建工作中，坚持以创造顾客价值为导向，借助质量管理体系、顾客满意度测评体系、服务标准质量管控体系等管理工具，推动精细化服务和服务精品建设，为顾客提供专业化的服务体验。2011 年 12 月 20 日，厦门国际航空港集团（已于 2012 年 1 月 1 日正式更名为“厦门翔业集团”）再次蝉联“全国文明单位”称号。

Xiamen International Airport Co., Ltd.

2011年10月22日，厦门高崎国际机场新候机楼奠基仪式

On October 22, 2011, the Foundation Laying Ceremony for the New Terminal of Xiamen Gaoqi International Airport Is Held

In 2011, Xiamen Airport safely handled 136 000 movements, representing a year-on-year increase of 16.3%, among which 133 000 were for transport aircraft, a year-on-year increase of 16.4%. It also recorded a passenger turnover of 15 757 000 and a cargo and mail turnover of 261 000 ton, representing year-on-year increases of 19.3% and 6.1% respectively.

I. Launching the First Intercontinental Route to Make Xiamen Closer to Other Parts of the World

The opening into service of the direct air route between Xiamen and Amsterdam on March 28, 2011 signified that Xiamen became the eighth mainland airport (following Beijing, Shanghai, Guangzhou, Hangzhou, Chengdu, Nanjing and Shenzhen) beginning to operate oceanic passenger air route, and also became the first city in China's Special Economic Zones and Western Taiwan Straits Economic Zone and among all the sub-provincial cities, having an air passenger route connecting Europe. This route further cemented Xiamen Airport's role as the central airport in the Western Taiwan Straits Economic Zone, served as a connecting airport for passengers flying to Europe, improved the regional influence of Xiamen Airport and made Xiamen closer to other parts of the world.

In 2011, three airlines began their operation at Xiamen Airport, namely KLM Royal Dutch Airlines, China United Airlines and Tianjin Airlines. In addition, a total of four new routes were added, and 17 flights were added each week. At present, Xiamen Airport has launched flights with 78 cities, of which 59 were domestic, 13 international and 6 regional. 118 air routes were opened into service, of which 94 routes were domestic, 17 international and 7 regional. There were 38 airlines operating at Xiamen Airport, of which 20 were national and 18 foreign. Currently, Xiamen Airport handled averagely 383 aircraft movements a day, of which 324 were national, 33 international and 26 were for flights to or from Hong Kong, Macao and Taiwan. With the continuous expansion of air routes and the increase in passenger throughput, the handling capacity of the existing T3 became saturated. To meet the increasing needs, Xiamen Airport launched in 2011 the projects of new terminal construction and T2 renovation.

II. Continuous Risk Control to Build Safety Culture

Building a comprehensive Safety Management System was the focus of Xiamen Airport's safety work in 2011, and an

effective approach to maintaining and improving the long-term effective safety management mechanism. In June 2011, Xiamen Airport successfully passed the follow-up audit of aviation security conducted by the aviation security audit expert team of CAAC East Regional Administration, signaling a higher standard being met by the Xiamen Airport's aviation security system.

On November 3, 2011, with the stable takeoff and landing of a testing flight by a B737-800 airplane at Xiamen Airport, the performance-based navigation (PBN) flight procedures of Xiamen Airport was validated successfully. Without the need for any additional ground navigation facilities, Xiamen Airport applied PBN procedures to eight departure routes and 11 arrival routes, covering over 300 kilometers along the south-north direction. In particular, with the application of PBN procedures to cover the southeastern area to the airport, the routes to the southeastern of Xiamen Airport were well coordinated with the Jinmen airspace, which has solved the long-standing problem of "one airport covering half a sky" that remained unsolved for 28 years since Xiamen Airport was opened to service.

Xiamen Airport continuously strengthened communication with CAAC, made full use of slot resources, increased the peak hour capacity from 25 to 26 movements in early March, and even to 28 during IATA summer season. The number of daily movements during summer season was increased to 370, compared with 380 movements a day during winter season.

III. Considerate Services for Passengers, Great Contributions to the Society

In 2011, Xiamen Airport was dedicated to boosting its soft power in service, enhanced service quality by innovation, supplemented tangible capacities with intangible strengths, strengthened the service brand boasted by Xiamen Airport and laid a solid foundation for building the best service airport.

After three years' efforts lasting from 2008 to 2011, Xiamen Airport has made pronounced achievements in basically meeting the requirements for international sanitary airport in terms of the establishment of airport's core competencies and the response to public health emergencies of international concern and in areas of personnel, mechanisms, management, facilities, health and services.

The Excellent Service Project Demonstration activities were carried out in the airport's pursuance of excellence in services provision. The demonstration helped check service quality and create a sound atmosphere of Advocating Refined Services and Innovated High-quality Services. Breakthrough efforts and QC programs were carried out in respect of corporate operation and management, operation processes, hotspot concerns of customers and bottleneck issues. A batch of entities was recognized as excellent performers at the provincial or national level.

Xiamen Airport made vigorous efforts in enhancing civility, as a main approach to improving corporate core competitiveness. Its civility efforts were oriented toward creating customer value. The quality management system, the customer satisfaction survey system, the service standard and quality control system and other management tools were employed to pursue refinement and excellence in services provision and provide customers with professional services. On December 20, 2011, Xiamen International Airport Group (formally renamed Xiamen Iport Group on January 1, 2012) was re-awarded the title of National Role Model Entity.

武夷山机场有限公司

武夷山机场于1994年正式通航，2002年与厦门开发有限公司合作重组，成立武夷山机场有限公司。

2011年，武夷山机场有限公司以资产重组为契机，大力深化公司内部改革，在安全生产、航线营销、机场改建等方面取得了可喜成绩。全年飞机安全起降5 249架次，完成年旅客吞吐量59.45万人次，创下历史最高纪录，并取得通航18年以来年年安全的良好业绩。

2011年6月1日，武夷山机场有限公司一届一次董事会会议召开

On June 1, 2011, Wuyishan Airport Holds Its 1st Meeting of the 1st Board

一、顺利完成公司重组，安全形势持续平稳

2011年5月，武夷山机场有限公司进行资产重组，由厦门翔业集团（原厦门国际航空港集团有限公司）出资1.95亿元购得公司65%股权，成为厦门翔业集团旗下继厦门高崎机场、福州长乐机场、龙岩冠山机场后的第四个机场。

公司始终坚持安全发展理念，持续推动安全管理体系（SMS）建设，深化安全隐患的排查治理，强化安全生产的责任落实，加强监督检查，确保了机场的飞行、空防、地面、消防等方面的全年安全，并以96.3%的符合率在福建省内，首家通过了空管安全管理体系（SMS）审核。

公司不断探索航空保卫管理体系（SeMS）建设，积极参加民航局组织的航空安保管理体系培训，并到试点机场对SeMS建设实践和风险管理先进经验进行学习，初步完成了公司航空保卫管理体系手册的编写，并进入试运行阶段。

二、引入市场竞争机制，航线营销成效凸显

2011年上半年，武夷山机场受重组影响航班减少，旅客吞吐量同比减少近20%。厦门翔业集团入主后，积极开展航线营销，成功引进山东航空公司在本场投放运力，并先后加密武夷山—厦门航线、增开北京—济南—武夷山往返航班，打破武夷山机场成熟航线由一家航空公司独飞的局面，形成良好的市场竞争机制。

在市场的推动下，航空公司纷纷打折，票价回落拉动机场客流量的大幅增长。从8月21日至12月31日，旅客吞吐量同比增长24.74%，其中，武夷山—厦门、武夷山—北京两条航线旅客吞吐量增长约50%。10月、11月，机场旅客吞吐量分别达到7.07万人次和6.01万人次，连创历史单月最好成绩。

Wuyishan Airport Co., Ltd.

Wuyishan Airport officially began operating in 1994, and Wuyishan Airport Co., Ltd. (referred to hereafter as the company) was established in 2002, through the restructuring with Xiamen Aviation Development Company.

In 2011, Wuyishan Airport Co., Ltd. took the asset restructuring as an opportunity to deepen its internal reform, and made pleasing achievements in the fields of safety in production, air route marketing and airport reconstruction. For the whole year, 5 249 aircraft movements were safely supported and 594 500 passengers were handled, which hit record high. The airport safety was assured for the 18th consecutive year since its opening to air service.

I. Restructuring Completed Successfully and Stable Safety Situation Sustained

In May 2011, the company was restructured through the payment of 195 million yuan for its 65% stake by Xiamen Iport Group Co., Ltd. (formerly as Xiamen International Airport Group Company), and became the 4th airport under Xiamen Iport Group Co., Ltd., following Xiamen Gaoqi, Fuzhou Changle and Longyan Guanshan airports.

The company adhered to the concept of safe development all the time, continued promoting the construction of safety management system (SMS), deepened the investigation and rectification of the hidden risks in safety and security, enhanced the responsibility of safety in production, strengthened the supervision and inspection, assured safety for the whole year in the fields of flight, aviation security, ground and fire fighting in the airport, and passed, as the first airport in Fujian Province, the ATM Safety Management System Audit at a compliance rate of 96.3%.

The company continuously worked on security management system (SeMS) building, actively participated in the trainings on SeMS organized by CAAC. By visiting the pilot airports, the company learned from their advanced experience in SeMS construction and risk control, initially completing the compilation of its SeMS manual and putting it into trial operation.

II. Market Competition Mechanisms Introduced and Achievements in Air Route Marketing Made

In the first half of 2011, Wuyishan Airport had fewer flights because of the restructuring, with its passenger volume nearly 20% less than that of the last year. After Xiamen Iport Group Co., Ltd. took the control, the company actively created air route marketing and successfully introduced Shandong Airlines to operate in the airport. It successively added flights on Wuyishan-Xiamen route and provided new round-trip flights on Beijing-Ji'nan-Wuyishan route, ending the situation that the mature routes were only flown by one airlines and creating a sound market competition mechanism.

Driven by the market, airlines gave discounts on air fares one after another, which greatly increased the passenger in the airport. From August 21 to December 31, passengers handled increased by 24.74% over those of the last year, of which the passengers handled on Wuyishan-Xiamen and Wuyishan-Beijing increased by about 50%. In October and November, passengers handled in the airport reached 70 700 person·times and 60 100 person·times respectively, both being the record high for the single month.

2011年8月21日，机场携手山东航空公司开通武夷山—厦门往返航班

On August 21, 2011, the Airport Launches Wuyishan-Xiamen Round-trip Flight Jointly with Shandong Airlines

青岛国际机场集团有限公司

一、运输生产

2011年，新增航线9条，保障飞行10.5万架次，旅客吞吐量1 172万人次，货邮吞吐量16.7万吨，同比分别增长1.73%、5.54%和1.70%。

（1）空域开发成果空前 努力与各方沟通取得了空域优化的重大突破：新开辟6条航线和1条临时航线，将“单进单出”的进离场航线结构改善为“三进四出”的进离场航线分流结构。高峰小时由22架次提升到28架次，本场容量提高了27%，每天可新增航班90余个。

（2）航线网络日臻完善 争取到市政府洲际航线补贴，与汉莎航空、沈阳机场联合开发的青岛—沈阳—法兰克福航线拟于2012年3月份首航，将成为我省首条洲际客运定期航线；与扬子江合作开通了浦东—青岛—洛杉矶洲际货运航线；与达美航空就青岛—东京—美国航线开发达成合作共识。

（3）保税油库投入运转 该项目每年可为执飞国际航线的航空公司节省约4 000万元运营成本，也使青岛机场成为继北京、上海、广州、深圳机场之后，全国第二批享受该政策的机场。

（4）中转功能得以加强 通过有计划的高层互访，与山航、东航等航空公司就支线业务开发、中转功能建设等事宜达成了合作意向。

（5）腹地拓展形势喜人 新增设东营、昌乐、荣成、文登、胶南城市候机楼及旅客班车。服务网络已延伸至省内17市（县），辐射范围达全省的40%。全年城市候机楼和异地旅客直通车共输送乘客38.8万人次，同比增长57.8%。开拓异地货运服务，在烟台、潍坊异地货站基础上，济宁、日照异地货站项目已进入实质性推进阶段。全年异地货站共发运货物1 630吨，同比增长15.6%。

（6）货运业务加快拓展 开通邮政航空快线，集聚了省内腹地快件至青岛分拨转运；吸引了顺丰快递、联邦快递等专业航空公司关注的目光。

二、安全管理

2011年安全工作顺利实现了“双零”目标。安检旅客约580万人次，查处危险和违禁品1 580件，维护飞机2.16万架次，发现和排除飞机故障55起。

（1）综合保障能力方面 重新修订了《机场使用手册》并获局方批准；制定完善《机坪运行安全管理规定》等18项制度。开展安全培训484项，参训人数达1.8万人次。强化设备及飞行区秩序管控，投入1 950多万元购置了平台车等设备；改造11～18号登机桥固定端和21、22号机位，并改进了保障流程，提高了登机桥、复合机位的利用率。

（2）安全防范能力方面 全面实施航空保安管理系统（SeMS）建设，设立专职内保机构，健全内保组织体系。开展了货邮运输检查、安全生产月等7次专项活动，整改隐患60余项。组织开展安全风险评估，采取加装防冲撞门、增设双围栏等措施，大大降低了风险指数。持续开展“打击盗窃托运行李、货物专项行动”，“平安机场”建设再上台阶。

（3）应急处置能力方面 修编《应急救援手册》、《应急管理实用手册》，实施预案动态管理。开展候机楼反暴力事件处置、突发事件紧急拉动等大规模演练，全年组织部门演练118次，参与人数达1 700人次。

三、服务质量

航空公司、旅客、货主满意率分别达到91.53%、91.66%、92.09%，全年航班正常率为99.34%。圆满完成重大保障任务41次，保障视察、合作来访等37批次。

（1）监管体系日益健全 成立了服务质量监督管理委员会，实施了服务质量绩效考核，服务监管实现常态化、体系化。

（2）不正常航班处置取得成效 建立了信息发布平台，统一了内外协调机制，优化了应急处置流程，强化了指挥调度力量，成立了“红马甲”等服务团队，

Qingdao International Airport Group Co., Ltd.

I. Air Transportation

In 2011, 9 air routes were added. 105 000 aircraft movements, 11.72 million passengers and 167 000 tons of cargo and mail were handled, with representing year-on-year increases of 1.73%, 5.54% and 1.70% respectively.

1. Unprecedented Progress in Airspace Development Made. Through diligent communication with all concerning parties, major breakthroughs in airspace optimization were made: 6 air routes and 1 temporary air route were newly opened, the one in/one out Pattern (one arrival and one departure) was replaced by the three in/four out diversified pattern (three arrivals and four departures) for arrival and departure routes. Aircraft movements at peak hours were increased from 22 to 28, the airport capacity was increased by 27%, and the newly added flights were over 90 per day.

2. Route Network Improved Gradually. The intercontinental routes subsidies were secured from the Municipal Government. The air route between Qingdao-Shenyang-Frankfurt, which was developed jointly with Lufthansa and Shenyang Airport, is the first intercontinental air route for scheduled passenger flights in Shandong province and is due to open in March 2012. The intercontinental air route between Pudong-Qingdao-Los Angeles for cargo flights was opened in cooperation with the Yangtze River Express, and a cooperation consensus was reached with Delta Air Lines on the introduction of an air route between Qingdao-Tokyo-U.S.

3. Bonded Oil Depot Put into Operation. 40 million yuan in operating costs can be saved by the project annually for those airlines operating international flights, making Qingdao Airport, following Beijing, Shanghai, Guangzhou and Shenzhen Airports, to be among the second group having this privilege.

4. Transfer Function of the Airport Strengthened. Cooperation intentions were reached, through scheduled high-level exchange visits, on the development of feeder routes and the construction of airport transfers function with Shandong Airlines, China Eastern Airlines and others.

5. Pleasing Outcome Achieved in Hinterland Expansion. The city terminals and passenger shuttles were newly established at Dongying, Changle, Rongcheng, Wendeng and Jiaonan. The service network extended to 17 cities (counties), covering up to 40% of the whole province. For the whole year, the city terminals and the through buses for the passengers from other places fulfilled a total number of 388 000 passengers, with a year-on-year growth of 57.8%. The off-site freight transport services were developed. Based on the off-site cargo terminals at Yantai and Weifang, the projects of off-site cargo terminals at Jining and Rizhao progressed substantively. In 2011, a total of 1 630 tons of cargo were forwarded from off-site cargo terminals, with a year-on-year increase of 15.6%.

及时增加物资储备，不正常航班处置进一步规范化、制度化。

（3）攻坚克难效果初显 深入开展第三方调查，通过部署实施“五个一工程”和“六场硬仗”，卫生间管理、外包单位服务、大件行李运输等服务难点得以改善，实现了服务的精细化、标准化。

（4）特色服务亮点频现 继自助值机和网上值机后，联合山航推出手机登机业务，成为省内首家开通此项业务的机场。无线上网、视听娱乐等功能得以丰富提升，特色服务彰显个性化、多样化。机场获得“全日空顾客满意度调查全球第一名”等多个奖项，服务工作广受好评。

6. Expansion of Freight Business Accelerated. The postal air express was opened. The express mails within the hinterland of the province were gathered to be transshipped to Qingdao in batches, attracting the attentions of S.F. Express, Federal Express and other airlines of the kind.

II. Safety Management

The safety goal of "zero zero" was realized in 2011. About 5.8 million person/times were security-checked, 1 580 dangerous and prohibited items were investigated and dealt, 21 600 aircraft/times were maintained, and 55 aircraft faults were found out and fixed.

1. Capabilities in Comprehensive Support. Airport Operations Manual was revised and approved by CAAC. 18 regulations including the Regulations on Safety Management for Apron Operations were worked out and revised. Safety trainings with 484 topics were carried out with up to 18 000 person/times involved. The control of the equipment and the flight area order was enhanced, more than 19.5 million yuan was spent on platform trucks and other equipment, the fixed ends of boarding bridges at Gate 11 to Gate 18 and the aircraft stands 21 and 22 were renovated, the support process was bettered, and the utilization of boarding bridges and aircraft stands was improved.

2. Capabilities in Ensuring Safety and Security. An overall construction of aviation security management system (SeMS) was implemented, and special internal security units were set up to strengthen the internal security system. 7 special activities such as cargo and mail checking, month of work safety were carried out and more than 60 hidden hazards were rectified. Security risk assessments were organized and measures such as installing anti-collision gates and adding double fences were taken, making risks greatly reduced. The special actions to combat the theft of checked baggage and cargoes were continued, with the construction of a safer airport being on a new step.

3. Capabilities in Emergency Response. Emergency Rescue Manual and Practical Handbook of Emergency Management were compiled and revised, and dynamic management of preplans was carried out. Large-scale drills for anti-violence and emergency evacuation at the terminal were conducted. For the whole year, 118 drills were organized with 1 700 person/times attended.

III. Service Quality

The satisfaction rates of airlines, passengers, cargo owners were up to 91.53%, 91.66% and 92.09% respectively, and the annual flight regularity rate was 99.34%. 41 major support tasks were fulfilled, and 37 flights were supported for those visitors on inspections and for the purpose of cooperation.

1. Supervision Systems Growing Robust. Supervision Committee for Service Quality was set up, and the performance appraisal for service quality was carried out, thus service supervision becoming regular and systematic.

2. Making Achievements in Irregular Flights Handling. Information publishing platform was set up, and the internal and external coordination mechanisms were unified, the emergency response process was optimized, the command and dispatch functions were strengthened, service teams named "Red Vests" were set up, and the supplies reserves were supplemented in a timely manner, so that the handling of irregular flight became further standardized and institutionalized.

3. Tackling Tough Issues Bearing Fruits. The tough service issues like toilet management, the services provided by outsourcing units, oversize luggage shipping, etc. were settled through deepening the third party investigation, and employing Five One Projects and Six Tough Actions, and as the result, the services were refined and standardized.

4. Featured Services Spackling. After the self-service check-in and online check-in, the airport introduced mobile check-in service together with Shandong Airlines, becoming the first airport to provide this kind of service within the province. The functions such as Wi-Fi access and audio-visual entertainment were richly upgraded, and featured services highlighted individuality and diversity. The airport was awarded the First Prize in ANA Customer Satisfaction Surveys and many other prizes, and the services were widely popular.

广东省机场管理集团公司

2011 年，广东省机场管理集团公司（以下简称集团公司）坚定不移地推进体制改革，实施“十二五”发展战略，在运输生产、基础建设、服务提升、航空枢纽建设等方面取得了较好成绩，为广东机场集团“十二五”期间的发展奠定了坚实基础。

一、确保持续安全，实现连续第八个安全年目标

狠抓安全生产责任制和规章制度的落实，加大安全基础设施设备和员工素质培训的投入，强化隐患排查治理工作。推进安全管理体系（SMS）和航空安保管理体系（SeMS）建设。圆满完成深圳大运会安全服务保障任务。召开安全专项工作会，全面分析安全与发展的关系，确立了集团公司持续安全发展的新理念。全年未发生机场责任原因造成的航空、空防和航空地面事故，保持了平稳的安全态势，为集团公司的改革发展打下了良好的基础。集团公司连续六年荣获全国“安康杯”竞赛优胜企业称号。

二、运输生产保持增长，白云机场航空枢纽建设成效提高

集团公司全年累计完成飞机起降 37.83 万架次、旅客吞吐量 4 749.26 万人次、货邮吞吐量 119.23 万吨，同比分别增长 6.1%、9.8%、3%。白云机场航空枢纽建设稳步推进。全年累计完成飞机起降 34.93 万架次、旅客吞吐量 4 504.03 万人次、货邮吞吐量 118 万吨，同比分别增长 6.1%、9.9%、3.1%。白云机场新开通 10 条国际航线，国际（地区）航线总数达到 103 条；国际旅客吞吐量同比增长 22.9%，国际旅客占旅客吞吐量比例上升至 14%；中转旅客吞吐量同比增长 15.7%，中转旅客比例占旅客吞吐量比例上升至 8.3%。联邦快递亚太转运中心货邮吞吐量达到 30.81 万吨，同比增长 0.7%，占白云机场全年国际货邮吞吐量的 56.7%，货邮吞吐总量的 26.1%。白云机场在

2011年4月25日，中国民用航空局和广东省人民政府签订《关于加快广东省民航科学发展的战略合作框架协议》

On April 25, 2011, CAAC and Guangdong Provincial Government Sign the Strategic Cooperation Framework Agreement on Accelerating Scientific Development of Civil Aviation in Guangdong Province

运输生产稳步增长的同时确保了服务质量的稳定，保持在“世界十佳服务机场”行列。白云机场综合交通枢纽整体交通规划已通过专家评审。圆满承办了第十届东亚机场联盟会议。

揭阳潮汕机场（汕头机场）、梅县机场都保持了较快增长，揭阳潮汕机场旅客吞吐量接近汕头机场历史最高水平。湛江机场组建商旅服务公司，创建“宜乘”商旅高端服务品牌，社会反响良好。梅县机场提升“飞翼”高端服务品牌价值，获得旅客好评。

三、基础设施建设稳步推进，揭阳潮汕机场重点工程项目建成通航

揭阳潮汕机场圆满完成了工程建设任务，2011 年 12 月 15 日成功转场启用后，设施设备运转良好，总体运作正常。努力推进白云机场扩建工程可研报批工作，第三跑道项目涉及的空域问题在各方协调下基本得到解决，二号航站楼方案设计工作全面铺开。白云机场中性货站道口及围界工程已通过竣工验收。汕头城市候机楼项目已开工。湛江机场航站楼附属楼工程顺利通过验收并正式投入运营。梅县机场飞行区扩

建工程场道工程进展顺利，场道主体工程已完工。惠州机场滑行道改造完工。

四、完成管理体制变革，承担起促进全省民航事业发展重任

2011年,集团公司实现了“省属市管”体制向“省属省管”体制的转变和新老班子平稳交接过渡。积极推进广东省与中国民航局签署《关于加快广东省民航科学发展的战略合作框架协议》。研究制订了促进全省民航事业加快发展指导意见和推进珠三角机场管理运营一体化工作方案。配合做好全省民用机场体系建设,《广东省民用机场发展规划》已通过专家评审。依托白云机场发展空港经济开始起步，广州新科宇航科技有限公司正式成立，第一个机库建设前期工作稳步开展。完成集团公司所属机场公安机构移交省公安厅工作。

五、加强资金筹措，取得良好经济效益

全年集团公司实现合并营业收入50.5亿元，同比增长8.8% 。其中,股份公司实现营业收入42.5亿元,同比增长10.1%；完成税前利润9.6亿元，同比增长15.4%。积极争取省市政府、民航局资本金及各类补助资金16.45亿元，发行10亿元中期票据、15亿元短期融资券，全年共筹集资金58.2亿元，在一定程度上缓解了资金压力。积极开展资本运作，中科白云基金共投资18个项目，总投资金额10.33亿元，目前已有一个项目上市，四个项目在审。

Guangdong Airport Management Corporation

In 2011, Guangdong Airport Management Corporation (shortened as GAMC) resolutely pressed ahead with institutional reform, implemented the development strategy for 12th Five-Year Plan, thus making good achievements in transport, infrastructure construction, service improvement, and aviation hub building, etc., and laying a solid foundation for the development of GAMC in the 12th Five-Year Plan period.

I. Sustained Safety Maintained and 8 Consecutive Years' Annual Safety Objectives Realized

GAMC made great efforts in the implementation of industrial safety responsibilities and regulations, increased the input in safety infrastructure and equipment and the quality training of employees, and reinforced the hidden hazards screening and rectification. It pushed ahead with the building of safety management system (SMS) and security management system (SeMS), and successfully accomplished the safety service and support for the Universiade Shenzhen 2011. It convened the special work conference on safety and comprehensively analyzed the relationship between safety and development, thus establishing the new concept of sustained safe development of GAMC. In the whole year, there was no aviation, aviation security or ground accident that occurred due to the airport responsibilities, maintained the steady safety momentum and laid a good foundation for the reform and development of GAMC. GAMC was awarded the outstanding enterprises in the national Safety and Health Cup Competition for six consecutive years.

II. Increase in Transport Maintained and Efficiency of Baiyun Airport Aviation Hub Building Uplifted

In 2011, GAMC witnessed 378.3 thousand aircraft movements, 47.492 6 million passenger traffic, and 1.192 3 million tons of cargo and mail turnover, representing year-on-year increases of 6.1%, 9.8% and 3% respectively. The aviation hub building of Baiyun Airport progressed steadily. The airport saw 349.3 thousand aircraft movements, 45.040 3 million passenger traffic and 1.18 million tons of cargo and mail turnover in the whole year, representing year-on-year increases of 6.1%, 9.9% and 3.1% respectively. 10 new international routes were launched in Baiyun Airport, adding its total to 103. The international passenger traffic increased, 22.9% higher than that of the previous year, and the percentage of the international passengers among all the passengers increased to 14%. The transit passenger traffic increased, 15.7% higher than that of the previous year, and the percentage of transit passengers among all passengers increased to 8.3%. The cargo and mail handled by FedEx Asia Pacific Hub hit 308.1 thousand tons, a year-on-year increase of 0.7%, accounting for 56.7% of the annual international cargo and mail turnover and 26.1% of all cargo and mail handled by the airport. While maintaining its steady increase in transport, the airport also ensured the stabilization of its service quality, keeping its qualifications to be in the league of World Top Ten Service Airports. The overall transport plan for the comprehensive transport hub of Baiyun Airport passed the appraisal of experts. GAMC undertook successfully the 10th East Asia Airports Alliance (EAAA) Annual Meeting.

Jieyang Chaoshan Airport (Shantou Airport) and Meixian Airport also maintained a comparative rapid pace of growth, and the passenger traffic of the former nearly attained its historical high. Zhanjiang Airport formed a business travel company and created the upscale service brand of Convenient for Taking business travels receiving good social feedback. Meixian Airport improved its high-end service brand value of Flying Wings, winning acclamation from the passengers.

III. Infrastructure Construction Steadily Pushed Forward and Key Construction Project of Jieyang Chaoshan Airport Completed and Opened to Service

The construction project of Jieyang Chaoshan Airport was successfully completed. On December 15, 2011, after its successful removal to the new one, all its facilities and equipment were operated well, and its overall operation was normal. GAMC pursued with vigor the feasibility report on development and submission of the expansion project of Baiyun Airport, basically solved, in coordination with various parties, the airspace problems involved in the third runway project and brought into full swing the plan design of the terminal 2. The road paths and fencing projects of neutral air freight terminals in Baiyun Airport received acceptance on examination. The project of city terminals in Shantou Airport was initiated. The project of affiliating building to Zhanjiang Airport terminal successfully passed the acceptance inspection and was officially put into operation. With its main body completed, the pavement construction of Meixian Airport aircraft movement area expansion project went on smoothly. The taxiway reconstruction project in Huizhou Airport was also accomplished.

IV. Management System Reform Accomplished and Important Task of Facilitating Provincial Civil Aviation Development Undertaken

In 2011, GAMC realized the system transformation from Belonging to the Provincial Government and Being Managed by the Guangzhou Municipal Government to Belonging to the Provincial Government and Being Managed by the Provincial Government, and smooth transition from the old leadership to the new one. GAMC actively push ahead with the signing of Strategic Cooperation Framework Agreement on Accelerating Scientific Development of Civil Aviation in Guangdong Province by Guangdong Province and CAAC. It studied and developed the guidance proposals on accelerating the civil aviation industry in entire Guangdong Province and the work plan for promoting integrated operation of airports in Pearl River Delta region. Coordination and support were given to the building of the airport systems in the province, and the Civil Airports Development Plan of Guangdong Province passed the appraisal by experts. Based on the practices of Baiyun Airport, airport economy was developed initially, STAG was officially established and the preliminary work of the first hanger went on smoothly. The management of aviation security bureau under GAMC was transferred to Guangdong Provincial Public Security Department.

V. Fund Raising Reinforced and Good Economic Effects Achieved

In 2011, GAMC garnered total revenue of 5.05 billion yuan, a year-on-year increase of 8.8%, among which the limited company realized 4.25 billion yuan revenue, a year-on-year increase of 10.1%, and its profits before tax stood at 960 million yuan, representing an increase of 15.4% over that of the previous year. In 2011, GAMC canvassed totaling 1.645 billion yuan of the provincial government, municipal government and CAAC capital and various subsidies, issued 1 billion yuan of medium term bills and 1.5 billion short term financing bonds, making the total amount of the raising fund to 5.82 billion yuan. This, to a certain extent, eased the capital pressure of GAMC. GAMC actively engaged in capital operation and China Science Baiyun Fund invested in 18 projects with a total investment of 1.033 billion yuan. Currently one project has been publicly listed and four have remained in the approval process.

安徽民航机场集团有限公司

安徽民航机场集团有限公司为省属国有大型航空运输企业。下设合肥机场分公司，黄山机场分公司，以及安徽民航客货销售有限责任公司、安徽民航机场建设发展有限公司和安徽民航蓝天实业总公司3个全资子公司。

集团公司所属合肥骆岗机场是我省连接东西部和沿海发达地区的重要航空枢纽。1977年11月竣工开航，1996年扩建完善为现代化航空港4D标准，2005年被正式升为国家一级航空口岸。目前，合肥机场开通航线50多条，有国内外18家航空公司投入了航班运力，航线网络辐射到全国40多个大中城市，每周执行计划航班460多班。同时开通了合肥—日本、新加坡、韩国、香港、澳门、台湾等9条国际及地区航线。为了全面改善合肥骆岗机场服务保障环境，2009年4月完成总概算为8 818万元的改扩建工程，可满足高峰小时1 800人次的旅客流量。

集团公司所属黄山机场，1959年10月建成通航，2004年5月完成现代化航空港4C标准扩建工程，设计年旅客吞吐量90万人次。2008年6月通过民航华东局验收批准，飞行等级提升为4D级，目前开通航线10多条，通航12个旅游城市。2010年升级为国际口岸，2011年韩国大韩、韩亚航空公司分别开通两条至韩国的定期航班。

淮南、铜陵、蚌埠、宿州、亳州、六安、巢湖、滁州、安庆、池州、芜湖、宣城、马鞍山、和县、淮北15个合肥机场异地城市候机楼和1个合肥市区候机楼的陆续开通，不仅有效解决了广大市民交通换乘困难，服务了地方经济的发展，也有效提高了各航空公司航班的客运率和载运率。

近年来，随着安徽经济的快速发展，省机场集团公司积极抢抓机遇，取得了较好的发展业绩，截至2011年，合肥骆岗机场连续23年保证航空安全无事故，空防安全连续实现第52个安全年。合肥机场的航空旅客吞吐量连续7年保持两位数快速增长，与周边航空市场发达地区的机场相比，在整体上呈现出良好的赶超势头并继续逐步缩小彼此间的差距，旅客吞吐量自2004年首次突破百万人次大关后，又实现200万、300万和400万人次的连续跨越，去年完成旅客吞吐量440万人次，旅客吞吐量和货邮吞吐量增幅分别位居全国民航机场的前列，实现了“十二五”的良好开局。今年合肥机场的旅客吞吐量有望突破500万人次大关。黄山机场通过口岸升级，已成为皖南及皖浙赣毗邻区域重要空中门户，2011年，旅客吞吐量达46万人次，创历史最好水平。集团公司先后荣获全国民航“安康杯”劳动竞赛优胜单位、全国“安康杯”竞赛优胜企业、全国民航五一劳动奖状、全国民航先进劳动关系和谐企业、全国民航抗震救灾先进集体、奥运安保特别贡献奖、安徽省文明单位等各类奖项和荣誉称号。

航空市场发达地区的机场相比，在整体上呈现出良好的赶超势头并继续逐步缩小彼此间的差距，旅客吞吐量自2004年首次突破百万人次大关后，又实现200万、300万和400万人次的连续跨越，去年完成旅客吞吐量440万人次，旅客吞吐量和货邮吞吐量增幅分别位居全国民航机场的前列，实现了“十二五”的良好开局。今年合肥机场的旅客吞吐量有望突破500万人次大关。黄山机场通过口岸升级，已成为皖南及皖浙赣毗邻区域重要空中门户，2011年，旅客吞吐量达46万人次，创历史最好水平。集团公司先后荣获全国民航“安康杯”劳动竞赛优胜单位、全国“安康杯”竞赛优胜企业、全国民航五一劳动奖状、全国民航先进劳动关系和谐企业、全国民航抗震救灾先进集体、奥运安保特别贡献奖、安徽省文明单位等各类奖项和荣誉称号。

重庆机场集团有限公司

2011 年，重庆江北国际机场完成旅客吞吐量 1 905.14 万人次，同比增长 20.56%；保障飞行 16.54 万架次，同比增长 14.69%；货邮吞吐量 23.74 万吨，同比增长 21.31%。在 2011 年度国际机场理事会（ACI）旅客满意度测评中得分 4.61 分，取得了世界同量级机场排名第二、国内同量级机场排名第一的好成绩。全年机场无空防、飞行、地面、消防等重特大事故，应急救援率 100%。全年无重大服务投诉事件，机场原因航站放行正常率 100%。

2011年5月，民航局局长李家祥（左五）率队视察重庆江北国际机场
Li Jiaxiang, Administrator of CAAC (fifth from the left), Inspects Chongqing Jiangbei International Airport in May, 2011

一、以与南航战略合作为契机，大力开拓航空市场，实现生产量全国排名的提升

2011 年，公司抓住重庆内陆开放高地建设和产业结构升级良机，积极开拓航空市场，全年旅客吞吐量增长近 21%，比全国主要机场平均水平高 13%，比西南地区主要机场平均水平高 7%，成绩显著。

一是国际客运航线开发取得实质进展，重庆市政府给予国际航线“3 年 10 个亿”的支持政策，相继开通重庆至普吉、河内、吴哥等 8 条客运航线，国际（地区）客运航线达到 13 条。

二是国际（地区）货运发展实现重大突破。新开通重庆至卢森堡、莫斯科、阿姆斯特丹等 7 条全货机航线，全货机航线达到 13 条，每周航班超过 20 班；全年国际货运量达到 5.5 万吨，同比增长 5 倍以上。

三是国内航线网络进一步完善，高原中转市场持续巩固。相继开通大同、攀枝花、潍坊等 9 条国内航线，正班通航城市达到 85 个。

四是创新推出“空轨联运”，完善重庆机场“空陆”、“空铁”、“空轨”联运的综合交通体系。

二、全面开展东区建设前期工作，实现基础保障能力持续提升

2011 年是东航站区及第三跑道工程的动工奠基年，完成了保税港区货库及通道工程，实现了市委、市政府确定的重庆机场工程建设目标。成功实现东北部空中交通分流，高峰小时由 29 架次提高至 42 架次。

三、强化经营管理，实现发展质量和效益水平持续提升

面对严峻的经营形势，公司从增加收入和控制成本两方面着手，加强经营管理，深挖资源价值。一是以业务外包为突破，加快推进机场管理转型；二是全面实施预算动态管理严格控制成本；三是积极推进节能减排工作，实施计量系统改造、登机桥气源装置及 400 赫兹电源改造等五大节能减排改造项目，预计每年能耗支出将节约 400 万元。单位旅客能耗实现了下降 10% 的目标；四是实施黔江机场一体化运营，兑现管理输出承诺。黔江武陵山机场相继开通至上海、

Chongqing Airport Group Co., Ltd.

In 2011, Chongqing Jiangbei International Airport witnessed an annual traffic of over 19.051 4 million passengers, safe aircraft movements of 165 400, and cargo and mail turnover of 237 400 tons, representing year-on-year increases of 20.56%, 14.69% and 21.31% respectively. In 2011 Annual Passenger Satisfaction Survey by Airports Council International (ACI), the airport got 4.61 marks, ranking the second among its peer airports of the same league in the world and the first among its peer airports of the same league in China. There were no major or extraordinary airport accidents in aviation security, flight, ground service or fire control, and the rate of emergency rescue reached 100%. In the whole year, there was no major service complaint against the airport. The regularity rate of clearance from the terminals of the airport stood at 100%.

I. Taking the Opportunity of Strategic Cooperation with China Southern Airlines, Making Great efforts in Expanding Aviation Market and Realizing the Upgrading of Nationwide Rank inTraffic Volume

In 2011, the company made good use of the opportune time when Chongqing was building itself into internal opening-up showcase and upgrading its industrial structure. The company actively expanded aviation market and made outstanding progress in passenger turnover, with an annual growth of nearly 21%, 13% higher than the average level of the major airports in China and 7% higher than the average level of the major airports in southwest area.

1. Substantive progress was made in developing international passenger transport routes. Chongqing Municipal Government adopted a support policy, offering "1 billion yuan in three years" in support of international routes. 8 passenger transport routes were launched one by one from Chongqing to Phuket, Hanoi, Angkor, etc., totaling to 13 international (regional) passenger transport routes.

2. Major breakthroughs were made in developing international cargo transport. 7 all-cargo aircraft routes from Chongqing to Luxembourg, Moscow, Amsterdam, etc. were newly launched, with all-cargo aircraft routes totaling to 13. Every week there were more than 20 flights and annual international cargo transport amounted to 55 000 tons, a year-on-year growth of over 5 times.

3. Domestic route network was further refined and plateau tranfer market was continuously reconsolidated. 9 domestic air routes were launched one by one to Datong, Panzhihua, Weifang, etc. and regular flights linked with 85 cities.

4. "Air-rail joint transport" was launched on an innovative basis, improving the integrated traffic system of "air-land", "air-railway", "air-rail" joint transport of Chongqing Airport .

II. Comprehensively Expanding the Preliminary Work of the East Area Construction Project and Realizing the Continuous Improvement of the Basic Support Capability

2011 marked the year for the foundation stone-laying of the east terminal area and the third runway project. Warehouse and

---

昆明的直飞航线，旅客吞吐量突破 2 万人。

2011 年是公司发展的重要转折之年，重庆机场全面确立了以“大型复合型枢纽”建设指引全局的发展思路，在重庆机场的发展史上具有重要里程碑意义。随着江北机场的持续快速发展，集团公司已经进入发展转型的关键时期。

corridor project in the bonded area was completed, realizing construction target of Chongqing Airport project set forth by Chongqing Municipal Party Committee and the Municipality. Air traffic flow diversion in northeast part was successfully achieved and flights at the peak hour were up from 29 to 42 flights.

III. Strengthening Operation Management and Continuously Uplifting Development Quality and Revenue Level

1. Facing the grim operation situation, the company set about to increase revenue and control cost in order to strengthen operation management and tap the potential value of resources. a) Taking business outsourcing as a breakthrough, it accelerated and promoted the management transformation of the airport; b) Implementing dynamic management of the budget comprehensively, it tightened control of cost; c) Vigorously promoting energy-saving and emission-reduction work, it implemented five retrofit projects, including metrological system retrofit, air supply installment to the boarding bridges and 400 Hz power supply retrofit, etc. It was estimated that every year's energy saving would be about 4 million yuan. The target of cutting 10% of per unit passenger energy consumption was achieved; d) Implementing integrated operation with Qianjiang Airport, it honored its management output promise. Qianjiang Wulingshan Airport launched direct air routes to Shanghai and Kunming, with a passenger turnover over 20 000.

2011 was an important turning year for the development of the company. Chongqing Airport set for itself a strategy of "large and integrated hub" construction in guiding all-round development, which was of major milestone significance in the development history of the airport. Along with constant and rapid development of Jiangbei Airport, the company has been ushered into a key period of development transformation.

2011年5月5日，民航局李家祥局长与重庆市黄奇帆市长出席重庆民航建设发展领导小组第一次会议

On May 5, 2011, Li Jiaxiang, Administrator of CAAC, and Huang Qifan, Mayor of Chongqing Municipality Attend the First Meeting of the Steering Group of Chongqing Civil Aviation Development

安全服务品质显著提升

重庆机场集团公司狠抓安全基层和基础工作。一是着眼主体责任和资质能力两个关键，深入推进安全管理体系（SMS）建设，完成航空安保管理体系（SeMS）编写。二是按照民航局要求，开展飞行区、货运区、内场交通及危险品运输等专项整治，成功承办首都机场集团飞行区管理经验交流会，得到集团及同行机场的好评。三是成立机坪运行管理委员会，搭建运行协调平台，启用机场运控中心，提升安全运行效率。四是推进风险管理，全年查找并消除高风险源7个，消除中低风险源102个。全年没有发生空防、飞行、地面、消防等重特大事故，应急救援率100%。

服务方面，在“践行中国服务”的总体指导下，率先建立服务管理体系，持续开展了服务流程优化、服务监察、旅客满意度测评及需求调查等基础工作，ACI旅客满意度测评取得年度亚太区最佳进步奖和全球旅客吞吐量1 500万~2 500万级最佳机场第二名的好成绩。品牌建设全面推进。成功召开“一秒服务”品牌新闻发布会，在成员机场中率先推出一秒服务品牌体系，得到了社会的广泛认可和关注，同时荣获首都机场集团公司品牌建设示范单位称号。

航空运输保持稳步增长

公司积极开拓航空市场，国际航线取得重大突破、航空货运逆势而上、客货运输快速增长。

国内航线网络进一步完善，高原中转市场持续巩固。新开大同、攀枝花、潍坊、义乌、通辽、淮安、长治、济宁、佛山等9条国内航线，正班通航城市达到85个。联手南航打造高原中转枢纽，高原通航点达到12个，九寨、拉萨等高原航班量同比增长30%以上。

国际（地区）航线快速增长。2011年，重庆至赫尔辛基航线也已正式开通。重庆机场还凭借近两年来国际航空货运业务的跨越式发展获得了最佳新兴机场奖的殊荣。

创新推介媒体和航空产品。利用“微博”等新兴网络平台，大力宣传航空服务产品；通过广告投放、优化空地一体化服务体系、建设

异地候机楼等举措，深度开发周边市场；联手市轨道集团，创新推出“空轨联运”产品，完善重庆机场“空陆”、“空铁”、“空轨”联运的综合交通体系。

东航站区项目建设扎实推进

按照重庆市政府“加快东区前期审批，力争2011年底开工，2015年建成投用”的工作要求，公司积极做好东区建设前期工作，全力推进工程建设。持续优化设计方案。瞄准国际一流目标，以绿色、可持续发展理念指导规划设计和建设实践，建设全行业的标杆和典范工程，为大飞机运营时代的到来做好充分准备。积极稳妥地推进工程进度。协调推动项目立项、可研、征地、初步设计等前期工作；狠抓工程招投标管理，选择一批资质高、管理强、技术硬的施工队伍；协调渝北区做好土地移交，确保建设进度和项目用地相适应，确保项目全面开工。建设阳光工程、廉洁工程。按照首都机场集团全过程跟踪审计“一四六一”基本原则，创新实践工程跟踪审计，建设廉洁工程。目前，顺利完成了第三跑道和东航站区工程奠基。实现了保税港区货库及通道工程竣工。重庆机场国际航空货运站暨专用货机坪正式启用，标志着西部唯一的保税港区与重庆江北国际机场实现了无缝衔接。白市驿军用机场搬迁工作取得进展。空域结构优化取得实质突破。成功实现东北部空中交通分流，高峰小时由29架次提高至42架次。

党建工作水平持续提升

坚持以人为本，全面兑现公司党委年初“五件实事”的承诺，共计投入4 000万元提高员工生活品质。创新宣传工作手段，积极利用新兴媒体，开通“重庆机场官方微博”；利用网站，宣传推介“西部游、重庆飞”、“便捷重庆飞”等航空产品；成立“重庆机场新闻危机处置委员会”，组建“新闻中心”。先后获得“全国民航文明单位”、“全国民航五一劳动奖状”等重大奖项近10项。

YAG 云南机场集团有限责任公司

一、运输指标有增有降

2011年，云南机场集团所属各机场共保障航班运输起降25.42万架次、旅客吞吐量2 868.64万人次、货邮吞吐量28.98万吨，分别比上年同期增长4.9%、9.1%，下降0.5%。其中，昆明机场保障航班运输起降19.12万架次、旅客吞吐量2 227.31万人次、货邮吞吐量27.25万吨，同比分别增长5.6%、10.3%，下降0.4%。

各机场新开、恢复航线共计52条，新增唐山、南通、百色、鄂尔多斯、榆林、台州、巴厘岛、岘港、苏拉塔尼、内比都、沙巴、高雄12个通航城市。新增河北航空公司、中国联合航空公司、印度尼西亚发达菲航空公司、柬埔寨通里萨航空公司、缅甸国际航空公司、泰国东方航空6家承运人。

二、安全态势总体平稳

2011年，各机场未发生飞行事故、地面事故、空防事故和事故征候，保证了集团安全平稳发展，巫家坝机场实现安全运行60周年。

昆明长水国际机场

Kunming Changshui International Airport

三、重点工程稳步推进

2011年，昆明长水国际机场建设共完成实物工程量投资50.74亿元，开工至今累计完成实物工程量投资187.88亿元，占概算批复总投资额的98.72%，12月底主体工程通过竣工验收；丽江机场改扩建工程已竣工验收，共完成工程投资10.92亿元，机场等级由4C提高到4D，获批国家口岸机场；西双版纳机场改扩建工程完成年度工程投资3.76亿元，累计完成工程投资6.26亿元；泸沽湖机场扩大试验段工程顺利竣工，专用公路全线路基土石方工程全部完工；红河、沧源、澜沧、怒江机场正在积极参与、协助政府部门开展选址、项目立项、可研、初设等前期工作。

四、统筹协调，加紧实施长水国际机场转场工作

2011年8月9日，中国民用航空局正式批复，同意将昆明新机场命名为“昆明长水国际机场”，英文名称为“KUNMING CHANGSHUI INTERNATIONAL AIRPORT”。9月25日，省市各有关部门和各转场演练工作组成功开展了昆明新机场第一次运行模拟演练，稳步推进转场培训和实物移交，确保建设与转场齐头并进；结合现场实物移交及成品保护工作，全面加强现场安全保卫工作。12月底昆明新机场项目主体工程共64项单位工程全部通过验收，标志着昆明新机场项目主体工程建设圆满收官，全面具备校飞、试飞条件并进入转场运行前准备阶段。

五、落实主体责任，完善安全体系建设

重点加强了机场运行质量控制，全面推行“检查单”报告制度，狠抓复杂天气条件下的飞行保障和特殊航班的运行保障“两个程序”，引入安全绩效监测机制，进一步实施动态风险管理；编制完成《“十二五”安全发展规划》，明确安全发展方向；完成全国中小机场安保管理体系（SeMS）建设试点相关工作，不断完善体系手册、程序文件和作业文件，深入开展“标兵班组”建设，有效提升基层班组的执行力；加强机场净空保护，进一步加大对特许经营单位安全服务工作的管理力度，开展治大隐患防大事故安全隐患排查治理专项行动，不断巩固安全平稳运行的态势。

六、坚持“两轮驱动”，大力推动产业发展

主业方面，推动各州市机场与当地政府成立了航空市场发展领导小组，初步建立起共同开发航空市场的工作机制。截至2011年12月，云南机场集团航线数量为323条，其中，国内航线277条，国际、地区航线为46条。建立了大面积航班延误新闻发布机制，推行“优质服务”班组评比考核，全面落实服务质量监督检查机制，航班正常率和顾客满意度均保持在较高水平；非航运方面，不断加强参控股企业治理，完善产权管理机制，促进企业间的业务、资金协同，各经营主体协同效应初步显现，腾冲航空旅游，新机场物流、酒店、机务维修资源整合等招商项目稳步推进；云南民航教育培训学院已完成组建并将投入试运行。■

Yunnan Airport Group Co., Ltd.

I. Traffic Indicators Showed Increases/Decreases

In 2011, the airports operated by Yunnan Airport Group handled in total 254 200 aircraft movements, about 28.686 4 million passengers and 289 800 tons of cargo and mail, representing increases of 4.9%, 9.1% and -0.5% over those of the previous year respectively. Of them, Kunming Airport accommodated 191 200 aircraft movements, about 22.273 1 million passengers and 272 500 tons of cargo and mail, representing year-on-year increases of 5.6%, 10.3% and -0.4% respectively.

52 routes were newly opened or resumed at the group's airports. 12 of the new routes connect the cities of Tangshan, Nantong, Baise, Erdos, Yulin, Taizhou, Bali, Danang, Surat Thani, Naypyidaw, Sabah and Kaohsiung. Six new carriers were added, namely Hebei Airlines, China United Airlines, Batavia Air, TonleSap Airlines, Myanmar Airways and Orient Thai Airlines.

II. Overall Safety Performance Kept Stable

In 2011, no airports recorded any air accident, ground accident, air aviation accident or incident, which ensured safe and smooth development of the group. Wujiaba Airport embraced its 60th consecutive year of safe operation.

III. Key Projects Made Steady Progress

In 2011, an investment of 5.074 billion yuan was completed in the construction of Kunming Changshui International Airport, adding the total investment put into the project to 18.788 billion yuan by now, accounting for 98.72% of the approved total investment. The principal part of the project was completed and passed the acceptance inspection late in December. The renovation and expansion project of Lijiang Airport with a total investment of 1.092 billion yuan was completed and passed the acceptance inspection, after which the airport was upgraded from 4C to 4D and approved as a national port of China. The renovation and expansion project of Xishuangbanna Airport completed an investment of 376 million yuan in the year, adding the total investment to 626 million yuan. The test section of the Lugu Lake Airport expansion project was successfully completed, with the subgrade earthworks fully completed for the dedicated highway; airports in Honghe, Cangyuan, Lancang and Nujiang are now involved in the preparatory work of site selection, project initiation, feasibility study, preliminary design, etc.

IV. Transferring Changshui International Airport Stepped Up with Coordination

On August 9, 2011, CAAC officially approved the naming of the new Kunming airport as "Kunming Changshui International Airport". On September 25, relevant municipal and provincial authorities and drill groups for the transferring successfully conducted the first operation simulation exercise at the new Kunming airport, steadily pushing forward the training of transferring and handover of physical assets to ensure construction and the transferring proceeded in parallel. Field security efforts were enhanced, having regard to onsite handover of physical assets and protection of completed works. Late in December, all the 64 items of the principal part of the new Kunming airport project passed the acceptance inspection, marking the successful completion of the principal part of the airport, which was ready for calibration and trial flights and entered the preparatory phase for official operation.

V. Responsibilities Clearly Assigned and Safety System Building Enhanced

Primary efforts were made to enhance quality control of airport operations by fully implementing the "checklist" reporting system, putting in place the "two procedures" for assuring flight services under complicated weather conditions and for providing operation supports for special flights, introducing the safety performance monitoring mechanism and further implementing dynamic risk management. The Safety Development Plan for the 12th Five-Year Plan period was formulated to define the direction of safety development. The pilot program for the building of security management system (SeMS) in national small and medium-sized airports were completed, system manuals, operating procedures and job documents were continuously improved, and the "Model Crews" campaign was carried out to effectively enhance the execution capability of crews. Protection of airport clearance was strengthened, management of the safety services of franchise entities was stepped up and special campaigns were launched to investigate and crack down on major safety hazards and prevent the occurrence of major accidents to continuously fortify the safety and stability of operations.

VI. Industry Development Aggressively Promoted by Adhering to "Two-Wheel Drive" Mechanism

With regard to principal business, the group promoted the setting up of aviation market development leading groups between its municipal and prefectural airports and local governments to preliminarily establish a working mechanism for joint development of aviation markets. By the end of December 2011, the group operated 323 routes, of which 277 were domestic ones and 46 international or regional. A press release mechanism was established for large-scale flight delays, the "Quality Service" crew assessment was introduced and the service quality supervision and inspection mechanism was fully implemented, keeping flight punctuality rate and customer satisfaction both at high levels. In the non-aviation dimension, the group continuously strengthened governance of its subsidiaries, improved the equity management mechanism and facilitated business and fund coordination among the subsidiaries, with synergies preliminarily produced among the operating entities. Tengchong air travel, the new airport logistics, hotel and maintenance resources integration and other investment attraction projects were advanced steadily. Yunnan Civil Aviation Education and Training College has been established and will be put into trial operation.

改扩建完工后的丽江机场新停机坪

The New Apron of Li Jiang Airport After Expansion

昆明机场第一代候机楼　　昆明机场第二代候机楼　　昆明机场第三代候机楼

昆明巫家坝国际机场位于昆明东南部，是中国最重要的国际口岸机场和全国起降最繁忙的国际航空港之一，是中国西南地区门户枢纽机场。

昆明巫家坝国际机场位于昆明东南部，在中国民用机场中巫家坝国际机场是离市中心最近的机场，仅为3公里，有多条公交线路直达市区。2010年民航机场业务量排名位居全国第七。昆明机场是中国历史上的第二个机场。

2010年，昆明机场结合“安全体系建设年”活动，认真总结体系运行经验，进一步修订和完善了体系内容，在继续做好对原有危险源风险管控的基础上，重新辨识和整理危险源782项，组织安全管理体系及危险源辨识培训9期，受训人数400余人，初步建立了以风险管理为核心的安全管理体系。同时，昆明机场还将集团公司相关参控股企业危险源管控纳入其安全体系运行范畴，进行统一指导和推进。

多年来，在昆明机场，涉及安全问题的事情没有大小之分，机场始终坚持做到有章可循、有人负责、专人检查、违章必究，对安全工作实行领导责任、工作任务、人员安排、部门配合、多方协调、责任追究六项落实。

与此同时，为促进机场安全与服务相结合、文化与制度相接轨的发展规划，昆明机场于2005年全面推进企业文化建设，明确将“展示航空旅游第一形象，打造航空强省第一平台”作为建设使命，推出了“天地之间人为本”的企业文化形象以及　　“安全为基、诚信为本、顾客为尊、创新为魂、绩效为先”的工作理念，以机场核心价值观凝聚人心，激励人心，共谋发展。自2005年以来，昆明机场在全国民航系统首家开展“创建诚信机场工程”，通过建设“云南大民航协作”四项联动机制，积极研究、探索并实现了对安全诚信的监管；通过“定期曝光制”、“通报奖惩制”、明察暗访以及“讲评考评制”等措施，考核、监管昆明机场安全诚信情况，完善安全诚信机制，提升了昆明机场的安全诚信度。

打开中国地图，云南省4 000多公里长的国境线清晰可见。作为国家西南地区区域枢纽机场，昆明机场承担着保障国家安全、云南对外开放安全、云南航空枢纽安全的重任，是云南第一门户窗口及“桥头堡”战略最直接、最重要的组成部分。

60年来，昆明机场将安全视为发展的根本、工作的重中之重，始终坚持将安全作为昆明机场科学发展的重要前提和必要条件，通过健全组织管理、完善规章制度、狠抓运行安全、加强资源配置、规范信息管理、提升应急能力、强化人员培训等卓有成效的举措，为保障云南经济社会发展、人民财产与生命的安全、社会和谐

昆明机场第四代候机楼

发展，为建设富裕、民主、文明、开放、和谐的云南作出了巨大贡献。

在“十二五”规划的开局之年，昆明机场即将转场至昆明新机场，并逐步完成从区域枢纽向国家门户枢纽的转变。可以预见，在此过程中，昆明机场的全体员工将面临新的环境、新的安全形势，承担更加繁重的安全任务。将面临新的环境、新的安全形势，承担更加繁重的安全任务。

为此，2011年，昆明机场提出了五项安全任务：一是进一步强化安全目标责任制和监督考核，严格执行“一岗双责”和“无后果责任追究”制度；二是结合安全管理体系（SMS）建设及运行实际，进一步完善风险管理，经常性地排查和监控安全隐患，对安全隐患进行分类管理，明确责任人、整改措施和完成时限；三是继续推进班组建设，在班组内部积极开展意识教育、岗位练兵、技能培训，促进班组间相互交流，推动班组建设向安全任务指标化、安全要求标准化、安全步骤程序化、安全考核数据化及安全管理系统化迈进；四是继续推进安保体系（SeMS）建设，强化空防安全；五是对员工继续开展安全文化教育，通过集中、转岗、特殊岗位、特殊工种的培训，加强从业资质管理，提高员工职业技能和整体素质。

同时，作为云南第一门户及“桥头堡”战略最直接、最重要的组成部分，昆明新机场将在优化中转流程、完善中转功能、建设大型枢纽机场的过程中，充分利用社会资源，构建机场综合交通运输体系；将通过合作方式，为基地航空公司提供更优质的运营环境，协助航空公司开辟、培育连接东南亚及南亚的航线；并继续提升机场服务能力和运营效率等，多方面打造机场品牌。

未来的昆明新机场，将开通至东南亚、南亚及中东中远程国际航线，将航线网络延伸至欧亚、非洲和北美洲，发挥其对南亚地区以及南太平洋、印度洋的区位优势，并在开放第五航权后，推出国际航班国内段中转衔接业务。新机场建设按照近期2020年、中期2030年和远期2040年，年旅客吞吐量分别达到3 800万人次、5 800万人次、6 500万人次，货邮吞吐量达到95万吨、170万吨、230万吨的目标，航空公司特别是基地航空公司的数量也将得到一定的增加。

时光荏苒，岁月如梭。走过波澜壮阔、催人奋进的60年，站在即将转入新机场运行的历史节点上，昆明机场人更加矢志不渝，信心满怀。展望未来，在彩云之南的大板桥上，昆明机场人将用勤劳与智慧，开创昆明新机场航空安全运营的新纪元！

西部机场集团有限公司

2011 年，西部机场集团所辖 13 个机场共计完成运输起降 24.8 万架次、旅客吞吐量 2 787 万人次、货邮吞吐量 21 万吨，同比分别增长 12.7%、16.8% 和 8.3%。实现汇总收入 31.5 亿元、利润 6 亿元，分别较上年增长 50% 和 70%，连续第五年实现整体盈利。

民航局李家祥局长参观“民航强国之路”主题展西部机场集团展位

Li Jiaxiang, Administrator of CAAC, Visits the Booth of China West Airport Group Co, Ltd at the “Road to Civil Aviation Power” Exhibition

一、深化安全管理，连续实现第八个航空安全年

一是建立健全安全监察体系。将生产链条和管理环节中存在的危险源、控制点纳入安全检查体系，运用风险管控工具，有效控制不安全风险。二是深入开展“安全生产年”活动。切实推进危险品运输和航空货邮安保专项整治，加大场区秩序、机坪运行、外来物防范和标志标识治理力度。三是狠抓空防安全。定期分析安全形势，及时提升空防等级，严格内部安全防范，坚持场区 24 小时巡逻，圆满完成春运、两会、世园会等重大保障任务。四是强化航务管理。召开集团首次空管工作会议，理顺工作关系，明确管理职责。与西北空管局合作建立管制员培训基地，创新培训模式，着力提高航务人员的专业技能水平。五是持续加强施工安全管理。严格程序审核，强化过程管控，落实现场监管，严肃责任追究，确保了机场的正常运行。六是加大安全投入。投资 1.36 亿元，增配航空器大型应急救援设备，新建银川机场应急指挥中心和围界报警监控系统，提升榆林机场消防保障等级，完成天水等机场通导及助航灯光设施建设。

二、加强市场营销，主业发展迈上新台阶

2011 年，集团运输生产和服务工作亮点纷呈。一是干线机场主业快速发展。咸阳机场年旅客吞吐量突破 2 100 万人次，稳居全国第八。银川、西宁机场年旅客吞吐量分别突破 300 万和 200 万人次，增幅远高于行业平均水平。二是国际（地区）业务稳步增长。运输起降架次、旅客吞吐量、货邮吞吐量比上一年分别增长 15%、21.8% 和 20%。咸阳机场新增 3 个国际通航点，开通济州等 5 个城市包机航线，西安至首尔、台北航班进一步加密。三是货邮业务实现新突破。在全行业货运业务同比下降的背景下，集团货邮吞吐量实现 8.3% 的增长。咸阳机场货邮吞吐量全国排名升至第十三位，榆林机场货邮吞吐量突破 1 000 吨，天水机场在阶段性停航 5 个月的不利情况下，货邮发运量突破 100 吨。此外，增开西安—南京—广州全货运航线，引入顺丰速运公司在咸阳机场设立快递分拨中心，助推了货邮业务的快速发展。四是机场运营和服务能力持续提升。西安至主要城市航线密度显著增加，地面运输网络逐步延伸，枢纽摆渡功能进一步增强。青海航空公司组建工作扎实推进。汉中、天水机场实现复航。安康机场引入金胜通用航空，设立飞行训练基地。五是政策环境更加有利。促成陕西省国际航线补贴额度从每年 3 000 万元提高至 1.5 亿元；宁夏自治区政府出台《加快宁夏航空运输发展的若干意见》，并与民航局签署《会谈纪要》；青海省人民政府出台《青海省民航运输专项资金管理办法》。六是服

务品质全面提升。以世园会保障为契机，进一步健全服务质量管理体系，扎实开展航班延误专项整治，创新服务产品，加强品牌建设。咸阳机场等单位荣获民航局“西安世园会航空运输服务保障和安全保卫工作先进单位”称号。

三、坚持机场建设理念，咸阳机场二期扩建工程基本完工

2011 年 12 月 28 日，空客 380 在咸阳机场新跑道成功试飞，标志着咸阳机场完全具备了保障全球最大型客机的能力。2012 年 5 月，随着二期扩建工程投运，咸阳机场将开启我国西北地区“双跑道运行时代”，机场综合保障能力将比肩世界大型枢纽机场。西宁机场二期扩建飞行区工程提前两个月完工，新建跑道已经投运。银川机场三期扩建工程进入全面实施阶段。青海德令哈机场开工建设，花土沟机场顺利奠基。

四、推进体制改革，发展活力进一步增强

一是抢抓机遇，主动作为，促成宁夏自治区政府将中卫机场资产整体移交集团管理，实现了产权关系和运营管理的统一。二是进一步壮大企业资本规模。完成咸阳机场公司增资 12 亿元，其中引进外资 5.88 亿元，有效降低了企业融资成本和财务压力。集团置业公司注册资本增至 1 亿元，企业实力和市场竞争力进一步提升。三是优化调整产权结构。回购地勤公司、咸阳机场保洁公司外方股权，转让艺格公司股权，强化对航空主业的服务保障功能。四是完成基地处公司化改制，实行市场化运作，理顺后勤保障机制，解决了西北民航遗留多年的历史问题。五是修订完善辅业管理规定，进一步扩大经营自主权，推动辅业公司健康发展。

五、主动适应市场变化，经济效益持续提高

2011 年，集团上下紧紧围绕年度预算目标，大力开拓市场，强化资金管理，努力增收节支，取得了良好的经营效益。咸阳机场公司实现利润 2.5 亿元，较去年增长 50%；宁夏机场公司实现收入 2.34 亿元，较上年增长 18%；青海机场公司实现收入 1.37 亿元，较上年增长 18%。置业、广告、建设、实业公司均实现收入过亿、利润过千万。物流、配餐公司创新营销模式，加大产品研发，利润也突破千万元。悦泰公司大力拓展外部市场，签订合同金额近亿元。迅邦达贵宾公司积极推进冠名业务，完成收入 6 400 万元；西安地勤公司开发增收项目，实现收入 8 351 万元。集团机场板块实现业务收入 14.15 亿元，较上年增长 35%；辅业板块实现收入 17.35 亿元，较上年增长 95%。

西安咸阳国际机场年旅客吞吐量突破2 000万人次庆祝仪式

A Celebration Is Held Marking 20 Million Passengers Traffic at Xi'an Xianyang International Airport

China West Airport Group Co., Ltd.

In 2011, 13 airports operated by China West Airport Group Co., Ltd. (hereinafter referred to as the group) handled 248 000 aircraft movements, 27.87 million passengers and 210 000 tons of cargo and mail, representing year-on-year increases of 12.7%, 16.8% and 8.3% respectively. The group recorded 3.15 billion yuan in gross income and 600 million yuan in profit, 50% and 70% more than those of the previous year respectively, being the fifth consecutive year of realizing overall profitability.

I. Deepening Safety Management and Achieving the 8th Consecutive Aviation Safety Year

The group carried out the following jobs: a) establishing and improving safety supervision system, including hazard sources and control points in the production and management into the safety examination system, and employing risk control tools to effectively control unsafe risks. b) carrying out in depth the activity of the Year of Work Safety, effectively implementing special rectification of dangerous goods transport and air cargo and mail security, and stepping up the rectification of airfield order, apron operation, foreign object prevention and the marking of airfield signs. c) enhancing earnestly aviation security, regularly analyzing safety situation, upgrading aviation security without delay, taking strict internal safety precautions maintaining around-the-clock airfield patrol, and successfully accomplishing the major safety support tasks during the Spring Festival, NPC & CPPCC and the World Horticultural Exposition 2011 Xi'an China. d) intensifying flight operation management, holding the first air traffic management working conference to clarify the work relationships and make clear management duties, creating the air traffic controller training base in cooperation with CAAC Northwest Regional Administration, innovating training modes and endeavoring to improve flight operation personnel's professional skills. e) continuously strengthening construction safety management, rigorously enforcing procedural review, intensifying process control, effectively implementing on-site supervision, stringently investigating and affixing responsibilities and ensuring the normal operation of airports. f) increasing the safety investment, investing 136 million yuan in purchasing additional large-scale emergency and rescue equipment for aircraft, building Yinchuan Airport's new emergency command center and fencing alarming monitoring system, upgrading the firefighting of Yulin Airport and accomplishing the communication, navigation and lighting facilities for Tianshui and other airports.

II. Strengthening Market Promotion and Making New Achievements in Principal Business

In 2011, the group demonstrated remarkable performances in transport and services. a) the principal business of trunk-line airports growing fast. Xianyang Airport handled more than 21 million passengers in the year, ranking the 8th nationwide. Passengers handled by Yinchuan and Xining airports broke 3 million and 2 million respectively, increment margin much higher than that of the industry average. b) the international (regional) business increasing steadily. Transport movements, passengers and mail and cargo handled increased by 15%, 21.8% and 20% respectively over those of the previous year Xianyang Airport added three international destinations and opened five charter routes including one linking Jeju. Flights connecting Xi'an to Seoul and Taipei were further increased. c) making new breakthroughs in cargo and mail business. Against the backdrop of industry-wide year-on-year drop in air freight, the group posted an 8.3% increase in cargo and mail transport. Xianyang Airport climbed to the 13th place nationwide in cargo and mail throughput, Yulin Airport expanded its cargo and mail throughput, exceeding 1 000 tons and Tianshui Airport handled over 100 tons of cargo and mail despite a five-month's suspension of service. In addition, the Xi'an-Nanjing-Guangzhou all-cargo air route was opened and S.F. Express set a distribution center at Xianyang Airport to fuel rapid growth of the air freight business. d) continuously enhancing the airport operation and service capacity. The density of routes between Xi'an and major cities was significantly increased, the ground transport network was gradually extended and the hub functions were further enhanced. Qinghai Airlines made a solid progress in its setup. Hanzhong and Tianshui airports resumed their flight operations. Ankang Airport hosted Jinsheng General Aviation Co., Ltd., a new airline, and established a flight training base. e) operating with more favorable policy environment. The international flight subsidy of Shaanxi Province was increased from 30 million yuan to 150 million yuan a year. The government of Ningxia Hui Autonomous Region promulgated the Suggestions on Accelerating Air Transport Development of Ningxia Hui Autonomous Region and signed Minutes of Talks with the CAAC. Qinghai provincial government issued the Methods on Special Civil Air Transport Fund Management of Qinghai Province. f) broadly improving the service quality. The group took the opportunity of the World Horticultural Exposition, further improving the service quality management system. It took special steps to rectify flight delays, innovated its products and services, and strengthened the brand building. Xianyang Airport and other entities were commended by CAAC as Excellent Air Transport and Security Service Entity for Xi'an World Horticultural Exposition.

III. Upholding the Concept of Airport Construction and Substantially Accomplished the Phase II Expansion of Xianyang Airport

On December 28, 2011, the successful test flight of Airbus 380 at the new runway of Xianyang Airport demonstrated that the airport was able to accommodate the largest passenger planes in the world. In May 2012, the operation of Phase II expansion project of Xianyang Airport will open the Dual Runway Era in Northwest China, providing an overall airport support capacity comparable to the world's largest hub airports. Xining Airport completed its Phase II expansion project of the movement areas two months ahead of schedule and its new runway was out into operation. The Phase III expansion project of Yinchuan Airport was in full implementation. The construction of Qinghai Delingha Airport was commenced and the ground-breaking ceremony of Huatugou Airport was successfully held.

IV. Precsing Ahead with Institution Reform and Further Strengthening Development Momentum

The group took the following measures: a) seizing the opportunities and taking initiatives in its work. It facilitated Ningxia Government to hand over the assets of Zhongwei Airport under the management of the group and thus harmonized the ownership and management. b) further expanding the capital scale. It injected into Xianyang Airport 1.2 billion yuan of additional capital, including 588 million yuan foreign capital, effectively easing the funding cost and financial pressure. The property company's registered capital increased to 100 million yuan, further boosting its strength and competitiveness. c) optimizing and adjusting equity structure. Foreign equity in the Ground Service Company and Xianyang Airport Cleaning Company was bought back and shares in Yige Company were assigned, with the aim of strengthening service supports for the principal aviation business. d) completing the company-based restructuring of base operations. It conducted market-based operation and streamlined the logistics supports mechanism, solving the long-standing problems in the northwest civil aviation sector.e) amending and improving the auxiliary business rules. It further expanded the managerial discretion and promoted healthy development of the auxiliary business segments.

V. Taking the Initiative to Adapt to Market Changes and Continuously Improving Economic Profit

In 2011, the group, closely adhering to the annual budget objectives, made great efforts to tap into markets, enhanced its fund management, and expanded its revenues and reduced its costs, thus making a preferable economic profit. Xianyang Airport produced a profit of 250 million yuan, Ningxia Airport earned 234 million yuan and Qinghai Airport realized 137 million yuan in income, increasing by 50%, 18% and 18% respectively over those of the previous year. Property, advertising, construction and industrial companies all recorded an income of over 100 million yuan and a profit of more than 10 million yuan. Logistics and catering firms, by innovating marketing modes and stepping up product research and development, also broke 10 million yuan of profit. Xi'an Yuetai Science & Technology Co., Ltd. made great efforts to tap into external markets and signed nearly 100 million worth of contracts. Simple Business Club promoted the title sponsorship business and generated 64 million yuan in income. Xi'an Ground Services diversified income avenues, earning 83.51 million yuan. The Group registered 1.415 billion yuan in income from the airport segment and 1.735 billion yuan in income from auxiliary business segments, increasing by 35% and 95% respectively over those of the previous year.

新疆机场（集团）有限责任公司

2011年8月16日，民航局副局长李健（左三）视察乌鲁木齐国际机场

On August 16, 2011, Li Jian (3rd from the left), Deputy Administrator of CAAC , Inspects Urumqi International Airport

2011 年，新疆机场（集团）有限责任公司全年旅客吞吐量、货邮吞吐量和航班运输起降架次三大经营指标均呈现出高速增长态势。截至 2011 年 11 月，乌鲁木齐国际机场年旅客吞吐量首次突破 1 000 万人次，使乌鲁木齐国际机场成功跨入国内第 17 个“千万级”大型机场行列；在主要生产指标保持高速增长的同时，在安全生产、基础建设、航线开辟、提高服务质量和经济效益等方面同样取得了显著成绩。

一、运输生产快速增长，保持了持续强劲的发展势头

2011 年完成旅客吞吐量 1 422 万人次、货邮吞吐量 11.6 万吨、飞机起降 14.9 万架次，分别完成年计划的 103%、101% 和 110%，同比分别增长 21%、14% 和 21%。其中乌鲁木齐国际机场完成旅客吞吐量 1 108 万人次、货邮吞吐量 10.8 万吨、飞机起降 9.8 万架次，同比分别增长 21%、13% 和 13%；疆内其他 15 个支线机场共完成旅客吞吐量 315 万人次，同比增长 23%。

二、空防安全形势平稳，安全生产管理水平显著提升

全年杜绝各类空防安全事故及事故征候；安全检查旅客 711 万人次、行李 2 071 万件、货邮 302 万件。同时，以开展深化“安全生产年”、“百日安全专项整治”活动为主线，及时制定、修订 12 部规章；组织编写支线机场航站区、飞行区岗位工作规范及操作规程，在伊宁、库尔勒机场先试先行。重点完善支线机场空管安全管理体系。重建航行情报系统，恢复 3 个支线机场气象台站，完成伊宁机场 RNP 验证飞行。投入资金 7 797 万元开展飞行区标识标线符合性整改、FOD 防范、鸟击防范、危险品运输等 11 项综合整治。先后 3 次开展综合安全自查，多次接受局方安全督察，通过持续整改，消除了安全隐患。扎实开展安全生产月活动，成功举办机场运行安全业务研讨会，促使各机场安全管理提高到新水平。全年杜绝了飞行事故、重大航空地面事故、航空器维修事故和航空器事故征候；未发生由于机场责任原因鸟击航空器的不安全事件。新疆机场集团以优异成绩通过新疆维吾尔自治区、民航新疆管理局年度安全生产目标管理考核，圆满完成了首届亚博会的保障任务。实现第 8 个运行安全年目标。

三、大力促进航空主业发展，继续拓展航空市场空间

主动开展市场营销，继续以对口援疆航线为重点引进运力，向航空公司重点推介伊宁、阿克苏、库车、克拉玛依等支线机场；借助国际航展平台，大力推介国际航线。积极引导和支持航空公司打造乌鲁木齐中转枢纽，打造疆内快捷航线，深入实施干线延伸支线、激活支线促进枢纽战略。南航、海航、天津航均不同程度加密了疆内航线；有 11 个支线机场每日

达到 2 个航班以上，其中 8 个支线机场实现 2 家航空公司运营；2011 年乌鲁木齐机场始发运力、国际旅客、中转旅客同比分别增长 14%、24%、11%；支线机场全年平均起降架次、货邮吞吐量增幅分别高出乌鲁木齐 29 和 25 个百分点。支线航空与乌鲁木齐门户枢纽初步实现良性互动发展。2011 年新引进 3 家航空公司运营乌鲁木齐机场，1 家航空公司延伸运营疆内支线。截至 2011 年底，运营新疆定期航班的航空公司达到 29 家，其中运营疆内航线的航空公司达到 9 家；共开通航线 141 条，同比新增 22 条，其中新辟国际航线、援疆航线各 3 条；已有 21 个国家、31 个国际（地区）城市、52 个国内城市与乌鲁木齐机场通航。乌鲁木齐枢纽航线网络不断完善，支线机场航班量快速增长。

四、稳步推进“十二五”建设规划，全力打造西部门户枢纽

截至 2011 年底，乌鲁木齐门户枢纽机场总体规划修编、第二跑道和北航站区改扩建工程预可研已完成；富蕴、且末机场迁建工程正在审批立项；塔中、莎车、楼兰机场新建工程，库尔勒、和田、哈密机场改扩建工程均已进入预可研审批程序；喀什区域枢纽、伊宁国际口岸改扩建工程已启动前期工作。同时，为满足安全保障及生产发展新形势需要，全年分三批下达固定资产投资计划 6 862 万元、大修理投资计划 1 998 万元；下达克拉玛依机场等四个专项投资计划 3 682 万元。喀纳斯机场航站楼扩建、乌鲁木齐等六机场安防设施、塔城等四机场仪表着陆及助航灯光系统等一批项目先后实施。

五、服务质量进一步提高，经营业绩显著

2011 年，乌鲁木齐机场国内航班放行正常率达到 81%，旅客满意度达到 87%，比上年提高 5%，有效投诉明显减少。新疆机场集团在保障航空运输业快速增长的同时，积极发展扩大延伸服务领域。从酒店、航站楼商业、贵宾服务、货运业务、广告、房地产等方面入手，积极拓展非航业务，取得明显成效。全年完成收入 100 412 万元，营业成本 103 197 万元，同比分别增长 21%、20.8%；非航收入占总收入比例的 51%；乌鲁木齐国际机场实现盈利。

2011年8月10日，“迎亚欧博览盛会 展空港文明风采”主题实践活动启动仪式隆重举行

On August 10, 2011, the Opening Ceremony for the Activity of “Embracing China-Eurasia Expo and Displaying Services of Airport” Is Held

Xinjiang Airport Group Co., Ltd.

For the whole year of 2011, three key operating indicators showed a rapid growth in the passenger, cargo and mail, and aircraft movement handled at Xinjiang Airport Group Co., Ltd. By the end of November 2011, Urumqi International Airport had, for the first time, handled more than 10 million passengers, successfully becoming the 17th airport in the country handling more than ten million passengers. In addition to the rapid growth of major work indicators, remarkable achievements were made in the fields of work safety, infrastructure construction, routes opening up, service quality improvement and economic benefits.

I. Transportation Grew Rapidly and Sustained Development Maintained Strongly

In 2011, 14.22 million passengers, 116 000 tons of cargo and mail, and 149 000 aircraft movements were handled, with 103%, 101% and 110% of the annual plans being completed, representing year-on-year increases of 21%, 14% and 21% respectively. Urumqi International Airport handled 11.08 million passengers, 108 000 tons of cargo and mail and 98 000 aircraft movements, representing year on year increases of 21%, 13% and 13% respectively. The other 15 feeder airports in Xinjiang handled a total of 3.15 million passengers, a year-on-year increase of 23%.

2011年11月22日，乌鲁木齐国际机场旅客吞吐量突破1 000万人次庆典仪式

On November 22, 2011, a Celebration Is Held for 10 Million Passengers Traffic at Urumqi International Airport

II. Aviation Security Situation Stable and Safety Management Improved Significantly

For the whole year, all types of aviation security accidents and incidents were eliminated; security check for 7.11 million passengers/times, 20.71 million baggage and 3.02 million cargo and mail was carried out. At the same time, activities of the Year of Work Safety, 100-Day Special Rectifications of Safety were carried out in an in-depth manner, and 12 regulations were developed and revised in a timely way. Working specifications and operating procedures were formulated for feeder airports' terminal and movement areas, which were experimented first at Yining and Korla Airports. While focusing on improving the safety management system for ATM systems at feeder airports, the group reconstructed the aeronautical information system, restored the meteorological stations at three feeder airports and completed RNP validation flight at Yining Airport. With 77.97 million yuan invested for the 11 comprehensive rectifications including rectifying non-compliance of signs and markings at airport movement areas, prevention of FOD, prevention of bird strike and transport of dangerous goods, the group eliminated hazards in safety through continuous rectifications, for instance, three times of comprehensive safety self-inspections and many times of safety inspections by CAAC. The activities of the Month of Work Safety were carried out solidly and safety seminars for airport operations were held successfully, impelling the safety management at all the airports to reach to a new level. For the whole year, there were no flight accidents, major aircraft ground accidents, aircraft maintenance accidents or aircraft incidents, and no bird strike events that ever happened due to airports, Xinjiang Airport

Group passed with honors the assessment for the annual work safety objective management by Xinjiang Uygur Autonomous Region Government and CAAC Xinjiang Administration, successfully completed the support task of the first China-Eurasia Expo, and realized the goal of the 8th year of operation safety.

III. Development of Principal Business in Air Transport Promoted Vigorously and Air Transport Market Expanded Continuously

Taking initiative in marketing, the group, with the routes launched by other provinces to support Xinjiang as priority, continued to introduce transport capacity and strongly recommended to the airlines the feeder airports of Yining, Aksu, Kuche, Karamay and others. With the help of the international air shows, the group made its efforts in promoting the international routes. Airlines were actively guided and supported to build Urumqi Airport into a transit hub, to create express routes within Xinjiang, to extend the trunk routes into feeder routes, and to activate feeder routes for promoting the hub by the group. With China Southern Airlines, Hainan Airlines and Tianjin Airlines all, to various extents, adding flight frequency on the routes within Xinjiang, there were 11 feeder airports having more than two flights a day, and 8 of them had two operating airlines. In 2011, the departure capacity, international passengers and transit passengers at Urumqi Airport had year-on-year increases of 14%, 24%, 11% respectively, and the annual average aircraft movements, and cargo and mail handled at feeder airports increased by margins which were 29 and 25 percentage points higher than Urumqi Airport respectively, indicating a good start of a virtuous circle of interactive development of feeder airports with the hub of Urumqi. In 2011, 3 new airlines were introduced to operate at Urumqi Airport with one extending its operation to the feeder routes within Xinjiang. By the end of 2011, there had been as many as 29 airlines operating scheduled flights to Xinjiang, 9 of them operating the routes within Xinjiang. 141 routes were opened, a year-on-year increase of 22, in which 3 were new international routes and 3 were the ones launched by other provinces to support Xinjiang. There had already been 21 countries, 31 international (regional) cities and 52 domestic cities having air transport service with Urumqi Airport. The Urumqi hub network was improved continuously, and flights at feeder airports were increasing rapidly.

IV. The 12th Five-Year Plan Pushed Forward Steadily and a Gateway Hub in the West Built through Efforts

By the end of 2011, the group had completed the revision of the master plan of Urumqi gateway hub airport and the pre-feasibility study on the renovation and expansion projects of the second runway and the north terminal area. The relocation projects of Fuyun and Qiemo airports were in the process of approval. The construction projects of Tazheng, Shache and Loulan new airports, and the renovation and expansion projects of Korlar, Hetian and Hami airports had entered into pre-feasibility study and project approval process. The preliminary work for renovation and expansion projects of Kashi regional hub and Yining international port had started. At the same time, in order to meet the needs of the new situation of safety support and development, 68.62 million yuan investment in fixed assets and 19.98 million yuan for overhaul had been made in three batches over the year, and 36.82 million yuan of four special investments had been issued to Karamay Airport. A number of projects such as the expansion of Kanas Airport terminal, security facilities at six airports including Urumqi Airport, and the instrument landing and lighting systems for four airports including Tacheng Airport had been carried out one after another.

V. Service Quality Further Improved and Remarkable Operating Achievements Made

In 2011, the regularity rate of domestic flights departed from Urumqi Airport reached 81%, the passenger satisfaction rate reached 87%, increasing by 5% over that of the previous year, and the valid complaints decreased noticeably. At the same time, in order to assure the rapid growth of air transport industry, Xinjiang Airport Group actively developed and expanded the services. The non-aviation business such as hotels, in-terminal concessions, VIP lounges, freight forwarding, advertising, real estate and others were actively promoted with significant results. A total revenue of 1.004 12 billion yuan was achieved for the whole year, and the operating cost was 1.031 97 billion yuan representing year-on-year increases of 21% and 20.8% respectively. The Non-aviation revenue was 51% of the total revenue, and Urumqi International Airport became profitable.

新疆机场（集团）有限责任公司于2004年4月16日挂牌成立。乌鲁木齐国际机场等10个机场正式移交自治区人民政府管理，标志着新疆民航机场实现属地化管理，新疆民航政企彻底分开。随着新疆民航事业步入崭新发展阶段，新疆机场集团迎来了新疆航空史上又一浓墨重彩的华丽篇章。目前，新疆机场集团管辖有乌鲁木齐、喀什、伊宁、库尔勒、阿勒泰、阿克苏、和田、塔城、库车、且末、克拉玛依、那拉提、喀纳斯、哈密、吐鲁番、博乐等16个在用运输机场，新疆为全国民用机场数量最多的省区。

作为新疆对外开放的“窗口”和“空中桥梁”，新疆机场集团八年来始终坚持为航空公司、旅客、货主提供卓越航空服务，助推新疆经济社会跨越式发展。得到了自治区、民航局和社会各界的表彰和赞誉。先后荣获全国文明单位称号、全国模范劳动关系和谐企业和全国劳动争议预防调解示范性企业称号、全国工会系统“五五”普法先进单位称号，5次获得全国“安康杯”竞赛活动优胜企业称号，连续八年保持乌鲁木齐市综合治理先进单位称号。为自治区对外开放、经济建设、国防建设和长治久安做出了积极贡献。

安全立本　服务强基

在构建新一代航空运输体系的征程中，新疆机场集团始终把安全视为机场生存与发展的基础，“安全第一，预防为主，综合治理”的安全方针在新疆各机场落地生根。乌鲁木齐国际机场自开航至今，已连续安全运行8周年；圆满完成北京奥运、首届亚博会等重大安保任务，多次受到自治区、民航局表彰奖励，机场安全形势总体持续稳固。

八年来，新疆机场集团始终坚持把安全保障工作放在首位。成立了机场集团安委会，完善了安全管理监督体系，建立健全了机场集团安全管理体系。同时各项安全保障工作逐步迈向规范化、制度化、系统化，安全管理水平逐年提高。八年间先后投入近二十亿元资金用于建设、改造、更新、购置各类安全生产保障设施设备。先后为各支线机场配备专职安全主管及安全员，保障安全生产的力量不断增强。同时坚持深入开展各类安全生产隐患排查整治和安全自查，有效消除和整改安全生产隐患700余项。积极推进安全文化建设，传播安全管理理念，增强人员安全意识；严格规范、严密细致、求真务实、精益求精的安全工作作风得到传承和发扬。在长期的工作实践中，形成了具有新疆机场鲜明特色的安全管理模式，连续实现八个运行安全年目标。2009—2011年，新疆机场集团连续三年获得自治区安全生产先进单位称号。

在空防安全方面，通过八年实践检验，新疆机场集团不仅在公安、安检、消防护卫、执勤、急救、防控、反恐等方面打造了一支过硬的安保队伍，而且专机、要客、朝觐等各项重大保障工作更加有力；机场集团空防安全保障体系更加稳固。由于地处边疆多民族聚集区，多年来，新疆各机场在国庆、节假日、重大事件、特殊运兵包机、急救、防控、反恐等方面，能够从容不迫，迅速及时启动应急处置预案，紧急动员机场一切资源投入安全保障中，为新疆的跨越式发展和长治久安做出了积极贡献。

在秉承“旅客至尊、客户至上”的服务理念下，新疆机场集团把服务工作当成是民生最主要的核心内容、把服务放到前所未有的高度来看待。新疆机场集团先后对12个机场进行了新建、迁建和改扩建，极大地改善了旅客候机环境；着力解决乌鲁木齐机场天气原因造成航班大面积延误的服务难题；加快完善乌鲁木齐机场中转服务功能，基本实现了国内、国际航班自由中转。同时开展服务品牌创建以及各类示范岗创建活动，以点带面提升服务水平。截至2011年底，各航空公司对乌鲁木齐国际机场设施完好率和各项服务满意度达到良好；乌鲁木齐国际机场航班放行正常率达到81.3%；机场地面服务顾客满意度达83.2%。

安全与服务两手抓，两手都硬，使得新疆机场集团各机场的运行保障能力得到极大提升。南航股份新疆分公司、海航股份新疆分公司相继落户乌鲁木齐国际机场，运营新疆定期航班的国内外航空公司达到29家，共开通航线141条；已有21个国家、31个国际城市、52个国内城市与乌鲁木齐国际机场通航。新疆民用机场“疆内成网、东西成扇、东联西出”的航线网络布局更趋完善和通达，有力促进了自治区以及各地州经济社会的发展和繁荣。

“两轮驱动”　科学发展

新疆机场集团成立之初，新疆航空市场初步开放，各机场运输生产总量小，增长慢；乌鲁木齐航空市场竞争不充分，疆内支线处于独家经营状态，适航机型及航班量十分有限；同时各机场基本形成单一依靠航空主业收入维持运行的局面。

为从根本上解决制约新疆机场发展的支线与干线、国内与国际、客运与货运、航空业与非航空业发展不协调的矛盾，新疆机场集团在正确判断形势和任务基础上，审时度势、科学谋划，适时提出了“把市场开发作为发动机，把做活做大做强市场作为实现新疆机场科学发展的重大举措”和“依托航空主业，充分利用现有优势资源，大力发展非航空业和与航空运输相关联的客、货延伸服务业务”的发展战略。

为加快新疆航空市场发展，新疆机场集团一方面充分挖掘各机场的时刻及航线资源，增加新疆航空市场总量；另一方面积极实施机场的改扩建和增容改造，尽可能满足航空运输市场需求；同时，通过价格机制调节航空市场资源，引导和鼓励各航空公司新开航线，扶持疆内落户航空公司发展，建立战略合作关系，共同构建疆内、国内和国际三个航线网络。努力实现了国内与国际、区外与区内两个市场、两个扇面协调持续快速发展。截至2011年，运营新疆定期航班的航空公司达到29家，运营疆内航线的航空公司达到9家。

19省市对口援疆是中央促进新疆跨越式发展的重要举措。为充分发挥航空运输安全、快捷、高效优势，同时抓住历史机遇进一步扩大新疆航空市场，中央新疆工作座谈会召开以后，新疆机场集团迅速与航空公司和机场所在地政府对接，全力支持协助19省市开通直达对口援疆航线。截至目前，已开通了12个省市对口援疆直达航线。

新疆机场集团运输生产已呈现跨越式发展态势，2004—2011年，新疆机场集团旅客吞吐量从516.4万人次增长到1 422.9万人次，是2004年成立前的4.2倍。其中乌鲁木齐国际机场旅客吞吐量从389.1万人次增长到1 107.9万人次，跻身全国第17个千万级大型机场行列。

经过八年探索，新疆机场集团逐步形成了依托航空主业，充分利用现有优势资源，大力发展非航空业和与航空运输相关联的客、货延伸服务业务的发展战略：重点发展酒店、广告、房地产等三大产业；同时积极开拓航空货运、贵宾服务、候机楼商业等业务。

伴随航空运输业的快速发展，2011年全集团收入首次突破10亿元；其中非航空业务收入连续三年超过航空主业收入，达到51%。2011年乌鲁木齐国际机场实现盈利，15个支线机场亏损额同比减少3 000多万元。初步形成机场主业和非航产业“两轮驱动”。

软硬兼施　增强后劲

新疆机场集团成立之初，由于体制等多种因素制约，新疆民用机场尤其支线机场基础设施陈旧简陋，设备落后，航站楼面积较小，安全等级较低，曾被外界形容为“像个县级火车站”。为从根本上改变这一局面，新疆机场集团坚持以建设促进发展，以发展带动建设，努力推动新疆民用机场跨越式发展。

为适应自治区旅游业发展需要，新疆机场集团分别于2004、2005年开工建设两个旅游支线机场——那拉提和喀纳斯机场，同时对阿勒泰机场实施改扩建。2005年10月，国家民航局与自治区人民政府共同签署《关于加快新疆民航发展的会谈纪要》。《会谈纪要》确立了乌鲁木齐机场为国家西部门户枢纽机场的定位；描绘了“十一五”新疆机场建设和发展的蓝图；明确给予新疆机场建设和发展优惠扶持政策。由此，新疆机场展开了有史以来最大规模的建设步伐，迎来了波澜壮阔的建设高峰。

乌鲁木齐国际机场三期改扩建工程是新疆机场“十一五”规划建设的标志性工程，也是打造乌鲁木齐西部门户枢纽机场的关键工程。工程总投资概算24.93亿元。新建航站楼11.5万平方米，货运站3.8万平方米，站坪和货机坪43.8万平方米。新建成的T3航站楼，突出国际、国内旅客中转服务及行李流程，不仅使旅客出行更加方便、快捷，其服务档次也实现了质的飞跃；重新布局客机带货服务和全货机货站服务，严格按照国际货物监管要求进行建设，使航空公司、旅客和货主倍感便捷。乌鲁木齐国际机场三期改扩建的竣工投产，使乌鲁木齐国际机场航站楼总面积达到18万平方米，客货站坪达到83个，近机位登机桥33座。保障能力可达年旅客吞吐量1 635万人次、货邮吞吐量27.5万吨、起降架次15.5万架次。同时，适应乌鲁木齐门户枢纽机场需要的吐鲁番、库尔勒、克拉玛依等备降场相继建成或改造完成。经新疆机场集团多方协调，《乌鲁木齐国际机场总体规划》（2011版）获中国民航局和自治区政府联合批复，“十二五”期间将完成北航站区和第二跑道建设，具备全球最大机型A380飞机的保障能力，为乌鲁木齐国际机场打造成我国西部门户枢纽机场进一步奠定了坚实基础。

以全面提高支线机场保障等级为目标，新疆机场集团“十一五”期间先后完成阿勒泰、喀什、伊宁、阿克苏机场改扩建，那拉提、喀纳斯、博乐机场新建，库尔勒、库车、吐鲁番机场迁建；哈密机场复航改扩建等重要工程。通过新一轮建设，新疆各支线机场的保障服务能力大幅提升，而且新增了5个支线机场，使疆内在用机场数量发展到16个。新疆机场的总体布局更加合理，设施设备全面更新，服务功能更加完善，配套设施更加齐全，机场基础设施落后于生产快速发展的矛盾明显缓解，适应自治区政治经济社会发展新形势需要的保障服务能力显著增强。

“先进的企业文化能够铸造优秀的企业和优秀的员工，是企业不断创新的源泉，制胜的法宝。新疆机场经过几代人的不懈努力，在艰苦创业过程中积累了许多宝贵的精神文化财富。能吃苦、肯奉献、敢打硬仗，聚人心、勇进取、争创一流的企业精神，使新疆机场不断发展壮大。新的时期、新的使命又赋予新疆机场人创业的新内涵，秉承和升华老传统，总结和提炼新观念，将成为新疆机场事业又好又快发展的核心动力”，新疆机场集团董事长、党委书记顾中秦表示。新疆机场集团将文化管理紧密地贯穿于安全、服务等各项工作的全过程，充分调动广大员工的主观能动性，激励他们立足本职岗位，为全集团的发展贡献自己的力量，以此为企业中心工作提供精神动力和智力支持。形成了富有新疆机场特色的安全文化和服务文化。

湖北机场集团公司

Hubei Airports Group Company

湖北机场集团公司成立于2004年3月，系首都机场集团公司全资子公司，总资产51.4亿元，员工队伍近3 000人。下辖武汉天河国际机场、恩施许家坪机场、襄阳刘集机场和宜昌航务管理站。

2011年以来，湖北机场集团公司坚持持续安全理念，落实“客货并举”工作思路，大力推进基础建设，努力实施各项改革，稳步提升服务水平，实现了突飞猛进的大发展、大突破。

战略引领，文化导航

湖北省出台了《关于加快湖北民航事业发展的指导意见》，同时民航局与湖北省在京签署了《关于加快湖北民航事业发展的会谈纪要》，共同致力于将武汉机场打造成为全国重要的枢纽机场。

从“区域性枢纽机场”到“全国重要的枢纽机场”，再到“国家重要门户机场”，得益于地方经济的飞速发展，武汉天河机场历经十七年建设发展，成功实现了发展目标的“三级跳”。

2011年，是国家实施“十二五”规划的开局之年，也是湖北机场集团公司战略持续推进、改革发展不断深化，实现跨越式品质化发展的关键之年。湖北机场集团公司紧紧围绕2010年制定的“五场硬仗”战略目标，狠抓战略落地，稳扎稳打，逐步深入，层层细化。164个行动计划应完成125个，实际完成144个，超额完成了年度目标。同时积极推动有利机场发展的法制环境建设，继《湖北省民用机场净空安全保护条例》颁布实施之后，已启动《湖北省民用运输机场管理条例》立法

程序，并顺利列入湖北省人大2012年立法计划项目名录。

2011年3月，湖北机场集团公司完成新一轮企业文化创新工作，形成了以“亚洲机场业的翘楚”为企业愿景，“中厚灵秀”为经营管理理念的具有湖北民航特色的企业文化理念体系，以文化引领企业发展。

创新营销模式，助推市场升温

2011年，在市场竞争加剧的情况下，面对运力短缺、基地公司削减运力及“高铁”、“高速公路”冲击的现实困难，积极创新营销方式。一方面争取民航中南局时刻虚占的清理，提高航班实际执行率，打通制约发展的时刻瓶颈；另一方面多方营销航空公司，扩运力、调网络、增航点，构建“米”字型航线结构，减少与“高铁”的正面竞争，成果丰硕。武汉机场航空主业从2011年4月份开始摆脱多重不利因素的阴影，迎来拐点，并一路上扬，成功实现了航空主业的“V型”反转，圆满完成了全年任务。

2011年，湖北机场集团公司全年共完成旅客吞吐量1 283.66万人次，货邮吞吐量12.46万吨，保障航班11.98万架次，同比分别增长6.1%、11.7%和2.4%。其中，武汉天河国际机场完成旅客吞吐1 246.2万人次，货邮吞吐量12.28万吨，航班起降11.54万架次；武汉天河机场全年新增、恢复国内外航点11个，加密12个航点航班。2011年，武汉—东京航线顺利首航，汉台航班增至每周18

班，全年国际及地区客流量首次突破40万人次。

2011年，武汉天河机场ACI旅客满意度测评值为4.45，进入全球同量级机场前十名，率先跨入世界百强；全年安全工作持续平稳，实现了第十七个安全年；

2011年，湖北机场集团公司大力落实“客货并举”思路，推动货运发展，友和道通全货运航空顺利开航，顺丰、东海航空在汉开通货运航线，货运增长全国领先。

建设紧锣密鼓，各有重大进展

2011年，湖北机场集团公司积极打造中部枢纽。按照“搭平台、顺流程、建体系”的思路，枢纽建设稳步推进。制定枢纽建设方案，与东航签订枢纽建设合作协议；明确计划，细化任务，各项重点建设工程紧锣密鼓，加速推进。T3综合交通体完成设计，明确了建设主体；A380改造工程顺利竣工；全力推进国际航站楼扩建工程并于2012年4月竣工；恩施机场二期扩建顺利进行；襄阳机场总规和扩建工程已获襄阳市政府批复；在建的神农架机场建设工程，克服重重困难，在海拔2 580米的神农架群山之巅，一座高原山顶机场的轮廓壮观呈现。

武汉天河机场三期扩建工程，以满足2020年旅客吞吐量3 500万人次、货邮吞吐量44万吨、年保障飞机起降31.26万架次为目标，将新建长3 600米、等级为4F的第二条跑道及平行滑行道、联络道和站坪，同时建设面积为37万平方米的T3航站楼，60个机位的停机坪，配套建设进场路、商业交通中心、货运区和其它公用设施等。

与此同时，武汉机场长途客运站已于2011年建成运行，异地城市候机楼在省内已设立6家，机场腹地延伸到了黄石、宜昌、荆州、孝感、随州、鄂州六地，湖北省内航空枢纽架构初步形成。

襄阳机场

宜昌航管站

恩施机场

严格经营管理，突出“两压两保”

2011年，面对市场竞争加剧、建设及人工等成本增加等现实困难，湖北机场集团公司审时度势，及时提出了“两压两保”经营工作方针。即压缩可控成本、压缩非紧急非增效投资,保证业务收入持续增长,保证员工待遇有所提高。

2011年，湖北机场集团公司严格内部管控，完善管理制度，继续深化绩效管理，编制《组织绩效管理手册》和《员工绩效考核办法》，认真组织半年和年度的组织绩效考核，员工绩效意识、成本意识普遍提高；深化全面预算管理，采取“以收定支”和“利润导向”，运用绩效监督机制压降成本，取得实效；节能减排指标也已纳入绩效考核，以技改促节能，申请节能补贴，天河机场全年保障性用电下降5%，超额完成年初预定目标。同时，湖北机场集团公司提出了支线机场管理的新导向，即现金流平衡与绩效考核挂钩，支线机场的现金流平衡与绩效考核挂钩，增强了压降投资的自觉性，开始积极向地方政府争取优惠和补贴。

在“两压两保”工作思路的积极带动下，湖北机场集团公司在2011年经营和成本控制十分困难的情况下，仍然下大力气解决了诸多关系员工切身利益的问题，解决了机场高速路收费难题，积极推进完善薪酬制度，构建和谐共赢企业。

German Technology-Asian Service

Ameco Beijing is a joint venture between Air China and Lufthansa German Airlines founded in1989.In the past 22 years,we combined German technical know-how and systematic thinking with superior Asian services.

As a mature comprehensive MRO provider,Ameco Beijing provides a wide variety of maintenance services to more than 100 domestic and international customers. Based on the accumulated rich experience,we are confident that Ameco Beijing is a reliable partner for airlines.

Word-Class Facilities

Ameco Beijing's hangar space is about 136 000 square meters,including a 35 000 square meters four-bay hangar and a 54 000 square meters "two-A380-sized" hanger close to Terminal 3. In addition,we have well-equipped engine and component workshops.

Talk To Us About All Your Maintenance Needs

Our range of services includes:

- ☐ B737,B747,B767,B777 and A340 maintenance and overhaul
- ☐ B747 section 41 and strut modification
- ☐ B767 strut modification
- ☐ Major structure repairs
- ☐ Aging aircraft corrosion prevention and control program
- ☐ Aircraft exterior painting
- ☐ Cabin refurbishment
- ☐ VIP cabin modification
- ☐ Winglet modification
- ☐ Engine repair and overhaul
- ☐ Component repair and overhaul
- ☐ Landing gear overhaul
- ☐ Line maintenance in Beijing,Shanghai, Guangzhou and Tianjin
- ☐ Training(EASA 147 certification)

STARCO 上海科技宇航有限公司

Shanghai Technologies Aerospace Company Limited

上海科技宇航有限公司（STARCO）是中国东方航空股份有限公司和世界上最大飞机机身维修公司——新加坡科技宇航有限公司共同投资成立的中外合资企业。作为新科宇航全球网络的一部分，为多种波音和空客飞机提供机身维修和改装服务，机型包括A300、A310、A320系列、A330、A340、B737、B747、MD80、MD90、MD11。

“我们保持飞机飞行安全”，是STARCO永恒的追求。在建立符合国际维修飞机行业质量管理体系（AS9100）的同时、STARCO已经获取国内外多项飞机维修许可证，包括了中国民用航空局（CAAC）、美国联邦航空局（FAA）、欧洲民用航空安全局（EASA）、日本民航局（JCAB）、澳大利亚民用航空安全局（CASA）及港澳地区颁发的维修许可证。并且顺利地通过了飞机生产商——法国空中客车公司的质量审核和资格认定，成为空客公司全球指定空客飞机系列的维修厂家之一。

STARCO秉承持续改善的维修理念，得到全球客户的高度赞赏。目前，STARCO已承接了中国东方航空、中国货运航空、上海货运航空、春秋航空、吉祥航空、深圳航空、海南航空、四川航空、成都航空及国外的日本ANA、俄罗斯Air Bridge货航、俄罗斯URAL航空、西伯利亚S7航空、印度AIR INDIA、越南SpiceJet、越南Jet Airway、澳门Air Macao 等26家中外客户的各类飞机高级别检修、改装工作，并顺利完成多家航空公司的飞机退租检工作,与相关的退租公司建立了良好的合作关系。

2010年3月1日，STARCO浦东国际机场新机库正式启用。作为国内唯一在上海浦东和虹桥国际机场同时拥有大型飞机大修机库的第三方维修机构，STARCO将继续努力为中外航空公司的飞机大修、部附件维修和航线AOG支援提供更完善的航空运输维修保障服务。

成都飞亚航空设备应用研究所有限公司

成都飞亚航空设备应用研究所有限公司成立于1994年，原址在青羊区黄田坝，毗邻成飞集团。2008年底，公司整体搬迁到温江海峡两岸科技产业开发园，现址占地63亩，总建筑面积约40000平方米。1995年取得中国民用航空局颁发的维修许可证，是西南地区创建最早的民营航空维修企业之一。公司主要从事航空机载产品维修与研制、航空地面设备设计与制造。

公司2006年被四川省经济委员会和四川省中小企业发展中心授予"诚信企业"称号，并被成都市总工会评为"成都市合格职工之家"；2007年被成都市总工会评为"成都市先进职工之家"，同年被评为"成都市劳动关系和谐企业"；2008年取得二级保密单位资格证书；2009年1月取得新时代质量管理体系认证证书，8月取得装备承制单位注册证书，12月取得四川省高新技术企业证书；2010年1月取得武器装备质量体系认证证书。

在质量管理体系上，按照中国民用航空规章《CCAR-145R3》、《CCAR-66R1》的要求，编制了《维修管理手册》及《工作程序手册》；按国家军用标准《GJB9001B-2009》的要求，编制了《质量手册》和《程序文件》。在维修生产过程中，严格执行相关规章及标准要求的程序，确保修理、开发、制造和服务全过程的质量得到控制和保证。

公司本着"质量是生命，适航是根本"的经营理念，秉承"团结、诚信、务实、超越"的企业价值观，贯彻既定的质量方针，弘扬团队精神，不断发展，持续改进，确保"安全、可靠、快捷"，更好地服务客户，服务社会。

地址：四川省成都市温江区海峡两岸科技产业开发园锦绣大道北段480号　邮编：611130

电话：028-67204783　67204781　网址：www.cdfeiya.com　E-mail：info@cdfeiya.com

CAH
中國服務

热烈庆祝
首都机场集团
成立
10
周年
首都机场集团公司
Capital Airports Holding Company

图书在版编目（CIP）数据

中国民航年刊．2011：汉英对照 / 中国民用航空局编．—北京：中国民航出版社，2012.8

ISBN 978-7-5128-0082-3

Ⅰ．①中… Ⅱ．①中… Ⅲ．①民用航空-中国-2011-年刊-汉、英 Ⅳ．①F562-54

中国版本图书馆CIP数据核字（2012）第173352号

责任编辑：唐 明

中国民航年刊（2011）

中国民用航空局 编

出 版	中国民航出版社
社 址	北京市朝阳区光熙门北里甲31号楼
广告代理	北京中媒富信信息技术中心
印 刷	中印集团数字印务有限公司
发 行	中国民用航空局国际合作服务中心
	中国民航出版社 新华书店
开 本	889×1 194 1/16
印 张	21.75
字 数	620 千字
版 本	2012年8月第1版 2012年8月第1次印刷
书 号	ISBN 978-7-5128-0082-3
定 价	160.00元